Asian Law Series
School of Law
University of Washington

Number 4

Asian Law Series
School of Law, University of Washington

The Asian Law Series was initiated with the cooperation of the University of Washington Press and the Institute for Comparative and Foreign Area Studies in 1969 in order to publish the results of several projects under way in Japanese, Chinese, and Korean law. The members of the editorial committee are: Herbert J. Ellison, Director of the Institute for Comparative and Foreign Area Studies; John O. Haley; and Dan Fenno Henderson, chairman.

Law and Politics
in China's
Foreign Trade

Edited by

Victor H. Li

University of Washington Press
Seattle and London

Copyright © 1977 by the University of Washington Press

Printed in Hong Kong

LIBRARY OF CONGRESS CATALOGING IN PUBLICATION DATA

Main entry under title:

Law and politics in China's foreign trade.

(Asian law series; 4)

Updated papers of a conference held at the Contemporary China Institute, School of Oriental and African Studies, London, 1971, and sponsored by the Subcommittee on Chinese Law of the Joint Committee on Contemporary China of the Social Science Research Council and the American Council of Learned Societies, and the University of Illinois, Edwardsville, with the cooperation of the Contemporary China Institute.

Includes bibliographical references.

1. Foreign trade regulation—China—Congresses.

2. China—Commerce—Congresses. I. Li, Victor H. II. Series.

Law   343'.51'087   76-7790

ISBN 0-295-95512-0

Foreword

This symposium grew out of a conference jointly sponsored by the Subcommittee on Chinese Law of the Joint Committee on Contemporary China of the Social Science Research Council and the American Council of Learned Societies as well as Southern Illinois University at Edwardsville. The Contemporary China Institute of the School of Oriental and African Studies at the University of London hosted the meeting in London on 13–17 September 1971. In addition to the staff members of the subcommittee and the Contemporary China Institute, about twenty-nine scholars, diplomats, and business executives from Denmark, France, Germany, Great Britain, Italy, the Netherlands, Hong Kong, Japan, and the United States attended the five-day session.

The planning and organizational work of the conference started in 1970 under the energetic leadership of Professor Victor H. Li, then with the School of Law at Columbia University. The need for such an international symposium arose from the fact that aside from the few articles prepared by Li, Professor Jerome A. Cohen of the Harvard Law School, and myself, there was virtually no other scholarly exploration of the foreign trade law of the People's Republic of China in the United States, which at that time had been out of contact with the Chinese mainland for twenty-odd years.

Admittedly, in international trade, law is not an end in itself but it is a technique to achieve certain goals determined by economics and politics. Nevertheless, once a contractual arrangement is made, law becomes an important criterion by which the performance of each contracting party is judged. Moreover, China came to know the Western world mainly through commercial intercourse. The West-oriented rules and regulations that governed the Celestial Empire's trade relations with foreign powers on the basis of the "unequal" treaties in the nineteenth century have left a permanent imprint in the memories of contemporary Chinese leaders. How the new China has formulated and applied its own rules and regulations in commercial transactions with other countries and how the new Chinese leaders have viewed the question of foreign trade in the context of China's diplomacy are undoubtedly points of interest to all those concerned with Chinese affairs. This volume, which offers rich insights into both China's trade system and her practical experience with individual countries, should serve as a useful guide to businessmen, lawyers, scholars, and government officials.

GENE T. HSIAO

Southern Illinois University
Edwardsville

Acknowledgments

The conference which produced the papers in this volume was sponsored by the Subcommittee on Chinese Law of the Joint Committee on Contemporary China of the Social Science Research Council and the American Council of Learned Societies, and by the University of Southern Illinois, Edwardsville, with the cooperation of the Contemporary China Institute. I am extremely grateful to Gene T. Hsiao, Director of the Asian Studies Program, Southern Illinois University, Edwardsville, and to Stuart Schram, Head of the Contemporary China Institute, for their tremendous support and assistance. In this regard, very special and personal thanks of the highest order go to David Wilson, then editor of the *China Quarterly,* for his invaluable substantive and organizational contributions. I also wish to thank the other members of the subcommittee for their guidance and help: Dan Fenno Henderson, who was the initiator of this project, and Jerome A. Cohen, valued mentor and friend, as well as Bryce Wood and John Campbell of the Social Science Research Council for their staff support and their perceptive and kindly guidance of a novice through his first experience as a conference organizer.

In addition to the contributors to this volume, other participants at the conference included: Rolf Audouard, Association of Machinery Manufacturers, Frankfurt/Main; Françoise Baetz, CEGOS Corporation, Paris; William E. Butler, University College, London; John Gittings, London School of Economics; Christopher Howe, School of Oriental and African Studies; Gene T. Hsiao, University of Southern Illinois, Edwardsville; Marinus J. Meijer, Ministry of Foreign Affairs, The Hague; Peter Nolan, London School of Asian Studies; Jon Sigurdson, University of Sussex; Eduard Solich, East Asian Association, Federal Republic of Germany; and David Wilson, *China Quarterly.* We are especially grateful to the "old China hands" who generously shared with us their unique knowledge and insights derived from many years of direct commercial and diplomatic dealings with China.

Victor H. Li

Stanford University
Stanford, California
May 1976

Contents

PART I. PATTERNS AND LEGAL ASPECTS OF TRADE BETWEEN
CHINA AND OTHER COUNTRIES

PART II.   METHODS AND CONTROL OF TRADE

CONTENTS

Introduction

Following the format of the conference, this volume is organized around a number of "country studies" which discuss the history and special characteristics of the trade between China and a particular country. We have tried to focus both on the practical how-to-do-it aspects of trade and on more general issues such as the relationship of politics to economics. These chapters are obviously not representative of China's total world trade. They deal primarily with industrialized countries, in part because of our own interests and in part because of the availability of suitable data and authors.

Dan Fenno Henderson and Tasuku Matsuo begin the volume with a discussion of the experience of Japan. They show the great importance of political considerations in Sino-Japanese trade, but also explain that both sides are sometimes willing to let form prevail over substance when politics threaten to unduly disrupt economic relations. On the other hand, George Ginsburgs' chapter on the rise and fall of Sino-Soviet trade is a prime example of the direct correlation between politics and economics. Perhaps of special interest to countries such as the United States are the harsh criticisms that came out in the 1960s concerning the conduct of trade in the 1950s. If political relations between China and the United States were to deteriorate at some future time, many of the seemingly routine petty annoyances of today's trade might be viewed later as major disturbances.

Some of the studies on other countries deal with situations where politics has not played an important role. One of the most striking aspects of the chapter on the Federal Republic of Germany by Arthur Stahnke is China's avoidance of stressing or creating political issues. Approaching the same problem from another angle, Poul Mohr's description of the Danish experience indicates that being an early and firm friend of China does not necessarily result in a boom in trade. The chapter on Sino-Italian trade by Gabriele Crespi Reghizzi raises the question of the extent to which recent major improvements in political relations will produce a corresponding increment in economic dealings. This is a complex issue since China is improving relations with many countries at the same time. The strongest case for demonstrating the separation of politics and economics is Hong Kong. Going beyond the fact that China tolerates a colony on its doorstep, Alan H. Smith shows the considerable extent to which China has penetrated the Hong Kong economic establishment and has used capitalist business forms. Finally, Stanley Lubman discusses the recent development of trade between China and the United States. Being a latecomer is a disadvantage since large parts of the China market have already been staked out by others; but this could be turned into an advantage if American traders would use the experience of their European and Japanese counterparts in dealing with China.

The other chapters in this volume present in a more systematic fashion a number of themes that run through the country studies. Anthony R. Dicks discusses the manner in which China, presently the world's largest charterer of ships, handles shipping and insurance matters, and also the procedures a foreign shipper must follow in dealing with Chinese port authorities and trading corporations. Frank Münzel describes the operation of the Chinese banking system, internationally and domestically, as it pertains to foreign trade. Both chapters show how closely China follows international practice.

Jerome A. Cohen deals with the question of the personal security of foreign businessmen in China and of Chinese commercial personnel abroad. He points out that the great majority of foreigners in China have not encountered any difficulty, although the risk of harassment is greater during periods of political radicalism. The chapter by Donald Klein describes the structure of the Chinese foreign trade apparatus, particularly the diplomatic and commercial establishments abroad. From studying biographical data, he also shows that the core of persons leading foreign trade work in China are highly experienced, and that there is considerable personnel interchange between governmental and "nongovernmental" trade organizations. I examine the operation of the trade apparatus within China. I treat the subject as a case study of the Chinese bureaucracy in action, paying particular attention to the balance between central control and local autonomy. Finally, Randle Edwards looks at Chinese efforts to control foreign trade and foreign traders with a historian's eye. He reminds us that many of the contemporary practices which appear novel and unique have counterparts in the eighteenth and nineteenth centuries.

The publication of this volume has been delayed. Several authors were prompt in submitting their articles. To these contributors the editor expresses his thanks. In other cases the authors were very late. The author apologizes to those who met the deadlines for himself and for those who did not.

But even when no unusual delays are encountered, scholars writing on current affairs face a seemingly insurmountable difficulty. There is always a substantial time-lag between the point at which research is completed and a paper is written, and the point at which the paper is actually published. During this period of time, however, events continue to take place and changes occur, often in fundamental ways.

The majority of the papers in this volume have been updated to cover developments up to 1972 or 1973. Where this has been done the appropriate cut-off date is indicated at the beginning of the chapter. The reader should note that some very important changes have taken place in Chinese trade patterns between 1973 and 1976. Total foreign trade, which remained at an annual level of around US $4–5 billion for a number of years, has increased sharply. By the mid-1970s, the trade volume as a percentage of GNP has begun to approach the levels of the 1950s. During that first decade, the import of foreign plants, equipment, and technology played a major role in China's industrialization effort. It appears that foreign technical goods might once again be an important part of China's modernization plans for the coming years.

CHINA'S FOREIGN TRADE
(billions US $)

	Exports	Imports	Total	Balance
1971	2.4	2.3	4.7	+ .1
1972	3.1	2.8	5.9	+ .3
1973	4.9	5.0	9.9	— .1
1974	6.5	7.5	14.0	—1.0
1975	6.8	7.2	14.0	— .4

In the mid-1970s China has developed a substantial trade deficit for the first time since the years immediately after Liberation. In partial response to this problem, China has begun exporting significant amounts of petroleum and has also increased use of short- and medium-term credits.

The developments in United States-China trade illustrate some of the concrete changes and constant patterns in Chinese trade practice.[1] The statistics are dramatic:

UNITED STATES TRADE WITH CHINA
(millions US $)

	Exports	Imports	Total	Balance
1971	0	4.9	4.9	— 4.9
1972	63.5	32.4	95.9	+ 31.1
1973	740.2	64.9	805.1	+675.3
1974	819.1	114.7	933.8	+704.4
1975	303.6	158.3	461.9	+145.3

---

[1] The following summary was written together with Stanley Lubman.

The high volume of Chinese purchases in 1973 and 1974, and the resulting large trade imbalance, is attributable mostly to heavy Chinese purchase of American agricultural products. Foodstuffs, for example, comprise over 60 percent of American exports to China in 1973, and over 40 percent in 1974. For a complex of reasons, such sales dropped sharply in 1975. China's own harvest improved after several years of drought in the early 1970s; long-term agreements with Canada and Australia for wheat deliveries will supply much of China's on-going needs. In addition, the presence of smut on some American wheat sold to China in 1972–73 may have influenced later Chinese cancellations. Dissatisfaction with the slowness of progress toward "normalization" probably also influenced the Chinese to treat the United States only as a residual supplier of foodstuffs.

During 1972–76 relatively limited Chinese purchases of American capital goods disappointed some observers who had thought that Chinese interest in high technology products might lead to sustained major purchases. By early 1976 the largest transactions were for a total of eight fertilizer plants purchased in 1972–73 from the M. W. Kellogg Corporation of Houston, Texas, and the ten Boeing 707's purchased in 1972. Thereafter, some of the more notable Chinese imports of United States manufactures were geophysical and oil field equipment purchased from several companies, mining equipment and heavy trucks for use in mining operations, and a quantity of iron and steel scrap and aluminum. In addition, there have been several licensing agreements in the petrochemical area which involve a transfer of American technology to China. On the whole, however, Chinese purchases of technical good have not been large. Some of the reasons for this low level may be the general decline in Chinese capital purchases in 1974–76, a growing Chinese concern over trade deficits, the restraining influence of American export controls, the competitive strength of Japanese and European producers, and the slightly cooler climate of United States-China relations.

Chinese exports to the United States, although limited in volume, have grown steadily despite the high American tariff and the existence of nontariff barriers such as legal standards concerning quality to which imports from China, like those from elsewhere, must conform. The leading imports from China in 1975 were tea, cotton piece-goods, antiques, rosin, raw silk, bristles, fireworks, and baskets of straw, bamboo, and willow. The amount of Chinese cotton piece-goods entering the United States has begun to arouse protectionist sentiments, as has the growing import of Chinese frozen shrimp and other foodstuffs. Buttressed by the import-inhibiting tendencies of the high American tariff, domestic protectionism in the United States could have a significantly negative effort on importation of many of the Chinese products.

The Canton Fair continues to attract Americans, of whom some six hundred were expected to attend the Spring 1976 Fair. The bulk of the transactions concluded at the Fair continue to be Chinese sales, and indeed China's trade deficit in 1974–75 was symbolized at the fair by the absence of Chinese negotiators interested in discussing machinery purchases. An increasing amount of business is being done between fairs by American exporters and importers who either go to China on special visits or who attend the growing number of specialized exhibitions of goods arranged by particular Chinese corporations. Travel has not only been in one direction. The Chinese remain very interested in studying American technology and in selling consumer goods to the United States, and have sent a series of technical and trade delegations here.

Chinese trade practices have not changed very much in 1972–76. They continue to adjust quite slowly to the American market. The stringent FDA standards remains a real obstacle to increased trade in foodstuffs, although in certain areas such as canned goods the Chinese have shown some movement toward adapting their products to the legal and practical requirements of the United States market.

The terms of Chinese export contracts also have changed very little, although in mid-1975 the Chinese began to sign contracts in U.S. dollars rather than insisting on RMB. Settlement of claims and disputes continues to be done through negotiations and compromise, and no institutional innovation has appeared in that respect.

In Chinese import contracts the most notable general development has been the purchasing of whole plants on credit or, as the Chinese put it, on "deferred payment" terms. Other Chinese purchases, however, continued to be for cash. There has also been considerable evolution of practice in negotiating the language of other contract clauses, such as the ones concerning *force majeure* and dispute settlement. On the latter point, the Technical Import and Machinery Corporations have agreed to clauses, sometimes quite detailed, providing for third-country arbitration. The Technical Import Corporation has also agreed to provide protection for patented technology and proprietary know-how in licensing agreements. No progress has been made on trademarks, however, and the Chinese continue to insist that under Chinese law foreign trademarks cannot be registered in the absence of a bilateral intergovernmental agreement. On the other hand, a Chinese trademark has been registered in the United States by an American distributor of the trademarked product, since United States law does not require reciprocity as a condition of registration of a foreign mark.

Perhaps the most important achievement among the past several years has been progress, albeit very slow, toward greater mutual understanding. American businessmen who care to do their homework need not regard China as *terra incognita*. There has been a growing number of sophisticated scholarly and technical books and articles published on Chinese trade, including a very informative journal published by the National Council for United States-China Trade, the *United States-China Business Review*. Presumably, continued travel to the United States and contacts with businessmen and other Americans have produced a corresponding increase in Chinese knowledge of the American scene. Many obstacles to mutual understanding remain, however, between these two very different societies.

V. H. L.

Abbreviations

CFJP: Chieh-fang jih-pao (Liberation daily)

CHINCOM: China Committee of the Consultative Group of NATO

CCPIT: China Council for the Promotion of International Trade

CCP: Chinese Communist Party

COCOM: Coordinating Committee of the Consultative Group of NATO

CMEA: Council for Mutual Economic Aid

FKHP: Chung-hua jen-min kung-ho-kuo fa-kuei hui-pien (Compendium of laws and regulations of the PRC)

TYC: Chung-hua jen-min kung-ho-kuo t'iao-yüeh-chi (Collection of treaties of the PRC)

FLHP: Chung-yang jen-min cheng-fu fa-ling hui-pien (Compendium of laws and decrees of the central people's government)

CB: Current Background

EEC: European Economic Community

ECMM: Extracts from Current Mainland Magazines

FEER: Far Eastern Economic Review

FBIS: Foreign Broadcast Information Service

FTAC: Foreign Trade Arbitration Committee

GATT: General Agreement on Tariffs and Trade

GAC: Government Administration Council

JETRO: Japan External Trade Organization

JMJP: Jen-min jih-pao (People's daily)

JPRS: Joint Publications Research Service

MFT: Ministry of Foreign Trade

MFN: Most favored nation

NCNA: New China News Agency

PR: Peking Review

PRC: People's Republic of China

RMB: Renminbi

SCMP: Survey of China Mainland Press

TKP: Ta kung pao (Impartial daily)

TPA: Trade and Payments Agreement

PART I

*Patterns and Legal Aspects of
Trade between China and
Other Countries*

Trade with China: An Introduction

VICTOR H. LI

I. THE CHINA MARKET

After languishing for more than twenty years, "China trade" is again capturing the American fancy. Books, articles, and symposia abound on this subject, with quality sometimes overwhelmed by quantity. A great many companies are vying to attend the Canton Trade Fair; and countless persons, out of some appreciation of the nostalgic or the exotic, are building new collections of chinoiserie.

This attention is due in part to the fact that trade is symbolic of the dramatic shift in relations between the United States and the People's Republic of China. While ping-pong was the icebreaker, trade is one of the principal means by which the policies of the new detente are being manifested and implemented. Traders will be major points of contact between the two countries, and in that sense will act as the initial "ambassadors." All this is very well, though we should note that symbols are passing things which tend to pale as the novelty wears off. One symbol replaces another, just as trade has displaced ping-pong and pandas in the public eye.

A far more important reason for the interest in trade is the expectation held by many persons that a great deal of profitable business could be done with China. This is only partially true: a certain amount of business will be done, but perhaps not as much as some people might hope for. The overly optimistic estimates of the volume of China trade often stem from the myth that China is a market with hundreds of millions of consumers who will pay for Western industrial goods with still largely untapped minerals and raw materials. Visions of sugarplums appear when one considers the quantity of goods needed "if

---

NOTE: Portions of this chapter are derived from Victor H. Li, "Ups and Downs of Trading with China," *Columbia Journal of Transnational Law* 13 (1975): 371.

each person in China would purchase but a single unit." A century earlier
some English textile manufacturers hoped to increase sales by convincing the
Chinese to lengthen their shirttails by a little bit. *Oil for the Lamps of China*
also reflected the belief that a little cup of oil multiplied several hundred
million times comes to a huge quantity of sales.

This belief persists even today, despite repeated demonstrations that it is
a myth and nothing more. In 1965 the Canadian minister of agriculture, Alvin
Hamilton, said that "China is the largest single stable market in the world.
It is not the market of the future—it is here now!"[1] Similarly, an officer of the
Australian Primary Producers Union came up with the idea that "if every
Chinese person used one woolen article a year, it would absorb the whole of
the Australian wool clip."[2] He also suggested that Australian visitors to China
might take along yarn and knitting needles in order to make the Chinese more
"wool conscious." And not to leave out Americans, an officer of a major pharmaceutical company observed, perhaps in jest, that if every person in China
with a headache would take two aspirin, that would consume all of his
company's aspirin production. Suffice it to say, there is no market of 800
million. Whether in absolute or in per capita terms, a total foreign trade of
even $10–15 billion a year is very small.

What then is a more realistic expectation of the volume of trade between
China and the United States? Prior to President Nixon's trip to China, a
number of studies were carried out in the United States and elsewhere that
tried to estimate the likely volume and commodity composition of future
Sino-United States trade.[3] Factors such as China's present economic capacity
and anticipated future growth, the past patterns of Chinese foreign trade, the
possible effects of Chinese acceptance of Western credits, and the probable
American share of China's foreign trade were examined. Several of the studies
concluded that trade might total several hundred million by 1975, and perhaps
reach the one billion dollar level by 1980—although all were careful to stress
the tentativeness of these figures.

---

[1] Henry S. Albinski and F. Conrad Raabe, "Canada's Chinese Trade in Political
Perspective," in Arthur Stahnke, ed., *China's Trade with the West, A Political and
Legal Analysis* (New York: Praeger, 1972), p. 92.

[2] Henry S. Albinski, *Australian Policies and Attitudes Toward China* (Princeton,
N. J.: Princeton University Press, 1965), p. 267.

[3] Robert F. Dernberger, "Prospects for Trade Between China and the United
States," in Alexander Eckstein, ed., *China Trade Prospects and U. S. Policy* (New
York: Praeger, 1971), p. 185; Victor H. Li, "Trade with China: A Cautionary Pro-
pectus," in Stahnke, ed., *China's Trade*, p. 209. See also Feng-hwa Mah, *The Foreign
Trade of Mainland China* (New York: Aldine, 1971); note 8 in the chapter by Henderson
and Matsuo. For a contrary view, see David C. Buxbaum, "American Trade with the
People's Republic of China: Some Preliminary Perspectives," *Colum. J. Transnat'l L.*
12 (1973): 39. The Japanese External Trade Organization estimated that Sino-United
States Trade might be $300 million by 1975. *Nihon keizai shimbun*, 4 August 1972, p. 9.

As things worked out the actual volume of trade exceeded even the rosiest of predictions. Trade increased at an almost exponential rate, growing from $5 million in 1971 to $96 million in 1972. In March 1973 Assistant Secretary of State Marshall Green said that trade might increase three- to four-fold that year. Even this estimate proved to be far too low. Actual trade for 1973 totaled $805 million, making the United States the second largest trading partner of China after Japan.[4] Chinese sales to the United States reached $65 million, mostly in agricultural goods, raw materials, and manufactured items. The United States sold over $600 million of agricultural goods to China, and more than $100 million of machinery and equipment, chemicals, and manufactured items. The last figure includes about $70 million from a contract for Boeing aircraft which was signed in 1972, but called for deliveries to be made in 1973 and 1974.

Clearly, something quite dramatic is happening here and poses many questions. What were the factors that contributed to the early estimates being so low and the actual figures being so high? Even more interesting, what will future Sino-United States trade be? Will it continue to increase at the present very rapid rate? One current estimate suggests that a 10 percent annual rate of growth is possible, leading to a total trade volume of $2 billion (in 1973 prices) by 1980.[5] On the other hand, might some of the constraints on trade suggested in the earlier studies still be correct? If so, the rapid expansion of trade during the past two years might not set the pattern for the future. There are already some indications that trade may be slowing down.[6]

In examining why the early projections were too low, some of the factors are fairly straightforward. These projections used fixed prices as an index; consequently, an upward adjustment must be made for the rate of inflation. In addition, the substantial devaluations of the dollar made American products much more of a bargain in the world market.

An important economic factor was that drought in both central and north China reduced the 1972 grain harvest by about 10 percent. The resulting deficit was further aggravated by the continuing efforts to build up grain stockpiles against the danger of war with the Soviet Union (a major slogan of this period has been Dig Deep Tunnels, Store Grain Everywhere), and to

---

[4] National Council for United States-China Trade, *Special Report No. 7—Sino-U. S. Trade Statistics 1972–1973 Including Agricultural Trade.*

[5] Alexander Eckstein and Bruce Reynolds, "Sino-American Trade Prospects and Policy," *Am. Econ. R.* 64 (May, 1974): 294; see also David L. Denny and Daniel D. Stein, "Recent Developments in Trade Between the U. S. and the P. R. C.: A Legal and Economic Perspective," *Law and Contemporary Problems* 38, no. 2 (Summer-Autumn, 1973), p. 260.

[6] See, e.g., Robert S. Elegant, "China Must Hustle to Pay for Imports," *Los Angeles Times,* 2 June 1974, part 8, p. 1; Christopher Lewis, "An End to the Bargain Days," *FEER,* 86, no. 39 (4 October 1974), p. 11.

convert grain lands to cotton lands. In any case yearly Chinese purchases of grain from abroad, which had averaged 5–6 million metric tons (mmt) in the early 1960s and had decreased to 3–5 mmt in 1967–72, grew in 1973 to over 7 mmt. This increased need combined with readily available American supplies produced the largest item in Sino-United States trade in 1973.

A number of political considerations also affected trade. Rapprochement between the two countries took place much faster than anticipated. The transition from hostility just prior to Mr. Kissinger's "Pakistani stomach ache" to the establishment of quasi-official liaison offices occurred in less than two years. As discussed in the chapter by Stanley Lubman, trade was an integral part of this normalization process; The initial gestures made by the United States to improve relations consisted of a series of steps that dismantled the American embargo. Thereafter, trade appeared to have been regarded by both sides as a manifestation of better political relations and a measure of how well things were going. One of the specific areas of agreement announced in the Shanghai Communique concerned the improvement of trade relations. The United States government has actively supported trade by facilitating the granting of export licenses, giving advice to businessmen, and helping form the National Council on United States-China Trade. By the same token, larger and larger numbers of Americans have been invited to visit China to do business.[7] American businessmen also may have benefited directly from the Chinese interest in building a sunny political climate by having been favored over "equivalent" foreign competitors.

The large volume of trade with the United States also reflected some basic policy decisions made in China. In the 1950s foreign trade played an important role in Chinese economic development, particularly in the effort to industrialize.[8] All this changed in the 1960s. Still burdened by the American embargo and by the International Coordinating Committee on Strategic Trade with Communist Countries (COCOM) restrictions, and seeing relations worsen with the Soviet Union, China emphasized even more strongly the principle of self-reliance. This was done in large part to avoid being overly dependent on other countries for goods, technology, and spare parts—an economic dependence that would limit China's ability to be politically independent and militarily secure. As a consequence the importance of foreign trade declined, and the annual volume of trade remained at a $4–5 billion level from 1958 until 1971. China also paid cash for all purchases, thus further reducing dependence on foreign countries.

---

[7] See National Council for United States-China Trade, *Special Report no. 5—U. S. Participants at the Spring and Fall Kwangchou Fairs, 1971–73.*

[8] See generally Alexander Eckstein, *Communist China's Economic Growth and Foreign Trade* (New York: McGraw-Hill, 1966); Eckstein, ed., *China Trade;* Feng-hwa Mah, *Foreign Trade.*

In late 1971 or early 1972 it appears that a basic decision was made to once again emphasize the importance of foreign trade in economic development. While the principle of self-reliance was still upheld, there was new stress on the idea of "exchanging needed goods." China began to buy large quantities of plants, machinery, and equipment from abroad. The volume of trade jumped to over $10 billion in 1973.[9] China also used medium term credits for a number of purchases and made fairly extensive inquiries about credit in general.

All the above factors contributed to the banner year for Sino-United States trade in 1973. If one takes a three- or five-year time prospective, what might the events of the past two years lead us to expect for future trade? I enter this area with considerable trepidation, both because forecasting is dangerous business and because past batting averages have not been good. I stress the speculativeness of this effort, the main point of which is to warn against over-optimistic expectations. I also am intentionally leaning toward a conservative point of view. This is due in part to the fact that I believe the conservative estimates to be more correct, and in part to balance the optimism that already abounds. For example, the volume of Chinese purchases of American grain may fall, perhaps as early as 1974. On the American side much less grain is available for sale and at considerably higher prices. The recent curtailment of wheat exports to the Soviet Union also must worry the Chinese buyers, although no comparable problems have yet arisen in Sino-United States trade.

More importantly, China may be wanting to buy much less grain. As mentioned earlier, China had a poor harvest in 1972. From both Chinese statements and Western estimates, however, it appears that the 1973 harvest matched or exceeded the output of the record 1971 harvest.[10] Moreover, as the danger of war subsides and as the stockpiling program moves forward, the amount of grain needed for storage will also decline. If this analysis is correct, then China's 1974 grain imports may not exceed the 1973 quantity and may even fall below that level. More specifically, some estimates made in 1973 suggested that China will import a total of 9 mmt of grain in 1974;[11] preliminary trade figures indicate that China probably will import only about

[9] Elegant, "China Must Hustle;" Wang Yao-ting, "China's Foreign Trade," *Peking Review,* 17, no. 41 (9 October 1974), p. 18. See also, "China's Role in the World Economy," *Stanford Journal of International Affairs* 10 (1975):1–82.

[10] "1973 All-Round Rich Harvests in China," *Peking Review,* 17, no. 1 (4 January 1974), p. 8; see also Peter Weintraub, "An Introduction to Chinese Agriculture," *U. S. China Business Review,* 1, no. 2 (March–April 1974), p. 38; Denny and Stein, "Recent Developments;" Leo Goodstadt, "Struggle Against the Elements," *FEER,* 86, no. 39 (4 October 1974), p. 15.

[11] "China's Agricultural Trade," *U. S. China Business Review,* 1, no. 2 (March–April 1974), p. 41.

7 mmt. Of this amount 4 mmt of wheat are being supplied through three-year contracts with Australia, Canada, and Argentina, leaving maximum American sales of approximately 2 mmt of wheat and 1 mmt of corn—figures that are below the 1973 level.

Possible losses in grain sales, which constitute 60 percent of American exports to China, might be offset by increases in other categories. Despite dwindling fiber reserves and rising prices cotton sales to China should continue to grow. China's need for cotton will not decline. This is a variation on an old theme: increasing each person's cloth ration by one yard would require 800 million yards of cloth, which in turn would require large investments of factories and land. It will also be some time before synthetic fibers can begin to overcome this problem. The largest increase in trade will be in American sales of plants, equipment, and other technical products. In 1974 sales of such goods is likely to be several times those of 1973.[12]

Chinese exports to the United States will also increase, especially if China receives most-favored-nation treatment. This rise, however, probably will be quite small. It appears that China is now exporting to near the limits of its economic capacity; some businessmen, for example, at times refer to the Canton Export Commodities Fair as the Canton Export Allocation Fair. As the economy grows more goods will be available. A substantial part of the increment, however, will be consumed within the country rather than used for export. In addition, almost three-fourths of China's exports are foodstuffs and textile products. Neither of these items will find a great market in the United States, and indeed may encounter resistance from American producers in the same areas.

Any substantial increase in Chinese exports is likely to come in the area of oil and other natural resources. China exported oil for the first time in 1973, selling a million tons of crude to Japan. The potential for oil sales is considerable. Present Chinese oil production is estimated at 50 million tons a year and exceeds refining capacity by over 10 million tons.[13] While China recognizes that "increasing oil exports have provided China with a greater possibility for further developing her foreign trade,"[14] the actual volume of oil exports has not been large. Japan, the principal purchaser of Chinese oil,

---

[12] See generally "Major U. S. Plant, Equipment, and Technology Sales to China" *ibid.,* p. 10; "Plant Sales to China 1973," *ibid.,* p. 36; "Plant Sales to China Under Negotiation," *ibid.,* p. 38; Elegant, "China Must Hustle."

[13] See, e.g., Christopher Lewis, "Outlook Bright for Oil, Coal," *FEER* 86, no. 39 (4 October 1974): 21. For slightly earlier figures, see Peter Weintraub, "China's Oil Production and Consumption," *U. S. China Business Review,* 1, no. 1 (March–April 1974), p. 29.

[14] Wang, "China's Foreign Trade."

will be able to buy 4 million tons of crude in 1974 and more in 1975.[15] Nevertheless, the potential for substantial Chinese exports remain.

The political issues affecting trade are even more interesting. For one thing, how permanent is the swing toward emphasizing foreign trade? It appears that important segments of the Chinese leadership feel ambivalent about the question of whether an increase in foreign trade, and therefore an increase in the dependence on foreign goods and technology, might imply a partial abandonment of the basic principle of self-reliance. For example, a recent article praised the growth of foreign trade as a means of "mutual economic development" based on "the principles of equality and mutual benefit and supplying each other's needs."[16] At the same time, however, the article also stressed "building the country independently, through self-reliance," and "relying on [the Chinese people's] own strength and wisdom and using their domestic accumulation funds and their own natural resources." Similarly, an article that proudly described the building of Shanghai's industry through self-reliance and without the aid of foreign ideas, capital, or goods also criticized as "superficial" the idea that self-reliance is equivalent to not importing.[17]

Self-reliance was born during the 1930s and 1940s when the Communist movement was weak and isolated. It came into full force after Liberation when first the Western embargo and later the Sino-Soviet split severely limited China's access to foreign goods and technology. Perhaps it is that habits and ideas of long standing are hard to change quickly, especially when they involve a principle that has been critical to China's political and economic development during the past quarter century. Or perhaps some people believe that the long-term benefits of self-reliance, such as the developing of domestic manpower skills and the avoidance of dependence on things foreign, outweigh the short-term economic benefits of getting access to foreign technology and goods.

There may also be some discomfort within the Chinese leadership about the process of normalization of relations with the United States. Some persons may still believe that American imperialism continues to be an active and aggressive threat which must be countered with equal force rather than through peaceful economic competition. Others might feel that normalization is proceeding too slowly; besides failing to formally recognize the People's Republic of China, the United States has sold additional arms to Taiwan and has even allowed Taiwan to open new consulates in Portland and Kansas City.

---

[15] *Ibid.;* Nicholas C. Chriss, "Offshore Oil—China Has Plenty For Lamps and Maybe For World," *Los Angeles Times,* 27 April 1974, p. 10; "Oil—China Has Plenty, Sells Little," *Christian Science Monitor,* 12 July 1974, p. 4; Lewis, "Bright Outlook."

[16] Wang, "China's Foreign Trade."

[17] "Taking the Road of Self-Reliance," *Peking Review,* 17, no. 42 (18 October 1974), p. 5; note 9, *supra.*

In order to induce the United States to proceed with normalization, China might move to restrict trade with the United States. Thus, just as trade has occupied a leading role in the development of the rapprochement, it could also bear the brunt of any disruption of the newly established political relationship.

I repeat that I am intentionally stating a bleaker case than I believe. I do so to point out the possibility that trade might level off, or even decline, as early as next year. The decline may be due to perfectly understandable economic reasons. It may also result, however, from changes in China's political policies, both domestic and international. That is, if rapidly rising trade were to be regarded as an indication of improving political relations, then decreased trade might be interpreted as a deterioration of the political climate. Such an interpretation would be a mistake if the reasons for the decline are economic. On the other hand, the decline might be a result of changes in Chinese political policies, changes first signaled in trade patterns.

The actual situation is much brighter. Despite the improved harvest and the export-import imbalance, the level of Sino-United States trade has kept up. And despite the renewed emphasis on self-reliance and the problems of political succession, there are no clear indications that present trade policies will not continue into the indefinite future. Sales of American technical and agricultural goods to China and continued promotion of Chinese exports to the United States will remain mutually beneficial.

In the longer range there are enormous opportunities for joint economic effort. For example, there appear to be very large oil reserves on the Chinese mainland and in the adjacent continental shelf.[18] In addition to domestic use China might sell a portion of this oil to obtain large amounts of foreign exchange which could purchase foreign technology and goods for China's economic development. The United States and Japan both have great oil needs, needs made even more clear by the recent events in the Middle East. It must be stressed, however, that I am speaking only of the potential for international cooperation in this area. Actual transactions concerning oil development have been quite limited.[19]

One cannot help but wonder whether these oil hopes are just another version of the myth of the China market which, like its many predecessors, may well produce far more expectations than results. For example, because of strategic considerations or a desire to maintain the principle of self-reliance, China might decide to reject, or at least severely limit, foreign participation in her oil development. This would mean that the entire project must proceed much

---

[18] Victor H. Li, "China and Off-shore Oil: The Tiao-yü Tai Dispute," *Stanford Journal of International Affairs* 10 (1975): 143; Nicholas Ludlow, "China's Oil," *U. S. China Business Review,* 1, no. 1 (January–February 1974), p. 21.

[19] "Oil Technology and Equipment to China," *ibid.,* p. 31; see also note 16, *supra*.

more slowly, but it also would mean that China can avoid repeating the past history of foreign intrusion into Chinese society. I may be sounding too sober a note in this discussion of the volume of China trade. Yet I do think that greater sobriety is needed here, for unrealistically high expectations will lead to disappointment and frustration. This in turn might lead to an effort to remove the "causes" of the frustration. Such a sequence of events is not a parade of horribles, but rather a partial description of the history of foreign influence in China during the past two hundred years.

Finally, while we should be pleased with the course of Sino-United States trade, we ought not let our optimism get out of hand. Some estimates made in 1973 suggesting that the 1974 level of trade would be $1.25 billion or more now appear to be overly optimistic. Preliminary trade figures indicate that total trade in 1974 is likely to be just under $1 billion. Still, a billion is an impressive figure for dealings between two countries that have considerable political and economic differences. At the same time, a billion is not a large figure, especially when one considers that it represents only about 1 percent of over-all United States foreign trade. Surely, a number of persons will do quite well in this trade, but equally surely, the total profits available are barely able to justify the quantity of high-priced business and professional talent that is presently turning its attention to this subject.

II.   THE STUDY OF CHINESE FOREIGN TRADE PRACTICES

Although I am suggesting that China's foreign trade is of passing symbolic interest and limited economic significance, there is still another reason that makes trade an important subject of study. Trade, after all, is not conducted in a vacuum or in the abstract. It is a part of the over-all activities of a society, and as such reflects the same concerns and attitudes that influence the society's actions in other areas. This is especially true of the PRC where trade is state-managed and centrally controlled. Thus, a careful examination of China's trade practices will help answer questions such as how trade is used as an instrument of foreign policy, or what contractual forms are favored by the Chinese. More than this, however, using foreign trade as a case study, we should be able to derive valuable insights into more general issues such as how central policies (here, central trade policies) are formulated and articulated, by what processes are these policies implemented, what political or bureaucratic problems arise in the course of implementation, and whether there are clearly preferred work styles or methods of implementation.

Indeed, focusing on trade as a means of studying China has some distinct advantages. For example, China specialists are concerned about the insufficiency of data for their research and about the need to rely heavily on Chinese sources and on interviews with refugees. In the area of trade, however, the "traditional" sources can be supplemented by information from China's trading partners, on both the governmental and the private levels. Not only are these new and independent sources of data, but equally important, they bring fresh points of view to the picture—points of view that were developed through actual dealings with real people in practical matters, and thus balance the more detached and theoretical approach of the academic community.

Despite the advantages, the study of trade practices is an academically under-developed area in Chinese studies. With the exception of several studies on the volume of trade and on the role of trade in economic development,[20] there is lacking a well-organized intellectual framework for analyzing the available information and for helping to expand our knowledge into broader and more far-reaching generalizations. Perhaps this situation is due to the fact that trade studies fall into the interstices among various academic disciplines such as economics, political science, and law, and consequently receive inadequate attention from all of them.

In this preliminary effort I am not able to propose a thorough and viable intellectual framework. Instead, let me sketch out several issues that arise in a number of the subsequent chapters and suggest what they might tell us more generally about China.

One striking feature of Chinese foreign trade practice is the manner in which disputes are resolved. The chapters by Gabriele Crespi Reghezzi (trade with Italy), A. R. Dicks (maritime law), Dan Fenno Henderson and Tasuku Matsuo (trade with Japan), Poul Mohr (trade with Denmark), and Arthur Stahnke (trade with West Germany) all deal with this issue at some length. They indicate that except for the import of complex and large-scale technical products, the Chinese generally insist on using their own standard form contracts for all transactions.[21] These contracts almost always contain a clause that urges the parties to try to settle all disputes through friendly negotiations; where this is unsuccessful, the dispute is to be submitted to arbitration—usually to a tribunal in Peking, but sometimes in the country of the defendant or a neutral third country. None of this is particularly unusual. What is unusual is that, with the exception of some maritime matters, *virtually no* trade cases have been arbitrated, in Peking or elsewhere. Indeed, several of the chapters cite instances where foreign traders seeking to arbitrate disputes in Peking were rebuffed by the Chinese and were occasionally even criticized for violating the "friendly negotiations" clause in attempting to bring the

---

[20] Eckstein, *Communist China's Economic Growth;* Samuel P. S. Ho and Ralph W. Huenemann, "Canada's Trade with China: Patterns, Policies, and Prospects" (Discussion paper no. 71, University of British Columbia, Department of Economics, 1972); and notes 2 and 3, *supra.*

[21] See the contract forms reproduced in the appendixes; see also, Alan H. Smith, "Standard Form Contracts in the International Commercial Transactions of the People's Republic of China," *International & Comparative Law Quarterly* 21 (January 1972): 133.

dispute to arbitration. In addition, except for some fairly specialized Hong Kong cases, there also have been no legal suits concerning trade. If nothing else, the arbitration clause effectively prevents a court of law from asserting jurisdiction.

Surely it cannot be that no disputes have arisen in a trade that totals several billions of dollars a year. How, then, are disputes resolved? The Chinese usually answer that since the parties to the dispute are reasonable men, "friendly negotiations" always produce a result that is satisfactory to all. This answer leaves the somewhat litigious and breach-minded Western lawyer— though perhaps not the performance-minded Western businessman—a little uncomfortable. Nevertheless, it makes good sense and works quite well in the context of Chinese trade.

An important factor in ensuring that negotiations alone will indeed produce satisfactory results is that the Chinese appear to be very careful in developing relations with their trading partners. The chapters mentioned above and the chapters by Jerome Cohen (status of businessmen), Stanley Lubman (trade with the United States), and Alan Smith (trade with Hong Kong) all stress the direct relationship between "friendliness" and successful trade. This may take the form of disfavoring foreign traders whose governments are not on good terms with the Chinese government, favoring foreign traders who themselves have proven to be friendly and reliable, or taking special care of "old friends" of China.

From this complex picture one of the basic patterns that emerges is that the Chinese try to develop trading relations very slowly. Although a foreign trader may wish to enter into substantial dealings right away, the Chinese prefer limited transactions in the beginning. There is a "feeling out" process, during which the amount of dealings is gradually increased. At some point friendliness and reliability are established; then the relationship advances to a higher level involving easier and more frequent contacts and substantially larger transactions.

How this affects dispute resolution is that during the "feeling out" period, either side can readily terminate the relationship if it feels that the other side is unreasonable or too difficult to deal with. The amounts of the transactions are still small enough so that termination does not result in undue loss. The Chinese appear willing to write off some of these losses rather than go through a lengthy and formal dispute resolution procedure. On the foreign trader's side the expectation of increased future dealings and profits often helps to foster a spirit of cooperativeness.

By the time the higher level of relationship is reached, presumably the more difficult trading partners have already been weeded out. The others now enter into a whole network of dealings with the Chinese trading corporations, a network that not only encompasses a large number of separate transactions but also continues over a long period of time. In such a situation the primary objective of both sides is to develop this ongoing, mutually beneficial relationship. If one aspect of the relationship encounters difficulty—for example, if a particular contract is not carried out—both sides will be more concerned with preserving the over-all relationship than with asserting one's "rights" under the breached contract to the fullest extent. And, since there are many other contracts present and future, the exercise of restraint by the aggrieved party in this instance helps ensure that the other party will act with equal restraint when the shoe is on the other foot. All this forebearance and understanding contribute greatly to the success of "friendly negotiations." Only in the most extreme cases when there is a breakdown in the overall relationship, such as the Vickers-Zimmer case cited by Mr. Cohen, does this method of dispute resolution fail. Then the parties involved must resort to arbitration or some other procedure.

I am not suggesting that establishment of the ongoing and mutually beneficial relationships described above is the sole reason why arbitration is not used in Chinese trade. One might also cite cultural factors such as the Chinese preference for mediation over adjudication.[22] Perhaps more to the point, the extensive negotiations that often precede the signing of a contract undoubtedly clarify the obligations and expectations of both sides, and thus reduce the chances for misunderstandings later on. The Boeing transaction, reportedly negotiated over several months and resulting in a book-length set of contracts, may be an example of where careful negotiations substituted in part for the lack of a pre-existing and more extensive relationship. Along a different line some foreign traders might add their own "China differential" to make up for the possible difficulties in carrying out "friendly negotiations." Despite all these considerations, I am suggesting that thinking of China trade within the framework of maintaining continuing relationships renders the absence of arbitration or judicial resolution of disputes more understandable.

We can try to press further into other aspects of Chinese studies by applying the framework of continuing relationships to nonforeign trade matters. For example, the Chinese use essentially the same "friendly negotiations" formula in describing how interenterprise and intraenterprise disputes within China are resolved.[23] The domestic situation is quite different, of course, since no aliens

---

[22] Stanley Lubman, "Mao and Mediation: Politics and Dispute Resolution in Communist China," *California Law Review* 55 (November 1967): 1284; Jerome A. Cohen, "Drafting People's Mediation Rules," in John W. Lewis, ed., *The City in Communist China* (Stanford: Stanford University Press, 1971), p. 29. See generally Jerome A. Cohen, *The Criminal Process in the People's Republic of China, 1949–1963: An Introduction* (Cambridge, Mass.: Harvard University Press, 1968).

[23] "A Brief Discussion of the Nature and Functions of Economic Contracts in Industry," *Ching-chi yen-chiu* (Economic research), no. 2, (1965), pp. 33–38, transl. in *JPRS*, no. 31, 033 (12 July 1965); Richard Pfeffer, "The Institution of Contracts in the Chinese People's Republic," *China Quarterly*, no. 14 (April–June 1963), p. 153;

are involved and since the participants presumably possess a far higher degree of shared values and understandings. Even so, we are basically dealing with transactions and processes where the parties have dealt with each other before and will continue to deal with each other over a wide variety of matters in the future. Consequently, the same arguments raised in the earlier discussion of foreign trade, concerning the exercise of restraint and the reliance on friendly negotiations, would apply. This, in turn, would help explain why virtually no disputes involving enterprises reach the courts and why, with some very limited exceptions, there is no Soviet-style system of *arbitragh.*

Going further, it seems clear that the process of friendly negotiations works best in simple repetitive transactions. It also works well in a highly decentralized system where most of the suppliers, producers, and consumers are local people in close and constant contact with each other. The question arises concerning what will happen as economic transactions cover larger geographical areas and face-to-face dealings become more difficult, or as greater economic diversity produces more one-shot transactions which are not part of a network of continuing relationships. It may be that in such situations the domestic contract negotiation process and the contract forms resemble what we find in foreign trade, or even that some third-party arbitration or adjudication is needed to resolve disputes.

The concept of continuing relationships can also be applied to the study of interpersonal dealings and disputes.[24] In this instance the concept is quite similar to describing relations within a village, a small town, or some other closely knit community in China or elsewhere. Most problems are handled through a form of "friendly negotiations" where differences are adjusted through discussions and social pressure. Again, only in extreme cases would outside agencies be called in. Thus, a very small percentage of "civil" disputes reach the courts, and the criminal process would not be invoked except in most serious circumstances.

An interesting Chinese contribution in this area is that they have managed, whether by design or by accident, to maintain the network of continuing

---

Richard Pfeffer, "Contracts in China Revisited with a Focus on Agriculture, 1949–1963," *China Quarterly,* no. 28 (October–December 1966), p. 106. See also three articles by Gene T. Hsiao: "Communist China's Foreign Trade Organization," *Vanderbilt Law Review* 20 (March 1967): 303; "Communist China's Trade Treaties and Agreements (1949–1964)," *Vanderbilt Law Review* 21 (October 1968): 623; "Communist China's Foreign Trade Contracts and Means of Settling Disputes," *Vanderbilt Law Review* 22 (April 1969): 503. Much can also be learned from studying the American experience in trading with the Soviet Union; Samuel Pisar, *Commerce and Coexistence* (New York: McGraw-Hill, 1970); James J. H. Giffen, *Legal and Practical Aspects of Trade with the Soviet Union* (New York: Praeger, 1969).

[24] Victor H. Li, "The Role of Law in Communist China," *China Quarterly,* no. 44 (October–December 1970), p. 66; Stanley Lubman, "Form and Function in the Chinese Criminal Process," *Colum. L. R.* 69 (April 1969): 535; note 7, *supra.*

relationships in urban areas. Rather than slowly building contacts as in the field of foreign trade, the Chinese have delegated a very wide range of responsibilities to neighborhood organizations. In carrying out these responsibilities, neighbors must deal with each other, and in the process, develop an extensive interpersonal network. A kind of "second village" has been established in the cities, which has helped to reduce some of the problems of urbanization, such as crime and a sense of isolation.

Speculating even further and along a different line, do the Chinese use the "feeling out" technique in their nontrade international relations? That is to say, during the initial period of dealings with another state, the principal issue may be the testing of each other's good faith. Sensitivities are particularly keen, and a relatively minor incident can jeopardize the entire relationship. Thus, after the 1956 agreement on repatriation of nationals between the United States and China, mutual suspicion and misunderstanding quickly led to a belief that good faith was lacking, and a breakdown in relations resulted.[25] Are we now in another period of testing for good faith? If so, we should tread particularly carefully; but we can also look forward to a substantial improvement in relations once this stage is past and the next higher stage is reached.

The above discussion of the "nonarbitration" clause should not lead one to think that Chinese and Western foreign trade contract terms and practices are vastly different. Indeed, I am struck by their similarity, all the way down to China's altering of some terms for import and export trade, so that the Chinese party would be favored in any case. Aside from the arbitration clause, some major differences that can be seen in the Chinese contracts reproduced in the appendixes are: a somewhat vague and variable *force majeure* clause, a strong preference for binding certification by the Chinese Commodity Inspection Bureau (which, incidentally, has a good reputation in the international trading community); and two political matters, the preamble in the Japanese contracts, and the refusal of Chinese banks to issue confirmed letters of credit on the grounds that the promise of a Chinese bank is totally reliable and hence need not be confirmed. None of these is especially significant. Moreover, the chapter on banking by Frank Münzel and the chapter on maritime law by A. R. Dicks show the great extent to which China uses internationally developed and accepted forms and customs, although Mr. Dicks points out that some shipping and insurance clauses have been "Sinicized." Both the contract forms and reports from Western businessmen indicate that the persons handling China's foreign trade possess considerable trade expertise.

The question of why China follows international trade practices to such a large extent is worth more thought. If the reason is that China has no other

---

[25] Kenneth T. Young, *Negotiating with the Chinese Communists: The United States Experience, 1953–1967* (New York: McGraw-Hill, 1968).

choice if it wishes to engage in beneficial trade, then does this suggest that adopting a hard line, at least in some areas, will yield good results? Or what is more likely, if China adheres to international practice because this is a convenient and effective way of conducting its affairs, then a major effort ought to be made to identify other substantive and procedural areas of potential agreement. This inquiry could be quite far-reaching. For example, Alan Smith's chapter on Chinese businesses in Hong Kong describes a Chinese willingness to use capitalist business forms that goes well beyond mere tolerance or accommodation.

One need not dwell on the subtleties of arbitration clauses and contract terms to find connections between foreign trade practices and Chinese attitudes and actions in other areas. The most obvious example of such a connection is the fascinating intertwining of political and economic considerations in Chinese foreign trade policy, including the manner in which trade is offered or withheld to encourage or chastise a given foreign government. Most decisions, of course, involve some combination of politics and economics, but the particular proportions seem to vary greatly over time and from place to place.

For example, the chapter on trade with the Soviet Union by George Ginsburgs gives a trade's-eye view of the development of the Sino-Soviet dispute. During the early years, the volume of trade was large and was conducted in an apparently amicable fashion. As the dispute heated up each side, with the benefit of hindsight, began castigating the other for the manner in which it had earlier carried out its trade and aid obligations. At the same time the volume of trade fell sharply from a high of about $2 billion in 1959 to only about $100 million in the late 1960s.

The Japanese case is the converse. Beginning with a total embargo on trade at Liberation, Japan is now China's foremost trading partner, handling over $2 billion of goods a year. This volume has increased with the recent establishment of diplomatic relations between the two countries. Even so, the growth of Sino-Japanese trade has not been a smooth process. Dan Fenno Henderson and Tasuku Matsuo describe how trade dropped from over $100 million to about $20 million after the 1958 Nagasaki flag incident, and how it did not fully recover for five years. This episode is a prime example of China's willingness to sacrifice economic benefits, its own as well as those of friendly Japanese traders, to make a political point. But it also illustrates Chinese economic pragmatism: the authors suggest that the improvement in Chinese attitudes towards trading with Japan during the early 1960s was due in part to a perceived need to find replacements for the dwindling Soviet export and import market.

Japan's experience also shows the limits to which China will go in trying to influence the governmental policy and even domestic politics of another state. These efforts include the imposition of a series of political principles and conditions of trade (which among other things bar from dealing with China

companies who trade with Taiwan or are associated with American imperialism), the inclusion in joint trade communiques and even in contract preambles
of denunciations of Japanese governmental policy towards China, and the
restricting of trade only to certified "friendly firms." Despite such extraordinary actions, however, China has refrained from pushing these efforts too
far. Thus, Chinese acceptance of "dummy" friendly firms enabled the major
Japanese companies to circumvent the political principles and conditions.
Even now, after the establishment of diplomatic relations between China and
Japan, trade and tourism between Japan and Taiwan continue to grow,
although governmental agencies have been converted to "private" bodies and
perhaps some new Taiwan trade "dummies" have been set up.[26]

Compare the Chinese treatment of Japan and of West Germany.[27] Both
countries are great industrial powers and major trading partners of China;
and both were World War II enemies and are now important allies of the
United States. Yet in contrast to the harassments and interferences detailed
in the chapter on trade with Japan, Arthur Stahnke's chapter describes a
straightforward series of dealings with West Germany, with the possible
exception of the arrest of some German businessmen during the Cultural
Revolution. There is neither a requirement that German businessmen
denounce the policies of their government, nor an imposition of political
principles of trade. Indeed, when public pressure by the Johnson administration in 1964 caused Chancellor Erhard to terminate discussions with China
concerning the signing of some kind of commercial "treaty," no complaint
was heard from the Chinese side. Even more striking, the 1964 "Yoshida
letter" which announced the policy of no credit from the Japanese Export-
Import Bank brought on a torrent of Chinese protests; yet the cancellation
(again under American pressure) of the Demag deal in 1966, which also
involved the extension of long-term German credit, produced no outcry.

It is not entirely clear to me why China tried so hard to influence Japan's
political stand, but essentially left West Germany alone. Perhaps China
believes that it has less stake in what West Germany does since the latter is
basically a European regional power. Perhaps out of a sense of cultural
affinity or a memory of Japanese occupation during World War II, China
thinks that it is able to sway Japanese public opinion in a way that would
not work on the Germans. Whatever the reasons, one question that arises is
where does the United States stand in this Japan-to-West Germany continuum
involving the degree to which political considerations figure into China's

---

[26] See, e.g., Tillman Durdin, "Japan-Taiwan Tie Is Still Strong," *New York Times,*
1 June 1973, p. 5.

[27] In addition to the chapter by Arthur Stahnke in this volume, see particularly
Arthur Stahnke, "The Political Context of Sino-West German Trade," in Stahnke,
ed., *China's Trade,* p. 135.

economic dealings? The United States clearly is an Asian power, although possibly not to the same extent as Japan will be in the near future. American public opinion is difficult to influence, but probably not as difficult as German.

The chapter by Stanley Lubman on trade with the United States discusses the manner in which trade relations have developed, paying particular attention to the lessons that the United States should learn from the experiences of other countries. Most of the major American trade restrictions have now been removed, although there still are a number of matters such as the limitations on credit imposed by the Johnson Debt Default Act of 1934 and by some of the rules of the Export-Import Bank concerning dealings with communist countries.[28] In the near future there should be a settlement of most of each country's outstanding claims against the other (claims for nationalized American property and for frozen Chinese bank accounts), further clarification of the sovereign immunity rules applicable to Chinese foreign trade corporations, and a resolution of the Chinese demand for most-favored-nation treatment. Some other problems are more difficult. For example, the Chinese appear to prefer dealing with an American counterpart to the China Council for Promotion of International Trade (CCPIT) which will "coordinate" the American side of the trade. But how compatible is an organization such as the recently formed National Council for United States-China Trade with the general structure of American business or with the relationship between the business community and the government? Along a different line, up until now Chinese domestic politics (and consequently also international relations) has gone through almost alternating periods of moderation and radicalism.[29] There is little reason to believe that this pattern will not continue. What will happen to foreign trade and other international dealings as the present moderation gives way to new radical policies?

III. A SURVEY OF CHINESE FOREIGN TRADE, 1949–1970[30]

Many of the "problems" of China trade appear less troublesome when viewed in light of the fact that China has had substantial and largely satisfactory trade relations with many countries for many years. This perspective

---

[28] For American trade restrictions, see John R. Garson, "The American Trade Embargo Against China," in Eckstein, ed., *China Trade Prospects,* p. 3; Thomas W. Hoya, "The Changing U.S. Regulation of East-West Trade," *Colum. J. Transnat'l L.* 12 (1973): 1; Denny and Stein, "Recent Developments."

[29] See, e.g., G. William Skinner and Edwin A. Winckler, "A Compliance Succession in Rural Communist China," in Amitai Etzioni, ed., *A Sociological Reader on Complex Organizations* (2nd ed., New York: Holt, Rinehart and Winston, 1969), pp. 410–38.

[30] Much of the research for this section was done by Celia Suk-chun Tang. The trade figures cited are taken from Eckstein, ed., *China Trade Prospects;* Eckstein, *Communist China's Economic Growth;* Mah, *Foreign Trade;* "China's Foreign Trade in 1968,"

is especially important for latecomers such as the United States. For example, we may not know exactly how an American seller can protect his patent rights and other industrial property, but surely such protection is available since European and Japanese producers have made many sales of complex technical goods to China. Similarly, other traders have found ways to cope with the Chinese trade bureaucracy and to conclude transactions without ever dealing directly with the ultimate Chinese user or producer.

China presently carries on a trade of approximately $14 billion a year with about a hundred countries. In general China sells agriculture-related and light manufactured products, and purchases metals, chemicals, and machinery and equipment. From 1954 until 1973 exports have exceeded imports by a moderate amount, although there has been considerable variation over time and for different parts of the world. In recent years until 1973, China has conducted a roughly balanced trade with Eastern Europe, but she has maintained a substantial trade deficit with Western Europe, Canada, Australia, and Japan, and a corresponding surplus with other Asian countries and with Africa. This section will briefly survey China's trade relations with a number of countries not discussed elsewhere in this volume and will focus on the period 1949–70.

In the early years after Liberation, due to the policy of "leaning to one side" and to the United Nations embargo, the bulk of China's foreign trade was conducted with the Soviet Union and Eastern Europe. As described in several other chapters, trade with nonbloc countries began to increase after the 1952 Moscow Conference, and especially in the mid-1950s as the embargo restrictions were relaxed and as China adopted much more moderate "spirit of Bandung" foreign policies.

The early trade pattern was entirely reversed with the development of the Sino-Soviet dispute. In recent years China's trade with the Soviet Union and Eastern Europe has amounted to only about one-fifth of China's total trade. As might be expected, decline of Sino-Soviet trade has been the most precipitous, dropping from 48 percent of China's total trade in 1959 to a scant 3 percent in 1967. Other Eastern European countries (which export a quantity of trucks, ships, and machinery to China) have been similarly affected, although to a lesser degree. For example, trade with East Germany and with Czechoslovakia totaled over $400 million in the late 1950s, but dropped to one-fourth that figure by the late 1960s.

As also might be expected, Sino-Albanian trade has blossomed during the past decade, growing from $9 million in 1960 to nearly $80 million in 1967. More than half of Albania's exports went to China. These sums (further

Current Scene, 7, no. 13 (1 July 1969); "China's Foreign Trade in 1969," *Current Scene*, 8, no. 16 (7 October 1970); "China's Foreign Trade in 1970," *Current Scene*, 9, no. 8 (7 August 1971). See also, Sidney Klein, *Politics versus Economics, the Foreign Trade and Policies of China* (Hong Kong: International Studies Group, 1968).

supplemented by Chinese foreign aid grants) are particularly impressive given Albania's small population of one and a half million—a figure possibly exceeded by the number of Chinese lining the airport-to-Peking route to welcome a visit of President Hoxha.

Other chapters in this volume deal in some detail with the Western European experience in trading with China, ranging from the case of Denmark (a small nation and one of the first nonbloc countries to establish diplomatic and trade relations with China), to Italy (the first NATO country to sign a formal trade agreement), to West Germany (China's largest European trading partner). Total trade with Western Europe has grown from a roughly balanced trade of $109 million in 1952, to $644 million (with Chinese purchases exceeding sales by $183 million) in 1959 during the height of the Great Leap Forward, to $881 million (with a Chinese deficit of $143 million) in 1968. In general Western Europe (and Japan) replaced Eastern Europe as the supplier of technical goods needed for Chinese industrial development in the 1960s.[31] At the same time purchasing from many countries has reduced China's dependence on any single source for technical inputs and spare parts. Such a dependence had existed in the 1950s vis-à-vis the Soviet Union, with unhappy results for China when the Soviet technicians left in 1960.

The experience of the United Kingdom is similar to those of the Western European countries discussed in other chapters. In addition to the usual technical products, the British have also sold a quantity of aircraft to China, including some recent sales of Tridents. Total trade in 1968 was $152 million, with a small balance in the United Kingdom's favor.

France presents a somewhat different picture. Although the establishment of diplomatic relations in 1964 was a major breakthrough for China, this did not result in significantly increased Sino-French trade. (The chapter by Donald Klein shows that the French experience in this regard was not unique.) That is, while trade has increased more than 50 percent since 1964, the rate of increase for trade with West Germany and Italy, two countries which did not recognize China in the 1960s, was even greater. One special characteristic of Sino-French trade is the Chinese purchase of wheat. In 1963–64, wheat sales represented about two-thirds of French exports to China. Indeed, the hope for a considerably expanded and relatively permanent wheat market may have been an important incentive to the French for normalizing relations. This hope has not materialized; after a drop in the mid-1960s recent French wheat sales have totaled about $20 million a year, a figure that is below the 1963–64 volume.

Wheat sales, however, have played a decisive role in China's relations with several other countries. Canada had been selling small quantities of wheat to

---

[31] S. Klein, *Politics versus Economics*, p. 62.

China since the early 1950s.[32] These sales jumped tremendously in 1961 when, in response to several years of bad harvests, China purchased over $100 million of Canadian wheat, or about 20 percent of Canadian wheat exports for the year. Sales have generally remained at that level in subsequent years, with $156 million sold in 1970. In 1973 China signed three-year contracts for substantial amounts with Canada and Australia.

These sales came at a particularly fortunate time for Canadian farmers. Rising costs and declining sales since the 1950s had produced a severe recession in the agricultural sector. The economic benefits resulting from the wheat sales helped foster a favorable attitude towards China in the conservative prairie states, and thus assured broadly based political support for the establishment of diplomatic relations with China in 1970.

The Australian experience, however, shows that the sale of wheat can be a two-edged sword.[33] Until diplomatic relations were established after the Labour Party victory in the 1972 elections, Australia had followed the hard American line on political and military policy towards China, but at the same time had actively promoted economic relations. The latter effort was quite successful; in the 1960s China was Australia's fifth largest export market. In the area of wheat China purchased over one-third of Australian exports; sales for 1970 totaled $112 million.

One can imagine the consternation of the wheat producers when China failed to respond to overtures of the Australian Wheat Board to begin the 1971 negotiations. The consternation was doubly felt since during previous years many farmers had converted their land to wheat production, and since Chinese purchases of Canadian wheat increased by some $60 million in 1971. It is not exactly clear why China suddenly stopped buying Australian wheat. Some of the likely contributing factors were economic. For example, a record Chinese harvest in 1970 reduced the domestic need for grain imports; and falling world rice prices made the wheat-for-rice substitution less attractive. China may also have preferred, for reasons of nutrition or taste, Canadian hard wheat to Australian soft wheat.

At the same time political considerations were also very much involved, although China's poor harvest in 1972 was undoubtedly a major factor. The years 1970 and 1971 were a time when many countries were changing their China policies. Canada had just recognized China, and a large number of other nations were beginning to follow suit. The United States was also negotiating the Nixon visit. Perhaps the stopping of wheat purchases was a means of urging Australia to reconsider its political policies. In this regard it is interesting to note that in 1971 Chinese purchases of Australian metals

---

[32] See particularly Albinski and Raabe, "Canada's Chinese Trade"; Ho and Huenemann, "Canada's Trade with China."

[33] Albinski, *Australian Policies.*

and ores reached a record high. Thus, China was not completely boycotting Australian goods, but rather was hitting a single highly vulnerable and politically influential portion of Australian society.

To pay for goods from Western Europe, Japan, the "wheat countries," and now the United States, China maintains a substantial trade surplus with other parts of the world. By far the largest foreign exchange earnings come from dealings with Hong Kong.[34] In the early years after Liberation, Hong Kong was especially valuable as an entrepôt for indirect trade with third countries, and in providing various commercial services and facilities. The importance of these functions declined as China established direct trade relationships with more countries. Instead, Hong Kong has developed into a major world center for light industry, with its own needs for supplies and consumer goods. In 1970 China exported about $470 million of goods to Hong Kong, about half of which was food and a fourth was items for reexport. Hong Kong sales to China totaled only $5 million; the result was an enormous Chinese surplus. In addition, China derives income from the business activities described in the chapter by Alan Smith, and also receives through Hong Kong perhaps $100 million a year in remittances from overseas Chinese to their relatives in China.

In part because of the foreign exchange earnings, China has followed a very moderate line regarding the political status and future of Hong Kong. Despite the fact that Hong Kong is a foreign colony actually situated on the China mainland (and periodically being reminded by the Russians about this), the Chinese position has consistently been that Hong Kong is "a problem left over from history" which will be taken care of at some point; until then, the status quo is maintained.[35] The only time this policy was shaken was during the 1967 riots, but even this episode was limited in duration and scope.

China also earns foreign exchange in Southeast and South Asia. For example, trade with Singapore resembles trade with Hong Kong on a smaller scale, and in recent years has yielded an annual surplus of about $150 million for China.

---

[34] In addition to the chapter by Alan H. Smith in this volume, see particularly Colina MacDougall Lupton, "Hong Kong's Role in Sino-Western Trade," in Stahnke, ed., *China's Trade,* p. 175.

[35] For example, in response to Khrushchev's references to the colony of Hong Kong in his speech of 12 December 1962 before the Supreme Soviet, the Chinese said: "[With respect to unequal treaties creating colonies] our government declared that it would examine the treaties concluded by previous governments with foreign governments, treaties that has been left by history, and would recognize, abrogate, revise or renegotiate them according to their respective contents. . . . [T]hey should be settled peacefully through negotiations and that, pending a settlement, the *status quo* should be maintained." "A Comment on the Statement of the Communist Party of the U.S.A.," *Peking Review,* no. 10/11 (1963). See also *New York Times,* 11 March 1972, pp. 1, 4 for a more recent Chinese statement at the United Nations on the same subject.

Dealing with this part of the world, however, has not been a simple matter for China. Obviously, the Vietnam War and the earlier Indochina War have been the great problems. In addition, there have been several staunchly anticommunist countries in this area, as well as organizations such as SEATO. There also have been a number of coups and changes in government, often with attendant changes in policy towards China. The border clashes with India, the formation of strong ties with Pakistan, and the establishment of the new nation of Bangladesh have created still more problems. Finally, people's liberation movements are active in several Asian countries. China is sometimes faced with the uncomfortable choice between refusing to support a "liberation" movement or else supporting a movement that attacks a government friendly to China.[36]

A less apparent but in some ways more interesting issue is the presence of about twenty million "overseas Chinese" in Southeast Asia, including about three-fourths of the population of Singapore and half of the people of Malaysia. These persons are in a most ambiguous and even contradictory position. Many have lived for generations in their host country, but have maintained Chinese customs and language and have not been assimilated into the local population. Traditional Chinese concepts of *jus sanguinis* have bestowed on these people the often dubious benefits of dual nationality. In response to some of the problems mentioned below, the PRC has been moving away from the use of *jus sanguinis* as a determination of nationality; in addition, no obligations are imposed on overseas Chinese and these persons are urged to obey the laws of their host country.[37] Still, the Chinese government on occasion has felt obliged to extend a kind of "diplomatic protection" by protesting discriminatory or oppressive actions taken by another country against overseas Chinese living there. (A further contradiction is that the objects of the discrimination are sometimes rich Chinese landlords and merchants.) Along a related line there is considerable competition between Peking and Taipei to win the support of the overseas Chinese. Propaganda and other efforts on the part of both sides have raised apprehensions about the extent to which Peking and Taipei may be interfering in the internal affairs of another country. Some anticommunist governments in the area also feared that the PRC might use the local overseas Chinese community as a point of infiltration.

Many of the factors discussed above can be clearly seen in Sino-Indonesian relations.[38] Diplomatic relations were established in 1950, but early Chinese

---

[36] Peter Van Ness, *Revolution and Chinese Foreign Policy* (Berkeley, Calif.: University of California Press, 1971).

[37] James C. Hsiung, *Law and Policy in China's Foreign Relations* (New York: Columbia University Press, 1972), pp. 131–51.

[38] Arnold C. Brackamn, *The Communist Collapse in Indonesia* (New York: W. W. North, 1969); see also Daniel Tretiak, "Changes in Chinese Attention to South-East Asia, 1967–1969: Their Relevance for the Future of the Area," *Current Scene,* 7, no. 21 (1 November 1969).

attempts to purchase rubber were rejected by Indonesia as violating the United Nations embargo. Two years later a new Indonesian government formed by an alliance of the Nationalist Party and the Communist Party (PKI) defied the embargo and entered into two trade agreements which called for the exchange of Indonesian rubber and forest products for Chinese textiles and machinery.

The 1955 Bandung Conference further improved relations. In addition to a third trade agreement, China began to provide credits to Indonesia: $16 million in 1955, $11 million in 1958, $30 million in 1961, and $50 million in 1965 (the last was not completely implemented). These were not large sums when compared to the Soviet Union's aid and credits of $368 million, but they still represented substantial commitments, given China's own limited economic capacity and great needs. The Bandung Conference also produced agreement on a dual nationality treaty, whereby Chinese living in Indonesia had two years in which to elect one nationality or the other. Ratification of this treaty was delayed for five years, however, by right-wing Islamic parties who did not want to grant Indonesian citizenship to the local Chinese.

Further problems arose in 1959 when President Sukarno passed a law that prohibited aliens, in effect the local Chinese, from carrying on commerce in the rural areas. The following year the Basic Agrarian Law limited private ownership of land to Indonesian citizens. During these two years trade between China and Indonesia dropped sharply. In December 1960 the dual nationality treaty was finally ratified, and relations began to normalize. Trade increased steadily, reaching a volume of over $100 million in 1964.

All this ended abruptly with the attempted coup by the PKI in September 1965. The PRC and the local Chinese community were accused of involvement in the coup. Numerous violent attacks were launched against local Chinese and also against the PRC embassy. After a series of heated exchanges trade was stopped, Chinese technical experts went home, and finally diplomatic relations were severed. Several thousand Indonesian Chinese left their country of birth to settle in China. In 1968 the dual nationality treaty was unilaterally revoked by Indonesia. There has been virtually no direct trade between the two countries since 1965, although a certain amount of indirect trade is carried on through Hong Kong and Singapore. In the early 1970s, however, Indonesian officials indicated an interest in the resumption of trade.

To balance the picture, the sharp turns in Sino-Indonesian relations should be contrasted with the almost unique steadiness of relations between China and Sri Lanka. Political changes within the island have not affected trade. The exchange of rubber for rice is based on five-year trade agreements (signed in 1953, 1957, 1962, and 1967) with annual protocols. Except for 1961–62 when China's bad harvests limited her export capacity, the volume of trade has been relatively steady at $50–70 million a year since 1956.

Chinese trade with Middle Eastern countries has been limited, totaling

$163 million in 1968 (with a surplus in China's favor of $73 million). This is due in part to China's self-sufficiency in oil and in part to the great Soviet influence in this part of the world. Generally, China buys cotton and sells foodstuffs and manufactured products. The recognition of China by Iran, Turkey, and Kuwait in 1971 should produce an increase in trade.

Trade with Africa also has been on a small scale, amounting to $125 million in 1968 (with a surplus in China's favor of $65 million). These figures, however, do not adequately reflect Chinese activity or interest in this continent. As a leader of the Third World, China has provided credits, equipment, and technical personnel to assist in the economic development of a number of African countries. These efforts have not always produced the desired results. Complaints about political interference and subversion led to a temporary severing of diplomatic relations with Ghana, Burundi, Dahomey, Tunisia, and the Central African Republic in the mid-1960s. (See the chapter by Donald Klein for further details.)

By far the most ambitious Chinese economic action in Africa has been the support provided for the construction of the Tanzam Railway after organizations such as the World Bank had refused to do so.[39] Obviously, few projects of this magnitude—$400 million—can be undertaken. Nevertheless, the Tanzam Railway is a dramatic demonstration to the Third World of Chinese capabilities and interest.

Even here, however, some serious problems are present. The three countries have agreed that 60 percent of the construction costs is to be paid out of profits derived from Chinese exports to Tanzania and Zambia. The question is how will these two countries be able to import $120 million of Chinese goods a year as provided for in the agreement? This may be too large a volume for the Tanzanian and Zambian economies to absorb. More specifically, a 1970 Zambian trade mission to China reported that the principal Chinese goods suitable for import to Zambia were chinaware, glassware, carpets, bicycles, and a small quantity of textiles (so as to avoid adverse competition with the new local textile industry); if this assessment is correct, one wonders how the total of $120 million could be reached.

Until recently American influence and the existence of a number of right-wing dictatorships have kept China's trade with Central and South America to a mere trickle.[40] The only two exceptions have been Chinese purchase of a substantial amount of Argentinian wheat in 1962–66, and trade with Cuba since 1960; otherwise, the total volume of trade with this area was only about

[39] George T. Yu, "Working on the Railroad: China and the Tanzania-Zambia Railway," *Asian Survey*, 9, no. 11 (November 1971); George T. Yu, *China and Tanzania: A Study in Cooperative Interaction* (Berkeley: Center for Chinese Studies, University of California, 1970).

[40] George Ginsburgs and Arthur Stahnke, "Communist China's Trade Relations with Latin America," *Asian Survey*, 10, no. 3 (July–December 1970).

$10 million a year in the 1960s. Recent improvement of relations with Chile, Mexico, Peru, and other countries indicate, however, that future economic dealings with this part of the world will increase rapidly.

More generally, in the past several years China has emerged as a principal spokesman and champion for the Third World. She has played this role in the United Nations and in international conferences concerning the law of the sea, population, and food. This trend is likely to continue for some time. With the growth of political ties with the Third World, trade should correspondingly increase.

Trade with Japan

DAN FENNO HENDERSON
and
TASUKU MATSUO

I. INTRODUCTION

The Nixon visit to Peking in February 1972 stimulated Japan's efforts to increase trade with the PRC by creating potential American competition in the China markets and by relaxing the general political atmosphere for dealing with the PRC. In July 1972 the new prime minister Tanaka Kakuei had replaced the anti-PRC Sato Eisaku. Tanaka visited Peking two months later; at that time he established diplomatic relations with the PRC, recognized that rights to Taiwan under the Potsdam and Cairo Declarations accrued to the PRC, and implicitly abrogated the peace treaty of 1952 with the Republic of China.[1] Diplomats and embassies were exchanged in January 1973. During the fall of 1972 diplomatic relations between Japan and Taiwan were severed, although recently both Japanese and Taiwan spokesmen have been hinting at the possibility of maintaining some kind of relations under the principle of "separation of politics and economics"—this time applied to Tokyo-Taipei dealings.

Since late 1971 the Japanese business community has been responding to the new climate by sending delegation after delegation to Peking. Included in these pilgrimages are many major companies that had theretofore traded with the PRC only through dummy subsidiaries. This peculiar arrangement was

---

NOTE: This paper attempts to present the Sino-Japanese trade experience up to the end of 1973.

[1] A convenient Japanese text of the joint communique may be found in *Tōzai bōeki report* (East-West trade report) (Tokyo: Ajia Bōeki Tsūshinsha, Autumn, 1972), 10: A-2.

devised because the PRC had required that Japanese applicants for entry into the China trade prove their friendliness (as opposed to the unfriendliness of the Sato government) by accepting terms known as Chou En-lai's "four conditions." Briefly this meant that the "friendly firm" *(yuko shosha)* would not deal with Taiwan, South Korea, or South Vietnam, or ally themselves with U.S. capital. Unusual as these conditions are (China has not imposed similar conditions for trade with any other country), they reflect a basic Chinese logic.[2] Since it was the Japanese traders who were applying for permission to participate and inasmuch as the Japanese government had not recognized Peking, these traders, as individual companies, had to accept the PRC policies regarding Taiwan, South Korea, South Vietnam, and U.S. imperialism. In other words, these companies had a choice between being friendly or being excluded from doing business.

Since these conditions were unacceptable to most major firms, a number of subsidiary "dummy" companies were established which would announce adherence to these policies, and hence could (on behalf of the parent) carry on trade with the PRC. Most of Japan's major companies shifted their positions, and they themselves appeared on the friendly list of fall 1972.[3] It is important to understand the background of this change, which flows from Nixon's trip and the normalization campaign of the new Prime Minister Tanaka.[4]

---

[2] See Tanishiki Hiroshi, *Nitchū bōeki annai* (Guide to Sino-Japanese trade) (Tokyo: Nihon Keizai Shimbunsha, 1964), pp. 1–44. A convenient summary sympathetic to the PRC may be found in Takahashi Shogorō and Tanaka Shūjirō, in the series *Gendai Chūgoku kyōshitsu* (Classroom Sino-Japanese trade), vol. 8 *Nitchū bōeki kyōshitsu* (Classroom Contemporary China) (Tokyo: Seinan Shuppansha, 1968), pp. 44–63, 155–228. See also Arai Takeo, "Satō seikenka no Nitchū kankei" (Sino-Japanese relations under the Sato government), *Sekai* (May 1971), pp. 59–82.

[3] *Chūgoku bōeki kankei kikan meibo ; Nitchū bōeki kankei kigyō dantai meibo* (List of organizations related to Chinese trade; list of enterprises related to Sino-Japanese trade; and list of groups [related to Sino-Japanese trade]) (Tokyo: Ajia Bōeki Tsūshinsha, October 1972), p. 2. (Hereafter, List for Chinese Trade.)

[4] Recent Japanese literature on the new problems and potentials of Sino-Japanese trade include: Okamoto Saburō, *Nitchū bōeki-ron* (Treatise on Sino-Japanese trade) (Tokyo: Tōyō Keizai Shimpōsha, 1971), 290 pp; Watanabe Tamao and Ogawa Kazuo, *Nitchū bōeki nyūmon* (Entrée to Sino-Japanese trade) (Tokyo: Nihon Keizai Shimbunsha, 1972), 311 pp; Nihon Kokusai Bōeki Sokushin Kyōkai, *Nitchū bōeki hikkei* (Essential guide for Sino-Japanese trade) (Tokyo: Nihon Kokusai Bōeki Sokushin Kyōkai, 1972), 203 pp; Suga Eiichi, Yamamoto Tsuyoshi, and Shiranishi Shinichirō, *Nitchū mondai* (The Sino-Japanese problem) (Tokyo: Sanseidō, 1971), pp. 247–330; "Nitchū shuno kaidan ni omou" (Thoughts about the talks between PRC and Japanese leaders), *Sekai*, no. 324 (November 1972), p. 69; Kimura Kihachiro, *Chūgoku wa Nihon o dō mite iru ka?* (How does the PRC view Japan?) (Tokyo: Zaisei Keizai kōhōsha, 1971), 282 pp; Hirai Hiroji, *Nitchū bōeki no kiso chishiki* (Basic information on Sino-Japanese trade) (Tokyo: Tabata Shoten, 1971), 315 pp; Hirai Hiroji, *Nitchū bōeki no jitsumu chishiki* (Practical information on Sino-Japanese trade) (Tokyo: Nippon Jitsugyo Shuppanoka, 1972), 238 pp.

As part of the peace treaty of 1952, Japan early recognized the Republic of China even though at that time the PRC was already firmly in control of all of China, except Taiwan. It appears that Japan attempted at the peace negotiations to limit her recognition by stipulating that it extended only to territory that Chiang then controlled. This move failed, however, and Japan became aligned with the United States line of "one China" in favor of Taiwan.[5] In exchange for this commitment, Japan has received several benefits (along with the disabilities): Taiwan's backing in the Security Council for UN membership; an easy reparations settlement ostensibly on behalf of all of China (apparently now a dead issue, since the PRC indicated on 29 September 1972 that it had no desire to assert reparations claims); and the opening of business opportunities with Taiwan, which has produced more trade ($923 million in 1971) than has business between Japan and the PRC ($901 million in 1971). In addition, of course, Japan has benefited from United States security arrangements, technological infusions, and membership in the "free world community."[6]

Unlike the United States, however, Japan did not refuse to trade with the PRC during the 1950s and 1960s, although she has observed the restrictions imposed by the Coordinating Committee (COCOM) of the NATO Consultative Group in Brussels, and has dealt only in nonstrategic materials. In fact, Japan has managed the improbable feat of becoming the second largest

---

[5] In connection with the peace treaty and the recognition of the Republic of China in 1952, Anthony Eden, former British prime minister, questioned American pressures on Japan as follows:

I thought that Japan's attitude towards the two Chinese governments should be entirely her own concern. Mr. Herbert Morison, who was then Foreign Secretary, and Mr. Dulles had, after discussion, agreed in June 1951 that neither would bring any pressure to bear on the Japanese one way or the other.

I shared these views, and held them all the more strongly for trade reasons. It was clear that if Japan was to have an outlet for her resurgent export trade, the Chinese mainland was the natural one. I thought it important that she should not be deprived of this by being led to adopt an inflexibly hostile attitude towards the Chinese People's Republic. If she did, she would regret it later, when her full sovereignty and independence had been restored by the ratification of the peace treaty.

When I discussed the matter with Mr. Acheson and Mr. Dulles, they explained to me the domestic political difficulties which the Administration faced on this issue. If Japan did not indicate that she intended to recognize Chiang Kai-shek's regime, the "China lobby" might be able to prevent ratification of the peace treaty by the Senate. I replied that I fully understood their position, but the view of His Majesty's Government had not changed.

Anthony Eden, *The Memories of Anthony Eden; Full Circle* (Cambridge, The Riverside Press, 1960), pp. 20–22.

[6] See Tōzai Bōeki Tsūshinsha, *1971 nenkan, Tōzai Bōeki* (1971 annual: a guide to East-West trade) (Tokyo: K.K. Tōzai Bōeki Tsūshinsha, 1971), 4: 29, for recent statements of the Chinese view of the arrangement between the United States and Japan.

trading partner of Taiwan and the leading trade partner of the PRC. This was achieved by applying her own special formula of "separation of politics and economics" *(seikei bunri)*, meaning that in political matters she recognized "one China" (Taiwan), but in economic matters she traded with both Taiwan and the PRC. This awkward posture has been maintained despite the fact that the PRC has asserted, just as forcefully and perhaps more successfully, the opposite formula of "inseparability of politics and economics" *(cheng-ching, pu-k'o-fen, seikei fukabun)*.

Still, as a credit to the practical flexibility of both governments, these political inconsistencies did not prevent trade. The ingenious vehicle that initially cut through the policy impasse was the "friendly firm." In this way certain leftist Japanese could do business with the PRC on a private basis, without Japan's officially abandoning its diplomatic ties with Taiwan and risking abrogation of the peace treaty. At the same time, Peking could claim the "inseparability of politics and economics" by requiring the friendly firms to accept the "four conditions" in opposition to their own government's foreign policy as a requirement for doing business.

In domestic Japanese politics, of course, the friendly firms, populated by members of the opposition Japan Socialist Party or the Clean Government Party (Kōmeitō), proved to be a source of difficulty for Sato. When larger companies first began to use dummy friendly firms and later began to accept friendly firm status directly (largely after the Nixon trip was announced), many Liberal Democratic Party (hereafter LDP) members joined a cross-party group seeking normalization of relations with the PRC. Because he was not welcome in Peking, Sato was unable either to resist or to yield. In this respect one must concede the success of the PRC's policy of *seikei fukabun,* which culminated in Sato's resignation in July 1972 and Tanaka's visit to Peking in September.

With this glimpse of the political background, we now review the characteristics of recent Sino-Japanese trade and the major events in its growth during the past two decades (1952–73). Thereafter, we take up the main subject of this paper—the specific structural, procedural, and legal practices[7] by which

---

[7] The latest forms on Sino-Japanese trade practices are found in: Nihon Bōeki Shinkōkai (JETRO, ed.) *Nitchū bōeki techo-Chūgoku ichiba e no approach* (Handbook on Japanese-Chinese trade, an approach to the Chinese market) (Tokyo: Nihon Bōeki Shinkōkai, 1971); English translation: JETRO, ed., *How to Approach the China Market* (Tokyo: Press Int'l, 1972), 277 pp. (Hereafter JETRO, *Handbook.*) For a pro-China presentation see Takahashi and Tanaka, *Nitchū bōeki kyōshitsu.* For a variety of actual forms used in the Sino-Japanese trade with versions in both Chinese and Japanese on opposite pages, see Sumida Teruo, *Chūgoku gendai shogyō tsūshinbun* (Forms for current Chinese commercial correspondence) (Tokyo: Daian, 1964; reprinted 1969). Some of the forms are now outdated.

trade has been transacted, and their relevance to the future after Sino-Japanese relations are normalized pursuant to the Chou-Tanaka communique.

II. THE VOLUME OF SINO-JAPANESE TRADE

Because some people may still think of China as a land of 800 million potential customers, it is necessary at the outset to place the volume of the PRC's foreign trade into proper perspective.[8] Japanese trade with Taiwan has always been, up through 1972, somewhat greater than Japanese trade with the PRC, and her share of the PRC trade (20 percent of China's total trade) has been only about 2 percent of her total trade and only 5 percent of Japan's trade with the United States. Indeed, it was not until 1969 that the Japan-PRC trade reached the prewar high ($630 million) of 1939.

From 1945 to 1949 and also from 1949 to 1952, Sino-Japanese trade was severely limited by allied occupation policies. From the conclusion of the peace treaty in 1952 until 1958, trade with the PRC grew to modest amounts, with a peak $150,986,000 in 1956. During this period the balance was in favor of China, reflecting her preference for leaning toward the Soviet Union and the severe limitations placed in 1952 on trade with the Communist bloc by Western nations through COCOM. During the Korean War a special China Committee (CHINCOM) was established by the same fifteen nations, which set up tighter restrictions on exports to mainland China than to the Soviet Union and Eastern European countries. These committees established lists that specified the *minimum* restrictions on exports to the Communist bloc.[9]

---

[8] JETRO predicted $300 million for United States-PRC trade in 1975. *Nihon keizai shimbun* (4 August 1972), p. 9. Earlier, Ishikawa Shigeru, a Japanese economist at Hitotsubashi University, in an article "Chūgoku keizai no chōki tembō" (Long-term projection of the Chinese economy), *Keizai kenkyū* 21 (July 1970): 140 projected a 6.2 percent annual growth in the PRC's GNP to 1980. Professor Robert F. Dernberger projected a 7.7 percent annual growth to 1980, with foreign trade being about 4 percent of the GNP. "Prospects for Trade Between China and the United States," in A. Eckstein, ed., *China Trade Prospects and U.S. Policy* (New York: Praeger, 1971), p. 185. More specifically, a balanced United States-Chinese trade is projected at about $250 million annually by 1980, or perhaps $650 million, if credits or three-way balancing becomes possible. But because of the thaw in the interim these figures are too pessimistic. For PRC trade in general see Feng-Hwa Mah, *The Foreign Trade of Mainland China* (New York: Aldine, 1971).

[9] See Ajia Seikei Kenkyū Gakkai, ed., *Chūgoku seiji keizai sōran, 1968 nenkan* (Survey of Chinese politics and economics, 1968 annual) (Tokyo: Shinkigensha, 1968), pp. 626–40; also see JETRO, *Handbook,* p. 137, and generally John R. Garson, "The American Embargo Against China," in A. Eckstein, ed., *China Trade Prospects,* p. 3. *Asahi shimbun* (12 September 1972) reports an agreement in Paris to relax 50 out of the remaining 167 items on the COCOM list.

While Japan has subscribed to them, in fact both the United States and Japan have applied, through their internal regulations, an even more restrictive trade policy.[10] Since the end of the Korean War, there has been some effort (usually initiated by the European members) to reduce these restrictions by occasional revisions of the lists and redefining of what products are "strategic."[11] One significant result was the abolition of the CHINCOM list in 1957.

The effect of the postwar shifts in Japanese trade can be shown by the following figures for percentage of Japanese imports from China and the United States during the mid 1950s:[12]

Item		*1934–36*	*1950*	*1951*	*1955*	*1956*
Iron Ore	China	34.0	18.7	1.3	1.1	0.1
	U.S.A.	...	...	...	...	...
Coal	China	64.4	58.8	1.1	2.9	15.1
	U.S.A.	...	13.9	70.9	85.5	80.1
Soybeans	China	71.3	56.5	2.6	27.4	23.1
	U.S.A.	...	43.5	97.3	56.9	74.7
Salt	China	38.6	8.6	0.2	26.1	37.1
	U.S.A.	...	2.8	10.6	4.9	2.3

Many have argued that this has placed severe burdens on Japan because of the higher prices of U.S. materials. For example, in 1956 the United States charged $26.50 for a ton of coal, while the PRC charged $12.20.[13]

In the 1950s about 80 percent of Chinese trade was with the Soviet bloc. The Sino-Soviet split reversed this pattern, so that 80 percent of her trade was with noncommunist countries in the 1960s. As one consequence Japan became China's single most important trading partner, despite the basic political differences.

After 1965 the comparative importance of Japanese trade to China and of Chinese trade to Japan can be seen as follows:

---

[10] See *Chūgoku seiji keizai sōran 1968 nenkan,* p. 636, for Japanese COCOM participation. Also see JETRO, *Handbook,* p. 137 for the Japanese internal restrictions including a special prior approval system applicable only to imports from China (p. 143). This system was finally lifted in August 1971.

See John R. Garson, "The American Trade Embargo Against China," in A. Eckstein, ed., *China Trade Prospects,* p. 396 for an excellent general treatment of COCOM and CHINCOM in the United States-China context.

[11] Allen I. Saeks, "East-West Trade: Time for a Reappraisal," *A.B.A.J.* 55 (1969): 1041.

[12] See George P. Jan, "Japan's Trade with Communist China," *Asian Survey* 9 (1969): 900, 904.

[13] *Ibid.* However, one must surely add to Japan's pre-World War II purchase price the huge cost of maintaining its military presence in China.

Unit: $1,000

Year	Japan to PRC	PRC to Japan	Total
1965	245,036	224,705	469,741
1966	315,150	306,237	621,387
1967	288,294	269,439	557,733
1968	325,438	224,185	549,623
1969	390,803	234,540	625,343
1970	568,878	253,818	822,696
1971	578,188	323,172	901,360
1972	608,921	491,115	1,100,036

SOURCE: *Nichu Boeki Tokei Kiho* (JETRO, 1973), pp. 155–56.

NOTE: 1975 figures are: 2,260,000; 1,530,000; 3,790,000. *Japan Econ. Journal*, 17 February 1976.

Despite the rapid rate of growth in the post-1965 Sino-Japanese trade, the volume is still modest because of China's policy of planned trade. Difficulties in the product composition of the trade have also arisen from recent fundamental changes in the basic industrial goals and structures of both Japan and China, as well as in the general world context. It is becoming more and more convenient for Japan to trade with the advanced Western countries (particularly the United States) and increasingly more difficult to take the products that China has to offer, except for oil and coal, in exchange for the industrial items that China desires. Canada, Italy, and West Germany have experienced similar problems.

The major Japanese export items to China have been fiber goods, chemicals (particularly fertilizer), steel, and machinery. In recent years steel products and chemical fertilizer have remained ranking Japanese export items, while fiber goods have decreased as China has begun to produce more such products domestically. Machinery exports were dampened by Japanese government support of the so-called Yoshida letter which denied long-term Japanese Export-Import Bank financing, although it appears that this impediment has been largely overcome by adjustments made in 1972 (see below).

In exchange for Japanese goods the PRC has been offering foods (soy beans, shrimp, jellyfish, etc.) and raw silk (*kenchū,* pongee). A serious imbalance in Japan's favor has arisen, however, from the fact that Japan is now self-sufficient in rice, and that despite a strong Japanese demand China has not been willing until recently to discuss exporting iron ore, oil, or coking coal, items needed for her own industrial development. In addition, 1972 marks the first time Japan has been willing to reconsider the ban on purchase of Chinese beef resulting from inspection problems regarding hoof-and-mouth disease.[14] Furthermore, advances in bulk shipping and port facilities have reduced the

---

[14] See *Kaidan yōroku* (Minutes Memo), 15 May 1969, in *1970 Shin Chūgoku nenkan* (Annual of New China), p. 345.

cost of distant hauls to the point where some Japanese buyers question the advantage of looking to the prewar Chinese sources for the major products needed by Japan. This is especially true since long-term contracting with the West seems more secure than with the PRC. Some progress may be expected, however, given the new climate developed since 1972.

The current trends are shown by the memorandum trade (hereafter MT trade) agreement signed in 1972, which was the last MT trade program as the PRC and Japan moved toward a government-to-government trading arrangement.[15] This agreement called for a two-way exchange of $120 million. Japan exported chemical fertilizers, special steel, ordinary steel, raw material for the chemical industry, machinery (including farm implements), and other items; China was to export soy beans, other beans, salt, eggs, noodles, corn, and other items.

In summary, Chinese trading policy, together with changes in both the Chinese and the Japanese industrial plans and shifts in the commercial markets of the West, have seriously called into question the simple economic complementarity, long assumed, between Japanese manufactured goods and Chinese raw materials. This difficulty may be solved in some degree by Chinese policy changes in the future, e.g., making oil, iron, and coal available to Japan. Still, the PRC is, understandably, practicing protectionism in pursuit of economic self-sufficiency and industrial development. This protectionism has held the PRC's total trade volume down to an annual average of four to five billion dollars for the past decade or more, a figure that is now increasing rapidly. At the same time, to balance some of Japan's foreign policies, the PRC has exercised political censorship over Japanese participants in the China trade to a degree not found anywhere else in the world. All of these factors have placed Sino-Japanese trade under such severe strains that it is remarkable that the volume of trade has been as large as it has been.

III. GROWTH OF THE FRAMEWORK OF SINO-JAPANESE TRADE

Great Britain dominated Chinese trade until after 1900, but by the 1920s Japan had displaced Great Britain as China's largest trading partner. With the occupation of parts of China in the 1930s, when Japan had as many as a million military men stationed there plus over a million civilians and dependents, China became Japan's leading trading partner, but on a colonial basis. Geographical proximity, economic factors, cultural and racial affinity, and Japanese aggressiveness thus led to the gradual growth of Sino-Japanese trade up to the end of World War II.

In the 1945–52 period Sino-Japanese trade was minimal because of the near collapse of the Japanese economy at the end of the war, and the loss of

---

[15] *Japan Times*, 2 November 1972.

trade autonomy to the Supreme Commander of the Allied Powers (SCAP).[16] Upon signing the San Francisco peace treaty in 1952, however, Japan regained control over her external trade. Nevertheless, her trade autonomy with respect to the PRC was still limited by her recognition of Taiwan and the attendant political tensions in her dealings with the PRC.

Despite these obstacles, during the 1950s several Japanese groups and the China Council for Promotion of International Trade (hereafter CCPIT) (on the Chinese side) represented by Nan Han-chen developed a modest trade on a semiprivate basis through four separate Chinese-Japanese trade agreements *(chu-nichi boeki kyotei)*, signed on 1 June 1952, 29 October 1953, 4 May 1955, and 5 March 1958 respectively.[17] The PRC (apparently with the support of the Japanese signers, which included several members of the incumbent LDP) wished to gradually upgrade the status of this arrangement and give it an official coloring. Consequently, the parties negotiated Article 11 in the agreement of 5 March 1958, which provided that each side will establish a private trade office in the other party's territory. These trade offices could use a secret code and fly the national flag over the buildings housing the respective offices, as well as exercise other privileges.

On returning home the Japanese signators found that the Ikeda government took the position that since Taiwan was recognized as the Chinese government, Japan could not protect the flag of the PRC on Japanese territory. On 2 May 1958 the government was forced to act in accordance with this policy during the famous Nagasaki flag incident, when a Japanese pulled down a PRC flag on display in a Nagasaki department store at a stamp collection exhibition sponsored by the Japan-China Friendship Association (Nitchu Yuko Kyokai). The Japanese was arrested, but he was given only a minor fine (500 yen) on the grounds that he had not violated the Japanese Criminal Code, Article 92, providing for punishment of persons who damage national flags or other national emblems.[18] In other words, the police's position was that the PRC

---

[16] We have relied on the following for a summary of the postwar growth of Sino-Japanese trade: JETRO, *Handbook,* pp. 57–89, and Takahashi and Tanaka, *Kyōshitsu,* pp. 44–63.

[17] The most convenient Japanese-language collection of primary documents on the early development of Sino-Japanese trade (1945–66) is: Nitchū Bōeki Sokushin Giin Remmei, *Nitchū kankei shiryō* (Collection of materials on Sino-Japanese relations) (Tokyo, 1967), which is not for general distribution. We were fortunate to be able to use this convenient compilation, hereafter cited as *NKS.* Unless otherwise cited, texts of Sino-Japanese trade agreements, joint communiques, and the like are from this source.

[18] Criminal Code Art. 92 (Damage or Destruction of Foreign Flag, etc.): "A person who, for the purpose of insulting a foreign state, damages, destroys, removes or defiles the national flag or other national emblem of that state shall be punished with imprisonment at forced labor for not more than two years or a fine of not more than two hundred yen but the crime shall be dealt with only on the request of the government of such state."

flag was simply private property and not entitled to protection under Article 92 because the Peking government had not been recognized by the Japanese government. This was entirely unacceptable to the PRC and caused a dramatic four-year break in trade relations with Japan.

Actually the 1958–62 period was not an entire trade vacuum because considerable trade continued through Hong Kong, and also because leftist Sino-Japanese "friendship groups," including elements from the Socialist Party, Communist Party, and Trade Union representatives, began visiting China soon after 1958. Some "consideration commodity transactions" *(hairyo busshi torihiki,* hereafter HBT*)* were arranged after Premier Chou En-lai enunciated his "three political principles" (1958) and "three trading principles" (1960) for trade on a "people-to-people basis." These principles together with the addition of four conditions in 1970 (see below)[19] became the virtual constitution for Sino-Japanese trade after 1960.

The "three political principles" for Sino-Japanese relations enunciated by Chou En-lai as early as 11 June 1958 were as follows.[20]

1. The Japanese should not regard China as an enemy.

2. The Japanese government should not follow the United States in constructing the two-China plot.

3. The Japanese government should not obstruct developments in the direction of normalizing Sino-Japanese relations.

These political principles were enunciated again in the *Peking Review*[21] in 1960 at the beginning of the HBT trade. Just before this, at a meeting on 27 August 1960 with Executive Director Suzuki Kazuo of the Japan-China Trade Promotion Association (Nitchu Boeki Sokushin-Kai), Chou En-lai laid down the "three principles of Japanese trade," which provided for three channels through which to develop Sino-Japanese trade:[22]

1. There should be agreements concluded by the governments covering trade (Liao-Takasaki trade grew out of this, hereafter LT trade).

2. Trade by private contract (the friendly firm trade grew out of this).

3. Trade by special consideration in case of special difficulties in the small and medium industries especially to benefit Sōhyo (Japanese Labor Union Federation) and Chinese labor. (This was the so-called HBT Trade.)

---

[19] JETRO, *Handbook,* p. 84.

[20] This is our translation; see text, *NKS,* p. 493. Also see the conditions reasserted in the joint communique after conclusion of the MT negotiations March 1971, *Tōzai bōeki yōran,* pp. 53, 55.

[21] *Peking Review,* no. 33 (14 September 1960), pp. 25–26.

[22] Our translation; see text, *NKS,* pp. 196, 493.

The timing of Chou En-lai's enunciation of the three principles of Japanese trade goes a long way toward explaining the rationale underlying them. At this time the Sino-Soviet breach was causing China to look to the noncommunist world for goods required by its economic plans. Consequently, the continuation of the 1958 rupture in Sino-Japanese trade became quite inconvenient.

The HBT trade was only of interim importance. It started in 1959 when members of the Socialist Party and Sōhyo visited China and beseeched the Chinese government to assist Japanese laborers and small merchants in obtaining items needed for "traditional" Chinese culture-related businesses, such as Chinese medical herbs and cooking materials.[23] This resulted in an agreement between Sōhyo and the Chinese labor group for direct individual importations. This trade was limited, and gradually faded out with the growth of LT and friendly firm trade.

Friendly firm trade began in late 1960 and early 1961. This trade was based on the second of Chou En-lai's three principles for Sino-Japanese trade which provided for transactions with private companies designated as "friendly firms" by the Chinese. Immediately, this trade was surprisingly brisk, and reached $47 million in 1961 and $84 million in 1962, with more than 80 Japanese friendly firms participating in the Autumn Canton Fair of 1962.

Despite these favorable developments, by 1962 Chou En-lai began to realize the limitations of the HBT and friendly firm trades. The HBT trade was always small. The friendly firm trade was populated on the Japanese side by insubstantial companies or "dummy companies" acting for mainline Japanese firms. In addition, this trade was capable of handling only spot transactions and lacked the financing, continuity, and planning necessary to insure a steady flow of the basic material that China needed. To fill this gap Chou En-lai apparently felt that a more structured, quasi-official trade agreement should be worked out to supply the substance and continuity lacking in the other forms of trade.

It was in this context that the former Minister of International Trade and Industry (hereafter MITI), Takasaki Tatsunosuke (LDP), visited Peking in November 1962 and concluded, on a semigovernmental basis, a five-year agreement signed by Takasaki and Liao Ch'eng-chih.[24] The agreement called for an annual average of £36 million of trade both ways for the years 1963 through 1967. This Liao-Takasaki Memorandum (Oboegaki) was imple-

---

[23] NKS, p. 196 for Sōhyo's Iwai Akira's report. An example of this kind of trade is the Japanese importation of sweet chestnuts, a favorite traditional sweet of children. Even today, the allocation of this item is based on the favors and loyalties developed out of HBT trade.

[24] Japanese text: Asahi shimbun, 10 November 1962.

mented by an annual "Detailed Agreement" *(Torikime jiko)* specifying the exact quantities of specific products and other terms.[25]

In no sense, however, was the LT trade to replace the friendly firm trade. Instead they became known as the "two wheels on the same cart." Indeed, the volume of friendly firm trade exceeded the volume of LT trade. As early as 27 December 1962 the Japan-China Friendship Association and the CCPIT signed an agreement[26] *(Giteisho)* calling for further trade and for a Japanese trade fair in Peking in 1963 and an exchange Chinese fair in Tokyo and Osaka in 1964. The friendly firm organizations sponsored additional Japanese fairs in Peking and Shanghai in 1965 and 1968, and Chinese trade fairs in Nagoya and Kita-Kyushu in 1966.

On the occasion of opening the Japanese fair in Peking, the LT trade office representatives (Okazaki and Matsumura) agreed with Liao on 19 April 1964 to try again for an exchange of offices in the two countries. These were actually opened in February 1965, symbolizing a significant advance in Sino-Japanese trade relations after the embarrassing rupture in 1958 over similar attempts to establish offices and to resolve the status of the PRC flag and personnel in Japan. So, in fact if not in form, the LT trade has had some official color since 1965.

In the process of negotiating the first contracts under the LT Agreement, arrangements were made for a Japanese company (Kurashiki) to sell a vinylon plant to China on five-year credit terms from the Japanese Export-Import Bank. Credit up to two years was also allowed in other instances. The Japanese government raised objections, but nevertheless approved these initial transactions with the understanding that they should not be regarded as precedents. The following year's trade (1964) included two more large transactions which were to be financed by the Export-Import Bank (a cargo ship by Hitachi Zosen, and another vinylon plant by Nichibo).

In the interim the Taiwan government had strenuously objected to the extension of governmental credit to the PRC, even to the point of threatening to break off all relations with Japan. To save the situation Prime Minister Ikeda had sent former Prime Minister Yoshida to Taiwan in February 1964 to celebrate Chiang Kai-shek's birthday. Upon his return Yoshida wrote a letter 30 May 1964 to Chang Chun, the secretary-general of the Presidential Office, which has been interpreted by some as binding Japan not to extend further Export-Import Bank credit to the PRC.[27]

---

[25] Japanese texts: *NKS*, pp. 199, 205, 214, 222, 229.

[26] *NKS*, p. 202.

[27] See Okamoto Saburo, *Nitchū bōeki-ron* (Sino-Japanese trade views), pp. 193–205 for the most detailed treatment of the Yoshida letter; JETRO, *Handbook*, p. 74 has a convenient summary. In English see "Communist China Cancels Big Contracts due to the Yoshida Letter," *Foreign Trade News*, no. 165 (1965), p. 11.

Perhaps no point raised more political and legal questions inside Japan. Even an important LDP member, Miki Takeo, then minister of foreign affairs, opined in 1965 that the Yoshida letter was no more than a private letter and not binding on the government. The legal issues are difficult to resolve because the text of the letter has never been publicly disclosed. The newspaper *Mainichi,* on 5 August 1965, revealed the background and a summary of the whole letter and published the purported exact text of the portion regarding Export-Import Bank credit:[28]

1. "We shall proceed to study along the lines of your position the use of a purely private base for credit for plant exports to the PRC."

2. "We have no intention of approving the export of the Nichibo Vinylon Plant to the PRC during this year (1964)."

The relationship between the letter's first statement to "study" purely private financing and the second specific assurance that the particular Nichibo plant would not be financed has led some to say that credit might still be granted in the future on a case by case basis. Others have focused on the phrase "during this year" and have suggested that credit might be available by 1965. Certainly as a legal matter it seems clear enough that under Japanese law such a letter could not be binding on the Japanese government; the most it could be is a personal commitment by Prime Minister Ikeda. In any case, Prime Minister Ikeda was soon replaced by Sato who, honoring the Yoshida letter, stopped Export-Import Bank credit on the sale of whole plants to the PRC. In 1971 the Sato government backed off from its prior position that the Yoshida letter was a commitment by his government, to the position that Japan will consider Export-Import Bank credit in each individual application that may come up. This issue was finally resolved after the Chou-Tanaka communique when Japan began to grant medium-term credits to the PRC (see below).

The volume of trade in 1966 and 1967 was not quite up to expectations, probably reflecting the Chinese reactions to the Yoshida letter, as well as the disruption from the incipient Cultural Revolution.[29] Nevertheless, over the five-year period LT trade was worth roughly $730 million. It also served as a channel for the exchange of news correspondents.

The LT trade agreement expired in 1967 and thereafter several annual memorandum agreements were negotiated, and the parties renamed their respective offices as the memorandum (MT) trade offices. Evident in the annual negotiations in the MT trade between 1967 and 1972 was the intensified political propaganda against Japanese militarism and the Sato government, and the insistence that assertions hostile to the Sato policy be included in the

[28] See *NKS,* p. 477 for a convenient reprint from which we made this translation.
[29] See Takahashi and Tanaka, *Kyōshitsu,* p. 176 for a pro-Chinese critique.

joint communication issued at the conclusion of negotiations.[30] The Japanese had become inured to accepting these tactics, and the MT trade continued at the same modest annual level of about $70 million. As a percentage of the total Sino-Japanese trade, however, it has dropped from about half in 1963 to 8.5 percent by 1970 and up to 10 percent in 1971.[31]

The role of politics in trade loomed larger after Chou En-lai introduced his four conditions of Sino-Japanese trade on 19 April 1970. This policy sought to bar those firms that were involved in American militarism in Vietnam or were doing business with Taiwan or Korea; it applied both to friendly firm transactions and to MT trade. Contracts that were concluded would be canceled if a violation of any of the four principles was later discovered. At the 1971 MT negotiations the Chinese required a Japanese reaffirmation of the four conditions.

The political importance of Taiwan can be seen from a statement made by Chou En-lai saying that China would trade with firms previously connected with the Japan-Taiwan Cooperation Committee (Nikka Kyoryoku Iinkai), if these firms would withdraw from this organization and publicly acknowlege their past errors. This statement caused some anxiety in the Japanese business world, and in mid-1971 several important companies, makers as well as traders, including Hitachi Electric, Nippon Steel, Toyota Auto, and others, absented themselves from the Japan-Taiwan Cooperation Committee, apparently in order to avoid violations of the four conditions.[32]

---

[30] See Shirai Hisaya, "Chūgoku ni kuzushita Mitsui Mitsubishi no uchimaku" (The inside story of Mitsui's and Mitsubishi's knuckling under to the PRC), *Zaikai* (15 July 1972), p. 96. JETRO, *Handbook*, p. 121 seems misleading in pointing out that the MT trade is free from obligations of the three trade principles.

[31] JETRO, *Handbook*, p. 122 shows the volume of both trades, 1963–70.

[32] The Japanese newspapers have carried frequent articles announcing that certain important firms have decided to avoid violating the four conditions. For example, the newspaper *Nikkei*, 28 April 1971, reported that Hitachi, Ltd., had decided not to invest further in Taiwan to avoid jeopardizing its chances in the PRC market; *Asahi shimbun*, 16 July 1971, reported Toyota Motors had decided not to participate in the Japanese-Korean Cooperation Committee to avoid violation of the "four conditions;" *Asahi shimbun*, 17 July 1971, reported that Japan's largest steel company's president, Inayama, had decided not to participate in the Taiwan and Korean Cooperation Committees, and the next day the same newspaper reported that the firm's affiliate, Daido Seiko, was sending its sales manager to the PRC; *Nikkei*, 23 April 1971, reported that Toray's (textiles) officers must have affirmed the four conditions in order to take the PRC trip. On the other hand, Isuzu Motors has decided to trade with Taiwan (*Nikkei*, 12 January 1971), and Japan Airlines was boycotted by the PRC (*Asahi shimbun*, 3 April 1971) (the boycott was lifted in August 1971). An interesting article appeared in the *Nikkei*, 21 July 1971, likening the PRC's oath against Taiwan, Korea, and the United States to the seventeenth-century *fumie* ordeal for Christians whereby they were forced to trample on a picture of Christ. The article was entitled "Atama itai Nikka Nichihan no fumie" (Headaches of "picture trampling" in Japanese-Taiwan and Japanese-Korean relations).

The Taiwan issue gradually became less important as the entire Japanese commercial and industrial community shifted toward compliance with PRC demands. In 1972 the biggest hold-outs, Mitsubishi Trading Company and Mitsui & Co., joined the friendly firms.[33] It appears that individual firms began to realize, contrary to the Sato cabinet's policy, that business and politics were not separate after all.

The replacement of Sato by Tanaka in mid-1972 prepared the way for the establishment of normal diplomatic relations and at the same time ushered in a new era of officially recognized trade channels. In October 1972 the two sides announced that the 1973 memorandum would be the last, and would thereafter be replaced by government to government arrangements. In March 1973 the "friendly firm" idea lost much of it formal meaning because since then all Japanese firms have been regarded as friendly, provided they have passed the screening to go to the Canton fair.

IV. THE STRUCTURE OF SINO-JAPANESE TRADE

As noted, the channels of Sino-Japanese trade grew into three kinds of trade based on Chou En-lai's "three trade principles" enunciated during discussions with Suzuki Kazuo on 27 August 1960. At the policy level this strategy reflected the practical penchant of Chou En-lai for pursuing concrete operational objectives, despite the existence of sharp political differences.[34] During the 1960s this approach produced a stormy but persisting semi-governmental LT or MT trade and a briskly growing nongovernmental friendly firm trade. (The HBT trade had soon dwindled to little significance.) We shall review below the organization of these two types of trade as they existed for doing business in 1972.[35]

A. The Memorandum Trade

Again, we emphasize that the MT trade operated at a level of only about $90 million annually, against a 1971 total of $901 million of over-all Sino-Japanese trade. The "two wheels of the Sino-Japanese trade cart" have developed quite disproportionately. However, the MT trade had characteristics that made it more important than its volume might indicate. First, because of the exchange of trade offices and the participation of LDP members, the MT trade has had an official coloring presumably pleasing to the PRC.

---

[33] See *Tōzai bōeki yōran,* p. 51.

[34] See Thomas W. Robinson, "Chou En-lai's Political Style: Comparisons with Mao Tse-tung and Lin Piao," *Asian Survey* 10 (December 1970): 1101.

[35] Most information on the organization of the MT and friendly firm trade has been gleaned by interviews and office visits or from personal experience, if not otherwise indicated in the notes below.

Also, permission to station journalists at these offices has greatly facilitated the gathering and dissemination of information.[36] Most significant of all is the allocation of government funds by MITI to JETRO (Japan Export Trade Organization) of roughly $180,000 annually which pays all expenses, including personnel and maintenance of the Japanese MT trade offices *(Nippon oboegaki boeki jimusho)*. The office was originally conceived in Japan as a sort of commercial attaché to be encompassed within the foreign service, if and when diplomatic relations are resumed. In fact, the staff consists mainly of government officials who have resigned (but with reserved rights to return) from MITI, the Ministry of Finance, or other government offices. In a sense, then, the MT trade approximates Chou En-lai's first principle which called for a trade agreement between the two governments.

Charts 1 and 2 show the leading personnel involved as of 1972 on both sides of the PRC-Japanese trade organization.[37]

The organizations responsible for the MT trade were renamed during the Cultural Revolution. The Japan office was called the Japan Sino-Japanese Memorandum Trade Office (Zaidan Hojin Nihon Nitchu Oboegaki Boeki Jimusho) headed by Okazaki Kaheita, former president of All-Nippon Airlines and at one time an official in the Bank of Japan and in the Shanghai Japanese Consulate. This office, as successor of the original LT trade offices, had a Tokyo headquarters and a liaison office in Peking in accordance with the agreement between Takasaki and Liao signed 18 April 1964. The Tokyo office had a small staff of three or four officers and as many clerks between 1967 and 1972.

Similarly, the Chinese office is called the China-Japan Memorandum Trade Office (Chung-Jih pei-wang-lu mao-yi pan-shih-ch'u), which in turn has a Tokyo liaison office as successor to the prior Liao office and is headed by Liu Hsi-wen. In 1972 the staff was increased to the pre-Cultural Revolution level of about seven officers.[38] The Tokyo and Peking offices are the parties to the basic annual agreements establishing the over-all scope of MT trade for that year.

On the Japanese side a rather complex organization had grown up to handle the transactions for each commodity. First, all makers of a certain commodity interested in the China trade form an association, such as the Sino-Japanese Commercial Fertilizer Association or the Special Steel Export Council.[39]

---

[36] *NKS*, p. 211.

[37] For a list of officials involved in PRC-Japanese relations see *Asahi shimbun*, 24 August 1972; for general PRC organization, see *Chūgoku yōran* (Survey of China) (Tokyo: Jiji Tsūshinsha, 1972), p. 31.

[38] *Asahi shimbun*, 20 June 1972.

[39] See *List for Chinese Trade* for a complete listing of Japanese makers' associations and the Chinese state corporations as of October 1972. See also the following section.

CHART 1

PRC AGENCIES CONCERNED WITH JAPANESE TRADE

(1972)

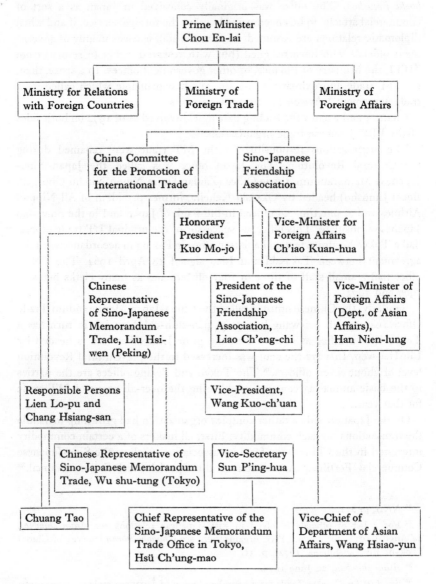

CHART 2

JAPANESE AGENCIES CONCERNED WITH PRC RELATIONS

(1972)

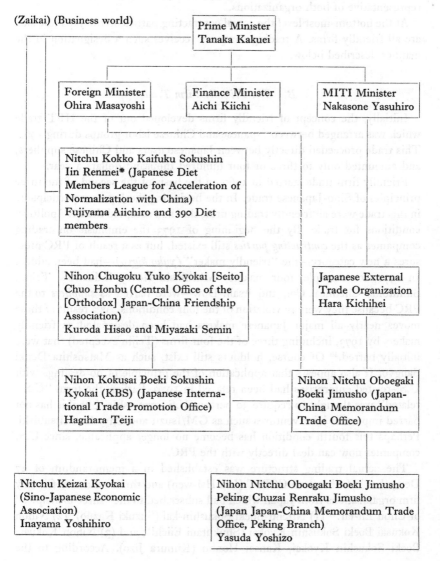

(Zaikai) (Business world)

Prime Minister
Tanaka Kakuei

Foreign Minister
Ohira Masayoshi

Finance Minister
Aichi Kiichi

MITI Minister
Nakasone Yasuhiro

Nitchu Kokko Kaifuku Sokushin
Iin Renmei* (Japanese Diet
Members League for Acceleration of
Normalization with China)
Fujiyama Aiichiro and 390 Diet
members

Nihon Chugoku Yuko Kyokai [Seito]
Chuo Honbu (Central Office of the
[Orthodox] Japan-China Friendship
Association)
Kuroda Hisao and Miyazaki Semin

Japanese External
Trade Organization
Hara Kichihei

Nihon Kokusai Boeki Sokushin
Kyokai (KBS) (Japanese Interna-
tional Trade Promotion Office)
Hagihara Teiji

Nihon Nitchu Oboegaki
Boeki Jimusho (Japan-
China Memorandum
Trade Office)

Nitchu Keizai Kyokai
(Sino-Japanese Economic
Association)
Inayama Yoshihiro

Nihon Nitchu Oboegaki Boeki Jimusho
Peking Chuzai Renraku Jimusho
(Japan Japan-China Memorandum Trade
Office, Peking Branch)
Yasuda Yoshizo

---

* Changed its name in 1973 to Nitchu Yuko Giin Renmei (Members League for
Japan-China Friendly Relations).

These groups of makers negotiate price and quantity with the Chinese side, and in turn allocate quotas to members of the groups. Finally, these associations form a federation called the Sino-Japanese Consolidated Trade Liaison Council (Nitchu Sogo Boeki Renraku Kyogikai). The council's offices are in the same building as the MT office, and Okazaki Kaheita is the chief representative of both organizations.

At the bottom-most level the actual contracting parties on the Japanese side are all friendly firms. A trading company receives such a designation in the manner described below.

B. The Friendly Firm Trade

Initially, the concept of friendly firms developed out of the HBT trade which was arranged between Japanese and Chinese labor groups during 1962. This trade proceeded directly between Japanese users and Chinese suppliers, and amounted only to three or four hundred thousand dollars a year.

Friendly firm trade started in 1960 on the basis of the second of the three principles of Sino-Japanese trade. In the beginning the Japanese participants in this trade were all friendly trading firms that had accepted the PRC political conditions for trade. By the beginning of 1973 the emphasis on trading companies as the *contracting parties* still existed, but as a result of PRC pressures a new category—the "friendly maker" *(yuko kigyo)*—had been added. In 1971, for example, four makers—Mitsubishi Heavy Industries, Teijin, Sumitomo Chemical Co., and Asahi-Dow—were barred as *suppliers* to the PRC because they were in violation of the four conditions. As a result of these moves nearly all major Japanese makers had been designated as friendly makers by 1973, including three of the four firms (Teijin excepted) that were initially barred.[40] Of course, holdouts still exist, such as Matsushita Denki Sangyo. It also appears that application of the principle of no dealings with U.S.-related enterprises had been relaxed in 1970. Earlier, the term "U.S.-related" was thought to require 30 percent U.S. ownership, but this has not barred important joint ventures such as GM/Isuzu and Chrysler/Mitsubishi. Perhaps this fourth condition has become no longer applicable, since U.S. companies now can deal directly with the PRC.

The actual trading structure was established in a memorandum of 27 December 1962 between CCPIT (Liu Hsi-wen) and three voluntary friendly firm organizations from Japan which had subscribed to the "three principles" of Chou En-lai:[41] (1) Nitchu Boeki Sokushin-kai (Suzuki Kazuo); (2) Nihon Kokusai Boeki Sokushin Kyokai (Shukutani Eiichi); and (3) Nihon Kokusai Boeki Sokushin Kyokai, Kansai Honbu (Kimura Jizo). According to the

---

[40] See *Asahi shimbun* 8 August 1972 for a recent tally of friendly makers.
[41] *Tōzai bōeki yōran*, p. 226.

memorandum, all firms wishing to engage in trade with the PRC must apply for membership in one of these organizations. The organization then investigates the applicant's background and certifies it to CCPIT. Upon receiving such nominations, the Chinese designate the trader as a friendly firm.

Without such a designation it would be impossible for a firm to trade with China. Because travel and advertising facilities were lacking, the only way for a Japanese to do business with China before 1973 was at the semi-annual Canton trade fairs. Only friendly firms were invited from Japan to the fairs, and only friendly firms could make the necessary arrangements for "visas," transportation, and accommodations in Canton.

Before 1973 there actually were two major types of friendly firms. First, there were many minor trading firms (*shosha* means "trading firm" and does not include manufacturing companies). Many of these were short of capital and trading know-how, but were leftist on the domestic political spectrum and willing to support the PRC foreign policy. The second group of friendly firms were called "dummy companies." They were subsidiaries of major companies and were set up for the specific purpose of enabling the parent to trade with the PRC without having to accept the trade principles announced by the Chinese. These dummies had the support and know-how of the parent companies, although they themselves were small and were separate legal entities.

The major dummy companies in turn may be divided into five groups.

Group 1. *Parent*   *Dummy*

         Mitsui Bussan   Daiichi Tsūshō

         Kanematsu Gōshō   Nikka Bōeki

Dummy corporations of this group could not function at all, because they got into trouble in China, with the result that some employees were detained (and later released). The details of what happened are not available.

Group 2. *Parent*   *Dummy*

         Mitsui Bussan   Keimei Kōeki

         Mitsubishi Shōji   Meiwa Sangyō

         Tōshoku   Tōyō Bussan

Although dummy corporations of this group were classified as friendly firms, they were not actually engaged in transactions with China because their parent companies belonged to the Japan-Taiwan Cooperation Committee and had not publicly approved Chou's four conditions.

Group 3. *Parent*   *Dummy*

         Itō Chū   Shin Nihon Kōeki

         Marubeni Iida   Wakō Kōeki

These dummy corporations severed connections with their parent firms immediately after Chou's four conditions were announced because the parents had not yet publicly approved Chou's conditions. The separation seems to have been rather thorough. Capital connections were severed; the dummy corporations moved their head offices away from their parent firms; and those employees who had been transferred from the parent firms returned to the parent firm or else resigned.

Group 4.

Parent	Dummy
Nisshō Iwai	Daihō Bōeki
Sumitomo Shōji	Taika Bōeki
Ataka Sangyō	Toyoshima Bōeki
Okura Shōji	Taiho Bōeki

These dummy corporations actively traded with China, because the parent corporations had approved Chou's four conditions.

Group 5.   Tōmen
                Nichimen Jitsugyō
                Chōri
                Itoman
                Nomura Bōeki
                Tokyo Bōeki
                Yuasa

This group was comprised of large trading corporations which, at an early date, were designated as friendly firms themselves. All of them still do considerable business with the United States but do not trade with Taiwan. The PRC is still very strict with Japanese firms who trade with Taiwan. Absolute secrecy is preserved as to the Taiwan dummies, except that it is generally known that Tōmen has a dummy (Nankai Kōygō) for the Taiwan trade.

Aside from designation as a friendly firm, manufacturing companies developed still another technique for dealing with the PRC. Such a company wishing to export to China could send one of its officers (shokoku) to be a nonregular staff member of a friendly firm. In this way he could sell goods to China indirectly through the friendly firm. This practice was curtailed when Wu Shu-tung, the Canton Trade Fair representative, announced on 2 May 1970 that the four leading Japanese manufacturers mentioned above would be barred from selling to China because of their Taiwan connections and for other reasons.

There were other changes in the friendly firm trade in the later years. We have already mentioned the growth of the concept of the "friendly maker." By the summer of 1971 there were some three hundred trading firms and another thirty-five banks, insurance companies, inspection companies, shipping agencies, and warehousing companies designated as friendly firms.[42] By the end of 1972, following the general shift in political atmosphere, nearly all major enterprises had accepted the four principles and had become friendly firms or friendly makers.

A third important change occurred in 1966 when a struggle between pro-Chinese and pro-Soviet (called *Yoyogi* and aligned with the Japanese Communist Party) groups took place in the friendly firm "certifying" organization Nitchu Boeki Sokushin Kyokai. Ten *Yoyogi* members were discharged, and they in turn locked out the pro-Chinese group and occupied the building for four months before the dispute was settled. Sometimes the Yoyogi/Maoist clashes were so severe that the groups or companies were dissolved or went bankrupt.[43] Several interesting labor law cases[44] have gone to court in the aftermath of discharges of one faction by the other. As a result of this leftist infighting the structure of a new friendly firm organization purged of the pro-Soviet faction has emerged. Operating under the general name of Japanese International Trade Promotion Office (Nihon Kokusai Boeki Sokushin Kyokai, hereafter KBS), it includes several local associations in major Japanese cities, each independent and financed by dues from members.[45]

V. Procedures for Dealing with the PRC

A. Memorandum Trade Procedures

There are three steps in the contracting process. First, as we have noted, the two permanent MT offices negotiate the annual memorandum. This memorandum specifies the over-all projected amount ($90 million for 1971; about $120 million for 1973), and indicates the kinds of products to be exchanged, as well as tentative quantities and prices. At first both countries tried to limit particular products to the MT trade channels, but this has not worked out in practice.

The second step is for the Japanese makers associations to send a mission

---

[42] An up-to-date list of friendly firms is found in *List for Chinese Trade*, together with addresses, telephone numbers, representatives, and date of designation as a friendly firm.

[43] For example, the bankruptcy of the book publishers K. K. Daian in October 1970 was caused by such a clash.

[44] E.g., *Yoshimura, et al. v. K. K. Nitchū Ryokōsha*, 90 *Hanrei jihō* (No. 599) [1970]; also see comment, 131 *Hanrei jihō* (No. 609) [1970] and 100 *Hanrei Taimuzu* (No. 247) [1970].

[45] JETRO, *Handbook*, p. 112 describes organizational details, as well as addresses, telephone numbers, etc.

to negotiate with the appropriate Chinese state trading corporation for actual prices and terms. For example, the *Asahi Shimbun* announced on 26 December 1972 that the six major Japanese steel manufacturers and the China National Metals and Minerals Import and Export Corporation had agreed to the sale of 1.4 million tons of regular steel for a total price of 67 billion yen, which is to be handled on the basis of yen/yüan settlement. As noted above, these associations are made up only of firms in a particular industry interested in Chinese trade. Perhaps their most important function is to allocate shares of the total trade to the several Japanese makers. Allocations to individual Japanese makers are not trade contracts with the Chinese as such. This presumably allows Japanese makers to use their own criteria in setting quotas among themselves, rather than having the quotas determined by the Chinese in accordance with the political performance of each maker (as occurs with friendly firms in the next step below).

In the third step the Japanese mission, with the approval of the Chinese, designates traders from the list of friendly firms to act as the *contracting parties* on behalf of the makers. It is here that the Chinese implement their policy of favoring the "friendliest" friendly firms. For example, in 1970 the Japanese mission decided that Sumitomo Chemical (manufacturer) should receive an allocation of 32.8 tons of fertilizer from the total fertilizer to be sold that year in MT trade. Thereafter, apparently following Chinese wishes, this amount was divided into subquotas to be handled by five friendly trading firms agreeable to China. Sumitomo's own dummy (by way of the Sumitomo Trading Company), Taika Bōeki, did *not* receive one of the subquotas; in similar dealings with other countries Taika (or Sumitomo Trading) would have handled the entire 32.8 tons on behalf of Sumitomo Chemical.[46] In this way China retains some commercial leverage with which to reward smaller friendly firms that have actively supported political demonstrations on behalf of Chinese causes in Japan and have faithfully adhered to pro-Chinese lines. In addition, this subdividing of the third step assures that there will be many friendly firms, and consequently many friendly individuals, to engage in pro-Chinese political activities in Japan.

To summarize, in a typical Japanese export transaction under the MT procedures, the Chinese state corporations contract only with friendly Japanese trading firms, never with Japanese manufacturers. The terms of the contract, however, are set by the manufacturers working through their industrial associations' missions. The mission also allocates quotas among Japanese makers; in this phase, the makers have not been required to affirm their

---

[46] *Tōzai bōeki yoran*, p. 202; see also pp. 198–99 for a discussion of the allocation of ammonium chloride sales. But cf. Appendix 9, Art. 17 which provides for a somewhat different arrangement for distributing subquotas to friendly trading firms. This is because of the peculiar nature of the goods involved in this contract.

support of Chinese political positions, as the friendly firms did. For Japan this arrangement has advantages of uniformity and reduced intramural competition. The Chinese benefit by being able to negotiate with Japanese manufacturers as a group and thus assure a stable supply, and also by parceling out rewards to many friendly firms. In addition, both sides may want to keep the price and amount bought from Japan a secret from other nations.

Exporting from China in the MT trade is relatively simple because China is not concerned with who are the ultimate users. The Chinese state trading corporations deal directly with friendly Japanese trading companies. As before, the "friendlier" friendly firms receive a greater portion of the trade. From the Japanese side, bulk quotas are allocated by the various Japanese business associations to interested ultimate users. These parties in turn acquire their share from the friendly firms who actually contract with the Chinese state trading corporations.*

B. The Friendly Firm Trade

Some procedures of the friendly firm trade, particularly the methods used in designating friendly firms, apply as well to MT trade. On the whole the friendly firm trade is not formally structured on a binational basis, except for the initial agreement signed in December 1962 between three associations of friendly firms and CCPIT, as described above. The key elements of this trade then are the Canton Fair and the friendly firm status based on acceptance of the whole PRC political catechism—the inseparability of politics and economics, the three political principles, the three trade principles, and the four trade conditions.[47] If a firm complies energetically with Chinese political wishes, it is favored with trade opportunities. If it does not, it may very well miss an invitation to the Canton Fair, or find its allocations cut down.

The following is an actual example. The T Trading Corporation is the only friendly trading corporation in Y city. If any other firm in Y city wants to visit China to do business, it must have an employee accepted by T as a nonregular employee (shukko), who then can visit China. Several years ago, T neglected to send its staff members to participate in demonstrations in Tokyo and Yokohama in support of the PRC program, thinking that such neglect would go unnoticed. However, the PRC was well aware of the facts and granted T a smaller quota than the year before. Before the next Canton Fair T employees attended demonstrations diligently; the following year the corporation was once again awarded its full quota.

Thus, appointment as a friendly firm is tantamount to a pledge of allegiance to PRC policy, as well as a commitment to support PRC political rallies and

---

* In 1973 the MT trade came to an end.

[47] Ample details are found in JETRO, Handbook, p. 128–31.

to represent Chinese commercial interests. Most significant, perhaps, is the fact that the friendly firm concept is peculiar to the Sino-Japanese trade and has not been used as a political instrument to influence domestic affairs of other countries, such as Canada, Italy, France, England, Germany, or the United States, that have traded extensively with the PRC even before recognition.

Once the Chinese have designated a company a friendly firm, the procedure for doing business with China is to write to China through KBS requesting an invitation to attend the Canton Trade Fair. If an invitation is received, the trader must submit a "letter of intention to travel to the Communist area" to the Japanese Ministry of Foreign Affairs and obtain approval which usually involves scrutiny by the Ministry of Justice, MITI, as well as the Ministry of Foreign Affairs. This is not a special requirement for the PRC; it applies to all travel to the Communist bloc. The procedure takes only about two weeks. For other travel arrangements there are several friendly travel firms set up in Tokyo and Hong Kong. These firms are indispensable since as of 1973 there were no Chinese consulates or other offices that could handle visas and other such matters.[48]

In the friendly firm trading process, it is difficult to exaggerate the importance of trade expositions, exhibitions, and particularly the Canton Fair. The fairs have been held every year since 1957, from April 15 to May 15 and again from October 15 to November 15. The Japanese have participated since 1961. Originally the foreign participants were largely overseas Chinese from Southeast Asia. In recent years many Europeans have also attended, and over a dozen Americans were invited for the first time in Spring 1972. The largest number of foreign participants have been the Japanese. In 1971 fourteen hundred Japanese businessmen were present, representing (presumably as nonregular employees of friendly firms) over one hundred machinery manufacturers.[49]

The fairs are important because they exhibit Chinese goods available for export. About one-third of each year's trade contracts are signed at each fair. The remainder is started in Canton and concluded by wire or trips to Shanghai or Peking. Much more than this, the fair serves as an important opportunity to make personal contacts and to exchange information and technology.

In addition to the fairs Japan has had exhibitions in China in 1956, 1958, 1963, and 1965. One scheduled for 1969 was canceled. China had an exhibition

---

[48] See the guide put out by KBS for the briefing of Japanese going to the PRC: Nihon Kokusai Bōeki Sokushin Kyōkai, *Nitchū bōeki hikkei* (Essential guide for Sino-Japanese trade) (Tokyo: KBS, 1972). In addition to giving essential information it warns about etiquette, language, photos, etc., p. 125.

[49] See JETRO, *Handbook*, p. 136 for further details of Japanese participation in the fair.

in Tokyo and Osaka in 1964 and 1966 and is presently making plans to hold others.[50]

VI. CONTRACTING TERMS

The practices and forms used in "contracts"[51] in the Sino-Japanese trade have changed rapidly in recent years, and several printed standard forms have been developed by the Chinese state trading corporations. There are significant variations between the friendly firm and the MT contracts, and between import and export contracts in both trades. Thus, there are four types of transactions with their respective forms, two in each of the major channels of trade. Furthermore, these Chinese forms, though rather standard within their type, do show some variations depending on the commodities and circumstances. Especially noticeable is the politicization of the MT trade in 1970, and resultant additions to the contract prefaces. In the appendixes 5, 6, 9, and 10 we have translated typical recent forms in each of the four types of transactions for reference. We will comment below on the differences between the friendly firm trade and the MT trade, as well as import-export variations.[52]

A. Memorandum Trade Contracts

The MT forms, whether for imports or exports, tend to favor the Chinese but to a lesser extent than do those for the friendly firm trade. This section deals basically with Japanese export transactions, because in Japanese import transactions the contracting forms are left to the friendly traders to a much greater degree. Thus, the Japanese import phase of MT trade resembles the purely friendly firm trade discussed in the next section.

1. Governing Law

Businessmen or lawyers approaching China for the first time need to remember that the PRC has postponed codification of its internal Chinese commercial law,[53] and that such rules and practices as exist for internal

---

[50] *Nihon keizai, shimbun,* 9 March 1971 and 13 May 1971.

[51] One hesitates to use the word "contract" for the Sino-Japanese trade because, to lawyers at least, "contract" implies promises enforceable at law; such is not the case with these agreements in any realistic sense. But the agreement is to be taken seriously, as advised by the KBS, *Nitchū bōeki hikkei,* p. 116.

[52] Through the generosity of friends, we have been able to examine many contracts of different kinds. Variations within each category are not often significant in recent Sino-Japanese trade except as required by the different kinds of goods.

[53] There is a brief text on civil law generally: *Basic Problems in the Civil Law of the People's Republic of China* (Institute of Civil Law, Central Political Judicial, Cadres School), *US Government Jt. Publications Research Service* (hereafter *JPRS*), no. 4879 (1961). See generally Victor Li, "The Role of Law in Communist China," *China Quarterly,* no. 44 (October–November 1970), p. 66.

relations are not necessarily apt or applicable for trading externally with non-Communists.[54] Furthermore, they must remember that the PRC has not generally participated in the international treaties for standardization, although she has joined in some conventions regarding shipping. Also, at present such PRC commercial law as there may be is still all but unascertainable by outsiders. The kind of legal precision that, for example, the Japanese have observed in their well-developed codified system or that American lawyers strive for in the Uniform Commercial Code simply does not exist.

This nonlegal approach explains why all of the PRC contract forms violate the competent transnational lawyer's first commandment: "Thou shalt not fail to establish a single law-of-the-contract by stipulation of the parties, or by shaping the transaction." Our experience in interviews with businessmen makes it entirely clear, however, that in both the MT and friendly firm trade, a litigated or even an arbitrated solution to a trade dispute is so far from their thinking that a "governing law clause" probably never crosses the minds of either party; it certainly seldom surfaces in Sino-Japanese negotiations and has never appeared in any of the contracts we have reviewed from this trade. Indeed it is said that the PRC favors arbitral clauses, not to arbitrate disputes, but to avoid jurisdiction of foreign courts.

2. Arbitration

There seem to be several levels of dispute settlement under Sino-Japanese import-export agreements.[55] Especially in the friendly firm trade where breaches have occurred because of political friction between the governments, Japanese parties have chosen to absorb the loss without claim. The key example was the wholesale cancellation of all contracts between Japanese traders and the PRC under the fourth Sino-Japanese trade agreement in 1958, in the aftermath of the Nagasaki flag incident. Export contracts valued at $44 million and import contracts valued at $53 million were abruptly canceled by the PRC. This caused damages (consequential as well as direct) estimated between $70 and $80 million to roughly 120 traders and 2,000 underlying suppliers in Japan.[56] Yet the PRC did not allege *force majeure* under the contracts, and the Japanese submitted no claims. Instead, Masanosuke Ikeda, representative director of the League of Japanese Diet Members for Sino-Japanese Trade Promotion, presumably speaking also for the injured traders,

---

[54] See Gabriele Crespi Reghizzi, "Legal Aspects of Trade with China; the Italian Experience," *Harv. Int'l. L. J.,* 85, no. 9 (1968), 97–125. See also Richard Pfeffer, "The Institution of Contracts in the Chinese People's Republic," *China Quarterly,* no. 14 (April–June 1963), p. 153; Pfeffer, "Contracts in China Revisited," *China Quarterly,* no. 28 (October–December 1966), p. 106; Gene Hsiao, "The Role of Economic Contracts in Communist China," *Calif. L. Rev.* 53 (1963): 1029.

[55] See JETRO, *Handbook,* pp. 117, 120, 145.

[56] *Ibid.,* p. 62.

immediately sent a telegram to Nan Han-chen, representative of the CCPIT, as follows:[57]

With regard to the incident concerning the flag of your country, we would like to express our sincere regrets to you. We are following the progress of the event, and we have made strong requests to the authorities that an endeavor be made to see that this kind of incident shall not occur again, and that they shall take every conceivable method to prevent it.

After this telegram no claims based on their contracts were submitted by the Japanese buyers, even though in international law it seems clear enough that Article 92 of the Japanese Criminal Code was properly interpreted as not applicable to the Japanese who destroyed the PRC flag, however much his conduct might be disapproved. The foregoing type of contract "breach," if it be one, is so extraordinary as to make claim procedures academic since there is no practical diplomatic or legal order to support justiciable claims in either country under such circumstances, and no real hope in international tribunals either.

The second kind of dispute settlement procedure, and the approach overwhelmingly favored by both the Chinese and Japanese, is a mutual settlement of disputes between the parties without third-party intervention, official or otherwise. Indeed this is the only practicable procedure available in the Sino-Japanese trade today.[58]

In the third procedure arbitration is provided in the "contract" clauses (e.g., Article 19 in Appendix 5) in addition to mediation between the parties themselves. In the friendly firm trade the place for arbitration has usually been fixed in China until recently, and procedures and facilities of the Chinese Foreign Trade Arbitration Committee (FTAC) were to be used. Also, in the early 1950s the initial agreements provided for arbitration only in China. It was not until the third Sino-Japanese Trade Agreement of 4 May 1955, that the provisions for arbitration in the country of the defendant were included.[59] This has been the practice in the LT and the subsequent MT trade ever since, and recently such terms are more and more frequently found in forms for the friendly firm trade. No third-country arbitration clauses have been found in any of the documents of the Sino-Japanese trade.

One might speculate that, lacking governing law clauses, a Chinese claim arbitrated in Japan might be governed by Japanese law, depending on interpretation of Article 7 of the Law on Governing Law (Hōrei) which states that if the intention of the parties regarding governing law is not clear, the place of contracting will govern. Since it seems that the place of contracting is almost always China, that fact might override the usual implication that a designation

---

[57] *NKS*, p. 18.

[58] Italian experience is the same. Crespi Reghizzi, "Legal Aspects," p. 116.

[59] *NKS*, p. 154.

of the defendant's country for arbitration would also carry with it the inference that defendant's law was intended to govern. Without all of the circumstances in each case before us, it would be difficult to say how Article 7 might apply. So if legal certainty were the goal, the clause is quite inadequate. But in fact it is quite unthinkable that a Chinese state corporation would seek arbitration as plaintiff in Japan, at least before recognition in September 1972.

So far, no arbitrations have been requested by either side in twenty years of trading. As noted, the Chinese would not likely submit a dispute to arbitration in Japan, nor are the Japanese likely to go to the mat before the Chinese FTAC. After all, the Japanese are no more litigious than the Chinese (nor more accustomed to arbitrate). Moreover, the relationship between Japanese friendly firms as parties to all these contracts (MT trade included) puts them in no position to insist on more than the Chinese wish to give them. Other experience indicates that FTAC arbitration would result in more mediation and would seldom go to an award. Lawyers acquainting themselves for the first time with this different kind of trading experience will realize by now that the function of law and lawyers in the PRC trade is in the areas of precise communication, thorough negotiations, and conflict prevention, rather than litigious resolution of disputes. The situation for Japanese before September 1972 was somewhat different from that for traders from countries that have diplomatic relations with the PRC.

3. Preface to MT Contracts

We have seen that after the four trade conditions of 1970, the MT trade became increasingly subject to the same kind of political affirmations found in the friendly firm trade, even for makers. Still, bringing friendly trading firms into the MT contracts at the signing stage insulated the Japanese makers from political oaths. Most of these makers found such politics unacceptable until the recent pressures caused them to cave in. The political preface in the MT contract forms for Japanese exports in 1970 was as follows:

In order to fulfill the details of agreement *(Kyogi jiko)* of the 1970 Memorandum Trade, based on the principle of inseparability of politics and economics and on the three political principles which both the Japanese and Chinese sides affirmed through representatives of their Memorandum Trade offices in the Conference Communique published April 19, 1970, and also based on the four conditions of Sino-Japanese trade enunciated by the Chinese government, both parties agree to the following terms by signing this contract form.[60]

---

[60] Appendix 5. Note that the Japanese Communist Party, which has resisted Maoist interference, in the JCP congress July 1970 emphasized that the "Mao clique" was joining hands with Japanese business in denouncing the JCP at the MT signing in Peking. Fuwa Tetsuzo called the attitudes of Japanese business "flunkyism," which encourages Chinese intervention in Japanese internal affairs. See *Asahi shimbun*, 14 February 1970.

This clause is much more than a mere recital. In some ways it is the essence of Sino-Japanese trade since it specifies the "political terms" which are conditions precedent to doing business with the PRC.

4. Inspection

The inspection procedures in the MT trade are roughly the same as those in the friendly firm trade, where the Chinese inspection is final whether China is the buyer or the seller.

5. Shipping Arrangements

In both trades the PRC forms require FOB terms for Chinese imports and CIF for exports, in order to give the PRC control of the insurance and shipping business. (See Appendix 19 for a PRC insurance policy.)

In the MT trade Japanese exporters in performing their obligations to make FOB shipping arrangements are not always required to obtain Chinese approval for the hire when chartering a Japanese ship, as has been required in their friendly firm trade.

6. Price Negotiations

Though a friendly trading firm signs the contracts, negotiations over price are handled by the entire Japanese industrial association for each commodity involved. In this sense the MT trade is more maker-oriented, and the Japanese position is somewhat stronger. These associations are more comparable to the monolithic Chinese buyer than in the case of the friendly firm trade, which is trader-oriented and populated mostly by minor Japanese trading companies dependent on the PRC.

There is a system of rebating on Chinese exports, by which the friendly trader profits even though he has to accede to a price proffered by the PRC which is not profitable. The Japanese buyer's letter of credit enables the Chinese corporations to get their price in China at the time of shipping. It then rebates (perhaps 2–3 percent) in pounds to the Japanese firms, as a reward for selling their full quotas. This arrangement does not appear in the contracts themselves, but in a side letter.[61]

7. Credit Terms

We have seen that long-term Export-Import Bank credit for sale of Japanese plants in the Sino-Japanese trade has been a major problem since 1964. Nevertheless, in the MT trade credit terms are allowed in exports of Japanese steel and machinery (20 percent down and the balance in two equal annual

---

[61] An example of this may be seen in Sumida Teruo, *Chūgoku gendai shōgyō tsūshinbun* (Forms for current Chinese commercial correspondence) (Reprint ed., Tokyo: Daian, 1969), p. 231.

payments) and fertilizer (price payable within one year).[62] For the above mentioned commodities credit is supported by the letters of credit or guarantees from the Bank of China, plus a note from the Peking branch of the Bank of China bearing interest at 5 percent as opposed to 7 or 8 percent charged by the Japan Export-Import Bank. As noted earlier, no credit is possible under the friendly firm trade because these petty firms lack credit resources themselves.

B. Friendly Firm Contracts

In the friendly firm trade there are marked differences in contract terms for Chinese exports and for Japanese exports. These differences all favor the Chinese because of their domination of the Japanese parties in both kinds of transactions. All friendly firm contracts are printed in Chinese and signed by whoever is in China for the Japanese firm, whether he is properly authorized by Japanese agency law or not.

1. Preface

We have noted that even the new MT trade contracts require that a friendly firm be the actual signing party and that the Japanese party make affirmations of political faith. The preface of the friendly firm contracts requires similar statements of allegiance to the Chinese policy (three principles and four conditions).[63]

2. Establishment of Letter of Credit

In the case of Chinese exports the L/C from Japan must be sent at least twenty-five days before loading date, whereas in the case Japanese exports the Chinese have to establish the L/C only ten days before loading.[64]

3. Remittance

In the case of Chinese exports the remittance provision requires telegraphic remittance and sight drafts, whereas in the case of Japanese exports there is no such obligation placed on the Chinese. L/Cs are to be irrevocable and transferable and expire fifteen days after the bill of lading date. The loading documents are not appreciably different from those required in other bilateral trade, but it is stipulated in the bills of lading that the ship may not call at United States or Taiwan ports.[65]

---

[62] JETRO, *Handbook,* p. 122; English, p. 130.

[63] *Ibid.,* p. 117.

[64] *Ibid.,* p. 118. Also see discussion on payment settlements below; Tanishiki Hiroshi, *Nitchū bōeki annai,* p. 94.

[65] One concrete example of a PRC legal enforcement is found in the Peking Municipal Intermediate People's Court judgment in the Vickers-Zimmers Ltd. case discussed in *Peking Review,* no. 28 (12 July 1968), p. 4. See Jerome A. Cohen, "Chinese Law and Sino-American Trade" in A. Eckstein, ed., *China Trade Prospects,* pp. 127, 168.

4. Chinese Approval of Charter Hire

In case the seller, arranging for FOB shipment, supplies his own ship, the Chinese require prior approval for the hire whereas this right is not afforded to the Japanese buyer.

5. Notice of Completion of Loading

The Japanese exporter has obligations to give notice immediately, whereas the Chinese exporter must do it within forty-eight hours.

6. Delays in Loading

Japanese exporters are liable for delays in loading, unless the opening L/C from China has been delayed or unless there is *force majeure*.

7. Inspection of Commodity for Quality and Quantity

In the case of Japanese exports the Chinese inspection is only final at discharge, and in the case of Chinese exports the Chinese inspection is also final at loading, except that the Japanese importer may reinspect and protest, usually within ninety days for textiles, within sixty to ninety days for machinery, and within thirty days for food products and the like.

8. Loading Allowances

In the case of Chinese exports the quantity loaded may vary about 5 percent and there are also impurity allowances (see Appendix 10, clause 4), whereas Japanese exports seem to have less leeway.

9. Acts of God or Force Majeure

In the case of both Chinese and Japanese exports somewhat vague provisions are made for excusing performance in case of Acts of God. Such acts are variously specified but usually cover war, fire or floods, frost, failure of refrigeration, or pests (also strikes in the case of Japanese exports). To claim an Act of God the Japanese exporter must send a notorial deed, whereas an unformalized notice is acceptable from the Chinese.

10. Delayed Delivery

For Japanese exports penalties are provided for delayed delivery, whereas no such penalties are provided for Chinese delay. This is a highly significant provision because of the rather general complaint about delays among PRC trading partners.

11. Arbitration

Disputes must be settled by mutual agreement, but if such negotiations fail, provision is made for arbitration. Recently this has been at defendant's place of business. As discussed earlier, given the Chinese domination and both parties' attitudes approving mediation, arbitration is a marginal "right," which is probably included to avoid jurisdiction of foreign courts.

The above summary of the differences between contracting terms in the two types of trade, and the differences between contracts for Japanese and Chinese exports in the friendly trade, shows clearly the disabilities suffered by Japan because of her relationship with Taiwan and the United States. Much more detailed legalistic gloss could be written on the various provisions listed above. We have left this for another day, because the points mentioned focus on the business context as it existed before establishment of diplomatic relations in September 1972. A more refined analysis of the meaning of these contracts in Japanese law or in Chinese law (to the extent that it is ascertainable) would seem to yield little of practical value at this time. Instead, in the next section we have undertaken to list some of the major problems of interest to lawyers and businessmen, which have occurred or still exist in the Sino-Japanese trade.

C. Payment Settlements

Until August 1972 Sino-Japanese trade transactions were posted in pounds and then settled in pounds in London (see chart 3), without the use of either yen or yüan directly. The Chinese required unequal treatment in that letters of credit for Japanese imports required payment remittance to London on telegraphic notice, while in the case of Japanese exports the Japanese seller was entitled to settlement only by ordinary mail remittance, which takes two or three weeks longer. Because of the weakening of the pound (and the franc) in the past, there was some risk in the added time required for London settlement. In addition, the time that had elapsed between contracting and performance often ran as long as a year or two, causing problems of quoting prices.

In March 1970 the United Kingdom, France, Switzerland, West Germany, Italy, and Canada established a system of direct settlement between their own currencies and the Chinese yüan, and in 1972 the initial deals with the United States were handled in dollars. Thus, vis-à-vis her major Western competitors, Japan has been at a disadvantage in having to settle in the currency of a third country.

As early as July 1968 Japan initiated talks with China suggesting that Japanese exports be posted in yen figures on contracts and shipping documents, and that Japanese imports be posted in yüan figures for settlement of both in pounds.[66] Though some progress was made in these negotiations, the Chinese

---

[66] "Nitchū mondai . . . kono jūdai ken'an wa dō naru?" (Sino-Japanese Problems . . . how will these ten major bending questions be answered?) *Shūkan Daiyamondo* (14 August 1971), pp. 69, 84. Also see Katherine Huang Hsiao, *Money and Monetary Policy in Communist China* (New York: Columbia University Press, 1971) for background on the yüan currency, and Tadao Miyashita, *The Currency and Financial System of Mainland China* (Tokyo: Institute of Asian Economic Affairs, 1966).

CHART 3

SINO-JAPANESE PAYMENT SETTLEMENTS BEFORE 1972

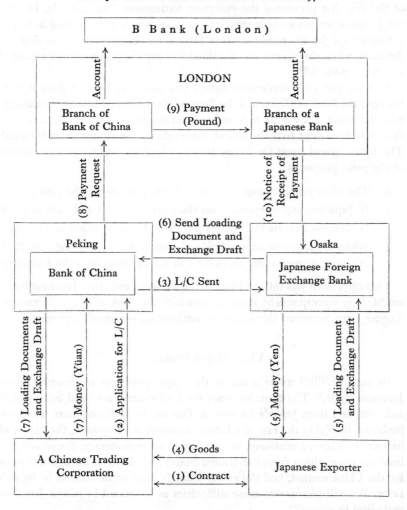

finally broke off the discussions. They preferred to leave the Japanese in their unequal position, because they distrusted the Japanese government and because the strength of the yen created risks for the PRC in case of revaluation.[67] Later, the Japanese suggested direct settlement and went so far as to retain the inequality of payment timing. The Chinese refused, even though they soon permitted direct settlement for yüan with the other countries mentioned above. Instead, the Chinese suggested that yüan be posted for both imports

---

[67] See *Nikkei*, 10 February 1971; *Asahi shimbun*, 21 July 1971.

and exports.[68] This was unacceptable to Japan since the custom in international trade is to use the currency of the exporter. In all, it was the strength of the yen that prevented the yen-yüan settlements. For example, in 1970 the Japanese export surplus was $160 million, which, if expressed in yen as a balance for Japan, would cause a loss to the Chinese upon revaluation. Actually, when the pound was devalued in 1967 the Japanese lost a total of about $20 million.[69]

A direct yen-yüan settlement accord was announced on 18 August 1972 between the Bank of China and the Bank of Tokyo.[70] The basic breakthrough was that Japan was willing to have her favorable balance stated in yüan, even though in the fall of 1972 the risk of yen revaluation looked rather substantial. The terms agreed upon for future trade settlements are interesting variants of the prior proposals:

1. The yüan-yen exchange was set at 1 yüan equals 135.84 yen.

2. In Japanese export transactions the price is posted and paid in yüan.

2. In Chinese exports the price is posted and paid in either yen or yüan.

4. When the Japanese accumulation of yüan builds up too high, the Bank of China agrees to buy them back in the currency of a third country.

This agreement was followed by the Sanwa Bank and other Japanese banks establishing correspondent arrangements with the Bank of China. Even after August 1972, however, third-country settlements remained important.

VII. Major Problems

In 1970 JETRO made a list of the major problems confronting Sino-Japanese trade.[71] The thorniest ones were, of course, not legal but political and stemmed from Japan's interest in Taiwan. In addition, there were also problems involving the rate of Chinese economic development, the nature of its socialist planned economy, the rigidity of its bureaucracy, the increase in business competition from the United States and Western European nations for the China market, and the embarrassingly large trade balance in Japan's favor. We will summarize these difficulties as expressed in recent Japanese periodical literature.[72]

---

[68] *Nikkei,* 10 February 1971.

[69] *Asahi shimbun,* 20 August 1972.

[70] *Asahi shimbun,* 18 August 1972 and 30 August 1972.

[71] JETRO, *Handbook,* pp. 73–89.

[72] In the wake of recent American moves toward rapprochement with the PRC, there has been a spate of symposia in the popular periodical literature in Japan: e.g., see "Sekai Sangoku jidai to Nihon" (Japan and the period of the "Three World Giants"), *Shūkan Daiyamondo* (Special Issue) (14 August 1971), p. 34; *Sandē Mainichi,* (Special

A. Political Disagreements

The political background of Sino-Japanese relations has been chronicled above. The policy of "separation of politics and economics" fell with the Sato cabinet,[73] and a new era began with the Chou-Tanaka communique. Even so, a number of political problems remain, including the need to conclude a treaty to replace the peace treaty of 1952 with Taiwan which was implicitly abrogated by Japan's shift of its "one China" policy in favor of the PRC.

Perhaps a more difficult question concerns Japan's future relations with Taiwan. As discussed earlier, diplomatic relations have been severed and embassies withdrawn. In addition, recent interrogatives in the Diet raised the question of whether Taiwan is a part of the Far East for purposes of the United States/Japanese Security Treaty provisions. Further, if American forces from Japan could be used to protect Taiwan, would such use constitute Japanese interference with domestic affairs of the PRC, since the Chou-Tanaka communique recognized that Taiwan is part of China.[74] The government position is that Japan's recent recognition of Taiwan as part of China does not affect Japan's position toward third countries, and that the United States Security Treaty stands; problems regarding the use of Japan-based American forces to defend Taiwan would be settled by consultation.

As for economic relations, Japan's trade with Taiwan increased 20 percent in the first half of 1972, despite the Chou-Tanaka communique. This trade continued to be larger than Japan-PRC trade. At this point little withdrawal of Japanese investment (estimated at $200 million) from Taiwan has occurred, apparently because that is not required by Chou's four conditions of 1970. New Taiwan investments from Japan, however, have virtually ceased, at least for the time being. The Japan-Taiwan Economic Cooperation Committee has been avoided by many Japanese companies since 1970, and resignations have sharply increased after Nixon's announcement in July 1971.

Thus, with trade still brisk and political disengagement under way, an exact

---

Issue), (23 August 1971); *Shūkan Gendai* (Extra Issue), 9 August 1971; "Nitchū keizei kōryū no kongo" (Future of Sino-Japanese economic exchanges), *Asahi shimbun,* (14 November 1972), p. 11; Okazai Kaheita, "Chūgoku no kokoro tsukande kōryū o" (For trade, understand China's feelings), *Nikkei,* 8 December 1972.

[73] The postwar Japanese press cannot be accused of coddling incumbent LDP governments. Speculation in 1971 was rampant in the Tokyo press about "post-Sato" developments in Sino-Japanese relations. Examples are "Sato naikaku taijin no hi made no dorama" (The drama until the day the Sato cabinet retires), *Shūkan gendai,* 9 August 1971, p. 80; "Sato-go" (After Sato), *Asahi shimbun,* 23 July 1971, speculating about the China views of possible LDP pro-China successors such as Tanaka Kakuei, Fukuda, or Miki Takeo; and "Posuto Satō, dono naikaku ga Chūgoku shonin sura ka" (Post-Sato, which cabinet will recognize the PRC?), *Shūkan Daiyamondo,* 14 August 1971, p. 70.

[74] *Nikkei,* 3 November 1972, p. 2.

reversal of the situation under the Sato cabinet seems to be developing whereby there is unity of politics and economics in dealing with the PRC and separation of them in new dealings with Taiwan. Perhaps dummy companies will be used for Japan-Taiwan transactions, although these companies might have to be organized outside of Japan in order to maintain a sufficient image of independence from the Japanese parent companies.

B. Settlement of Payments

Although not entirely resolved, the currency problem has been vastly alleviated with the agreements of August 1972 reached between Japanese banks and the Bank of China to settle accounts on the yen/yüan basis. Settlements in third-country currencies remains important, in part because of the need to convert balances resulting from the lopsided trade in Japan's favor. Nevertheless, the agreement marks an important breakthrough in this area.

C. Japanese and International (COCOM) Restrictions
on Sino-Japanese Trade

A major restriction on trade generally has been the COCOM list. Several factors have made these restrictions particularly important in the Sino-Japanese trade. Among these are the fact that: (a) Japan is the leading trader with the PRC, so that on the basis of sheer volume alone the restrictions make a bigger difference to Japan; (2) the unusually high degree of dependency upon American technology, security, and trade has meant that Japan has been constrained to follow the American lead in applying a higher degree of restrictions than COCOM requires; (3) the American rules against both transshipment and, until 1969, American entities residing in Japan shipping or transshipping from Japan have borne heavily upon Japanese trade; and (4) since so much of Japanese industry is based on American technology, the provisions of American law prohibiting the sale to China of goods produced by American technology have also been an onerous burden on the Sino-Japanese trade.[75]

Two recent developments are significant in that they look toward a reduction of such restrictions. First, the COCOM list is reviewed every four years or so. Since the fall of 1972 Japan together with several European countries has spearheaded a drive to decontrol 68 of the 167 items still restricted by COCOM. This has resulted in a compromise arrangement with the United States and the United Kingdom favoring retention of restrictions and in

---

[75] Note a former official concerned with the controls, Alfred P. Rubin, "U.S. Exports Controls: An Immodest Proposal," George Wash. L. Rev. 36 (1968): 633, 642 says that these barriers against outflow of technology are practically unenforceable.

Japan and others pushing for reduction. Some fifty items were decontrolled,[76] including many goods of particular importance to Japan, such as optical instruments, large fishing boats, many chemical products, and synthetic rubber; computers and certain telecommunications equipment, however, remain on the restricted list.

Second, a judicial decision of 8 July 1969 by the Tokyo District Court, *Association for the 1969 Peking-Shanghai Japanese Industrial Exhibition* vs. *Japan (MITI)*,[77] found that the enforcement of COCOM regulations through the Japanese foreign exchange control law was illegal. The association had applied on 13 November 1968 to the defendant (MITI) for an export license for goods to be sent to a trade exhibition in China in 1969. The application was made under the Foreign Exchange and Foreign Trade Control Laws (FECL, Article 48) and the Export Trade Control Order (*Yushutsu boeki kanri-rei,* Article 1). It was denied with respect to nineteen specific items which were covered by the COCOM list. The plaintiffs went to court seeking a cancellation of the denial, but because of the strong reaction in Peking and the ongoing Cultural Revolution, the entire exhibition was canceled. Instead, the plaintiff shifted the suit to an action for damages under the Administrative Case Litigation Law (*Gyōsei jiken sosho-ho,* Article 21).

The plaintiff lost the case because the court did not find the requisite evidence of intent or negligence necessary to support recovery of damages against the Japanese government. However, the reasoning of the court is interesting in that it did find that the enforcement of COCOM regulations under the FECL and its dependent regulations was illegal. The underlying premise of the court was, as the Japanese government had been saying, that "politics and economics are separate," and that the FECL was a law with purely economic objectives. The court then decided that the COCOM arrangement could not be properly considered a self-executing treaty since, among other things, the COCOM regime is still for all practical purposes secret. It also found that the Japanese Diet had not passed any special statute to support enforcement of the COCOM. Instead, the bureaucracy had chosen to use the FECL to enforce COCOM, a purpose for which the statute was not intended. Also of interest was the court's reference to Article 22 of the Constitution, saying that freedom of export is one of the fundamental human rights that must not be abridged without specific legislative justification.

Since this decision denied plaintiff's claim on the grounds of insufficient evidence to prove defendant's intent or negligence, the case is not likely to be reviewed by the Japanese Supreme Court. Consequently, its value as precedent

---

[76] *Asahi shimbun,* 12 September 1972, and 12 December 1972.

[77] *1969 Peking-Shanghai Nippon kōgyō tenrankai* v. *Kuni* (Japan), *Hanrei jihō* (No. 560) 7 (1969); also see comment *Hanrei Jihō* (No. 572) 133 (1969). In English, see Chin Kim "The COCOM Case," *J. of World Trade* 4 (1970): 604-7.

is speculative, as is all lower court case law in Japan. Nevertheless, it illustrates the point that the restrictions on exports to the PRC, both the Japanese national restrictions and the international burdens of COCOM, still remain a major problem in Sino-Japanese trade.

D. Long-Term Credit Problems

We have already mentioned the Yoshida letter of 30 May 1964, which cut off Export-Import Bank credit for PRC trade. As a result, Japan has supplied only one of at least thirty-three plants sold to the PRC in recent years.[78] This has been a sore point with friends of the PRC because of loss of these important trade opportunities.[79] (We should remember, however, that since the Cultural Revolution, the PRC has discontinued the purchase of whole industrial plants from European countries as well.) The importance of the Japanese Export-Import Bank credit was magnified by the fact that there was no other source of such credit in Japan—in Europe credit was available through various commercial banks, consortia, and syndicates.

In 1971 the Sato government adopted the position that Export-Import Bank credit might be granted on a case-by-case basis if the PRC applied.[80] Nothing happened since the PRC would not apply, saying that it is incumbent upon the Japanese government to take affirmative action to cancel and nullify the Yoshida letter and any effect it may have had.[81]

Recently, there has been a Japanese plan to establish a separate credit organization, but so far the PRC appears unimpressed with that idea.[82] The Mitsubishi Bank also has indicated that credits might be extended.[83]

The long-term credit problem symbolized by the Yoshida letter was finally resolved in late 1972 when the export of an ethylene plant by Toyo Engineering was cleared for a thirteen billion yen, five-year credit from the Japanese Export-Import Bank at an ostensible rate *(hyōmen kinri)* of 6.25 percent per annum. The Chinese requested 5.5 percent, and rumors have it that the actual interest will be reduced to something between 6.25 percent and 5.5 percent

---

[78] A breakdown by country of all complete plants sold to the PRC may be found in *Shin Chūgoku nenkan* (The new China annual) (Daishukan shoten, 1968), pp. 280–81.

[79] *Nikkei,* 7 April 1971.

[80] *NKS,* (18 March 1972), p. 1. See also Gene T. Hsiao, "The Role of Trade in China's Diplomacy with Japan" in Jerome A. Cohen, ed., *The Dynamics of China's Foreign Relations* (Cambridge: Harvard U. Press, 1970), pp. 41, 45. Also "Communist China Cancels Big Contracts due to Yoshida Letter," *Japan Foreign Trade News,* no. 165 (1965), p. 11.

[81] *Nikkei,* 18 March 1972.

[82] *Nikkei,* 7 February 1971.

[83] *Nikkei,* 18 March 1972, p. 1; see also *Japan Economic Journal* (14 November 1972), p. 2; *Asahi shimbun,* 26 December 1972; *Nikkei,* 14 November 1972.

by behind-the-scenes accounting adjustments. Four other plant export negotiations (Toray, Kuraray, Asahi Kasei, and Mitsubishi Yuka) are nearing completion with assurances of Export-Import Bank financing. Thus, a major stumbling block to trade with the PRC apparently has been removed.

E. Unbalanced Trade

Though the period 1950–63 showed a consistent trade balance in the PRC's favor, since 1964 Japan has had a high favorable balance. In 1970 it amounted to a $160 million excess on a $822 million trade total. This is partly because Japan has about a four-to-one advantage over European competitors on freight. More importantly, Japanese agricultural protectionism has excluded a great deal of China's export goods. The same protectionism occurs in the Japanese fishing industry. On the other hand, China, in attempting to build up its own heavy industries and use its own raw materials, has weakened its chance to export to Japan by withholding many of the raw materials and ores that Japan would very much like to obtain. Recent PRC attitudes indicate that some raw materials may be exported henceforth.

The Japanese have also complained of other problems with Chinese imports, including (1) Chinese insensitivity to price fluctuations, (2) delayed delivery, and (3) inability of suppliers and users, particularly of machinery, to by-pass the state trading corporations and deal directly with ultimate Chinese producers and users. Still another problem has been the very high Japanese tariff rates on many Chinese products, because these rates were not ameliorated in the case of the PRC by concessions to developing countries which were spelled out in the Kennedy-rounds. A move beginning in April 1972 favors PRC imports by a special customs device, but the name "preferential tariff" will be avoided in deference to PRC pride, as that term is now applied usually to underdeveloped countries.[84]

Even more interesting are recent indications that the PRC might again offer to sell fuel coal to Japan, though that commodity was not included in the last MT trade accord of October 1972. Coal and oil could become a substantial Japanese import and greatly improve the trade balance.

F. Continuing Difficulties

While many of the problems mentioned above are in the process of being resolved, some will persist into the future. One difficulty shared by most PRC trading partners from Europe has been the frustration of dealing with a massive bureaucracy in a socialist economy, a bureaucracy that plans and operates trade and at the same time is largely divorced from market forces and the

---

[84] *Nikkei*, 3 January 1972.

usual commercial techniques and motivations that assist businessmen in understanding and predicting the behavior of their counterparts in other countries. There is little indication that the Japanese have encountered problems much different from those that have been described by other Western traders, except that the past lack of diplomatic relations plus the special fears and enmities persisting from the Sino-Japanese past have surely aggravated the intensity, if not the kind, of problems encountered.[85]

Much more serious is the question of the future psychological climate for Sino-Japanese trade. The initial excitement felt by most Japanese over prospects for normal relations between the two countries has already begun to subside with the realization that China, though courteous and friendly, nevertheless has a memory. Key Japanese figures in Sino-Japanese affairs are cautiously reminding the business community that rather than engaging in flights of romanticism, what is needed are careful business practices and realistic goals. No one knows to what extent a binational trading program can be expanded to mutual benefit. Such a program certainly will not emerge along the prewar pattern, because China will jealously nurture her resources for national development and political advantage.

A second imponderable with deep political overtones concerns the current Japanese argument over unification of outlets *(madoguchi iponka-ron)* in the China trade. The idea is that Japan should organize on a national scale to match the size and coordination of the Chinese trading structure. In practice this could very well mean that the mainstream business circles *(zaikai)* would monopolize the China trade, with official sanction, and that the old friendly firm organizations would be relegated to a peripheral role. In November of 1972 Japanese big business moved to organize an entirely new entity for that purpose, the Sino-Japanese Economic Association (Nitchū keizai kyōkai), headed by the prestigious Inayama Yasuhiro, president of Nippon Steel Corporation. Only the future can tell whether the PRC will attempt to intervene on behalf of the many smaller friendly firms, who without some external help would be no match for the new "unified access" to Chinese trade.

VIII. CONCLUSION

Our study has shown that recent Sino-Japanese trade has been a rather special creature of complementary economics and differing politics. Confronted by Japan's one-China (Taiwan) policy, the PRC has imposed rather severe political conditions on the terms of trade with Japan, up until 1973. These terms included organizational strictures—the memorandum trade and

---

[85] The Japanese press often referred to James Reston's reports from the PRC of anti-Japanese emotions in the PRC, for example, *Asahi shimbun,* 11 August 1971. See generally Kimura Kihachirō, *Chūguku wa Nihon o dō mite iru ka?* (How does China view Japan?) (Tokyo: Zaisei kaizai koho sha, 1971); see also, note 8, *supra.*

the friendly firm system. The memorandum trade represented the Chinese preference for official government-to-government dealings, implying some degree of recognition for the Peking government. The friendly firm trade was a method of insuring that transactions were handled by Japanese firms (usually small ones), which favored the PRC's political position over the policy of the Japanese government. Citizens of no other country have been required to comply with such political terms as a condition of transactions.

The Japanese answer to the friendly firm interposed by the PRC was the dummy firm—a minor friendly firm actually controlled by a larger Japanese firm unwilling itself to accede to PRC political demands (*i.e.,* unfriendly). This flexible mode of trade was thus devised by the PRC and modified by Japan in the 1960s to take advantage of the economic opportunities and circumspect the sharp political differences between the two countries.

In fact, the friendly firms, including the dummies, were able to do enough business to make Japan the PRC's largest trading partner in the 1960s and early 1970s. But this unusual mode of trade was not without its practical problems. Advertising and the usual salesmanship were outside the rules of the game; third-country currency and banks had to be used; government credit was unavailable and friendly firms were usually insubstantial and had little credit; visas, travel, and information services could not be rendered by regular channels, until diplomatic relations were established in 1973 and the friendly firm requirements for trade were relaxed.

In the contracting process the legal devices of international sales have been generally followed in the Sino-Japanese trade. But the weakness of the friendly firm's bargaining position, vis-à-vis the PRC state trading corporations, has produced several special provisions as noted above. Also, the use of arbitration clauses may be intended more to avoid law suits than for arbitration purposes—in fact these clauses have not been invoked to date. In the MT trade, up through 1973, the Japanese makers associations have fixed the prices and other terms on a more equal footing (compared to friendly firms) with the PRC state corporations. However, the volume of MT trade had become (by 1973 when it ended) a very minor portion of total Sino-Japanese trade. Most of the trade flowed through friendly trade channels on predominantly PRC terms; these terms were, however, generally—but not always—standard. Except for extraordinary situations such as the Nagasaki flag incident, the PRC record for contract performance is said to be very good.

Compared to other bilateral trade experiences, our study shows that the PRC-Japanese trade has had its own strains and successes flowing from the special relationship of these two countries in Asia and in history. The strains have been caused by political differences and, perhaps, by memories of the past; the successes have flowed from the logic of location, pragmatic flexibility on both sides, and a cultural affinity that makes it easier for the PRC to communicate with Japan than with the rest of the "West."

Trade with the Soviet Union

GEORGE GINSBURGS

I. BACKGROUND

The experience of Soviet trade with Chinese Communist quarters antedates the establishment of the People's Republic. Active commercial contacts developed independently at both extremities of the long continental frontier shared by the two countries. From the second half of 1943 the once brisk exchange of commodities between the Soviet Union and Sinkiang Province ceased almost entirely in those portions of the region that remained under Nationalist control. Simultaneously, trade relations were initiated with individual merchants and trading companies in the areas where the "people's democratic" administration held sway, primarily in the districts around Chuguchak, Kuldja, and A-lo t'ai. Local trade between Sinkiang businessmen and "Sovsintorg" was conducted on a barter basis. During 1946 and 1947 the level of Sinkiang border trade was low and involved but a small group of petty Chinese merchants residing in towns lying close to the Soviet frontier. Beginning in 1948 and particularly in 1949 Chinese merchants located in towns in the interior of the province were also drawn into these operations, and the volume of trade turnover with the Soviet Union rose visibly.

At the far eastern end of the border regular commercial ties between Soviet import-export agencies and the "liberated" zones of the Northeast (Manchuria) and the Liaotung Peninsula were instituted right after the close of the war. In a rather unusual move, as early as November 1945, several Soviet foreign trade organizations acquired the shares of I. Ya. Churin and Co., a former émigré commercial corporation with outlets throughout Manchuria, and during 1946–47 re-established its vast network of large department stores servicing all the important local urban centers, backed by its own extensive chain of food-processing enterprises. Because of the isolation of Manchuria from the industrial resources of North and Central China and the sorry state of economic affairs in Manchuria proper in the aftermath of the war, the company had to purchase the required raw materials and manufactured goods in the Soviet Union and pay for them by deliveries of native food produce. The value of this bilateral trade was always relatively low; nevertheless, it mounted steadily between 1947 and 1949.

On 21 December 1946 the All-Union association Eksportkhleb and the Chinese trade company Tunsin concluded the first contract for reciprocal deliveries of goods. Tunsin sold Eksportkhleb a million tons of grain and soy beans and ten thousand tons of meat; in return, the Soviet Union supplied the Northeast provinces with cotton textiles, yarn, paper, sugar, salt, benzine, kerosene, industrial lubricants, hard coal, machinery, and equipment. In the following years, as more and more of Manchuria fell to the Communists and they consolidated their hold on the region's economy, trade between the local Chinese companies and Soviet foreign trade entities continued to grow.

In 1946 trade relations also began developing between the Chinese companies on the Liaotung Peninsula (the Dal'dok factory, the trade and industrial company Dal'energo, the fish-processing company Kwantungryba, the local locomotive and railroad-car construction plant, and so forth; in 1947–48 Liaotung still was cut off from North Manchuria) and Soviet foreign trade agencies. A signal event was the trip to Moscow in July 1949 of a trade delegation appointed by the "people's democratic" authorities of Manchuria, which resulted in a one-year trade agreement between the Soviet Union and Manchuria. The fact that the mission was invited to travel to Moscow to sign what sounded like a merely local trade accord indicates that the episode had much greater political significance than would appear on the surface. Indeed, the contingent was headed by Kao Kang, a leading Party figure known for his pro-Russian sympathies who was purged in 1955. One of the charges against him may have been that he was seeking to set himself up as czar of an autonomous entity in Manchuria (probably with covert Soviet encouragement and support). Hence, it is possible to suspect that ulterior political calculations motivated the Soviet move, quite apart from the traditional interest in playing a major role in Manchuria's economic life. Concurrently, Soviet specialists were dispatched to the area and in record time managed to help repair railroad communications, rebuild bridges and several industrial enterprises, organize city services, and stem an epidemic of plague. All this assistance was reportedly rendered *gratis*.

Finally, at the beginning of 1949, after Liberation, the "people's democratic" regime likewise took steps to revitalize foreign trade in North China. That spring a North China Foreign Trade Company was created in Peking. Thanks to the restoration of railway links between Peking and Mukden, trade contacts could now be maintained with Northeast China as well as the Soviet Union. In September 1949 the first commercial transactions were concluded between this company and Soviet foreign trade organizations (Dal'intorg, Eksportkhleb) providing for the mutual delivery of thirty-one million rubles worth of goods. This arrangement was effectively implemented during the last quarter of 1949,

Although the size and value of the above exchanges never surpassed modest proportions, it is in a sense a cause for wonder that these ventures on the whole did so well, given the immense logistical and political difficulties which attended their execution.

II. TRADE AND AID RELATIONS, 1950–51

The signature in Moscow on 14 February 1950 by the governments of the Soviet Union and the PRC of a series of important agreements ushers in a new phase in the history of contemporary Sino-Soviet diplomacy. Foremost among these documents was the treaty of friendship, alliance, and mutual assistance. Despite their predominantly political character conventions of this type are considered by Soviet scholars as "seminal interstate juridical acts for the establishment and broad development of mutual trade and other economic relations" on grounds that the climate of trust and intimacy thus generated on the political plane automatically stimulates collaboration in the commercial and economic spheres. Thus, Article 5 of the treaty records the parties' resolve,

in the spirit of friendship and cooperation and in conformity with the principles of equality, mutual interest, and also mutual respect for the state sovereignty and territorial integrity and non-interference in the internal affairs of the other High Contracting Party—to develop and consolidate economic and cultural ties between the Soviet Union and China, to render each other every possible economic assistance, and to carry out the necessary economic cooperation.

In tangible proof of the "fraternal sentiments" animating the two sides, the Soviet government further acceded to the PRC government's request for credits. In a companion agreement the Soviet Union now granted the PRC a US $300 million credit, at the rate of 35 American dollars to one ounce of fine gold on favorable terms of 1 percent annual interest. The credit could be drawn upon in the course of five years, starting 1 January 1950, in equal portions of $60 million per annum, to cover the cost of deliveries of equipment and materials from the Soviet Union. Credits that remained unused in the course of one annual period could be added to successive annual installments.

The credits and interest on them would be repaid by the PRC through deliveries of raw materials, tea, gold, and American dollars. The terms of trade would be fixed by special agreement, with prices for raw materials and tea geared to world market prices. Repayment of credits was distributed over the course of ten years in equal annual parts at the rate of one-tenth yearly of the sum total of received credits. The first scheduled payment fell due by 31 December 1954, and the last by 31 December 1963. Payment of interest on credits, calculated from the day of drawing the respective fraction of the credits, was to be effected semiannually. The State Bank of the Soviet Union and the People's Bank of the PRC would open special accounts and jointly establish procedures for clearance and accounting under the present agreement.

On an absolute scale U.S. $300 million (converted to 1,200 million rubles) is not an enormous amount as international aid programs run. Yet, as Soviet sources explain, it was the largest economic credit ever granted China by a foreign nation and the low 1 percent interest rate was not only "unprecedented" by international standards but also unparalleled in both Soviet and Chinese practice. An extra attaction was the power given China to decide whether to extinguish the loan through transfers of bullion and convertible currency or through shipment of traditional export items at normal commercial prices.

There were two other credit arrangements between the two countries. On 12 October 1954 the Soviet Union granted the PRC a long-term credit of 520 million rubles and again, in 1961, at a time when China was experiencing acute food shortages, the Soviet authorities offered the CCP leadership a loan of 1 million tons of grain and 500,000 tons of sugar. On 7 April 1961 an agreement was reached whereby China accepted the Soviet proposal to deliver by the end of that August as an interest-free loan 500,000 tons of sugar which China undertook to replace in kind during 1964–67. In his report to the plenary session of the CPSU Central Committee on 14 February 1964, Suslov revealed that the Soviet Union had extended to the PRC long-term credits on favorable terms to the total sum of 1,816 million rubles.

The bulk of the credits took the form of commodity loans, together with some investment credits that were allocated for the construction of specific industrial projects selected by the Chinese government. Credits in gold or freely convertible currency were not employed on a wide scale in Sino-Soviet economic transactions, and, as noted earlier, a typical feature of these relations was that China amortized the Soviet investment and commodity credits and the accrued interest charges through deliveries of traditional Chinese exports. The great advantage of this method, the Russians maintain, lay in that it provided China with a stable and secure market for the sale of her wares, enabled China to save gold and hard currency reserves and liquidate its indebtedness through delivery of commodities which could be spared from domestic consumption, ensured that many sectors of the national economy functioned to capacity, raised the level of employment, and consolidated the country's currency and finances. The terms of the Soviet Union's credit to the PRC have also been described by Soviet spokesmen as "very easy" since the interest rate did not exceed 2 percent per annum (presumably on the 520 million ruble loan; 1 percent on the original US $300 million loan) and some of the credits were granted without any interest fee at all (i.e., the 1961 sugar loan).

On 19 April 1950 the government of the Soviet Union and the government of the PRC signed their first trade agreement. Animated by the desire to expand commercial exchanges, the High Contracting Parties stipulated that the delivery of goods from the Soviet Union to the PRC and vice versa would be carried out in conformity with the lists which would be jointly drawn in the form of a special protocol. Both governments would guarantee deliveries of the merchandise in accordance with that protocol. Soviet and Chinese foreign trade organizations would then conclude contracts for the delivery of the commodities featured on the aforementioned lists, in which they would set the quantities, prices, dates and places of delivery, and other terms of trade. These agencies were also empowered, pursuant to the existing regulations in their respective countries concerning the import and export of goods, to conclude contracts for the delivery of wares on the conditions prescribed by the present agreement above and beyond the contingents established by the lists referred to. In every instance the prices of the goods would be determined on the basis of world market prices computed in rubles. Payments would be effected in the Soviet Union through the State Bank and in the PRC through the People's Bank. To that end these institutions would open in each other's name special, interest-free accounts in rubles.

Soviet and Chinese foreign trade entities were also authorized, with the prior sanction of the competent state organs, to conclude contracts for the delivery of goods calling for payment in gold, American dollars, or pounds sterling, as well as arrange for barter transactions. Payments on such contracts would take place through the above banks without being recorded in the accounts in question. These rules applied to payments for items delivered in execution of the agreement, payment on expenses connected with the trade turnover between the two countries as well as payments for the repair of vessels and transit expenses, and other payments approved by the banks.

The sums of all payments by each side (with the exception of those not entered on the accounts) had to balance semiannually for the duration of the agreement. A difference of less than 6 million rubles for a six-month period would not be considered a violation of the principle of equivalence. Any indebtedness shown on these accounts could be liquidated through deliveries of goods or transfers of gold, American dollars, or pounds sterling by mutual consent of the parties. The conversion of rubles into U.S. dollars or pounds sterling would follow the rate fixed by the Soviet Union State Bank on the day of payment, and the conversion of rubles into gold would be pegged to the gold content of the ruble.

The two governments instructed their trade representatives to check every six months on the progress of implementation of the agreement and, in case of need, to draft appropriate recommendations improving deliveries and achieving equivalence of payments in line with the agreement. In order to ensure timely deliveries of goods, both principals bound themselves to guarantee favorable conditions of railroad transportation and utilization of ports. Customs duties on the territory of each signatory on goods imported or exported pursuant to this agreement were to be paid by that party's trade organizations. Upon the expiration of the accord the designated banks would continue to accept bills against the accounts and issue payments on contracts concluded before the agreement lapsed. Any indebtedness remaining thereafter had to be extinguished within three months through additional deliveries of goods or by transfer of gold, American dollars, or pounds sterling, as determined by the parties. The agreement was scheduled to run from 1 January 1950 (i.e., retroactively) to 31 December 1950 and was subject to ratification.

A curious picture emerges. To begin with, what the Soviet Union and the PRC signed on this occasion was a trade agreement, whereas in the Soviet repertory trade treaties constitute the highest juridical form of economic modus vivendi between states. The latter provide a definite legal basis for the whole complex of trade and other economic relations between the parties, establishing the trade and political regimen that the signatories grant each other in respect to customs levies, commercial navigation, transport and transit, and the activities of juridical and physical persons of one on the territory of the other. Furthermore, they regulate a wide circle of questions connected with the development of mutual trade and economic exchanges, recognize the right of the Soviet Union to maintain a trade mission in the country involved, and spell out its juridical status. In general, documents of this genre are broad in scope and address themselves to topics which ordinary trade agreements do not deal with, for example, the assessment of internal taxes and imposts on merchandise, the carriage of goods by internal railroad and water transport, freedom of temporarily imported items from customs duties and levies, privileges and immunities afforded to vessels and cargoes in the event of shipwreck, mutual collaboration in the exchange of technical experience, and the execution of arbitral awards. All the trade treaties of the Soviet Union, whatever their titular designation, contain clauses governing these matters of principle—customs procedure, most-favored-nation rule, questions of navigation and transit, the legal condition of juridical and physical persons, the legal status of the trade missions of the Soviet Union, and so forth.

The formal elements likewise underscore the superior rank occupied by trade treaties vis-à-vis trade agreements. In the practice of the Soviet Union and the "people's democracies," the treaties are concluded on behalf of the supreme organs of state power (the Presidium of the Supreme Soviet in the case of the Soviet Union) and enter into force upon the official exchange of acts of ratification. By comparison the Soviet Union's trade agreements with its "socialist" colleagues (as the Sino-Soviet specimen indicates) are signed by the respective governments. Even so, China received preferential treatment on two particulars: most trade agreements dispense altogether with the business of ratification, whereas the Sino-Soviet version expressly required that extra safeguard; though the text said nothing about an exchange of acts of ratification, such a ceremony was in fact staged in Peking on 30 September 1950. Both gestures were doubtless calculated to enhance the PRC's prestige and dramatize the affair.

Lastly, trade treaties are concluded by the Soviet Union either for an indefinite period or for a term of several years, with an option of automatic prolongation by tacit acquiescence of the signatories, and thus in essence terminate upon denunciation by either side in accordance with established procedure on filing prior notice to that effect. The Sino-Soviet agreement, it should be noted, specifically spanned a single year and contained no proviso for extension. Actually, of course, the agreement remained in force until 1958, being renewed on an annual basis after its appointed year ran out by a succession of supplementary protocols which fixed the level and composition of trade between the two countries for the current year within the cadre of its technical rules on the negotiation of individual contracts, schedules and methods of payment, etc.

As the summary of its provisions makes clear, the 1950 agreement was a skeleton instrument which concentrated almost exclusively on the proposed system of accounting. It enunciated no general principles of commercial policy and even left the concrete modalities of trade operations to be worked out separately. (Although a secondary source reports that coincidentally an understanding was reached concerning the transit of goods through the territory of both states, and the legal status of the Soviet trade mission in China and the staff of the commercial counselor attached to the PRC embassy in the Soviet Union was defined.) This meant that (as further discussed below) in a formal sense between 1950 and 1958 Soviet-Chinese trade was conducted without benefit of a long-term trade agreement and through a series of ad hoc annual arrangements designed to take care of immediate exigencies in piece-meal fashion. Not surprisingly, therefore, some Western analysts have described the mechanics of Sino-Soviet trade during this stage as lacking a firm legal foundation and have speculated that in reality it was the Soviet Union which did not wish to commit itself by long-term commercial treaties or agreements to China.

The Soviets have reacted strongly to the implied criticism. Soviet-Chinese trade in the period 1950–64, they retort, included not only ordinary commercial shipments of goods, but also deliveries under the economic and the military assistance programs. By the same token Chinese exports to the Soviet Union comprised ordinary commercial deliveries of commodities along with deliveries in payment for Soviet economic and military credits. Economic assistance, military assistance, and credits were, it is emphasized, granted to China on the basis of long-term agreements.

More to the point, Soviet publicists further claim that the Soviet Union did repeatedly suggest the conclusion of a long-term agreement, but, allegedly, the Chinese side always avoided the topic. If this claim is true—and there is some reason to believe that it is—one possible explanation for the Chinese attitude may have been Peking's unhappiness with the prevailing system of fixing prices for the goods entering the Sino-Soviet trade stream (see below). These prices remained relatively constant from 1950 to 1958, and the arrangement ostensibly worked to China's detriment. It is noteworthy that the prices were revised in 1958 and that the conclusion of the long-term trade treaty on 23 April 1958 coincided with an exchange of letters that defined the new principles for determining such prices. The conjuncture of events could easily mean that until the Chinese got the Soviets to adopt a fairer price scale, they ducked all Soviet invitations to sign a regular trade treaty.

Despite these underlying tensions (of which little or nothing was suspected in the outside world), the record shows that in quantity as well as in quality the commercial exchanges between the Soviet Union and the PRC during this period grew at an unprecedented pace. The sharp upswing, according to Soviet analysts, cannot simply be explained by the Western embargo on trade with China. The chief reason presumably lay in the Soviet Union's ability and readiness to supply the PRC with all the indispensable modern industrial machinery and material the country needed on economically favorably terms. Indeed, industrial equipment led the parade of Soviet exports to the PRC. Deliveries of turnkey plants and plants being rebuilt—consisting of machine-tools, machinery, and instruments—mounted with every year. In addition, the Soviet Union also supplied the PRC with many other goods to tide it over the difficult initial stage of reconstruction.

Between 1953 and 1956 the size and substance of Sino-Soviet trade continued to augment and diversify and the composition of the trade flow underwent constant overhaul to reflect supervening changes in the social and physical infrastructure. With the revival of the PRC's own productive capacity, certain select commodities no longer had to be purchased abroad: hence, Soviet deliveries of cotton textiles and of yarn, paper, automobile tires, and sugar ceased almost entirely, and imports of cruder manufactured items (e.g., beams, small diameter pipes, and rails) dipped. The Chinese also drastically reduced the importing of some industrial items, such as simple-model machine-tools and textile equipment, as domestic production capacity improved.

Internal shifts in the make-up of Chinese imports from the Soviet Union meant stricter selectivity and heavier emphasis on more advanced models of industrial equipment and higher-grade materials for the operation of a more sophisticated industrial plant. While China could begin to fulfill national requirements in certain items through domestic efforts, its needs for a multitude of other products to sustain the current tempo of rapid and "massive" industrialization raced far ahead. Thus, notwithstanding individual cutbacks, the range of Soviet commodities exported to the PRC kept expanding and by 1957 comprised some twenty thousand titles. Pride of place went to modern equipment, precision instruments, laboratory equipment, large-diameter pipes, equipment for oil and geological survey work, and so forth. Turnkey industrial facilities now became the chief article of Soviet export to the PRC, with deliveries multiplying six-fold between 1952 and 1956. Even so, a bigger proportion of China's exigencies in this domain was met out of domestic production; initially 80 percent of the machinery installed in Chinese industrial plants was of Russian provenance, and the rest was manufactured locally; by the end of 1956 the ratio had dropped to 70:30, and in individual cases only 50–60 percent of the equipment originated in the Soviet Union.

A parallel trend may be observed in the structure of Chinese exports to the Soviet Union. Given the country's wartime devastation and the lack of communications between north and south, the bulk of exports to the Soviet Union at first featured agricultural products from the north and northeast regions. The gradual restoration of normal conditions throughout the mainland prompted both an increase in the value of Chinese exports to the Soviet Union and a change in their content. By 1952 nonferrous metals from the south and southwest areas occupied top place in the roster of Soviet imports from the PRC, and the list of agricultural products now also expanded as the resources of China's central and southern provinces were tapped.

More important, central planning and efficient organization had a positive impact on China's ability to sustain a higher export level. Since the development coincided with an increased interest on the part of the Soviet Union to obtain foodstuffs and industrial raw materials from foreign outlets, conditions were ripe for a joint attempt to coordinate Peking's desire to boost its exports with Moscow's import exigencies. This often meant mobilizing new export commodities not familiar to Russian consumers. The Soviets claim that they and the other "socialist" countries gave China an ideal opportunity to promote its exports in the desired fields, in spite of encountering an occasional hitch in introducing Chinese commodities to a Soviet clientele that called for special measures to resolve the difficulty. For example, in the past the Soviet Union had only imported fresh eggs from China, whereas such products as powdered eggs were supplied to England and Western Europe. These channels were no longer open to the PRC after the onset of the Korean War, so Soviet organizations adapted their techniques to utilize Chinese powdered eggs.

The parties strove for mutual accommodation. Soviet agencies were seeking suppliers of cork bark, previously not exported by China. Nevertheless, Chinese foreign trade companies managed in short order to organize the collection of stocks of the needed item for export to the Soviet Union. In some instances, where the export of certain goods or their utilization in the Soviet Union required specific arrangements or heavy capital investment, Soviet and Chinese foreign trade aggregates concluded *inter se* corresponding long-term agreements and in this manner the efforts and expenses of each side were economically justified.

In closing, several other aspects of the physical profile of Sino-Soviet trade during the 1953–57 period merit brief comment. First, from 1955 through 1957 the value of Soviet exports to China receded with each passing year. The curve registered a modest upswing in 1958, but not until 1959 did it again catch up and surpass the 1954 peak. On the other hand, in 1955 and 1956 the value of imports from China continued to rise and for these two years the growth of Chinese exports to the Soviet Union managed to pick up the slack in Soviet exports to the PRC, so that the gross turnover showed a net increase.

The fluctuations can be attributed to several elements. The large Soviet credit granted in 1950 ran out in 1954, and the smaller 1954 credit could not sustain the large Chinese purchases of Soviet goods which its predecessor had made possible. In addition, an undertone of tension was beginning to creep into the Sino-Soviet dialogue around this time over both political and economic issues: the Chinese had virtually strong-armed the Russians into liquidating their joint stock corporations and had evinced an unseemly interest in Mongolia; the Twentieth Congress of the CPSU and Peking's annoyance over Khrushchev's de-Stalinization speech precipitated another cold spell. Further-more, the Kremlin faced a difficult situation in Eastern Europe and funds were hurriedly diverted in that direction to stem the tide of popular discontent in the satellite states. Finally, Moscow had woken up to the realization that a large bloc of uncommitted nations was parked on its doorstep, just waiting to be cultivated and promising dramatic diplomatic victories in return—but that, too, cost money. Since the pie was finite and in the post-Stalin era the long-repressed appetites of the consumer on the home front also had to be accommodated, adjustments had to be made elsewhere. Apparently, "aid" to China was judged to be expendable under the circumstances, especially since the key Chinese imports—machinery and equipment—weathered the cutback with little adverse effect.

By coincidence the Chinese had by now launched their own public campaign to sing the virtues of national "self-reliance." Stressing the use of domestic resources and native manpower and ingenuity, the regime strove to improvise local substitutes for goods formerly purchased abroad.

Second, the combination of the spirit of Bandung and the relaxation of Western trade restrictions encouraged China's emergence as an increasingly active and independent participant in international economic and political affairs. This, of course, gave the Chinese a chance to look around for more attractive opportunities to buy and sell, which they were not slow to do. Soviet spokesmen, citing extensive statistical data, tend to downgrade the significance of the impact of this development on the course of Sino-Soviet commercial exchanges and point to the continued predominance of the Soviet Union as an importer of Chinese products. Yet, by 1957 seventy-one capitalist countries had established trade relations with the PRC and accounted for 33.9 percent of China's foreign trade turnover that year. As the PRC markedly expanded its purchases from capitalist suppliers, it also sought to promote exports to these countries in order to defray the attendant cost. Given the objective limitations on China's import-export capability, this partial reorientation required a concomitant shift of resources and the sprawling Sino-Soviet trading empire was a natural storehouse from which to draw such reserves.

Third, both governments were fully aware that one way for the Chinese to extinguish their current debt to the Soviet Union was to reduce Soviet imports while expanding Chinese exports. Spurring them on must have been the knowledge that meantime the consequence of their other mutual initiatives had acted to push the amount of Chinese indebtedness to the Russians steadily upward.

The picture would not be complete without at least alluding to the related subject of noncommercial debts. A series of agreements provided for the training of Chinese citizens in civic and technical institutions of higher education in the Soviet Union. A part of the expenses connected with these programs was to be reimbursed by cash payments and a part offset by accepting Soviet citizens for training in China, although the number of Soviet visitors to China never matched that of the Chinese traveling to the Soviet Union: by Soviet count, between 1951 and 1962 more than eight thousand Chinese citizens received industrial and technical training in the Soviet Union, more than eleven thousand Chinese undergraduate and postgraduate students attended Soviet educational establishments, and about one thousand scientific workers of China's Academy of Sciences studied at research institutes of the Soviet Union Academy of Sciences. Add to this the fact that in the period from 1950 to 1960 over ten thousand highly qualified Soviet specialists were posted to China for more or less protracted tours of duty. One can only conclude that the cost of the scheme must have been quite impressive. The money for payment had to be earned somehow, which essentially entailed the sale of extra goods and services to the Russians through established trade channels.

III.   PROBLEMS IN THE PERIOD 1950-57

Ironically, all this efflux of good will somehow managed to breed its own quota of discordance. For example, the Soviet credit grants have sparked a fair share of controversy in the framework of the protracted Sino-Soviet polemics. First, the Chinese have repeatedly drawn attention to the fact that these were just ordinary loans which they had to, and did, repay in full, with interest. Thus, Soviet generosity involved neither gifts nor donations and, by inference, entailed no self-sacrifice on the part of the Soviet Union. To this the Russians retort that Soviet credits to China meant that a part of the surplus product created by the Soviet people was siphoned off from the

Soviet economy. Greater advantages could have been derived if, instead of sending to the PRC in the form of credits industrial equipment and machinery, these were used at home to increase production so as to export the increment to foreign states in exchange for commodities required by the Soviet Union. The interest on Soviet credits, to boot, was far below the rates prevailing on the world capitalist market and only partially compensated for the losses incurred by the Soviet economy by the withdrawal of the material values embodied in these credits.

Allegedly, then, "guided by the principles of proletarian internationalism," the Soviet Union extended credits to China from funds that could have been profitably expended on the development of its own national economy and on raising the Soviet people's living standards. Hence, to the Russians, thinking of the Soviet credits to China in the same terms as the money-lending practices of the capitalist powers smacks of either ignorance or bad faith. According to them, their credits had nothing in common with the so-called aid administered by the capitalist states, because they were not for the purpose of exploitation, economic aggrandizement, or maximum profit, nor were they used to extort political or military concessions. The Soviet credits, it is contended, were designed to help the Chinese people build socialism at home.

Second, the Chinese have, on a number of occasions, made disparaging remarks about the amount of the credits that the Soviet Union had granted China and have commented adversely on the rapid increase in recent years of Soviet financial commitments to various members of the Third World, India in particular, obliquely implying that the money lavished on the latter group of countries could more wisely be spent within the socialist family proper. (Indeed, Soviet sources now admit that even the initial US $300 million credit met with instant criticism by prominent members of Mao's immediate entourage as woefully inadequate.) For political, ideological, and moral reasons the Chinese may well be right, of course, and justifiably unhappy about the tenor of Soviet behavior on this score, but at the same time there are no valid legal or technical grounds for their complaints on this specific issue. The primary decision on whether to extend credits and how much to extend is, after all, a purely discretionary matter and is not in itself subject to legal regulation or constraint under the current norms of interstate relations.

Nevertheless, the Soviets seem to have been deeply stung by these charges of niggardliness. Their defense has been that, in assessing the extent of Soviet financial assistance to the PRC, the Soviet Union never claimed that the furnishing of credits would ensure that the Peking regime would be fully supplied with the means necessary for carrying out its entire industrialization program. The purpose of the loans was merely to help the Chinese nation to establish, through the maximum use of internal resources and reserves, the initial foundation for socialist industrialization and to acquire a seminal complex of industrial enterprises. With this nucleus as a basis China could then be catapulted from a backward agrarian society into an advanced and powerful industrial socialist state. According to Soviet analysts such a launching pad was in fact created on the mainland in short order with the devoted help of the socialist countries, chief among them the Soviet Union. Glossing on the statement by Li Hsien-nien, the PRC's finance minister, to the effect that the share of revenues from Soviet credits in the total volume of financial receipts during the first decade of the PRC's existence amounted to a bare 2 percent, Soviet spokesmen insist that this ostensibly small fraction played a disproportionately large role in the industrialization of the country and in boosting its defense potential by equipping China with a hard core of modern industries consisting of the largest and most up-to-date processing and manufacturing plants.

On the same principle Soviet military credits were not intended for building barracks or providing local military personnel with food and uniforms. The money was used to modernize the People's Liberation Army, and the Soviets see in the PLA's ample stocks of new materiel, armaments, and equipment shipped from the Soviet Union or produced under Soviet licenses at Chinese enterprises built with Soviet help conclusive evidence of the scope, effectiveness, and importance for China of the Soviet credits she received.

In brief, Peking may have felt disappointment. The Soviets, however, have maintained throughout that the credit operations between the Soviet Union and China contributed significantly to the success of their economic relations, while accelerating the building of socialism in the PRC and strengthening that country's economic and defense capability.

This brings us to the third item, namely, the whole sensitive business of credits reputedly earmarked for routine commercial use being applied instead to fulfill military exigencies. For there is no doubt that a portion of the original credits that the Soviet Union granted the PRC was indeed diverted in this manner. The exact fraction is unknown, but independent estimates run quite high; according to official Chinese sources, Soviet loans to China were "used mostly for the purchase of war materiel from the Soviet Union, the greater part of which was used up in the war to resist U.S. aggression and aid in Korea."

In addition to technical assistance in building defense establishments and providing them with modern equipment, the Russians also delivered equipment, armaments, supplies, and material for the PLA's stores. A substantial segment of China's imports from the Soviet Union thus consisted of goods intended for bolstering China's defense system. The big share of military deliveries occurred in the period 1950–53 to satisfy the immediate requirements of the Korean War effort. Even following the end of the hostilities, the level stayed comparatively high when China strove to modernize her armed forces and replenish depleted stocks. Only after 1957 did it drop sharply as the modernization program was completed and the defense industry installations built with Soviet assistance entered the production phase.

To the Russians the military assistance aspect of their dealings with China was a fair substitute for the more mundane brand of economic aid since this solution purportedly allowed China to mobilize her available material and manpower resources for civilian economic construction. Had the Chinese elected to focus on meeting their own military needs, they would have had to depend on the Russians to assist them in the civilian domain. For these services they were expected to pay; therefore, the inference goes, reversing the situation in no way alters the picture.

The Chinese have taken a rather dim view of this interpretation. True, they profess to be proud of what they did for the common cause in standing up to American "aggression" in Korea, and they ask for no thanks for having merely "performed their proletarian duty." Nevertheless, in light of their heavy sacrifices in Korea in human life and national wealth, they quite obviously resent having to pay the Russians for weapons which, they believe, were used for the defense as much of the interests of the Soviet Union as of the PRC or North Korea—even as a free gift to the Chinese, these arms were cheaper than what it would have cost the Soviet Union to send an expeditionary corps to Korea in order to safeguard the integrity of the North Korean regime.

In fact, such sentiments were aired openly at the time of the Hundred Flowers campaign: that it was unreasonable for China to bear all the expenses of the "resist-America aid-Korea" war; that during the Second World War, the United States granted loans and leases to her allies and some of them later refused to pay back while others were excused from repayment; and that it would take the PRC ten years to reimburse the Soviet Union, and the loans also carried interest. The authorities quickly moved to suppress the critics, but the incidents are enough to suggest a profound and persistent sense of grievance among the better informed Chinese over the ethics of the Soviet conduct in this episode. The irony of it is that the early dissidents and their current successors are only echoing the arguments that the Soviets themselves advanced against United States' demands for payment for the lend-lease deliveries to the Soviet Union during the Second World War. The Russians, too, could not then understand, or pretended not to understand, how an ally could exact monetary compensation for aid that contributed to the common victory. The memories of statesmen and politicians, the historical record shows, can be extremely short, and practical expediency can often be trusted to trigger a most convenient fit of amnesia: the disease does not defer to ideological boundaries.

Another problem related to the issue of credits concerned the characterization of the exchange of goods between the two countries. The Chinese viewed this process as an exchange of value for equal value, and in recent years have voiced strong objections to the persistent Soviet habit of indiscriminately designating the mass flow of Soviet goods to China as "aid." Yet, the Soviet position in this regard does have some merit.

First, the Russians adduce the subjective element. The assistance that the Soviet government undertook to furnish China at a crucial juncture in that country's history did not, as they put it, signify that the Soviet Union possessed internal surpluses of some kind which could be spared at home. Thus, the Soviet Union shared with China, in a truly fraternal spirit, materials that it sometimes badly needed itself. In doing this it was guided by a desire to help the Communist Party of China and the Chinese people to turn China as quickly as possible into an industrial socialist power, and not by commercial motives. All this, in the Soviet mind, stamps the venture as a manifestation of selfless aid (even if money did change hands in the process) rather than an incidence of "ordinary business ethics."

Second, Soviet sources note that from 1949 to 1955 China's imports from the Soviet Union exceeded her exports to that country by a total of 947.3 million rubles. In concrete terms the phenomenon meant that the Soviet Union thereby allocated from its national income and lent to China for a considerable period of time substantial resources which the latter applied toward the solution of urgent local economic and other tasks. Not until 1956 did China begin to amortize her debts with the Soviet Union, and the job was not completed until 1964. To be sure, interest accrued on the sums involved and ultimately the money had to be repaid, but in the meantime the "loan" helped finance China's program of economic reconstruction. Again, to the Soviets this readiness not to insist on an immediate settlement of accounts spelled aid, not a straightforward entrepreneurial deal.

Finally, the Russians contend that the very pattern and character of Soviet deliveries to the PRC amounted to aid. The nature of the exports was calculated to enhance China's economic welfare and promote its independence. The capitalist universe would never dream of selling China machinery and equipment embodying the latest discoveries in science and technology and allow it to escape from the toils of economic thralldom to the western monopolies. According to the official version the thrust of Soviet exports ran diametrically counter to what up until now had been considered in "bourgeois" quarters as sound business practices vis-à-vis weak and underdeveloped states and, for that reason also, de facto represents a variety of aid.

Add to this the Soviet claim that the PRC as a young, emerging state found it very hard, owing to the range and quality of its export goods, to secure a foothold in the world market and handle the competition of other developing nations as well as of the technically advanced capitalist powers. Presumably, it was solely thanks to its close ties with the socialist community and primarily with the Soviet Union that the PRC was able to export large quantities of agricultural and industrial raw materials and other commodities at stable prices. Implicit in the theme is the suggestion that the Chinese exports to the Soviet Union were of but marginal utility to the Soviet economy and were purchased more to help the Chinese finance their imports than for their intrinsic value. Soviet willingness to accept as quid pro quo whatever the Chinese had to offer and could afford to spare sprang, so the story goes, from a noble sentiment of generosity and not from crass expectations of material enrichment.

The majority of Western commentators agree with the Soviet thesis that the Chinese derived more benefit than the Russians from the structure of their mutual trade. Still, Chinese spokesmen are prompt to respond, if Soviet exports to the PRC deserve to be called "aid" on grounds that they comprised articles vital to China's economic progress, the exact same label fits Chinese deliveries to the Soviet Union. For example, many of the substantial mineral exports to the Soviet Union, the Chinese emphasize, are raw materials which are indispensable for the development of the most advanced branches of science and for the manufacture of rockets and nuclear weapons.

Actually, much of the argument is a problem of semantics. The Soviets do acknowledge that they received in return important "aid" from China, citing identical data. The shipments of nonferrous and rare metals, oils, industrial crops, fruit, and consumer goods from China have been openly hailed in the Soviet literature as significant contributions to the rapid economic development of the Soviet Union and to the improvement in the standard of living of the Soviet population. In particular, when the Soviet Union suffered a serious tin shortage because England, which had previously supplied it, deliberately short-circuited trade with the Soviet Union after World War II, China came to the rescue and provided enough tin to meet all of the Soviet industrial requirements. What it really boils down to is that, while the Soviets admit that the "aid" program worked both ways, they nevertheless maintain that they did more for China than vice versa. They are probably quite right, but the Chinese today resent that attitude and seek to redress the picture by extolling instead the positive role they themselves played in the episode and thus win the recognition they feel they are properly entitled to. The legitimacy of this ambition cannot be denied either.

Lastly, to the foregoing elements of doctrinal discord a technical element must be added, revolving around the question of the conversion rate of the two currencies. There is some evidence for instance, that in the 1950s the Soviet Union and China feuded over the issue of the conversion rates of their currencies, with the nontrade rate of exchange between the ruble and the yüan lying at the heart of the protracted dispute. According to a Soviet source, when the Soviet Union and the PRC first moved to set the ruble-yüan rate of exchange, the PRC had still not overcome its inflationary problem and the agreement signed on 1 June 1951 noted that "the parties unanimously consented to use as a basis for determining the rate of the ruble to the yüan of the People's Bank of China the official price of gold." As of that date, the nontrade rate was fixed at 6,754 old yüan to 1 ruble. The present agreement was to stay in force until "the completion of the currency reform in the PRC and the establishment of the gold content of the PRC currency."

On 23 September 1953, allegedly "at the initiative of the USSR," another protocol was concluded in Peking, and the ruble-yüan exchange rate was revised, to 5,000 yüan to 1 ruble. The Soviets claim that the new conversion rate was intended to have a positive effect on the PRC's pending currency reform as well as on the determination of the rate of the yüan to other currencies. After the implementation of the currency reform in China in March 1955, during which 10,000 old yüan were exchanged for 1 new yüan, the ruble-yüan rate remained the same: 0.5 yüan to 1 ruble (2 rubles for 1 yüan). The Soviet explanation is that because the gold content of the yüan had not yet been set, the governments of the Soviet Union and the PRC decided to keep the existing exchange rate.

The Chinese, however, maintained that the nontrade rate of 0.5 yüan to the ruble greatly undervalued the yüan and since the salaries of the Soviet advisers, experts, and technicians stationed in China were converted on that scale, their local buying-power was artificially inflated. The reverse was true of Chinese students and visitors to the Soviet Union: they suffered a severe loss in acquiring rubles for yüan at the official rate. Under the circumstances it is not surprising that the Chinese continued to press the Russians to make the necessary adjustments. Renewed negotiations resulted in the protocols of 23 October 1956 and 30 December 1957. The latter document imposed a 200 percent surtax, effective 1 January 1958, on ruble payments for a limited category of noncommercial transactions (the vexing situation of the preferential treatment afforded Soviet personnel in China was not cured, for example). This meant that henceforth 16.67 yüan equaled 100 rubles (or 600 rubles for 100 yüan). "The rate of the ruble to the yüan for nontrade payments was established on the basis of the prices in the PRC for representative industrial and consumer goods and prices for services in comparison with prices for similar goods and services functioning in the USSR."

When on 1 January 1961 the Soviet Union decreed an increase in the gold content of the ruble, its buying power rose, and the rate between the ruble and foreign currencies in general, and the yüan in particular, had to be revised. By arrangement between the State Bank of the Soviet Union and the People's Bank of China, a ratio of 45 rubles for 100 yüan in trade transactions and 77.52 rubles for 100 yüan in noncommercial transactions was arrived at. To the Russians these facts show that "the currency relations between the Soviet Union and the PRC rested on an objective economic basis, on the basis of mutual agreement, and that the Soviet Union did not derive any unilateral economic benefits from currency transactions with China." The record would indicate that the Chinese thought quite differently.

There was a similar difficulty concerning the question of the conversion rate utilized in computing Soviet credits to China. For these purposes a special conversion rate was derived from the prevailing ruble-dollar and yüan-dollar exchange scales, different from any existing trade rate between the ruble and the yüan. The practice apparently was a source of considerable aggravation. From explanations volunteered by Soviet spokesmen, one gathers that in a majority of cases Soviet credits to the PRC were expressed in rubles, at the rate of 4 rubles to $1.

This situation lasted until 1 January 1961, when a new exchange rate was fixed between the ruble and foreign currencies, which "significantly narrowed the gap between the levels of world prices and domestic wholesale prices for goods featured in international trade." One American dollar was now worth 0.9 rubles. The rise in the gold content and value of the ruble required a recalculation of the indebtedness incurred by the PRC and other recipients of Soviet credits, which was effected by reducing the amount of the unpaid balance by 77.5 percent and by lowering by the same fraction the prices of commodities under the existing trade agreements and all other classes of deliveries. Hence, the Soviets claim, the volume of deliveries against outstanding credits and the real cost of their repayment did not fluctuate, no changes supervened in the terms of the trade and credit agreements previously concluded between the Soviet Union and the PRC, and the PRC lost nothing on the deal from the Soviet Union's switch to the new monetary standard.

True or false, the perceived need in responsible Soviet circles to mount a formal apologia for the Soviet Union's record in this domain would tend to indicate that Peking did not match Moscow's enthusiasm in its endorsement of the virtues of these policies. If Peking were of the same mind as Moscow, the protestations and assurances would be superfluous.

The difficulties encountered during this period should not be overemphasized. Whatever frictions were at work underneath the official surface of Sino-Soviet relations, Soviet comments as 1957 drew to a close exuded genuine optimism about the prospects for commercial cooperation between the twin giants of the communist world. In recent years agreements had been signed on regular air communications, on navigation on the border lakes and waterways, and on direct rail service. Railroads, in particular, were viewed as a crucial factor in the continued expansion of economic contacts between the two states because they shared such a long land boundary, all the more so since these routes were immune to external influences and not susceptible to hostile interference. New trunk-lines, along with older facilities that had been renovated and modernized, facilitated the mass movement of wares, shuttling approximately six million tons of goods annually across the international frontier. Additional spurs were under construction and were expected to improve traffic further. Outwardly the scene looked rosy indeed.

IV. The Terms of Trade

The 1950 trade agreement, as previously noted, only fixed the general framework within which the process of Sino-Soviet commercial exchanges was designed to function. The elaboration of the concrete modus operandi was consigned to subsidiary documents, principally to the instrumentality of the so-called general conditions of deliveries of goods. This device plays so central a role in the mechanics of Soviet trade activities with its socialist allies that it merits detailed attention. It sets the following commercial standards of contracts: form; place of delivery; schedule and date of delivery; packing and marking; appendixes to the contract; technical documentation; testing; guarantee; claims; procedure of payment; sanctions; *force majeure*; and arbitration. Only a few of the salient traits will be examined here.

Before proceeding to an analysis *in substantia*, two preliminary remarks are in order. First, the PRC, North Korea, North Vietnam, and Cuba are the only socialist states left whose relations with the Soviet Union in this sector are still regulated by bilateral agreements. The remaining members of the "commonwealth" have all by now been integrated into the multilateral scheme introduced under the auspices of the Council for Mutual Economic Aid in 1958 and revised in 1968 (hereafter referred to as "CMEA general conditions of deliveries"). Second, while the bulk of the provisions of the bilateral protocols on "general conditions of deliveries" which operated between the Soviet Union and its socialist allies at the initial stage followed a uniform pattern, occasional divergences do occur in the texts. Soviet commentators treat these as "minor discrepancies" attributable to the geographic location of the countries concerned and, in individual instances, to the peculiarities of the circumstances of delivery. Exactly the same has been said of the relationship between the current batch of bilateral protocols on "general conditions of deliveries" and the "CMEA general conditions of deliveries" and, it is stressed, the few cases where the language of the respective agreements does not coincide are in no way the outgrowth of distinct "commercial-political principles."

To put the Sino-Soviet experience in this field in proper perspective, the major differences between the Soviet Union-PRC version of the "general conditions of deliveries" and the parent (Eastern European) model as well as the "CMEA general conditions of deliveries" will be duly noted. Furthermore, the nature and thematic distribution of these "deviations" may prove interesting in their own right.

Agreements (protocols) on "general conditions of deliveries" are concluded by the Ministries of Foreign Trade of the respective parties for an indefinite period and can be terminated by either signatory by filing a three months' prior notice to that effect. As interdepartmental documents, intended to be easily updated to accommodate changing practices, they have been frequently revised. The first such protocol between the Soviet Union and the PRC was signed on 19 April 1950, the same day as the trade agreement, and amended on 29 March 1952. Later editions date from 12 February 1955 (amended 27 December 1955) and 10 April 1957.

Use of the "general conditions" is predicated on the proposition that deliveries of goods will be implemented in accordance with their provisions "unless a different procedure has been established in individual contracts in light of the peculiarities of the delivery." In concluding contracts, therefore, the interested foreign trade organizations have the right, by virtue of the specific character of the goods or on other grounds, to introduce supplementary stipulations that depart from the formulations incorporated in the "general conditions." Unless modification of the norms prescribed by the "general conditions" is justified by the special nature of the deliveries concerned, the arrangements may be struck down by the corresponding ministries as violative of the imperative instructions of the apposite "general conditions." Furthermore, the applicability of the "general conditions" to contracts signed by the corresponding foreign trade associations does not depend on whether the contract specifies that in all matters not covered by its articles the "general conditions" govern. Even without an explicit reservation on that point the "general conditions" are considered controlling for these purposes.

The contracts themselves as well as diverse enclosures (technical conditions, specifications, instructions on packing, marking, loading, etc.) must without exception be in writing and signed by authorized persons. All the correspondence and negotiations preceding the signature of the contract or confirmation of an order lose force at the moment the contract is signed. To be sure, the parties may enter into deals orally—in face-to-face conversations or by phone—but the transactions must still be formalized in writing. The procedure pertaining to the signing of foreign trade contracts by the competent agencies is regulated by the domestic legislation of the respective parties. The problem of the mechanics and date of formation of the contract is treated in detail in the "CMEA general conditions of deliveries." By contrast, in concluding contracts with the foreign trade organizations of the Asian socialist countries (as well, interestingly enough, as with the companies of capitalist countries), the question of when the contract is considered to have been concluded is decided by reference to the domestic civil law of the country which is recognized as applicable to the given case.

The trade agreements in general anticipate the delivery of goods during the corresponding year covered by the agreement and very rarely direct that some particular item must be delivered by a given date before the expiration of the year in question (e.g., in the first half of the year, in the first or third quarter, etc.). The "general conditions" indicate that the concrete time limits for the deliveries of goods are settled in the contracts. This, in fact, means that the contracts merely arrange the timetable to pinpoint when and in what quantities during the period governed by the agreement the respective articles will be delivered.

When concluding contracts, the foreign trade organizations are not entitled to appoint terminal dates beyond those prescribed by the applicable trade agreement. Within these bounds, however, the delivery periods may be prolonged if, for example, the buyer has failed to furnish the seller the necessary data required by the terms of the contract, thus causing serious inconvenience to the deliverer, or if performance has been delayed because of unforeseen circumstances or *force majeure*.

Questions connected with the price of the goods, in particular the price scale, possible discounts, etc., are taken care of by the parties when each concrete foreign trade transaction is concluded. The quality of the goods is, as a rule, also designated in the contract. The "general conditions" require that the quality of the articles satisfy the technical conditions and standards envisaged in the contract, and that this fact be confirmed through suitable documentation in the contract itself. In the Sino-Soviet experience the practice has been that in the absence of a contract stipulation, the quality of the goods must fulfill the state standards of the country of the seller.

The "CMEA general conditions of deliveries" address themselves in considerable detail to the question of the seller's obligation to furnish technical documentation and the manner of the subsequent utilization of this data. The Sino-Soviet "general conditions" are silent on this point. Hence, all matters pertaining to the procedure and deadlines for the transfer of technical documentation, its scope, etc., are ironed out by the buyer and the seller at the time of the conclusion of the contract.

The "CMEA general conditions of deliveries," just as the old European bilateral model of "general conditions of deliveries," deal *in extenso* with the business of preshipment verification as well as guarantee of the quality of the goods earmarked for export. The "general conditions" presently in force between the Soviet Union and the Asian socialist countries, on the other hand, shun these topics completely. They are regulated in the contract proper. If the contract does not establish any special procedures concerning a prior check on the quality of the goods slated for shipment, then the seller can act at his own discretion. However, quality must in every case be confirmed by a corresponding certificate. Similarly, if the contract fails to define the terms of the guarantee, the seller is obligated to guarantee the appropriate quality of the goods for the appropriate period in accordance with the state standard under which the article was produced.

The character of the tare or packing may depend on the nature of the goods, the method and distance of transportation (e.g., marine packing), climatic conditions (e.g., tropical packing), the commercial customs prevailing in the sales market, the exigencies of the customs administrations, etc. That is why the "CMEA general conditions" and the USSR-PRC "general conditions" confine themselves to establishing general principles and leave the details to be determined in the individual contracts. The prescriptions of both these documents on the subject boil down to stipulating that if the contract does not feature explicit instructions concerning tare and packing of the goods, the seller must then ship the items in the tare and packing such as would ensure the safety of the goods en route, taking into account duration and methods of transportation and possible transhipments under circumstances of proper and ordinary handling of the cargo.

Both the "CMEA general conditions" and the "general conditions of deliveries" between the Soviet Union and the Asian socialist countries assume that, unless otherwise indicated in the contract, each piece must be clearly inscribed in indelible paint with the contract number, the package number, the name of the receiver, the net and gross weight in kilograms, as well as special (precautionary) signs should these be required by virtue of the character of the goods. Furthermore, since not only the buyer but also the carrier is interested in the correct marking of the cargo, the "general conditions" direct that the marking must meet the specifications of the Agreement on International Railway Freight Communication or the standards set for other modes of transportation.

In order to eliminate potential sources of dispute, the "general conditions" establish that the number of pieces and/or the weight delivered by the seller is determined by the data entered on the bills of lading issued by the railroad station or shipping company that receives the goods. Any claims concerning shortages from the quantity of pieces and/or weight shown on the bill of lading must be submitted by the buyer not to the seller but to the responsible railroad administration or shipping company.

A central role in foreign trade operations is assigned to the terms of notification. The "general conditions" obligate the seller and the buyer to inform each other of the readiness of the goods and the dispatch of contingents in the manner and time spans specified in the contract. In particular, the buyer must communicate to the seller in writing the shipping details if the data is not listed in the contract. The seller, in turn, must let the buyer know that the merchandise has been sent off, indicating the number of pieces or the weight, the buyer's order number, the number of the bill of lading, etc. Where the commodities are being delivered FOB, the seller must notify the buyer that the goods are ready for shipment so that he may have a vessel waiting in port on schedule. If the buyer has failed to have a vessel ready to receive the cargo despite timely notice, he bears the cost of storing the cargo beyond the twenty-one-day period of grace. The "general conditions" enjoin the foreign trade organizations to set firm deadlines for the various mutual notifications, and impose responsibility on the delinquent party for all losses and expenses incurred through nonobservance of the established timetable.

The contract also fixes the terms and place of delivery. These have considerable legal importance since they serve to determine when title to and risk and responsibilities for the merchandise is transferred from the seller to the purchaser. Pursuant to the "general conditions," deliveries by water are conducted exclusively on FOB terms between the Soviet Union and the PRC, whereas vis-à-vis most of the socialist states the contracting parties may opt for either FOB or CIF terms.

The concept of FOB, in Sino-Soviet practice, has also acquired a specific meaning. The seller is liable for loading the goods on board the ship, but in addition he must bear the cost and risk of stowing the merchandise into the hold of the ship and must furnish the necessary padding material. This is distinct from the provisions of the "CMEA general conditions of deliveries" where risk passes to the buyer from the moment the cargo is aboard ship.

Deliveries by railroad are effected at the state frontier of the seller. The buyer pays the transportation cost from that point and any expenses connected with switching the cars from a broad to a narrow gauge or vice versa.

Between the member-states of CMEA, two sets of terms of delivery of goods by highway transportation are available: FOB site of transfer of goods to the buyer's means of transportation; or, if the goods are being delivered by the seller's means of transportation, FOB site of inspection of the goods at the frontier customs office of the country adjacent to the country of the seller. In the Sino-Soviet "general conditions," however, all deliveries by highway transportation are effected at the Sino-Soviet frontier where the goods are transferred from the transportation facilities of the seller to those of the buyer. Deliveries by air between the Soviet Union and the PRC observe the principle of FOB on board the plane in the airport of the country of the deliverer. Where postal services are employed, the seller absorbs the expenses stemming from the conveyance of the parcel as far as the state frontier of his country.

Relations between the foreign trade organizations of the Soviet Union and the other socialist states rest, if Soviet sources can be believed, on the principle of strict and honest performance by the parties of their obligations. The practice of many years of experience is said to attest to the success of the enterprise. Foreign trade institutions within the "community" conduct large-scale exchanges, and during all this time there have been only a few instances of resort to arbitration to settle a disputed point. Of course, this does not exclude the possibility of reciprocal submission of various sorts of claims arising out of their contractual ties, and for that reason the "general conditions" feature a special section devoted to claims procedure.

Claims may be filed solely as regards the quality and quantity of the goods involved in a transaction. Thus, shortages noticed at the time of receipt of a shipment are protested by drawing up a corresponding commercial document witnessed by a third party. The "general principles" further provide that the seller is not liable for any changes in the quality of the goods after they cross the frontier, as long as the deterioration does not occur through the seller's fault.

In the early bilateral protocols on "general conditions" concluded between the Soviet Union and the European socialist states, the deadline for filing claims concerning quantity was fixed at three months and for those concerning quality at six months, computed from the date of delivery. The same rule was adopted by the "CMEA general conditions of deliveries." In the parallel agreement with the PRC, however, the time limit is uniformly set at six months in both cases. For merchandise carrying a guarantee, claims must be submitted not later than thirty days following the expiration of the period of guarantee. In the Sino-Soviet context, even if he misses the deadline, the buyer still retains the right to seek relief through arbitration subject to the restrictions of the statute of limitations. In short, no sanction attaches for filing a claim too late. While this was also true under the terms of the original bilateral agreements between the Soviet Union and the European people's democracies, the "CMEA general conditions of deliveries" consummated a major change by providing that a violation of the established deadlines entails forfeiture by the buyer of the right to resort to arbitration.

All submitted claims must be dealt with within a forty-five-day period. Under the CMEA, if the seller does not reply to a claim within the set deadline, he must bear the costs of the ensuing arbitration, regardless of the outcome of the proceedings. Pursuant to the "general conditions" between the Soviet Union and the Asian socialist countries, however, failure on the part of the seller to respond to the buyer's claim is tantamount to its acceptance.

Payments for goods and services connected with trade exchanges are effected through the central banks of the contracting parties and to that end the respective banks open special clearing accounts in each other's name. According to the official version, because the relations between the foreign trade organizations of the Soviet Union and the people's democracies are based on total mutual trust, the standard form of accounting between them is "incasso" and only in very rare instances, primarily involving payments for bulk cargoes delivered throughout the year (ores, coal, etc.), is the accrediting form employed.

In an earlier variant of the incasso system the seller submitted an "incasso" order for collection together with the invoice-bill and other commercial and transportation documents and the buyer had to pay for the goods within ten days of receiving the designated order from the bank of his country. The Sino-Soviet arrangement espoused a different technique, which has since been extended to Soviet trade relations with virtually the entire bloc. Under this formula the bank of the country of the seller, upon receiving from the seller a complete set of the commercial documents specified by the "general conditions" and the respective foreign trade contract, immediately pays the seller from the clearing account of the bank of the country of the buyer. On receipt of the debit notice and commercial documents the latter bank in turn deducts that amount from the account of the buyer, forwards him the accompanying commercial documents, and credits the amount to the clearing account of the bank of the country of the seller. This new form of payment, which did not call for prior certification of acceptance by the buyer, reportedly speeded up considerably the execution of payments. Distances and long delays may explain the practical need to introduce a scheme of "payment on demand" in the case of the PRC (and, incidentally, of North Korea as well) aimed at easing the extra financial burden imposed on the seller by the long wait.

Subsequently, if while verifying the relevant commercial documents the buyer discovers a violation of contractual obligations by the seller, he has ten days after the bank of his country has received these documents to refuse to endorse the invoice-bill paid by the bank, i.e., to demand the return of the amount paid from his account. This right is said to represent a very important aspect of the present payments system in that it guarantees the importer the possibility of exercising control over his trading partner and fully protects his interests as a payer.

Such refusal may be total or partial. The importer has the right to refuse endorsement in the full amount if the bill is presented for goods not specified by the contract, if the goods have not been shipped to their proper destination, if the appended documents contain discrepancies that preclude precise determination of the quantity, assortment, quality, and cost of the goods, as well as for a number of other reasons. Partial refusal is permitted when the price fixed by the contract has been exceeded, when expenses not foreseen by the contract have been included in the bill, when an arithmetical error occurs in the bill or the attached documents, and so on. The bank's function boils down to checking whether an authorized reason is cited for the refusal. If so, the amount deducted from the buyer's account is reinstated forthwith, and the bank of the country of the seller is notified accordingly. After this all disagreements between the buyer and the seller are settled by them directly. In that connection if the buyer's refusal to pay subsequently is found to be groundless, he must, in addition to restituting the money owed, pay a fine of 0.1 percent of the amount concerned for each day of delay counting from the day the objection was communicated to the bank.

Soviet sources report that in practice refusals by buyers to confirm payments and shipments by sellers of unordered or improper items occur extremely rarely, which safeguards the accuracy of interstate accounts in foreign trade.

To ensure promptness and discipline in making payments, the "general conditions" establish specific deadlines for the execution of payments and prescribe penalties for violating these conditions. In the event the buyer does not pay on schedule, he is required to pay a fine amounting to 0.1 percent of the value of the goods delivered per diem. Should the delay run to over ten days from the date payment is due, the seller has the additional right to suspend further shipment of goods until the bill is settled.

For similar reasons the "general conditions" contained a separate chapter on sanction incurred for delays in the delivery of goods. Pursuant to these rules the supplier has a thirty-day grace period in case of a delay. Beyond this period a fine for each day of delay is computed in proportion to the value of the undelivered goods. The rate is the following: during the first month, 0.05 percent; during the second month, 0.08 percent; and after that, 0.12 percent. However, the total sum of the fine may not exceed 8 percent of the price of the goods.

With delays of over four months (or over six months where large pieces of equipment of special manufacture are concerned) the buyer has the option of canceling the entire remainder of the contract, or that portion on which the deadline has expired. In doing so he foregoes the right to file a claim for breach of contract, except for the aforementioned fine for unjustified delays; the supplier must then return to the buyer all advance payments, plus 4 percent interest per annum. Soviet sources note that the "general conditions" between the Soviet Union and the PRC differ here from the "CMEA general conditions of deliveries." First, two different grace periods are envisaged— thirty days for ordinary goods and forty-five days for machinery equipment —instead of a uniform thirty-day grace period. Second, the penalty is computed on a weekly (not daily) basis, on the following scale: if the extra delay runs less than four weeks—the penalty is calculated at the rate of 0.3 percent per week; from the beginning of the fifth week—0.6 percent per week; and from the ninth week—1 percent per week. On the other hand, in the Soviet Union-PRC case too, the global sum of the fine is limited by a ceiling set at 8 percent of the total value of the delayed goods.

The "general conditions" free the parties from liability for complete or partial nonperformance of a contract on a plea of *force majeure;* in that eventuality the side faced with the impossibility of fulfilling the contract must at once let its opposite know both when such circumstances arise and when they terminate. The "CMEA general conditions of delivery" provide that if the unforeseen circumstances last more than five months for goods destined for delivery within a year or more than eight months for goods due for delivery in more than a year, either party has the right to refuse further performance of the contract and cannot then demand from the other reimbursement for possible losses. As against this, the Soviet Union-PRC "general conditions" contain no such clause and shed no light on the question of how long a party must wait before he can cancel a contract whose performance is being delayed by circumstances of insuperable force. The matter is therefore resolved in the contract itself, or by reference to the civil law of the country whose law is recognized as governing the given case.

What constitutes *force majeure* is left undetermined in the text of the agreements. In the opinion of Soviet jurists an *a priori* definition is not really necessary, given the fact that the municipal legislation of the Soviet Union and the people's democracies treats the concept in an identical fashion. (The "CMEA general conditions of deliveries" do not specifically enumerate the circumstances that would qualify as an incidence of insuperable force either, but they do furnish a general description of what the principle embraces: "circumstances arising after the conclusion of the contract as a result of unforeseen and unavoidable events of an extraordinary character.") The question is thus left to be resolved by the parties themselves at the time of the conclusion of the contract. Should they fail to do so, disputes on the subject are settled pursuant to the general legal norms of the country whose law is recognized as governing the given contract. According to Soviet authors foreign trade contracts usually do feature a list of such contingencies and, for example, in those signed by Soviet foreign trade organizations references to strikes are normally excluded from the catalogue inasmuch as they are deemed to be phenomena that an owner could prevent from happening.

The complex of bilateral protocols on "general conditions" also stipulates that all disputes related to foreign trade contracts be submitted to arbitration and *eo ipso* exempt from the jurisdiction of the regular courts. The proceedings are to be conducted before permanent arbitral bodies, when such agencies are available. In some of the documents, the signatories designate the appropriate organ where the respondent is located to hear the case (the principle of so-called mixed, or parity, arbitration at the locus of the respondent); otherwise, they prefer to entrust the whole business to the Foreign Trade Arbitration Commission of the All-Union Chamber of Commerce sitting in Moscow.

Initially, Poland and Czechoslovakia alone among the people's democracies possessed a standing arbitration board and, hence, the "general conditions" between the Soviet Union and each of them featured the "parity" formula. Yet, curiously enough, from the very start China too enjoyed in this respect a privileged position. Though a permanent national arbitral tribunal was not created on the mainland until 1954, the applicable article of the 1952 set of "general conditions" already provided that, if the respondent was a Soviet organization, arbitration would take place in Moscow, and if the respondent was a Chinese organization, in Peking or some other city in accordance with the law on arbitration currently in force in the PRC. Presumably, once a fixed arbitration panel was established in Peking, this entity would exercise sole jurisdiction in the latter contingency.

The unique extent to which China was favored in this affair may be appreciated from the fact that, until the rest of the people's democracies acquired comparable agencies, their respective protocols on "general conditions" with the Soviet Union simply envisaged the settlement of all such disputes in Moscow. China was treated as an equal right away.

Finally, the "CMEA general conditions of deliveries" take the precautionary measure of enunciating the applicable conflict of law rule. The pertinent clause directs that those questions that are not fully settled by either the contract or the "CMEA general conditions" are resolved in accordance with the law of the country of the seller. The inclusion of this norm is said to have helped appreciably to eliminate possible misunderstandings. Similar dispositions referring the matter to the law of the country of the seller or to the prevailing practice in the country of the seller occur elsewhere in the text of the "CMEA general conditions of deliveries." By contrast, the bilateral Sino-Soviet version contains no specific conflict of law rule.

In the past Soviet commentators treated the ostensible advantages of the "general conditions" system as essentially self-evident. In the wake of the recent political polemics between Moscow and Peking, however, some aspects of the mechanics of enforcement of the "general conditions" program during this period have also come under fire, particularly as regards the elements of price determination and quality control. In its letter to the CPSU Central Committee of 29 February 1964, the Chinese leadership touched on an extremely sore spot when it publicly charged that the prices of many goods hitherto imported from the Soviet Union were much higher than the world-market prices. To hear the Soviets talk about it, the claim made no sense. The Soviet-Chinese commercial agreement of 19 April 1950 spelled out that prices "will be set in rubles on the basis of the prices existing on the world market." During the 1950 talks on trade the prices on the world capitalist markets in the preceding year served as an index for fixing prices in Sino-Soviet trade. These figures continued to be followed, in the main, until 1958, a long time in which to operate with old data in a dynamic situation. The Soviet explanation for this singular phenomenon is that the principle of stable prices for goods delivered on a reciprocal basis pursued the aim of safeguarding prices in trade among the socialist countries from the harmful influences of fluctuations of the capitalist market.

Soviet spokesmen themselves conceded, of course, that on occasion this resulted in the Soviet Union and the PRC selling each other goods at prices which were lower or higher than the current prices on the world capitalist market. PRC sources are quoted to demonstrate that during and in the immediate aftermath of the Korean War prices on sundry machinery imported from the Soviet Union were 20–30 percent less and, on certain types of equipment vital for heavy industry, 30–60 percent less than prices for analogous pieces of equipment on the British and American markets. Conversely, somewhat later, as a consequence of changes in prices on the world capitalist market, the Soviet Union could for a while buy such staple commodities as wool, rice, jute, tung oil, black tea, raw silk, tin, wolfram concentrates, etc., at less than world market prices. Even so, the net benefits of this approach presumably outweighed the attendant inconveniences.

At any rate, price adjustments for some particular articles were effected by joint consent between 1950 and 1958. By mutual accord the prices were next revised in 1958 and new prices were fixed by the two partners in line with the average annual prices for 1957 on the principal world markets. The principle governing the fixing of prices was laid down in letters exchanged by the competent authorities on 23 April 1958 and 26 February 1959, and was then, on the proposal of the Chinese side and with Soviet agreement, reaffirmed each year during the signing of the annual protocols on trade exchanges. Thus, as far as the Soviets are concerned, this proves that the Chinese statements voiced after 1960, that the prices of many kinds of Soviet goods and equipment were much higher than the prices on the world market and that, consequently, commercial relations with the Soviet Union often worked to China's detriment, are not true to the facts. Indeed, they point out that to this very day Sino-Soviet trade is conducted in accordance with the prices accepted by both sides in 1958.

Technical quality has cropped up as another bone of contention, and the Soviets have attempted to counter Chinese criticism on that score by arguing that, given the huge amount of machinery, equipment, and other commodities that the Soviet Union exported to China over a period of many years, it was inevitable that the shipments would include a few items that were not quite up to the prescribed standards. Furthermore, China was supplied with large quantities of the latest equipment, including some which up to that time had not even been supplied to Soviet enterprises. While this was favorably regarded by the Chinese, on occasion, nevertheless, the delivery post-haste of experimental models of equipment also caused problems, for shortcomings requiring additional improvements came to light when this equipment was put to regular use. Reportedly, in all such cases the faulty equipment was either replaced or brought up to the proper technical standards by Soviet experts *gratis,* in full conformity with the recognized practices in international trade. What is more, the Soviets say, the same difficulty was sometimes experienced with Chinese goods imported into the Soviet Union. Notwithstanding, so runs the clear implication, the Soviets for their part did not choose to stir up a fuss over a thoroughly routine issue.

In general, though, the Soviets insist that the caliber of Soviet goods shipped to China was high, and to corroborate the point evidence is cited indicating that more than 250 large-scale industrial enterprises, factory shops, and other plants built with the help of the Soviet Union and fitted out with machinery and equipment delivered from the Soviet Union were still in operation as of 1969. Scores of thousands of machine-tools, machines, and instruments produced under Soviet licenses and by Soviet equipment continue to this day to serve in every important sector of Chinese industry.

V. Trade Relations and the Sino-Soviet Dispute

On 23 April 1958 the governments of the Soviet Union and the PRC signed a Treaty of Trade and Navigation. To reproduce in detail here the contents of the accord would serve little purpose, since the text of the document is readily available in English, and since the agreement merely formulated the broad legal principles applicable to the conduct of trade. Suffice it to note, then, that the Contracting Parties now pledged themselves to take all necessary measures to develop and strengthen common trade ties "in a spirit of friendly cooperation and mutual assistance and on the basis of equality and mutual benefit." To that end they undertook to conclude agreements, including long-term ones, ensuring the development of trade in accordance with the requirements of the national economies of both countries. The treaty was concluded for an indefinite period and either party could terminate its operation by filing a notice six months in advance to that effect.

In order to promote the flow of trade between them, the Soviet Union and the PRC granted each other most-favored-nation treatment in all matters relating to trade, navigation, treatment of corporate entities and individuals, and other aspects of economic intercourse. They likewise consented not to impose on imports from or exports to each other's territory any restrictions that did not affect all states, and they also agreed to recognize the validity of the nationality papers, tonnage certificates, and other ship's documents issued by the competent authorities of either side. Products of one Contracting Party in transit through the territory of the other were not liable to any duties, taxes, or other charges.

The treaty also featured a guarantee for the enforcement of arbitral awards in commercial cases. Orders for the execution of such awards were to be made and implemented in compliance with the laws of the state enforcing the award.

Each of the Contracting Parties had the right to maintain in the capital of the other a trade delegation whose legal status was defined in an annex to the treaty in terms more or less standard for Soviet practice in this field. Thus, the trade delegate and his deputies enjoyed all the rights and privileges of members of diplomatic missions, and the premises occupied by the trade delegation and its branches enjoyed extraterritoriality. In commercial matters the delegation possessed all the immunities to which a sovereign state was entitled, save that: 1) disputes regarding foreign trade contracts concluded or properly guaranteed by the delegation in the territory of the receiving state would, in the absence of an arbitration or other clause limiting jurisdiction, be subject to the jurisdiction of the local courts, barring, however, in this connection interim court orders for the provision of security; and 2) final judicial decisions against the delegation could be executed solely against the goods and claims outstanding to the credit of the delegation.

The signature of the treaty itself represents, of course, a significant event which both symbolized and enhanced the new warm spell in Sino-Soviet relations that followed the relative chill of 1957. Perhaps even more important in a concrete sense was the accompanying exchange of notes that recomputed the prices charged on the principal commodities and, in so doing, removed—or at least alleviated—a prime source of past grievance stemming from Peking's conviction that the old price scale openly profited the Soviet side. The improved atmosphere was confirmed by the tenor of the trade protocol for 1958 of the same date which set the annual goal at a record high of 5.2 billion rubles and next led to the signature on 8 August 1958 of a fresh agreement on Soviet technical aid to the PRC under which the Soviet Union promised to assist its confederate in the construction and expansion of forty-seven industrial enterprises.

Finally, in the second half of the year, the original trade figure for 1958 in fact proved inadequate and was revised sharply upward (ending up with an extra increment of 600 million rubles) to meet the mounting pressures of the Chinese Great Leap Forward campaign. Both Soviet and Chinese contemporary press accounts described at length how entire branches of the Soviet industry successfully reorganized their production system and altered their plan priorities so as to fulfill urgent Chinese orders for a large assortment of equipment, machinery, and supplies for delivery ahead of schedule. It should be noted, though, that while the total of the Sino-Soviet trade turnover rose steeply in 1958, Chinese exports to the Soviet Union registered a greater fractional increase than did imports and hence the gap in China's favorable trade balance grew even wider. By the end of 1958 the Chinese net trade surplus thus amounted to one-fourth of the loans received from the Soviet Union in 1953–57.

The pace accelerated in 1959. On February 7 the two governments signed a new agreement providing for five billion rubles' worth of Soviet financial and technical aid for Chinese industrial expansion over the next nine years, calling for the construction by 1967 of seventy-eight enterprises (the forty-seven covered by the August 1958 accord and thirty-one additional objectives). The PRC would manufacture a considerable proportion of the equipment for these projects and, as hitherto, pay for the cost of Soviet equipment and technical aid through deliveries of goods. Reflecting the heavy Chinese commitment to Russia for its industrial assistance and possibly rumored internal economic difficulties as well, the PRC's exports to noncommunist countries dropped badly at the beginning of 1959. Food and other staple commodities were reported to be scarce in many parts of China, and one explanation offered for this situation was that China had stepped up exports to the Soviet Union and the other communist countries in an effort to foot the Soviet bill.

Nevertheless, the trade curve continued to climb: the annual trade protocol for 1959, signed on February 26, announced that the projected value of two-way trade that year would reach an unprecedented 7.2 billion rubles. Soon after, it was reported that preparations were in progress for the conclusion of a long-term trade agreement between the Soviet Union and the PRC to correct the glaring anomaly whereby China was the only member of the "socialist commonwealth" still without such an arrangement with the Soviet Union (as it turned out, the accord never did materialize).

Behind the facade of the spectacular upswing in Sino-Soviet trade in 1958–59, however, several disruptive forces were busily at work. In the long run these forces proved a fatal stumbling block to this massive bid to engineer a lasting rapprochement between the twin giants of the communist world. A fundamental flaw in the Chinese position on this score must bear a share of the blame for the final outcome. Indeed, the commune and Great Leap Forward concepts were essentially predicated on the three-fold principle of substitution of labor-intensive for capital-intensive construction, emphasis on small units and native methods of production which would help diminish dependence on Soviet deliveries and technical aid, and substitution of intensified political and ideological stimuli for material incentives as a means of improving the country's foreign trade capacity by cutting down on home consumption.

In that light the appreciable increase in the Chinese export surplus to the Soviet Union in 1958–59 can be explained as a logical corollary to the spirit of "self-reliance" that underlay this program combined with a wish to escape as quickly as possible from economic mortgage to the Soviet Union. If so, the aspiration was torpedoed by the then current necessity to incur further financial commitments vis-à-vis the Soviet Union to feed the momentum of the commune and Great Leap Forward campaigns. The rise also can be attributed to Soviet insistence (a contingency the Chinese should have anticipated, even if they could see no way out of the dilemma) that China amortize earlier indebtedness in conjunction with the recent pledges of expanded technical assistance. This in fact meant that much of the impact of this aid was neutralized and China was not able to achieve the critical concentration of reserves required for the supreme attempt to break out of the vicious cycle of chronic capital deficiency. In that case, too, the fault would be ascribed to the Soviets and Sino-Soviet relations would suffer as a consequence. Either way, then, given excessive Chinese expectations and a Soviet performance that was helpful without being quixotic, disillusionment was bound to result, and did.

Meantime, various political factors contributed mightily to fostering a general climate of discord and malaise from which Sino-Soviet economic interaction could not, of course, long be kept insulated. The commune experiment and what it implied in the important field of ideology posed a serious challenge to Russia's leadership in the communist universe. Other factors were persistent friction over Khrushchev's manner of handling the Yugoslavs, the official policy line of the bloc on the Geneva talks for banning

atomic tests, and Soviet behavior in the Middle East crisis in the summer of
1958. A significant effort to achieve a détente at the Twenty-First Congress
of the CPSU in January 1959 produced no permanent improvement: Chinese
claims on behalf of the people's communes and the Great Leap Forward
scheme had a doctrinally disturbing and militant connotation to which Moscow
simply could not adjust. In addition, the opponents openly clashed over the
respective merits of the Chinese espousal of the dictum of national autarky
versus Soviet advocacy of the theme of "increased productivity through
international division of labor," i.e., regional integration through CMEA.

Gradually, prospects of a compromise faded away, and by August 1959
things had reached a point where China's economic isolation from her former
friends looked like a real possibility. Thereafter, the situation steadily deteriorated and in 1960 the political controversy flared up anew, with spiraling
economic difficulties now making matters worse. Nevertheless, the practical
impact of this mounting chorus of dissension was not immediate: the trade
protocol for 1960, signed on March 29, projected a fresh 10 percent increase
in annual trade over the record high posted in 1959; the Soviet Union continued to furnish the PRC with technical assistance up to late summer of
1960; and until 1961 the Soviet Union still served as China's chief purveyor
of investment goods.

The overt act that seems to have brought all the pent-up resentments to a
head and precipitated the confrontation that finally snapped the thread of the
laborious Sino-Soviet quest for an amicable modus vivendi in the sphere of
economic relations was Khrushchev's abrupt decision in August 1960 to recall
all Soviet technical specialists from China. Why Khrushchev took the dramatic
step has never been satisfactorily resolved. Whether in a fit of pique over China's
"demonstrative" gestures of independence or fully aware of the grave problems besetting the Chinese economy at the time, he either sought to bring
China to heel by applying a massive dose of economic pressure, or he figured
that this tactic could wreck the commune and Great Leap Forward experi-
ments and discredit Mao's "ideological innovations," thus, at a single stroke
confirming Moscow's primacy within the camp and putting the Chinese in
the humiliating position of having to choose between making political concessions to Soviet leadership or seeing their economic edifice tumble in ruins.

What is quite clear, however, is that if he hoped by this means to compel
the Chinese to return to the Soviet fold, the gambit failed. The Chinese
response to the "blackmail" was swift and harsh, for the Soviets later complained how "even on the eve of the [November] 1960 Moscow conference of
fraternal parties, the Chinese government demanded from the Soviet Union
a revision of all the previously concluded agreements and protocols on economic
and scientific-technical cooperation, refused a considerable part of the planned
deliveries of Soviet equipment and reduced the volume of Soviet-Chinese
trade to a minimum."

The decline in Sino-Soviet trade in subsequent years was drastic. The Soviet Union's share in China's foreign trade stood at 50 percent in 1959, at 40 percent in 1960, at 31 percent in 1961, at 28 percent in 1962, and at 21 percent in 1963. In 1965 her share in China's foreign trade slipped to 15 percent; in 1966 it fell to 7 percent; and in 1967 it slumped to a mere 2 percent.

Can this downward course of Sino-Soviet economic exchanges be ascribed to the particular withdrawal-of-technicians episode, or does the true reason for this rapid decline lie elsewhere? Predictably enough, the Chinese heap all the blame on Khrushchev and his acolytes and portray the incident as a traumatic experience, with themselves cast as innocent victims forced to take appropriate countermeasures literally in self-defence. By their account the Soviet personnel employed in China "were invariably made welcome, respected and trusted by the Chinese government and people." Even as late as 1964 the Chinese insisted that "we have always highly appreciated their conscientious work and still miss them to this day," and seized the opportunity to remind the Russians that "when the leaders of the CPSU unilaterally decided to recall all the Soviet experts in China we solemnly affirmed our desire to have them continue their work in China and expressed the hope that the leaders of the CPSU would reconsider and change their decision."

However, the CPC letter to the CPSU of 29 February 1964 then charged,

in spite of our objections you turned your back on the principles guiding international relations and unscrupulously withdrew the 1,390 Soviet experts working in China, tore up 343 contracts and supplementary contracts concerning experts, and scrapped 257 projects of scientific and technical cooperation, all within the short span of a month. You were well aware that the Soviet experts were posted in over 250 enterprises and establishments in the economic field and the field of national defence, culture, education, and scientific research, and that they were undertaking important tasks involving technical design, the construction of projects, the installation of equipment, trial production, and scientific research. As a result of your peremptory orders to the Soviet experts to discontinue their work and return to the Soviet Union, many of our country's important designing and scientific research projects had to stop halfway, some of the construction projects in progress had to be suspended, and some of the factories and mines which were conducting trial production could not go into production according to schedule. Your perfidious action disrupted China's original national economic plan and inflicted enormous losses upon China's socialist construction.

"The sudden withdrawal of all Soviet experts working in China," Peking contended, "upset the schedules of construction and the production arrangements of many of our factories, mines, and other enterprises and establishments, and had a direct impact on our need for the import of complete sets of equipment." The next logical step presumably was a cutback in Chinese orders for these items, since, as the CPC note sarcastically remarked, "such being the case, did you expect us to keep on buying them just for display?"

The Russians, of course, took the opposite view. To them the need for foreign specialists was only temporary because of the rapid pace at which the "fraternal socialist countries" acquired their own skilled cadres and they pointed out that in 1956 and 1958 the Soviet government had already raised the question of the recall of Soviet personnel. The rest of the socialist states reportedly agreed forthwith; the PRC alone "requested that the Soviet specialists remain for a certain time," and the Soviet Union in the end consented. However, the Soviets claimed, during the Great Leap Forward the professional advice of the Soviet specialists was systematically disregarded, leading to numerous mishaps and some loss of life. The Chinese authorities also tried to agitate among these people and turn them against their government and party, provoking "legitimate indignation" in their midst and causing many of them to ask to be allowed to go back home. In the face of efforts by Moscow to get the Chinese government to correct the situation and to "create normal conditions for the work of the Soviet specialists," the latter's attitude allegedly became even more hostile and the harassment of Soviet personnel reached a pitch that their evacuation was seen as the "only solution."

As for Chinese assertions that the precipitous recall of the Soviet specialists resulted in widespread damage to the PRC's economy, the Russian spokesmen dismissed these accusations as utter nonsense, citing as common knowledge the fact that economic hardships arose in the PRC long before any such move was contemplated and emphasizing that the "biggest difficulties arose precisely in those branches in which no Soviet specialists at all, or at most very few, were working." Thus, Suslov, in his report of 14 February 1964 to the Plenum of the CPSU Central Committee, asked:

how, for example, could the recall of the Soviet specialists have affected the work of the coal, petroleum, lumber and light industries and other branches of industry and agriculture if in 1960 just two specialists were working in the coal industry, three in the Ministry of State Farms and Virgin Lands and one each in the systems of the Ministries of Agriculture and Forestry? Meanwhile, the greatest failures occurred in precisely those branches of industry and particularly in agriculture.

The obvious conclusion, as far as the Russians were concerned, was that "the Chinese leadership did not need the specialists themselves as much as it needed an issue about them that it could use in the struggle against the CPSU."

It should be mentioned, however, that subsequently the Soviet hierarchy modified its position on this score and expressed a guarded willingness to sanction the return of its technical specialists to the PRC, provided they were guaranteed an ambiance that would enable them to function properly. From Soviet sources we learn that this suggestion was made by Mikoyan in November 1960, during official talks with members of the Chinese delegation to the Moscow conference, and by Khrushchev in a conversation with Chou En-lai at the Twenty-Second Party Congress in October 1961. It was repeated at the bilateral meeting of representatives of the CPSU and CPC in July 1963, and in the CPSU's letter of 29 November 1963. These moves were in vain, since the Chinese did not even deign to respond to the Soviet proposals.

In broaching the subject the Soviet may have hoped to exact a suitable quid pro quo or, anticipating a rejection of the overture, they may simply have sought a means to demonstrate China's unfriendly and intransigent conduct. Be that as it may, when the Chinese did answer in February 1964, it was to let the Russians know that the Chinese people were not willing to be duped a second time. The Russians were told that no country had the right unilaterally to annul or scrap any agreement or contract concerning the sending of experts, that any country guilty of behaving in this manner should, in accordance with international practice, compensate the other side for the resultant losses, and that only thus could there be an interchange between China and the Soviet Union. The message ended with a taunt: the leaders of the PRC, basing themselves on the internationalist principle of mutual assistance among countries in the socialist camp, professed a deep sense of anxiety about the present economic situation in the Soviet Union and hastened to assure their Russian comrades that if they should feel the need for the help of Chinese experts in certain fields, the Chinese government would be glad to send them.

This is the documented record. The official stories stand poles apart, making it hard, if not impossible, to determine wherein lies the kernel of truth in this whole complicated business. Most foreign observers are convinced that the unexpected withdrawal of Soviet experts from China seriously impaired the performance of the PRC's economic mechanism. Granted even that the magnitude of the injury may have warranted the reprisals to which the Chinese resorted, were there also certain ulterior motives behind the prompt Chinese retaliatory thrust on the economic front in response to the Soviet "provocation," so that the latter emerges as both a genuine stimulus and an expedient pretext for Peking's reflexive action? Several sound possibilities along those lines do suggest themselves.

Quite illuminating in this respect are the contents of the declaration attributed by the Russians to Ku Cho-hsin, leader of the PRC government delegation at the Soviet-Chinese negotiations, dated 10 February 1961, in which the reasons for Chinese insistence on an immediate curtailment of economic ties with the Soviet Union were explained as follows:

First, thanks to the aid of the Soviet Union preliminary foundations for modern industry and technology have been created in China; therefore in the future the construction and design of the majority of projects will be carried out with our own forces. We want to lighten the efforts of the USSR with respect to aid to China. However, in the future we shall have to turn to the Soviet Union for aid on those projects that we cannot design, build and equip on our own.

Second, the CPC Central Committee and the Chinese government have deemed it necessary to concentrate forces on the construction of the most important projects, reducing the total number of capital construction projects and nonurgent projects in order to implement more fully the principle of socialist construction in the PRC: "Better, more, faster and cheaper." The scale of construction in the country will continue to be big and the tempos fast.

Third, as a result of the calamities in agriculture resulting from the weather in the past two years, certain difficulties have arisen with respect to the balance of payments. Therefore, by reducing the number of projects being built with the aid of the Soviet Union, we hope to create conditions for more favorable cooperation between our countries.

The first two propositions are not novel. Applying these priorities would automatically lead to a curtailment of the volume of Chinese purchases from the Soviet Union. At the same time, bureaucratic mismanagement and natural adversities drastically reduced China's potential to maintain a sufficiently high level of exports to finance mass imports from the Soviet Union while amortizing accumulated debts. For all that, the Chinese still managed to eke out a modest export surplus which would suggest a firm resolve on the part of Peking to keep liquidating its arrears to the Soviet Union, regardless of the difficulties. Such a commitment would be a powerful motivation to cut back heavily on imports from the Soviet Union, irrespective of any alleged "causal" insult.

The year 1961 brought only a little relief. A trade protocol for 1961 was duly signed on April 7. Simultaneously, an agreement was concluded on the postponement (at no interest) of repayment by the PRC of debts stemming from 1960 trade deals. China was now scheduled to liquidate its latest 288 million ruble quota of indebtedness over the next four years through deliveries of goods. Finally, in a companion accord the Soviet Union undertook to supply China with 500,000 tons of raw sugar to be shipped before the end of August 1961, and to be repaid (again at no interest) through shipments of Chinese sugar during 1964–67.

The trade figures for 1960 indicate that about 62.3 percent of the gross value of Chinese exports to the USSR in that year was applied to earlier debts, because of the small export surplus; the remainder did not cover current imports. The result was that a fresh increment of 288 million rubles was debited to the PRC's account. The immediate effect, as outside observers were quick to point out, was that the trade deficit operated as an unplanned loan; thus, China received more economic aid from the Soviet Union than any other nation had received to date during a single year. Repayment, however, posed a serious problem. Since China was presently not even in a position to sustain the past level of exports to the Soviet Union, to say nothing of stepping up the tempo of deliveries, a drastic paring of purchases from the Soviet Union seemed the sole safe answer at the moment to balance the books once again.

In their private conversations the Soviets must have reproached the Chinese for this sorry turn of events, for the latter felt called upon to retort that from 1959 to 1961 their country had "suffered extraordinary natural disasters for three years in succession," and as "the result of factors beyond human control," it had to reduce trade levels. The defense is only partially valid. First, the Soviet contention that the Chinese aggravated the economic situation by their head-long plunge into the commune and Great Leap Forward schemes is sound, and the leadership in Peking must bear responsibility for some of the adverse consequences of its own behavior rather than heap it all on the shoulders of Mother Nature.

Second, deliberate policy calculations played a crucial role in the decision too. The new emphasis on agriculture meant a more selective approach to industrial development, namely, fewer projects and concentration on simpler machinery that could either be manufactured at home or, if bought abroad, could be obtained more cheaply elsewhere than in the Soviet Union. Moreover, since these purchases would have to be paid for in hard cash in any case because of the shortage of available export commodities, shopping for equipment in the Soviet Union no longer offered any special inducement. An extra incentive may have been the 1961 revaluation of the gold content of the ruble which necessitated a thorough revision of the existing pricing-system and exchange ratio between the ruble and the yüan. Soviet spokesmen insist that China lost nothing through the reform, but the very compulsion to justify the episode would suggest that the Chinese took a dim view of the affair and, hence, would be apt to look elsewhere for more attractive bargains.

Lastly, plain politics also enter into the picture. When, for example, the loan of 500,000 tons of raw sugar was being negotiated, the Russians expressed their willingness to furnish in addition 1 million tons of grain to ease China's food crisis. Perhaps no single incident illustrates so vividly the degree of estrangement to which the two erstwhile friends had come than the fact that the Chinese spurned the proposal and preferred rather to spend the bulk of sums of scarce foreign currency in the next several years to purchase grain from major Western producers, principally Canada and Australia.

Two themes dominate the scenario of subsequent Sino-Soviet polemics over economic issues. The first item involves the question of who is actually responsible for the catastrophic decline in the sheer volume of Sino-Soviet trade. Publicly, both parties have consistently claimed that they have always made every effort to encourage trade and improve economic contacts. Each has accused the other of deliberately wrecking its efforts at reconciliation and each has reaffirmed its commitment to restoring normalcy in their commercial relations.

In his report to the Plenum of the CPSU Central Committee on 14 February 1964, Suslov said that the Soviet government could not be indifferent to the sharp reduction in Soviet-Chinese cooperation and had proposed a number of concrete steps to avert the process, to which the Chinese hierarchy had turned a deaf ear. The fault lay squarely with the Chinese. Referring to ongoing Soviet assistance to China in the construction of 80 industrial enterprises, the presence in the Soviet Union of Chinese engineering and technical workers, scientists, and students enrolled in production practice and instruction, the shipment of 500,000 tons of sugar in 1961 and the simultaneous offer of a loan of 1 million tons of grain, and the moratorium on the repayment of China's 288 million ruble trade indebtedness for 1960, he demanded to know how all this fit the Chinese assertion that the Soviet Union strove to curtail its economic ties with China. If so, he asked rhetorically, "why did it have to take all these steps, to continue to render aid in the construction of industrial enterprises and to make proposals again and again on expanding mutually profitable trade and economic cooperation?" The Chinese leaders, he declared, had not and indeed could not supply a valid answer to this question since "it is the Chinese leadership itself that brought about the reduction in cooperation between our countries."

Soviet sources have since cited additional evidence of the tactics allegedly used by the Chinese to keep Sino-Soviet trade at its current low level. To quote just one report:

> Soviet representatives repeatedly proposed that exports of Soviet commodities to China should be increased. The Chinese side did not accept those proposals. At the same time, it went on refusing to increase deliveries to the Soviet Union of many commodities which the latter needed, including goods which China was exporting in large quantities to capitalist countries and which in previous years had figured as traditional Chinese exports to the USSR. In this situation, deliveries of those goods to the Soviet Union shrank abruptly. As compared with 1959, China had reduced her deliveries to the USSR in 1965 by the following percentages: tin, 97.5 percent; mercury, 96.9 percent; molybdenum concentrate, 95.8 percent; tungsten concentrate, 76.8 percent; raw silk, 97.2 percent; wool, 84.6 percent; bristle, 81.8 percent.
>
> The Chinese representatives disguised their policy of curtailing Soviet-Chinese economic relations by talk about a desire on China's part to increase the volume of trade with the Soviet Union. With this end in view, they annually offered the Soviet foreign trade bodies, in ever-increasing quantities, goods which China was finding it hard to sell on the world market, while reducing their sales of goods which had previously been China's main exports to the Soviet Union. Such actions on the part of the Chinese leadership could not fail to result in a sharp reduction of Soviet-Chinese trade in the years preceding the so-called "cultural revolution" in China. China's trade exchange with the Soviet Union decreased by nearly 85 percent in the period from 1959 to 1966.

The Chinese script sounds almost identical, *mutatis mutandis*. The CCP letter of 29 February 1964 to the CPSU states the case succinctly:

> In pursuance of your policy of further imposing restrictions on and discriminating against China in the economic and commercial fields, since 1960 you have deliberately placed obstacles in the way of economic and trade negotiations between our two countries and held up or refused supplies of important goods which China needs. You have insisted on providing large amounts of goods which we do not really need or which we do not need at all, while holding back or supplying very few of the goods which we need badly. For several years you have used the trade between our two countries as an instrument for bringing political pressure to bear on China. How could this avoid cutting down the volume of Sino-Soviet trade?
>
> Indeed, but for China's efforts the volume of Sino-Soviet trade would have decreased

even more. Take this year for example. China has already put forward a list of 220 million new rubles' worth of exports to the Soviet Union. But you have been procrastinating unreasonably, continuing to hold back goods we need while trying to force on us goods we do not need. You say in your letter [of 29 November 1963] "In the course of the next few years the USSR could increase its export to China of goods in which you are interested. . . ." But your deeds do not agree with your words.

The verbal volley prompts several observations. To begin with, there is ample reason to believe that both the Soviet Union and Communist China on different occasions did in fact seek to deny certain valuable trade articles to one another as a means of exerting pressure for political ends. Next, on balance it would seem that while Moscow did resort to this weapon on a selective scale, the initiative for a general reduction in the volume of Sino-Soviet trade came from Peking: *inter alia,* China was the partner that was determined to achieve economic emancipation from the senior associate; and, after all, the Chinese were the ones who were disgruntled by the terms of trade they had so far been able to get from the Russians. Finally, the single most curious aspect of the tenor of the foregoing dialogue is that neither the PRC nor the Soviet Union was prepared to admit that perhaps their chief motivation for preferring to sell various goods to capitalist countries rather than to each other was simply the prospect of larger profits: higher prices for their merchandise, a chance to earn hard currency, and therefore greater freedom to shop around for assorted items to fill their own economic exigencies.

Did such a pitch strike the Soviets and Chinese as too crass to inject into relations between fellow socialist states? Or did Moscow and Peking, after years of advertising how much benefit both derived from their commercial exchanges, now find it inexpedient to acknowledge that more could be gained from trading with the capitalist world than with one another? In short, did the Soviet and Chinese hierarchies end up here as prisoners of their doctrinal oratory, which postulated that trade between socialist states must, by definition, serve their mutual interests better than trade across international class lines? Were the two countries bound by their past insistence that Sino-Soviet trade had indeed operated in exactly that fashion, so that a confession to the contrary at this late date entailed excessive risk for the respective office-holders who deemed it safer to blame extraneous human failings for their present predicament than to cast doubt on the validity of the basic theory on which the whole system was built? These are tantalizing questions on which the principals have yet to shed light. At a guess, the answers are yes.

The second object of dispute hinges on the record specifically of Chinese purchases of Soviet machinery and equipment in the post-1959 period. If Sino-Soviet trade in toto slumped, Chinese imports of Soviet capital goods virtually plummeted, and by 1962 deliveries of sets of equipment and industrial materials stood at only one-fortieth of the 1959 figure. This particular phenomenon appears to have especially incensed the Russians. At first an effort was made to patch up the differences and the CPSU letter of 29 November 1963 took extra pains to remind the CPC that "the Protocol of 13 May 1962 concluded by the governments of our two countries provides for the renewal next year of negotiations concerning the delivery to the People's Republic of China of whole sets of equipment the manufacture of which was postponed for two years at the request of the Chinese side." It then went on to add:

If your side shows interest, it would be possible in our view to come to an understanding on the broadening of technical aid to the PRC in the building of industrial enterprises and specifically to discuss the possibility of aid in the development of the petroleum industry and the building of enterprises in the mining and other industries on terms beneficial to both our countries.

The bid was in vain, and in 1964 the Russians switched to a tougher stance. Suslov himself publicly berated the Chinese for "concocting the slander that the Soviet Union allegedly delivered obsolete equipment to China" and voiced the accusation *ex cathedra* that "striving to erase Soviet aid from the memory of the people, the Chinese are not even shrinking from knocking the plant trade-marks from Soviet machine tools and machines. . . ." Today, the standard Soviet interpretation of the experience is that:

In accordance with instructions received from the Mao group, the Chinese representatives in Soviet-Chinese negotiations reduced the volume of orders for Soviet goods and refused to buy many kinds of commodities which had long been among the Soviet Union's main exports to China. Thus, in December 1961 the Chinese representatives announced a 78–80 percent reduction in imports of complete sets of plants from the Soviet Union as compared with the previous year, and a complete end to those imports in 1962–63. The political background to this step taken by the Chinese leadership becomes completely obvious if we bear in mind that in those years China was importing large numbers of complete sets of plant from capitalist countries. For instance, China purchased in Britain, Italy, the Federal Republic of Germany, and Japan complete sets of plants for 20 enterprises.

That politics played a role in this connection is undeniable, of course. But, as had been suggested earlier, sound economic calculations exerted at least an equally important influence, and maybe even a superior one, on the Chinese decision not to rely blindly on what was available from Soviet stocks and instead to engage in a bit of bargain-hunting abroad—with gratifying results in the opinion of most outside observers. Yet, the Russians will recognize none of these elements and point to politics alone.

Three possible explanations of this attitude recommend themselves: 1) the Russians simply cannot afford to concede that their equipment is not the finest and most reasonably priced on the world market, so the Chinese must have an ulterior motive for buying from the capitalist competitors; 2) as a matter of prestige, the Soviet Union prides itself on being the chief purveyor of modern industrial equipment to the socialist community, and if a member of the "fraternity" regularly takes its business elsewhere the Kremlin can only square such deviant behavior with its self-image by attributing it to political "perversity"; 3) Soviet equipment could not readily be sold in the West, and plain ordinary spite may well account for the violent Soviet reflex in the face of Chinese refusal to buy en masse machinery which the Soviet Union knew it would have a hard time unloading on less complaisant customers.

Since then the core pattern here has persisted. Every year the volume of two-way trade between them has dipped lower: in 1967 for the first time it fell beneath the 100 million ruble mark and by 1970 constituted a minuscule 41.9 million rubles. Within the framework of this general trend, minor fluctuations have occurred, of course: brighter spots have alternated with thoroughly grim moments. Thus, thanks to sizable export surpluses in 1963 and 1964, the Chinese succeeded in wiping out their entire indebtedness to the Soviet Union by the end of 1964. This was a full year ahead of schedule and was an eloquent testimonial to the depth of Peking's anxiety to settle its accounts with the Kremlin as soon as possible. At that time PRC spokesmen revealed that the sum total of the reimbursement had amounted to 1.4 billion rubles.

Controversy over the transit of Soviet goods to North Vietnam via the PRC's railroad grid led to the conclusion of an agreement in 1965 which provided, *inter alia,* for the free transport on Chinese freight-lines of military aid whereas unspecified fees in rubles were to be levied for the transit of civilian articles. Nevertheless, in 1966 the Soviet Union was again reported to be experiencing major difficulties in transporting supplies to North Vietnam because of the recurrence of the previous year's dispute over transit arrangements. The railroad link had assumed increasing importance since Peking meanwhile was said to have rejected Soviet requests for landing rights in Yunnan and Sinkiang that would permit delivery by air to the DRV—carriage by sea had proved slow, cumbersome, dangerous, and expensive.

China also broadened its criticism of the Soviet Union's economic objectives by attacking it for pursuing an "imperialist" trade policy toward the other socialist states. Without mentioning the PRC by name, official Chinese documents indicted the Russians for systematically exploiting their allies, claiming that:

You infringe the independence and sovereignty of fraternal countries and oppose their efforts to develop their economy on an independent basis in accordance with their own needs and potentialities.

You bully those fraternal countries whose economies are less advanced and oppose their policy of industrialization and try to force them to remain agricultural countries and serve as your sources of raw materials and as outlets for your goods.

You bully fraternal countries which are industrially more developed and insist that they stop manufacturing their traditional products and become accessory factories serving your industries.

Moreover, you have introduced the jungle law of the capitalist world into relations between socialist countries. You openly follow the example of the Common Market which was organized by monopoly capitalist groups.

By 1969 the Chinese would graduate to excoriating the Council for Mutual Economic Aid as a "Soviet revisionist tool for pushing neocolonialism" and depicting Soviet aid programs to the Third World in cold print as a means used by "the Soviet revisionist new tsars . . . to stretch their claws into Asia, Africa, and Latin America."

The outbreak of the Cultural Revolution on the mainland brought with it fresh headaches. The Soviets blamed the Chinese delay in sending a mission to Moscow in early 1967 to negotiate the annual trade agreement for contributing to a further decline in commercial turnover that year. For once, however, the Soviets could derive a measure of satisfaction from the knowledge that Western merchantmen who had recently been busy picking up the growing slack in Chinese trade with the socialist community now fared no better as the turmoil of the Cultural Revolution engulfed the country. No Sino-Soviet trade protocols were signed at all for either 1968 or 1969: yet, even during this period bilateral trade still managed somehow to limp along—albeit in negligible quantities.

Factional strife in the port cities and the provinces added to the tribulations as the movement of Soviet merchandise found itself severely hampered by widespread railway dislocations and disturbances on the docks. In June 1967 two Soviet trade officials were manhandled and put on trial by Red Guards in Shenyang on charges of stealing information from posters while walking around the town. Incidents involving Soviet vessels in Chinese ports, culminating in the seizure of the *Svirsk* in Dairen and the arrest of its captain, finally prompted Kosygin to send a telegram (12 August 1967) to Chou En-lai accusing the Chinese authorities of "violation of the elementary standards of international law," demanding the immediate release of the ship and the crew, and warning the Chinese that their behavior showed that

the Chinese side is intentionally bringing matters to a further aggravation of Soviet-Chinese relations, and is placing in doubt the fulfillment of existing trade relations between the Soviet Union and the People's Republic of China.

On August 20 the Foreign Ministry of the Soviet Union followed up the démarche with a formal note which described the Chinese treatment of Soviet ships and personnel in Dairen as a "violation of universally-accepted standards of international law and the existing Soviet-Chinese agreements on trade and navigation" and again put the Chinese on notice that by such "wanton and lawless actions . . . they place in question the implementation of the trade and navigation agreements between the USSR and the People's Republic of China."

The situation calmed down a bit after that, although in April 1968 the Kremlin was compelled to file another protest over the "unlawful detention of the tanker *Komsomolets Ukrainy*" in the harbor of Canton, which the Soviet government characterized as a "flagrant violation of international law." Oddly enough, also at just about that time, Chen Chi-hsien, member of a trade delegation visiting the Soviet Union in connection with an aircraft order, was expelled for taking photographs of the Tashkent airport, an episode which the Chinese diplomatic reply—in an obvious tone of quid pro quo—greeted as *prima facie* evidence that served "to fully reveal once again the sinister motives of the Soviet government to deliberately sabotage the trade agreement between the two countries and further aggravate their relations."

By the end of 1969 the worst of the storm had blown over. In the fall a new commercial counselor to the Chinese Embassy in Moscow was appointed to take up a post which had stayed vacant for more than two years. Reportedly, his principal assignment was forthwith to instigate talks aimed at securing some sort of trade protocol. It was not until 22 November 1970, however, that the corresponding agreement was finally signed; that year, too, had virtually elapsed without an appropriate trade accord between the two countries. Not surprisingly, the volume of annual commercial exchanges continued on a downhill course and reached a nadir at the close of 1970.

VI. CONCLUSIONS

Such is the picture to date. Paradoxically, the period of heaviest commercial traffic between the Soviet Union and the PRC coincides with a phase of extensive improvisation in the technical modalities of trade exchange. Experimentation, *ad hoc* arrangements, short-term solutions mark the *modus operandi* prevailing at this stage of economic relations between the two countries. Even so, from the very beginning China has occupied a special place in the constellation of people's democracies—it receives preferential treatment and unique privileges as compared with the lesser members of the camp, insignia designed to convey an impression of near equality of the Soviet Union and the PRC in their mutual dealings. To be sure, some of these concessions only have symbolic significance, but they do have the effect of singling China out from group anonymity and, quite possibly, reflect Peking's own perceptions of its rightful rank within the official hierarchy of the international communist system.

The irony of the whole story is that the formal signing of the 1958 treaty of trade and navigation, which was expected to usher in an era of intense economic cooperation between the two great Communist powers, fails to accomplish that mission because, *inter alia*, it soon runs afoul of rampant political dissension. After a rapid expansion in the volume and value of the Sino-Soviet trade turnover in 1958 and 1959, a peak year in the annals of Sino-Soviet commerce, the widening political rift between Moscow and Peking takes its toll in the economic sphere as well and figures for Sino-Soviet trade begin their long slide toward the bottom. Today, trade with the Soviet Union plays an altogether minor role in China's total foreign trade activities and *vice versa*.

Phase I (ca. 1950–57). The dominant theme of this phase is the revolutionary regime's drive to consummate the rapid and massive industrialization of China. Given the current hostile international environment, the country's shortage of precious metals and hard currency, and the lack of ready export outlets for China's products, the success of such an ambitious program automatically hinged on guaranteed access to vast amounts of credit and technical assistance from the socialist community, principally the Soviet Union. This virtually exclusive dependence on one source, plus the relative inflexibility of Chinese versus Soviet import needs in the context of their commercial association, in fact meant that the Russians, if they so wished (and seemingly they did), could manipulate the terms of reciprocal trade for their own profit.

In an ideal state, i.e., a situation bereft of the foregoing (or kindred) handicaps, Peking doubtless could have obtained more favorable trade conditions elsewhere on a piece-meal basis. Absent these circumstances, however, the Chinese still managed, on balance, to derive unparalleled economic gains from the liaison—true, at a certain economic price (optimally speaking) and at an extremely high political cost to themselves.

Conversely, the scheme imposed a hefty economic burden on the Soviet Union, though a burden which was more than compensated for by the immense concomitant political and ideological advantages of permanently acquiring China as a junior partner, and which also was partially alleviated even in the economic sense by systematically juggling figures to overcharge the Chinese for imports from the Soviet Union and underprice Chinese exports. In the final Soviet equation, important political dividends matched accompanying economic expenses which, in practice, amounted to much less than what the official books showed.

Given their known priorities, then, both parties could attribute appreciable benefits to the cooperative venture: the Soviet Union won politically, and paid for it in cash; the PRC profited economically, and incurred political liabilities. On the other hand, in a way neither side did as well on the bargain as it might have hoped to: Moscow's political reward soon turned out to be essentially ephemeral; and the Chinese felt that they never got enough assistance from the Russians and paid an inflated price (both economic and political) for what they did receive. On the whole, though, one is tempted to say that the subsequent disenchantment stemmed more from unfulfilled excessive initial expectations than from particular lapses in the actual record of performance, i.e., was rooted in subjective rather than objective causes.

Phase II (ca. 1957–60). Here the *leitmotiv* is greater equilibrium in the profile of China's external trade. The recent thaw on the post-Bandung international scene and the relaxation of the earlier Western embargo on trade with the PRC conspire to create fresh opportunities for Peking to pursue a more independent foreign policy and to establish economic contacts with an increasing number of countries, especially in the Third World. Political considerations call for a more active economic image abroad and in the process the Chinese leaders discover that tangible economic advantages can be reaped on occasion which surpass the material benefits of a comparable operation with the Soviet Union or a socialist partner. Still on a small scale, and without fundamentally affecting the intensity of China's economic intercourse with the "socialist commonwealth," this modest shift nevertheless foreshadows Peking's growing interest in extricating itself in some measure from the too tight political embrace of its senior associate, and mounting awareness that in select instances China could strike a better deal by shopping around than by blandly sticking to precedent and *ex principio* keeping all its business confined to the family circle. By no stretch of the imagination has China at this juncture ceased to "lean to one side": both heels are squarely planted in the socialist camp, even if a couple of toes henceforth manage to straddle the fence.

Phase III (ca. 1960-present). Now the refrain is self-reliance, gradual and balanced industrial development, and foreign trade operations based on solid economic incentives. Having abandoned, at least for the moment, its dream of modern industrialization "overnight," China need no longer subordinate economic desiderata to political dicta, and can move away from a buying spree that was beyond its means or in any event had various strings (economic and political) attached to it which greatly diminished its end value. In these circumstances a marked decline in the size of Sino-Soviet trade was only to be expected, for the original volume of exchanges owed its *raison d'être* to a peculiar plexus of stimuli that has since ceased to apply.

What some observers have noted, however, is that the pendulum has as of late tended to swing too far in the opposite direction and that in several cases during recent years the Chinese have deliberately preferred to buy from capitalists what they could have obtained from the Soviet Union at cheaper or identical rates and at no sacrifice of quality. Whether this stratagem was intended to serve extra notice on the Russians of China's firm resolve to maintain her newly won independence, or whether it rested on the calculation that China had to seize every possible opportunity to cultivate her "bourgeois" contacts for fear they might otherwise wither away, is not quite clear. The current record does seem to indicate that where the Chinese encounter difficulties in purchasing certain items on the open market (e.g., civilian air-craft), they will seek delivery from the Russians. All things being equal, however, they would rather (on political grounds) do business either with capitalist companies or deviant socialist governments. The final score? The economic hemorrhage that the Soviet Union suffered as a result of China's drain on its resources has stopped, although the cure entailed a high political price; the PRC made dramatic political gains and put its foreign trade transactions on a sound financial footing, except that to do so the regime has had to jettison its pet plan to transform China into an industrial giant in the space of just a few years. Again, each party won and lost something in the shuffle. By contrast, at the technical level the phenomenon of Sino-Soviet commercial collaboration has left a more enduring impression. There is little doubt that the PRC's foreign trade cadres were weaned on the corresponding Soviet experience and learned their craft from Soviet mentors. The successive protocols on "general conditions of deliveries" concluded between the Soviet Union and China, started shortly after the latter was established, contain the most comprehensive and elaborate code of regulations on the routine procedures of foreign trade ever in force between the PRC and any foreign nation. The young Chinese officialdom striving to grasp the essence of a socialist system of foreign trade and understand its *modus operandi* must have treated the text of the "general conditions" much as a breviary, whose guidelines offered a basic model, adaptable to suit different circumstances.

It has already been mentioned that several changes were introduced at the outset into the standard version of the "general conditions" to take into account the special features of Sino-Soviet trade. For that matter, some of these devices represented important innovations which were later extended to the rest of the socialist community. Subsequently, the situation was reversed: relations between the Soviet Union and its East European allies reached a new level of intimacy which was forthwith reflected in the tenor of the latest canons on the mechanics of economic intercourse within the group designed to secure the gains already achieved and speed further progress on the road to full integration; meantime, on the Sino-Soviet front, the economic and political temperature dropped sharply and, as a consequence, the juridical channels remained frozen.

The result has been that, by comparison with the current generation of "general conditions" adopted among the members of the Council for Mutual Economic Aid, the pertinent regulations to which the Soviet Union and China adhere *inter se* are relatively primitive. They are less methodical, precise, refined, coordinated, and symmetrical, they display major technical gaps, and they perpetuate the old and outmoded concept of legal decentralization. In particular, whereas the latest crop of "general conditions" attempts to promote the regional unification of the basic norms governing trade between the local socialist countries, their Sino-Soviet counterpart in the main still follows the stock "conflict of laws" principles and contains the many deficiencies inherent in the traditional approach with its accent on merely identifying the effects of spontaneous collision between rival jurisdictions rather than preventing its incidence through advance synchronization and the positing of common rules. The fluid and incomplete state of Chinese law may, of course, have been responsible in part for the decision to eschew a premature bid at synthesis.

Although the quality of Sino-Soviet economic and political relations has deteriorated almost beyond the point of recognition in the past decade, the "general conditions" have been spared that fate and to this day function as the institutional infrastructure for the ongoing commercial operations. If the substantive elements of these agreements have proved virtually immune to the raging political storms, this may very well be prima facie evidence of the vital importance both parties attach to their technical merits, *stricto sensu*. Such a record of invulnerability to political passions may, in turn, suggest the wisdom for Western businessmen seriously to explore the prospect of invoking the optimal terms of these accords on their own behalf. To be sure, Peking may respond that generically the Soviet Union and the PRC both perceive themselves as socialist political and economic organisms and that their organizational fabric sanctions the use of an ensemble of formulas that would simply not fit the hybrid complexion of East-West trade across international class lines. Nevertheless, there is no harm in trying, and the Chinese may yet be prevailed upon to appreciate the logic of the contrary argument.

Finally, lest ending on an upbeat note create an illusion of undue optimism, let me cite just one more cautionary example from the tortuous history of Sino-Soviet commercial experience. Communist writers on economic affairs, of whatever stripe, have always drawn a rigid distinction between trade protocols signed by a socialist state with a capitalist state and analogous agreements entered into by two socialist states. While both types of documents usually fix the target figures for the proposed annual trade turnover, capitalist states by their very nature can only exhort their private sector to fulfill these goals, while socialist states are in fact bound to honor the commitment and, ostensibly, never fail to live up to their vows. A slight caveat may here be in order. Thus, the Soviet Union-PRC trade protocol for 1960 originally provided for a 10 percent increase in that year's trade over 1959: in reality, according to official computations, trade in 1960 fell by 19 percent measured by 1959 indices. Similarly, the Sino-Soviet trade protocol for 1967 set the value of trade for that period at 228 million rubles; in fact, the value plummeted to 96 million rubles.

True, in 1960 China had suffered from widespread natural calamities and in 1967 the Cultural Revolution had swept the country, sowing strife and disruption, and the plea of *force majeure* might *in extremis* serve to justify both defaults. However, one may also see a different moral to the story. Either the somewhat flamboyant claims by communist experts on foreign trade that where there is a socialist will, there is always a way, perhaps have to be scaled down a bit. Or, we may have to conclude that, past communist contentions to the contrary notwithstanding, the vaunted socialist will can on occasion turn out to be as fickle as Woman in the Duke of Mantua's celebrated opinion.

Bibliographic Note

A number of essays on problems of Sino-Soviet trade and economic cooperation have been published over the years in the journal *People's China*.

This body of literature has been consulted and found to be marginally useful: the tone is invariably positive and the treatment impressionistic, although individual pieces do contain a certain amount of hard data which helps round out the picture. Russian literature of comparable quality, published in a variety of journals, has also been checked but has not been catalogued below. Only major items are included in the list that follows, and the documentation of the present article is drawn almost exclusively from these sources, except for current materials (e.g., correspondence involved in the ongoing Sino-Soviet polemics) which have been obtained from English and Russian-language newspapers and such mass circulation periodicals as the *Peking Review, New Times,* etc. A complete listing of Russian-language literature on USSR-PRC economic relations for 1949–57 may be found in P. E. Skachkov, *Bibliografiya Kitaya* (Bibliography of China) (Moscow: 1960), pp. 276–82.

1. BOOKS

Borisov, O. V., and Koloskov, B. T. *Sovetsko-Kitaiskie otnosheniya 1945–70, kratkii ocherk* (Soviet-Chinese relations 1945–70, short outline). Moscow, 1971.

Cheng Chu-yuan. *Economic Relations between Peking and Moscow : 1949–63.* New York and London, 1964.

Chervyakov, P. A. *Organizatsiya i tekhnika vneshnei torgovli SSSR* (Organization and technique of the foreign trade of the USSR), 2nd ed. Moscow, 1962.

Desyat let Kitaiskoi Narodnoi Respubliki (10 Years of the Chinese People's Republic). Moscow, 1959.

Genkin, D. M., ed. *Pravovoe regulirovanie vneshnei torgovli SSSR* (Legal regulation of the foreign trade of the USSR). Moscow, 1961.

——*Pravovye voprosy vneshnei torgovli SSSR s evropeiskimi stranami narodnoi demo-kratii* (Legal questions of the foreign trade of the USSR with the European People's Democracies). Moscow, 1955.

Griffith, W. E. *Sino-Soviet Relations 1964–65.* Cambridge, Mass. and London, 1967.

Kapelinskii, Yu. M., et al. *Razvitie ekonomiki i vneshneekonomicheskikh svyazei Kitaiskoi Narodnoi Respubliki* (Development of the economy and foreign economic ties of the Chinese People's Republic). Moscow, 1959.

Kapitsa, M.S. *Sovetsko-Kitaiskie otnosheniya* (Soviet-Chinese relations). Moscow, 1958.

Koloskov, B. *The Soviet Union and China : Friendship or Alienation?.* Moscow, 1971.

Korolenko, A. S. *Torgovye dogovory i soglasheniya SSSR s inostrannymi gosudarstvami* (Trade treaties and agreements of the USSR with foreign states). Moscow, 1953.

Lebedev, S. N. *Mezhdunarodnyi torgovyi arbitrazh* (International commercial arbitration). Moscow, 1965.

Leninskaya politika SSSR v otnoshenii Kitaya, sbornik statei (Leninist policy of the USSR toward China, collection of articles). Moscow, 1968.

Mnogostoronnee ekonomicheskoe sotrudnichestvo sotsialisticheskikh gosudarstv (sbornik dokumentov) (Multilateral economic cooperation of socialist states, Collection of Documents). Moscow, 1967.

Obshchie usloviya postavok tovarov mezhdu vneshnetorgovymi organizatsiyami stran— uchastnits Soveta Ekonomicheskoi Vzaimopomoshchi (General conditions of deliveries of goods between the foreign trade organizations of countries members of the Council for Mutual Economic Assistance). Moscow, 1958.

Pozdnyakov, V. S., ed. *Eksportno-importnye operatsii, pravovoe regulirovanie* (Export-import operations, legal regulation). Moscow, 1970.

Pyn Min. *Istoriya kitaisko-sovetskoi druzhby* (History of Chinese-Soviet friendship). Moscow, 1959.

Ramzaitsev, D. F. *Vneshnetorgovyi arbitrazh v SSSR* (Foreign trade arbitration in the USSR), 2nd ed. Moscow, 1957.

Sbornik normativnykh materialov po voprosam vneshnei torgovli SSSR (Collection of normative materials on questions of the foreign trade of the USSR), vol. I. Moscow, 1970.

Sladkovskii, M. I. *Ocherki ekonomicheskikh otnoshenii SSSR s Kitaem* (Essays on the economic relations of the USSR with China). Moscow, 1957.

Sovetsko-Kitaiskie otnosheniya, 1917–57, sbornik dokumentov (Soviet-Chinese relations, 1917–57, collection of documents). Moscow, 1959.

Suslov, M. A. *O borbe KPSS za splochennost mezhdunarodnogo kommunisticheskogo dvizheniya* (On the struggle of the CPSU for the unity of the international Communist movement). Moscow, 1964.

Vaganov, B. S., ed. *Organizatsiya i tekhnika vneshnei torgovli SSSR i drugikh sotsia-listicheskikh stran* (Organization and technique of the foreign trade of the USSR and other socialist countries). Moscow, 1963.

Vneshnyaya torgovlya SSSR s sotsialisticheskimi stranami (Foreign trade of the USSR with socialist countries). Moscow, 1957.

Zagoria, D. S. *The Sino-Soviet Conflict 1956–61*. Princeton, N.J., 1962.

2. ARTICLES

Baginyan, K. A., and Lazarev, M. I. "Mezhdunarodnyi dogovor istoricheskogo znacheniya" (International treaty of historic significance). *Sovetskoe gosudarstvo i pravo* 4 (1950): 68–78.

Efimov, G. V. "Sovetskii Soyuz—velikii drug kitaiskogo naroda" (The Soviet Union—great friend of the Chinese people). *Voprosy ekonomiki*, no. 3 (1951), pp. 68–85.

E Tsi-chzhuan. "Vneshnyaya torgovlya nashei strany za desyat let" (The foreign trade of our country during ten years). *Vneshnyaya torgovlya*, no. 10 (1959), pp. 10–17.

Ginsburgs, G. "Execution of Foreign Commercial Arbitral Awards in Post-War Soviet Bilateral Treaty Practice." *Canadian Yearbook of International Law* 9 (1971): 59–101.

Goldmann, M. I. "Sino-Soviet Trade: A Barometer." *Problems of Communism*, no. 6 (1962), pp. 47–50.

Golubkov, A. "Ispolzuya opyt drug druga . . ." (Using each other's experience . . .). *Novoe vremya*, no. 7 (1957), pp. 30–31.

——"Sovetsko-kitaiskoe nauchno-tekhnicheskoe sotrudnichestvo" (Soviet-Chinese scientific-technical cooperation), *Vneshnyaya torgovlya*, no. 7 (1957), pp. 2–6.

Hoya, Th. W. "The COMECON General Conditions—A Socialist Unification of International Trade Law." *Columbia Law Review*, no. 2 (1970), pp. 253–326.

Kang Chao. "Sino-Soviet Exchange Rates." *The China Quarterly*, no. 47 (1971), pp. 546–52.

Kleimenov, M. "Plodotvornoe sotrudnichestvo" (Fruitful cooperation). *Vneshnyaya torgovlya*, no. 2 (1960), pp. 15–19.

Lysenko, I. A. "Nauchno-tekhnicheskoe sotrudnichestvo Sovetskogo Soyuza i KNR" (Scientific-technical cooperation of the Soviet Union and PRC). *Kratkie soobshcheniya Instituta Vostokovedeniya* 21 (1956): 3–14.

"Novaya industriya Kitaya i Sovetskii Soyuz. Beseda s zam. nach. Glav. upr. po delam ekon. svyazei N. A. Smelovym" (The new industry of China and the Soviet Union. Talk with the deputy director of the main administration on questions of economic ties, N. A. Smelov). *Novoe vremya* no. 12 (1957), pp. 17–18.

Pekshev, Yu. "Ekonomicheskoe sotrudnichestvo Sovetskogo Soyuza i Kitaiskoi Narodnoi Respubliki" (Economic cooperation of the Soviet Union and Chinese People's Republic). *Vneshnyaya torgovlya*, no. 2 (1955), pp. 1–6.

Sladkovskii, M. I. "Nerushimaya sovetsko-kitaiskaya druzhba" (Indestructible Soviet-Chinese friendship). *Vneshnyaya torgovlya*, no. 2 (1957), pp. 2–4.

—— 'Razvitie torgovli Sovetskogo Soyuza s Kitaiskoi Narodnoi Respublikoi" (Development of the trade of the Soviet Union with the Chinese People's Republic). *Vneshnyaya torgovlya*, no. 10 (1959), pp. 2–10.

——"Razvitie torgovykh putei mezhdu Sovetskim Soyuzom i Kitaem" (Development of trade routes between the Soviet Union and China). *Sovetskoe vostokovedenie*, no. 1 (1957), pp. 118–28.

——"Uspekhi sovetsko-kitaiskoi torgovli" (Successes of Soviet-Chinese trade). *Vneshnyaya torgovlya*, no. 10 (1957), pp. 2–6.

Vladimirov, Yu. V. "K voprosu o sovetsko-kitaiskikh ekonomicheskikh otnosheniyakh v 1950–1966 godakh" (On the question of Soviet-Chinese economic relations in 1950–66). *Voprosy istorii*, no. 6 (1969), pp. 46–62.

Trade with West Germany

ARTHUR A. STAHNKE

I. Introduction

Since the early 1960s, when China's foreign trade was significantly reoriented away from the socialist bloc, Sino-West German trade has been comparatively substantial. As shown in table 1, West Germany has been China's leading European trading partner for most of the years since 1965. Before then a brief flurry of trade took place in the late 1960s, and minimal exchanges were recorded from 1950, often indirectly through third states.

This trade has taken place despite some minor political handicaps.[1] During its first years as an actor in international affairs, the Bonn government was extremely cautious about antagonizing Washington on most matters, and Washington, needless to say, was easily antagonized by any actions its western allies undertook that ran counter to its own vigorous policy of containment. It was largely concern over the likely American reaction, for example, that led the Adenauer cabinet up to late 1956 to resist domestic pressures and Chinese overtures designed to bring about a normalization of trade relations between the two countries. Even after that date the government would go only so far as to support the efforts of the semiprivate Ostausschuss der Deutschen

NOTE: The author wishes to thank the American Philosophical Society and the Graduate School of Southern Illinois University (Edwardsville) for their financial assistance which made possible a visit to the Federal Republic of Germany in March 1971. The information in this paper is based largely on interviews held with members of the trading community and government officials, as well as on materials supplied to the author by these individuals.

[1] For an extended analysis of the political aspects of China's relations with West Germany, see: "The Political Context of Sino-West German Trade," in Arthur A. Stahnke, ed.. *China's Trade with the West: A Political and Economic Analysis* (New York: Frederick Praeger, 1972).

TABLE 1

TRADE BETWEEN THE PRC AND PRINCIPAL
WEST EUROPEAN PARTNERS, 1965–70
(In U.S. $ million)

Exports to China (FOB)

European Partner	1965	1966	1967	1968	1969	1970
West Germany	79.8	129.4	286.5	174.1	158.9	168.6
France	60.1	92.1	93.2	67.7	43.2	61.2
Italy	56.4	62.7	73.6	61.1	31.7	56.9
United Kingdom	72.3	93.6	187.3	69.8	124.5	107.0

Imports from China (CIF)

European Partner	1965	1966	1967	1968	1969	1970
West Germany	72.7	92.5	76.5	85.3	84.2	85.1
France	43.7	53.9	48.1	53.3	69.6	69.8
Italy	38.4	56.5	57.8	48.0	37.2	63.1
United Kingdom	62.2	94.7	81.6	82.3	90.6	80.5

SOURCES: For the years 1965–68 *U.S. Department of State Research Memo. 85U 67,*
15 December 1969. For 1969 and 1970 *China Trade Report* (September 1970 and April
1971).

Wirtschaft (The German Committee on Trade with the East) to reach a
nongovernmental trade agreement with the China Committee for the Promotion of International Trade (hereafter CCPIT).[2]

Bonn remained sensitive to attitudes of the United States in the 1960s.
After the French government extended recognition to the PRC in early 1964,
German Chancellor Erhard began to speak hopefully and vaguely about
"new approaches" to China[3]—until he met with President Johnson in June
of that year. Immediately after that conference the chancellor announced that
no substantial moves toward the People's Republic would be made in the
immediate future.[4] In 1966, when the U.S. vigorously protested a decision
by the German government to guarantee credits for the much publicized
Demag deal that was being negotiated then with Chinese counterparts, Bonn's
spokesmen conceded that "a special relationship" existed between the United

---

[2] In debate before the *Bundestag* in 1956, a Government spokesman said that the
Ostausschuss had had official support for the development of trade with China for
several years. However, it was only in late 1956 that the government actually gave that
committee sufficient official standing to convince its Chinese counterpart that an
"unofficial" agreement would have the German government's blessing. This information was obtained by the author from interviews with several of the persons directly
involved.

[3] See, for example, *New York Times,* 10 June 1964, p. 1.

[4] *New York Times,* 14 June 1964, pp. 1, 24. See also *Die Welt,* 1 July 1964.

States and the Federal Republic, and that Washington had been and would be kept fully informed of all German decisions relating to China.[5] It may be, too, that the collapse of these negotiations a year later was in part a result of intervention on the part of the United States.

There is little evidence to suggest that Sino-German trade levels have been affected much by Bonn's consistent practice of tailoring its China policies to fit the imperatives of its relationships with Washington and/or Moscow. Despite the Erhard about-face in 1964 and the *Demag* flap of 1966, Sino-West German trade rose sharply in the years 1965–67; and recent modest reductions in the exchange totals can be explained as primarily a function of currency revaluation and other economic factors rather than as negative Chinese reactions to Brandt's *Ostpolitik*. At the same time substantial trade has been conducted without the exchange of diplomats, the establishment of permanent trade missions, or even the existence of formal treaties establishing the conditions of trade.

The fact that the Chinese have shown a certain indulgence—on political matters—toward both the West German government and the West German business community is curious, especially to the Japan traders whose relationships with China have been highly charged with political overtones. Why should Germans wanting to buy and sell in the China market not be required, as a precondition for completing a deal, to condemn their own government for its dependence on Washington or its *Ostpolitik*? Also, as French and British traders must occasionally wonder, why do the Chinese seem to favor German companies over competing firms from countries that have extended recognition and "normalized" relations? Finally, why has China not used its trade with West Germany as a political lever either to obtain or to deny political favors?

The probable reasons for China's treatment of West German traders and their government are several. First, the Federal Republic is not an obstacle to the achievement of any fundamental Chinese objective. Bonn has never recognized Taiwan[6] and has no real stake in its continued separation from the Mainland. More generally, West Germany's interests have been almost exclusively regional in scope, and China is well outside any definition of Europe or the West. By the same token, since China is essentially also a regional power, it in turn poses no threat to the Federal Republic. Hence,

---

[5] See: "Bonn Press Release" (New York: German Information Office, 19 March 1966), and *Archiv der Gegenwart vom 31 März 1966*: 12429. For a more thorough treatment of the *"Demag* deal" see: "The Political Context of Sino-West German Trade."

[6] In the early 1950s Washington encouraged Bonn to extend recognition to the Nationalist regime, but the step was never taken. According to sources in the German Foreign Ministry, the major German consideration was the presence of German nationals on the mainland until 1955. See also: Bernhard Grossmann, "Peking-Bonn: Substantial Non-Relations," *Pacific Community*, 2, no. 1 (October 1970), pp. 224–26.

each can comfortably ignore—and each has—the other on most matters without fear of adverse repercussions. How different this is from the Sino-Japanese case!

Second, as the discussion below will show, the German government has informally but effectively supported trade with China by permitting trade delegations to come and go, by maintaining liberal licensing practices, and even by providing credit guarantees and risk insurance. These rather technical steps might not receive the attention from the press accorded high-level policy statements, but Peking seems to have found them significant indicators of Bonn's serious interest in the Chinese market and lack of hostile design.

Third, there have been commercial inducements for a substantial Sino-German trade. The two economies are complementary in many ways, though the potential market for Chinese goods in West Germany is somewhat questionable.[7] In addition, until the revaluation of the Deutsch mark in 1969, German exports were priced very favorably in the world market. Finally, a tradition of economic contacts has existed between German and Chinese traders. Several of the leading trading houses in Hamburg and other German ports that do a major portion of the current business with the PRC have been active in Asia since the nineteenth century. Many of their directors have spent long periods of time in China and are fluent in the language. With reason they think they understand the Chinese market even with the revolutionary changes of the past twenty years. Then, too, German manufacturers have a prestigious reputation because of the performance of products delivered to China before 1949, and because their new machines and replacement parts are known to be of high quality.

Fourth, though in relative terms the German share of the China market has been significant, in absolute terms Germany's trade with China is insignificant compared to Germany's total trade with all other countries. As a result fluctuations in trade levels with China would not have much impact on the German economy overall, though, of course, individual firms might suffer seriously or benefit greatly. Presumably, Chinese leaders understand that their commercial position cannot sustain the use of trade as a major lever for political concessions from West Germany.

As a final consideration, it should be noted that West German traders do have to conform to some noncommercial standards if they wish to buy or sell with the Chinese. They must be "friendly firms," i.e., they must not trade with Taiwan. And, many have reported that they often are strongly encouraged to participate in political discussions in which their opinions about their

---

[7] As shown in table I, Chinese exports to Germany have consistently lagged behind German exports to China. On the other hand, some German traders are of the opinion that with proper sales techniques an increased demand for Chinese products in Germany could be generated.

government's policies are solicited. Hence, it is not quite accurate to suggest that politics and economics are kept entirely separate in the Sino-German relationship. Nevertheless, trade has developed in response to commercial forces, and with it has come a set of quite adequate legal or quasi-legal arrangements.

II. THE ROLE OF GOVERNMENT

The structures and processes of China's foreign trade organization have been examined by Professor Hsiao and others both in previous publications and in this volume.[8] From their work it is evident that the Chinese government's role in trade is pervasive. At the policy level the total amount and composition of foreign trade is calculated as a part of the regime's basic economic objectives. At the operational level Chinese agents, though some may technically be labeled "nongovernmental," act under and are controlled by the Party/State. The relationships may be complex, but they are not ambiguous.

In the German case the role of the government is considerably vaguer. The Bonn Foreign Ministry insists, as have spokesmen for each successive cabinet, that West German trade with China is not a public concern. At the same time, of course, routine governmental provisions for allocating quotas, granting licenses, or simply registering exported or imported goods admittedly bring the trader under the jurisdiction of public agencies. Similarly, special COCOM restrictions on the sale of strategic goods also reflect official interest in this "private" matter.

Beyond this area of rather ordinary regulation of German trading circles dealing in the China market, Bonn cabinets from 1949 to the present have aided in creating the conditions for trade with the PRC and other socialist states through unofficial encouragement, private assurances, and administrative decisions. Taken together, these actions have created real, if not legal obligations for the state toward its trading community. They have also given some measure of added prestige and standing to German spokesmen in their contacts with Chinese counterparts and have provided assurances to the Chinese that Bonn would aid rather than hinder the execution of "semi-official" trade agreements and contracts.

A. The Creation of the Ostausschuss der Deutschen Wirtschaft

One of the earliest and most important governmental actions with respect to the China trade came in the early 1950s in the form of official encouragement

---

[8] See especially Gene T. Hsiao's articles: "Communist China's Foreign Trade Organization," *Vanderbilt Law Review* 20 (March 1967): 303–19; "Communist China's Trade Treaties and Agreements: 1949–1964," *Vanderbilt Law Review* 21, (October 1968): 623–58; and, "Communist China's Foreign Trade Contracts and Means of Settling Disputes," *Vanderbilt Law Review* 22 (April 1969): 503–29.

and even pressure on the leading German economic circles to establish an ostensibly private body to facilitate trade with the socialist bloc. The organization that emerged in 1952 was the Ostausschuss der Deutschen Wirtschaft.

The formal responsibilities assumed by the Ostausschuss included:[9] (1) providing information and advice to German firms on trading opportunities and hazards with socialist countries; (2) advising the government on any matter pertaining to Eastern trade; (3) participating in government negotiation with agents from the socialist bloc on pertinent subjects; and (4) negotiating with socialist bloc counterparts where for one reason or another the government could not. Its structure is comprised of a main committee (Hauptausschuss) and six subcommittees (Arbeitskreisen), one of which is responsible for the China trade.

Given the absence of formal diplomatic recognition and the caution shown by both Bonn and Peking about negotiating directly, the last of the four functions of the committee has been of particular importance. In 1953–57 negotiations were carried on by its representatives in East Berlin, Berne, and finally Peking with spokesmen of the CCPIT which led to a 1957 trade agreement between these two bodies.[10] The role of the German government in these negotiations is clear. Its leaders have acknowledged that the committee was encouraged to reach the agreement and also was delegated the competence to conclude all agreements except formal state-to-state treaties.[11] According to knowledgeable sources the Chinese team would not agree to anything until it had hard evidence that the German government stood behind the Ostausschuss. Late in 1956 that "guarantee" was apparently given, and armed with it, a delegation of German leaders journeyed to Peking in 1957 and promptly concluded the accord.

In addition to conducting negotiations on that agreement, the committee has maintained contact with the CCPIT for purposes of providing and obtaining commercial information for governmental as well as private use. Moreover, it has expressed an interest in, and also has participated in, solving problems that have developed in Sino-German trade, such as disputes over contract performance.

Finally, the committee has used its access to the government to obtain authoritative decisions affecting the China trade. On its advice the government refused until after 1961 to license contracts that stipulated Peking as the site of arbitration, at which time a change in regulations eliminated the need for

---

[9] The information upon which this section is based was obtained from interviews with Ostausschuss officials and from the memoranda and materials they provided.

[10] The text of the agreement can be found in: *Verträge der Volksrepublik China mit anderen Staaten* (Hamburg: Institut für Asienkünde), 12/13: 4–9.

[11] See Bundestag, 2nd el. pd., 177th Session, 6 December 1956: 9811–32, in Gerard Braunthal, *The Federation of German Industry in Politics* (Ithaca: Cornell University Press, 1965), p. 315.

special governmental approval of each sale. Again, the committee actively and successfully sought the liberalization of credit terms in 1965–66 when the opportunities for the sale of complete plants to Chinese corporations greatly increased. In sum, this body has performed a variety of functions with some degree of public authority and had a substantial effect on Germany's China trade.

B. *The Government and Export Guarantees and Insurance*

The Federal Republic has provided several forms of insurance for manufacturers and dealers in international trade. The legal basis for export guarantees was laid in 1949 and became effective before the end of the year.[12] It was not until 1955, however, that the Military Control Commission ceased reviewing requests for export licenses. Even then, China trade remained outside the range of insurable ventures until Germany, following Britain's lead, dropped its "China differential."[13] From that time manufacturers could obtain insurance against the risks of production of goods designated for the China market. In 1965 insurance covering the risks of extending credit to Chinese buyers was made available.

The agency established to provide these several services was the Hermes Kreditversicherungs Aktiengesellschaft (Hermes). Structurally, routine decisions on requests for insurance are made by a committee composed of representatives from the Ministries of Finance, Foreign Affairs, Economics, and Economic Cooperation. Advising this group are twelve to twenty spokesmen from commercial circles, including bankers, traders, and manufacturers.

The Hermes instructions and application forms set rather precise conditions, thus giving the impression that little discretionary authority rests with the committee. In practice, however, the group has been known to consider informally additional factors which have been important for its final decisions. It also has referred sensitive questions to another, higher interministerial committee at the subcabinet level, or even to the cabinet itself.

China trade, of course, has seldom been entirely devoid of political ramifications, and at times it has posed rather delicate problems for the government. As a result, the discretionary element in granting Hermes guarantees has been important and decisions not infrequently have been made in subcabinet or cabinet sessions. For example, the cabinet itself made credits available for

---

[12] The information upon which this section is based was obtained from officials of Hermes and from traders who have insured their goods with that agency. Particularly helpful was a mimeographed memorandum: "Ausfuhrgasantien und ausfuhrbürgschaften der Bundesrepublik Deutschland," which is available upon request from Hermes.

[13] See John R. Garson, "The American Trade Embargo Against China," in Alexander Eckstein, ed., *China Trade Prospects and U.S. Policy* (New York: Praeger Publishers, 1971).

China-bound goods in a March 1965 session.[14] And incidental to the *Demag* controversy of the following year, it became clear that the specific applications for credits also were being approved at that level.[15] Though the evidence is not conclusive, it may be that the cabinet also set the present Hermes policy which prohibits guarantees for contracts that entail the sending of technical personnel to China. Interestingly enough, these restrictions are not to be found in writing; "Telephones are useful devices!" the author was told by one interviewee when he commented on these "regulations."

The importance of Hermes guarantees to Germany's present China trade is substantially less than it was in earlier years. For one thing, the fees assessed are hardly negligible. This plus the reliability demonstrated over time by Chinese buyers has led exporters to seek private sources of insurance to cover risks of production, or even to forego insurance protection altogether. Even more important has been the changing composition of China's purchases and the modifications in the terms of payment. At the present time individual contracts are for smaller amounts than they were for the mid-1960s. The terms of payment are typically cash (full payment upon receipt of documents), and the goods involved are usually standard in design. Cash payments obviously render credit insurance unnecessary, and standard products often need not be specially insured against the chance that a certain buyer may cancel his order. In the future should the Chinese call for goods with unique properties or for credit, Hermes doubtless would again become a more significant factor in Sino-West German trade.

C.   The Legal Status of Chinese and German Nationals while Engaged in Trade in the Other Country

Since West Germany and People's China have had no formal relations and maintain only limited direct diplomatic contact, persons from one country visiting the other on whatever mission do so as private individuals. That is, German traders, bankers, or Ostausschuss delegations going to the Canton fairs or to Peking, as well as Chinese buyers visiting the Ruhr or the Hanover fair have traveled on nondiplomatic passports, at least within the jurisdiction of the host country. Similarly, the press correspondents based in the other country under a "semi-official" agreement reached in 1964 are issued ordinary visas. Only the representative of the German Consulate in Hong Kong, who has gone by invitation to the Canton fairs each year since the early 1960s,

---

[14] See *Die Welt*, 18 March 1966.

[15] *Ibid.* In this report, it was noted that a second, smaller credit application also was approved by the Cabinet.

has traveled to China on a passport and with a visa recognizing his official status.[16]

Nevertheless, both governments have shown a more than casual interest in the itineraries and activities of visiting delegations and individuals—for obvious reasons. Should embarrassing incidents occur, whatever the cause, the political consequences could be substantial. More positively, governmental cooperation could facilitate the successful conclusion of "private" trade agreements or contract negotiations.

In the case of a Chinese delegation visiting Germany, the formal procedures for the entry of its members are fairly routine, with visas usually issued in Berne or Paris. Before this apparently simple act, however, a series of favorable decisions must be made by several government departments, including both the legal and the political departments of the Ministry of Foreign Affairs as well as the Ministry of Interior.

Ordinarily, Chinese teams visit the Federal Republic only by invitation. As a result, the German hosts enter into consultations with these governmental agencies at the time the visa requests are made. Assuming that a legitimate commercial purpose is present, that the necessary precautions for the group's safety and welfare have been taken, and that the visit will occasion no unacceptable political consequences, the visas will be granted. How closely the government is involved in observing or even overseeing day-to-day activities of the guests is understandably difficult to determine. Yet its participation in the planning phase has probably been one reason for the conclusion of numerous missions without adverse political or legal complications.

The manner in which the Bonn government would treat a violation of German domestic law by a visiting Chinese trader is an open question. The author was informed by a highly placed official that the New China News Agency correspondent in Bonn would be directed to leave the country rather than be prosecuted for any serious illegality. Whether this would be the course followed with errant traders is not known. All parties concerned prefer to think that adequate preparation for each visit can keep the question strictly academic.

Germans visiting China for commercial purposes have obtained their visas in essentially the same fashion as their Chinese counterparts: applications are made in Berne and are granted only to applicants who have been properly invited by a host agency. This would-be visitor may request an invitation, of course; for example, a banker might inquire of the London branch of the Bank of China whether "he would be welcome" if he attempted to pay a courtesy call to the bank's main offices in Peking.

---

[16] This information was obtained from an official of the German Foreign Ministry. The official also noted that when he personally was once sent to Taiwan on a semi-official mission, he traveled on a regular nondiplomatic passport.

Traders wishing to attend the fair in Canton also must obtain invitations as well as visas. The former may be requested through the Chinese agency with which the individual has had previous contact. An individual without previous contacts might ask an experienced dealer to write on his behalf. The invitation, of course, is sent out by the fair officials and the details of each person's visit are prescribed—often in some detail—by the Chinese travel agency.

While there has been no known case in which Chinese nationals in Germany have been prosecuted for violations of German domestic law, Germans in China have not always been so fortunate. Indeed, several were detained and at least two were imprisoned during the Cultural Revolution. German traders view these incidents as products of peculiar circumstances, however, since the persons who were arrested or detained were technicians living in China for lengthy periods while erecting plants ordered from German (or British) firms. Moreover, German sources readily admit that the technicians sometimes behaved improperly, if not in clear violation of Chinese law. The general tension of the Cultural Revolution probably exacerbated several of these cases. Thus, the circumstances surrounding these instances of Chinese sanctions against German nationals were unique in important respects.

Nevertheless, detentions and imprisonments have not been without their effects on the German trading community. Because of these past troubles, many Germans in the China trade are convinced that they could be arrested while in China for real or alleged offenses against the Chinese state, particularly in periods of turmoil like the one just past. They see their position as somewhat more vulnerable than that of their counterparts visiting the Federal Republic. Even so, German traders also feel a certain protection from the fact that China desires to preserve its trading relationship with West Germany. Since arbitrary arrests of visiting traders are hardly an encouragement to amicable commercial ties, they are not seen as likely.

III. The Conditions of Trade: Trade Agreements and Contracts

A. The 1957 Trade Agreement

Since China and the Federal Republic of Germany have neither recognized each other nor reached any formal agreements on trade, individual contracts have been virtually the only instruments for setting the agreed-upon conditions for exchange. As noted above, the Ostausschuss and the CCPIT did negotiate an "unofficial" agreement which went into effect in October 1957 for a period of one year.[17] However, it was not renewed in 1958 nor has it been renegotiated since.

---

[17] According to German sources, the Chinese took the position that any new agreement should be on an official, government to government basis.

The 1957 accord is of interest, however, for it provides us with a convenient base against which to compare the provisions of more contemporary contracts It also has served and may still be used occasionally as the basis of contract negotiations even though it is not in effect.

The document is composed of eleven articles, two commodities lists, and two exchanges of letters. Its provisions treat many of the subjects covered in contracts (e.g., with clauses on arbitration, inspection, and *force majeure*) so that its effect, intended as well as actual, was to reduce the number of points at issue in contract negotiations. Even where it specifies that the agreement is to be applicable only if a contract includes no alternative provisions, neither contracting party would ordinarily accept terms more unfavorable to itself than are found in the more general document.

Compared with current practice, the 1957 agreement includes several provisions that are relatively favorable to the German side. For example, Zurich is designated the site for arbitration unless otherwise agreed to by both parties. Moreover, in an exchange of letters made part of the document itself, detailed procedures for arbitration are set out. These are in accord with current German preferences: each party chooses an arbitrator; the two, in turn, choose the third member who acts as umpire. Should one of the parties to a dispute fail to select an arbitrator within thirty days, or should the two arbitrators fail to agree on the choice of an umpire, the chamber of commerce at the site of arbitration names that member of the body.

The payments clause also reflects German preferences, for payment is to be made in Deutsch marks or other currencies agreed to in the contracts. Even the inspection clause, which appears to give a slight advantage to the Chinese, affords more protection to the German buyer than do most current contracts. It provides that goods exported from China are to be inspected by the Chinese Commodity Inspection Bureaus and may be reinspected by an agency agreed to by the buyer and seller. (German exports are to be inspected by an agency similarly agreed to by the parties and may be reinspected by the Chinese Commodity Inspection Bureau upon its arrival in China.) Under current practice Chinese exports to Germany usually are not reinspected (under the terms of the contract) after they have left the Chinese port.

The provisions apparently reflect the Chinese desire at that time to break into Western markets. Also important was the German concern to obtain as much protection as possible. Over the years, as the trading relationship has matured, some of these stipulations are no longer viewed as necessary—or even desirable.

No consideration of the 1957 agreement would be complete without some mention of the political context in which it was reached. Peking was interested from the beginning in a formal trade agreement with West Germany as one indication of its general acceptance in the international community as the legitimate government of China.[18] It seems to have viewed the 1957 accord as a temporary compromise or first step toward more official political contact. While the Bonn government pursued a trade policy conducive to increasing its commercial exchanges with the PRC, the larger objective was to separate trade from a general political settlement or formal relations.

This is not to say that Bonn sought no political payoff in the discussions between the Ostausschuss and the CCPIT. In the second exchange of letters attached to the agreement, trade involving West Berlin was brought under the provisions of the document. This has been a rather standard technique of the Federal Republic to obtain an implied recognition of Bonn's claims *vis-à-vis* Berlin, and Peking's adherence to a "Berlin Clause" was at least a mini-political triumph of the sort China now seeks by demanding the inclusion of a "Taiwan clause" in its agreements to exchange diplomatic missions.

Finally, political considerations were largely responsible for the failure to renew the agreement in 1958. Since Germany was not willing to move toward more formal contacts, Peking saw no reason to agree to an extension, especially when the accord included provisions less favorable than it could obtain in individual contract negotiations. Though Bonn would probably have preferred to renew the trade agreement, no great efforts were made to that end. By the mid-1960s government spokesmen found the contractual basis of Sino-German trade entirely adequate to protect German interests.[19]

B.   *Terms of Contracts in Sino-West German Trade*

The processes by which contracts are negotiated in the Sino-German trade vary considerably, though perhaps not so much as do the products exchanged. Procedures for purchasing Chinese goods are often very simple: a telegrammed order from the German firm which is acknowledged by a sales confirmation. The documents are brief and the entire transaction is standardized. The agreement is but one part of a continuing relationship, and both buyers and suppliers know that adjustments can be made the next time around. Simplicity in the contract is also possible because the goods usually are standard and not very complex. The commodity might be "Chinese white goose feathers" whose specifications are given in the seller's pamphlet on "Chinese Feathers and Down." Weight, unit price, and packing are similarly uncomplicated.

In contrast Chinese purchases have tended more often to be isolated

---

[18] According to Ernst Majonica, a member of the German Bundestag who had access to the German Foreign Office archives, the PRC first sought normalization of relations with West Germany in 1955. See "Bonn ohne eine eigene China Politik," *Suddeutsche Zeitung,* 9 March 1971.

[19] In a 17 April 1967 interview with the *Deutsche Welle,* State Secretary Schütz stressed the level of Sino-German trade as evidence of the adequacy of individual contracts in permitting and promoting such exchanges.

individual acts which are not easily related to previous or subsequent orders. Moreover, the products involved often have been highly technical and complex. The specifications in the contract must be followed exactly if the goods are to be of any use to the purchaser. Often too, the seller has had no great experience in dealing with Chinese buyers and may in fact have relied on the advice of his banker or trade association in contract negotiations. For all these reasons German export contracts tend to be more specific, formal, and comprehensive.

The provisions of typical Chinese export contracts generally reflect both Chinese preferences and German confidence in their partners. Most significant is the fact that an arbitration clause might not be included in the agreement. Even if it is, several traders agreed, there is an informal understanding that there are other and better ways to settle any problems that might arise. Second inspection by the Chinese Commodity Inspection Bureau prior to loading in the Chinese port is final. Should reinspection in Germany reveal a variance between the order and the goods as delivered, the buyer's claim is to be made against the insurance company or the shipping firm—or else it will be settled amicably and informally.

Other provisions are less startling. Insurance is effected by the sellers with the People's Insurance Company of China. Under the terms of those contracts and insurance certificates the author was permitted to see, the coverage included: "All Risks" as outlined in the Ocean Marine Cargo Clauses of the People's Insurance Company of China, dated 9 January 1963; "Warehouse to Warehouse" coverage; and "Risks of War, Capture and Seizure" as per Ocean Marine Cargo War Risk Clauses. Protection is for 110 percent of the value of the cargo. Finally, payment (in RMB) is made by irrevocable letter of credit opened before the date of shipment with the Bank of China.

In Chinese import contracts only the most elementary provisions are similar to those found in the arrangements just described. The buyer and seller, design specifications, quantity, and price of the goods are explicitly stated. Also similar are the insurance provisions that obligate the buyers to insure the products as of the time the goods are stowed on board the ship.

Beyond that a significant difference emerges: the definitions of responsibility are detailed, as are the procedures for making claims. Even the packing instructions not only may prescribe (and in great detail) the process the seller is to follow, but also may include the following type of stipulation:

The sellers shall be liable for any damage to the commodity and expenses incident thereto on account of improper packing and for any rust damage attributable to inadequate or improper protective measures taken by them in regard to packing.

The directions for the inclusion of technical documents, where they are relevant, and the quality and performance warranties are also apt to be lengthy, if not always very precise. For example, one contract provided that the goods were to be of the "best materials" and made by the "finest workmanship" and that they were to be guaranteed for a period of twelve months. Likewise, the contract provided detailed directions for the placing of shipping marks on the packaged goods.

The terms of payment provided in Chinese import contracts vary considerably from case to case. The provisions might call for cash payment, as is standard at the present time, or they might provide for credit arrangements. In the former case the provisions normally stipulate that a letter of credit shall be opened three to six weeks prior to the date of delivery and shall be valid until the fifteenth day after shipment.[20] In some cases the letter may be opened right after the contract is signed and remains in effect until after shipment or for 180 days. German exporters have reported that this time limitation has posed difficulties on occasion, for tie-ups in production or shipping have forced delays over which they had little control. An extension may be granted upon request, however, or even may be provided for in the contract itself. In cases where payment is made in installments over a period of time, the letter of credit is used as before and the timing of the payments is explicitly stated.

The German seller, of course, must present documents for payment which almost always include copies of the following: bill of lading, invoice, packing lists, certificates of quality and quantity, and certified copies of cables advising shipment. In addition, the seller usually is directed to send copies of these documents (excluding the last) to the China National Foreign Trade Transportation Corporation at the port of destination. The place of payment may be in China, Germany, or a third country. Likewise, the currency used may be Deutsch marks or RMB (earlier, Swiss and British currencies also were used).

Chinese import contracts also provide in detail for the terms of delivery. The seller has the obligation to inform the buyers or their agent thirty days prior to the time of delivery as set in the contract of the specific date of delivery and to send a description of the goods and a copy of the invoice. The buyers, in turn, must give the seller shipping instructions fifteen days before the declared date of delivery. Should the seller fail to follow these instructions (e.g., due to delay in delivery), he is liable for the expenses incurred. Storage and insurance costs for goods at port are assumed by the seller until thirty days after the ship's arrival date set by the buyers. Thereafter, the buyers assume the costs of further storage.

Immediately after the goods are loaded, the seller must advise the buyer by cable of the contract number, description, number of packages loaded, invoice value, the name of the vessel, port of departure, sailing date, and port of destination. If the delay of such advice should make it impossible for the buyer

---

[20] See the chapter by Frank Münzel on Chinese international banking practices.

to obtain insurance for the goods, the seller is held responsible for all resulting damages.

The inspection provisions vary according to the type of goods involved. Yet, like most elements in the contract, they attempt to establish precisely the elements of responsibility. With machinery, the seller must carry out a thorough inspection and testing, and not only must certify that the goods conform to the contract provisions, but also must describe the procedures followed and results of these tests. After arrival in China the goods are re-inspected by the China Commodity Inspection and Testing Bureau and a survey report is issued. In cases of discrepancies in regard to specifications or quantity, the buyers have the right (which remains operative for sixty days) to reject the goods or to make a claim against the sellers. Further, the buyers may request the Commodity Inspection Bureau to conduct an additional survey for the determination of performance failures during the period of guarantee. The bureau's findings are final in making a claim against the seller.

When the buyer files a claim, he ordinarily has the following options. (1) He can reject the goods; in this case the seller must refund the value of the goods and accept all direct losses and expenses. (2) He can request a reduction in the price of the goods. (3) He can ask for the replacement of defective items; in this case, too, the seller bears all costs and direct losses. Under most contracts claims are regarded as accepted if the seller fails to answer within fifteen days after they have been received.

Normally, the seller also is obligated to pay a penalty (usually up to 5 percent of the total net invoice value) for late deliveries. The rate of penalty assessment is .5 percent per seven days. When the delay is longer than ten weeks, the buyer has the option of canceling the contract; if he exercises that option, the seller's obligation to pay the penalty remains.

Chinese import contracts with German firms generally include a *force majeure* clause. When the seller seeks to invoke this clause, he must immediately inform the buyer and supply a certificate of confirmation from the competent governmental authority within fifteen days. Moreover, a delay in delivery of more than ten weeks gives the buyer the option of canceling the contract.

The provisions for arbitration in German export contracts are of especial significance for both parties, and a real difference between Chinese and German preferences has clearly emerged. The Chinese, not surprisingly, prefer Peking as the site of arbitration and would have any cases taken before the Arbitration Committee of the CCPIT. Procedures of the Arbitration Committee would be followed. The German preference is for the inclusion of arbitration provisions as found in the 1957 agreement: the location of the proceedings should be Zurich, Berne, or Stockholm; the arbitration commission should be specially selected for each dispute, with one person nominated by each party and an umpire chosen by the other two; and the requirement that each party must name its arbitrator within a reasonable period of time.

In actual cases both extremes as well as compromises between them have been written into contracts. The Germans appear to be most concerned with the composition of the arbitration commission and the procedures it is to follow; they will concede to provisions for arbitration before the CCPIT committee only where they must. If, however, they can have their way on these points, they have shown some willingness to accept Peking as the site of arbitration. One fairly common compromise, unusual in international practice,[21] sets the place of arbitraton in Peking if the Chinese party is the plaintiff and in Stockholm or Berne if the seller initiates the case. Whatever the provisions on these points, the contracts generally stipulate that the arbitral decision is final and that the losing party shall be assessed the costs of the proceedings.

IV. BANKING IN SINO-WEST GERMAN TRADE

While German traders and manufacturers agree that the China trade involves real risks as well as rewards, bankers are almost unanimously of the opinion that their part in the enterprise provides modest but nearly certain profit. Their involvement is not usually complex, and the Chinese are thought to be thoroughly reliable. Only one irritant seems to mar an otherwise ideal business: as is well known, the Chinese object to the practice of confirming letters of credit. When German clients seek such confirmations, the bankers are placed in a dilemma from which they cannot always easily escape. Yet, even when the German banks give confirmations, their Chinese counterparts apparently have done no more than voice complaints.[22]

The most common banking functions in the China trade are the opening of irrevocable letters of credit and making currency exchanges. The provisions of the contracts largely determine the manner in which these functions are executed. In many cases contracts identify the bank with which the account will be opened, and invariably also stipulate the currency, place, and conditions of payment.

While payment under a contract might be made in marks or RMB and payable in Peking, London, or Frankfurt, the German trader generally wants his bank to act as his agent. The importer, for example, will have his banker

---

[21] See Hsiao, "Communist China's Contracts and Means of Settling Disputes," p. 514 for a discussion of arbitration clauses in contracts negotiated by the Chinese. According to German sources, the Chinese have been willing to accept the compromise outlined in the text above because they have assumed that they would be the more likely to make claims which could conceivably lead to arbitration.

[22] One German banker informed the author that when he was reproached for having confirmed a letter of credit, he satisfied his critic with the argument that to have failed to confirm would have been construed by the seller as evidence that the bank had no confidence in the reliability of the Chinese.

open the letter of credit with the Bank of China in Peking or Shanghai, or make payment directly to his supplier. Likewise, the German exporter has evidenced a preference for contracts that oblige the buyer to open an account with a German bank. As noted above, when Chinese buyers have opened letters of credit with the Bank of China in Peking, the sellers sometimes have sought confirmations from their own banks. Only experienced German traders involved in both imports and exports have few misgivings about delivering goods for shipment and then sending documents for payment to the Bank of China.

The Chinese, of course, have taken great pride in the stability and strength of their currency. One means they have used to preserve these qualities is the strict regulation of currency exchange. According to informed sources, each German bank involved in the China trade has an agreement with the Bank of China on exchange procedures which includes at least the following provisions:

1. RMB may be purchased only for uses directly related to trade.

2. German banks may obtain Chinese currency only for the use of German firms.

3. RMB to be used in the settlement of a trade account can be obtained only after the contract for which the currency shall be used has been signed.

4. Exchange transactions and letters of credit must extend for no more than 180 days, though renegotiation is possible.

5. The rate of exchange is fixed. Any changes affect only new contracts.

6. The German bank must have a RMB account in Peking which is sufficient to cover all accounts outstanding.

In addition to these standard and routine banking functions, German bankers also may provide a number of ancillary services to German firms involved in the China trade. For example, a bank might provide assistance in the initiation of contracts with Chinese trading corporations and in supplying expertise needed to establish fruitful commercial relations. The banks most heavily involved in the China trade regularly send delegations to the Canton Fair, and their representatives pay courtesy visits to Peking as well. While their presence at the fairs may be useful to the traders as they finalize contracts, "making contracts" and gaining current information about the Chinese market for their customers are also important inducements to attend. Armed with such information, they can then advise their clients of marketing opportunities and may even participate in contract negotiations insofar as financial arrangements are concerned. In an exceptional case where the contract is unusual or when the German firm is small or inexperienced in negotiating with the Chinese, the bank may act as virtually one of the parties in the contract talks.

Finally, German banks may finance the costs of production for exporters or assume some or all of the risks of production. Alternatively, they might prepare or support requests for risk or credit insurance from Hermes.

V. Shipping

Only one German shipping firm is involved in the China trade. For over one hundred years this liner company has been operating its own services to and from China. In addition, it acts as agent for the two major Chinese business corporations concerned with shipping, the China Ocean Shipping Company and the China National Chartering Corporation. Generally speaking the relationship between the German shipping company in both of its capacities, as liner operator and as agent, and the Chinese corporations appears to be relatively simple and routinized, though the author quite possibly was not given all the relevant information because of its sensitive nature. With respect to cargo allocation, the German firm executes the directives received from Peking. Because the Chinese import on FOB terms and export on CIF terms, the procedures followed are essentially the same whether the ships involved are German, Chinese, or merely chartered by the latter.

The author was not able to determine the exact nature of the agreement between the German and Chinese shipping organizations. Nevertheless, it appears that the Chinese are comparatively straightforward in setting their terms, conditions, and fees, and that they leave the German agent little or no room for bargaining. That freight rates in the China trade are not particularly favorable might be inferred from the fact that other Western shipping lines have in the past few years dropped their services.

VI. The Sino-West German Trade Relationship in Practice

So much has been written of the shrewd, business-like behavior of the Chinese trading community that any such generalization offered here is redundant. Nevertheless, so universal and strongly held is this opinion among the German traders of their Chinese counterparts, and so important is it to an understanding of the milieu in which Sino-West German trade takes place that a restatement of the point is useful. Put simply, the Germans interviewed by the author seem to greatly admire and trust the Chinese and have approached trade opportunities accordingly. In addition, they generally claim to understand the "Chinese mentality" to the point that they know when to make concessions and when to stand firm on a point of disagreement. Given this set of attitudes, they enter into contract negotiations with confidence, tempered by the caution possessed by any successful entrepreneur.

The general provisions of contracts as well as the banking and shipping arrangements reflect German willingness to accept the Chinese on their own terms. When the Chinese insist that their export contracts need not be precise and detailed, that they must be paid in RMB, and that inspection in China must be final, German importers agree with surprising alacrity. On the other hand, when the Chinese import German goods and press for detailed and lengthy contracts in which the seller's responsibilities are set out in very explicit fashion, the German party again agrees, though sometimes not without hesitation. And, almost without exception, the contracts have been implemented without significant difficulty.

In spite of the general amicability, there have been disputes over contract performance, some of which have reached quite serious proportions. Virtually every German importer interviewed by the author said that he had made claims against his supplier and had received compensation in one form or another. The strong preference of the Chinese, all agreed, was to "make adjustments" in a succeeding contract, usually by reducing the price of the goods in the next shipment. When possible the buyers have accommodated themselves to this arrangement.

Occasionally, however, the German losses due to late delivery or damaged goods cannot be met by this means of settlement, and buyers have sought to obtain cash payment from the seller or the insurance company. Reportedly, this course of action has often involved complications to the point that some traders admitted that they "invariably lose" when they try it. They note that negotiations (which might last several years) are always difficult, for the buyers' rights are not clearly spelled out, the procedures are not well defined, and the sellers side more with their insurance company than with the buyer. In one case the German party allegedly made an original claim for only 100 percent of the invoice value (rather than 110 percent as was provided for in the sales confirmation) in order to receive speedy consideration and settlement. More than two years later, during which time scores of letters were exchanged, he settled for 30 percent of the invoice value and got that, apparently, because he threatened to go directly to the Ministry of Foreign Trade.

The standard explanation given by the German trading community for these difficulties in claim adjustment is that "loss of face" results when any Chinese official or agency is made formally responsible for an error or failure. Chinese exporting corporations, for example, allegedly do not want the insurance company to become involved in a claim settlement in the first place, and are even more opposed to its making a settlement in favor of the German importer; it would look bad on the record. Hence, if a means of reconciling the differences can be worked out without pinpointing responsibility, the Chinese will accept it promptly without worrying about technical details.

German importers have also reported a recurring problem for which they have no ready remedy: delays in delivery. The standard contract stipulates only the time of shipment and makes no provision for allowances due to shipping problems. Yet, the Chinese shipping fleet is not noted for its speed and promptness, and goods at times have not arrived as needed. During the Cultural Revolution delays of up to six months occurred. The traders who have experienced these difficulties generally have assumed that their Chinese suppliers themselves have been unable to effect more rapid delivery and cannot admit to their ineffectuality.

While the Chinese exporting corporations prefer a rather unstructured nonlegalistic approach to the settlement of claims, Chinese importing bodies have shown a pronounced tendency to make their claims in a formalistic fashion and to interpret the contract strictly. According to informed sources there have even been instances where the German manufacturer has built additional safeguards into ordered machinery at his own expense only to be sent a claim based on the deviation of the final product from the contractual specifications. The contracts themselves, as was noted above, are comprehensive and detailed; they also usually provide explicit mechanisms for making claims. German exporters find this approach acceptable, for they are protected by the contract as well as responsible under it. That they are not entirely trusted by the Chinese is taken as a given.

While Chinese buyers are determined to make detailed provisions for assigning responsibility and making claims in their purchase contracts, and to follow these provisions precisely, the actual process of claim settlement they seem to prefer is similar to that described above for Chinese export contracts. Arbitraton is to be avoided, and negotiations for adjustments in price or specifications is much preferred. According to some German exporters, the Chinese would prefer not to arbitrate even if they are certain to receive the award.

German traders have indicated that knowledge of this Chinese attitude toward arbitration is a real advantage, especially if the contract in question calls for arbitration in Stockholm or Zurich. They can threaten to seek a settlement by arbitration if they are the partner making a claim, or they can negotiate on a Chinese claim knowing that they are not apt to be taken before an arbitration commission themselves.

Actual cases of arbitration most probably have been initiated in Sino-West German trade. According to one informed source, at least two disputes were settled in this way, and another observer was quite certain that there had been three or four such settlements. A third source noted that an arbitration case was pending in Stockholm at the time German nationals were detained in China in 1969. Yet, their occurrence and the nature of the settlements involved are among the best kept secrets of the trading relationships; no one interviewed by the author admitted to having direct knowledge of an actual case of arbitration. Such secrecy is probably related to the known attitude of the Chinese about that kind of dispute settlement.

VII. CONCLUDING STATEMENTS

As the above survey indicates, the legal framework within which Sino-West German trade has taken place had been rudimentary, informal, and unintegrated by a general government to government accord. And yet, somehow it has adequately fulfilled the needs of the parties concerned. This adequacy has not been a function of the easy availability of legal protections or sanctions. The German importer, for example, has had no effective legal recourse if the Chinese insurance company should refuse to honor his claim. More fundamentally, neither party to a contract has had the legal means to obtain its fulfillment beyond the terms of the contract itself.

Adequacy of the legal instruments, rather, has resulted from the generally consistent practice of voluntary compliance with the terms of each agreement. When the German exporter ships his goods to China and then sends his documents to Peking for receipt of payment, the Bank of China complies promptly. And, when the Chinese Commodity Inspection Bureau reports that machinery parts have been damaged, the German seller has settled the resultant claim.

At best, however, voluntary compliance, even though based upon a very substantial mutuality of interest, is a fragile foundation upon which to base economic intercourse, and a feeling of uncertainty is clearly discernible among the members of the German trading fraternity. Conceivably, contracts could be canceled, payments could be delayed, or manifestly unfair awards could be rendered by arbitration commissions. Should these unlikely eventualities occur, the German concerns affected would have no means of protecting themselves. Presumably, the Chinese have similar misgivings.

In the last analysis the major German fear relating to the China trade is that political considerations will somehow intrude in the future. While it is commonly believed that Peking has "played politics" with trade only in special circumstances, it is also widely held that unforseen or dimly perceived political factors could seriously jeopardize the German trading position.

This general uncertainty reflects the difficulty of attempting to assess the role of politics in Chinese trade practices. Perhaps the one generalization that can be made with some confidence on this subject is that the Chinese have treated their trading relationship with each state on an individual basis, each with its unique circumstances, problems, and opportunities. As a result one cannot say with much confidence what the German experience indicates regarding either the possible future trading relationship of China with the United States, or even for the future of Sino-West German trade.

Looking to the future, the German trading community hopes that Bonn's relations with Peking will be regularized. In this way the level of political uncertainty could be reduced and the possibility of a more substantial legal framework would be increased.

Trade with Denmark

POUL MOHR

The context of Denmark's trade with the People's Republic of China (PRC) differs in certain respects from that of some other West European countries. Denmark, unlike most other European countries, has had relations with the PRC almost from the beginning. France was facing a critical situation in Southeastern Asia that hampered relations with the PRC, and the Federal Republic of Germany had not yet celebrated her first anniversary when Denmark, as part of a joint Scandinavian action, recognized the government of the PRC in January 1950. A few months later regular diplomatic relations were established which have remained unstrained ever since. Three government agreements have been concluded, and a fourth—a cultural agreement (*ad modum* similar Danish agreements with a number of Eastern and Western European states)—has been discussed from time to time since the mid-sixties.[1]

NOTE: The author is indebted to Danish authorities, trade organizations, and a number of private traders for their readiness to answer his questions and meet his importunate wishes for documents and other written material. He wants to thank Professors Jerome A. Cohen and Ole Lando for putting him on the track and the editor, Professor Victor H. Li, and Professor Randle Edwards and Mr. Stanley Lubman, Attorney at Law, for valuable suggestions. Mrs. Caroline Ralston, Ph.D., furnished a most necessary assistance in avoiding stylistic pitfalls. All errors, of course, are the responsibility of the author.

[1] (1) Trade and Payments Agreement of 12 December 1957, between the government of the Kingdom of Denmark and the Government of the PRC, including exchange of letters of 12 December 1957, concerning most-favored-nation treatment (hereinafter referred to as TPA); (2) exchange of notes of 12 April 1958, concerning trade mark registration; (3) exchange of notes of 9 September 1961, concerning tax exemptions for students. See Rudolf Herzer and Wolfgang Mohr, eds., *Verträge der Volksrepublik China mit anderen Staaten.* Vol. 3, *Die nichtkommunistischen Länder Europas und die*

Finally, and not irrelevant to the evaluation of the Danish experience, the trade has been extremely limited and marginal to both economies.[2]

I. THE VOLUME AND DISTRIBUTION OF TRADE

The volume of Sino-Danish trade has fluctuated greatly. Table 1 gives the value of Danish imports from and exports to the PRC and for purposes of comparison, Danish imports from and exports to Taiwan and Hong Kong in the period 1947–70.

Table 1 must be adjusted. A substantial part of Denmark's imports from the PRC comes via a third country, mainly Hong Kong, whereas the bulk of the exports is shipped directly to the PRC. This is illustrated in table 2. Detailed information is not available after the rearrangement of official statistical reporting methods in 1967.

Some of these oscillations are a reflection of the PRC's internal economy and also are manifestations of the over-all shift of China's trade from the communist world to the noncommunist world.[3] In addition, the 1950–51 boom in Danish imports probably is due in part to a special effort by Danish traders to reestablish traditional connections with China, and in part to the favorable effect of the early Danish recognition of the PRC. The boom ended abruptly in 1952, in large part because of the Korean War trade embargo.

There was another substantial increase in trade in 1958–59. This was aided by the abolition of the CHINCOM list[4] and by the signing of the Trade and Payments Agreement (TPA) of 1 December 1957. The significance of the TPA is substantiated by parallel trends in Sino-Swedish and Sino-Norwegian trade.[5] In addition, these years coincided with the beginning of one of the biggest booms in the Danish economy and with the gradual abolition of import restrictions that gained momentum around 1958–60.

Länder Amerikas (einschliesslich Kubas) (Frankfurt am Main: Alfred Metzner Verlag, 1965), pp. 12 ff; and Douglas M. Johnston and Hungdah Chiu, eds., *Agreements of the People's Republic of China, 1949–67* (Cambridge, Mass.: Harvard University Press, 1968), pp. 241–42.

[2] In 1969 Danish exports to the PRC amounted to less than 0.1 percent of the PRC's total imports and to about 0.05 percent of Denmark's total exports, while the PRC's share of Denmark's total import was less than 0.3 percent. In 1970, which is a more normal year for exports, Danish exports to the PRC were little more than 0.1 percent of Denmark's total exports.

[3] Alexander Eckstein, *Communist China's Economic Growth and Foreign Trade* (New York: McGraw-Hill, 1966), pp. 186–87.

[4] John R. Garson, "The American Trade Embargo Against China," in Alexander Eckstein, ed., *China Trade Prospects and U.S. Policy* (New York: Praeger Publishers, 1971), pp. 60–66.

[5] Robert F. Dernberger, "Prospects for Trade Between China and the United States," in Eckstein, *China Trade Prospects,* pp. 284–85.

TABLE 1

DENMARK'S IMPORTS FROM AND EXPORTS TO THE PRC, TAIWAN,
AND HONG KONG, 1947–70
(in 1,000 D.Kr.)*

	China		PRC		Taiwan		Hong Kong	
	Im	Ex	Im	Ex	Im	Ex	Im	Ex
1947	1.821	335	...	...	...	...	...	...
1948	4.591	1.891	...	...	...	...	...	...
1949	2.348	699	...	...	...	...	...	...
1950	19.249	831	...	...	...	...	...	...
1951	59.468	618	...	...	...	...	...	...
1952	53	1.190	...	...	...	...	...	...
1953	14.464	2.093	...	...	...	...	7.013	36.303
1954	1.915	924	...	...	...	...	10.016	18.302
1955	...	...	1.103	451	204	544	7.238	7.587
1956	...	...	9.584	21.566	315	1.078	6.794	8.803
1957	...	...	3.340	4.912	100	1.645	8.977	18.736
1958	...	...	27.409	29.474	74	1.337	6.831	13.156
1959	...	...	49.429	24.341	724	4.066	9.675	10.777
1960	...	...	70.442	14.444	2.987	2.391	14.406	14.304
1961	...	...	45.740	26.500	1.569	2.054	17.698	25.896
1962	...	...	26.418	25.206	2.553	3.629	26.252	23.520
1963	...	...	29.215	3.983	2.385	1.840	35.227	23.588
1964	...	...	52.693	7.291	1.030	4.268	51.436	31.177
1965	...	...	44.272	13.096	1.657	4.200	54.552	27.887
1966	...	...	47.455	17.073	1.869	3.428	66.337	32.666
1967	...	...	61.665	41.460	3.332	8.870	79.405	57.617
1968	...	...	62.052	15.791	2.999	12.502	83.194	55.419
1969	...	...	68.518	9.732	4.279	17.636	139.481	75.028
1970	...	...	79.136	28.371	8.401	21.498	166.784	80.420

* Imports in CIF prices, exports in FOB prices.

SOURCE: Statistisk Årbog/Statistical Yearbook (Copenhagen: Denmarks Statistik, 1948–71).

NOTE: The official Danish statistics have no information on the trade with Hong Kong until 1953 and do not separate the figures for the PRC and Taiwan before 1955. From 1947 to 1966 the import figures are based on country of purchase and the export figures on country of sale. From 1967 the figures are based on country of origin and country of destination respectively.

Notwithstanding the figures in table 1, it can be shown by means of interpolation from table 2 and other data that total imports from the PRC dropped in 1967. This decline most likely was due to the economic effects of the Cultural Revolution. The considerable increase in exports in 1967 is related to the first Danish Industrial Exhibition in Peking in March 1967.[6]

---

[6] *Tan-mai kung-yeh chan-lan-hui* (Industrial Trade Exhibition) (Copenhagen, 1967).

TABLE 2

DENMARK'S IMPORTS FROM AND EXPORTS TO THE PRC, 1960–66

(In 1,000 D.Kr.)*

	Imports			*Exports*		
	O	P	Via third country (O-P)	D	S	Via third country (D-S)
1960	117,158	70,442	46,716	14,968	14,444	524
1961	92,962	45,740	47,222	27,845	26,500	1,345
1962	64,736	26,418	38,318	25,683	25,206	477
1963	45,519	29,215	16,304	3,933	3,983	50
1964	75,259	52,693	22,566	7,566	7,291	275
1965	72,532	44,272	28,260	14,356	13,096	1,260
1966	81,097	47,455	33,642	17,111	17,073	38

* Imports in CIF prices, exports in FOB prices.

SOURCE: Statistisk Årbog/Statistical Yearbook, Copenhagen 1961–67.

NOTE: The import figures are specified with respect to country of origin (O) and purchase (P), and the export figures with respect to country of destination (D) and country of sale (S).

This exhibition was arranged by the Danish Government Committee on Exhibitions Abroad in cooperation with various Chinese government organizations, notably the Chinese Committee for the Promotion of International Trade (hereafter CCPIT) and the Ministry of Foreign Trade, and thirty major Danish exporters participated. Although some participants were disappointed by the 1968 trade figures when export volume was back to normal, the effect of the Cultural Revolution did not hit the export trade until 1969.

It stands to reason that the relative instability of the trade has certain self-propagatory effects that evade the control of the authorities. Confidence in a market once lost is hard to regain. This is especially true of larger firms that work on the basis of long-term planning, whereas smaller traders more or less operate on a hit-and-run basis.

Since 1959 the considerable Danish import surplus has created a substantial balance in the PRC's bank accounts in Copenhagen. This balance is convertible into hard currency, including American dollars. The Chinese are well aware of Danish wishes here. Chou Hua-min, vice-minister of foreign trade, and head of an official trade delegation to Denmark in October 1971, mentioned as one of the purposes of the visit the mutual interest in reducing the Chinese export surplus.

This issue was mentioned again in the Chinese speeches at the opening of the Danish Industrial Exhibition in Peking in March 1972. According to the Danish press, it was a subject of negotiation between the Chinese Ministry of Foreign Trade and the Danish minister of trade who spent a week in the PRC in connection with the exhibition. It would be unrealistic, however, to imagine that the surplus will be eliminated in the near future. Thus, after the termination of the Canton Fair in November 1971, the Copenhagen daily *Politiken* reported from Peking that the Chinese foreign trade corporations were instructed to favor the Scandinavians, at competitive prices, but that the Danish traders as usual bought more than they sold.[7]

Besides being very limited in scale, Sino-Danish trade involves a relatively large number of commodity groups,[8] which fact indicates that it is carried out mainly by means of fairly small contracts. This is especially true of Danish exports, where most of the commodity groups (in 1967 21 out of 34, in 1968 13 out of 26, in 1969 17 out of 28, and in 1970 15 out of 26) represented sales of less than D.Kr. 10,000, roughly corresponding to US $1,400.

The number of Danish traders involved is also small, probably numbering about a hundred. Most of these are not small traders. Some of them, particularly importers having exclusive sales agreements or other agency arrangements with the Chinese foreign trade corporations, have done comparatively good—if not always stable—business. Considering the low frequency of disputes in overseas trade, the nature of the business connections, the reputation of the Chinese traders, and the minimal risks connected with minor contracts which to the average trader are not worth more than a few letters in case of breach, the reader is warned against jumping to conclusions on the basis of the Danish experience.

II. DIPLOMATIC RELATIONS

A diplomatic interregnum followed the assumption of power by the Communists in 1949. Before that time, the Danish envoy extraordinary and plenipotentiary was accredited to the Nationalist Government in Nanking. Owing to housing problems in Nanking during the Civil War the legation resided at the Danish Consulate General in Shanghai. In April 1949, shortly

---

[7] *Politiken*, 30 November 1971, p. 16.

[8] The twelve main imported articles in 1970—which was a fairly representative year—were (value in D.Kr. 1,000): tin: unwrought, unalloyed (16,486); bed feathers: uncleaned (8,497); apricots, peaches (7,725); dish towels (2,765); cotton: unbleached, undyed (2,684); shirts: cotton (2,562); carpets, mats, and rugs (2,373); skin, Persian lamb (1,778); pineapple: canned (1,424); pajamas for men (1,188); pig's hair (1,158); and alarm clocks (1,019). Together these articles made up 63 percent of the total imports from the PRC. Imports of miscellaneous manufactured articles amounted to D.Kr. 3,286 million. Cf. *Udenrigsministeriets Tidsskrift*, no. 27 (16 July 1971), p. 501. The four main export commodity groups in 1970 were: chemical elements and compounds (5,144); electrical machinery and equipment (3,524); non-electrical machinery and equipment (2,635); paper and paperboard and articles thereof (384). Miscellaneous manufactured articles amounted to D.Kr. 478,000 and a used tanker (some claim that it was a dry-cargo ship) to D.Kr. 15,953,000. Cf. *Kina. Vejledning for Eksportører* (Copenhagen, 1971), p. 52 and *Udenrigsministeriets Tidsskrift*.

before Shanghai was abandoned by the Nationalists, the Nationalist government requested the Danish minister to remove the legation to Canton. This request was disregarded, probably on instructions from the Danish government. Although the legation remained in Shanghai, there was no contact whatsoever with the PRC government between May 1949 and late spring of 1950. Letters to the Chinese authorities were returned stamped "no diplomatic relations." After the Danish recognition of the PRC government in January 1950, the minister was ordered by his government to go to Peking where, upon the establishment of diplomatic relations in May, he was received not by the Head of State but by a vice-foreign minister.[9]

The Danish Consulate General in Shanghai was reopened in February 1950 and functioned until 1963. From 1950 to 1952 it was led by a secretary of legation, in 1954 by an archivist, and from 1955 to 1957 by a vice-consul.[10] However, it was without Danish staff during part of 1953, and continuously from 1958 till it was formally closed down. Under a treaty with the Republic of China, in 1949–50 there were Danish honorary consuls in the following Chinese cities: Harbin, Tientsin, Tsingtao, Hankow, Amoy, and Canton.[11] A consulate in Dairen was abolished in 1947–48, while the others continued to function during the Civil War and the diplomatic interregnum. With the exception of Tientsin all the consulates were suspended in 1952, and in 1953 they were formally closed down, including the one in Tientsin.

Since 1960 Denmark has only been represented by an ambassador and a diplomatic staff consisting of one secretary of embassy. As a seafaring nation with a considerable number of ships calling in at Chinese ports, some of them

---

[9] Announcement of 9 January 1950 of the Danish Ministry of Foreign Affairs, and exchange of telegrams of 9 and 14 January 1950 between the foreign ministers of Denmark and PRC. The text of the telegrams is rendered in German in Herzer und Mohr, *Verträge*, pp. 11–12. The Danish text of the announcement is found in Alf Ross and Isi Foighel, *Studiebog i Folkeret* (Copenhagen: Munksgaard, 1954), p. 110. See also Herzer und Mohr, *Verträge*, p. 12. n.

[10] Information about the diplomatic representations is mainly based on *Udenrigsministeriets Kalender* for the years 1946–71. The *Kalender* does not give the dates when the various appointments took effect. The author is indebted to Ambassador Alex Mørch for information concerning the diplomatic interregnum. In addition to the formal contacts, in the early 1950s, an unofficial delegation of Danish traders visited the PRC on the initiative of a few "old China hands."

[11] Cf. Treaty between the Kingdom of Denmark and the Republic of China for the Relinquishment of Extraterritorial Rights in China and the Regulation of Related Matters (signed in Nanking on 20 May 1946). Article 7, section 1 reads "The Government of the Kingdom of Denmark and the Government of the Republic of China agree that the consular officers of each country, duly provided with exequaturs, shall be permitted to reside in such ports, places, and cities of the territory of the other country as may be agreed upon. . . . and, in general the consular officers of each country shall be accorded the rights, privileges, and immunities enjoyed by consular officers under modern international usage."

chartered by the China National Chartering and Transportation Corporation, Denmark is presumably interested in resuming consular relations with the PRC.

In 1949 the Chinese Legation in Copenhagen was closed down, although the Chinese consul-general, a Danish citizen, apparently, continued to act as such until some time in 1950 when consular business was transferred to the PRC's Legation in Copenhagen. This legation was opened in May in connection with the establishment of regular diplomatic relations. It was manned with a first and a third secretary of legation, a military attaché, and an assistant military attaché. An envoy extraordinary and plenipotentiary, principally accredited and domiciled in Stockholm and co-accredited in Copenhagen, was appointed Head of Legation. In late 1950 or early 1951 a chargé d'affairs *ad interim* was accredited in Copenhagen.

In 1956 the Chinese chargé d'affaires in Copenhagen was replaced by an ambassador. At the same time the staff was increased by a cultural attaché, a commercial attaché (only from 25 April to 5 June 1956), an attaché without portfolio, and a first secretary. The next commercial attaché arrived in September 1956 and stayed until January 1958. His successor was appointed in September 1959, and since then the embassy has constantly had one commercial attaché, except for the period from August 1964 to August 1970 when there were two. This may be connected with the division of the embassy into a chancellery and a commercial department in 1961–62. In 1963 a commercial attaché was appointed. Unlike the Chinese embassy in Stockholm, the embassy in Copenhagen has never had a commercial counselor.

The commercial attaché handles a wide variety of matters. He collects information on Danish products, industries, and traders (and probably keeps an eye on similar matters in the neighboring countries[12]). He provides Danes with material and information about China and looks after the connections between the various Chinese foreign trade corporations and Danish firms, including paying regular visits to those companies that have agency arrangements for Chinese products.[13] He also acts as an intermediary in less pleasant matters. More than one Danish trader has forwarded complaints concerning nonperformance or delayed performance by Chinese exporters via the commercial attaché. "It takes time," one interviewee said, "but sometimes it works." The complaint is probably sent from the embassy to the Ministry of Foreign Affairs, or possibly to the Ministry of Foreign Trade, and from there to the head or branch office of the corporation in question. The traders

---

[12] For example, contact between a Danish exporter and a Chinese foreign trade corporation was established after an inquiry from the PRC's Embassy in Oslo.

[13] The commercial attaché (or the Commercial Department) probably has capacity to sign contracts (see *Kina. Vejledning for Eksportører,* p. 30), but it is unclear whether this has actually happened. None of the interviewees had ever heard of an instance, although they also would not exclude the possibility in an exceptional situation.

seem to prefer this procedure to advancing their complaints via the Danish Embassy in Peking, although there is no doubt that the embassy is anxious to be informed on such matters so that it may take them up during the regular visits to the foreign trade corporations or, if need be, with higher authorities.

In addition to the regular diplomatic establishment, from time to time Denmark is visited by general and special trade delegations from the PRC. Special trade delegations usually come in order to negotiate more substantial transactions, such as purchases of complete plants and ships. The latest general trade delegation arrived in October 1971. During a one-week stay it visited fifteen major export houses and industries, including shipbuilders, engineering, construction, and electronic industries. The delegation was not expected to and presumably did not sign contracts, since this is usually done by special trade delegations to Denmark, by Danish traders visiting Chinese foreign trade corporations, or by correspondence.

According to Danish law, members of special missions are not entitled to diplomatic privileges unless they are vested with credentials (which they are not known to be). The members of the Chinese delegations travel on diplomatic passports; Danish visas are needed, but this is only a matter of form.

Except for activities of the delegation members outside their official functions, the question of diplomatic status is not particularly important. Danish courts are not likely to accept a plea of sovereign immunity from state-owned foreign trade corporations or any other state-operated companies.[14] In addition, the issue is not likely to arise since practically all Sino-Danish contracts contain an arbitration clause or (as in the case of the standard Chinese bill of lading) a jurisdictional agreement which states that Danish courts are not competent to deal with disputes arising out of the contracts. The courts are extremely reluctant to declare such agreements invalid.

III. INTERGOVERNMENTAL AGREEMENTS

Since the 1930s bilateral trade agreements have undergone considerable change, and new types of agreements have emerged. The traditional treaty of friendship, commerce, and navigation, containing elaborate clauses on most-favored-nation treatment regarding customs duties, rights of citizens, shipping, etc., has largely been replaced by the more concise commodity exchange agreement. That agreement is usually confined to reciprocal concessions concerning the administration of import and export licenses for specifically listed commodities. The commodity lists may be indicative or binding

---

[14] Cf. Alf Ross, *Laerebog i Folkeret* (Copenhagen: Munksgaard, 1967), pp. 229–30; and Allan Philip, *Dansk international privat- og procesret* (Copenhagen: Jurist Forbundets Forlag, 1971), pp. 86 ff. Cf. also the principle laid down in Article 31, section 1, subsection C, of the Vienna Convention on Diplomatic Relations of 18 April 1961.

(maximum or minimum quotas). The commodity exchange agreement is usually supplemented by a payments agreement. The latter is sometimes laid out in a special protocol, which stipulates the method of payment and the currencies to be used, usually the currencies of the contracting parties and one or more third-party currencies.

Since the liberalization in the 1950s and especially after the introduction of the "external" convertibility in 1958, the importance of the Danish bilateral trade and payments agreements has gradually decreased, except in relation to the trade with state-trading countries which is still subject to control.[15] The predominant type of agreement between Denmark and the state-trading countries is a long-term agreement which is valid for a number of years, with annual protocols fixing the annual quotas. It differs from the commercial treaty mainly in that it is more concise, and that—like commodity exchange agreements in general—it need only be submitted to the Exchange Control Committee of the Folketing (the Danish Parliament) for its information, while the commercial treaty must be formally approved by the Folketing.[16] In recent years Denmark also has established a number of agreements regarding economic and technical cooperation with the Eastern European countries.

The TPA is a short-term commodity exchange and payments agreement subject to automatic annual renewal. It consists of an agreement proper, two indicative lists of commodities, and an exchange of letters providing for most-favored-nation treatment with respect to the levying of customs duties and other charges, customs clearance formalities, and navigation (see Appendix 2).

Compared with agreements with other state-trading countries, the TPA contains several striking features: the vagueness of the principal agreement, the use of commodity lists that merely indicate what might be traded without fixing minimum or maximum quotas, and the highly atypical exchange of letters which lay down a fairly detailed agreement concerning most-favored-nation treatment, matters usually arranged for by most states through more solemn instruments in the diplomatic hierarchy of forms. Exchange of notes or letters are usually employed in order to confirm principles or matters agreed upon by the parties during the negotiation of the main agreement. It is thus interesting to note that the Sino-Finnish most-favored-nation agreement also is found in a separate exchange of letters, whereas the corresponding Sino-Norwegian and Sino-Swedish agreements are included in the main agreements.

As it is, the TPA looks like a compromise between a Chinese wish for a

---

[15] A license is always required for trade with Albania, East Germany, Southern Rhodesia, Taiwan, the PRC, the People's Republic of Mongolia, North Korea, and North Vietnam.

[16] Cf. P. Nyboe Andersen, *Udenrigsøkonomi* (Copenhagen: Nyt Nordisk Forlag, Arnold Busck, 1969), p. 204.

more substantial or classic, i.e., slightly old-fashioned, trade agreement, and a certain Danish resistance to entering an agreement whose formality is out of proportion to the actual commercial intercourse. In this connection it is worthwhile noting that the Soviet Union is the only Eastern bloc country with which Denmark has concluded a treaty of commerce and navigation (in 1946), and that the Danish trade with Poland, which is almost five times larger than the trade with the PRC and more than 25 percent larger than the trade with the Soviet Union, is based on a long-term commodity exchange agreement and a separate payments agreement. In addition, unlike the Danish trade with Poland and the Soviet Union, the China trade has not yet found a reasonable stability. The exchange of letters seem to reflect a bargain. The Chinese are known to insist on most-favored-nation treatment in major trade agreements in order to protect Chinese exports and to defeat embargoes against the PRC,[17] but the most-favored-nation agreement has long been outdated as seen from a Danish point of view.

A. Trade and Payments Agreement

The TPA proper consists of five articles: Articles 1–3 constitute the trade agreement,[18] Article 4 contains the payments agreement, while Article 5 deals with questions of coming into force, expiration, and interpretation.

The trade agreement does not establish a plan for regulating the volume and value of trade within the framework of a quota system subject to revision as the trade develops. Without committing themselves to specific measures the parties merely assure each other that they will "accord one another as favorable a treatment as possible with respect to the issue of import and export licenses," and "in accordance with rules in force permit the exportation [to each other] of the commodities specified [in Lists A and B] . . . and give favorable consideration to the license applications for such commodities." In addition, they also will "give sympathetic consideration to applications for the import and export of commodities which are not mentioned in Lists A and B."

Both countries have quantitative restrictions on trade[19] and thus require

---

[17] Cf. Luke T. Lee, *China and International Agreements: A Study of Compliance* (Leyden: A. W. Sijthoff, 1969), p. 88, n. 56.

[18] The Danish title, *vareudvekslingsaftale*, means "commodity exchange agreement."

[19] Danish imports from the PRC are subject to free licensing. Thus, a license is mainly a matter of form, but may be refused if (1) the annual quota fixed by the Ministry of Trade for the commodity in question has been exhausted; (2) the import inflicts unreasonable competition on Danish trade; (3) the import is contrary to Danish political-commercial interests. Annual quotas are fixed for a number of commodities and published in *Meddelelser fra Handelsministeriets Licenskontor*. In such cases a *pro forma* invoice must be forwarded with the license application because it has happened that traders, who do not want foreign competition, have applied for and been

licenses for individual transactions. In principle the trade agreement binds the parties to facilitate the granting of licenses; but owing to vagueness in language, it may not be possible to invoke the agreement successfully against isolated refusals of license applications. The trade agreement is useful in dealing with obviously discriminatory actions in the administration of licenses. Here the Chinese are in a relatively strong position, since they may claim that (unpublished) economic plans do not provide for a particular transaction— even though Danish traders have not known Chinese foreign trade corporations to have ever acted without being able to provide the necessary licenses. In the reverse situation the Danish authorities may adduce considerations regarding politico-commercial interests, such as the securing of reasonable competition or the exhaustion of annual quotas, to warrant the denial of a license. It may even be possible at some point to regard the remarkable Danish import surplus as a contravention of the presumption laid down in the preamble that trade will be reasonably balanced.

The trade agreement is more striking for what it omits than for what it includes. Denmark's long-term agreements with the European state-trading countries (except for the Soviet Union and Albania) are designed to secure both the balance and the stability of the trade. Trading of nonliberalized commodities is based on annual quotas, and the issue of licenses for the value or volume indicated in the commodity lists is guaranteed. Problems that arise are referred to negotiation by mixed commissions which are appointed by the governments and which meet once a year. Some of the agreements also contain a provision stating that the parties will do their best to expedite the conclusion of contracts concerning the delivery of commodities offered on the lists.[20]

The payments agreement was drafted while the convertibility of the currencies of the Organization for European Economic Cooperation (OEEC) countries was still limited to the sterling area.[21] In December 1958 complete convertibility was established among the currencies of the Western world whereby the currency of each country was made exchangeable into any other's, including U.S. dollars and—until recently—gold.

---

granted licenses for the total quota only to store them in the safe until the end of the quota period. The authorities have, for instance, maintained an attitude of reserve toward import of manufactured textiles from the PRC.

In the PRC a license is required for all foreign trade activities. Victor H. Li, "Legal Aspects of Trade with Communist China," *Colum. J. Transn'l L.* 3 (1964): 58.

[20] Cf. Trade and Payments Agreement of 7 December 1949 between Denmark and Poland, Article 4: "Afin de faciliter l'utilisation des contingents prévus, les deux Gouvernements s'engagent à faire leur possible pour hâter la conclusion des contrats concernant la livraison des marchandises mentionées dans les listes A et B."

[21] The author is indebted to Mr. Jørn Knudsen, Head of the Foreign Department of Denmark's National Bank for details concerning the significance of the payments agreement.

In accordance with Article 4, section 2, the Chinese People's Bank and Denmark's National Bank agreed in early 1958 that the Chinese People's Bank would open kroner accounts in the principal banks in Copenhagen, the so-called transferable China accounts, on which all payments should be entered and the balance of which should be transferable to other currencies within the sterling area.

This arrangement became obsolete at the end of 1958 after the reorganization of the foreign exchange system. Since then all payments between Denmark and the PRC may, subject only to the foreign exchange laws in the respective countries, be effected in Danish kroner or any other mutually acceptable and convertible currency.[22] There is no need for special arrangements between the two central banks. Payments are now effected via accounts kept by the Bank of China and the principal Danish banks. The Chinese accounts in Denmark are kept in D.Kr. and the Danish accounts in the Bank of China are kept in RMB.

Sterling, together with D.Kr., was the currency preferred by the Chinese until the sterling crisis in 1968. Since then sterling has to a certain extend been replaced by Swiss francs, German marks, and RMB. RMB bought in London by Danish banks and transferred to the Bank of China is preferred by the Chinese because of the elimination of the exchange risk.

B. *The Most-Favored-Nation Agreement*

The agreement contained in the Sino-Danish Exchange of Letters falls into two parts: a customs agreement, see Appendix 2, paragraph (a) of the letter of the Chinese delegation (not to be confused with a tariff agreement) and a navigation agreement, see paragraphs (b), (c), and (d). The former is a pure most-favored-nation agreement, while the latter is a combined most-favored-nation and equality-of-treatment (or nondiscrimination) agreement.

The customs agreement accords "unconditional and unrestricted most-favored-nation treatment in all matters concerning customs duties, surtaxes, and other subsidiary charges as well as customs clearance formalities, regulations, and procedures." "Unconditional" means that favors granted to any third country by either of the contracting countries automatically applies to the other party without special consideration. The meaning of "unrestricted" is not quite clear. The Danish text has *ubegraenset* which means "unlimited" rather than "unrestricted." The author has not had access to the Chinese text. The unlimited form is supposed not to impose any restrictions on the scope of the application of the most-favored-nation clause to certain specified objects or territories.[23]

---

[22] Cf. Trade Agreement between Denmark and Albania of 23 June 1971, Article 3.

[23] Cf. Andersen, *Udenrigsøkonomi,* p. 162; and Hungdah Chiu, *The People's Republic of China and the Law of Treaties* (Cambridge, Mass: Harvard Univ. Press, 1972), p. 51.

According to the exemption clauses (par. b, sec. 1–4) the customs agreement does not apply to favors granted by either country to adjoining third countries to facilitate frontier traffic or favors "resulting from any existing or future customs union or similar international agreement to which either of the Contracting Parties is or may become a Party." These are standard reservations present in a great number of bilateral agreements. The latter is especially relevant to Denmark which, besides being a General Agreement on Tariffs and Trade (GATT) member, was, at the time of the TPA, negotiating a Nordic Tariff Union and, within the framework of the then OEEC, a large European free trade area. Both plans came to naught, but in 1959 Denmark became a member of the European Free Trade Area (EFTA) and later, on 22 January 1972, a signatory to the Treaty of Accession to the Common Market.

The frontier traffic clause applies to the PRC and Denmark equally. A similar clause is found in the exchange of letters of 31 March 1956 between Finland and the PRC concerning most-favored-nation treatment with respect to customs and navigation,[24] but not in the PRC's agreements with Norway and Sweden.

Section 2 exempting favors that the PRC "has granted or may grant to any neighbouring country" seems to be the counterpart of section 3, the so-called Scandinavian reservation clause which is inserted in a considerable number of most-favored-nation treaties or agreements concluded by Denmark, Finland, Iceland, Norway, and Sweden. Thus, it is found in the PRC's agreements with Norway and Sweden, but strangely, not in the exchange of letters with Finland. This section may become important in the long run, depending on how the PRC will define the concept of "neighboring country."

The exemption clauses apply to paragraph (b) ("treatment of crews from ships of either Contracting Party during stays in ports of the other Contracting Party"), but not to paragraph (c) (treatment of ships "entering into, berthing at, and sailing from the ports of the other Party"). The exemptions also do not apply to the equality of treatment agreement in paragraph (d) ("the liberty of ships of either country to take part in normal competition with ships of any third country"). This is an extremely practical provision (and entirely in the spirit of the Convention on the International Regime of Maritime Ports of 31 October 1924), since a restraint in trade in favor of ships flying the flag of any third country might make the service unattractive to others. Paragraph (d) has not yet been invoked, although during the Cultural Revolution the Chinese corporations sometimes refused to ship goods to several Danish importers in certain ships belonging to one Danish shipowner the Chinese declared "imperialist."

Paragraph (b) is not found in the PRC's agreements with Norway and Sweden.

---

[24] Herzer and Mohr, *Verträge,* pp. 32–34.

It may have been inserted at Danish request, possibly because of certain unpleasant adventures experienced by some Danish sailors in Chinese ports.

Paragraphs (b) and (c) do not provide unconditional most-favored-nation treatment. It is generally believed that a conditional most-favored-nation agreement is of extremely limited value.[25] Nevertheless, the most important aspect of the present agreement is that it does not explicitly include quantitative restrictions, and the fact that these are included in the TPA proper in the form of mutual concessions excludes liberal interpretation of the exchange of letters.

Finally, it should be noticed that the most-favored-nation agreement does not itself contain an expiration clause nor does it incorporate by reference the expiration clause in Article 5 of the main agreement. Since the corresponding Finnish, Norwegian, and Swedish agreements are all subject to the respective expiration clauses, the omission here is likely to be an oversight, probably due to the unusual nature of the form of the agreement.

C. The Trade Mark Agreement

During the early years the Chinese government had not been amenable to the question of registration of foreign trade marks. A number of applications from Western firms were left unanswered. Gradually it became the practice to forward individual trade marks for registration through the respective embassies in Peking. The advantages of this procedure were problematic, however, and various countries, including Denmark since 1953, kept pressing for general agreements. There was a certain breakthrough in 1956–57 when agreements were made with the United Kingdom and Switzerland.[26]

A lengthy correspondence led to a Danish-Chinese trade mark agreement in 1958.[27] In a note of 4 October 1956 the Chinese Ministry of Foreign Affairs informed the Danish Embassy that (1) the 1950 Provisional Trade Mark Act of the PRC did not—as asked for in a Danish note of 24 July of the same year—provide protection for collective marks, and (2) "according to Chinese legislation it is not a condition for a foreign firm to run a commercial enterprise

---

[25] Cf. Andersen, Udenrigsøkonomi, p. 162. The reader is referred to Martin Domke and John Hazard, "La clause de la nation la plus favorisée," in René David, ed., *Aspects juridiques du commerce avec les pays d'économie planifiée* (Paris: R. Pichon and R. Durant-Auzias, 1961) for a general evaluation of the most-favored-nation clause as a means of increasing the volume of trade between the free market and the state trading countries.

[26] Exchanges of notes between the Chinese Ministry of Foreign Affairs and the British and Swiss Legations in Peking of 13 April and 1 June 1956, and 14 April 1956 and 8 March 1957, respectively. Cf. Herzer and Mohr, *Verträge*, pp. 81–82 and 100–1.

[27] Cf. Danish note of 25 March 1958 *in fine*, Herzer and Mohr, *Verträge*, p. 18. A copy of the Danish Trade Mark Act of 7 April 1936 was forwarded with a note from the embassy in Peking on 4 August 1953 informing the Chinese authorities of the conditions for registration of foreign trade marks in Denmark.

in China in order to be entitled to have their trade marks registered." The note further says that "to register trade mark in China, it can only be for one individual or one cooperative to apply for the registration. After approval, the individual, business concern, or cooperative will obtain the exclusive right to use the trade marks."

As the next step, a Danish royal ordinance was then issued on 15 October 1957. It stated:

> ... Whereas information has been laid before Us that persons, firms and companies belonging to this Kingdom, are granted the right, subject to reciprocity, to register trade marks in the People's Republic of China, We hereby, under the provisions of sec. 14(2) of the Trade Mark Act No. 101 of April 7th, 1936, order and ordain as follows:

> that any person, firm or company belonging to the People's Republic of China and who is carrying on industry or handicraft, agriculture, mining, commercial activity or other trade in the said Republic, shall be entitled to acquire by registration the exclusive right to use trade marks in this Kingdom, provided that it is proved that a corresponding trade mark is registered for the party concerned in the People's Republic of China for the commodity in respect of which the trade mark is notified for registration in this Kingdom.

This ordinance was forwarded to the Chinese Ministry of Foreign Affairs with a note of 25 March 1958. The ministry replied in a note of 12 April 1958 which confirmed that "as Chinese citizens, enterprises and cooperatives are entitled to acquire by registration in accordance with Danish law the exclusive right to use trade marks in Denmark, Danish citizens, companies and co-operatives, according to Chinese law, are granted the same right in the PRC."[28]

IV. THE TRANSACTIONS

Owing to the lacunae in the Chinese legal system and the almost total absence of reference to other legal systems, the contract itself is a principal source of knowledge of the private law aspects of the PRC's foreign trade.[29] From it data can be gleaned concerning the topology of transactions, the

---

[28] "Provisional Trade Mark Act" and "Detailed Regulations for the Execution of the Trade Mark Act," n.d. According to *Kina. Vejledning for Eksportører*, p. 25, the Chinese rules in force on the registration of trade marks are found in regulations of 25 April 1963; cf Tao-tai Hsia, *Guide to Selected Legal Sources of Mainland China* (Washington D.C.: Library of Congress, 1967), no. 1642. Application forms and further information may be obtained at the Trade Mark Registration Agency of the CCPIT. The registration fee is at present about D.Kr. 430, and renewal is not requested. According to C. M. Schmitthoff, *The Export Trade* (London: Stevens and Sons, Ltd., 1969), pp. 338–9, the trade mark acts of Denmark and the PRC both belong to the system of ownership based on priority of registration. Information that both countries have registered trade marks with each other has not been verifiable.

[29] According to the Chinese Ministry of Foreign Trade no statutes or regulations concerning foreign trade have been issued since 1963.

development of the foreign trade contract, and no less interesting, the differences among the practices of different foreign trade corporations and between head offices and local branches. Other documents that throw light on Chinese practices and attitudes are draft agreements submitted by the parties prior to negotiations concerning the sale of nonstaple commodities (e.g., complete plants, ships, and machinery manufactured according to the specifications of the buyer), and postcontractual correspondence concerning alterations and breaches of contract.

Unfortunately, it is extremely difficult to gather adequate materials in this area. Far from all traders are prepared to open their files to the student of Chinese law, and even when they are willing to cooperate, competitive and other considerations set limits to how much can be revealed. In interviews with Danish traders I collected some twenty-odd contracts and documents including various types of sales confirmations, individual (nonstandard) and standard sales and purchase contracts, charterparties, ocean bills of lading, and standard and nonstandard agency and exclusive sales agreements. This material is too limited to support anything but some preliminary observations. First, it does not—at least as far as the sales and purchase contracts are concerned—differ from the material that has formed the basis of other publications on the subject.[30] Second, the need to protect the identity of the sources sometimes reduces the usefulness of the material.

A. Sales and Purchase Contracts

The sales and purchase contracts may be divided into the following groups: Chinese export and Danish export. There are two kinds of Chinese export contracts: the sales confirmation (SCF) and the sales contract (SCT). The Danish export contracts are of three kinds: the purchase order, the standard purchase contract (SPC), and the individual purchase contract.

There are two varieties of SCF, "simple" and "extended," depending on whether or not it contains a set of general provisions. The simple SCF seems to prevail in minor transactions between parties who have firmly established business relations. It consists typically of one sheet with highly concise information concerning commodity, quality, quantity, unit price, total value, packing, shipping terms, and payment terms. The extended SCF further specifies terms of payment (including the consequences of delay in payment) and insurance, and fixes procedures to handle quantity/quality discrepancy, delay in delivery, or failure to deliver.

[30] See, G. Crespi Reghizzi, "Legal Aspects of Foreign Trade with China: The Italian Experience," *Harvard International Law Journal* 9 (1968): 85; Gene T. Hsiao, "Communist China's Foreign Trade Contracts and Means of Settling Disputes," *Vanderbilt Law Review* 22 (1969): 503; Li, "Legal Aspects of Trade"; Alan H. Smith, "Standard Form Contracts in the International Commercial Transactions of the People's Republic of China," *International and Comparative Law Quarterly* 11 (1972): 133.

The SCT usually is used in connection with first or "once-only" transactions or in connection with more substantial transactions even between parties who know each other well, e.g., principal and agent. (The practice seems to differ from one foreign trade corporation to another and within the same corporation from one branch or local office to another. There appears to be some effort at rationalization, since at the fall 1971 Canton Fair a number of corporations used common forms very similar to the simple SCF.) The major difference between the extended SCF and the SCT is that the latter contains an inspection clause, a more elaborate *force majeure* clause, and sometimes an arbitration clause. The claims clause of the SCT is identical with or similar to the quality/quantity clause of the SCF. On the whole the SCT is still a much briefer document than the SPC and, as such, is silent on a number of problems that may arise during the transactions, e.g., the passing of the risk, the distribution of costs between buyer and seller.

The SCFs and the SCT are issued in acceptance of cable or letter orders and in confirmation of transactions concluded in China. In case of cable or letter orders it is customary within some trades that the buyer signs one copy of the document and returns it to the seller. The procedure is a little more complicated under agency agreements. After receiving an order from the agent the principal returns three copies of an SCF (or SCT), one of which is signed by the agent (or, according to the practice of the corporation or branch in question, by the buyer) and is returned to the principal.

One variant of the extended SCF contains the following provision:

> The Buyer is requested to sign and return one copy of this Sales Confirmation immediately after receipt of the same. Objection, if any, should be raised by the Buyer within five days after the receipt of this Sales Confirmation, in the absence of which it is understood that the Buyer has accepted the terms and conditions of the Sales Confirmation.

This clause occurs—in the contracts I have seen—only in transactions regulated by agency agreement. Thus, it is in keeping with Danish law, which provides that the buyer who has regular business with the seller is bound if he does not complain immediately in the event of nonconforming acceptance, unless he can prove that his offer was different. It happens now and then, especially under exclusive sales arrangements, that the Chinese seller takes the initiative in a transaction by forwarding a favorable offer in the form of an SCT that the Danish agent can sign and return if he is interested. In such cases the corporations do not seem to apply the above provision.[31]

The purchase order is widely used in minor transactions (D.Kr. 10,000 and less) involving parties having well-established business relations.[32] This document is very similar to the extended SCF and is a far cry from the

---

[31] Smith, "Standard Form Contracts," pp. 137–38.

[32] Cf. *Kina. Vejledning for Eksportører*, p. 20.

elaborate SPC which dominates the Chinese import trade. (See Appendix 7 for a copy of a SPC.[33]) In contrast to the individual contracts, which usually are products of long and hard negotiations, the purchase order and the SPC may be issued on acceptance of letter and cable orders.

The initial reaction of many Danish traders when discussing Chinese contracts is that these contracts contain the usual international trade terms and that nobody examines them very carefully—until it is too late, as one trader thoughtfully added. There are, however, a number of differences among the terms of standard Chinese contracts and other contracts used in international trade.

Danish export to the PRC is practically always on FOB terms, while import from the PRC is on CIF terms.[34] The SCF and the SCT usually incorporate the term CIF in the printed text, without further specification of the duties of the seller and the buyer. However, the term FOB is rarely—if ever—found in the printed text of the SPC; rather it is added under price and/or port of shipment terms. On the other hand, the SPC specifies in detail the responsibility of the parties (see Appendix 7, sections 11–13), although it is silent on some important problems concerning the distribution of expenses between the buyer and the seller.[35] The individual contracts clearly demonstrate that this is not irrelevant to the Danish exporter, since some of these contracts come close to, and a few go beyond, the Incoterms in specifying who is going to pay for what.

Section 19 of the SPC gives the seller a kind of *délai de grâce* of ten weeks in the event of late delivery and, unlike the SCF and the SCT, stipulates liquidated damages for delays. The maximum—and heavy—penalty is 5 percent of the total price, corresponding to 0.5 percent per week for ten weeks, after which time the buyer may cancel the contract. The individual contracts tend to fix a penalty-free period of one or two months, to lower the weekly penalty, and to restrict buyer's ability to cancel the contract.

According to the SPC sections 18 and 19 the seller is liable for delay in delivery except in the event of *force majeure*. The SPC does not define the ambit of *force majeure*, but it may be inferred from the individual contracts

---

[33] The author is indebted to the Danish Ministry of Foreign Affairs for permission to print the standard purchase contract published in *Kina. Vejledning for Eksportører*.

[34] There are some recent instances of Chinese c. & f. imports from Denmark; See *Kina. Vejledning for Eksportører*, p. 33. It is significant that the c. & f. terms secure the insurance premiums for the People's Insurance Company. Incidentally, the insurance claims are a constant source of trouble which some Danish importers try to eliminate by taking out subsidiary insurance; exporters can protect themselves to a certain extent against production and credit risk through the Danish Trade Fund *(Eksportkreditrådet)* which undertakes to provide guarantees for commercial and political risks that are not covered by commercial insurance.

[35] See Incoterms 1953 A: 3, 8, and 9.

and from discussions during negotiations that strikes (and lockouts) are not included. It is therefore interesting to note that strike by officers or crew is inserted in the suspension-of-hire clause of charterparties by demand of the Chinese charterers, and that according to one Chinese standard bill of lading "[n]either the carrier [n]or the ship shall be responsible for loss or damage arising or resulting from: (a) *Force Majeure* . . . [and] (e) Strikes, lockouts, stoppage or restraint of labour from whatever cause whether partial or general."

The inspection clause of the SPC does not occur in any of the individual contracts I have seen. It is replaced by various agreements whereby the buyers are allowed at their own costs to send one or more supervisors to Denmark to follow the production and testing of the goods, and even to certify that the goods are packed according to the packing regulations of the foreign trade corporation in question. One contract further agreed that in the event of disagreement between the supervisor and the seller, the parties shall accept as final the ruling of a certain expert third party who shall supervise the testing and issue a final test certificate. Other contracts give the Danish seller a possibility to re-inspect the goods after delivery by linking the inspection clause with the guarantee clause.

Underneath the almost proverbial phrase about the punctuality of the Chinese foreign trade corporations lurks a basic feeling of uncertainty concerning the consequences of a possible breach of contract. This is most clearly revealed in the notorious anxiety of Danish (and other Western) traders to have the place of arbitration removed from Peking to one of the arbitration institutions in Western Europe, preferably Berne, Hamburg, London, Stockholm, or Zürich. There are no examples of arbitration through the International Chamber of Commerce. Chinese resistance to arbitration outside the PRC has led to various forms of compromise such as "arbitration in Peking or London on the option of the defendant," "arbitrators (one appointed by the seller and one by the buyer) to agree upon a place of arbitration," and "the umpire (appointed by the arbitrators) appoints a place of arbitration in case the arbitrators fail to agree." Clearcut clauses like "arbitration at institution X in Zürich" occur infrequently. Equally unusual is the "bullet-proof" clause which stipulates the maximum duration of the phase of friendly negotiations, a deadline for the appointment of the arbitrators, directions for the appointment of an arbitrator for the party who fails to do so himself, directions for the appointment of an umpire in the event the arbitrators cannot agree, place of arbitration, and a set of rules concerning arbitration procedure, distribution of expenses, and execution of the award. There is only one example of an arbitration clause containing all these provisions in the contracts I have examined.

One of the shrewdest devices for minimizing the risks of the overseas trade is the confirmed letter of credit according to which the seller need not release the goods until he has assurance of payment and by which, conversely, the buyer assumes control over the goods as soon as he pays. In order to protect the buyer against the risk of defective goods, the contract often stipulates that the seller cannot collect payment unless he presents an appropriate inspection certificate, issued by a third party.

The standard contracts give the Chinese the best of both worlds: the final word concerning the condition of the commodity is always with the Chinese Commodity Inspection Bureau; and the letters of credit issued by the Bank of China are never confirmed, whereas those opened by Danish importers must always be confirmed, irrevocable, assignable, and divisible. This is customary practice even when not explicitly stipulated by the simple SCFs.

The Chinese refusal to confirm letters of credit may be explained *in terms of prestige*: an irrevocable letter of credit issued by the Bank of China is as good as an irrevocable, confirmed letter of credit issued by a Western bank. It may also be explained *in terms of cost*: for the time being Danish banks charge 1/8 percent to confirm. In addition, *a matter of international civil procedure* may be involved, since irrevocable and unconfirmed credits "have the grave disadvantage that they do not localize the performance of the contract of sale in the seller's country; if the correspondent bank refuses to pay tender of the documents, the seller might be compelled to institute proceedings overseas—a situation which largely defeats the main purpose of the commercial credit."[36]

With the exception of transactions under agency and exclusive sales agreements, which apparently have been dominated by the letter of credit for more than ten years, the use of documentary credits is a fairly recent mode of payment where Danish imports from the PRC are concerned. It was introduced shortly before the sterling devaluation in 1968—very much to the annoyance of the importers as it makes heavier demands on capital than the terms of cash against documents and sight payment which were common before 1968.

B. *Breach of Contract*

The widespread use of the Chinese standard contracts is a tangible proof of the confidence the Chinese foreign trade corporations enjoy among Danish and other Western traders, and of these corporations' ability to preserve their outstanding reputation. Nevertheless, there have been cases of Chinese breach of contract. This is not surprising considering the number of transactions concluded during the past twenty-two years. The cases can be divided into three groups: late delivery, nondelivery, and defective goods.

Late delivery was a common phenomenon during the Cultural Revolution and was a most difficult problem to handle. Some Danish importers tried to

---

[36] Schmitthoff, *The Export Trade*, p. 213.

stipulate exact dates of shipment and even specific (preferably Danish) ships in their contracts, but very often without success. Complaints remained unanswered, and so the Danish traders saw no other recourse except advancing their complaints through the Chinese Embassy in order to speed deliveries. It is, however, difficult to tell whether the remarkable change for the better that began in 1969–70 was due to the efficiency of the embassy or to the return to normal conditions after the Cultural Revolution.

In the material I have seen there is one case of nondelivery. At a Canton Fair a few years ago a Danish importer was offered certain goods at a rather favorable price on condition that he make up his mind at once. He did so and a SCF was signed. Upon returning to Denmark he immediately resold these goods. A couple of weeks later the seller informed the Danish importer that the contract had to be canceled since the price had been quoted incorrectly. Some of the importer's customers claimed compensation and were paid. The importer tried without success to recover from the seller compensation for this loss and for costs, but not for loss of profits. After a long correspondence the seller stopped answering letters, whereupon the importer then tried to pursue the matter through diplomatic channels, with the result that the seller has sent some evasive letters.

The Chinese seem to be more amenable in cases where they have delivered defective goods. Their reaction is said to be prompt whether the Danish importers have asked for compensation—which is usually given in the form of a deduction of the amount on the next invoice—or for new spare parts. No cases, however, are reported in which the compensation has been paid in cash or the goods have been totally replaced.

For additional information see the discussion on the role of the Chinese Commercial Attaché in dispute resolution in section II.

C. *Agency and Exclusive Sales Agreements*

Commercial parlance does not always distinguish clearly between the agent and the agency agreement, on the one hand, and the sole agent *(Alleinvertreter)* and the exclusive sales agreement, on the other. This is illustrated by the frequency of agreements which are entitled agency agreements but which really are some form of exclusive sales agreements.[37] Both variants and at least

---

[37] According to continental European law the agent is an independent trader who is employed to conclude contracts in the name and on the account of the principal *or*—as is the case in the Chinese agency contracts—to effect the conclusion of contracts for the principal. The sole agent is an independent trader whom the manufacturer or supplier has designated the exclusive seller of his products within a certain geographic area. The sole agent is not a middleman; he buys from the manufacturer and resells on his own account. In contrast to the agent, he is not remunerated by way of commission. Cf. Ole Lando, *Udenrigshandels Kontrakter. Udenrigshandelsret I* (Copenhagen: Munksgaard, 1969), pp. 117, 143.

one hybrid form occur in Sino-Danish trade; the last goes back to the beginning of the 1960s, whereas the pure forms are more recent. The Chinese foreign trade corporations have not been generous with such agreements. One way to avoid committing themselves has been to give Danish traders verbal or *de facto* agreements, notably agency agreements, which only recently have been put into writing. Another way is to limit the validity of written agreements to one or two years, and to insist that renewal must be negotiated in China. Until recently it has been impossible for the agents to receive commission on transactions concluded directly between the principal and other Danish importers. The standard agency agreement which appeared in 1971 still differentiates between directly and indirectly concluded transactions. Still another problem is that most, if not all, agency and exclusive sales agreements have been concluded with the local branches and not with the head offices of the corporations. This fact—theoretically—has made it possible for the corporations to have more than one agent for the same commodity in Denmark. Whether this has actually happened is difficult to ascertain. Two interviewees claimed to be agents for the same commodity, but only one of them was willing and able to substantiate his assertion. However, it appears that the corporations will begin in 1972 to enter into such agreements only through the head office.

The terms of these agreements gradually became more severe during the 1960s. The corporations have insisted on stipulating an increasingly high annual minimum volume of trade. Further, the standard agency agreement has a clause providing that the principal shall not be bound by the agreement "should Party B [the agent] fail to pass on their orders to Party A [the principal] for a period of six months for a minimum 60 percent of [the stipulated minimum volume]." Another issue has been the place of arbitration which in the earlier agreements was the country of the defendant but in the standard agreement has been removed to Peking.

These agreements lack many of the usual protections.[38] They are also strongly biased in favor of the Chinese party. According to the standard agency agreement the commission is only due after receipt of payment; the agent shall—presumably at his own expense—forward "samples of similar commodities offered by other suppliers, together with their prices, sales position, and advertising materials," bear all expenses for "advertising and publicity," and also "submit drafts and/or drawings intended for such purposes for prior approval."

D. The Contracts of Carriage by Sea

The standard contract by which Danish ships are chartered by the China National Chartering and Freight Broking Corporation (as agents for the China

---

[38] Schmitthoff, *The Export Trade,* pp. 135–42.

National Foreign Trade Transportation Corporation) is the Uniform Time-charter, better known under the code-name Baltime 1939, which was drawn up by the Baltic and International Conference, Copenhagen, and adopted by the Documentary Committee of the Chamber of Shipping of the United Kingdom. Voyage and demise charter parties are not known to occur.

In contrast to another well-known charter party form, the American Produce, the Baltime is slightly more favorable to the owner than to the charterer. This balance is completely overthrown by the Chinese "amended" version of the Baltime by means of dozens of deletions and additional clauses, sometimes to the disadvantage of both parties, e.g., the deletion of the reference to the York-Antwerp Rules as the basis for the adjustment of general average. The chartering conditions have gradually been tightened during the 1960s. The Chinese have had difficulties with some Western, notably Greek, shipowners, and the various concrete issues have given rise to a series of additional and rather casuistic clauses which have changed the nature of the Baltime from a clear charter party to an overloaded and confused hire and labor contract. The burdens of the shipowners have been drastically increased. The place of arbitraton in reality has been removed from Hamburg or London to Peking notwithstanding the usual formulation of the arbitration clauses: "arbitration in Peking or London on the option of the defendant." General average must always be adjusted in Peking. It is worth noting that neither the Foreign Trade Arbitration Committee nor the Maritime Arbitration Commission of the CCPIT is mentioned in the arbitration and general average clauses.

Danish shipowners are divided into two groups. Some readily admit that difficulties cannot be avoided in as complicated a trade as shipping, but claim that it is always possible to reach a reasonable solution to problems on a "give and take" basis and that experience has shown that the risk is nil. Others are not prepared to accept the Chinese "amendments." They claim that the charter parties as formulated invariably mark the beginning of an endless series of disputes concerning upkeep and damage to the vessel, suspension of hire, responsibility of the owners, etc. American bunkering controls have added significantly to the over-all problem.

The bill of lading is one of the few cases in which the Chinese to a certain extent—namely, when goods are carried by Chinese owners operating from Hong Kong, i.e., on ships not owned or chartered by the PRC—have had to accept Western standard contracts without any alterations whatsoever, including the reference to international conventions to which the PRC is not a party (the Hague Rules and the York-Antwerp Rules). In all other cases a Chinese standard bill of lading (SBL) is used which differs from the typical international bill of lading in a number of respects. The general average clause of the SBL is identical with that of the charter parties. The SBL contains no paramount, or proper law, clause; this means that it is not governed by the

Hague Rules or by any municipal enactment thereof. The SBL simply stipulates that all disputes shall be determined and general average adjusted in the PRC. It does not prescribe "amicable settlement," nor does it specify whether disputes shall be settled by arbitration or litigation. The words "unless suit is brought" in the notice of claim clause might indicate that disputes are not subject to arbitration, except that the rule in question is a verbatim quotation of the Hague Rules, Article 3, rule 6.3. Clauses based on important precedents and international custom like the both-to-blame-collision, the salvage, the scope of voyage, the optional cargo, and—less remarkably considering the nature of Sino-American relations—the amended Jason clauses are also left out. To what extent these provisions, as suggested by Anthony Dicks,[39] are replaced by Chinese legislation remains to be analyzed in detail.

The absence of the paramount clause is offset to a limited extent by the incorporation into the SBL of some of the Hague Rules. It is symptomatic of the Chinese suspiciousness of foreign standard contracts that the Hague Rules are only partially incorporated into the SBL and very often with a different wording; this is apt to create uncertainty and confusion.[40] We should note that the charter parties often in an additional clause incorporate Articles 3 and 4 in blank ("owners to be responsible as carrier for shortage, loss and/or damage to goods as per bills of lading in accordance with Articles 3 and 4 of the Hague Rules") and that the SBL does not refer to the conditions of the charter parties, possibly because this would invariably cause trouble for the issuing of documentary credits.[41]

---

[39] See the chapter in this volume by Anthony Dicks.

[40] The SBL omits Articles 1 (with the exception of subsection (e)), 2, 5-9, and a number of important rules of Articles 3 and 4, e.g., 3, 2 (the duty of the carrier to properly load, handle, stow, carry, keep, care for, and discharge the goods), 3, 5 (the shipper is deemed to guarantee to the carrier the accuracy of marks, number, quantity, and weight), 3, 6, subsection 2 (notice in writing concerning loss or damage need not to be given if the state of the goods has at the time of their receipt been subject to joint survey or inspection) and subsection 4 (the carrier and the receiver shall give each other all reasonable facilities for inspecting and tallying the goods), 3, 8 (the invalidity of any clause relieving the carrier or the ship from liability for loss or damage to the goods arising from negligence in the duties provided in Article 3), 4, 1 (neither carrier nor ship is liable for loss or damage resulting from unseaworthiness not caused by want of due diligence on the part of the carrier) and 4, 3 (the shipper is not responsible for loss or damage sustained by the carrier or the ship which is not due to the neglect or fault of the shipper). In the catalogue of expected perils of Article 4, 2 one notices with interest that the SBL does not contain rules (f) and (k) concerning loss or damage resulting from "act of public enemies" and "riots and civil commotions" respectively, and that the wording has been adapted to revolutionary usage.

[41] Cf. the Uniform Customs and Practice for Documentary Credits, 1962 (UCPDC), Article 17, section 1, subsection (b). Notwithstanding the fact that the PRC has not acceded to or informally recognized (as, e.g., North Vietnam) the UCPDC, there is

V. CONCLUSION

The over-all impression of the commercial intercourse between Denmark and the PRC is very favorable indeed. The general mood of the trouble-is-my-business-minded lawyer examining trade relations may best be characterized as one of increasing disappointment. Apart from minor incompatibilities, the trade presents an idyllic picture of no disputes, no litigation, and no arbitration. And yet, if he is patient he may eventually find isolated cases of nonperformance or inadequate performance on both sides.

In cases of Danish breaches of contract the Chinese party has confined himself to severing the relationship if the defaulter has not complied, while in the reverse situation the Danish party has overlooked the incident, complained (with or without result), or severed the relationship. There may have been a number of instances where the Danish party would have reacted differently if the other party had been a Western firm, or where a Western trading partner would have acted otherwise to begin with, conscious that the Danish party had different means at his disposal, ranging from litigation in the defaulter's own country to international commercial arbitration and various other mercantile measures. In other words, there were some situations in which disagreements could have become disputes with readily evident commercial or legal consequences had the other party not been Chinese.

The average international trader is not known to be litigious, and the Danish trader is no exception. But like most reasonable people he has a fondness for predictability. It helps him to draw up a contract and thereby to estimate the amount of protection available as well as the risks and costs of nonperformance. The more he knows about the proper law of the contract, the less time he will lose in negotiating the terms of the deal. In the trade with countries of planned economy, and especially with the PRC where records of and legal bases for formally settled disputes are virtually inaccessible, the Danish trader must accept a considerable element of uncertainty. This is offset by a general confidence in Chinese trading practices and, to a certain extent, by careful and very often time-consuming formulation of the contracts.

There are instances where Sino-Danish contract negotiations have lasted as long as three months, with daily sessions of one or two hours' duration, with one group of negotiators dealing with the technological and another with the commercial side of the contract. Asked about the competence of the Chinese representatives and whether he found it worth while to spend so much time on a single contract, one interviewee said that he respected them for their skill and remarkable ability to split hairs over every period of the text. He also found that the time spent at the beginning was inversely proportional to the

---

no reason to believe that the Danish banks are eager to deviate from the UCPDC if they can help it, and one Danish bank has explained that the Chinese nonrecognition of the UCPDC is of no practical importance whatsoever.

annoyance saved at the end. It is widely held among Danish traders—at least among those handling substantial transactions—that since it is difficult to identify the proper law of the contract, the contract has to be "the proper law of the parties." The rest is confidence.

The author, when questioning people, was told repeatedly that the Chinese are exceedingly clever businessmen, tough in negotiation and extremely reliable in performance. One reply that summarizes the general feeling among Danish traders is that if Danish firms have trouble in their dealings with China, nine times out of ten it is their own fault.

The ideal of the contract as "the proper law of the parties" is, of course, far from being realized. First, it is a fact that the Chinese standard contracts are not acceptable to the Danish traders when large amounts are at stake.[42] Second, only a few traders have the expertise to avoid the countless pitfalls of the ordinary sales contract or the patience to conduct protracted discussions. In the contracts I have examined, only *one* is worthy of serving as a model. One of the negotiators of this contract pointed out that the art of the Chinese foreign trade contract consists in understanding the political issues behind the words. If this is clearly perceived by the foreigner and if he is prepared to replace his notion of the contract as the ultimate basis for the transaction by the concept of the contract as a point of departure for adjustment according to the demands of the situation, he is likely to leave the conference table without losing much of the protection he wants from the contract and yet still having arranged the transaction to his own satisfaction.

Finally, Danish trade with the PRC is to a certain extent conducted in a legal void: disputes proper are carefully avoided by both parties; and should they nevertheless arise, it would be extremely difficult to discover the pertinent law of the contract. As there are no institutions between the Chinese corporation and the individual Danish trader, the last resort for Danish traders in the event of real trouble is protest through diplomatic channels—channels kept open presumably because of Chinese interest in preserving the present harmonious relations between the two countries.

There is no reason to believe, however, that the Danish traders are anxious to institutionalize their relations with the PRC, although this attitude may change overnight if the Chinese fail to maintain their reputation for reliable performance. Owing to notorious difficulties with trade offices of the East European countries (whose reputation among Danish traders is far behind that

---

[42] It should be borne in mind that the trade between the industrialized and the developing countries, especially in Africa, to a large extent is carried on by means of standard contracts drawn by the Western importers and exporters or their organizations stipulating arbitration in Western countries by Western arbitrators and in accordance with Western legal systems. Some of the reasons why Western traders accept the Chinese standard contracts are the prospects of the Chinese market and the margin of profit on Chinese commodities.

of the Chinese corporations), it was suggested a couple of years ago that an extra clause be added into contracts with the state-trading countries. This clause provided that dishonored contracts shall be subject to negotiation between the respective chambers of commerce, that the result of such negotiations shall be binding on the parties, and that the matter shall not be deferred to arbitration unless the chambers of commerce fail to reach a reasonable solution. Nothing has, as yet, come of this initiative, but it shows that under normal economic circumstances traders cannot be pushed beyond a certain point.

It is doubtful whether a private Danish attempt to organize trade would be successful. The Chinese corporations have consistently tried, with general success, to penetrate the organizational structure of trade of various European countries. A couple of years ago a non-Danish delegate to a meeting of the Special Committee on East-West Trade of the so-called Stockholm Club complained that the Chinese always attempt to evade the export houses by addressing the manufacturers or friendly firms directly. And it remains to be seen whether the Chinese government in case of a renewal of the TPA will be willing to accept the establishment of a joint committee *ad modum* the Danish trade agreements with the Eastern European countries, a device the Danish government is likely to insist upon with the backing of the trade organizations.

Trade with Italy

GABRIELE CRESPI REGHIZZI

I. INTRODUCTION

The purpose of this paper is to carry forward the work initiated in an article written several years ago which discussed the legal aspects of trade between Italy and China.[1] Since that time two important events have greatly changed the institutional framework for economic relations between the two countries: diplomatic relations were established on 6 November 1970, and a trade and payments agreement was signed in Rome on 29 October 1971.

In spite of the enthusiasm of the press and the joy of many businessmen new to the China trade, expert opinion among politicians, academics, and veterans of Sino-Italian exchanges is that one should not expect immediate results of great importance.[2] These changes do, however, create a legal framework and

---

NOTE: This essay covers basically the period to the end of 1972 and the first half of 1973.

[1] Gabriele Crespi Reghizzi, "Legal Aspects of Trade with China: the Italian Experience," *Harvard International Law Journal* (1968): 85–139.

[2] For example, Mr. Dino Gentili, Chairman of COGIS, a large Italian trading company, says that one must not expect a fantastic boom in Sino-Italian interchange because Peking's foreign trade is closely tied to the general development of Chinese production and also to the principle of maintaining a balanced trade. Similarly, Mr. Vittorino Colombo, chairman of the Italian-Chinese Institute for Economic and Cultural Exchanges and of the Italian Chamber of Commerce with China, believes that the political optimism that often has existed has not always been translated into the economic sphere. See also: "Il Sogno di Aprire un Negozio a Shanghai," *L'Espresso-Economia/Finanza*, 15 November 1970, p. 46; "Non Vogliono Fare Debiti," *Il Mondo*, 15 August 1971, p. 15; the reports presented during the seminars "Esperienze della prima missione commerciale alla Fiera Autunnale di Canton" (Milan, 8 February 1972), and "Sviluppo degli Scambi con la Cina" (Milan, 12 December 1972), and particularly the introduction by Mr. Vittorino Colombo; Galeazzo Santini, "Una

a set of general principles for future relations. In particular, when the attempt to modify the present trade imbalance is undertaken, the legal instruments for this effort will be ready, at least partially. These are the most interesting consequences of the diplomatic recognition and the signing of the trade agreement. In addition, these events potentially enable Italian businessmen to deal more directly, and therefore presumably more efficaciously, in the Chinese market. I stress "potentially" because Sino-Italian trade statistics from 1963 to the present do not justify excessive optimism. The data presented in table 1 and in appendixes 1, 8, 14, and 15 clearly demonstrate this point. Suffice it to say in this short introduction that Italian trade with China in 1971, for example, consisted of little more than 0.4 percent of total Italian trade. In addition, some sources have suggested that except for the building of monetary reserves in an amount ranging from U.S. $150–400 million, it appears that from 1965 until 1972 China has not made major efforts to increase her export trade.[3] Finally, the statistics cited in table 1 show that trade increased from 24 billion

TABLE 1

ITALIAN-CHINESE TRADE (1963–71)
(in billion liras)

Year	Total trade 1963 = 100	%	Imports from China	%	Exports to China	%	Italian Balance
1963	24.0	100	11.9	100	12.0	100	+ 0.1
1964	26.4	110	14.8	125	11.5	96	− 3.3
1965	59.4	247	24.1	203	35.3	294	+11.1
1966	74.4	310	35.2	292	39.1	325	+ 3.8
1967	82.0	342	36.1	301	45.9	382	+ 9.8
1968	68.1	284	29.9	250	38.1	317	+ 8.2
1969	75.3	314	40.1	334	35.2	293	− 4.9
1970	75.0	312	39.4	329	35.6	294	− 3.8
1971	76.3	318	39.7	333	36.6	298	− 2.9

SOURCE: Istituto Nazionale di Statistica.

Grande Muraglia filosofica," *Successo,* special issue (November 1971), 94–182; F. Carbonetti, "Le Relazioni Economiche e Commerciali della Cina," in *Italia-Cina* (1972) 2, pp. 14–17.

[3] An excellent and important reference series of news and statistics data on the foreign trade of China is *Il Portolano del Mondo Economico-cifre e notizie sistematicamente ordinate Paese per Paese—Paesi Socialisti,* compiled by the Study Bureau of the Banca Commerciale Italiana, Milan, 1972; see also Feng-hwa Mah, *The Foreign Trade of Mainland China* (Chicago and New York: Aldine, 1971); Alexander Eckstein, ed., *China Trade Prospects and United States Policy* (New York: Praeger, 1971); Samuel Pisar, *Coexistence and Commerce—Guidelines for Transactions between East and West* (London: McGraw-Hill, 1971).

liras in 1963 to 76.3 billion liras in 1971. But the situation looks less favorable if we consider that the trade peak of 82 billion liras was reached in 1967; the ensuing slump is due mainly to the decline in Italian exports from 45.9 to 36.6 billion liras while imports remained relatively constant.[4]

Two dates are particularly important in the recent history of Sino-Italian trade: 1965 and 1971. In 1965 the China Committee for the Promotion of International Trade (CCPIT) and the Italian Institute of Foreign Trade (ICE) signed an agreement for the exchange of permanent commercial delegations. In the absence of formal diplomatic relations this agreement could only be semiofficial and nongovernmental. Neither ICE nor CCPIT are formally organs of their respective governments but they do carry sufficient official backing to ensure governmental support without, at the same time, floundering on the shoals of technical legalities.[5]

---

[4] See also, Crespi Reghizzi, "Esportiamo Meno in Cina," *Il Mondo,* 17 March 1972, p. 25; ICE," Cina—Repubblica Popolare: Struttura Economica—Commercio Estero —Scambi con L'Italia," *Informazioni per il Commercio estero,* no. 40 (1970), pp. 545–51. The decrease seems to have been a direct consequence of the Italian market's incapacity to absorb some Chinese goods. It also seems that during 1970/71, several Italian firms failed to carry out some contractual obligations. The Chinese minister of foreign trade reportedly complained about this disruption of China's economic plans to an Italian politician. Year 1972, however, indicates a favorable reversal of this trend, with a marked increase both in total trade and in Italy's export to China. This is possibly a consequence of the coming into operation of the new legal framework of Sino-Italian trade.

It may be of interest to note that from 1963 to the present Italy has supplied China with at least eleven industrial plants: a petroleum refinery, a fertilizer plant, a synthetic ammonia plant, a plant for the construction of oil pipelines, a thermoelectric power station, etc. Six of these were supplied by Montedison, a leading Italian chemical corporation that alone makes up almost one-third of total Italian exports to China. It also signed with the Chinese an agreement of technical-scientific cooperation. See the special issues of *Il Sole—24 Ore,* 24 September, 30 September and 3 October 1972, entirely devoted to Sino-Italian trade.

During the past four years Italy also exported to China machine tools (Italy was the first supplier of such goods to China), iron and steel laminates, synthetic fibers, chemical fertilizers, plastics, synthetic resins, and motor vehicles. (Motor vehicle exports dropped to zero in 1969, probably in retaliation for a regulation—now abolished—of the Italian Health Authority prohibiting importation of Chinese pork.) Italian imports for the same period have been, in their order of importance: silk and silk waste yarns, raw hides not used for furs, fresh and frozen meat, oil bearing fruits and seeds, various chemical products, clothing, and furs.

[5] Crespi Reghizzi, "Legal Aspects," pp. 92–93. After the establishment of the Chinese Embassy in Rome, the permanent commercial delegation of the CCPIT became an office or section of the Chinese diplomatic mission in Italy, possibly enjoying full diplomatic immunity. Cf. the discussion of the legal status of trade delegations in the chapter by Jerome Cohen.

As has been noted in some other cases, the exchange of resident trade missions represented "a way station on the road to diplomatic relations."[6] In fact, recognition was announced in a joint communique issued simultaneously in Rome and Peking on 6 November 1970.[7] This communique was followed by the following declaration of the Italian government:

During negotiations, which took place in Paris, to establish diplomatic relations between the Italian Republic and the People's Republic of China, it has been stressed to the Chinese negotiators the Italian interest in the development of trade and cultural relations between the two countries and *desire to reach an agreement concerning consular matters and to solve the problems concerning rights and reciprocal interests pending between the two countries.*

The establishment of diplomatic relations will contribute to all this in a significant way. The Chinese side agreed upon the desirability of what was said above, and also agreed that the *two Governments will continue diplomatic consultations* to reach reasonable solutions of these problems as soon as their respective embassies take up their duties. [Emphasis added.][8]

On 26 May 1971 another joint communique was issued which stated:

The two parties agreed to stipulate, in conformity with the procedures existing in the two countries, a trade and payments agreement between the governments of the Italian Republic and of the People's Republic of China. Some principal aspects are that the agreement will be valid for a period of three years and that the two countries have

---

[6] Cohen, "Chinese Law and Sino-American Trade," in Eckstein, ed., *China Trade,* p. 158. See also Hsiao, "Communist China Foreign Trade Organization," *Vand. L. R.* 20 (1967): 303 "Communist China Trade Treaties and Agreements," *Vand. L. R.* 21 (1968): 623, and the chapter by Donald Klein in this book. See also, in general, James T. Haight, ed., *Current Legal Aspects of Doing Business with Sino-Soviet Nations* (Chicago: American Bar Association, 1973).

[7] For a discussion and interpretation of the diplomatic recognition see Giorgio Melis, "Le Recenti Aperture Diplomatiche Cinesi," *L'Est* 1 (1971): 7–23. Note the wording of this communique on the Taiwan question: "The Chinese Government confirms that Taiwan is an inalienable part of the People's Republic of China. The Italian Government takes note of *(chu-i tao)* the declaration *(sheng-ming)* (and not position *[li-ch'ang]* as in the Sino-Canadian communique) of the Chinese Government. The Italian Government recognizes the People's Republic of China as the only legal government of China."

[8] The complete text of this statement may be found in *Italia-Cina,* no. 1 (1971), p. 5. The Taiwan issue once again was prominently mentioned. "Negotiations were carried out over a long period of time, and it is known that the main difficulty encountered was the problem of the status of Taiwan. The government of the PRC has always insisted that Taiwan is an inalienable part of its territory, while the Italian government has always maintained that it did not consider itself competent to fix the borders of another country. In the joint communique Italy has taken note of the declaration made by the Chinese government concerning the status of Taiwan, and it is clear that the Chinese government attaches importance to this declaration. The Italian government continues to maintain that it is not its task to express any opinion on this matter."

discussed and approved the creation of a mixed commission for the study of the development of commercial relations and cooperation.[9]

The communique also expressed the desire of the two countries to increase "the organization of shows and commercial exhibitions, the exchange of persons, and the beginning of the reciprocal sending of specialized missions and commercial delegations.

Diplomatic recognition also resulted in the signing of a formal trade and payments agreement in Rome on 29 October 1971 (see Appendix 1).[10] The signing of this agreement was not unexpected. The Italian side apparently submitted a draft proposal which was discussed during the visit of an Italian delegation led by Minister of Foreign Trade Mario Zagari, in May 1971, and which also was the subject of further diplomatic contacts and exchanges of notes.

According to the Treaty of Rome which set up the European Economic Community (EEC) and subsequent EEC regulations and decisions, the Italian government had to inform the community authorities of the progress in the negotiations with China, as well as to submit a draft of the final agreement for Community approval.[11] During its session of 26 July 1971 the EEC Council authorized Italy to open negotiations for a commercial agreement with China.[12]

---

[9] See "Con la Cina Popolare possibili scambi piu intensi," in *Corriere della Sera*, 27 May 1971. On the Italian trade mission to Peking see: "Missione economica italiana nella Repubblica Popolare Cinese," in *Italia-Cina*, no. 2 (1971), pp. 11–12; Fracassi, "Scambi economici italo-cinesi nella prospettiva di espansione economica," in *Italia-Cina*, no. 3 (1971), pp. 11–16; Motta, "Impressione di un operatore economico sulla Cina," *ibid.*, nos. 4–5 (1971), pp. 16–19; Arena, "Il mercato cinese: prospettive e vincoli," *ibid.*, pp. 20–22; Rogers, "Appunti sulla Cina," *ibid.*, no. 6 (1971), pp. 30–32; Osio, "Impressioni di un uomo di banca," *ibid.*, pp. 35–37; "La Cina è dunque più vicina?" in *Il Sole—24 Ore*, 13 June 1971 (a round table with six participants to the May mission); "Lo spiraglio della porta cinese," *ibid.*, 28 May 1971 (another interview with Italian traders and officials from the Foreign Trade Ministry).

[10] "Firmato ieri l'accordo tra l'Italia e la Cina," in *Il Sole—24 Ore*, 30 October 1971; "In Italia il Ministro cinese del commercio estero," *ibid.*, 29 October 1971; "Intanto i piccoli cercano di vendere," in *L'Espresso*, 7 November 1971.

[11] See Preamble and Art. 110 ss. of the Treaty of Rome, the decision of the EEC Council n. 69/494 of 16 December 1969, and regulation of the EEC Council n. 109/70 of 19 December 1969 (in *Gazzetta Ufficiale delle Comunità Europee*, 26 January 1970, p. 1), which establishes a "common regime that can be applied to imports from countries engaging in State trade." This regulation contains an appendix listing goods that fall under its jurisdiction. The appendix has been updated from time to time. See also, Regulations 2406 and 2407/71 of 9 November 1971, the commission decision of 30 November 1971 (in *Gazzetta Ufficiale delle Comunità Europee*, 20 December 1971, p. 29), and the commission decision n. 72/455 of 19 December 1972 (in *CEE Informazioni, Notizie e Documenti*, 30 January 1974, p. 2).

[12] *Bollettino delle Comunità Europee*, nos. 9–10 (1971), p. 152. Until now, this authorization has not been formalized by a council decision, although such a procedure has been followed in dealing with some other socialist countries. See, for example, the

The duration of this agreement, similar to that of any agreement concerning commercial relations concluded between EEC members and countries having a state commerce system, cannot extend, in theory, beyond 31 December 1974, the end of the treaty's transitional period. That is, as of 1 January 1975 all such agreements will expire, and the negotiation and conclusion of all subsequent similar treaties will be handled by the Community institutions.[13]

The ECC's authorization to Italy basically meant that according to the judgment of the Brussels institutions, the Sino-Italian agreement would not hinder or delay the coming into force of a uniform commercial policy towards countries with state commerce systems. In other words, this particular agreement was found to be quite similar to other existing agreements between member countries and socialist countries.

Once authorization from Brussels was obtained, the agreement was signed in Rome by Mr. Zagari and Mr. Pai Hsiang-kuo, then heading a large economic delegation visiting Italy.

II.   THE TRADE AND PAYMENTS AGREEMENT[14]

The text of the agreement (hereafter TPA) itself is quite short—nine articles and two lists of goods. As often happens when there is no generalized trade treaty between the parties, the agreement deals both with questions of fundamental principle and with the details of implementation; it also concerns both long-term problems and questions of immediate interest.

---

decision of 29 September 1970 (in *Gazzetta Ufficiale delle Comunità Europee,* 12, October 1970, L/225/22), authorizing the German Federal Republic to conclude a commercial agreement with the People's Republic of Poland. See also: "Sì Europeo agli scambi fra l'Italia e Pechino" in *Corriere della Sera,* 22 July 1971; "Ramoscello d'ulivo del MEC," *ibid.,* 28 July 1971; "Il MEC autorizza l'Italia a commerciare con Pechino," *ibid.,* 27 July 1971. On recent Chinese overtures to EEC see "Vigilia di negoziati tra Pechino e MEC" in *La Stampa,* 23 February 1972.

[13] Article 1 of the 9 October 1961 decision "regarding the information on the duration of commercial agreements with third parties" (*Gazzetta Ufficiale delle Comunità Europee,* 4 November 1961, p. 1274/61). See note 11, *supra.* Already during the transitional period a series of EEC regulations and decisions adopted according to procedures provided in Articles 111 and 113 of the Treaty of Rome have led to some standardization of the commercial policy of the EEC towards countries with state trading systems. Most of these provide for the application of "conventional" custom tariffs on imports, that is, for application of most-favored-nation treatment. Efforts for further standardization are continuing. Derogatory and exceptional regimes by which member countries may be authorized to bilaterally negotiate commercial agreements with socialist countries should have ended 31 December 1972; in fact, however, a further postponement was decided. On 31 December 1974 all bilateral commercial agreements concluded between member countries and state trading countries will expire, and the development of a common policy will be completed.

[14] Cf. the discussion of a similar Sino-Danish agreement in the chapter by Poul Mohr.

The TPA is valid for one year, and can be extended by the agreement of the two sides (subject to the above-mentioned expiration date of 31 December 1974). The TPA states as its general aims the promotion of commercial exchange and the strengthening of economic relations between the two countries "on the basis of equality and mutual benefit."[15]

The TPA also contains a clause that provides for most-favored-nation treatment in matters "of customs rights, additional taxes, and any other supplementary burdens, as well as in matters concerning customs, formalities, regulations, and procedures." This law does not apply, however, to "the advantages, favors, privileges, and immunities allowed or which will be allowed by each of the contracting parties to its neighboring countries (border traffic included)" or "to present or future member countries in customs unions or similar institutions." (Article 4.) It appears that the border traffic exception is principally for the benefit of China (similar clauses are quite usual to Western-Chinese treaties), since that country traditionally has maintained a specialized and privileged regime of trade with its border countries. The customs union exception affects principally the obligations incurred by Italy because of its participation in the Common Market. In any case it appears that these various visible and invisible exceptions to the concept of most-favored-nation, particularly when included in a bilateral context, considerably

---

[15] The concepts of equality and mutual benefit are two of the fundamental principles of peaceful coexistence enunciated by Chou En-lai in the 1955 Bandung Conference. These principles were reaffirmed at the third session of UNCTAD (United Nations Conference on Trade and Development) at Santiago, Chile. See: "La position de principe de la Chine dans les relations économiques et commerciales entre nations," in *Pékin Information*, no. 17 (1972), pp. 12–17; "A la CNUCED: la voix puissante du tiers monde," *ibid.*, no. 22 (1972), pp. 15–18.

The emphasis on the principles of peaceful coexistence also can be seen in the joint communique on diplomatic recognition:

The Italian and Chinese Governments after consultations decided, on the basis of *equality* and *reciprocity of advantages* and in compliance with *international customs*, to render each other all assistance necessary to establish Embassies in their respective capitals and to carry out the duties of these Embassies. [Emphasis added.]

Note that the Chinese are reluctant to refer to international law, but prefer to refer to international customs or practice. See generally on this and similar questions: James Chien Hsiung, *Law and Policy in China's Foreign Relations—a Study of Attitudes and Practice* (New York and London: Columbia University Press, 1972); Hungdah Chiu, *The People's Republic of China and the Law of Treaties* (Cambridge, Mass.: Harvard University Press, 1972); Hungdah Chiu and Shao-chuan Leng, eds., *Law in Chinese Foreign Policy: Communist China and Selected Problems of International Law* (Dobbs Ferry, N.Y.: Oceana Publications, 1972); Jerome A. Cohen, ed., *China's Practice of International Law—Some Case Studies* (Cambridge, Mass.; Harvard University Press, 1972); and Franco Florio, *La Cina all' Organizzazione delle Nazioni Unite* (Milano: Alcione, 1972).

reduce the efficacy of this concept and are evidence of the general decline of this concept in the field of international relations. Even more striking, when dealing with socialist countries and other countries engaged in state operated commerce, this clause becomes completely altered and offers only an illusory advantage to a trader from a market-economy country. The reciprocity concept is only apparent since competitive conditions can be easily altered through the various manipulations of economic plans, price, quota, subsidies, etc.—all done in the name of commercial competition, but actually reflecting governmental policy positions.[16]

In light of the above discussion one is somewhat surprised to learn—although the source of information is not 100 percent reliable—that it was the Italian side that insisted upon the inclusion of the most-favored-nation clause in the trade agreement. In the past, some socialist countries have insisted upon the inclusion of such a clause for purposes of international prestige. In still other cases involving agreements with socialist or state-economy countries, various alternative instruments and techniques were tried to ensure the equitable implementation of trade exchanges. Often this takes the form of specifing the quantity and kinds of goods each side will purchase from the other within a specified period of time. This is one reason why the trade agreement is preferred over the trade treaty in dealing with such countries. While the latter usually states a set of general principles regarding trade, the former can specify in greater detail the price, volume, and commodity composition of trade.

In this context it must be noted that the TPA merely expresses the desire of the two countries to carry out the specified exchanges. It does *not* obligate either side to "guarantee" that this trade in fact will be carried out, since the implementation of particular transactions is left to the initiative of the businessmen or trading corporations of each side. At the same time, in the absence of some positive restriction the kinds and quantities of goods specified in the agreement do not constitute an upper limit which may not be exceeded, but rather target figures which both sides would like to attain. Consequently, it is quite possible, and perhaps even quite usual, that the figures stated in the TPA are underfulfilled or overfulfilled.

Much of the above discussion applies generally to trade agreements signed between Italy and other socialist countries. The Sino-Italian agreement contains several additional peculiarities that deserve mentioning. First, the obligations assumed by each side are stated in more broad and vague terms

---

[16] See, for example, R. David, *Les grands systèmes de droit contemporains (droit comparé)*, 3rd ed. (Paris: Dalloz, 1969), pp. 310–12, and S. Pisar, *Coexistence and Commerce. Guidelines for Transactions between East and West* (London: Allen Lane, The Penguin Presse, 1971), pp. 194–98 and *passim*.

than is usually found in similar agreements with other socialist countries.[17] For example, the "A" and "B" lists (which describe the goods to be imported by Italy and China respectively) do not require that these goods must be imported, but rather act only as reminders *(pro memoria)* for interested traders. Furthermore, for purposes of carrying out specific transactions, the agreement states that "each of the contracting parties undertakes to give, as far as possible, favorable treatment *in conformity with regulations actually in force in their own countries*" (emphasis added; Article 1). The parties also promise "to make all possible efforts to ensure that the prices of goods exchanged under this agreement are fixed according to the prices for similar goods on the major international markets" (Article 5). But this article, like all other provisions of the agreement, is imperfect, since no legal sanction is provided in case of nonfulfillment.

We might ask why such a "nonbinding" agreement was adopted. More generally, the question can be phrased as what are the real effects of bilateral commercial agreements in the light of a general liberalization of world-trade policy and a rapid growth of multilateral arrangements (such as GATT). One answer is that the major significance of such bilateral agreements is really political rather than commercial. This is especially true of the Sino-Italian case. Even a quick glance at the nine concise articles of this agreement show that they establish not so much a specific program and set of rules for the conduct of trade, but rather state a set of fundamental principles and an organic framework that will act as a springboard for further positive political development. This is not to say that the agreement does not create real commercial advantages, or that Italy will not reap, at least temporarily, benefits for having the "political courage" to be the first member of the Common Market to conclude a trade agreement with China.[18] This agreement is becoming a model for other countries.

This advantage is becoming real rather than potential when the most important clause of the Sino-Italian TPA is implemented. Article 6 calls for the creation of a Mixed Commission which will meet at least once a year, alternately in Rome and Peking, and which has "the duty of examining the application of this agreement and of studying the development of commercial

---

[17] See, for example, the long-term trade agreement signed by Italy and Bulgaria in Rome on 21 January 1970, in P. Gramatica, *Le Economie di scambio con i paesi dell' Est* (Milan, Cisalpino, 1971), p. 268. See generally, Luke T. Lee, *China and International Agreements* (Durham, N.C., 1969); *Vertäge der Volksrepublik China mit anderen Staaten,* part V *(Verträge mit Kommunistichen Staaten)* (Hamburg, 1972). See also, for a general frame of reference, M. Giuliano, *La cooperazione degli Stati e il commercio internazionale* (third edition, Milan: Giuffre, 1972).

[18] See Colombo, *Prolusione,* "Atti della giornata di studi: Incontro con la Cina," Milan (8 February 1972), pp. 7–9; see also Colombo, *"La realtà economico-sociale della Cina,"* in *Italia-Cina,* no. 6 (1971), pp. 5–17.

exchanges and of cooperation between the two Countries." This kind of commission has been established in almost all the bilateral commercial agreements with Eastern European countries. It has proved to be a useful mechanism for conducting negotiations at the subgovernment level. Consequently, the Sino-Italian Mixed Commission very likely will produce a series of agreements that, from the point of view of the Italian trader, will clarify the conditions for trade and thereby promote trade. In this regard it is interesting to note that the Mixed-Commission clause as well as the mention of "cooperation" between the two countries seems to have been added at the request of Italy.

Until the Mixed Commission acts and in order to ensure the continuity of exchanges between the two countries, Italy is taking a number of unilateral steps to remove restraints on trade between the two countries. In general the Italian system of regulation of foreign trade creates two categories of goods. The import or export of "license goods" require a specific ministerial authorization. On the other hand, "customs goods" may be traded without a particular license, although sometimes they are subject to quotas imposed by the customs administration or by the Ministry of Foreign Trade. In recent years most items have become "customs goods." That is, all goods can be freely imported and exported, except those listed on particular "tables."

In trade with socialist countries "license goods" are listed in the Table B/Import and by the Export Table. Bilateral agreements, however, often provide that certain "license goods" should become "customs goods" or "controlled customs goods" so that they may be freely traded within the limits fixed by the two countries. Moreover, in order to facilitate trade with European socialist countries, Italy has taken a number of steps to remove particular items from the Table B/Import; such departures from this table at various times have been extended to China.[19]

---

[19] The latest circular (No. A/220527 of 29 December 1972) of the Italian Foreign Trade Ministry, in regulating trade with China for the year 1973, liberalizes further import products. This circular has been enacted as a result of the first meeting of the Sino-Italian Mixed Commission in Peking on 10–12 April 1972. During this meeting the Chinese turned down the Italian proposal to sign a complementary yearly protocol to the commercial agreement (as is the rule in commercial agreements between Italy and other state-economy countries: see, for example, the 1972 trade agreement with Albania, in *Il Sole—24 Ore*, 15 November 1972, p. 8) and proposed instead a further liberalization of imports in an autonomous way.

On the Italian system of foreign trade regulation see Mario Morales, *Commercio Estero—Guida practica per gli operatori con l'estero*, 2nd ed. (Milano: Pirola, 1968); Leo Dal Maso, *La practica del commercio con l'estero* (Milano: Pirola, 1970); Paolo Grammatica, *Le economie di scambio*; ICE, *Scambi con l'estero* (Rome: 1971). See also P. DeGiorgis, "Favorevoli prospettive per lo sviluppo degli scambi italo-cinesi: regolamentazione doganale e valutaria," *Italia-Cina*, nos. 4–5 (1972), pp. 10–11; V. Pagliuzzi, "L'Italia si introduce nel mercato cinese," *Italia-Cina*, nos. 4–5 (1972), pp. 7–9 and, in general, Marie Lavigne, *Les économies socialistes* (Paris: Armand Colin, 1970).

After the conclusion of the Sino-Italian TPA, the Italian Foreign Trade Ministry in May 1972 stated that "in the framework of the commercial Italian-Chinese Agreement" but "in an autonomous and experimental way" (i.e., outside engagements entered into through the TPA) all the liberalizations concerning import of goods from European socialist countries would also apply to China. Consequently, Chinese goods now fall into four categories:

1. a small number of goods listed in Table B/Import (D.M. 10 July 1963, published in *Gazetta Ufficiale* No. 12, 16 January 1964, and subsequent amendments) which require an import license from the ministry;

2. "controlled customs goods" which may be imported through Venice or Genoa, in a temporary and exceptional way, subject to various quota limitations (circular no. A/317755 of 12 December 1970);

3. agricultural products which are subject to the special regulations of the European Common Market; and

4. "free customs goods" which include all other kinds of goods and which may be imported without limit to quantity or value. (In all four cases the Italian customs authorities must check that the goods have been "originally addressed to Italian firms.")

Quite apart from the expected accomplishments of the Mixed Commission, it is clear that these recent unilateral measures have had immediate and positive effect on Sino-Italian trade. They have abolished all differences of treatment between Chinese products and goods originating in other socialist countries, and have also stimulated the import of Chinese goods by placing more items on the free and controlled customs categories. Presumably, increased Italian purchases of Chinese goods will lead to an increased amount of sales to China.

III. THE SEA AND AIR NAVIGATION AGREEMENTS

The TPA has also been the basis of two bilateral agreements concerning navigation by sea and by air. An agreement on maritime transport (hereafter MTA) was laid down in Peking in April 1972 at the time of the first meeting of the Sino-Italian Mixed Commission, and signed there on 8 October 1972 by the Italian minister of merchant marine, Giuseppe Lupis, and the Chinese minister of communications, Yang Chieh. The complete text of the MTA has twelve articles and is written in three languages (Italian, Chinese, and English), all being equally authoritative.

The agreement is valid until one party has given the other a twelve-months' written notice (Article 12). Like the TPA, the MTA makes clear its own general and specific goals: the development of friendly relations between the two countries and the strengthening of cooperation in the area of transportation by sea, on the basis of equality and mutual benefit. The central idea of the MTA is expressed in Article 1, whereby ships flying the two parties' national flags are authorized to navigate between the harbors of the two countries that are open to foreign trade, and to transport merchandise and passengers between the two countries or between each of the two countries and a third country.

In a manner similar to the TPA, the maritime agreement contains two clauses (Articles 2 and 3) which provide for the mutual most-favored-nation treatment for national-flag ships and their crews in all matters concerning the fulfilment of customs, health, and harbor formalities and regulations, harbor anchorage and moorings, the displacement of moorings, the loading and unloading of merchandise, freight transportation, necessary supplies for the ship, the crew, and the passengers, access to all harbor assets, and navigation assistance and pilotage services. As in the case of the TPA, however, the most-favored-nation treatment does not apply to the advantages, privileges, and immunities that are allowed or will be allowed by each of the contracting parties to present or future member countries in customs unions or similar institutions (Article 2, paragraph 2). The same observations were made concerning the TPA.

The maritime agreement does not have the same broad and vague wording of the TPA. It does not deal mainly with questions of principle, but dictates concrete norms capable of immediate execution once the agreement has been ratified. One need only consider the clauses that establish the validity and reciprocal recognition of the crew-identification documents, of navigation certificates, and of other possible national documents (showing the tonnage, etc.), as well as the right of the captain (or of his representative) of a newly arrived ship to visit the diplomatic and consular authorities of the country whose flag the ship flies. These clauses are of special interest in light of China's refusal—unlike the Socialist countries in Europe—to sign, at least for the time being, a consular convention with Italy.

Like the TPA, the MTA also contains at least one imperfect norm, in which it is hard to predict the legal consequence in the case of nonexecution. According to Article 5 both parties are obliged to give each other all possible assistance and protection to ships, crew, load, and passengers finding themselves in danger while in the territorial waters of the other party. In addition, one major difficulty for the interpreter is caused by the many articles of the MTA which refer to "regulations in force in the host country" (Article 6), to "statutory norms of the country" (Article 7), to "norms of the country where the ship taxes and burdens are paid" (Article 8), or to "laws and regulations effective in the harbour of one side" (Article 9, concerning ways of payment of expenditures and burdens encountered by the ships of the other side). All these articles raise once more the unresolved problem of insufficient access to Chinese statutory and regulatory sources.

Because of the operative character of the MTA, there is less need for a continuous debate over the best ways of implementation than there is with the TPA. The MTA does not set up, therefore, a permanent mixed commission, but only a less formal consultation device: the meeting of *ad hoc* representatives of the parties at a time and place agreed upon, upon request of any of them, in order to deal "with all question of common interest resulting from carrying out of the MTA" (Article 11).

A Sino-Italian air agreement was signed in Peking on 8 January 1973 by General Felice Santini, head of an Italian aeronautical delegation, and Kuang Jen-nung, general director of the Chinese Administration for Civil Aviation (CAAC). Since China is not a member of the ICAO (International Civil Aviation Organization), the agreement is coupled with a protocol concerning all procedures relating to radioelectric assistance, meteorological services, exchange of messages, etc., between *Alitalia* and the CAAC. This agreement provides that planes of the Italian National Civil Aviation Company will be able to fly to Shanghai and Peking, and Chinese airplanes will be allowed to land in Rome and Milan. Each company is authorized to fly three times a week with passenger and freight on any kind of plane, although supersonic craft require special authorization. Moreover, both companies are granted the so-called "five freedom rights," i.e., the right to continue to fly beyond the port of destination. Alitalia may fly to Tokio and other airports in Asia, and CAAC may fly to Paris and other airports in Europe.

IV. RECENT DEVELOPMENTS

A. Contracts

There is little new in the area of foreign trade contracts. Contract formation and negotiation still require an inordinate amount of time and still go through the rites and rhythms described in the literature elsewhere. It does appear, however, that difficulties referred to as "indirect legal restraint on trade"[20] have practically disappeared.

There also has been virtually no change in the contract forms since 1968. The Italian businessman is nearly always presented with a standard Chinese contract (usually bilingual, in English and Chinese, and occasionally in Italian and Chinese) which he is expected to agree to with few or no alterations.[21]

---

[20] For discussion of these restraints, see Cohen, "Chinese Law," pp. 141–47. For a curious case, however, see "Un rappresentante di commercio italiano incarcerato in Cina cita lo Stato per mezzo miliardo," in *Corriere della Sera,* 20 January 1972.

[21] On the "inequality" of contract terms when the Chinese are buyers instead of sellers, see Alan H. Smith, "Standard Forms Contracts in the International Commercial Transactions of the People's Republic of China," *International and Comparative Law Quarterly,* 21, pt. 1 (January 1972), pp. 132–50.

Of course, the possibility of changing some standard clauses or imposing a different contractual scheme is considerably greater when the Italian party is selling whole plants or complex producer goods.

One item of interest has been the fairly common sales contract which gives to one (and sometimes two) Italian buyer an exclusive right to sell in Italy certain specified goods for a fixed period of time. (See Appendix 13.) The Chinese foreign trade corporations have occasionally violated this agreement by selling the same goods directly in Italy or to other Italian buyers. No adequate justification has been given for this practice; in one case the Chinese side spoke vaguely about how the Italian side, out of a spirit of friendship and cooperation, should understand the Chinese actions. I enclose in Appendixes 17 and 8 two more items I believe to be of special interest: a certificate of quality and quantity, on which the Chinese insist so much, and the text of a rare contract between the China National Machinery Import and Export Corporation and a large Italian trading corporation that specializes in East-West transactions. According to the latter contract, a vibrating roller, built by an Italian factory and sold by the Italian corporation to the Chinese Corporation, must be sent directly to Albania.

B. Dispute Resolution

The Foreign Trade Arbitration Committee and the Maritime Arbitration Committee of the CCPIT have never been active in the fifteen or so years of their existence.[22] As is well known, the Chinese prefer to use extralegal and informal means of settling disputes that arise in the course of trade.

In the past several years some Italian businessmen have felt that greater use of arbitration would facilitate Sino-Italian trade relations.[23] This subject was studied during a symposium organized by the Italian Chamber of Com-

---

[22] See Crespi Reghizzi, "Legal Aspects," Cohen, "Chinese Law," and S. Fabro, "Appunti sul sistema cinese di arbitrato per il commercio estero," in *Rassegna dell' Arbitrato* 5 (1972); 1–12. *Contra* Cohen, "Chinese Law at the Crossroads," *American Bar Association Journal* (January 1973), p. 44.

[23] Some of the other difficulties in Sino-Italian trade mentioned by Italian businessmen are: (a) the irregular pattern of Chinese purchases from Italy; (b) the Chinese practices of not responding to Italian offers, and of not giving any indications of why an offer was refused; (c) the Chinese refusal to sign long-term contracts and joint ventures of the kind signed with European socialist countries; (d) the difficulty in identifying the sectors of greater interest and in making contact with the ultimate user or supplier; and (e) the inability to alter standard Chinese contract conditions and terms of payment and delivery. Of course, the behavior of some Italian firms sometimes hinders trade. See, for example, Giuseppe Orlando, "Il ruolo delle Case Import Export nella promozione degli scambi con la Cina," proceedings of the Study Meeting "Prospettive e sviluppi degli scambi con la Cina," Milan, 23–24 March 1971 (unpublished papers).

merce for China in Milan on 4 October 1971 to discuss "Businessmen and the Italian-Chinese Commercial Treaty." The group urged that in negotiating the TPA, "special regulations should be agreed upon concerning arbitration which apply the (arbitration) procedures provided for in the Regulations of the International Chamber of Commerce." They further sent a memorandum to the Ministry of Foreign Affairs which stated:

Confirming the need that both parties must agree on the rules of arbitration, we hope that at the least the PRC will periodically and systematically make known the rules regulating the work of the arbitral commissions of the CCPIT. . . . Regarding the possible supplying of machinery, complete plants, and technical assistance, it is hoped that the Chinese government would adopt standard international contracts which generally include an arbitration clause.[24]

The memorandum also included a list of standard contract forms published by the United Nations.

The Ministry of Foreign Affairs, possibly at the urging of the Chinese side, ignored these requests so that the TPA contains no provision regarding the resolution of trade disputes or the use of arbitration. Presumably the question can be reopened in the discussions of the Mixed Commission.[25] In any case the present situation is one where the Chinese have not explicitly rejected the principle of arbitration, but where their attitude is such that extensive use of arbitration would be unlikely.[26] The difficulty might be psychological rather than technical, but we ought not underestimate the importance of the psychological factor.

In terms of actual practice, most contracts include a clause calling for arbitration by one of the arbitral tribunals in Peking. The few exceptions concern sales of complete plants or complex machinery by Italy; in these cases the inclusion and wording of an arbitration clause depends in large part on the bargaining strength of the two sides.[27]

Even when a contract contains the standard Chinese arbitration clause, this clause is almost never invoked. Thus, from 1965 to 1971 no disputes arising from Sino-Italian trade have been submitted for arbitration, or even mediation. Where disputes have arisen, the parties attempt to resolve it themselves through an endless exchange of correspondence. This procedure fulfills the spirit of a clause present in many standard Chinese contracts: "Any dispute

---

[24] Proceedings of the Study Meeting "Gli operatori economici e il trattato commerciale italo-cinese," Milan, 4 October 1971 (unpublished papers).

[25] Some businessmen have tried privately to urge the Chinese to make greater use of arbitration. These efforts have not been successful. See, e.g. Vincenzo Pagliuzzi, "Rapporto sulla missione nella Republica Popolare Cinese per l'accreditamento della Camera di Commercio Italiana per la Cina," Milan, 25 June 1971 (unpublished paper).

[26] Orlando, "Il ruolo."

[27] Crespi Reghizzi, "Legal Aspects," p. 115. For the special case of confirmation sales, see Smith, "Standard Form," pp. 147-8.

arising from the execution of or in connection with this contract shall be settled in accordance with the terms stipulated above *between the signers of this contract only, without involving any third party"* (Emphasis added).

Even the suggestion that a dispute be submitted to arbitration in Peking is met with disfavor. Such an act would break the bond of friendship and thrust that underlies all exchange relations, particularly long-term ones. In a manner similar to traditional practice the Chinese prefer that the disputants arrive at some mutually acceptable solution rather than seek third-party adjudication In order to preserve good relations the foreign trader often must give up some apparently legitimate claim or must accept some apparently groundless Chinese claim.

Excessive insistence that one is "right" can produce undesirable consequences. For example, an Italian company had sold benzene to a Chinese corporation which was to be shipped on a Chinese vessel. Before shipment satisfactory inspection samples were taken from the tanks of the ship which held the benzene in the presence of officers of the Chinese corporation and its freight agent. Upon arrival in China it was discovered that dirt from the ship's tanks had polluted the goods contained therein. The Chinese noted the damage and admitted their responsibility. Some time later, however, they filed a complaint stating that the benzene contained in the tanks did not meet the agreed technical specifications (see Appendix 18). This began a long correspondence in which the Chinese demanded compensation while the Italian firm insisted that the Chinese were responsible for the damage. In addition to letters, discussions were also held in Canton and in Italy. On several occasions the Italian firm suggested arbitration; this was resisted by the Chinese corporation, which expressed the desire to settle the dispute in a friendly manner. The final conclusion was that after four years the Chinese gave up their claim.

In a second case a Chinese corporation sold colophony to an Italian firm on CIF Genoa terms, with the People's Insurance Company of China as the insurer.[28] While in transit the leakage of some cement that was also being shipped spoiled the entire load of colophony. When the goods arrived in Italy, a portion was stored in Genoa, while for the sake of convenience another portion was stored in Milan. The insurance company was willing to pay for the goods stored in Genoa, but was unwilling to pay for goods sent to Milan since the insurance policy made no reference to further shipment to that city. The Italian firm insisted on full payment since all the goods were ruined during the shipment. Once again, a series of negotiations between the two

---

[28] See Appendix 21 for a sample insurance policy. Some Italian businessmen say that the People's Insurance Copany is very slow in making payment, and also demands so many certificates and documents that the Italian trader is discouraged from asking compensation for minor claims.

parties was conducted over a course of three or four years with the result that full payment was made by the insurance company.

These cases illustrate the great reluctance of the Chinese to enter into arbitration. In addition, they also illustrate that while the Italian firms may have "won," theirs may have been Pyrrhic victories. They saved or recovered a sum of money, but they also may have jeopardized the "friendly relationship" upon which further dealings must be based.

C. Industrial Property

There have been very few developments in the areas of trademark and patent registration. Contracts make no mention of these matters, and China still is no party to any international convention for the protection of industrial property.[29] So far as I know, there have been no attempts by individuals or corporations of one country to register patents in the other country.[30]

It appears, however, that Italian businessmen are paying more attention to this area. Based on some earlier incidents and on the warning issued by British trade officials, the Italians have expressed concern over the fact that their goods may be "copied" by the Chinese. Recently, the Italian Ministry of Industry and Trade asked the Italian Group of the International Association for the Protection of Industrial Property (AIPPI) to make suggestions concerning a possible agreement with the PRC concerning the protection of industrial property.[31]

The special committee formed within the Italian Group of AIPPI pointed out that in the field of patents, a Chinese citizen, even though not residing in Italy, can obtain an Italian patent. The reverse is not true: the residence qualification imposed by Chinese law precludes an Italian citizen from registering a patent in China.

As for trademarks, Chinese law (like Italian law) does not treat Chinese and foreigners differently, provided the foreigner is a national of a state having diplomatic relations or a commercial agreement with China. Consequently, the special committee suggested that the principle of reciprocity in registration of trademarks be regularized by means of an exchange of private notes between the two countries. It also asked that the appropriate Chinese governmental

---

[29] It appears that there was a confidential exchange of notes between China and England in the mid-1950s, which was revised in 1963, concerning trade mark protection. In order to register British trade marks in China, the trade mark must be registered in the United Kingdom, and the Chinese chargé d'affaires in London must be notified.

[30] In striking comparison, in 1971 alone aliens have applied for over 5,000 patents (2,336 of which were granted) in the Soviet Union.

[31] Also China and France have reportedly negotiated a trade marks registration agreement. (Source not to be quoted.)

organs make available the legal texts and other materials that regulate the protection of inventions and trademarks.

On 5 January 1973 an agreement on the reciprocal recognition of trademarks was signed between Italy and the PRC, which entered into force on 8 January 1973. In substance this agreement simply formalized the existing situation.

D. Banking

All experts agree that the Chinese banking apparatus continued to operate in an effective manner even during the most difficult period of the Cultural Revolution.[32] In July 1969, however, there was a major shift in Chinese monetary policy: in that month the *renminbi* (RMB) became the preferred accounting unit for foreign trade. (See Article 5 of the sales confirmation in Appendix 14.)

Several considerations underlie this new policy. First, the Chinese wanted to protect themselves against the possible devaluations and revaluations of various western currencies during the current international monetary crisis. The Chinese had already been hurt in the sterling devaluation in 1967 since they held a certain amount of sterling reserves and since many foreign trade contracts were quoted in sterling. The RMB will not fluctuate because its value is fixed by governmental authorities without reference to any gold parity or to the internal price system.[33] Second, the use of RMB may help reduce the trade deficit that China has with most industrial countries. Sellers from these countries will be paid in RMB, and consequently will be more inclined to purchase Chinese goods in order to use up a portion of this money. Finally, the Chinese sphere of political and economic influence may increase

---

[32] See, e.g., the statement of Giuseppe Osio, Central Director of the Milan seat of the Banca Commerciale Italiana, "Esperienze di una visita nella Repubblica Popolare Cinese," delivered orally at the Centro Pirelly, Milan, 14 June 1971.

[33] 1 RMB = 278 Italian liras (as of January 1973 for commercial transactions). Only the Bank of China fixes the exchange rate of RMB for Western currencies, thus preventing any influences by the world market. Italian exporters, in particular, receive payments at an exchange rate laid down by the Bank of China, this being carried out through convertible foreign currency, even though invoice amounts are made out in RMB. In case of considerable uncertainty of exchange, the Bank of China quickly suspends transactions in RMB until the situation becomes clear. In the spring of 1972, for instance, the Bank of China suspended until the month of August transactions on terms in RMB for liras both in buying and selling, while the selling of RMB for cash was subjected to restrictions. See G. P. Casadio, "I problemi monetari negli scambi con la Cina," *Il Sole—24 Ore* (special issue), 30 September, 1972, p. 18; G. Bazani, "Il Renminbi," *Italia-Cina* no. 2 (1972), pp. 20–25; see also generally *Chinas Renminbi—Eine Äusserst stabile Währung auf der Welt* (Peking: Foreign Language Press, 1969); K. Huang Hsiao, *Money and Monetary Policy in Communist China* (New York and London: Columbia University Press, 1971).

during the coming years with the development of a "RMB area" in South East Asia.[34]

In order to give foreign buyers access to RMB, in 1969 the Hong Kong branches of the Bank of China began to open RMB accounts for Italian traders. These accounts were payable either in RMB or in dollars and yielded an interest of 7 percent. During the next two years many Western European banks opened RMB accounts (yielding 5 percent interest) and began operating in Chinese currency. As a general rule these accounts can be used only in conjunction with definite sales or purchase contracts. (See Appendix 3 for a draft of an agreement between the Bank of China and a major Italian bank concerning regulations on the use of RMB accounts.) In addition, Article 3 of the TPA provides that all payments should be made "according to the rules actually in force in the two countries and to the usual practice."[35] In effect this clause incorporates into the TPA the banking regulations of the two countries and the customary international banking practices.

Finally, a reference should be made to trade financing and to export credit. Sino-Italian trade is normally financed by letters of credit. These instruments, however, differ when the Chinese are sellers and when they are buyers. In the former case the Italian party's letter of credit must always be at sight, confirmed, irrevocable, and normally transferable and without recourse. Very little is said about the document that the Chinese party must produce in order to receive payment. Various Italian trade groups have urged the use of letters of credit with drafts good for ninety or one hundred and eighty days, or even letters of credit against documents; these efforts have not met with success so far. When the Chinese are buyers, much less emphasis is placed on their obligation to open promptly a letter of credit, whereas the contracts specify in great detail all the documents the Bank of China must receive before making payment.

The 4 October 1971 symposium on "Businessmen and the Sino-Italian Trade Agreement" suggested that the TPA should make provision for "a system of credit lying grants" and "a system of supplier's credits." This proposal was not incorporated into the actual TPA. Recently, however, the Chinese have made enquiries about the use of credit lines by Italian banks. It is possible that this question will be discussed at future meetings of the Mixed Commission. At this point all that can be said is that while the Chinese

---

[34] This is, for example, the opinion of Alessandro Mennini of the Banco Ambrosiano di Milano in his report, "Missione Economica in Kwangchow, October 22–November 7, 1971," Milan, 1971, pp. 19–20.

[35] A similar rule is to be found in Article 9 of the 1972 Sino-Italian Agreement on Maritime Transports. That particular article speaks, however, of "laws and regulations in force in the harbour." According to Article 10 of the same Agreement, all collections and payments by one party in the territory of the other must be made "in convertible currencies agreed upon by both Parties."

do not want long-term indebtedness, they are showing a cautious but growing interest in short- and medium-term credit arrangements.

V. CONCLUDING REMARKS

Hopes that a solid legal basis will help to build up and develop trade relationships with China and change them from precarious into permanent relationships are reasonably shared by every Italian businessman, although economists and China experts may have a different opinion. Optimistic as merchants are, however, they probably prefer to believe the words of Kao Chu-feng, the commercial counselor of the PRC Embassy in Rome:

At present the volume of Sino-Italian trade is not very large but it is increasing. Last year witnessed an increase compared to that of 1970. A further increase will be obtained this year in comparison with that of last year. All the more important is that both China and Italy have a common desire to expand further their bilateral trade.

Recently, *through friendly negotiation,* several big transactions have been concluded between the Chinese corporations and the Italian companies. *The prospect for the development of Sino-Italian trade is bright.* We believe that through our common efforts, based on equality and mutual benefit, constant new development will be achieved in the Sino-Italian economic and trade relations. [Text in English, emphasis added.][36]

---

[36] "Friendly Collaboration in Mutual Interest," *Il Sole—24 Ore* (special issue), 24 September 1972, p. 1.

Trade with Hong Kong*

ALAN H. SMITH

I. INTRODUCTION

Economic relations between the People's Republic of China and Hong Kong are significantly different in nature from the PRC's relations with most other countries, including all those discussed elsewhere in this volume. Hong Kong's role as the purchaser of a substantial amount of Chinese exports, and consequently as a supplier of much needed hard currency, is well known.[1] In

NOTE: This essay covers material up to January 1973.

* I am pleased to acknowledge the support that I received in this research from the Centre of Asian Studies, Hong Kong University.

[1] The volume of Hong Kong's imports and exports from the PRC, rounded to the nearest HK $ million is:

Year	Imports	Exports	Re-exports	Total Exports	Trade Balance
1948	$ 461	Not available		$ 280	$ 181
1949	$ 593	„		$ 585	8
1950	$ 858	„		$1,461	−603
1951	$ 863	„		$1,604	−741
1952	$ 830	„		$ 520	310
1953	$ 857	„		$ 540	317
1954	$ 692	„		$ 391	301
1955	$ 898	„		$ 182	716
1956	$1,038	„		$ 138	900
1957	$1,131	„		$ 123	1,008
1958	$1,397	„		$ 156	1,241
1959	$1,034	$ 9	$105	$ 114	920
1960	$1,186	$ 13	$107	$ 120	1,066
1961	$1,028	$ 8	$ 91	$ 99	929
1962	$1,213	$ 8	$ 77	$ 85	1,128
1963	$1,487	$ 8	$ 62	$ 70	1,417

the early 1950s when the Coordinating Committee (COCOM) and China Committee (CHINCOM) restrictions[2] made it difficult for China to purchase goods from the West, Hong Kong also played an important part as the middleman in China's purchases. Today, Hong Kong continues to provide valuable services to facilitate China's economic dealings with other countries. These include the entrepôt trade, historically the *raison d'être* of the British Crown Colony, banking, shipping, and other commercial services.

In addition to the above activities China is involved in the economic life of Hong Kong by having considerable capital investments in Hong Kong. Through a variety of means, China supports, controls, or is associated with an increasing number of Hong Kong enterprises whose activities range from banking, shipping, and department stores to land investment, manufacturing, and heavy industry.

There are, for example, thirteen PRC associated banks with over sixty branches throughout Hong Kong. These banks constitute the very core of China's interests in Hong Kong and provide Hong Kong importers with credit facilities in China to enable them to make their purchases. The agreement between the bank and the Hong Kong importer often will provide that the imported goods are the property of the bank until the importer has paid off the money advanced. When the goods arrive in Hong Kong they may be stored in godowns in the importer's name, but the godown will be instructed to hold them "to the order of" the bank; in this way the bank, and indirectly the PRC, will retain a considerable degree of control over the goods, even after they have left China.

Year	Imports	Exports	Re-exports	Total Exports	Trade Balance
1964	$1,970	$ 13	$ 47	$ 60	1,910
1965	$2,322	$ 18	$ 54	$ 72	2,250
1966	$2,769	$ 15	$ 54	$ 69	2,700
1967	$2,282	$ 6	$ 42	$ 48	2,234
1968	$2,429	$ 9	$ 36	$ 45	2,384
1969	$2,700	$ 7	$ 30	$ 37	2,663
1970	$2,830	$ 30	$ 34	$ 64	2,766

SOURCES: Hong Kong Government Gazette and Hong Kong Annual Reports; Hong Kong Government. (Until 1959 exports were not broken down into exports and re-exports.)

For a detailed discussion of Hong Kong's trade relations with the PRC, see Colina MacDougall Lupton, "Hongkong's Role in Sino-Western Trade," in Arthur Stahnke, ed., *China's Trade with the West: A Political and Economic Analysis* (New York: Praeger, 1972).

[2] For a discussion of these trade restrictions see John Garson, "The American Trade Embargo of China," in Alexander Eckstein, ed., *China Trade Prospects and United States Policy* (New York: Praeger, 1971).

The accounts of the Hong Kong-incorporated PRC-associated banks are of interest. They show that there is considerable interbank lending among these banks, and that only comparatively small accounts are kept with non-PRC banks. During the dispute in 1969 between the Singapore branch of the Bank of China and the Singapore government, the PRC banks in Hong Kong were reported to have been ordered by China to give unlimited support to the Bank of China "to make sure that it survives . . . the crisis."[3] The Hong Kong banks are said to have responded to this call by transferring tens of millions of dollars to the credit of the Singapore bank.

Large amounts of U.S. dollars, both notes and bills, are held by these banks despite the earlier efforts of the United States Foreign Assets Control Regulations to prevent this. Furthermore, fluctuating amounts of unexpected currencies such as South Vietnamese piastres and South African rands also are held, presumably evidencing trading relations with those countries.[4]

Less well known than the department stores, banks, and newspapers are numerous land investment companies that have strong connections with China. Most of these investment companies, which were incorporated in Hong Kong, keep out of the news and would not be known to the great majority of Hong Kong residents. Some of the land on which PRC-associated companies carry on business or on which their employees live is held by other associated companies. For example, in 1947 the Bank of China acquired a renewable seventy-five year Crown lease on the land on which its building now stands and also purchased a number of houses for the use of its senior employees. The Nanyang Bros. Tobacco Co., Ltd.,[5] a company incorporated in the PRC but carrying on business as a manufacturer in Hong Kong, is the owner of

---

[3] The Singapore Government prosecuted the Singapore branch of the Bank of China for infringements of the Singapore Banking Ordinance. The bank was fined US $128,000; when it refused to pay its property was seized, and the government withdrew clearing-house facilities. See Jayakumar Am. J. Int'l L. (1970), p. 371. Also *Straits Times*, 24 May 1969.

[4] The PRC supplies, by means of re-exports from Hong Kong, significant quantities of Chinese herbal medicines and textiles to South Vietnam, the Khmer Republic, etc. In South Vietnam, in particular, sales rose from HK $4.45 million in 1970 to HK $20.3 million in 1971: The re-export trade with South Africa rose from HK $8.56 million to HK $12.6 million over the same period. Hong Kong Government External Trade Statistics; Census and Statistics Department; April 1972. See also *South China Morning Post,* Hong Kong, 1 and 2 May 1972.

[5] This company is something of an enigma and, being basically a manufacturing concern, it does not fit into the pattern of the normal PRC-incorporated company. It may be that China finds it convenient to permit this company to maintain its separate identity in order to preserve or increase the investments which the company holds. In 1971 the company acquired, through purchases from other shareholders, the majority interest in Wing Fat Printing Co., Ltd., one of the few public companies in which the PRC has an interest. It is also a shareholder in China Products Co. (HK), Ltd., and Wen Wei Po, Ltd., a local left-wing newspaper.

the land on which the Nanyang Theater stands. The Ko Shing Cinema at which patriotic films are shown is owned by Kiu Fat Investment Corporation, Ltd., a company that has strong links with the PRC. The Chinese Merchandise Emporium, Ltd., leases its Queen's Road premises from one of its shareholders Wang Tat Enterprises Co., Ltd. The shareholders of Wang Tat Enterprises Co., Ltd., include the Hua Chiao Commercial Bank, Ltd., and Kiu Kwong Investment Corporation, Ltd., both of which themselves have shareholders in the PRC.

Despite this, however, it seems that a considerable part of the land from which the PRC-associated firms conduct their business is owned by Hong Kong landlords who have no particular connection with China; e.g., Chinese Arts and Crafts (HK), Ltd., in Shell House and Star House, China Travel Service (HK), Ltd., in Queen's Road, the Bank of Communications in Prince's Building, and the China National Aviation Corporation, the tenant of a prime site in the center of Hong Kong.

This paper will focus primarily on these business enterprises, particularly on the structure and form of their relationship to China. As part of the inquiry this paper will consider how correct it is to say, as one author has written, that "in Hong Kong and neighboring areas there are 'private' Chinese corporations importing and exporting goods for the mainland of China. But these so-called private corporations are, in Peking's view, agencies of the state and thus part of the state trading system."[6] I have chosen this general topic not because these enterprises constitute the largest or most profitable section of China's economic relations with Hong Kong,[7] but rather because the extent of these enterprises make Hong Kong unique, and because it is possible that, in the future, China may wish to extend its Hong Kong experience to its economic dealings with the West.

This paper will not discuss, except in passing, two related and important topics: the legal aspects of individual contracts and transactions,[8] and the role

---

[6] Gene Hsiao, "Communist China's Trade Treaties and Agreements (1949–64)," *Vand. L.R.* 21 (1968): 623, 645.

[7] Reliable estimates of the value of China's investment in Hong Kong are not available and its full extent is difficult to ascertain. But see Goodstadt in *Far Eastern Economic Review* (hereafter *FEER*) (1967): 41, who put China's earnings from Hong Kong in 1966 at:

Exports to Hong Kong, less imports	2700
Profits from importing and distribution	690
Profits from banking	50
Water charges	14
Other economic activities	540
	HK $3994 million

[8] For a more detailed discussion of Chinese contract terms, see Alan H. Smith, "Standard Form Contracts in the International Commercial Transactions of the People's Republic of China," *Int'l & Comp. L. Q.* (1972): 133.

played by these companies, particularly the banks, in providing an easy and informal means by which Western and Chinese businessmen can come into contact. Both of these are substantial topics calling for a different point of view and approach and should be treated in separate papers.

II. CAPITAL INVESTMENT BY THE PRC IN HONG KONG BUSINESSES

A. *The Businesses Studied*

Any attempt to examine the legal structure of the Hong Kong businesses associated with the PRC must face at the very outset the problem of deciding what degree of control, support, or interest by the PRC is required before the enterprise can properly be labeled "PRC-associated." The spectrum through which PRC interest ranges is from total control by 100 percent shareholding in Peking, to indirect control through one of Hong Kong's "fat cats," i.e., Chinese businessmen of considerable wealth who have from early days supported and acted as informal spokesmen of the PRC.[9] For the purposes of this study, I have concentrated on the following businesses:

1. Those that were incorporated in the PRC itself and registered in Hong Kong as a foreign company under Part XI of the Hong Kong Companies Ordinance,[10] e.g., Bank of China and China Merchants Steam Navigation Company, Ltd.

2. Those that are the Hong Kong representatives of any of the Chinese national trading corporations, e.g., China Resources Co. and Ng Fung Hong.

3. Those that have substantial or important shareholders in China, e.g., Kiu Kwong Investment Corporation, Ltd., and Hua Chiao Commercial Bank, Ltd. (In these cases it is necessary to be selective and omit, for example, large and long-established Hong Kong corporations which had shareholders who were in China before 1949 but who have not been able to leave China or influence the corporation since then, e.g., Amoy Canning Corp. (HK), Ltd.)

4. Those that are controlled by local "fat cats" or that have as shareholders or directors the companies, or the directors of companies, listed in the first three categories, e.g., China Travel Service (HK), Ltd., and Chinese Merchandise Emporium, Ltd.

---

[9] They include people such as K. C. Wong, Chairman of the Chinese General Chamber of Commerce, and Ho Yin the "representative" of China on the Macau Legislative Council.

[10] Chap. 32 of the *Laws of Hong Kong* (1964 Revised Edition).

B. Methodology

In the course of this research in 1972, I examined over 500 Hong Kong companies, but I concentrated my interest on some 160 companies which I was satisfied had more than just a casual business relationship with the PRC. Thus, I excluded those companies that merely advertised in (and thereby contributed funds to) local communist newspapers on the October first celebrations, or which were included on the list of "designated nationals" under the United States Foreign Assets Control Regulations because, for example, they may have purchased human hair from China for wig-making. However, I treated several companies as being substantially associated with the PRC where there was a combination of indications of involvement, each of which, taken individually, would not have persuaded me to treat the company as PRC-associated. The scope of this research was restricted mainly to limited companies incorporated or registered under the Hong Kong Companies Ordinance.

To obtain incorporation in Hong Kong companies are required to file with the Registrar of Companies, Memorandum and Articles of Association, which set out the objects and powers of the company and the rules for its internal organization, and which correspond to American articles of incorporation and by-laws. Each year every company must make an annual return which will state the size of its issued share capital, and give the names, addresses, and occupations of all persons who were shareholders or directors during that year. Furthermore, all companies are required to deliver to the Registrar particulars of all debentures, mortgages, or other charges created by the company. Moreover, public companies, but not private companies, must file their balance sheets and annual accounts. All the above documents are available for public inspection on payment of a nominal fee and thus, in the case of the PRC-associated companies that are incorporated in Hong Kong, considerable information is available for the researcher.

Companies incorporated in the PRC but establishing a place of business within Hong Kong must deliver to the Registrar of Companies a certified copy of their charter, statutes, or memorandum and articles, together with a certified translation; the names of, and other information relating to, their directors; and the name and address of a person, resident in Hong Kong, who is authorized to accept service of process on the company's behalf. Each year these companies are required to file copies of their balance sheets and accounts, whether or not they are public companies, but they are not required to give details of their shareholders. Again, therefore, a large amount of useful information is available.

One cannot be entirely satisfied, however, that all PRC-associated companies have been included in the research because there may, of course, be companies whose connections were not apparent even after checks at the Companies Registry.

For the purposes of this research I examined very few partnerships or other unincorporated businesses because these are not regulated by the Companies Ordinance and the information available on them is very limited. They are required by the Business Registration Ordinance[11] to disclose the nature of the business and its commencement date, the names and residential addresses of the partners, and the address of the principal place of business and of all other places in Hong Kong at which business is carried on. All this information is open to public examination, but details of the internal management, the financing of the business, and the annual accounts are not available.

C. Companies Incorporated in the PRC Which Have a Place of Business in Hong Kong

According to Hong Kong government records the number of these companies leveled out to twenty-four after the closing of ten registrations in 1957–58. The reduction in number is a result of the rationalization and consolidation of business enterprises within China itself. This reduction may be contrasted with the steady increase in registrations in Hong Kong of companies incorporated in countries other than the PRC (see table 1).

While the total number of these Chinese companies is small, it includes some of their major companies operating in Hong Kong.[12] For example, nine of the thirteen PRC-associated banks in Hong Kong were incorporated in China. Many of these banks do not appear to operate anywhere else and their status and, indeed, their continued existence inside China is extremely doubtful. It is unclear whether they would be entitled to claim sovereign immunity in a suit instituted against them in a Hong Kong court. The better view is that since they are joint state-private enterprises, such a defense would not be open to them. Furthermore, in 1956 in *Midland Investment Co., Ltd.* v. *The Bank of Communications*[13] that bank conceded that it did not (at that time, at any rate) represent the government of China in the sense of being the accredited representative of that government.

---

[11] Chap. 310 of the *Laws of Hong Kong*.

[12] Among the more important PRC-incorporated companies are: Bank of China, Bank of Communications, China and South Sea Bank, Ltd., China Insurance Co., Ltd., China Merchants Steam Navigation Co., Ltd., China National Aviation Corporation, China State Bank, Ltd., China Vegetable Oil Corporation, Chung Hwa Book Co., Ltd., Commercial Press, Ltd., Kincheng Banking Corporation, Ltd., Kwangtung Provincial Bank, Ltd., Nanyang Bros. Tobacco Co., Ltd., National Commercial Bank, Ltd., Sin Hua Trust, Savings, and Commercial Bank, Ltd., Tai Ping Insurance Co., Ltd., and Yien Yieh Commercial Bank, Ltd.

[13] *HKLR* 40 (1956): 42.

TABLE 1

FOREIGN COMPANIES WITH PLACE OF BUSINESS IN HONG KONG

Year Position in April 1955*	Companies incorporated in China 38		Companies incorporated in all other countries 439	
Change since April 1955	No. of new registrations	No. of regis- trations closed	No. of new registrations	No. of regis- trations closed
1955–56	1	2	37	147
1956–57	—	1	32	15
1957–58	1	10	36	25
1958–59	1	—	28	15
1959–60	—	—	36	19
1960–61	1	1	43	16
1961–62	—	—	46	26
1962–63	—	—	55	11
1963–64	—	2	52	22
1964–65	—	—	54	28
1965–66	—	—	49	29
1966–67	—	2	50	23
1967–68	—	—	34	26
1968–69	—	—	46	37
1969–70	—	—	62	16
1970–71	—	—	91	33
Position in April 1971	24		689	

SOURCE: Registrar-General's Annual Departmental Reports; Hong Kong Government.

* Date from which records were first published.

The continued existence of large numbers of seemingly separate PRC-incorporated banks in Hong Kong seems to be due to the fact that each bank caters to its own group of clients. These clients may be different groups of overseas Chinese who traditionally have made remittances to relatives in China through one of these banks, or they may be businessmen in Hong Kong who have been long-term customers of the bank. Instead of rationalizing and reducing the number of these banks as has been done internally, the PRC seems to have preferred to maintain the status quo and not upset its customers in Hong Kong.

The PRC-incorporated businesses are important not only because of the direct profits which they make in Hong Kong and remit to China, but also because, through their offices, control is obtained or support given to a large number of smaller Hong Kong enterprises. As shown in subsection E below various persons affiliated with these directly owned corporations are the registered holders of many millions of dollars worth of stock in other Hong Kong companies.

The head offices of these companies are either in Peking or Shanghai, and the majority of their directors are resident there, although most of these companies also have at least one Hong Kong resident director.[14]

The article of association of these companies normally recite the fact that they are organized as joint state-private enterprises, though this is not invariably the case.[15]

It was not until 1962[16] that most of these companies drew up new articles of association to supersede their old regulations which had been in force since Nationalist days.[17] Under their new articles shareholders in these companies are given various rights though, of course, it is not known how far shareholders in China would actually seek to enforce them. The quorum for meetings is generally 50 percent of the shareholders, which is a very high figure and, if insisted upon, would probably require the private shareholders to attend meetings. It is common for the regulations to provide for less than equal voting rights, with the small shareholders being favored. For example, Article 17 of the China and South Sea Bank, Ltd., provides:

At a meeting of shareholders, a shareholder who holds up to one hundred shares shall have one vote for every ten shares he holds and one vote for the remainder of less than ten shares. A shareholder holding less than ten shares shall have one vote. A shareholder who holds more than one hundred shares shall have one vote for every twenty shares above one hundred shares.

The regulations of the Bank of China and the Bank of Communications currently registered with the Hong Kong Registrar of Companies fix the dividend on shares at 7 percent, in accordance with the Chinese law governing joint state-private enterprises.[18] The China State Bank, Ltd., fixes its dividend

---

[14] Cf. the China and South Sea Bank, Ltd., which has four directors and two supervisors in Hong Kong.

[15] For example, the 1962 articles of the Nanyang Bros. Tobacco Co., Ltd., are silent on this point. For a description of joint state-private enterprises, see Hsiao, "Communist China's Foreign Trade Organization," *Vand. L.R.* 20 (1967): 303, 307.

[16] It is surprising that there was no uniformity in the timing of these alterations. While the Bank of Communications drew up new articles in 1954, the Bank of China did not change its pre-Liberation articles until 1962. Moreover, the Chung Hwa Book Co., Ltd., is still operating under pre-1949 articles, and does not therefore acknowledge being a joint state-private enterprise.

[17] The minutes of an extraordinary general meeting of the Nanyang Bros. Tobacco Co., Ltd., held in Shanghai in June 1962 and attended by sixty-eight members, records: "Matters Discussed: The existing Articles of the Company contained certain Articles the wording of which is no longer suited to present circumstances and require alterations. The amended Articles were submitted to the Shareholders for their discussion and approval. Resolution: Resolved unanimously that the amended Articles be adopted."

[18] State Council Regulation of 8 February 1956 in *FKHP* 3: 282, and decree of 28 July 1956, *FKHP* 4: 355, 358. Note that this has been reduced to 5 percent and it is uncertain whether this is currently being paid.

at 5 percent, while other companies such as the Kincheng Banking Corporation do not deal with the question of fixed dividends.

Examples of minor infringements of Hong Kong statutory requirements by these companies may from time to time be found. The China National Aviation Corporation (whose head office is in Shanghai and in which Pan American Airways is a shareholder) faced a creditors wind-up petition in 1950, but this apparently was discontinued. The company would still appear to be in existence in Hong Kong, as it is the lessee of a shop in Hong Kong's Central District, which is used as a news and propaganda display center. However, no annual accounts or other records have been put on file at the Companies Registry since 1950, despite the requirements of section 336 of the Hong Kong Companies Ordinance. Moreover, it was widely reported, especially during the 1967 riots, that PRC-controlled banks were used for purposes other than those normally associated with the banking profession.[19]

It would be very wrong, however, to give the impression that many PRC-incorporated businesses frequently flout Hong Kong law merely because some of them do not strictly comply with it. The reason why these corporations do not follow the letter of the law in Hong Kong is no doubt partly because it would, in some cases, be extremely difficult to do so. The China National Aviation Corporation, for example, does not appear to have a continuing existence inside China itself, and it would therefore be impossible for it to file annual returns and accounts. Notwithstanding, however, it was clearly felt desirable to maintain the status quo and retain the low rent lease which the company held on valuable office space in central Hong Kong.

The Hong Kong government must certainly be aware of a number of irregularities involving the PRC-incorporated companies. The government sensibly has no desire to provoke a confrontation with the PRC over technical and usually relatively minor infringements and presumably, as a policy decision, has taken no action.

Moreover, the Hong Kong-incorporated PRC-associated businesses probably have a better record of full compliance with the Companies Ordinance requirements than does the average Hong Kong company. Even at the height of the 1967 riots, for example, the local PRC enterprise continued to file company returns with the Registrar in the normal way.

---

[19] See, e.g., *FEER* 10 August 1967, p. 304 *et seq.* Another potential problem, though not the concern of the government, arises out of the fact that the PRC-controlled banks close for business on October first. If a check were presented for payment on this unofficial "bank holiday," it might be held to have been dishonored by nonpayment, and this could have serious consequences for both the bank and the drawer. It is understood, however, that the banks still participate in the clearing-house facilities on this day, so that this risk is not a real one.

D. *The Hong Kong Agents of the Chinese State Trading Corporations*

China Resources Co., Ng Fung Hong, Hua Yuan Co., Teck Soon Hong, Ltd., Peace Book Co., and Southern Film Corporation are described by the China Committee of the Promotion of Internation Trade as the Hong Kong agents of the PRC state trading corporations. It seems clear that from the legal point of view these companies sometimes act as agents *stricto sensu,* but generally they are traders selling goods of Chinese origin on their own account. To determine in what capacity they are acting at any given time it would, of course, be necessary to examine each transaction on a case to case basis.

One of the main functions of these "agents" is to act as wholesalers for the numerous small traders in Hong Kong who market Chinese teas, foodstuffs, medicines, textiles, toys, and so on. In this capacity they often sell on their own account. For example, the import of vegetables from China

is organized by the Choi Luen Hong (United Vegetables Co.) through the Ng Fung Hong, which is actually the Chinese exporter stationed in Hong Kong. It is known that the Choi Luen Hong from time to time enters into contracts with the suppliers in China, lasting for about a season, and covering a rough quota of vegetables to be imported to Hong Kong. Then the Choi Luen Hong regulates the volume of daily supply which comes to Hong Kong mostly by sea (about 80 percent). Under the Choi Luen Hong are the thirteen closely supervised *laans* (collection depots), which again deal with *chaak kas,* a kind of chief representative for a group of retailers.[20]

China Resources Co. and Ng Fung Hong (for foodstuffs) are, however, also important as agents in the legal sense, for they do help negotiate contracts on behalf of the Chinese corporations. In this respect the part played by Ng Fung Hong in the wheat purchases made by the China National Cereal, Oils, and Foodstuffs Import Export Corporation in the 1960s is well known.

When dealing on their own account, the contracts of these agents are brief, in contrast with the standard forms used by the Chinese corporations.[21] The contracts generally are entirely in Chinese and may provide that payment will be made by check drawn on a Hong Kong bank and not by letter of credit in favor of the Bank of China, and insurance, if any, will not necessarily be handled by the People's Insurance Company of China, as would normally be the case in PRC standard form contracts. There would also generally be no provision for arbitration. (See Appendix 12.)

The majority of Hong Kong agents are unincorporated partnerships. Only Teck Soon Hong, Ltd., which specializes in teas, medicines, and pottery and which has a very long history of trading with China, is a limited company. It has an issued capital of almost HK $3 million. Four of its nine shareholders and two of its seven directors are resident in China, and it is connected through

---

[20] Dr. J. Wong, formerly of the Department of Economics, Hong Kong University, 'The Dynamics of the Vegetable Market in Hong Kong" (unpublished manuscript).

[21] See Smith, "Standard Contracts," note 8, *supra.*

its shareholders with other PRC-associated companies. The articles of association provide in considerable detail for the division of profits among staff and shareholders. (See subsection E for details on the division of profits.)

The largest and most important of these agents is China Resources Co. The legal status of the partnership, the extent to which it is governed by the Partnership Ordinance of Hong Kong, and the nature of its role in China's foreign trade network is not entirely clear. The partners, all twelve of whom reside in Hong Kong, are not entitled to protection under the Diplomatic Privileges Ordinance,[22] and probably are not immune from suit in Hong Kong as agents of the government of China, although the authorities in this area of law are not well settled.[23] In the documents it has filed in accordance with the Business Registration Ordinance, the firm does not claim to be in any way an organ of the Chinese government; it merely states that it commenced the business of importing and exporting in December 1948, and gives its principal place of business as the Bank of China Building, Hong Kong. When it does act an agent, *stricto sensu,* for one of the state-trading corporations it is undoubtedly entitled to the same protection as the corporation itself,[24] but when dealing with local Hong Kong traders on its own contractual terms the inference is that it is trading on its own account and is not entitled to immunity from suit.

So far as the other agents are concerned, the partnerships often appear to be formed entirely in Hong Kong, or to be in the nature of joint ventures between people resident in China or people resident in Hong Kong but holding Chinese service passports, on the one hand, and local Hong Kong traders, on the other. Southern Film Corporation (which releases the patriotic films shown at the Ko Shing and Nanyang Theaters) has a partner whose address is the Canton Theater, 428 The Bund, Canton, as well as partners who are residents of Hong Kong. Hua Yuan Co. (which is agent for many of the Chinese light industrial products and is particularly active in registering Chinese trade marks in Hong Kong) has five partners, three of whom hold Passports de Service and two of whom are identified only by Hong Kong identity card numbers, though this is not a clear indication that they are Hong Kong-born Chinese since these cards are issued to British subjects and aliens alike.

---

[22] Chap. 190, of the *Laws of Hong Kong.*

[23] *Krajina* v. *The Tass Agency* [1949] 2 All E.R. 274; *Baccus S.R.L.* v. *Servicio Nacional del Trigo* [1957] 1 Q.B. 438; and see J. K. Wedderburn, "Sovereign Immunity of Foreign Public Corporations," *Int'l. & Comp. L. Q.,* (1957): 290; Clive M. Schmitt-hoff, "The Claim of Sovereign Immunity in the Law of International Trade," *Int'l. & Comp. L. Q.,* (1958): 452.

[24] *Rahimtoola* v. *The Nizam of Hyderabad* [1958] A.C. 359; but note the extent of the corporation's protection is also doubtful; see note 23, *supra.*

E. The PRC-Associated Companies Incorporated in Hong Kong

These PRC-associated companies are involved primarily in the retailing and service industries rather than in manufacturing or heavy industry. The communist product department stores, for example, are well known to almost every Hong Kong tourist, and perhaps to none better than the American. The local PRC-associated newspapers also are conspicuous, as are the PRC-associated banks.

The nature and degree of association between the companies being discussed and the PRC can vary considerably, and it would be a mistake to imagine that they are all controlled in the same way or that they make up a monolithic business structure. In the case of the department stores, some (such as China Products Co. (HK), Ltd.) are very substantially controlled by China; others (such as Yue Hwa Chinese Products Emporium, Ltd.) have apparently far weaker associations; and still others (such as Chung Kiu Chinese Products Emporium, Ltd.) have little visible legal association with China at all. Many of these companies could be described as joint ventures between the PRC and sympathetic overseas Chinese; where this is so, the overseas Chinese often have their roots in Indonesia, Singapore, Malaysia, or Thailand and are not drawn exclusively from Hong Kong.

In many cases the association with the PRC is quite open. For example, a small group of land investment companies formed in 1963 (none of which would be well known by name to the Hong Kong public but including Kiu Kwan Estates, Ltd., Kiu Nam Investment Corporation, Ltd., and Kiu Yip Investment Corporation, Ltd.) has as principal shareholder, Tsa Ping, of 108 Hsi Chiao Ming Hsiang, Peking. From the address Tsa Ping appears to be a government employee. Along a different line the China Products Co. (HK), Ltd., lists some of the shareholders as:

Chiao Kee, Tong Kee, Jong Kee,
Kwok Kee, Yin Kee, Hong Kee,
Hsiang Kee, Kong Kee, Feng Kee

These names are merely parts of the Chinese characters forming the words, Bank of Communications (or) Bank of China, Hong Kong Branch.

In other cases the involvement of the PRC is less apparent or has only recently been made known. Thus, the Chiyu Banking Corporation, Ltd., a small Hong Kong incorporated bank, for a long time showed as principal shareholders the Chip Bee Foundation and the Chip Bee Private Institute, both of which gave as their address an exclusive residential area in Hong Kong. In the annual return filed in July 1968, however, these organizations showed a change of address, and they are now registered as c/o the Bank of China, Hong Kong.

In many ways it is difficult to understand why the PRC's interest is as obscure as it sometimes is. It would be interesting to know why the shares of the Hong Kong companies are normally held in the name of individuals in the PRC whose occupations are given as banker and whose addresses indicate government offices and not in the name of a state corporation. Why, if the PRC wants to act through nominees, have a host of different people been used when one or two would suffice? And why not, in the case of China Products Co. (HK), Ltd., reduce the number of shareholders by amalgamating various small shareholdings, since if this were done the company would not have to be a public company and would not then have to disclose its accounts to public view?

The relationship between the associated companies and the PRC can be described in various ways. The companies under review fall into the following categories:

Shares held by people resident in PRC	44%
Interlocking shareholdings with other associated companies	36%
Officials of the Bank of China, etc., as shareholders or directors	26%
Shares held by local "fat cats"	13%
Shares held c/o the Bank of China, etc.	11%
Miscellaneous	23%

(The total percentage exceeds 100 percent because a number of companies fall under several categories.)

Only five of the companies examined were public companies, the majority being small to medium-sized private companies,[25] with an issued capital of HK $1 million, or less; only eight had issued capitals in excess of HK $5 million. Two-thirds of the companies had ten or fewer shareholders, and of these the majority had five or fewer. The great majority had five or fewer directors, and as there is commonly a share-holding qualification for directors, in most cases the directors were also shareholders.

Twenty percent of the companies associated with the PRC were formed before October 1949 and have a long history of involvement in China trade. Of those formed since 1949 one-third were registered in the years 1960–64, which was a period of considerable expansion of PRC interests in Hong Kong.[26]

---

[25] By section 29 of the Companies Ordinance, a private company must (1) restrict the right to transfer its shares, (2) limit the number of members to fifty, and (3) prohibit invitations to the public to subscribe for its shares or debentures.

[26] These include Chinese Merchandise Emporium, Ltd,, Hua Chiao Commercial Bank, Ltd., Kiu Nam Investment Corporation, Ltd., Po Sang Bank, Ltd., and Wang Tat Enterprises Co., Ltd.

CHART

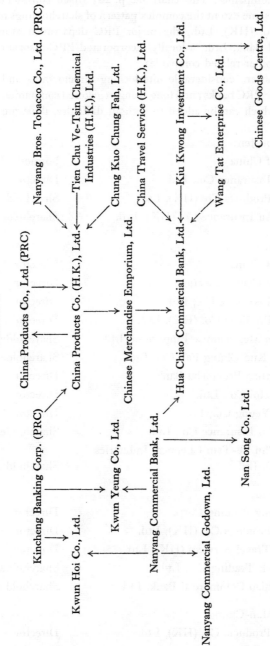

There is often a great deal of interlocking shareholding among PRC-associated companies. The chart on p. 203 (itself considerably simplified) indicates to some extent the complex pattern of shareholdings involving China Products Co. (HK), Ltd., the major PRC department store, Hua Chiao Commercial Bank, Ltd., a locally incorporated PRC-associated bank, and a number of other related companies.

There also are considerable interlocking directorships and shareholdings involving the PRC banks and Hong Kong-registered companies. The following examples, which can be added to without difficulty, illustrate this point:

Chen Shou Jen:

Bank of China	Formerly Manager
China Insurance Co., Ltd.	Director
China Products Co. (HK), Ltd.	Shareholder/director
Ming An Insurance Co. (HK), Ltd.	Shareholder/director

Cheng Mou-huo:

Bank of China	Director
Bank of Communications	Director
China Insurance Co., Ltd.	Director
China Products Co. (HK), Ltd.	Director
Chinese Merchandise Emporium, Ltd.	Shareholder/director
Chung Kuo Chung Fah Co., Ltd.	Shareholder/director
Kwangtung Provincial Bank	Director
Kwun Hoi Co., Ltd.	Director
Kwun Yeung Co., Ltd.	Director
Ming An Insurance Co., Ltd.	Shareholder/director
Tien Chu Ve-Tsin Chemical Industries (HK), Ltd.	Shareholder/director

Chan Pei-lu:

Kincheng Banking Corp.	Director
China Products Co. (HK), Ltd.	Director
China Travel Services (HK), Ltd.	Director
Dah Yeh Trading Co., Ltd.	Shareholder/director
Hua Chiao Commercial Bank, Ltd.	Shareholder/director

Cheong Man-Chung:

China Products Co. (HK), Ltd.	Director
Chinese Goods Centre, Ltd.	Shareholder/director

Cheong Man-Chung *(cont'd.)*:

Chinese Merchandise Emporium, Ltd.	Shareholder
Kwangtung Provincial Bank, Ltd.	Director
Kiu Kwan Investment Corp., Ltd.	Shareholder/director
Kiu Kwong Investment Corp., Ltd.	Shareholder/director
Kiu Nam Investment Corp., Ltd.	Shareholder/director
Kiu Wing Investment Corp., Ltd.	Shareholder/director
Kiu Yip Investment Corp., Ltd.	Shareholder/director
Ming An Insurance Co., Ltd.	Shareholder/director
Nanyang Commercial Bank, Ltd.	Shareholder/director

Chuang Shih-ping:

Hua Chiao Commercial Bank, Ltd.	Shareholder/director
Kiu Kwan Investment Corp., Ltd.	Shareholder/director
Kiu Kwong Investment Corp., Ltd.	Shareholder/director
Kiu Nam Investment Corp., Ltd.	Shareholder/director
Kwangtung Provincial Bank	Director
Kwun Hoi Co., Ltd.	Shareholder/director
Kwun Yeung Co., Ltd.	Shareholder/director
Nan Song Co., Ltd.	Shareholder/director
Nanyang Commercial Bank, Ltd.	Shareholder/director
Nanyang Commercial Godown Co., Ltd.	Shareholder/director
Wei Wen Estates, Ltd.	Shareholder/director

Despite the interlocking relationships it would be misleading to suggest that the PRC-associated companies have identical, or even consciously similar organizational structure or rules of operation.

In hardly any respects do their memoranda and articles of association differ from those of normal private enterprise companies. This in itself means that a large number have clauses which are surprising to find in PRC-associated companies. For example, almost half of them have a clause specifically empowering them: "To carry on business as capitalists, financiers, concession-aires and merchants and to undertake and carry on and execute all kinds of financial, commercial trading and other operations."[27]

It is hard to think why such an emotive word as "capitalist" is used when the same effect could be achieved by using different words. The probable explanation is that the firms of solicitors that were given the task of incorporating these companies merely followed normal Hong Kong precedents and

---

[27] Memorandum of Association of Kiu Nam Investment Corporation, Ltd.

inserted this clause without much thought as to its appropriateness; and the Chinese clients probably accepted the draft without a close reading. (This would not explain, however, the action of Tien Chu Ve-Tsin Chemical Industries (HK), Ltd., 90 percent of whose shares are held in China, which applied to the Supreme Court in 1959 to alter the objects set out in its memorandum to include a clause permitting it to carry on business, *inter alia,* as capitalists.)

One difference between PRC-associated companies and normal private enterprises in Hong Kong is that the former often make provision in their articles for supervisors as well as directors. This institution is unknown to English or Hong Kong company law, and appears to have been borrowed from Chinese models. The following clause is taken from the articles of the China Mutual Trading Co., Ltd.:

Article 100. The duties and powers of a Supervisor are as follows:

a. To examine and audit the accounts of the Company.

b. To investigate the Estimates and Statements of Accounts of the Company.

c. To inspect and ascertain the assets of the Company.

Article 101. A Supervisor in performing his duties and exercising his powers shall sign his name and affix his seal to the account books examined and audited by him and shall also make a report to the Shareholders' General Meeting.

A small but significant number of companies provide in their articles for the division of the profits in fixed proportion among the shareholders, the directors, and the employees.[28] For example, until 1968 the articles of the Tien Chu Ve-Tsin Chemical Industries, Ltd., stated:

Article 49. The profits of the Company in each year shall be applied first in setting aside 10 percent thereof as a reserve fund and secondly in paying a dividend for such year at the rate of 8 percent per annum on the paid up capital of the Company, and such dividend shall be paid next after the amount so set aside as a reserve fund but in priority to any other payments out of such profits.

Article 50. Subject to clause 49 hereof, the balance of the profits of the Company in each year shall be dealt with as follows:

a. In equally distributing 50 percent thereof amongst the shareholders as further dividend in proportion to the capital held by them respectively.

b. In setting aside 3 percent thereof towards the formation of a special reserve fund.

c. In distributing 5 percent thereof to the Directors of the Company to be distributed amongst them in such manner and proportion as the Director or a majority of them may decide.

---

[28] For example, China Products Co. (HK), Ltd., Chung Kiu Chinese Products Emporium, Ltd., Teck Soon Hong, Ltd., and Tien Chu Ve-Tsin Chemical Industries, Ltd. Some, such as Chinese Merchandise Emporium, Ltd., used to have a similar provision but have altered or removed it.

d. In distributing 7 percent thereof to the Managing Directors, General Manager, Factory and Business Managers and the Executive Officers of the Company in such proportion as the Directors may decide.

e. In setting aside 15 percent thereof towards the formation of a Health and Security Fund to be applied in such manner as the Directors may from time to time decide.

f. In setting aside 10 percent thereof as a Labour Welfare Fund to be applied in such manner as the Directors from time to time decide.

g. In distributing 10 percent thereof to the Staff of the Company in such manner and proportion as the Directors may decide.

The existence of such profit-sharing schemes may foster harmonious labor relations and may be in accordance with modern Western thinking, but in this respect the PRC-associated firms are probably leading the way in Hong Kong, rather than following the practice of the normal private enterprise company. It is, moreover, scarcely consistent with the view quoted earlier that "these so-called private corporations are, in Peking's view, agencies of the state and thus part of the state trading system," since there is no suggestion that this is common practice inside China.

Since most of the companies associated with the PRC are private companies, they are not, as pointed out earlier, obligated to file their accounts, and thus little solid information is available on their profitability. Regular Japanese visitors to the Canton Trade Fairs have the impression that the PRC increases the profitability of these Hong Kong firms by selling to them at prices lower than they sell to Japanese or European buyers. It has been reported that in the case of Chinese arts and crafts, which are sold through numerous small traders, profit mark-ups on wholesale prices are limited to from 5 to 10 percent, but prices to the final buyer are between 50 and several hundred percent above the wholesale price.[29]

The degree to which (if at all) these companies remit profits to China is also a matter of some speculation. Of course, where there is direct shareholding in the PRC, or through the Bank of China or one of its nominees, then the PRC will be entitled to a share of the profits when dividends are declared. Furthermore, the PRC-associated companies are members of and make contributions to the Chinese General Chamber of Commerce. On October 1 they also spend money on advertisements in the local left-wing newspapers, and since these often have shareholders in the PRC China stands to benefit.

One of the few companies on which information as to profits is available is China Products Co. (HK), Ltd. Its 1970 accounts are set out in Appendix C. This company is the principal PRC-associated department store, and its accounts probably give a good indication of how many of the smaller stores have fared. Nearly 200,000 out of its 300,000 shares are held by companies or individuals in China, or by bankers at the Bank of China, Bank of Com-

---

[29] *South China Morning Post* (Hong Kong), 5 December 1970.

munications, or other PRC banks. Its articles make provisions for dividing the profits among its shareholders, directors, supervisors, and employees. The accounts show that while the net profit against turnover ratio is small, compared with the issued capital of HK $3 million, the 1970 profits of HK $2.3 million are very satisfactory. Moreover, half of the issued capital is made up of bonus shares issued on the capitalization of profits in 1965. Until 1967 the accounts used to show separate figures for cash at banks of China (HK $39,000) and in Hong Kong (HK $193,000). In 1968 these figures were consolidated, and it is thus no longer possible to see to what extent the PRC benefits by prepayments, loans, or deposits. The company has granted mortgages to the Bank of Communications, secured on its flats and office accommodations, to obtain general banking facilities up to HK $1,540,000. Its 1967 accounts show that as a result of the riots of that year, which led to a boycott of communist merchandise shops,[30] the company showed its first recorded loss of HK $360,000. The accounts for the years before 1968 used to show credits in respect of goods returned to China. In 1967, for example, there were returns of nearly HK $1 million, out of purchases of HK $15 million. It is not clear if these credits represent defective or surplus goods, but it does indicate, contrary to what many businessmen often report, that the PRC will in some circumstances make cash adjustments for returned goods.

III. Two Aspects of Doing Business in Hong Kong

A. Trademarks

China has for some time recognized the importance of trademarks and has made provision for protection of foreign trademarks in China.[31] It has also been active in registering its own trademarks in Hong Kong. From 1953 (when records of countries of first origin were first published) until 1970, 198 such trademarks were registered, including 95 in the years 1958–61.[32] Most were registered in the name of local Hong Kong agents. Only 13 were registered in the name of the China National Cereals, Oils, and Foodstuffs Import and Export Corporation, compared with 105 in the name of Hua Yuan Co., 55 in the name of China Resources Co., and 38 in the name of Ng Fung Hong.

---

[30] See, *e.g.*, *FEER*, 6 July 1967; 16 November 1967.

[31] See "Provisional Arrangements for Foreign Enterprises to Entrust the China Council for the Promotion of International Trade with the Application for the Registration of Trade Marks in China"; G. Crespi Reghizzi, "Legal Aspects of Trade with China: the Italian Experience," *Harv. Int'l L. J.* 9: 85, 131 *et seq.* (Winter, 1968); Hsiao, "Communist China's Foreign Trade Organization," p. 317.

[32] Registrar General, *Annual Departmental Reports* (Hong Kong Government).

The trademarks covered over thirty classes of goods ranging from foodstuffs to vehicles. The main categories were "textiles (piece goods)" with twenty-eight registrations, "paper and paper articles, office requisites" with twenty-one registrations, and "small domestic utensils and containers" with nineteen registrations. Foodstuffs made up the largest number of registrations, but these were broken down under various headings such as "coffee, tea, cocoa, sugar, rice, etc." (fifteen registrations); "meat, fish, poultry and game, meat extracts, etc." (thirteen registrations); "beer, ale, and porter, mineral, and aerated water, etc." (twelve registrations); "wines, spirits, and liquors" (eleven registrations).

Section 9(1) (d) of the Trade Marks Ordinance prevents the registration of geographical names as trademarks because this might interfere with other traders who carry on business in the area designated by the geographical name or who wish to describe the place of manufacture of their goods. In the case of China, however, the Hong Kong government appears to have taken the sensible view that since private enterprise does not exist to any significant extent in the export trade of China, no harm would be done by permitting the registration of such trademarks as the "Pearl River Brand."

During the 1967 disturbances China Resources Co. applied to register a number of trademarks bearing quasi-political slogans. After some consideration the registrar of trade marks decided to permit their registration. For example, Trade Mark No. 660 of 1968 (for cotton and woolen piece goods) consists of a label featuring a mountain range in the background, the Chinese characters and English transliteration "HSIN-AN KIANG," the representations of a reservoir and dam on which appear the Chinese slogan Long Live the General line! Long Live the Great Leap! Long Live the People's Commune! and Raise High the Great Red Flag of Mao Tse-tung's Thoughts and Step Forward Fearlessly![33]

B. Litigation

It is almost axiomatic to say that resort to litigation is contrary to Chinese tradition and that even the use of relatively informal arbitration proceedings is rare.[34] In Hong Kong, however, this axiom has little validity. Firms associated with the PRC have been involved in a considerable volume of litigation, and many cases have been pursued to judgment rather than settled out of court. It is true, of course, that many of the early cases arose out of the change

---

[33] NB: All the Chinese characters and the words *Hsin-An Kiang* were subject to a disclaimer and no trade mark protection was granted in respect of them.

[34] See, e.g., J. A. Cohen, "Chinese Mediation on the Eve of Modernization," *Calif. L. R.* 54 (1966): 120; S. Lubman, "Mao and Mediation," *Calif. L.R.* 55 (1967): 1284.

of governments in 1949, and they were not the normal sort of civil litigation.[35] They involved, for example, claims to possession of Chinese aircraft and ships, or to the delivery of goods destined for China but caught by the United States' embargo. In a number of these cases the PRC did not enter an appearance and was not represented. Indeed, in *Civil Air Transport Incorporated* v. *Central Air Transport Corporation* a special Order in Council was made to give the Hong Kong Supreme Court jurisdiction to hear the action notwithstanding the PRC's failure to appear.[36]

In recent years litigation by the PRC-associated enterprises has run along more normal commercial lines. In the year 1969–70, for example, the Sin Hua Trust, Savings, and Commercial Bank, Ltd., issued five writs, four of which were pursued to judgment for sums varying from HK $55,000 to $5,000. The Nanyang Commercial Bank, Ltd., issued four writs, three of which were pursued to judgment and one settled out of court. The China Insurance Co., Ltd., has taken proceedings to recover insurance premiums and the PRC-associated land investment companies have been to court to obtain possession, arrears of rent, and mesne profits in respect of their land holdings.

As a yardstick for comparing the volume of litigation engaged in by these companies, one may look at the Hong Kong and Shanghai Banking Corp., which is the colony's largest bank by far, and which might be expected to have had a correspondingly larger number of court cases. It will be seen that in both relative and absolute terms this bank is normally involved in less litigation than many of the smaller PRC-incorporated banks.

Why is it, then, that in Hong Kong the PRC does engage in litigation, whereas in its international trade elsewhere it does not? There would seem to be a number of explanations. There is clearly less scope for negotiation or compromise over the refusal to repay an overdraft than there is where the dispute concerns an allegedly defective machine. Customers of the PRC banks are often small businessmen who cannot always supply the necessary security to make litigation unnecessary. Moreover, there are in Hong Kong a number of lawyers with whom the PRC has, over the years, established a relationship, and in whom they place confidence.

Undoubtedly, however, one of the reasons must be that the commercial atmosphere of Hong Kong has encouraged the PRC businesses to develop a more normal commercial attitude to litigation, and to use it as a means of putting pressure on recalcitrant debtors. In *Go Yet Wah* v. *The China State*

---

[35] *Civil Air Transport Inc.* v. *Central Air Transport Corp., HKLR* 35 (1951): 215. *Fisheries Dept., Kwangtung Provincial Government* v. *Fishing Trawler "North Carolina," HKLR* 35 (1951): 72; *Civil Air Transport Inc.* v. *China National Aviation Corporation, HKLR* 36 (1952): 302; *China Mutual Trading Co., Ltd.* v. *American President Lines HKLR* 37 (1953): 38.

[36] *HKLR* 35 (1951): 215; and Supreme Court of Hong Kong (Jurisdiction) Order in Council, 1950.

Bank,[37] for example, the bank had one of its debtors put in prison for nonpayment of a civil debt, and took action to oppose his release before payment of the debt.

Litigation may also be used by PRC firms, not so much to determine an individual case but to test the validity of current practice, and this again would be in keeping with Western commercial attitudes. This was undoubtedly one of the reasons, and possibly the predominant reason, behind *The China State Bank* v. *Leung Lin Yan*.[38] In this case the bank was suing as the holder in due course of a number of checks. The checks in question were drawn by the defendant in favor of the Seng Kee Co., an importing firm with connections in China. In late 1969 the Seng Kee Co. informed the defendant that, as a result of the Cultural Revolution in China, importers of twill in Hong Kong were being allotted a quota, and that in consequence materials might be more difficult to obtain in future. Thereupon the defendant agreed to take up the whole of Seng Kee's quota of 80,000 yards for delivery between June and September 1970. The contracts stipulated that payment was to be effected by postdated checks, which were to be delivered by the defendant to the Seng Kee Co. upon receipt of notice that the goods were packed and ready for shipment from the Chinese manufacturers. When the Seng Kee Co. received the checks from the defendant it endorsed them to the plaintiff bank in order to secure its existing overdraft. Because the Seng Kee Co. was in financial difficulties, the goods never reached Hong Kong and the defendant stopped his checks. The plaintiff bank subsequently commenced action and succeeded as a holder in due course of the endorsed checks, regardless of the fact that the defendant had not received the Chinese goods for which he thought he was paying. The bank quite clearly regarded itself as being in the position of an ordinary lender of money enforcing a security in the normal way. The defendant sought to show that since the bank was part and parcel of the trading system of the PRC, it was in some way associated with what went wrong, and that it should not be entitled to succeed against the defendant, who was himself clearly an injured party so far as the Seng Kee Co., a customer of the bank, was concerned. If the bank had not resisted successfully this line of argument and established its commercial independence, this would have had fundamental repercussions for the PRC-associated banks in Hong Kong.

IV. Conclusion

As this paper shows, the PRC's investments in Hong Kong extend far beyond a few banks and department stores, although they do not appear to be

---

[37] *HKLR* 42 (1958): 45.

[38] An unreported decision; Original Jurisdiction Action No. 1983 of 1970, in the Supreme Court of Hong Kong.

greatly involved in the manufacturing capacity of Hong Kong. The control exercised by the PRC over its vast and wide-ranging business interests in Hong Kong is neither total nor uniform; there is considerable flexibility in the form of association which is acceptable to the PRC. Indeed, the surprising thing is that there is not greater or more direct control over some firms than there appears to be. I have described the businesses, in appropriate cases, as joint ventures because there are numerous instances where private (though no doubt sympathetic) overseas Chinese provide part of the capital and much of the local expertise. In return these individuals share in the profits, possibly by way of dividends or in accordance with a profit-sharing scheme laid down in the articles of association.

Placed in a private enterprise and common law environment the PRC-associated companies, especially those incorporated in Hong Kong, find little difficulty in operating within the system, though a pragmatic Hong Kong government also assists by avoiding head-on clashes. As regards the use of the law to protect and promote their business interests, it seems clear from what has been said about trademarks and litigation that this is not an area in which the PRC businesses lack experience or know-how.

Appendix

APPEN

CHINA PRODUCTS COM

Balance Sheet as of

1969   *H.K. Currency*

Capital and Surplus

Share Capital
Authorised:
500,000 shares of $10.00 each   . $5,000,000.00
Issued:
300,000 shares of $10.00 each fully

$ 3,000,000	paid	$3,000,000.00
1,000,000	Development Fund	3,000,000.00
968,304	General Reserve	1,205,303.95
1,065,203	Special Reserve	1,065,203.09
302,002	Unappropriated Profit	19,190.88
6,335,509		8,289,697.92

Current Liabilities and Provision

1,388,954	Bank Overdrafts (Secured) . . .	$3,749,900.65	
3,311,329	Sundry Creditors (as per Schedule No. 3)	2,711,123.69	
264,533	Bills Payable	713,306.42	
9,305	Gifts Coupons	10,225,20	
319,622	Accrued Expenses	444,728.05	
297,000	Provision for Corporation Profits Tax 1971/72	332,000.00	
52,257	Dividend Payable	70,674.04	
360,000	Proposed Dividend	360,00.000	
296,686	Staff Welfare Fund	309,428.56	8,701,386.61

NOTE: There are contingent liabilities
amounting to $108,000.00 ap-
proximately in respect of letters
of credit established.

$12,635,195 $16,991,084.53

DIX A

PANY (H.K.) LIMITED

31ST DECEMBER 1970

1969			H.K. *Currency*
	FIXED ASSETS; at cost less depreciation		
$ 2,022,957	(as per Schedule No. 1)		$1,836,486.02
	UNQUOTED SHARE INVESTMENTS, at cost		
2,196,754	(as per Schedule No. 2)		2,196,753.71
	CURRENT ASSETS		
	Stock, at the lower of cost and net realisable value as certified by the		
7,814,931	Manager	$11,847,325.12	
87,953	Unused Supplies	66,626.77	
81,579	Utility and Sundry Deposits . .	97,135.90	
188,712	Sundry Debtors	613,008.98	
3,386	Post-dated Cheques	6,290.95	
34,269	Prepayments	54,412.34	
204,654	Cash at Banks and in Hand . .	273,044.74	12,957,844.80

$12,635,195 $16,991,084.53

APPEN

CHINA PRODUCTS COM

TRADING AND PROFIT AND LOSS ACCOUNTS

1969			*H.K. Currency*
$ 7,677,489	Opening Stock	$ 7,814,930.65	
21,047,739	*Add :* Purchases . . .	27,383,386.24	$35,198,316.89
	Inward Expenses:		
63,510	Landing and Loading Charges . $	61,417.29	
20,496	Bank Charges	24,023.67	85,440.96
$28,809,234			$35,283,757.85
(7,814,931)	*Less :* Closing Stock		11,847,325.12
20,994,303	Cost of goods sold		23,436,432.73
6,517,082	Cross Profit carried down		7,584,116.18
$27,511,385			$31,020,548.91

ESTABLISHMENT EXPENSES

$ 585,463	Rent, Rates and Property Tax . $	633,795.41		
213,252	Light and Water	195,989.09		
59,408	Cleaning	62,427.10		
66,494	Repairs and Replacement . .	175,756.25		
	Depreciation:			
127,962	Land and Buildings $130,302.39			
260,954	Equipment, Furniture, Fixtures and Fittings 154,686.85			
58,022	Air Conditioners 21,936.08	306,925.32	$ 1,374,893.17	

ADMINISTRATION AND SELLING EXPENSES

21,000	Directors' Fees and Bonus . . $	21,000.00	
2,256,737	Salaries, Wages and Allowances .	2,813,664.30	
413,377	Provisions	508,809.50	
101,174	Staff Welfare Expenses . . .	116,982.30	
23,649	Delivery Charges	37,812.57	
150,515	Packing Expenses	176,549.50	
20,328	Prizes and Samples	1,068.08	
73,558	Advertisements	104,818.78	
$ 4,431,893	Carried forward . . $	3,780,700.03	$ 1,374,893.17

DIX B

PANY (H.K.) LIMITED

<small>FOR THE YEAR ENDED 31ST DECEMBER 1970</small>

	1969							*H.K. Currency*
		Sales	.	.	.	.	.	$31,089,311.18
		Less : Returns	.	.	.	.		61,544.72
								31,026,766.46
$27,511,385		*Less :* Discounts	.	.	.	.		6,217.55 $31,020,548.91

$27,511,385		$31,020,548.91

$ 6,517,082	Gross Profit on Sales, brought down	$ 7,584,116.18
—	Interest Received	2,376.48
423,000	Dividend Received on Investments	249,000.00
22,500	Sundry Income	8,315.01
3,200	Profit on Sale of Equipment, Furniture, Air Conditioners and Motor Vehicle	930.00
—	Profit on Sale of Land and Building . . .	397,232.50

$ 6,965,782	Carried forward . . .	$ 8,241,970.17

APPEN

CHINA PRODU

TRADING AND PROFITS AND LOSS ACCOUNTS

1969			*H.K. Currency*
$4,431,893	Brought forward	$3,780,700.03	$1,374,893.17
	Administration and Selling Expenses (Continued)		
2,631	Storage	10,777.15	
21,515	Insurance	26,830.32	
3,066	Commissions Paid	382.25	
9,868	Shortage and Spoilage	9,998.25	
9,853	Telephone, Postage and Telegrams	11,005.85	
1,611	Revenue Stamps	2,358.05	
37,577	Printing and Stationery . . .	32,178.82	
1,012	Newspapers and Periodicals . .	1,324.55	
8,277	Licences and Business Registration Fee .	8,458.00	
28,996	Travelling and Transportation .	40,121.04	
3,388	Uniforms	16,375.28	
303,415	Interest Paid	229,981.19	
20,031	Entertainment	18,978.35	
550	Legal Fees	1,075.00	
7,000	Audit Fee	7,000.00	
—	Loss on Furniture and Fixtures written off	1,033.40	
6,202	Sundry Expenses	7,659.05	
15,930	Depreciation of Motor Vehicles . .	15,920.40	4,222,156.93
297,000	Provision for Corporation Profits Tax 1971/72 .		332,000.00
1,755,967	Balance, being Net Profit for the year carried down		2,312,920.07
$6,965,782			$8,241,970.17
$ 175,597	Amount transferred to General Reserve . .		$ 237,000.00
1,000,000	Amount transferred to Development Fund . .		2,000,000.00
360,000	Proposed Dividend on 300,000 shares at $1.20 per share		360,000.00
302,002	Unappreciated Profit		19,190.88
$1,837,599			$2,616,190.88

DIX C

CTS COMPANY

FOR THE YEAR ENDED 31ST DECEMBER 1970

1969		*H.K. Currency*
$6,965,782	Brought forward	$8,241,970.17

$6,965,782			$8,241,970.17
$80,605	Balance at 1st January 1970 . . .	$302,001.81	
1,027	*Add:* Over-provision of Corporation Profits Tax 1970/71 written back	1,269.00	$303,270.81
1,755,967	Net Profit for the year ended 31st December 1970 brought down .		2,312,920.07
$1,837,599			$2,616,190.88

Trade with the United States

STANLEY LUBMAN

The efforts of China and the United States to develop a new political relationship have brought about a renewal of trade between the two Pacific giants, which has grown dramatically since late 1971. That relationship has imparted some special characteristics to the legal and practical business aspects of the two countries' trade. At the same time significant new trends have appeared in China's approach to international trade. However, institutions and practices that American businessmen encounter in China also have to be seen in the long-range perspective of China's trade with other economically developed nations. While relations with the United States were suspended for over twenty years, China traded elsewhere, establishing patterns that Americans have just begun to discover and that they must not ignore. This paper examines the early experience of Americans doing business in 1972–73 in light of both past Chinese practices and current developments.

I. RAPPROCHEMENT AND THE AMERICAN BUSINESSMAN'S RUSH TO CHINA

Before President Nixon's visit to Peking in February 1972, no American businessman traveling under an American passport had attended the Canton Fair or otherwise visited China to transact business since 1950. The Shanghai communique issued at the close of the Nixon visit announced the two countries'

NOTE: The author has used as the basis for writing this chapter interviews with knowledgeable businessmen, bankers, and diplomats in Hong Kong, Japan, Canada, France, England, and Germany at various times in 1969–72, and personal experience and observations during negotiations on behalf of clients and discussions of US-China trade generally with Chinese officials at the Canton Fair, Peking, and Shanghai in October–November 1972 and April–May 1973.

agreement to "facilitate the progressive development of trade on a basis of equality and mutual benefit."[1] Much of the American regulatory apparatus forbidding or restricting trade with China had already been dismantled before the Shanghai communique. By the time of the Nixon visit United States passports were no longer being issued under restriction forbidding their bearers to travel to China; currency controls had been relaxed to permit dollars to be used in business transactions with China; vessels carrying cargo to and from China were again permitted to refuel at American-owned facilities; prohibitions had been removed on shipping United States-made components of nonstrategic foreign-manufactured goods to China; the embargo had been lifted to the extent that many nonstrategic United States products could be exported to China and virtually all Chinese products could be imported into the United States.

Additional significant changes in policy were announced just before the President's visit to Peking. Among them were the ending of the requirement of a Treasury license for the export of nonstrategic goods and technical data to China by United States-controlled firms in COCOM countries, and placing China on the same basis as the Soviet Union for export control purposes. The partial relaxation allowed some trade to begin in 1971.[2]

Thus, by the time the President had set foot in Peking he had removed many American-created impediments to renewing trade with China. The visit brought about American acceptance of essential Chinese postures on Taiwan and an American commitment to withdraw American forces from that island. With the semblance of agreement reached on the thorniest problem in United States-China relations, China was soon to demonstrate publicly that direct trade was again possible.

Almost immediately after the President left China, Assistant Secretary of State Marshall Green predicted that American companies would be represented at the Spring 1972 Canton Fair.[3] Altogether, approximately thirty to forty firms were invited to the fair, and about forty Americans attended. At about the same time COCOM approved the $3.2 million sale by RCA of a satellite ground station which had been set up in Shanghai for the Nixon visit.

---

[1] Text of communique, *New York Times*, 28 February 1972.

[2] The United States Department of Commerce states that approximately five million dollars worth of goods of Chinese origin were imported into the United States in 1971. United States Department of Commerce, Domestic and International Business Administration, "Trading with the People's Republic of China" (Overseas Business Reports 73–16, May 1973), p. 2. No figures are available for the indirect export of American goods to China before the embargo was lifted, but Monsanto, General Motors, and American Optical are among American corporations known to have made sales. "The China Trade: U.S. Concerns Export Mainland-Bound Goods as Embargo Loosens," *Wall Street Journal*, 11 March 1971.

[3] "U.S. Foresees Americans at Next China Trade Fair," *New York Times*, 1 March 1972.

The American contingent at the Spring 1972 Canton Fair was heavily weighted in favor of importers. Several large department stores were represented, but most of the importers were small and some were trading companies newly established specifically to engage in China trade.[4] A number of organizations responsible for promoting trade were also represented, such as the Chicago Board of Trade, the San Francisco Chamber of Commerce, and the California Council for International Trade. The Commerce Department estimated that approximately five million dollars worth of orders were placed for Chinese goods, which were chiefly metals and minerals, agricultural raw materials, light manufactures, chemicals, and canned and frozen foodstuffs.[5] No American sales were reported at the fair.

Sales to China soon appeared, however. The most dramatic event of the first full year of United States-China trade was Boeing's sale of ten 707 jet airliners to China for $150 million, which was announced in September 1972.[6] This sale was followed in the same month by the first of a series of Chinese purchases of American agricultural products, which were not, however, sold directly by American entities but by third-country dealers. The Louis Dreyfus Corporation of Paris made the first wheat sale, of 800,000 metric tons.[7] Three hundred thousand metric tons of soft "noodle wheat" were purchased through a Japanese trading company later in the year,[8] as were 300,000 tons of corn.[9] Another sale of 970,000 bushels of wheat, again through Louis Dreyfus, was also reported.[10]

In the meantime Chinese exports to the United States were also growing slowly. To the Autumn 1972 Canton Fair came a larger number of Americans, perhaps a hundred in all, mostly to buy.[11] Once again, relatively small importers and specialized China trade firms were represented, but so too were a greater number of large American importers. In addition, a number of larger American corporations that wanted to sell to China were also represented.

---

[4] "Canton Trade Fair is Spurring Enthusiasm," *New York Times,* 6 May 1972.

[5] United States Department of Commerce, note 2, *supra,* p. 8.

[6] "China Purchasing 10 Boeing Liners for $150 Million," *New York Times,* 11 September 1972. See also "China Seems to Eye Global Tourist Traffic with Its Purchase of 10 Boeing Transports," *Wall Street Journal,* 13 September 1972, and "Boeing Expects 6 Million from Chinese in a Week," *New York Times,* 13 September 1972.

[7] "Peking's Purchase of American Wheat is Confirmed by Louis Dreyfus Corp," *New York Times,* 19 September 1972.

[8] "Chinese Purchase Scarce U.S. Wheat to Produce Noodles," *New York Times,* 25 October 1972.

[9] "China Buys Corn on U.S. Market," *New York Times,* 28 October 1972.

[10] "Chinese are Buying More U.S. Wheat," *New York Times,* 2 November 1972.

[11] The total includes spouses and journalists; the Department of Commerce estimates that approximately seventy-six American firms were represented at the fair, United States Department of Commerce, note 2, *supra,* p. 7.

Contracts for twenty million dollars worth of Chinese imports were signed, and for the first time contracts for American sales to China were also signed at the fair, in the value of nine million dollars.[12]

The first full calendar year of resumed United States-China trade was thus an active one. It exceeded most expectations and presaged even more business thereafter. The over-all value of American exports to China in 1972 was sixty million dollars, while thirty-two million dollars of Chinese imports entered the United States. Early in 1973 Assistant Secretary of State Green estimated that the over-all value of bilateral trade in that year would be between three and four hundred million dollars.[13]

By the middle of the year his prediction seemed too conservative. An eighty million dollar cotton purchase (like the wheat deals, arranged through Louis Dreyfus) was announced.[14] State Department officials predicted that this was only one of a series of Chinese purchases of agricultural products which might reach a total value of two hundred million dollars in 1973.[15] In heavy industry a direct licensing agreement involving a process for the manufacture of acrylonitrile was signed between the Chinese and an American oil company in the value of eight million dollars,[16] and the first complete plant sale from the United States was announced by a company which for seventy million dollars would design, engineer, and supply materials and equipment for three ammonia plants.[17] It appeared likely that over-all trade volume in 1973 would probably be close to one billion dollars. With the news of these transactions and of visits to Peking by representatives of numerous American corporations,[18] it seemed that China trade was fast becoming big business in the United States.

Some of the small trading companies that had gotten to China first have been overshadowed by these developments. As noted above, among the most visible American participants at the first Canton Fairs attended by Americans were smaller importers and firms set up specially to enter the China trade. Also, the first year of United States-China trade was characterized by considerable hucksterism, publicity-seeking, and a few downright frauds as individual entrepreneurs tried to get on the road to Peking before large corporations began

---

[12] *Ibid.*, p. 8.

[13] *China Trade Report,* 11, no. 3 (March 1973), p. 9.

[14] "China is Reported to Be Buying U.S. Cotton Worth $80 Million," *New York Times,* 31 January 1973.

[15] "200-million in Grain Sale to China Seen," *New York Times,* 19 May 1973.

[16] "Sohio, Mainland China Set Royalty Agreement," *Wall Street Journal,* 7 May 1973.

[17] "U.S. Concern in China Deal," *New York Times,* 6 July 1973.

[18] Among the American oil companies and oil field equipment manufacturers known to have had representatives at the Spring 1973 Canton Fair, for instance, were EXXON, the Continental Oil Company, the Chevron Chemical Company (a subsidiary of Standard Oil of California), and Baker Oil Tool.

to move. Persons with no previous knowledge of Chinese affairs suddenly set themselves up as China trade specialists and consultants both in the United States[19] and in Hong Kong.[20] In addition, the American businessmen who did get to China understandably sought to make the most of their accomplishments upon their return. For example, one trader asserted that he had been authorized to act as the Chinese "liaison man with the American chemical industry."[21]

While the Chinese have sold some of their products to such firms, they also have given some indications that they prefer to purchase directly from American manufacturers rather than through trader intermediaries. Thus when American companies have tried to sell equipment through American traders or third-country intermediaries such as Japanese licensees or partners, the Chinese have sometimes tried to seek alternative routes so that they could deal directly with the seller. The Chinese have been inviting representatives of larger corporations to China to engage in direct negotiations rather than using the services of newly established China traders who want to sell as well as buy. In conversations at the Canton Fair, Chinese trade officials have indicated that on occasion they have been given false or misleading information by Americans. It appears that the difficulty in collecting reliable information on the vast American economy and the Chinese desire to deal with America's largest corporations have prompted them to welcome the establishment of a new American-China trade promotion group whose board of directors represented America's largest corporations and banks, although Chinese trade officials also continue to request other organizations and individuals for information.[22] By mid-1973 it appeared that a new stage was beginning in United States-China trade, at least so far as the participants were concerned, and the share of American exports to China which was to be sold via intermediaries was clearly very limited.[23]

---

[19] "Instant Authority: The China Trade Lags, but Consultants Hawk Expertise to Hopefuls," *Wall Street Journal*, 24 February 1972.

[20] "China Trade Experts Exploit U.S. Firms," *South China Morning Post*, 20 March 1972; for an exposé of one organization see "How clear is the 'Chinese Connection'?" *Newsday*, 31 August 1972.

[21] "Model for Acupuncture," *New York Times*, 18 June 1972.

[22] Thus the first meeting of the National Council on United States-China Trade in Washington on 31 May 1972 was greeted by a senior official in the newly established Chinese Liaison Office, whose speech, apparently not quoted in the media but heard by this writer as a participant, clearly indicated that the Chinese regarded the new group as potentially very significant in promoting United States-China trade.

[23] Obviously when the Chinese have no choice—as when a trading company or sales representative is the exclusive agent of the manufacturer of a product that China needs—they will buy even though an intermediary participates in the transaction. Some American companies are being represented by reputable European firms. See, e.g., "Why U.S. Companies Chose East Asiatic as Their China Agent," *South China*

Changes were also apparent in the channels through which commercial information flowed and contacts made. Until the liaison offices were established in Peking and Washington, the principal point of commercial contact with China for Americans was the Commercial Office in the Chinese Embassy in Ottawa. The office was overwhelmed by an enormous volume of letters and visits from American businessmen. Moreover, it did not seem equipped to operate a full-fledged effort to collect commercial information on the United States and on the American firms and individuals who beseiged the office seeking invitations to China.

It might be noted that these difficulties were apparently typical of the problems encountered everywhere by the Chinese foreign trade apparatus in collecting and in assessing information on the American economy. Members of the Chinese Commercial Office in Ottawa quizzed American visitors about many details of American commercial law and the structure and operation of American economic institutions. Often the same questions were repeated by Chinese trade representatives in Hong Kong, Canton, and Peking. Some difficulties have been created because, as indicated above, the Chinese were misinformed by some Americans to whom they had previously spoken. At any rate, the establishment of a Chinese commercial office in the Chinese Liaison Office in Washington will be a convenience for Americans and a benefit to the Chinese, who will now have additional facilities for gathering commercial information on the United States. Also, Chinese scientific and technical groups have visited American companies, and trade promotion missions seem likely in the near future.

II. Patterns in American Purchases from China

A. Some characteristic aspects of negotiation

Like those who have done business with the People's Republic before them, the American newcomers have had to undergo the rituals of the semiannual Canton Fair, at which most of China's export transactions and some routine import transactions are consummated. Many of the Americans have been surprised at the differences between conducting business there and in other

---

Morning Post, 24 March 1972. Other companies have looked to Japan, perhaps erroneously. Many of the trading companies which make up the Sino-Japanese "friendly firm" trade were very small, or were simply extensions of manufacturers rather than genuinely independent entities, Henderson and Matsuo, pp. oo, oo. After the Spring 1973 Canton Trade Fair this author was informed by a Japanese diplomat that in the wake of the establishment of normal Sino-Japanese relations the Chinese had noticeably cooled in their dealings with the "friendly firms" and were ending the preferential treatment that had long been accorded them for political reasons.

countries. Perhaps the most vivid description of what Americans have found is in one observer's account of the Spring 1971 Fair:

[T]he bored businessmen, compelled to loiter long hours in bleak corridors awaiting appointments with the Chinese, revert to a way of life reminiscent of boarding school or the army. Despite their reluctance to talk about business, they cling to their compatriots with boozy camaraderie in the bar of their hotel, the Tung Fang (The East). The bar closes very firmly at midnight, however, and looking for nightlife in Canton is something of a sick joke.

The Chinese, who use the fair as a prime source of commercial intelligence, do little to lift the businessmen from their slough of infantilism. The morning ritual when the fair opens at 8:00 each day presents a comic sight. The businessmen gather behind a tape stretched across the fair entrance. They pace and paw the ground as a little girl cadre carefully rolls up the tape. Then there is a breathless silence until suddenly the "East is Red" blares from the loudspeakers. This is the signal for dignified captains of commerce to rush pell-mell for the lifts in a race to be first to make an appointment with the Chinese corporations.

It is a depressing experience to be crammed into a Canton hotel lift with raucous, yelling businessmen-turned-schoolboys. Their boisterous, often impolite behavior must horrify the Chinese who, when all is said and done, are usually a quiet and dignified people. Their prejudices against the crude and hairy foreigners may be confirmed during the twice-yearly Canton fair interlude. There is a case for putting every Canton trader through a crash course in modern China and the Chinese psychology. Such courses would represent a valuable long-term investment to the firms attending the Canton Fair.[24]

Alien though Canton may be to Americans, they uniformly seem to have found their Chinese hosts friendly and hospitable. In their discussions with Americans Chinese trade personnel make plain their pleasure at the resumption of commercial relations with the United States. At the same time, Chinese warmth is by no means reserved for the Americans. European veterans of the China trade have stated that the atmosphere of the most recent fairs has been noticeably more friendly than any time since before the Cultural Revolution.

Regardless of the quality of Chinese hospitality, Americans discovered that the Chinese negotiators were tough bargainers who transacted business with them in certain characteristic ways that had long marked negotiations with the West Europeans.

The Chinese practice of collecting market and technical information from their customers, for instance, has long been known to the European veterans of the trade. Buyers of Chinese products often find that they are expected to provide more assistance to their sellers than is customary. Thus, a buyer of tung oil or cassia bark from the China National Native Produce and Animal By-Product Corporation would be expected to supply negotiators from that agency with current quotations on the commodity in the major markets at

---

[24] Ilsa Sharp, "No Carnival in Canton," *Far Eastern Economic Review*, 29 May 1971, pp. 6–8.

TRADE WITH THE UNITED STATES

227

which it was sold. Americans were treated the same way. They also found, like the Europeans before them, that they were expected to inform the Chinese of how they planned to distribute the goods they bought.[25]

In addition, the Americans, coming from a huge nation so long isolated from China, found that the Chinese had much more to ask them than most other businessmen. Americans were asked to discuss numerous aspects of the structure of the American economy, particularly banking and tariffs. The Chinese have commonly collected information by asking the same questions to many businessmen, determining the accuracy and reliability of the information by comparing the responses. They have unquestionably come to regard some Americans as more "sincere" than others and favored them by asking them more questions and occasionally directing bits of commercially useful information back in return. The American so favored, however, would be wrong to assume that he was the only person commissioned to gather information in a particular area of inquiry.

The probes conducted by the Chinese negotiators probably have another purpose besides collecting information. The Chinese are also trying to gauge the "sincerity" of the new American participants. European traders have found that the manner in which substantive commercial issues between them and the Chinese are settled is affected by the quality of the parties' over-all past relationship, as will be discussed below in connection with dispute settlement. But lacking a previous relationship with American companies, the Chinese state trading corporations now have to choose how and with whom to establish new relationships. The manner and thoroughness with which an American responds to Chinese queries probably contributes appreciably to Chinese estimates of his reliability.

As useful as this questioning may be to the Chinese, it does retard the pace of negotiations, which many Americans have found to be too slow for their taste. It may be noted parenthetically that most of the Americans whom the author has encountered in Canton had not known what to expect, and some had been downright misinformed. One China specialist had written in late 1971, for instance, that foreign businessmen in China are "insulted, harangued, kicked, but they just blink and take it. You're not going to have that with American businessmen. They have much shorter fuses."[26] The "harangues"

---

[25] In the past the Chinese have used such inquiries in aid of efforts to study Western processing of Chinese raw materials or semifinished products. Over the years these efforts have helped them learn to process products that in the past their Western purchasers had processed and sold in finished form. This has been true particularly with respect to leather; the Chinese have progressed gradually from exporting untreated skins to treating the skins themselves and then manufacturing wallets, suitcases, and other small leather products.

[26] Professor Lucian Pye of M.I.T., quoted in "The China Trade: U.S. Concerns Export Mainland-Bound Goods as Embargo Loosens," note 2, *supra*. Unpleasant

and insults of the Cultural Revolution days are over, but the need to accept slow negotiations is not—and most American businessmen in China have had to adjust to Chinese ways, just like other businessmen before them.

Mr. Stanley Marcus, representing Dallas' Nieman-Marcus department store, wrote after the Spring 1972 Canton Fair that he "found out very quickly that one does not take the direct Western approach of pricing merchandise and inquiring about deliveries."[27] First a preliminary meeting had to be held at which an appointment for a conference would be made; the conference would be held "before the buyer even knew whether he wants the merchandise or can get satisfactory delivery." In Marcus' experience the conferences were attended by a large number of Chinese, and "it took the full team's cooperation to provide prices, delivery dates, minimum quantities and shipping specifications." Negotiations attended by this author have not been so heavily attended; perhaps the number of Chinese negotiators encountered by Marcus was large out of respect to his position as his store's chief executive officer.

In addition to the slow pace of negotiations, Americans discovered other characteristics of Chinese sales methods which surprised them. The same department store executive quoted above also states:

> Probably the most frustrating experience I had was the difficulty encountered in meeting their minimum requirements. Not only are minimum quantities by style postulated, but after these are met you must buy enough to fill up their packing cases, the size of which is apparently predetermined. It was only after much persuasion and an indication of willingness to pay extra for a smaller case that certain orders were accepted. The rigid adherence to minimum requirements obviously eliminated consideration of any sample orders—and, by extension, indicated that at the present time China is no market for the small quantity buyer.[28]

This last described difficulty, which is well known, illustrates the kind of rigidity which Americans encountered when they first went to China, but to which Europeans had long ago grown accustomed. Americans also sometimes encountered problems not when their orders were too small, but when they were too large. Several representatives of potentially large American buyers have left Canton having bought little (by their lights) or nothing after discovering that the Chinese output of products they wanted was too small for the Chinese to be able to sell them the quantities they desired. The inadequacy of supply may prove to be one of the key difficulties in American purchases of Chinese goods.

---

treatment of businessmen, which had occurred during the Cultural Revolution, had long since ceased by 1971, when Professor Pye made his statement. See the chapter by Jerome A. Cohen in this volume.

[27] "Marcus Polo at China Trade Fair; Adventures of a Dallas Executive in Canton," *New York Times*, 4 June 1972.

[28] *Ibid.*

The limited quantities of Chinese products available for export, together with the increasing number of invitations which the Chinese have extended to foreign buyers, have combined to make the Canton Fair a gigantic exercise in the allocation of Chinese exports. Americans are often told that because the Chinese have many "old friends," European customers to whom they have been selling for many years, the Americans must realize that quantities available for the United States are limited. Yet those same "old friends" have often been simultaneously told that they cannot have the quantities *they* desire (and, indeed, have in some cases been accustomed to purchasing for years) because some must be sold to China's "new friends." The result seems to be that most purchasers come away from the fair having bought less than they wanted. Some buyers spend an entire month at each fair in the hope of increasing their purchases; the need for such patience is discouraging to American businessmen accustomed to a faster pace of doing business. The relatively long duration of the stay in Canton necessary to bring about substantial business, and the consequent possible loss of other opportunities elsewhere, also add cost of buying from China.

The difficulties of doing business with China are lessened by some recent indications of Chinese willingness to accomodate to the demands of the Western consumer market. For example, in the past Western European buyers of Chinese manufactures have had much reason to be discouraged by Chinese unwillingness to style, package, and label Chinese exports with their particular markets in mind. Western merchandising techniques emphasize brand names and distinctive packaging and labeling to capture the customer's attention, but Chinese sellers have hitherto not been very sensitive to those tactics. The average English or American shopper, for instance, is not likely to be arrested by the "Mount Elephant" brand on cans of chicken or duck.

West Europeans have only with difficulty obtained Chinese agreement to change design, packaging, and labeling. The Chinese have been cautious about abandoning customary practices, and sometimes they have also had good reason to regret making adjustments to Western markets. In furs and textiles they have found that Western fashions had changed by the time they had gotten around to adapting, as they thought, to Western tastes. During the Cultural Revolution ideology also played a role; accomodations to Western markets, criticized within China as too bourgeois, ceased for a time.

However, recent years have seen renewed Chinese willingness to make concessions in order to sell more Chinese products abroad. Large buyers of Chinese canned goods, especially those of which the Chinese happened to have a surplus, found the Chinese willing to consult on the design of labels and even agreeable to letting buyers print labels abroad and then send them to China to be affixed in the cannery. For a time after the Cultural Revolution buyers found conflicting trends in Chinese attitudes. Even though Chinese trade negotiators were sometimes willing to cooperate with buyers along the lines indicated above, some Westerners were also told by negotiators (some-times with apparent genuine regret) that revolutionary committees at Chinese enterprises were unwilling to affix Western customer-designed labels to garments or canned goods.

The Americans came along at a time when China's leadership had decided to strongly emphasize foreign trade as an adjunct to Chinese domestic develop-ment efforts. In years past the Maoist emphasis on Chinese self-reliance combined with China's limited capacity to produce for export limited China's foreign trade. Beginning in 1971–72, however, the Chinese evidenced a new interest in importing capital goods and technology, which is discussed more fully below. At the same time, they have increased their efforts to enlarge their export markets.

Consequently, Americans at the Canton Fair have found Chinese negotiators particularly interested in learning about what might sell best on the new American market. Chinese negotiators have expressed willingness to copy samples of various types of light industrial and textile products submitted to them by Americans, although they are not presently able to provide the iron-clad guarantees of exclusivity which the Americans usually also want.

To some extent, this new tendency to accommodate to the needs of Western customers is a general phenomenon, but it is also partly a response to the potential profitability which the Chinese see in the American market, particu-larly in the politically sunny atmosphere of 1972–73. Aware of the new American interest in China and the genuine rapprochement that has dramati-cally taken shape within so short a time, Chinese trade negotiators have sometimes been optimistic, occasionally unrealistically so, about the prospects for Chinese sales. For the most part they seem unable to grasp how faddish is much of American interest in China. The fickleness of American consumer tastes and trends is also difficult to understand. For instance, several conver-sations, in Ottawa as well as in China, have made clear the expectation of some Chinese trade officials that sales of Chinese garments to the United States would continue to rise after "Mao-suits," as they were dubbed in the United States, first made their appearance in American clothing-stores to be purchased by Americans who wanted to be chic. But even as such predictions were being made, the garments themselves were disappearing from the racks, not to be reordered in quantity—if at all.

It is too early to predict the size of the American market for Chinese goods. Some importers find the Chinese inflexible and too expensive to deal with. Each fair has seen at least several Americans leave Canton unhappy because the Chinese did not have goods available in desired quantities or because the Chinese seemed slow and hesitant to redesign their products. Long accustomed to dealing with accommodating manufacturers elsewhere in Asia, who are eager to cooperate with American importers, these persons have been too impatient to wait for the Chinese to make the changes or adaptations desired. Some will probably turn to other markets, while others have reduced their investment in China trade and have looked to other sources even while continuing to keep an eye on China.

There are other difficulties. Companies attending one Canton Fair cannot know if they will be reinvited (unless they place a very large order), and so are not assured of continuity in business relations. Because the number of invitations is still limited retailers are severely hampered, since they are unable to bring the large number of specialized buyers on whom they usually rely. Wholesalers, however, are limited in their purchases because the Chinese do not ordinarily distinguish between wholesalers and retailers, so that all must buy at identical prices. Yet the prices are so high that wholesalers have difficulty in making their customary mark-up when selling to retailers.

The speed with which the new Chinese interest in exports will be reflected in actual accommodations to the American market is difficult to predict. Assuming that the policy remains constant—always a difficult assumption—it will probably not be until late 1973 or mid-1974 that Chinese goods designed specifically for the American market will begin to appear on that market. Quite apart from having to decide which American customer's recommendations and needs to heed, the Chinese have to make adjustments in their production process. At the moment of writing little movement appears to have been made in rectifying some of the other difficulties mentioned above. Present evidence suggests no decisive Chinese response to the needs of the American market, but rather a series of tentative accommodations cautiously reached.

B. Contract terms

Experienced European traders have long been familiar with the fact that Chinese sales contracts are usually brief documents which do not spell out Chinese obligations in detail. Over the years the Chinese had evolved their standard sales documentation, centering on the standard sales confirmation and the standard sales contract. The standard sales confirmation is a one-page document which summarizes information on the commodity, quality, quantity, unit price, total value, packing, and terms relating to shipping, insurance, and payment. Some versions also contain a clause providing for inspection of the goods by the Chinese Commodities Inspection Bureau.[29] The standard sales contract is identical, except for a boilerplate clause requiring the shipper to notify the buyer by cable after a shipment is made, and clauses on *force majeure* and dispute settlement which are discussed below.[30]

The terms of American contracts seem generally to be identical with the standard terms used in contracts signed with Europeans, but there have been

---

[29] The document is also described in Mohr, "Trade with Denmark."
[30] *Ibid.*

some variations. Most contracts signed with Western Europe have been on CIF terms, but from the beginning of their renewed trade with the United States the Chinese corporations have signed C and F contracts. (They also acted quickly to appoint a well-known American firm to act as their agents on marine insurance claims.)

Perhaps of greater though academic interest is the dispute settlement clause in the standard sales contract. Most contracts provide for inspection of the goods by the Commodity Inspection Bureau, with that agency's findings to be final, although several contracts signed by this author and others with the Light Industrial Products Import and Export Corporation omit such a stipulation. The usual dispute settlement clause provides that disputes shall be settled through negotiations and, should the parties be unable to reach a settlement, by the Foreign Trade Arbitration Commission (hereafter FTAC). But another alternative is provided for, namely, referral of the dispute to "a competent Arbitration Committee in a third country approved by the two Contractual Parties for arbitration." Chinese willingness to agree to third-country arbitration of a dispute arising out of a Chinese sales contract is rare, although some Chinese sale contracts have provided for arbitration in the country of defendant. It is possible that the change in Chinese procedure is related to the resumption of United States-China trade.

A noteworthy sticking-point in negotiations for American purchases from China has been the problem of rejection of Chinese foodstuffs by Federal Food and Drug Administration (FDA) inspectors. American buyers have repeatedly requested Chinese negotiators to insert a contractual clause under which the Chinese seller would accept responsibility for such rejection, as is common in transactions in which such risks occur, but the Chinese have consistently refused. Chinese negotiators at first argued that they were "not clear" about the regulations or their enforcement; more recently, now that they have been given copies of the relevant regulations by their American customers, they have complained of unevenness in enforcement of the regulations and of unwarrantedly rigorous standards. For instance, one product over which problems have arisen is frozen shrimp, to which the standard applied by the FDA is purely olfactory; if a cargo smells bad to an inspector it is rejected. Chinese foreign trade officials feel aggrieved by the discretion given to individual inspectors. Faced with Chinese unwillingness to accept responsibility in the event of FDA rejection, American buyers have either refused to purchase any goods or have insured themselves against possible rejection. The latter practice has occurred in the importation of foodstuffs but it does raise the buyer's costs.

The issue of FDA rejection has caused Chinese trade officials much concern. Evidently anxious to expand exports to the United States as part of a general export drive and also to help offset the expense of purchases from the United States, the Chinese have quizzed many Americans about the FDA.

They have indicated a willingness to adjust their canning and labeling of foodstuffs to meet American legal requirements. For example, representatives of the China National Cereals, Oils, and Foodstuffs Import and Export Corporation and the Legal Affairs Section of the China Council for the Promotion of International Trade (hereafter CCPIT) have expressed to this author and others willingness to change the labels on Chinese canned mushrooms so that they meet the complex requirements of federal law. Also, CCPIT officials stated in conversations in Peking in April 1973, that a cannery was going to be outfitted with special machinery so that its output would conform to "North American" requirements. All officials with whom these matters have been discussed have also stated, however, that the transition to manufacture of products designed to conform to American law will be slow, because existing stocks must be sold first and also because the process of adaptation is necessarily slow.

C. *Unsolved Problems*

If 1972–73 saw the beginning of revived United States' imports from China, during that first period the problems impeding the further growth of such imports were also clearly apparent. Some are common to China's trade with other developed countries, but others are unique to the United States.

1. Delayed delivery

First, delays in Chinese delivery of goods has inhibited knowledgeable Americans from purchasing seasonable goods or some goods in rapidly fluctuating markets. Late delivery, the most common complaint of West European traders, has already occurred in the United States. Not only has the buyer had to postpone processing or resale of the Chinese goods, but he also may have incurred additional costs. The Chinese usually have expected him to extend his letter of credit until the goods were ready for shipment, without reimbursing him for the additional costs or any other losses, thereby causing him to tie up his money.

The reasons for delay are difficult to define, but many delays stem from the fact that Chinese exports are principally derived from the agricultural sector, where the vagaries of weather and harvests are impossible to control. Also, China's internal transportation network is very limited, and China lacks a large merchant marine. The Chinese try to get as much use as possible out of their own or chartered vessels. Thus, goods are sometimes carried on vessels that call at may ports before delivery.

These universal difficulties are compounded by the lack of direct United States-China shipping service. In the first stage of trade the Chinese shipped goods on third-country, often Japanese vessels with transshipment at a Japanese port or Hong Kong. Direct shipping connections seemed destined to await the settlement of Sino-American disputes over Chinese assets frozen in American banks since 1950 and American claims for property seized in the early years of the People's Republic (although there have been recent reports of direct US-PRC service offered by Japan's "K" lines). An agreement in principle was reportedly reached by the United States and China in early 1973,[31] and when that agreement is implemented Chinese vessels will again be able to call on United States ports without fear of attachment by an alleged Chinese creditor.

One of the more delicate aspects of relationships between Western buyers and the Chinese is the consequences of late deliveries. Evidently if buyers are loyal, extend their letters of credit, and return to make further purchases even after serious delays in prior years, ad hoc adjustments in subsequent transactions are made by the Chinese. The buyers may be rewarded for their loyalty by being allowed to purchase more of the products they desire than are some of their competitors; buyers of manufactured goods may find the Chinese willing to copy Western samples submitted to them, or to follow buyers' specifications on packaging or labeling to which the Chinese have previously refused to conform. It appears, then, that a variety of adjustments can be made to offset losses caused by Chinese delays, but only in the over-all context of subtle and enduring business relationships over a long period of time.

2. Dispute settlement

A second cluster of problems likely to occur will concern dispute settlement. The usual Chinese inspection clause provides that inspections by the Commodity Inspection Bureau are final. West European traders have often found the Chinese adamant in refusing to recognize or compromise their claims for defects which appeared evident when the goods arrived, if the certificate of the Commodity Inspection Bureau states that the goods met contract specifications.

West European traders and the Chinese have very different perceptions of the method by which these disputes are settled. The former complain that the Chinese only rarely settle claims by making payment or reducing the contract price.[32] They also say that the Chinese trading corporations are sometimes tardy in corresponding about claims and defer action until the buyer comes to the next Canton Fair.

---

[31] In February 1973 Mr. Henry Kissinger announced that the United States and China were preparing to negotiate settlement of the claims "on a global basis in the immediate future"; see "U.S. and China Set Up Office in Capitals for Liaison; Peking to Free Two Americans," *New York Times*, 23 February 1973. Talks began several days later; see "Rogers Initiates Talks with China on Asset Claim," *New York Times*, 26 February 1973.

[32] See, e.g., the discussions by Poul Mohr and Gabriele Crespi Reghizzi in this volume.

At the fair, frustrated claimants say, they often have to present and argue over the claim as if there had been no previous correspondence at all. Even if the claim is recognized by the Chinese as having some validity, they prefer to reach a compromise solution that does not involve payment. For example, they may give a discount on a subsequent purchase, increasing the quantity of a particular commodity allotted to the purchaser-claimant, or they may agree to make some other concession such as manufacturing a product according to the purchasers' specifications.

The Chinese have expressed very different views of the dispute settlement process. In November 1972 this author met several times for lengthy sessions with members of the Legal Affairs Department of CCPIT. During these talks the Chinese indicated that the FTAC, which in theory has arbitral jurisdiction under most Chinese export contracts, should not be viewed as a standing body. When CCPIT receives a foreign complaint either directly or through another Chinese agency such as a state trading corporation or a Chinese commercial office abroad, it does not immediately refer the matter to the FTAC. Rather, it appoints a foreign trade expert, not necessarily one listed on the roster of the FTAC, to review the matter with the purpose of proposing a compromise solution. Only in the event that he cannot propose a solution acceptable to both sides will the matter be turned over to the FTAC, and even then the FTAC is most likely to appoint not three arbitrators as its rules provide, but one member who will try to "mediate" between the two parties.

The Chinese officials with whom dispute settlement was discussed also gave several examples of compromise solutions. In one case a foreign buyer of plush complained that because of improper packing the plush had been flattened and lacked the necessary texture; CCPIT appointed a textiles expert, who reported that if the plush were steamed it would regain the desired texture. FTAC members witnessed a demonstration and then approved the solution and proposed it to the buyer, who withdrew his claim. In another case a Chinese corporation received a cabled request for an offer on a particular commodity and quoted a price. The buyer made a counteroffer. The corporation, intending to quote a price lower than the original offer but higher than the counter offer, by error quoted a price *lower than both*. The buyer immediately accepted that price—and increased the quantity desired. After the error was discovered the buyer was notified, but he argued that he had already sold the goods and would have to bear the resulting loss; he asserted a claim. The FTAC decided that the Chinese corporation should bear some responsibility for its error, although it reasoned that the buyer should have known that a mistake had been made; why else had the buyer *increased* the quantity? The compromise solution fixed the contract price at the level of the buyer's counteroffer, but only for the original amount requested. The common-sense reasoning behind this result was that the Chinese side had been negligent and should bear some responsibility, but at the same time the buyer should not be allowed to take advantage of the seller's error to snap up a larger quantity than he originally sought.[33]

The near future will no doubt see problems arise occasionally out of American buyers' allegations that goods purchased from the Chinese have not been up to contract specifications. At present the experience of West Europeans suggests that the Chinese insistence on bilateral negotiation may sometimes prove frustrating to claimants. On the other hand, the Chinese may also possibly be willing to modify their dispute settlement practices. Chinese trade officials have been very interested in learning about American attitudes toward, and institutions for, trade dispute settlement. It may be that in the context of a bilateral Sino-American agreement suitable arrangements can be made for third-party inspection of the goods on arrival and for third-party arbitration.

3. Payment and other banking problems

Banking and financial relations also present problems that await settlement. Most immediately the means for arranging payment for Chinese exports to the United States have been unsatisfactory. At present European purchasers are more favorably treated in one important respect than are their American competitors. In recent years the Chinese have insisted on Chinese currency, the Ren Min Bi (RMB), as the medium of payment, in this way trying to avoid losses through international currency fluctuations. European traders have been able to obtain limited protection against a revaluation of the RMB by purchasing RMB forward up to a period of six months. This they are permitted to do by the Bank of China upon proof of the existence of a purchase contract.[34] However, the Chinese have not permitted American purchasers to buy RMB forward in the same amounts, but appear to have limited such purchases to commercially almost insignificant sums. Even then the purchase cannot be made—by the third-country banks in the United States which have been handling financial arrangements—unless the American purchaser prepays the credit, thereby tying up his money for months.

Presumably this problem will be solved when direct Sino-American banking relationships are established. Both sides are ready for this move, which only awaits settlement of the Sino-American claims.[35] Already American banks

---

[33] The result was probably more favorable to the buyer than that which would have been reached by an Anglo-American court under the rule that "If the receiver of the telegram ought to have known that there must have been a mistake in the wording of the telegram, from his knowledge of the market, or for other reasons, he cannot under any view by accepting bind the offeror." Williston, *Contracts,* §94 (Student ed., New York: Baker, Voorhis & Co., 1938).

[34] See, e.g., the discussion of the German-Chinese payments agreement in the chapter in this volume by Arthur Stahnke.

[35] After a visit to Peking by Mr. David Rockefeller, chairman of the board of the Chase Manhattan Bank, it was announced that Chase would be a correspondent of the Bank of China—after the claims were settled.

have been engaged in limited financing of trade with China, by lending to both American sellers and buyers. At present American banks may be barred by the Johnson Act from lending to the Chinese government. The Act has been interpreted, however, as permitting private credits to finance commercial export sales.[36] When banking relations are established, American banks may also be able to assist the Chinese in their exporting efforts by offering advice on American markets for Chinese products and by providing other forms of useful information.

4. United States Tariff Treatment of Chinese Imports

Perhaps the most substantial problem affecting American imports from China is the lack of most-favored-nation (MFN) treatment for Chinese goods, which as a result of Congressional legislation are assessed at the levels of America's highest tariff, the Smoot-Hawley Tariff of 1931. It is unnecessary here to go into the details of the chilling effect on United States-China trade of this unwelcome relic of the Cold War, but the relevance of the MFN issue to existing practical problems of United States-China trade should be clearly perceived. Bilateral agreements on MFN usually involve mutual tariff concessions. The Chinese can give some such *quid pro quo* for American lowering of tariffs on Chinese goods, but this is limited since in purchasing from abroad they need not distinguish import licenses, customs formalities, and tariffs from other processes that form part of the negotiation of contracts. Yet nontariff Chinese concessions are possible which would facilitate American purchases from China, such as agreement on dispute settlement, payments, and banking. The trade agreements which some West European nations have signed with China dealing both with tariffs and with nontariff matters suggest that such agreements may contain suggestive analogies for structuring the United States-China relationship; this thought is examined briefly below. Suffice it to say here that agreement on the problems reviewed immediately above could much improve the new American trade relationship with China by increasing the possibility of Chinese exports to the United States and by strengthening commercial ties.

---

[36] The Johnson Act, 18 USC §955 (1972), prohibits American banks from lending to nationals and corporations of countries whose governments are in default on debts and to the United States government. Among the issues that would have to be resolved is the question of whether the government of the People's Republic of China should be considered the successor government of the Republic of China for these purposes, when the United States has consistently treated the present Taipei government as the successor for other purposes. Opinions by two recent attorneys general suggest that private credits to finance American export sales are not barred by the Act. 42 OPS Att'y Gen. No. 15 (9 October 1963); 42 OPS Att'y Gen. No. 27 (9 May 1967).

III. Patterns in American Sales to China

American sales to China are more difficult to discuss and to compare with similar transactions between the Chinese and West Europe because more secrecy surrounds Chinese imports than exports, the transactions are less uniform, and the number of contracts is still relatively small. This is a subject of some importance, however, since the beginning of major Chinese purchases from the United States coincided with some major changes in China's policy on imports of capital goods.

Some of the problems of sales to China center around the negotiation process. On the whole the seller is in the frustrating position of dealing with representatives of the Chinese state-trading corporations rather than with their "end-users." These representatives are not especially forthcoming about their purchasing interests. At the Canton Fair, for instance, they know their "shopping lists," the results of long and complex negotiations within the Chinese economic bureaucracy, which represent the purchases that have been approved and for which foreign exchange has been allotted. Thus, Americans, like their competitors, have discovered the difficulty of selling the Chinese products they had not already decided to purchase.

Although the Canton Fair is primarily devoted to export sales, considerable discussion does take place there about Chinese imports. These discussions can serve useful functions even if they do not lead directly and immediately to contracts. The American businessman can use the fair as an occasion to educate the Chinese about the products he wishes to sell and to make quasi-technical presentations. He can sometimes acquire useful bits of information about Chinese purchasing interests and attitudes toward proposed transactions. The fair also gives Chinese negotiators an opportunity to look over not only American products but American businessmen as well. After each fair a few have been invited to Peking for further discussions.

Not much information is available about the experiences in Peking of the still relatively small number of American businessmen who have gone there to negotiate. (All American sales seem to have been negotiated at Canton or Peking, except for Western Union's sale of its ground satellite station, which was discussed in Shanghai.) Both in private conversations and in rare public statements such Americans have indicated that they were treated with great politeness and hospitality although their negotiations were arduous and often long.

Like Europeans who have been there in similar circumstances, the Americans found that the Chinese asked for particularly detailed cost and price breakdowns to probe the price stated by the Americans and to seek opportunities to substitute cheaper domestically or foreign-manufactured components for some offered by the seller. Interruptions of negotiations may take place at insistence, often without explanation being offered. On some occasions, during a deadlock, the Chinese have proposed outings or excursions the next day, evidently so that the Chinese negotiating team's superiors could decide the Chinese position that would be taken on a critical issue when negotiations resumed. Although some of the interruptions may not have been welcome, on the whole American groups have yet to encounter suspensions that they considered unduly long. Some interruptions of negotiations with West Europeans have been known to last a week or longer, causing the European negotiators some discomfort and tension.

IV. STANDARD CONTRACT CLAUSES

A. *Payment*

The standard Chinese contract provides for payment by the Chinese buyer after advice of shipment by means of an irrevocable letter of credit opened by the Bank of China and payable against presentation of a draft together with the usual shipping documents. The Chinese practice of refusing to allow the Bank of China's letters of credit to be confirmed is well known and has undoubtedly been extended to Sino-American trade.[37]

Over the years considerable variation has occurred in the currency of payment, but recently the Chinese have insisted on the use of their own currency. The major transactions with Boeing, RCA, and Western Union provided for payment in dollars. With the decline of the dollar since those contracts were signed, the capital goods purchased under those agreements have come to the Chinese considerably cheaper than they were at the time the contracts were signed. A percentage of the price was of course paid soon after the signing of the contract, but the balance is to be paid in two installments: when the goods are shipped and then after acceptance of the goods by the Chinese purchasers.

B. *Force Majeure*

Outside the China trade general international practice with regard to drafting *force majeure* clauses is not uniform in the approach taken to defining the parties' rights and duties if supervening circumstances not attributable to the parties delay or prevent performance of the contract. Nor is Chinese practice uniform. Generally it can be said that the Chinese have resisted defining all these circumstances in advance. One standard clause provides only that "the seller shall not be responsible for the delay in shipment or nondelivery of the goods due to *force majeure* which might occur during the process of manufacturing or in the course of loading or transit." The clause further requires the seller to notify the buyer within fourteen days of the occurrence and to send a certificate from "the competent government authorities where

---

[37] See the chapter by Frank Münzel on banking.

the accident occurs." Another standard clause used by the China National Chemicals Import and Export Corporation excuses the seller from responsibility "for late delivery or non-delivery of the goods occurring to *generally recognized* 'force majeure' causes."[38] In contrast, a clause used in the Japanese memorandum trade specifies events "such as war, damage from severe wind or flood, snow or earthquake" as circumstances that may be considered as *force majeure.* A useful survey of clauses in contracts signed by Italian traders with the Chinese in recent years provides additional evidence of these variations.[39]

Scattered and fragmentary evidence from Americans who have negotiated contracts in Peking suggests that they have encountered the same Chinese reluctance met by Europeans to define in advance the circumstances which excuse the seller from liability for delay or nonperformance. "Strikes" and the term "Acts of God" are never allowed by the Chinese for obvious (but different) ideological reasons. One clause in an American contract refers to "Force Majeure as *agreed upon by both parties,*" with friendly negotiations to be held "to decide upon the further execution of the contract" if the delay is longer than a specified period of months. Another American contract only refers to *Force Majeure* without any further attempt to define the term or the process by which it might be clarified by the parties.

C. Delivery

In contrast to the considerable ambiguity of Chinese sales contracts regarding delivery dates, Chinese purchase contracts impose definite and heavy burdens on the tardy seller. A standard clause provides for a penalty for late delivery which is fixed at a percentage of the contract price for each seven days up to a stated maximum, with a right given to the buyer to cancel the contract (as well as to claim the penalty) if delivery is delayed beyond ten weeks. The maximum varies but does not usually exceed 5 percent.

Americans have been presented with and have agreed to sign such clauses, although at least one contract signed by an American corporation, in late 1972, contained a clause which set no maximum on the penalty for which the seller would be liable because of late delivery. Such a concession is perhaps partly explainable by the American seller's eagerness to begin business with the Chinese, but the clause must be considered unusual and not one which many other sellers, American or not, would be likely to agree to.

Of great practical interest in this connection is the wide variety of experience which Western European sellers to China have had under penalty clauses.

---

[38] See Appendix II.

[39] Gabriele Crespi Reghizzi, "Legal Aspects of Trade with China: The Italian Experience," *Harvard Journal of International Law* 9 (1968): 85, 109–11.

Some, particularly steel sellers, have found the Chinese to be unyielding in their insistence that the penalty be paid. Others, however, have found the Chinese willing to agree to extend the delivery time without a penalty. The differences may depend on how needed the foreign import may be and, of course, on the prior relationship of the parties.

D. Quality and Inspection

Sellers to China have had to be particularly careful in their negotiations with the Chinese on clauses relating to quality. The Chinese have a reputation for being most exacting in seeking the highest quality Western goods. They meticulously inspect the goods on delivery and try to hold the seller to the highest possible standards of quality. The standard clause requires the seller to "guarantee that the commodity is made of the best materials, with first-class workmanship, brand new, unused and complied in all respects with the quality, specifications and performance as stipulated in the Contract. The Sellers shall guarantee that the goods, when correctly mounted and properly operated and maintained, shall give satisfactory performance for a period of————months counting from the date on which the commodity arrives at the point of destination."

The Western seller who finds the Chinese demanding on quality and performance standards has even greater cause for concern when he discovers that Chinese standard contract forms not only provide for inspection of Chinese imports by the Commodity Inspection Bureau, which has branches in every major Chinese port, but also provide that the certificates issued by the bureau are to be regarded as final.

In the case of turnkey transactions including recent American sales of complicated equipment such as the satellite ground station, the Commodity Inspection Bureau is not usually explicitly given a prominent role in inspection, presumably because special tests out of the ordinary run of the bureau's activities are required. In such contracts it is customary to specify in detail the standards that the plant must attain. It is also common for contracts for large turnkey plants to permit Chinese buyers to send inspectors at their own expense to the seller's plant to participate in inspection and testing of equipment, although it is also usual for the Chinese to expressly refuse to permit such inspectors from countersigning any certificates approving equipment. Conversely, sellers usually send representatives to the site of the plant who are required to be present at the inspection of equipment delivered there. When such inspectors are present any details of lost, missing, or damaged equipment must be countersigned by both buyer's and seller's inspectors.

It is difficult to generalize as yet about American experience in these matters. Chinese personnel have come to the United States in connection with the Chinese purchase of the Boeing 707s and jet engines from United Aircraft.

Most of these personnel are evidently to be trained in operation and maintenance, but some may have had duties connected with inspection. Contracts for the sale of such complicated equipment as the satellite stations probably do not employ the standard Chinese clauses on quality, but are tailored to the particular technical circumstances of such complex equipment. It can be expected, however, that the contracts are rather vague on the procedure to be followed in the event of disagreement over quality. They probably leave the matter undefined in advance except to express a commitment to engage in bilateral consultations if differences arise.

Chinese practice in conducting the most detailed inspections has caused some annoyance to Western Europeans and Japanese sellers and may create occasional difficulties in Sino-American trade as well. Sellers of steel report that where other purchasers of steel pipe X-ray at random on delivery, the Chinese X-ray the entire shipment and complain of hairline cracks usually ignored by other purchasers. Sellers of vehicles and machinery report that although it is customary to ship small screws and other such items by weight, the Chinese count them all. Very minor variations from specifications which might be disregarded by other buyers may give rise to Chinese claims.

Unfortunately, the present framework of Sino-Western trade (including Sino-American trade) is not conducive to easy face-to-face contact between representatives of buyers and sellers, in the absence of which informal dispute settlement of a type common in the West is impossible to bring about. Arranging to have the seller's personnel at the site to engage in joint inspection with Chinese personnel may be of some assistance in this respect. However, the operation of the Chinese bureaucracy may be expected to continue to prompt Chinese officials to be reluctant to accept responsibility for accepting goods which do not conform exactly to contract specifications.

E. Dispute Settlement

Chinese tenacity in resisting third-party settlement of trade disputes is well known. The Chinese avoid not only litigation, but any third-party adjudication, including arbitration in Peking. The usual clause provides that disputes arising out of the contract "shall be settled amicably through negotiations," and that only if such negotiations fail will the parties resort to arbitration before the FTAC in Peking. In some instances the Chinese have reluctantly agreed to accept arbitration in Sweden or Switzerland. But regardless of the forum named in the contract the Chinese have evidenced extreme reluctance to become involved in arbitration.

Some European traders who are aware of these Chinese attitudes say that they will never request arbitration because the Chinese regard such a request as "unfriendly." Several traders have stated that they themselves have requested or know of others who have requested, or hinted that they were about to request, arbitration. The Chinese have responded in various ways. Sometimes they have settled their claims quickly, but in other cases the Chinese have not responded at all. In one instance they continued to correspond with the seller on matters arising out of the contract. It has been impossible to obtain a reliable account of an arbitration proceeding to which the Chinese were a party, either in China or abroad.

American sellers seeking to negotiate arbitration clauses have undoubtedly encountered Chinese resistance to choosing a forum other than Peking. Some have succeeded, however, in getting such a forum. Third countries have already been named in contracts with American companies. Despite the forum chosen, however, the Chinese can be expected in trade with the United States to avoid formal third-party adjudication of trade disputes and to insist on bilaterally negotiated compromise solutions.

F. New Developments in Chinese Purchases

Of great significance for American trade with China is the fact that the Sino-American rapprochement comes at a time, and is indeed part, of an apparent change in the Chinese leadership's approach to China's economic development. For many years policy has stressed the virtues of Chinese economic self-reliance, which has been manifested internationally in Chinese reluctance to expand foreign trade. China's over-all trade has remained in the vicinity of four billion dollars for many years, reflecting Chinese limitations on imports as well as the limitations on the goods that could be exported. As is well known, too, the Chinese have avoided purchasing Western capital goods on credit. The withdrawal of Soviet technicians in 1960 no doubt dramatized the need for self-reliance and apparently further buttressed Peking's determination to restrict China's trade.

However, recently China has appeared to be more eager to engage in foreign trade than at any time since 1949. To supplement the policy of self-reliance, a new stress has been placed on "exchanging needed goods." The reestablishment, in late 1972, of a state corporation exclusively concerned with importing technology reflects Chinese interest in looking to the developed nations more directly and on a larger scale than in recent years. Chinese willingness to enter into conventional licensing agreements has recently been manifested in several large transactions and has been discussed by Chinese trade officials. Large purchases of machinery, equipment, and whole plants from Europe, Japan, and the United States further demonstrate current heightened interest in imports, as do extremely large purchases of agricultural products from the United States and Canada.

Along with these developments have come other indications of changes in Chinese policy which, if they are carried out, will necessarily involve China in a considerably larger web of international commercial relationships than it has known before. In 1972 the then Minister of Foreign Trade publicly expressed Chinese willingness to purchase Western goods on credit, and some recent transactions with Japan have been on a five-year credit basis. Moreover, the Chinese have showed some signs of recognizing the importance of agreeing to protect foreign industrial property. CCPIT officials in Peking indicated in conversations in April 1973 that they were giving "serious consideration" to measures to protect foreign patents. The number of Chinese bilateral agreements recognizing protection of trademarks continues to grow.[40]

These developments clearly portend further considerable Chinese interest in purchasing American capital goods and licensing American technology. In certain areas the Chinese have already manifested strong interest, particularly in oilfield equipment, petrochemicals, electronics, scientific instruments, telecommunication, and air transport. The fact that the Chinese will be engaged in more transactions of a type in which sellers have usually been more able to negotiate firmly for desired contract clauses than buyers from China, together with the expansion of Chinese commercial contacts, suggests that sellers or licensors from all developed nations, not only the United States, may find negotiating in Peking somewhat easier than before.

V. CONCLUSIONS

As propitious as the beginning of United States-China trade has been, significant obstacles remain to be overcome at the time this paper is being written, of which the most prominent are settlement of the outstanding claims each nation has against the other and the question of granting most-favored-nation treatment to Chinese goods imported into the United States. Others obviously include the lack of direct banking relations, the absence of bilateral agreement on protection of industrial property, and the need for trade arbitration mechanisms and improvement in communications and facilities available to American businessmen. Here again the European experience has lessons for the United States and suggests that serious consideration should be given to negotiating an over-all trade agreement.

The Chinese have concluded trade agreements with a number of European nations, including several with which no formal diplomatic relations existed at the time.[41] Some of these agreements are very general, providing for most-favored-nation treatment, means of payment, and targets for the sale by each country to the other of categories of commodities. However, agreements with West European nations have sometimes included features apart from those mentioned immediately above that may be useful analogies for the United

---

[40] China presently has agreements with the United Kingdom, Sweden, Switzerland, Denmark, Finland, Italy, and Canada.

[41] See the discussions by Mohr, Stahnke, and Crespi Reghizzi in this volume.

States. The Sino-Italian agreement concluded in 1972, for instance, provides for a Mixed Commission which will meet yearly to study the development of trade between the two nations. It is possible the commission will adopt rules which would be generally applicable to all contracts between the two countries or to contracts for certain products such as machinery.[42] Such general conditions are not only common in Chinese trade agreements with other socialist countries but have also been established between Chinese corporations, particularly the China National Machinery Import and Export Corporation, and some European sellers.

The German-Chinese agreement of 1957, which was concluded between CCPIT and a 'non-governmental German body which had strong support from the government,'[43] is particularly instructive, although it expired after only one year. For instance, the agreement contains a clause providing for joint inspection by Chinese purchasers and German sellers of German exports before shipment, as well as after arrival in China. The agreement also contemplates that German importers could arrange for inspection of Chinese goods on arrival by an inspecting entity agreed upon by buyer and seller. A *force majeure* clause provided that contractual clauses on that issue could enumerate illustrative examples of circumstances deemed to be *force majeure*. Moreover, the Chinese and Germans also agreed on Zurich as the site for any arbitration needed if friendly negotiations failed to resolve a controversy and further agreed on the procedure for choosing arbitrators. These clauses were more favorable to Germans in some respects than are current contracts, evidently for political reasons—China was seeking to fortify its international position and the trade agreement may have been viewed in Peking as a preliminary to further Sino-German ties.

Not only do these agreements between China and European nations suggest patterns that may be followed and improved on, but there is a real need for some United States-Chinese trade agreement soon. Quite apart from the claims question, already settled in principle, most-favored-nation treatment remains a matter of genuine importance to the Chinese, and an agreement on trade that is addressed to nontariff issues as well as to tariffs seem to be the most appropriate vehicle to settle the issue.

The Chinese, eager to increase their export earnings, especially in the United States, have criticized the lack of most-favored-nation treatment as an obstacle to trade and a relic of the Cold War. They have objected to the prejudicial treatment of Chinese goods, which at present often enter the United States under severe handicaps. Moreover, they have sometimes implied that China would purchase more from the United States than at present if most-favored-nation treatment were granted.

---

[42] See Crespi Reghizzi, pp. 177–78.

[43] See Stahnke, p. 126.

But considerable difficulties stand in the way of a Sino-U.S. commercial agreement. Bilateral agreements on most-favored-nation treatment usually involve bargained-for *concessions,* and a Chinese agreement to extend most-favored-nation treatment to American imports is no concession at all, since China is a state-trading nation. In the Trade Reform Act of 1974, Congress enacted legislation which *requires* the President to receive concessions from any Communist nation in return for an agreement to extend most-favored-nation treament to that nation's products. The Act requires bilateral commercial agreements to provide for arrangements for the promotion of trade, settlement of commercial disputes, and protection of the industrial and literary property of U.S. citizens. Congress also made Chinese policies toward emigration into a trade-related issue by enacting general language applicable to all Communist countries, which restrains the President from negotiating an agreement unless he certifies that the emigration policy of the country in question meets certain standards.

Quite apart from the importance of commercial issues, events since the signing of the Shanghai Communique demonstrate that although U.S.-China trade has developed faster than most observers had originally believed possible, trade will be heavily influenced by the Sino-American political relationship. Watergate and the withdrawal of U.S. military forces from Southeast Asia, followed by the imminence of the 1976 Presidential elections, prevented United States from "normalizing" relations during 1973–75 by ending diplomatic relations with Taipei and establishing formal diplomatic relations with Peking. The Chinese leadership has clearly signaled that further movement must come from the United States. Until relations are normalized, commercial relations between the two countries will evolve cautiously and slowly. If and when normalization does occur, the prospects would still be for slow evolution rather than a dramatic leap forward. But normalization would signal the commencement of a new stage in Sino-American relations which would probably be reflected in trade as well, both in volume and in the articulation of an institutional framework for trade. Yet, even then, the commercial practices which China has developed in the course of long years of trade with Western partners and Japan are unlikely to be dramatically altered.

PART II

Methods and Control of Trade

Some Aspects of Maritime Law and Practice

A. R. DICKS

I. THE CONTEXT OF CHINESE MARITIME LAW AND PRACTICE

China's foreign trade can be very roughly classified into three geographical categories, which have not, of course, remained constant over the years. Much of the export trade is concentrated on a few relatively close territories where fresh produce and Chinese manufactures find a ready market. Of these, Hong Kong, Macao, North Korea, and North Vietnam can be classed as within the range of coastal vessels; it should not be forgotten, however, that Macao is also accessible to motor traffic, and the other three have rail as well as road communications with China. Southeast Asia, Japan, and Korea are accessible to small seagoing vessels. For the rest of the world, long-distance shipping is required. Prior to the Cultural Revolution, which led to sporadic but severe dislocation of China's maritime trade, these needs were supplied partly by foreign-owned liner services, partly by Chinese flag vessels, and partly by chartered tonnage of foreign registry. Some of the foreign-operated liner services, under economic strain since 1958[1] as a result of China's refusal to participate in the international freight conference system and her withholding of cargo to force reductions in freight rates, felt little incentive to ride out the storms of the Cultural Revolution period. Consequently, since that time the majority of oceangoing ships serving Chinese ports have been either of Chinese registry or under charter.

---

[1] In that year China severed commercial relations with Japan. As a result Chinese foreign trade began to develop with a wider range of countries, not all of which were served by existing shipping lines. It became necessary, therefore, to establish new routes, and in order to accomplish this the Chinese authorities began to charter foreign tonnage on a much larger scale than previously. See Audrey Donnithorne, *China's Economic System* (London: George Allen and Unwin, Ltd., 1967), p. 264.

It is clear that, since 1958 at least, Chinese policy has been directed toward total control of the country's seagoing trade. Ultimately, no doubt, the objective is that all such trade will be carried by Chinese flag vessels; this would be a complete reversal of the position in precommunist days when the lion's share of the trade was in the hands of foreign liner companies. This objective will in the long term be served by the growing Chinese shipbuilding industry, which without doubt represents one of the most impressive industrial achievements since 1949. There are already a significant number of Chinese-built vessels of all sizes up to 17,000-ton cargo liners and a new 22,000-ton tanker in the Chinese merchant fleet,[2] and this number may be expected to increase in both quantity and tonnage at an accelerating rate.

In the shorter term the objective of Chinese control has been served partly by the purchase of both new and older vessels for the Chinese flag fleet, and partly by the chartering of foreign registered tonnage. Many ships were bought in the post-1958 period (particularly in the advantageous years 1958–61 when the world market was seriously depressed) from both West and East European sources. New buildings came mostly from Polish or East German yards. Another source of older bottoms came from the extensive refloating of ships wrecked during the Sino-Japanese war; 120,000 tons of shipping had been sunk in the Yangtze alone. Some of these vessels were made serviceable and others were used for scrap.

Chinese participation in the international chartering market has been of importance since the mid-1950s and has at times reached dramatic proportions, particularly in the era of massive wheat shipments from Canada and Australia and large-scale rice exports to Ceylon. There were several years in which the Chinese National Chartering and Shipbroking Corporation (formerly known to foreigners by its old telegraphic code name SINOFRACHT, now altered to ZHONGZU) was the world's largest tonnage charterer. Indeed, there have been suggestons that the Chinese authorities have at various times over-chartered to an uneconomic extent, partly perhaps with the object of putting pressure on the foreign liner companies and conferences.

Some of the legal aspects of Chinese chartering will be mentioned subsequently. It is pertinent to point out here that a considerable amount of foreign-flag tonnage chartered by Chinese charterers is in fact beneficially owned or partly owned by Chinese state enterprises or their nominees. There are a number of shipping companies in Hong Kong that are under Chinese control; many of the ships belonging to these companies fly the British flag and thus are necessarily manned by officers holding British certificates. This pattern of ownership was at first coincidental, in the sense that like a number of other Hong Kong corporations, these companies came under the control of

---

[2] Of some two hundred seagoing vessels listed in *Lloyd's Register of Shipping,* *1970–71.*

the Chinese government or of Chinese state enterprises as the successors, by nationalization, "socialist transformation"[3] or otherwise, of majority shareholding interests. However, these British flag carriers have proved extremely useful, if not vital, to China's shipping trade as a whole, for they have enabled the Chinese to maintain good communications in circumstances where the use of Chinese flag vessels would have been politically or militarily impossible (e.g., in the Taiwan strait or in North Vietnamese waters), and where prudent independent owners would have hesitated to risk their vessels.[4] There is also a management company, Ocean Tramping, Ltd., which acts as a charterer and managing owner on behalf of these Hong Kong companies.

From this all too brief account of some of the practical arrangements for the marine carriage of China's foreign trade it is obvious that any discussion of the legal aspects of the subject must take place against a variegated background. Different shipping arrangements raise different problems, and in particular the involvement of foreign interests varies in nature and extent. Those who buy goods from China CIF may be concerned about the terms of a Chinese bill of lading, particularly if the carriage is in a Chinese flag vessel. Foreign shipowners (whether liner or tramp operators) and their shipmasters may face a whole host of legal problems in their use of Chinese ports and shipping facilities, quite apart from their contractual relations with Chinese enterprises in respect of employment of their vessels. From both types of situation other interests become involved: underwriters (whether of cargo, hull or freight), protecting and indemnity associations, banks and other mortgagees, classification societies, surveyors, average adjusters, and lawyers. Finally, owners of ships of Chinese registry or Chinese charterers of foreign tonnage may become involved with problems of "mixed law" when their vessels are in foreign waters, so that neither the Chinese nor the foreign side in all these transaction can avoid contact with each other's legal system.

Given the complexity of the subject matter, this paper must be confined to a study in outline of the more important legal aspects of Chinese marine transport. This complexity could be reduced to some extent by making arbitrary distinctions. For example, it would be possible to write solely on Chinese shipping law, disregarding all aspects of China's ocean trade which fall outside the rubric of Chinese legislation or practice. The present purpose, however, is better served by the examination in broad terms of the organization and legal basis of China's maritime trade, in the sort of context in which these matters are likely to be of practical interest to foreign traders.

---

[3] Under the "Provisional Regulations for State-Private Jointly Operated Enterprises," *FLHP*, no. 5 (5 September 1954), p. 65.

[4] It seems unlikely that this use of British registry for "flag of convenience" purposes will last indefinitely, for once the political and military difficulties disappear, the more commonly so-called flags of convenience are likely to prove more attractive from a commercial point of view.

The scope of the present study is based largely on the content of the maritime law or shipping law as those expressions are commonly used among English lawyers, to whom they connote a whole congeries of public or administrative law (the public control of ships, navigation, and harbors) and private law (the law of property as applied to ships and cargo, and the contractual and delictual obligations which arise from their commercial operation). It will at once appear to anyone familiar with Chinese law in its civil aspects that these classifications cannot be applied to the present subject without some distortion of what is known about Chinese legal classification. It is true that Chinese sources occasionally make mention of "maritime law" *(hai-shang fa)*, "marine transport law" *(hai-yün fa)*, and other similar phrases, but these expressions do not seem to carry any great conceptual weight, and they are unknown to the statute book. Nor is there in any sense a *corpus* of law relating specifically to shipping; rather, as with other branches of Chinese law, there is a partly comprehensive set of statutes and regulations—only partly comprehensive because many important aspects of shipping practice which are covered by statute or case law in other countries are left out of the Chinese legislation. However, these aspects often fall within the scope of the various contracts made between Chinese and foreign enterprises, so that where there is no statutory provision there nonetheless may be a contractual stipulation. In view of the difficulties that surround the precise legal status of many of these contracts, the foreign lawyer may be forgiven for regarding these as areas of legal uncertainty, although it will be suggested below that such pessimism may often be unwarranted.

Although these "gaps" in the maritime law often coincide with those parts of Western shipping law which are within the contractual competence of the parties, this demarcation between *lex cogens* and *lex dispositivum* does not always hold good. To take one example, the conditions under which the ship is exempted from liability in respect of damage to cargo is traditionally a matter of contract in Western legal systems, although in many countries shipments covered by bills of lading are usually subject to a special statutory regime based on the Hague Rules. In China, which is not a party to the relevant conventions, while the Hague Rules or their equivalent may be and often are incorporated into contracts of carriage, the law primarily to be applied in Chinese courts or other dispute-settling agencies is contained in a series of supplementary rules to the "Regulations Governing the Conduct of Investigations into Marine Casualties,"[5] and it accordingly has a quasi-administrative character. It would be impossible to make a neat demarcation between the "public" and "private" law relating to shipping, even if such a distinction were recognized by Chinese lawyers. Still less would such a demarcation correspond with Western classification. Nonetheless, it is convenient to con-

---

[5] *FKHP*, no. 10 (19 July 1959), p. 331.

sider the legal regulation of shipping under headings which roughly correspond to foreign practice.

The dearth of Chinese publications in the legal field since the beginning of the Cultural Revolution has made it difficult to estimate the extent to which the law and the legal system may have changed since that time.[6] It is true that the Cultural Revolution made its impact on the administration of shipping and ancillary services, and that during the more hectic periods shipping operations were sometimes considerably hampered by the activities of zealots. Nevertheless, there are some solid indications that most of the maritime law in force in 1966 is still in force today, and that the earlier statutes which governed shipping in China are still the basis for the administration of shipping.[7]

II. The Public Administration of Marine Transport

In common with all other aspects of China's industrial and commercial life, ultimate administrative authority for transport is vested in the State Council, and the more important legislation in respect of shipping is promulgated in the form of State Council decrees. Before 1959, when the State Council departments were reorganized, there was a special bureau for the supervision of the various ministries concerned with transport and communications, the Sixth General Office. Subsequently, over-all supervision of these fields passed to the Office of Industry and Communications.

While the control of the railways was formerly in the hands of a special ministry, and civil aviation has been placed under the supervision of a series of special commissions directly under the State Council, shipping, together with road transport, has always been under the aegis of a general transport ministry which since 1954 has been designated the Ministry of Communications. The ministry appears to be organized in two divisions, usually translated as the General Bureau of Highways and the General Bureau of Marine and River Navigation.

It should be noted that despite its crucial importance to the nation's foreign trade, ocean shipping is not under the immediate control of the Ministry of Foreign Trade. Furthermore, ocean shipping is controlled through the same organization, at the higher levels, as are coastal and inland navigation. This is of considerable importance for the substantive maritime law, for the principal legislation for both branches of the industry is evidently framed within the same department. It is not surprising, therefore, to see that the

---

[6] For developments since this paper was written in 1970, however, see A. R. Dicks, "A New Model for Chinese Legislation: the 1972 Shipping Regulations," *The China Quarterly*, no. 57 (January–March 1974), p. 63.

[7] The same organs appear to exercise the same functions and powers as previously, and particular statutes have been recently reprinted.

clear legal differentiation between marine and inland carriage by water which is to be found in many countries is not always evident in Chinese practice. By way of example, the regulations, mentioned above, on liability for marine casualties contain certain exemptions from liability for cargo damage to which shipowners may have recourse. The majority of these exemptions (which closely reflect some of those contained in the Hague Rules) enure to the benefit of owners in both marine and inland navigation. The one exception is the exemption for any act or default of the master, crew, or pilot in the navigation or management of the vessel, which does not cover Chinese vessels carrying Chinese-owned cargoes in coastal or inland waters. This position contrasts with the law in most countries, for although the Hague Rules themselves may be extended to inland navigation, the majority of signatories to the Hague Conventions apply the Rules compulsorily only to international shipments under ocean bills of lading.

Little is known of the division of responsibility between the ministry and the Office of Industry and Communications. The latter is doubtless responsible for coordinating the joint activities of the various other ministries that often have to cooperate with the Ministry of Communications in matters touching shipping—the Ministries of Trade, Foreign Trade, Marine Resources, Railways, and Machine Building, to name the most obvious. In 1964 there was established a State Maritime Bureau *(Kuo-chia hai-yang chü)*[8] under the aegis of the State Council, but its activities have remained obscure. It may be that the establishment of this bureau reflected a growing awareness of the increasing importance of shipping to the national economy, particularly in the period when massive foreign purchases of food grains necessitated special large-scale chartering arrangements. On the other hand, it may have no direct connection with maritime transport at all—it may, for example, be concerned primarily with ocean resources.

While general policy and legislation is formulated in the Ministry of Communications, the bulk of the detailed administration of shipping and navigation is delegated to a network of local authorities, and the commercial operation of ships and their cargoes is under the control of a number of state-owned corporations. It should be noted that certain types of decisions have to be referred to the ministry for final approval, for example, the attribution of liability in the course of investigations into marine casualties, when these are conducted through administrative channels. Again, such services as the maintenance of a register of shipping, which depend for their effectiveness on unified control, appear to be directly subject to the central ministry.

The local organs of the Ministry of Communications concerned with shipping and port control have a somewhat complex nomenclature, which has

---

[8] *Jen-min shou-ts'e* (People's handbook), *JMJP* (6 June 1964): 274.

undergone changes over the course of time. They appear to have been consistently divided into two broad categories: "shipping administration organs" *(hang-wu kuan-li chi-kuan)* and "port administration organs" *(kang-wu kuan-li chi-kuan)*.[9] Only the latter seem to be of significance to this study since all the ports open to foreign shipping are subject to the control of these bodies. Shipping administrative organs seem to be concerned largely with inland and possibly coastal traffic, although they may also have jurisdiction in smaller seaports and in coastal districts outside the areas of the major ports.

Space does not permit an attempt to trace all the changes in the terminology applicable to various port authorities; it is enough to note that their powers were first set out comprehensively in the "Provisional Regulations for the Administration of Sea Ports in the People's Republic of China,"[10] a law which appears still to be in force. The principal ports such as Shanghai, Tientsin, and Canton were placed by that law under the control of "port affairs administration bureaus" *(kang-wu kuan-li chü)*.

As constituted under the "Provisional Regulations," the port authorities are saddled with a multiplicity of duties and armed with a formidable array of powers. Many of their functions fall within the conventional duties of port authorities everywhere—for example, maintenance of navigational aids, dredging of channels, and public health arrangements. Pilotage and vessel control within the harbor is under a special department of the port authority known as *kang-wu chien-tu* which is specifically translated as "harbor superintendency administration."[11] Others sometimes fall within what would be the commercial sector in a differently organized economy—the provision or control of stevedorage, lighterage, warehousing, and all the other facilities for the shipment, receipt, and forwarding of goods and for the embarkation of passengers and the arrangement of ships' supplies and services and of salvage and towage facilities.[12]

---

[9] The two terms are generic in the sense that they have been used in legislative texts and elsewhere to denote a series of administrative bodies, the titles of which have varied both in accordance with their importance and over the course of time. For instance, in the "General Regulations Governing Joint Inspection of Ships Entering or Leaving Sea-ports," *FKHP*, no. 12 (24 October 1961), p. 99, port offices of different levels are alike referred to as "port administrative organs." On the other hand, both types of organs are designated "shipping administration organs" for the purposes of the "Provisional Regulations for the Registration of Ships," *Chung-hua jen-min kung-ho-kuo fa-kuei hsien-chi* (Selected laws and regulations of the PRC [hereafter FKHC]) (Peking: Fa-lü ch'u-pan-she 1956): 655 (28 November 1951; amended 29 April, 1953).

[10] *FLHP*, no. 5 (23 January 1954), p. 133.

[11] For example, in the translations that accompany ships' protests authenticated by the authorities of large ports such as Shanghai and Canton.

[12] "Provisional Regulations," Article 14; note that the appointment of surveyors for foreign vessels is now handled by a separate body; see pp. ooo *infra*.

In addition, the port authorities have important administrative functions not related to their immediate physical control of the harbor, such as the examination of ship's officers and pilots and the registration of ownership of Chinese vessels. They also perform the notarial function of receiving and authenticating protests by the masters of ships which have sustained weather damage or other losses.

The port authorities are of great importance to foreign shipowners. They enjoy judicial as well as executive and even legislative competence in certain fields. In addition to a general power to take whatever action is necessary "to prevent and put an end to all acts which may violate the laws and regulations in force," port authorities may issue, within the scope allowed by the principal legislation, various by-laws and regulations. This power has been widely used, and all the ports open to foreign trade have specific regulations applicable to foreign vessels. Failure to observe these regulations may prompt the port authorities to exercise their power to "initiate investigation or prosecution, or inflict a fine or penalty in respect of the violation of the shipping or harbor laws or regulations of the State by any organ, enterprise, vessel or person"[13]—a police power which gives them in some respects concurrent jurisdiction with the public security border control authorities. It is the port authorities, moreover, that take the leading part in the joint inspection procedure which applies to incoming and outgoing vessels, in cooperation with the customs, border control, and public health authorities.[14]

In addition to the obligation to provide salvage services on a contractual basis, the port authorities have important powers of wreck removal, all expenses of which are for the account of the vessel concerned.[15] The borderline between civil salvage and wreck removal is not always easy to discern, a fact which has sometimes proved embarrassing to foreign owners. There are also emergency powers to take immediate action against and to require immediate action from any vessel, organ of government, enterprise, or individual within the harbor to ensure the safety of life, property, or navigation.[16] Likewise, there is a specific power to require the removal or destruction of property for the preservation of the "safety and efficiency" of the port.[17] These powers, which by necessary implication must exempt the port authority from liability in respect of acts done in their exercise (unlike the provisions of Article 20,

[13] *Ibid.,* Article 15(3).

[14] "General Regulations Governing Joint Inspection of Ships Entering or Leaving Sea-ports," *FKHP,* no. 12 (24 October 1961), p. 99.

[15] "Administrative Rules for the Reclamation of Sunken Vessels of the PRC," *FKHP,* no. 6 (11 October 1957), pp. 413, 416.

[16] "Provisional Regulations for the Administration of Sea Ports in the PRC," Article 15(5).

[17] *Ibid.,* Article 15(7).

which create a right of action against the port authority for wrongful arrest), are very widely framed. So long as their use is confined to military or civil emergencies they are scarcely objectionable (and doubtless they could be justified in international law by reliance on the right of angary), but taken at face value they could cover a multitude of sins, and the foreign observer might be forgiven for thinking that they erode the safeguards for shipowners which are incorporated into the wreck-removal legislation.

Beyond maintaining a legal and physical environment in which ships may efficiently and safely operate, the port authorities have the duty of providing many services for which foreign ships pay on a commercial basis. Within the jurisdiction of each port authority, particular services are often organized as separate enterprises and accounting units. While some of these enterprises are still designated state-private joint enterprises and often continue to bear their old names, all were taken under full state control in accordance with the "Provisional Regulations." Thus, there are in each port open to foreign vessels stevedoring companies, tally companies, repair dockyards, and professional salvage and towage organizations. In addition, there are separate companies which own the smaller vessels for inland or coastal transport into which cargo is often transshipped at Chinese ports, and which provide harbor lighterage.

It is a matter of surprise to some foreign shipowners that foreign surveyors are excluded from carrying out their duties in China. Instead, surveyors are provided by the Register of Shipping of the PRC, which was established in 1963. This body, the Chinese name of which could be more literally translated as "Ship Survey Bureau of the PRC," has much broader functions than the mere casual provision of surveyors. Its principal function is to serve as a national classification society, and all Chinese-owned ships are now believed to be under this classification, although some vessels were still in class at Lloyd's as late as March 1968. Technically the register is under the direct control of the Ministry of Communications and not under the jurisdiction of the port authority, but the nature of its service to foreign shipping makes mention of it convenient at this point.

Pilotage is under the direct supervision of the port authorities and appears to be governed by the "Provisional General Rules on Harbor Pilotage."[18] Each port is bound to establish a "pilotage organ," and the qualifications and duties of pilots are set out in considerable detail together with their relationship to the master of the ship under pilotage.

The fees charged for the services offered by the port authorities to foreign vessels are prescribed by statute. They are as various as the services in respect of which they are payable, but they are all based on a sliding scale in accordance with the size of the vessel or the work performed. It is not known how

---

[18] *FKHP* (5 December 1953): 675.

far the commercial or quasi-commercial enterprises, e.g., such enterprises as the Canton Ocean Shipping Supply Corporation, are expected to make a profit, though clearly they are important earners of foreign exchange. Some Chinese port services are regarded by foreign owners as rather highly priced, and this contention is certainly true of the sums claimed by Chinese salvors, which are often well above world levels.

In addition to the charges for specific services and supplies, all of which are payable to each enterprise, harbor dues are payable to the port authority itself at the rate of RMB .30 per net registered ton on entry to, and also departure from, the port by all vessels which enter for a commercial purpose. They may be reduced in special circumstances on proof that freight earned is below a specific level per ton. Tonnage dues are also payable to the Customs on a sliding scale, with a reduction of up to almost 40 percent for ships belonging to states enjoying most-favored-nation treatment under a commercial treaty.[19] As will be seen below, the port authorities have a power of detention in respect of vessels which fail to pay any of these charges or dues, a power that they may exercise on their own initiative or at the instance of another organ or enterprise.

III.   THE COMMERCIAL OPERATION OF OCEAN SHIPPING IN CHINA

Despite the wide scope of their responsibilities, the port authorities do not appear to have any direct control over the operation of international shipping to and from Chinese ports. The ownership of ocean-going vessels, and their chartering, employment, and insurance are all functions of a number of nationally organized corporations. These are in many respects equivalent to the foreign trade corporations except that some are subordinate to the Ministry of Communications rather than to the Ministry of Foreign Trade. (The People's Insurance Company of China, which is responsible for all marine insurance matters, is subject to the overriding control of the Ministry of Finance.) Like their foreign trade counterparts, each of these corporations has independent legal personality and contractual capacity, and most of them are also organized into branch companies and branch offices throughout the coastal region of the country.[20]

---

[19] "Provisional Regulations for Ships' Tonnage Dues," Articles 2 and 3, *Chung-hua jen-min kung-ho-kuo hai-kuan fa-kuei* (Customs laws and regulations of the PRC) (Peking: Fa-lü ch'u-pan-she, 1960), p. 144 (16 September 1952). Since this paper was written, a "consolidated tax," an enterprise income tax, and a local supplementary industrial and commercial tax have been applied to the gross earnings of foreign vessels from shipments out of Chinese ports by regulations introduced on 1 July 1974. The standard rate of tax is 3.03 percent.

[20] See also the chapter by Victor H. Li on the organization of the foreign trade apparatus.

One major corporation, the China Ocean Shipping Company, is a ship-owner. It is by no means the only organization owning ships in the country. In the field of foreign trade, for example, the China Resources Company, a trading corporation with offices in various South China cities and in Hong Kong and Macao, which specializes in trade with those two territories, owns certain vessels for the special purposes of the Canton-Hong Kong trade; the Pearl River Navigation Company is in a similar position. The great majority of sea-going ships are thought to belong to the China Ocean Shipping Company. It is difficult to obtain precise information on the point, however, and there is also a growing tendency for Chinese ships to be described in foreign registers as belonging simply to the PRC.

The ownership of ships in China is governed by several statutes, detailed discussion of which is impossible here.[21] Apart from various technical regulations, particular statutes regulate the registration of acquisition, ownership, sale, and mortgage of ships, as well as their port of registry and nationality certification. Chinese registry (i.e., nationality) is based on 100 percent ownership by Chinese citizens, a consideration which even today is not of purely academic interest. The Chinese-Tanzania Joint Shipping Company of Dar-es-Salaam is shown in Lloyd's Register, 1970–71, as "owning" two vessels, one of which flies the Chinese, one the Tanzanian flag. It seems likely that in fact each ship is owned by a state corporation in each country, and that the joint company is simply a "managing owner,"[22] as is, presumably, the Sino-Albanian joint company, to which no specific vessels are known to be ascribed. The same may well be true of the Sino-Polish Line, for all the vessels employed in the service appear to be of Polish registry.

Most of the existing legislation was promulgated in the early days of the PRC when a significant proportion of the national fleet was in private hands. Many of the vessels in inland waters still belong to relatively small scale owners, e.g., specialized enterprises, fishing communes, and conservancy authorities. It is therefore not altogether surprising to find that the statutory regime for shipping presupposes a multiplicity of owners. Nevertheless, it is sometimes unclear to what extent these provisions are still of importance today. For example, a set of regulations for the registration of ownership is plainly a necessity, but how far the provisions for mortgage of ships are still of any significance is an open question. There is little doubt that the loans which finance the building in China or purchase from abroad of new additions to the fleet must be amortized in some way over a period of time from the

---

[21] See in particular the "Provisional Regulations for the Registration of Ships," note 3, *supra*, and the "Provisional Rules for the Issue of Certificates of Nationality for Ships," *FKHC*, p. 670 (1 September 1951, amended 29 April 1953).

[22] See Sir William McNair et al., eds., *Scrutton on Charterparties and Bills of Lading* (17th ed., London: Sweet and Maxwell, Ltd., 1964), 17: 38.

vessel's earnings (particularly where these include foreign exchange). It is not known whether the security represented by a mortgage is still employed in this connection, although in other branches of Chinese financial practice, hypothecation seems still to be very much alive.

A point of more practical significance to the foreign shipping community is the extent to which the PRC as such is an owner of commercial tonnage. Clearly the state must own directly many public vessels, but there seems to be too little evidence to hazard an opinion on the question of merchant ships. The question is of some importance since many jurisdictions, particularly those where English law applies or was formerly applied (including many in the "Third World"), afford broad jurisdictional immunity when the effect of legal proceedings is to implead a foreign sovereign or its property, whether or not this property is being used for commercial purposes.[23]

Affreightment

The commercial employment of Chinese flag vessels is a somewhat mysterious matter, because the vessels tend to trade principally with Asian and African countries and they carry their own insurance risks so that information is not readily available outside the countries concerned. While some ships operate on a liner basis, many are clearly booked for specific voyages. No doubt in some cases an export corporation fixes a whole ship by charterparty or freight contract for a voyage, or conceivably on time charter (for example, in the case of rice exports). However, the majority of Chinese exports are probably shipped on a bill-of-lading basis. The business of procuring space for export cargo on Chinese vessels (and on foreign liners in Chinese ports), together with the forwarding, storage, and loading and the customs clearance, is largely in the hands of the China National Foreign Trade Transportation Corporation (ZHONGWAIYUN)[24] which has branches in all the main Chinese ports.

The chartering of foreign tonnage, on the other hand, is carried out entirely by ZHONGZU,[25] which also negotiates the purchase of foreign vessels

---

[23] See, e.g., G. C. Cheshire and F. M. North, eds., *Cheshire's Private International Law* (London: Butterworths, 1970), p. 97–104. It should be noted that the interest of a time-charterer in a vessel is not adequate to sustain the plea: *Juan Ysmael & Co. Inc.* v. *Indonesian Government* [1955] *A.C.* 72 (P.C.). The rule stated in the text must now be modified in the light of the recent decision of the Judicial Committee of the Privy Council in *The Phillipine Admiral* (1975) (unreported at the date of going to press).

[24] ZHONGWAIYUN is a contracted form of the Chinese name of the corporation, and is used as telegraphic address. Formerly the corporation was known as SINOTRANS.

[25] Formerly the China National Chartering and Shipbroking Corporation, often known as SINOFRACHT.

for both trading and scrap. ZHONGZU usually fixes charters as agent on behalf of a principal. Generally the identity of the principal is undisclosed, in which case it appears that it is almost invariably ZHONGWAIYUN which is designated as the charterer (it is significant that ZHONGZU shares offices with ZHONGWAIYUN in most ports). ZHONGWAIYUN then presumably "puts the vessel up as a general ship" and books space for its various foreign trade corporation customers. There are, however, direct charters on behalf of the foreign trade corporations as principals in some trades; for example, ZHONGZU fixes vessels directly on behalf of the China National Chemical Import Corporation in the North African phosphate trade.

ZHONGZU does not itself negotiate in the market, for it has no offices outside China. Instead it acts by cable or telephone through two or three regularly employed brokers on the Baltic Exchange in London and other brokers in Hong Kong and elsewhere. Increasingly, it tends to insist on the use of its own *pro forma* charterparties, which are in fact modifications of established international forms. These are "Sinicized" by the deletion of certain clauses which are not in conformity with Chinese commercial requirements or general policy and by the insertion of more favorable terms. Examples of provisions of a purely functional kind which are found in most ZHONGZU charterparties are the prohibition on payments through American banks and restrictions on navigation in the Taiwan Straits. On the other hand, such requirements as Peking arbitration (or as is much more common, the negative position where no particular place is named for arbitration, which is adopted when a deadlock is reached between brokers on the issue of Peking arbitration) are part of a deliberate policy with regard to foreign trade law which will be familiar enough to the reader in other contexts. To date, China has not been as successful in her arbitration policy with regard to shipping as she has in other branches of foreign trade. A majority of Chinese charters probably still call for London arbitration, a situation which is likely to continue so long as the majority of protecting and indemnity clubs are reluctant to underwrite Peking arbitration. However, the pressure in favor of changes in arbitration practice will continue to be strong, may well gather weight as Chinese flag tonnage grows and Chinese chartering needs decrease, and may be hard to resist at times when the market is depressed.

Another provision which is usually inserted in ZHONGZU charterparties is the requirement that the vessel employ its own agents in Chinese ports, whether ports of loading or of discharge. This obliges the owners to have recourse to a further corporation under the umbrella of the Ministry of Communications, the Chinese Ocean Shipping Agency (PENAVICO). Whereas ZHONGWAIYUN acts as a forwarding and receiving agent for cargo owners, PENAVICO acts as the agent of the vessel. It does so on the basis of a quasi-statutory, quasi-contractual set of regulations which govern the relationship of vessel and agent. Ships may employ PENAVICO either on a long-term basis or on a voyage basis; in the latter case a request to the corporation to act must precede the ship's arrival at a Chinese port. Without an agent the vessel cannot be cleared for entry, except in emergency, and even then the request still has to be made in due course.

PENAVICO undertakes all the regular business of ship's agents. It attends to port and customs formalities, arranging for pilotage, berthing, loading and discharge (when it is the vessel's responsibility), tallying, survey, and transshipments; it procures provisions, stores, and labor for cleaning holds and arranges for painting or repairs; it provides cash for disbursements; it collects freight, draws up laytime statements, computes demurrage, and deals with cargo claims; it arranges for salvage and towage and settles marine casualties; and it acts as broker when the ship requires further charters on the spot, as well as arranging delivery and redelivery in terms of the charter. As will be seen, one result of this wide range of activity is that the vessel has very little or no direct contract with the various enterprises or organs which actually provide the services in question, although contracts are carefully drawn to make it clear that these latter are the principals. Even in legal matters such as the settlement of cargo claims, PENAVICO normally negotiates on behalf of the ship unless the dispute goes to arbitration or the owners regard the claim as of sufficient importance to send special representatives to China.[26] It seems probable that insulation of foreigners from direct contact with the sometimes competing interests within the national economy is an important aspect of PENAVICO's functions.

A further term which has at times proved burdensome for foreign owners is the habitual provision in ZHONGZU charterparties that stevedores are to be agents of the vessel, or, as it is often put, stevedorage is for vessel's account. The effect of such a provision (which has a well-established construction in English law) is to put upon the owners the liability for damage to cargo in the course of unloading, a liability which is particularly unwelcome where, as in China, there is no real choice in the employment or dismissal of stevedores. It may be noted that the normal standard of stevedore labor in Chinese ports is fairly high. During the Cultural Revolution, however, standards fell, and much of the work was in the hands of overenthusiastic amateurs. This resulted in a good deal of stevedore damage to ships as well as to their cargoes, in circumstances quite beyond the owners' control.

Similar provisions sometimes place on the vessel the responsibility for finding lighterage. Apart from possibly enlarged liability for cargo damage in

---

[26] There is no inherent reason why PENAVICO should not find itself representing both parties to a dispute, and in fact this sometimes happens in collision cases, when both vessels find that they have the same agents. In such cases the pressure for a negotiated settlement is particularly strong. The cargo interests are normally represented by ZHONGWAIYUN in disputes over carriage, however, because on Chinese sale terms the cargo is usually in Chinese ownership during shipment.

these cases, both stevedorage and lighterage can involve considerable delays, which often are not fully compensated for by the charter rate of demurrage. This is particularly true in geographically large harbors such as Canton. Lighters are centrally allocated from Canton itself by the harbor superintendency, and, even at the best of times, if a vessel is berthed at Whampoa, a considerable period may elapse before lighters are actually alongside.

Liner operators, of course, have fewer of these problems, since they have a greater degree of control over the terms of the carriage contracts contained in their own bills of lading. For them the main problem in the China trade has been to secure an economic freight.

It would be quite wrong to suggest (as a survey of legal problems must always be in danger of doing) that loading and discharge are sources of exceptional difficulty in China. There are many Asian, European, and American ports where labor problems, poor handling facilities, or sheer inefficiency make for problems just as serious as any encountered in China.

IV. SETTLEMENT OF MARITIME DISPUTES

It is impossible to discuss more than a small proportion of the legal problems which have arisen from the commercial aspects of the operation of shipping to and from Chinese ports. Many of them are eventually of less concern to shipowners than to their mutual insurance clubs and other underwriting interests. As a rule, with a measure of patience over the delays which invariably seem to attend the deliberations of the Chinese authorities, they can be settled without undue dissatisfaction on either side. There are, however, disputes which cannot be settled between the parties so easily, and it remains to consider some of the problems that confront the foreign enterprise when this pathological stage of commercial intercourse is reached.

Under the Chinese legal system there are three principal types of tribunal available for the settlement of maritime disputes to which foreign persons or enterprises may be parties. Litigation may be initiated in the people's courts; recourse may be had to arbitration in accordance with the procedure of the Maritime Arbitration Commission of the China Council for the Promotion of International Trade (with its heavy emphasis on conciliation); or certain cases may be resolved on the basis of findings made in the course of the investigation of a marine casualty by a port authority. In exceptional cases other forms of dispute settlement may be resorted to within China, for example, an *ad hoc* arbitration may be conducted by the diplomatic staff of an uninvolved foreign state in Peking.

Both litigation and arbitration may also be pursued in other countries at the instance of either Chinese or foreign parties. The Chinese authorities have had extensive experience of London arbitration in maritime matters, although they have never availed themselves of the device long used by the

Soviet Trade Delegation in the United Kingdom, whereby it is tacitly agreed that a designated member of the delegation shall be regarded as a "commercial man" for the purposes of the standard Baltic arbitration clause. Instead, the Chinese have regularly made use of one or two local professional arbitrators.

On the whole, the Chinese have proved reluctant to litigate in Western countries. As far as the English (and Hong Kong) courts are concerned, this reluctance is understandable, given the somewhat shameful[27] way in which the celebrated aircraft case was made the subject of almost nakedly political interference at the beginning of the Korean War.[28] A later adverse decision against a Chinese corporation was legally defensible but unhappily contrary to the obvious merits of the case.[29] However, more recently Chinese charterers have been indirectly involved in litigation in the English High Court in which their colleagues were successful, and it is to be hoped that eventually the Chinese will conclude that the courts of capitalist states are not necessarily biased against the PRC. Chinese vessels in foreign ports are in principle subject to admiralty actions *in rem,* and the widespread adoption in common law states of the "sister ship" rule[30] might well make such proceedings attractive to potential litigants. In practice, however, the utility of such proceedings is likely to be circumscribed. As mentioned above, most common-law countries also confer a wide immunity on vessels which can be shown to be the property of a foreign sovereign, and the availability of the action *in rem* would thus depend on the extent to which the shipowning corporation could be said to be identified with the PRC as a sovereign state.[31] The status of the various legal entities which own ships in China is of importance in this connection.

The extent to which the people's courts in China are currently used for the resolution of economic disputes is uncertain. It would be unwise, however, to assume that the wide use of less uncongenial and formal methods of dispute resolution has produced a situation in which the formal jurisdiction of the people's courts has fallen into anything like desuetude. Certainly, the various statutes affecting jurisdiction in maritime matters have always made it clear that ultimate jurisdiction is vested in the people's courts. Although the various means of settling maritime disputes—litigation, arbitration, or conciliation, and determination by the port authority—are in general mutually exclusive

---

[27] See Sir Alexander Grantham, *Via Ports: from Hong Kong to Hong Kong* (Hong Kong: Hong Kong University Press, 1965), pp. 161–63.

[28] *Central Air Transport* v. *Civil Air Transport* [1953] *A.C.* 70 (P.C.).

[29] *China State Bank* v. *Dairy Farm, Ice and Cold Storage Co. Ltd., HKLR* 51 [1967]: 95.

[30] See, for example, the (United Kingdom) Administration of Justice Act, 1956, S.3(4).

[31] See Cheshire and North, *Private International Law*, pp. 106–7.

and no appeal lies from the less formal agencies to the courts, compulsory measures of execution (including the sale of ships arrested by way of security) are still under their ultimate control. (It has been said that this power has never been invoked in respect of decisions of the Arbitration Commission.)[32] It is in the people's courts, moreover, that the specific remedy for abuse of legal process by the port authority which is provided in Article 20 of the "Provisional Regulations on the Administration of Sea Ports in the People's Republic of China" must presumably be sought.

The jurisdiction, in the international sense, of the people's courts in maritime matters was discussed in 1964 by Ni Cheng-ao, at that time a senior legal adviser to the Foreign Ministry.[33] He took the view that the people's courts had a jurisdiction coextensive with that conferred on port authorities by the "Regulations for the Conduct of Investigations into Marine Casualties," an opinion which is in itself of significance.

There are doubtless a number of sound reasons why the theoretical powers of the people's courts appear to be invoked only sparingly, one of which may be the shortage of suitable judicial personnel. If litigation appears to the Chinese authorities to be a blunt instrument for the purposes of foreign economic relations, there seems little reason for foreign parties to disputes in China to invoke the jurisdiction of the courts when other means, such as the port authorities or the Maritime Arbitration Commission, are available.

Although the Maritime Arbitration Commission is available to Chinese parties *inter se* as well as to foreign ones, by contrast with the people's courts and the port authorities, the commission was specifically constituted for the purposes of foreign trade. As such it plays an important part in what may be termed the "legal strategy" of the People's Republic, which, among other things, calls for the progressive abrogation of such "monopolistic" practices as the inclusion of London arbitration clauses in most charterparties fixed in the London market.

Space does not permit an analysis of the constitution and rules of the commission, which contain some interesting features.[34] One peculiarity which marks the commission off from purely voluntary tribunals in Western countries is the power of the chairman to make decisions before the hearings regarding security. These decisions are enforceable at the suit of one party by the courts,

---

[32] Wang Wen-lin, "People's Republic of China," in P. Sanders, ed., *International Commercial Arbitration: a World Handbook* (The Hague: Martinus Nijhoff, 1965), pp. 127, 133.

[33] Ni Cheng-ao, *Kuo-chi-fa chung-ti ssu-fa kuan-hsia wen-t'i* (Problems of jurisdiction in international law) (Peking: Shih-chieh chih-shih ch'u-pan-she, 1964), pp. 90–92.

[34] See Wang Wen-lin, "People's Republic of China"; "Decision to Establish a Maritime Arbitration Commission," *JMJP* (24 January 1959), translated in *SCMP*, no. 1948; see also, "Regulations Governing the Maritime Arbitration Committee," *JPRS*, no. 14335.

or, as is the actual practice, by the relevant port authority which would, if necessary, detain a vessel at the commission's instance until security requirements were met. (The same result can often be achieved by different means in the West, but it is no part of a Western arbitrator's function to take these measures; instead, the party seeking security has to start entirely separate proceedings in the courts.)

The jurisdiction of the commission is based on consent in writing, whether expressed before the occurrence of the dispute or for purposes of the particular dispute. The subject matter within the commission's purview is set out in its constitution and rules. The categories are widely drawn; they include salvage and collision disputes, in respect of each of which the commission has a standard form of reference agreement. In the case of salvage services this is based on a simplified version of Lloyds' open form and it creates what is, in effect, a lien in respect of salvage services independently of the chairman's power to enforce security. Also within the competence of the commission are "disputes arising from chartering seagoing vessels, agency services rendered to seagoing vessels, carriage by sea in virtue of contracts of affreightment, bills of lading or other shipping documents, as well as disputes arising from marine insurance." This clause seems wide enough to cover carriage disputes of all kinds and would, for example, include disputes arising out of general average adjustments in Peking. The reference to "agency services rendered to seagoing vessels" is somewhat obscure; it might cover all disputes over services procured by agents and embrace disputes between principals, i.e., between ship and service enterprises; or it might be read as including disputes with the agents themselves (PENAVICO), in which case a question arises as to the nature of a rather startling provision in the latter corporation's standard ship's agency agreement whereby "the authority to interpret these Regulations rests with this Company."

Formidably difficult questions could arise in respect of the conflict of laws before the commission, although in carriage cases the use of standard forms of contract, in which the majority of expressions have a well-established construction in terms of the law of England and other major maritime countries, makes the task of construing such contracts much easier. A responsible official of the commission has stated that "internationally accepted rules of law" are applied by the commission "when not unreasonable,"[35] and this appears to accord with the objective intention which courts or arbitrators in many countries would probably attribute to the parties to these transactions.

In practice the most important form of dispute settlement from the point of view of the foreign owner appears to be the special jurisdiction which is exercised by the port authorities in respect of the investigations which they are

---

[35] In conversation with the writer in Peking, May 1965.

bound by law to undertake in certain classes of marine casualties.[36] Shipping inquiries are, of course, an important institution in most maritime states, but the Chinese investigation regulations confer a wider jurisdiction than is usual in the common law world, in that they permit the attribution of civil liability as well as the factual finding of fault. Acceptance of this civil jurisdiction is optional in the sense that the parties may choose to apply to the people's court or to the Maritime Arbitration Commission instead. From the "Regulations for the Conduct of the Investigation of Marine Casualties," it appears that the parties may apply to the court or commission to entertain the civil proceedings up to fifteen days after issue of the first report by the port authority. However, this convenient option may be eliminated for foreign vessels by Article 1 of the "Supplementary Rules of the Ministry of Communications for the Investigation of Marine Casualties involving Foreign Ships."[37] This article permits the port authority to require the parties to choose their forum within a certain time. If they choose adjudication by the port authority, they may, after receiving the report, apply for a re-examination by a higher organ or by the ministry; but the results of the re-examination are final, and no appeal can be made to the court or commission.

Even if the civil dispute is transferred to another tribunal the casualty investigation must proceed. This is a matter of great importance since the report of this investigation, with its specific findings of fact, is likely to be of great, if not conclusive, value in other proceedings, whether in China or elsewhere. In suitable instances it even may be the basis of a criminal prosecution, and in the case of Chinese vessels, of professional disciplinary proceedings against the ship's officers.

The competence of the port authority extends to all collisions and perils of the sea, as well as to fires and explosions, which cause loss of life or damage to property. In respect of foreign vessels, jurisdiction may be exercised when the casualty occurs in Chinese waters, where there is damage to property in Chinese ownership, or when a consul of the state to which the ship involved belongs requests an investigation. Since the port authority has a power under the casualty regulations and under the "Provisional Regulations for the Administration of Sea Ports" to arrest property for the purpose of obtaining security, it may well be that the mere presence of a ship within territorial waters is a

---

[36] The investigatory function is set out in the "Provisional Regulations for the Administration of Seaports," article 14, and is elaborated in the "Regulations for the Conduct of Investigations into Marine Casualties," *FKHP*, no. 10 (19 September 1959): 331, which replace a set of provisional regulations made in 1952 and published in *CFJP* (6 August 1952).

[37] These regulations are at present available only in an unofficial translation, the exact provenance of which is unknown. They have every appearance of authenticity, however, and the sense of this particular provision is confirmed by Ni Cheng-ao, *Problems of Jurisdiction*, p. 90.

foundation of jurisdiction, in a manner similar to the English admiralty jurisdiction *in rem*. This is the tentative view of Ni Cheng-ao, who also raises the possibility of arrests of vessels by Chinese men-of-war following collisions in which Chinese lives or property are injured; he does not specify whether such arrests should be confined to territorial waters, or whether they might lawfully extend to the high seas.[38] He also asserts that foreign companies may always be subject to proceedings if they have an agent in China, a rule which may include all the customers of PENAVICO.

The Provisional Regulations on the Administration of Sea Ports do confer on the port authority a power to arrest any vessel which contravenes the law or where harbor dues, fines, penalties, ships' debts, or compensation for damage to property within the harbor and payable in respect of that ship remain unpaid. The Regulations for the Conduct of Investigations into Marine Casualties confer similar powers with regard to vessels involved in casualties where any interested party requests that security be furnished. Under the former regulations, there are provisions of great interest that give a right of action against a port authority which uses these powers wrongfully, and also a right of indemnity for the port authority when a wrongful arrest is made at the instance of some other party.

Once security is given, a vessel is always released. Nevertheless, the practice as to arrest in China is particularly burdensome to foreign owners and their protecting and indemnity associations since only cash can be accepted by way of security, bonds and bank guarantees being regarded as inadequate. This practice probably is due to the many and intricate payment restrictions which have been directed against the PRC; a natural reluctance to litigate abroad on the Chinese part can only have been strengthened by the possibility that defenses of this kind might be raised by a foreign guarantor sued on a bond.[39]

In discussing the arrest of ships as a basis of jurisdiction for casualty investigations, Ni Cheng-ao refers to the possibility of attaching property belonging to a foreign party other than the vessel immediately concerned.[40] This suggests that the "sister ships" rule operates in China. It also seems to indicate that ships' stores and funds in Chinese banks which represent freight, charter-hire or demurrage payable in China may be attached to found jurisdiction, as well as being subject to execution after judgment. In respect of all claims arising out of shipping casualties, however, liability is limited, except for loss of life, to the value of the defendant vessel, and presumably other property would not be at risk beyond this sum.

---

[38] *Ibid.*, pp. 90–91.

[39] Since the time of writing the Chinese authorities have somewhat relaxed this rule of practice, and a bank guarantee is now usually an acceptable form of security.

[40] Ni Cheng-an, *Problems of Jurisdiction*, pp. 90–91.

In the wreck-removal legislation, the port authority is given explicit power to sell property detained, but the other regulations which confer the power of arrest on the port authority omit all mention of sale. Rather, execution is specifically left to the people's court. The practice followed in recent years appears to be that a port authority can itself order sale in certain circumstances, and such orders, very much in the style of court judgments, have been made for this purpose. This apparent extension of power, which is probably justifiable on the basis of liberal or "functional" principles of statutory construction, is one of many problems associated with the partly judicial, partly ministerial, partly commercial activities of the port authority. Such problems might eventually be of great significance for a foreign court called upon to consider an arrest and sale of a ship in terms of an insurance policy.[41]

Where sale is ordered, the prices realized are usually in accordance with world-market rates. The actual process of sale is not known, but the price is presumably based on appraisement by experts. Once the ship's debts have been satisfied from the proceeds of sale, the balance, less procedural costs, is returned promptly to the owners. Although arrest is not uncommon in Chinese ports, the authorities have given the impression of being very reluctant to order sale.

41 See The "Anita," [1971] 1 W. L. R. 88a.

Ways of Payment in Foreign Trade

FRANK MÜNZEL

For much of the little I am able to say below, I am indebted to several merchants and bankers in Hong Kong, who suffered my uninformed questions with—for the most part—very good grace. Regrettably because of the Hong Kong love of secrecy, I may not name them. But I hope that they and I, through this paper, will contribute a little bit to the development of Sino-Western friendship. For relations between China and the West are still hampered by the old prejudice that the Chinese are all very peculiar people who do everything in a quite different way and can therefore be neither understood nor trusted. In the legal field this has taken the form of the belief that China has "no law in the Western sense" or "no socialist legality" at all—and who would want to have anything to do with a lawless country?

The problem is further aggravated by the fact that this concern with legality will seem disagreeably familiar to the Chinese. They will remember those respectable British merchants who complained about Chinese lawlessness when the Chinese imperial authorities confiscated the opium those gentlemen wanted to smuggle into China. They will recall that German emperor who wanted the Shantung coal mines and in the process developed great anger over the supposed state of lawlessness in that province which required his intervention. They will think of Lenin's heirs, who disregard Lenin's declarations on Russia's unequal treaties with China, but lament the absence of socialist legality in the Chinese People's Republic.

So, the Chinese are understandably skeptical about big words like "law" and "legality." They talk very little about such concepts and they make research into their legal system unreasonably difficult. But if, nevertheless, we do take the trouble to find out about Chinese law—and as this volume shows, this is by no means impossible—we will be disappointed if we had hoped for exotic chinoiseries. Instead, we will find what seems to be quite a sophisticated system of rules (though perhaps not sophisticated enough to strangle the economy with rigid plans and a rigid bureaucracy administering them) and, in foreign trade practices, a general conformity with international practice.

I. BANKING ARRANGEMENTS

Banking arrangements in foreign trade must include payment relations between two countries (and/or two banks) on the one side, and between individual buyers and sellers on the other. In payment arrangements with other countries, China formerly was usually represented by the People's Bank, and the other side, by its own state bank. Now the Bank of China usually appears on the Chinese side.

With most socialist countries[1] each bank opens an account with the other for one year. All payments between the two countries during this year are then made through these accounts. In the cases of the CSSR, the GDR, Poland, and Mongolia, however, there are several accounts—one main account for trade payments and one or several for other purposes. For example, in the case of Poland both banks also establish separate accounts for the cost of fairs, postal services, and provisions sold to the other side's ships, and other accounts in connection with the Sino-Polish Shipping Company.

All these accounts (with the exception of those of the Sino-Polish Shipping Company) are closed at the end of the year, though in some cases payments for contracts executed during that year may be made through them until the end of the following January. Surpluses from the nontrade accounts are usually transferred to the main trade account at the end of the year. A surplus on the (main) account must be transferred to next year's account, until the end of January (Soviet Union) or March (Korea, Mongolia) or February (all others) of the following year. For some countries, the agreements stipulate that the surplus must be balanced during the following year.

With the state banks of some capitalist countries, similar accounts are kept,

---

[1] Cf. the most recent available trade and payments agreements (TPA): with Albania, of 5 December 1971, *TYC,* 18:34, and the long-term agreement of 16 October 1970, *TYC,* 17:11; with Bulgaria, of 9 April 1971, *TYC,* 18:66; with the CSSR, of 18 May 1971, *TYC,* 18:77; with the GDR, of 18 May 1971, *TYC,* 18:94; with Hungary, of 28 April 1971, *TYC,* 18:30; with Korea, of 30 December 1971, *TYC,* 18:84, and exchange of letters of 10–20 April 1971, *TYC,* 18:81; with Mongolia, of 5 June 1971, *TYC,* 18:90; with Poland, of 31 May 1971, *TYC,* 18:60; with Romania, of 28 February 1971, *TYC,* 18:52, and the long-term agreement of the same day, *TYC,* 18:51; with the Soviet Union, of 5 August 1971, *TYC,* 18:49; and with Vietnam, of 5 December 1971, *TYC,* 18:75. (No recent agreements are available for Cuba and Yugoslavia.)

but usually for periods longer than one year. However, in some cases these accounts have to be balanced against each other after one year.[2]

Often there are restrictions on overdrafts of these accounts, i.e., mainly on the differences between the amounts paid for imports and the funds earned by exports. With some countries interest must be paid on overdrafts exceeding certain amounts. For example, 2 percent interest is to be paid on overdrafts exceeding 5 percent of the total amount traded under the relevant trade and payments agreement (TPA) in the case of the GDR, or exceeding certain sums, in the cases of the Soviet Union, CSSR, Poland, and Romania. (Up to these amounts—and in the cases of the other socialist countries and a number of other countries, entirely—the accounts are kept free of interest and charges.) In some cases the overdraft exceeding a certain amount has to be paid on demand of the creditor, after varying periods of time (e.g., at once in the case of Egypt; after six months in the case of Algeria; in the case of Finland, after the overdraft has existed for four months, the creditor may demand its repayment within one month).[3] In one case, the allowed overdraft was described as two loans—one of each country to the other—which the two countries might draw upon.[4] In the case of Cambodia, the creditor of the overdraft was allowed to stop exports to, or the debtor, imports from the other side when the overdraft exceeded the allowed amount.[5]

In these accounts RMB are used with Albania and Vietnam. With Mongolia and Romania the currencies of both sides are used at a fixed rate of exchange. With most countries, however, a convertible currency is used. In older agreements, the £St appears most often. Since the devaluation of the £St, the Chinese have preferred the Swiss franc (e.g., in all recent agreements with socialist countries, the four countries listed above excepted).

Under nearly all these agreements,[6] the amounts of the accounts as well as the sums to be paid under the individual trade contracts have to be changed as the official rate of exchange of the currency against gold fluctuates. Consequently, the "currency" used with most of those capitalist countries is gold. In the case of Ceylon Ceylonese rupees were used for account A which covered "guaranteed" deals, i.e., deals concluded under the trade agreement which provided for balanced trade. But a convertible currency had to be used for

---

[2] E.g., cf. agreements with Syria, of 21 February 1963, *TYC*, 12:169; with Burma, of 9 January 1961, *TYC*, 10:71; with Ghana, of 18 August 1961, *TYC*, 10:252.

[3] Cf. the agreements with Egypt, of 17 March 1962, *TYC*, 11:64, and of 2 August 1971, *TYC*, 18:45; with Algeria, of 19 September 1964, *TYC*, 13:293, and of 27 October 1971, *TYC*, 18:36; with Finland, of 5 June 1953, *TYC*, 2:37, and of 18 November 1971, *TYC*, 18:48.

[4] TPA with Mali, of 22 September 1961, *TYC*, 10:327.

[5] Agreement of 24 April 1956, *TYC*, 5:106.

[6] The agreements with Albania, Vietnam, and Mongolia seem to be exceptions.

account B, which covered the payments for other, unplanned transactions. We might call this a mixed capitalist-socialist payments agreement.[7]

Most TPA provide for payments between China and only one other country, but there has been one tripartite agreement involving China selling to the Soviet Union, the Soviet Union to Finland, and Finland to China—with corresponding special accounts of the three state banks and an allowable overdraft of two million rubles.[8] Also, some agreements with capitalist countries provide for the repayment of an overdraft "by ceding the claim of the debtor bank against the state bank of a third country,"[9] i.e., by ceding the surplus that the debtor country has acquired in its trade with a third country.

With some capitalist countries, especially those with which there are no payments agreements (and China's most important trading partners belong to this group), payments are made through mutual accounts of the Bank of China (*not* the People's Bank) on the one side and several private banks on the other. In these cases (and also in some of the capitalist countries using the system of two state banks opening mutual accounts described above), merchants may also bank directly with Chinese banks operating overseas (hereafter called overseas banks),[10] including the Bank of China, without going through a bank of their own country.

The case of Japan, where payments were formerly made through a British bank in London, is described in the chapter by Henderson and Matsuo. Generally, however, the Chinese tend to avoid going through a third bank. The main reason probably is their earlier experience in such instances as the Banque Belge case.[11] The Hong Kong branch of this Belgian bank opened "letters of credit" (in reality, authorities to purchase) for a Chinese company.

---

[7] TPA of 3 October 1962, *TYC*, 11:115.

[8] TPA of 21 September 1952, *TYC*, 2:174. This was one of a series of Finland-Soviet Union-third socialist country transactions. Cf. R. F. Miksell, J. N. Behrmann, *Financing Free World Trade with the Sino-Soviet Bloc* (Princeton, N.J.: International Finance Section, Department of Economics and Sociology, Princeton University, 1958), pp. 54–55.

[9] E.g., agreement with Egypt of 22 August 1955, *TYC*, 4:127. (This agreement is now superseded by the agreements cited in note 3.)

[10] There are at present about ten such banks in Hong Kong. The most important of these is the Bank of China, followed by the Bank of Communications, the Sin Hua Bank, and the China and South Sea Bank. Most were established many years ago (the Bank of China in 1904, the Bank of Communications in 1906) and have been joint state-private enterprises since their foundation. Now all of them are jointly owned but in fact entirely state-controlled, the smaller banks through the Bank of China. Outside China these banks handle all kinds of banking business; inside China they are employed only in transactions abroad and in handling foreign remittances. Cf. the chapter by Alan H. Smith on PRC-related enterprises in Hong Kong.

[11] *China Mutual Trading Co. v. Banque Belge pour l'Étranger (Extrême Orient) S.A., Hong Kong Law Reports* 39 (1955): 144.

Under these "L/C," the bank ordered its American agent, a United States' bank, to purchase from the American sellers drafts up to the amount of the contract price for certain imports to China. To that end, the Banque Belge established a "margin" with the United States bank whereby up to that margin, drafts would be purchased by that bank. Later, the United States government blocked the accounts of Chinese firms in the United States, including the account of the Chinese company in question. The United States government then induced the Banque Belge to pay the amount of that margin into the blocked account of the Chinese company, and to charge this payment against the security given by the Chinese company. Of course with mutual accounts of a Chinese bank on one side and either the Banque Belge or the United States bank on the other (accounts of the type described above), the Chinese would have been better off.

II. FOREIGN TRADE PAYMENTS IN THE BOOKS OF THE PEOPLE'S BANK

Before discussing methods for individual payments, we should take a short look at the general purpose of those mutual accounts established by the People's Bank with other state banks. From the Chinese point of view, these accounts not only help to control the balance of trade with individual countries, but they also constitute an important means of gathering information on the overall state of China's international financial situation.

In the books of the People's Bank, international payments are covered under a number of titles of accounts.[12] In 1962 foreign trade payments to and from central units—presumably the import-export corporations—appear under the number 26. To this we may add the titles covering movements of foreign currency: numbers 193 (buying and selling of foreign currency and foreign currency bills by the People's Bank), 184 (payments to and from the banks representing the People's Bank abroad, which probably was the surplus of the balance of payments with foreign state banks), and 192 (the same for the "special banks" abroad, probably the overseas banks), as well as the movements of foreign currency between different branches of the People's Bank under numbers 186 and 187.

Among the liabilities we find the foreign currency accounts with the People's Bank (number 169—much of which were, of course, the accounts of foreign state banks as described above) and those accounts (of foreign merchants and representatives) with the People's Bank that were calculated in RMB, but were paid in and reconvertible into foreign currency (number 141). On the other hand, there are the bank's holdings of foreign currency (number 145) and its acquisition of foreign currency and foreign currency bills (number 151).

---

[12] Lo Yü-fu et al., *Jen-min yin-hang k'uai-chi ho-suan* (Accounting of the People's Bank) (Peking: Chung-kuo ts'ai-cheng ching-chi ch'u-pan-she, 1964), pp. 35–36.

Payments connected with imports seem to be covered specifically by numbers 174 and 175 (sums received respectively returned as security deposits, presumably for the acquisition of imported goods). Liabilities of the People's Bank under deferred payment clauses for imports to China are listed under number 150; similar liabilities of the Bank's debtors who have bought Chinese exports are listed under number 147.

Foreign aid payments are covered by numbers 155 and 156 (for Soviet loans to China) and 164–167 (for Chinese aid payments).

All these titles evidently cover only transactions through the People's Bank. Therefore, it seems at first sight that an important part of Chinese foreign trade payments is left out, namely, those transactions between Import-Export Corporations and their partners in capitalist countries which are carried out through the overseas banks. However, these transactions have to correspond to deals between the Import-Export Corporations and buyers or sellers inside China. These deals are paid through the People's Bank and accounted for, presumably, under number 26, central foreign trade payments. Moreover, it seems that for all imports the units buying from the Import-Export Corporations have to pay the security deposits covered by titles number 174 and 175. (We shall discuss in more detail later the relations between the Import-Export Corporations and their partners inside China.)

III. INDIVIDUAL PAYMENTS

In the early days there were some instances of straight barter trade that did not involve bank payments, and also some cases where no individual transactions were carried out. The trade agreements with Korea of 18 August 1950[13] provided for nearly all particulars of the Sino-Korean trade for one year so that no individual contracts were considered necessary. Accounts were drawn up quarterly at meetings of the two sides, and surplus due to one side, if any, was carried over. Similarly, in the Sino-Vietnamese border trade between the "trade companies" (perhaps identical with the foreign trade companies described below) of the respective border provinces, sales of the two sides to each other have to be balanced, and accounts are kept to ensure this. Thus, it seems, perhaps wrongly, that banks are not involved.[14] Otherwise, such nearly straight barter is not used anymore. Individual payments are made for individual deals, even if the trade with the partner's country has to be balanced as a whole.

During the early 1950s, individual payments were usually made by "authority

---

[13] *TYC*, 1:84.

[14] Agreement of 7 July 1955, *TYC*, 4:157.

to purchase" (A/P) for imports (to China), and by letters of credit (L/C), documents against payment or documents against acceptance for exports.[15]

An A/P is opened by one bank, on the application of the importer, and addressed to another bank, usually in the country of the exporter. The opening bank authorizes the other bank to purchase the exporter's drafts, drawn on the importer, up to a certain amount, provided they are accompanied by the necessary sales and shipping documents. Such an A/P may be revocable and with recourse (from the drafts against the exporter); or it may be irrevocable, without recourse, and confirmed by the bank to which it is addressed. The A/P seems to have been developed in East Asia, where, to quote a 1964 Chinese textbook, the first of the two forms (revocable with recourse) was "used by the United States and British imperialistic countries' merchants as an instrument of credit provided by the banks of their countries (for buying from) exporters in Asian countries. . . . The second form (irrevocable, without recourse) was used only by the local capitalist importers of Asian countries . . . because the banks of the local capital were too weak to open L/C or revocable without recourse A/P."[16]

More specifically, the opening bank, and through it the negotiating bank, usually had to be given substantial security. The interest on the amount of the drafts was borne by the importer under the A/P, and by the exporter under the L/C.[17] Hence, the A/P—at least in the revocable with recourse form—really did not provide any "credit"; its continued use after 1949 was, apart from being traditional in East Asia, a consequence of the fact that the Chinese firms and banks had not yet gained the international reputation which they enjoy today of always meeting their financial obligations. Another reason probably was that an A/P practically restricted the negotiation of the drafts to the bank to which the A/P was addressed, a bank usually well known to the Chinese side. A third reason may have been that the early barter trade regulations did not allow the use of L/C's (except with special permission), but were silent on the use of A/P's. A/P's still were used, at least occasionally, up to the Cultural Revolution. Today, apart from the "immediate payment" method used with socialist countries, only L/C's are used for individual trade payments.[18]

The exclusive use of L/C's both for exports and imports occurred first in

---

[15] Wang Tan-ju, *Yin-hang k'uai-chi* (Bank accounting) (Shanghai: Li-hsin k'uai-chi yung-p'in-she, 1951), pp. 318 ff.

[16] Tseng Hsi, *Tzu-pen chu-i kuo-chia ti kuo-chi chieh-suan fang-shih* (International ways of payment of the capitalist countries) (Peking: Chung-kuo ts'ai-cheng ching-chi ch'u-pan-she, 1964), p. 121. I am far more indebted to this book than appears from these notes.

[17] An Tzu-chieh, *Kuo-chi mao-i shih-wu* (Foreign trade practice) (2nd ed., Shanghai: Shang-wu yin-shu kuan, 1951), p. 185; also cf. the Banque Belge case, note 11.

[18] Cf. the graph describing the use of L/C, in the chapter by Henderson and Matsuo.

China's trade with socialist countries.[19] These L/C's seem to have differed from the L/C's used in the trade with capitalist countries only in one point: like the L/C's used in the internal trade of socialist countries, they did not involve drafts.[20] Nevertheless, we shall treat them together with the "capitalist" L/C's.

Before discussing the L/C's more thoroughly, we have to describe the developments in China's trade with socialist countries. Here, in a manner similar to trade among the European socialist countries, the L/C soon was replaced by the so-called payment according to accounts. (This, as well as the later developments described below, was introduced by the Soviet Union.)[21] Under the rules of payment according to account, the seller applied to his bank for an "order for collection" (roughly corresponding to our bill for collection) of his bill; the application had to show date and number of the contract, price, quantity, specifications, etc. The seller had to add the relevant documents—in particular, the bill of lading in the case of transport by sea—and both the seller's and buyer's state banks checked these documents for discrepancies. After finding none, the seller's bank would credit the seller's account, debit the account of the buyer's bank and notify this bank. The buyer's bank, after also finding no discrepancy, would pay within five days, i.e., credit the account of the seller's bank and debit the account of the buyer.

The buyer's bank was not allowed to withhold payments because of complaints about the merchandise that were not based on discrepancies in the documents but rather upon an inspection of the actual goods. Claims arising out of such complaints had to be made separately by a protest from the buyer to which the seller had to reply within forty-five days; protest and reply normally led to an agreement on which payment had to be made, usually within five days.[22]

From 1955 onwards the socialist countries all switched to the method of

---

[19] Agreement on General Terms for the Exchange of Goods (hereafter GT) with the Soviet Union of 19 April 1950, *TYC*, 1:51; GT with Hungary of 19 February 1951, *TYC*, 1:38.

[20] Except for Sino-Yugoslav trade, where the same kinds of L/C's are used as in China's trade with capitalist countries. Payment Agreement with Yugoslavia, of 17 February 1956, *TYC*, 5:115.

[21] GT with the Soviet Union of 29 March 1952, *TYC*, 2:40; with the GDR of 28 May 1952, *TYC*, 2:156. For the Eastern European developments, cf. A. Vaganov et al., *Organizacija i tehnika vneshney torgovli SSSR i drugih socialisticheskih stran* (Organization and techniques of the foreign trade of the USSR and other socialist lands) (Moscow: IMO, 1963), p. 123.

[22] Cf. the 1953 GT's with Hungary, Romania, the CSR, and Bulgaria, in vol. 2 of the *TYC*.

278 FRANK MÜNZEL

"immediate payment."[23] Under this method only the seller's bank checked for documentary discrepancies. The buyer's bank merely credited and debited the appropriate accounts as described above immediately after receiving what was called the "payment notice" from the seller's bank. For documentary discrepancies as well as for other complaints the buyer had to protest as described above.[24]

Finally, the reasons for which such protests could be made were standardized,[25] and the procedure for these claims was simplified. Under the new rules within ten days after the buyer received the documents, the buyer could refuse payment wholly or partially if he thought there were documentary discrepancies of certain standard types. His bank would check his claim on the basis of the documents he produced and either reject it or else debit and credit accordingly, and then notify the seller's bank which also would immediately credit and debit accordingly.

If the buyer's bank rejected a claim for payment or repayment, this was not the end of the matter. The creditor could pursue his claim through an ordinary order for collection, or he could obtain the written agreement of the other side (or of the other side's trade attaché) to pursue his claim under immediate payment rules. In fact, the general terms of trade between China and other socialist countries sometimes contain a clause making it a duty of the rejected creditor to settle the claim directly within a certain period.

Claims arising not out of documentary discrepancies but out of deficiencies of the merchandise not apparent on the face of the documents still had to be made by order for collection. Even here, immediate payment could be used if there already was an agreement between the parties on the claim. If such an agreement had been reached, the debtor also might pay by immediate payment without a previous request by the creditor; in that case, the documents were checked by the debtor's bank.

At the beginning of the 1960s, these methods were used uniformly between China and the other socialist countries with a few exceptions. In trade with

[23] Among the European socialist countries (except Yugoslavia) the immediate payment rules became part of the "General Delivery Conditions of the COMECON" of 1958 (as well as of the revised 1968 edition). These conditions are not applied in trade with and among the non-European socialist countries (even though Mongolia became a COMECON member in 1962), but there are nearly identical bilateral agreements with and among them, which include the immediate payment rules. Cf. Vaganov, *Organizacija*, p. 133; Tseng Hsi, *Tzu-pen*, pp. 12–14; and the text of the bilateral conditions for the trade of the GDR with non-European socialist countries, in *Die Allgemeinen Lieferbedingungen der Länder des sozialistischen Wirtschaftsgebietes* (The General Delivery Conditions of the countries of the socialist economic area) (Berlin: Kammer für Außenhandel der DDR, 1966).

[24] Cf. the 1955 GT's with the Soviet Union, Romania, and the GDR, *TYC*, 4:47, 97, 180; the 1957 GT with Albania, *TYC*, 6:117.

[25] This first occurred in the 1955 GT with the Soviet Union.

Cuba, L/C's were employed until 1963; thereafter, a procedure nearly identical with the old payment according to accounts was introduced. That is, payments were made after the documents were checked by both the seller's and the buyer's bank. However, for a number of standardized reasons, including both documentary discrepancies and undocumented deficiencies, an agreement on the buyer's claims had to be reached within a certain short period of time, whereupon the buyer, with this agreement, could obtain immediate payment.[26] Another exception was the border trade between the Chinese and Vietnamese provincial trade companies which we had already described. A third was the small border trade carried on by individuals in the Sino-Vietnamese border region, where payments were made in cash.[27] (This was, of course, a peculiarity of border trade rather than of trade with socialist countries: cash also was paid to agents of the import-export corporations selling directly to people in some areas of Hong Kong as well as to Nepalese merchants operating in Tibet.[28])

In the trade with capitalist partners, forms similar to immediate payment are sometimes used in penalties for delayed delivery by the foreign seller which, according to a standard contract form, may be deducted from the amount of the L/C by the negotiating bank. Similarly, the premium for additional insurance demanded by a foreign buyer must be paid immediately upon receipt of the seller's "debit note." Apart from these peculiarities, however, only L/C's are used.

All Chinese overseas banks use the Uniform Customs and Practices for Documentary Credits (1962 revision) of the International Chamber of Commerce. However, even when standardized by the Uniform Customs, the L/C still is a very flexible instrument with a great number of different types answering a large variety of needs. Not all of these varieties are used by the overseas banks. For example, except sometimes with Japanese partners, they do not use or accept straight credits, i.e., L/C's where no drafts are used and the exporter will be paid only by the advising bank. (Formerly, straight credits were used in trade with socialist countries and also as "traveler's L/C" for visitors to China.[29] In the latter case various forms of drafts are now used.) In other words, L/C's in China's trade with capitalist countries except Japan are probably always used together with drafts.

Generally speaking, drafts under L/C's may serve three purposes. They

---

[26] 1963 GT with Cuba, *TYC*, 12:125.

[27] Cf. the Sino-Vietnamese agreements of 25 August 1953, *TYC*, 2:138, and of 7 July 1955, *TYC*, 4:154.

[28] Sino-Nepali exchange of letters of 7 October 1956, *TYC*, 5:33.

[29] Ching-ch'ang hui-k'uan, hui-hsiang chih jen k'o yung ting-ch'i ling-k'uan fang-shih" (Persons who regularly transfer money, or who return to their native areas can now use vouchers with fixed periods of validity), *Ta-kung-pao* (Hong Kong), 3 January 1962.

are a receipt for the money paid to the exporter; also, the negotiating bank uses them to get refunded by the opening bank. Both these purposes could be served as well, or better, by simpler techniques. The third reason, the use of drafts to finance the transaction, is generally regarded as the main *raison d'être* for the use of drafts under L/C's. Do the Chinese, then, use drafts to gain access to the international monetary market?

As a rule, drafts of Chinese exporters seem to be drawn without recourse, i.e., excluding the responsibility of the drawer; Chinese import contracts do not, at least, prohibit such drafts. But many banks, especially the large reimbursing banks, do not accept drafts drawn without recourse. Hence these drafts are not especially useful for tapping international financing.

Moreover, while the Chinese do not use straight L/C's, they frequently use restricted L/C's, that is, L/C's restricting the negotiation of the drafts and the documents to a certain bank, usually the local branch of the Bank of China. This practice probably developed to ensure that the documents are properly checked. While it does not completely bar other banks from negotiating the beneficiary's drafts and documents, negotiability is reduced since these drafts and documents must be approved by the Bank of China.

Moreover, while usance (i.e., deferred payment) credits do occur, the vast majority of the L/C's used in the China trade and the L/C's asked for in the standard contracts are sight credits. It certainly would be possible to use drafts under such L/C's to finance the deal in spite of all these difficulties. It could be done, for example, through "refinancing" whereby the importer's bank opens a sight credit, but the importer pays with a draft endorsed by his bank and drawn on the advising bank; the 1964 banking textbook cited above describes these and similar techniques in detail.[30] However, there seems to be no indication that the Chinese actually use such techniques. In fact, indications are otherwise. The overseas banks, on principle, do not open or ask for red or green clause credits wherein the buyer prefinances the deal. They regard this problem as the sole responsibility of the seller. Moreover, in the rare cases where usance credits are involved, these banks will not use banker's acceptance credits.[31] Rather, the overseas banks will use deferred sight credits whereby the exporter simply has to present a sight draft against documents for acceptance and, after a certain period of time, for payment.

Some techniques of financing also might be hampered by time limits for the validity of the L/C. When the Chinese are the buyers, the standard contracts limit the period of the validity of the L/C (issued by a Chinese

---

[30] Tseng Hsi, *Tzu-pen*, p. 78.

[31] Under these acceptance credits the exporter draws a draft on the opening or the advising bank or on some third bank, usually a big reimbursing bank. This draft is then accepted by the bank upon which it is drawn, in exchange for the documents. Then the exporter or his bank will negotiate the accepted draft.

overseas bank) usually to a month or less—starting from about twenty days before and ending fifteen days after shipment. When the Chinese are the sellers, the date for sending the L/C may be set somewhat earlier or be left to negotiation, but the time limit for negotiation of the L/C usually also is fifteen days after shipment.[32]

While China does not seem to take advantage of international financing through the use of L/C's, she has, to a probably modest extent, used other, "straighter" ways to finance her trade. The overseas banks do a great deal of business and consequently hold foreign currency. Moreover, people outside China, especially overseas Chinese, are encouraged to place foreign currency into RMB accounts with Chinese overseas banks. There are several different kinds of such accounts. Overseas Chinese and foreigners may open RMB savings accounts. Money is paid into and out of these accounts in the local currency—say Hong Kong dollars— converted at the rate of exchange prevailing at the time of payment. The rate of interest is lower than that paid by the local banks—including the Chinese overseas banks—on normal savings accounts, but the absence of the danger of devaluation of the RMB is supposed to make up for the difference.

Formerly, foreigners—at least overseas Chinese—also could open two other kinds of RMB accounts with the branches of overseas banks *inside* China, the so-called A and B accounts. Foreign currency was paid into both. Only RMB, however, was paid out of the B accounts; nor could B accounts be reconverted into a foreign currency without special permission. B accounts were opened by overseas Chinese for the benefit of relatives living in China.[33] The A accounts, on the other hand, could be reconverted into foreign currency at will. They were meant for overseas Chinese merchants who could use them to buy merchandise in China. Why merchants would use such accounts with a bank inside China, instead of simply opening an account with an overseas bank abroad, is not clear. Today, such accounts would be superfluous and are no longer used. All foreign buyers deal with one of the Chinese Import-Export corporations, all of which are sufficiently large and experienced not to require their foreign partners to open an account with a bank branch in the

---

[32] In Sino-Japanese friendly firm trade the validity of the L/C for Chinese exports may begin twenty-five days before shipment, and for Chinese imports may begin fifteen days before shipment, cf. Nihon bōeki shinkōkai (JETRO), *Nitchū bōeki handobukku* (Tokyo, 1971), p. 117; or twenty-five days before the month of shipment, or after conclusion of the contract (contracts reported by Henderson and Matsuo); or thirty days before the month of shipment, cf. Yano Harutaka, *Shinkō Nitchū bōeki tsūshinbun* (Tokyo: Koseikan, 1971), p. 41. But in *all* of these cases, the validity of the L/C ends fifteen days after shipment.

[33] Now money can be sent to China through all the overseas banks. A standing order for payments to relatives in China may be placed with the China and South Seas Bank in Hong Kong.

Chinese city where they have their offices. Perhaps in 1957, when these A accounts were first established, foreign merchants still were able to establish a more direct contact with the producers of the goods they bought from China or, at least, with the local foreign trade companies; and these companies may have been too inexperienced in foreign trade not to require the security of a local bank account.[34]

Even today, foreign merchants can open a RMB account with the RMB they have obtained by selling goods to China, instead of converting these amounts into foreign currency, provided that the payments agreements between China and their own country do not prohibit this. They may open such accounts with the overseas bank that handles payment on the transaction, or even with their own bank, if the Bank of China, by special agreement, has allowed this bank to open such RMB accounts. These accounts may be used later to purchase Chinese goods.

Since a large part of the China trade now is conducted in RMB, foreign merchants also may buy RMB if they can prove—usually by presenting a copy of the contract—that they need it to purchase goods from China. They may buy RMB up to six months in advance and may also sell in advance (without a time limit) RMB earned from sales to China.

To return to the L/C's, they may be revocable (until negotiated) or irrevocable, and confirmed (i.e., have their payment guaranteed by the advising bank) or unconfirmed. The L/C's *demanded* by Chinese sellers have to be irrevocable and confirmed "by a prime bank" (or the L/C has to be opened by a bank agreed upon in the contract). L/C's *opened* by Chinese banks also are nearly always irrevocable ("we won't deal with partners so unreliable as to make revocable L/C's necessary") but nowadays almost never confirmed ("a promise by a Chinese bank needs no confirmation"). But Chinese overseas banks take care to obtain sufficient security from capitalist clients for whom they open L/C's. Under Hong Kong practice, the application for the L/C will contain a pledge of the documents to the bank.[35] With reliable clients, the bank also will engage in trust-receipt financing. Where necessary, the bank also will demand a guarantor. However, no security is demanded from the Chinese Import-Export corporations.[36]

---

[34] Cf. "Wai-pi ts'un k'uan tsai Kuang-chou" (Foreign currency accounts in Canton), *Ta-kung-pao* (Hong Kong), 21 February 1957.

[35] A fairly thorough description of this practice can be found in the scandalous Dairy Farm decision. Cf. *The China State Farm, Ltd.* v. *Dairy Farm, Ltd., Hong Kong Law Reports* 51 (1967): 95–115.

[36] Under the Liao-Takasaki memorandum Chinese firms buying on credit in Japan may give a special form of security: the Bank of China may issue a "letter of guarantee" that is "to be based on the L/C" for the transaction. There are many different forms of letters of guarantee; this might be the bank guarantee for payment of a draft accepted by the importer or his bank, as described by Tseng Hsi, *Tzu-pen*, pp. 125–26. But the

Again, I am afraid that, in all this, one seeking the bizarre or the devious will be disappointed. There are no inscrutable Oriental tricks here. In their trade with capitalist countries the Chinese are quite content to use the ordinary methods and instruments developed and standardized by international business practice. They complain only that these methods are not yet standardized enough, and so leave too much leeway for the legal tricks that are such typical consequences of the turmoil and unreliability of capitalism. Consequently, they welcome every attempt at standardization.

However, there are two peculiar forms of the L/C that, though not restricted to the China trade, occur here more often than elsewhere: namely, revolving and reciprocal credits. In the case of the latter, the trading partners have to open alternating credits—A as importer for B as exporter, then vice versa, always for the same amount. If a somewhat more elastic procedure is needed, the beneficiary of the first L/C may sign a "letter of undertaking" to open the second L/C. Reciprocal L/C's may be used to safeguard a balanced trade between two partners. Consequently, they were the only form of L/C allowed by the early barter trade regulations although they are still in use today.

A revolving credit, in the form opened by Chinese overseas banks, allows its beneficiary to use the credit up to a certain amount during a certain period of time. After this period has elapsed, the beneficiary can use the credit again, up to the same amount, and so forth, with the credit renewed automatically.

Both these credit forms are used for steady, long-term business connections. The Chinese Import-Export corporations prefer this kind of connection and have developed several types of agency arrangements to further such connections. These agency contracts occur particularly in Southeast Asia. Revolving credits seem to be used mostly in connection with such contracts.[37]

IV. THE ENIGMATIC INTERMEDIARIES

Ordinary though the L/C's used by the Chinese may be, there is one apparently ordinary clause that is rather a mystery to me. When the Chinese are the sellers, their standard contracts often ask for a transferable L/C.[38] In international trade such L/C's are used when the seller himself still has to obtain the goods and wants to use the L/C to finance the deal by which he acquires the goods. In the Chinese case such L/C's might be used by the (selling) Import-Export Corporation to buy the goods to be sold from another

Memorandum also allows the use of only an appropriate L/C. The drafts (drawn on the Chinese firm buying on credit) have to be accepted by the Peking branch of the Bank of China. Cf. *Nitchū bōeki handobukku*, pp. 88, 120, 122.

[37] *Tao Kuang-chou tso sheng-i* (Going to Canton to do business) (Hong Kong: *Ta-kung-pao*, 1958), chap. 1. For an example of such a contract, cf. Yano Harutaka, *Shinkō*, p. 56; this contract, however, stipulates separate ordinary L/C's for each shipment.

[38] E.g., cf. the contract cited in note 37.

country. Occasionally, Chinese trade agreements provide for transit trade (e.g., with Albania[39]), but the clause appears too frequently to be explained by these rare cases. Another purpose of the clause might be to allow delivery by a different branch of the Import-Export Corporation other than the one that concluded the contract. That, however, should be possible even without such a clause. Finally, the Import-Export Corporation might use such an L/C to obtain the merchandise from inside the country. This, however, would be unlikely. While L/C's are used in China's internal trade, their form is quite different (and they are, of course, in Chinese). Hence, the use of international L/C's probably would confuse people involved in internal trade. Moreover, the import-export corporations generally do not deal directly with the ultimate internal producers and users; rather intermediaries, as a rule the local foreign trade companies, perform their function. (In 1955 these foreign trade companies were established as provincial companies.[40] Recent reports describe them as local companies (below provincial level), operating under provincial or lower level foreign trade bureaus.[41]) These foreign trade companies might be less confused by international L/C's.

---

[39] TPA of 5 December 1971, *TYC*, 18:34.

[40] This appears from the ordinance of 9 December 1954, *Chung-yang jen-min cheng-fu fa-ling hui-pien* (Compendium of laws and decrees of the Central People's Government), 1954:253.

[41] For example, cf. "Hsieh-shang chieh-chüeh ch'ang-ch'i wei chieh-chüeh ti wen-t'i" (Problems that have remained unsolved for a long time are solved by discussion), *Ta-kung-pao* (Peking), 28 May 1964; text to the picture on p. 2 of the *Jen-min jih-pao* of 21 August 1973. Little information is available about these companies. Their establishment in 1955 coincides with the introduction of immediate payment between China and the other socialist countries. In those countries there exist similar intermediaries "to allow the Import-Export Corporations to concentrate on foreign trade"; but there they usually are not units specializing in foreign trade, but parts of the general internal trade apparatus. Cf. Vaganov, *Organizacija*, pp. 51–53. In the Soviet Union the Import-Export Corporations issue plan orders but do not conclude contracts with their suppliers; this probably does not make the supply very elastic. The use of local rather than central units in China, on the other hand, may serve to provide more elastic supplies; many important export items, like the so-called native products, are only locally planned anyway. Moreover, the local foreign trade companies may have had something to do with the rules (abolished during the Cultural Revolution) which gave the provinces a share in the foreign exchange earned by their exports, cf. the ordinance of 5 November 1957, *Chung-hua jen-min kung-ho-kuo fa-kui hui-pien* (Compendium of laws and regulations of the People's Republic of China), 6:355, transl. by Chao Kuo-chun, *Economic Planning and Organization in Mainland China* (Cambridge: Harvard University Press, 1964), 2:47. However, as is usual with Chinese adaptations of Soviet institutions, the whole system is probably very flexible and full of exceptions. Cases have been described where import-export corporations even buy directly from producers, cf. "Fa-tung chih-kung chien-ch'a wen-t'i, kai-shan ching-ying kuan-li" (Mobilize workers and employees to study problems, improve ways of doing business and management), *Ta-kung-pao* (Peking), 14 February 1963; on the other hand, goods already packed with labels of the foreign trade corporations are also on sale inside China.

As discussed above, the existence of foreign trade companies probably enables the People's Bank to control foreign trade payments, even though payments between the Import-Export corporations and their foreign partners go through the overseas banks rather than the People's Bank. These payments must correspond to payments between the Import-Export corporations and the foreign trade companies which are made through the local branches of the People's Bank. In fact, it may be that, for internal purposes, the Import-Export corporations are regarded as mere agents of the foreign trade companies and not as firms trading on their own account. Consequently, payments between the Import-Export corporations and foreign firms actually are payments between the foreign trade companies and the foreign firms, and may be equated with the payments between the Import-Export corporations and the foreign trade companies.

The transactions between the Import-Export corporations and their foreign partners on the one hand, and between the Import-Export corporations and the foreign trade companies on the other, are quite closely linked, as can be seen from a 1954 ordinance on payments for imports from socialist countries.[42] According to this ordinance, the People's Bank was to send the documents it had received from the foreign seller's state bank to the Import-Export Corporation. (At that time all transactions in trade with socialist countries were made through the People's Bank. Now, as a rule, the Bank of China would take its place.) The corporation then would make out an order for collection of the amount due to the seller from the foreign trade company. One copy of this order was sent directly by the corporation to the foreign trade company; several others were sent back to the People's Bank. The bank would in turn order its branch at the place of business of the foreign trade company to collect the amount from that company. Then the People's Bank (now an overseas bank) would pay the amount to the foreign exporter. If the foreign trade company did not pay in time, the People's Bank would provide the corporation with a loan and make immediate payment to the foreign seller. In other words, it appears that the Import-Export Corporation did not have enough financial leeway to pay the foreign seller independently of the payments from the foreign trade company. This, too, indicates the former's dependent role.

The close connection between the foreign trade company and the Import-Export Corporation also might explain the titles of accounts in the books of the People's Bank (numbers 174 and 175) concerning security deposits for transactions with abroad. These titles cannot be explained if one considers only the Import-Export corporations. As mentioned earlier, the overseas banks do not ask these companies for security when opening an L/C. Hence, these companies do not have to give security in trade with capitalist countries;

---

[42] I.e., the ordinance of 9 December 1954, cited in note 40.

and in the trade with socialist countries, under immediate payment rules, there is even less need for security. But, security always has to be provided when L/C's are opened in China's internal trade. Therefore security probably also must be given by a foreign trade company when it wants the People's Bank to open an L/C for it so that it may buy from an Import-Export Corporation. As this amounts, practically, to buying from a foreign firm, this security will be accounted for as a security paid for a transaction with abroad, just as the L/C will be transformed into an international L/C opened for the same imports by an overseas bank for an import-export company.

However, this is, of course, mostly guesswork, and therefore I had better stop here. The interesting border area between internal and foreign trade still is one of the least known parts of China's legal-economic system. We can here, as always, only hope for more light from the East in the future.

The Personal Security of Businessmen and Trade Representatives

JEROME ALAN COHEN

Literally hundreds of West European, Japanese, and American technicians are scheduled to reside in China to aid in the installation of a variety of manufacturing plants which the People's Republic of China has recently contracted to buy from the capitalist countries. Chinese technicians are already living in many of those countries in order to learn the skills required for the successful operation of the PRC's capital imports. Some foreign businessmen spend months in China negotiating contracts, and today Chinese trade representatives can be found virtually everywhere in the world. In addition, thousands of businessmen visit China annually for brief periods, and an increasing number of Chinese trade delegations are traveling abroad.

The activities of these trade personnel are vital to the development of economic relations with China. Yet, in view of China's political relations with the rest of the world, even so basic a problem as the personal security of trade personnel cannot be taken for granted, either in China or abroad. To what extent do such persons court the risk of arbitrary arrest and imprisonment? Are they subject to other forms of harassment? What arrangements have been made to assure their protection? The essay that follows will discuss these questions, first dealing with the problems encountered by foreigners in China and then discussing the problems encountered by Chinese abroad.

I. THE SECURITY OF FOREIGNERS IN CHINA

Shortly before its demise the "Committee of One Million against the Admission of Red China to the UN" brought to the United States one George

NOTE: This essay covers material up to the end of 1973.

Watt, a British employee of the Vickers-Zimmer Company. Watt had been released in mid-1970 after serving a three-year sentence in a Chinese prison following an espionage conviction.[1] Although the committee failed in its effort to have Watt appear before the Committee on Foreign Relations of the United States Senate, which was holding hearings on China policy, it did manage to publicize his views in the American press. Watt's message concerning Sino-American relations was a simple one: "If any American businessmen contemplate profits out of the approaching détente," he said, "I will give them a flat prediction: They will encounter disaster and will be lucky to escape without imprisonment of their representatives."[2]

Watt's experience was not an isolated one during the Great Proletarian Cultural Revolution of 1966–69. For his participation in the same case another Vickers-Zimmer employee—a West German named Peter Deckart—was lucky enough to have been deported, rather than sentenced to prison.[3] Other business representatives were reported to have been arrested; these included a Belgian banker and twelve Japanese trade representatives, as well as journalists and ship's officers from Great Britain and other countries.[4]

In addition to those who were actually imprisoned, some personnel of foreign companies were subjected to other forms of harassment during the Cultural Revolution. For example, three British engineers, whose firm had sent them to Peking to supervise the installation of machinery, were kept under virtual house arrest for a number of weeks while the Chinese threatened to treat them as prisoners or hostages until a Chinese claim against their company was satisfactorily settled.[5] Moreover, refusal to grant exit visas was commonplace. British banking personnel in Shanghai, for example, had by mid-1968 been waiting a year to leave China, even though their replacements had already arrived.[6]

---

[1] "British Spy Case Broken in Lanchow," *Peking Review,* 11, no. 12 (22 March 1968), pp. 14–15; "Briton Held Three Years Is Free, Peking Says," *New York Times,* 31 July 1970, p. 5. See also George Watt, *China 'Spy'* (London: Johnson, 1972), pp. 200–8.

[2] "The Week," *National Review,* 10 August 1971, pp. 843–44.

[3] "British Spy Case Broken."

[4] See Jerome Alan Cohen, "Chinese Law and Sino-American Trade," in Alexander Eckstein, ed., *China Trade Prospects and United States Policy* (New York: Praeger, 1971), pp. 145–46. With the release in April 1973 of five Japanese trade representatives, only one Japanese businessman, who was sentenced to a twenty-year prison term, remained in Chinese custody; see "Freed Japanese Arrive in HK," *Mainichi Daily News* (Japan), 15 April 1973, p. 1. The last British subjects in Chinese prison were released in January 1973; see "China to Free Last Detained Britons," *London Times,* 29 January 1973, p. 1.

[5] See Derek Davies, "Twisting the Lions' Tails," *Far Eastern Economic Review* [hereafter *FEER*] 68 (28 July 1968): 228, 232–33.

[6] "Traveller's Tales," *Ibid.,* p. 223.

Infringement upon the personal security of foreign businessmen did not originate with the Cultural Revolution, of course. During the early 1950s, while China was participating in the Korean War and conducting a series of campaigns to eliminate counterrevolutionary activity at home, some business-men were convicted of espionage. In July 1970 the People's Republic provided a tragic reminder of that era by announcing the suicide a few months earlier of Hugh Redmond, an American who had been a businessman in Shanghai until he began serving a life sentence following his conviction in 1951.[7] Not only did the newly established Communist government imprison certain foreign businessmen during the early 1950s, but it also denied exit permits to a large number of employees of foreign firms, as part of what the United Kingdom charged was a "deliberate policy of the Chinese Government to render it impossible for most British and foreign firms to remain in China and to force them to surrender their assets."[8]

Harassment of foreign businessmen was muted from the mid-1950s until the Cultural Revolution, but still continued, and refusal to grant exit visas remained a principal sanction. An extreme case was that of a Belgian bank official in Shanghai, Frans Van Roosbroeck, whose bank had transferred $30 million to the United States on behalf of Chinese depositors as the Com-munists were taking over China in 1949; from 1952 until his arrest in 1968, Van Roosbroeck was refused permission to leave China.[9] In interviews several other representatives of foreign firms have reported that in the early 1960s the Chinese government made it clear that their freedom to leave the country was contingent upon their company's satisfactory compliance with its obliga-tions under Chinese law as expounded by the local authorities.

These are unpleasant but undeniable facts. The problem is how to assess their significance. In order to do so, one must consider other facts that are equally compelling but more attractive. Since 1949 tens of thousands of businessmen and company employees have visited China, many of them repeatedly and some of them for considerable periods of time. Relatively few have experienced any invasion of their personal security either by Chinese authorities or by the masses. Indeed, many of these foreign visitors have emphasized that they are actually safer on the streets of Peking, Canton, and Shanghai than they are in the crime-ridden urban centers of their own countries. Stories of lost wallets

[7] Tillman Durdin, "China Frees U.S. Bishop; Says One Captive Is Suicide," *New York Times,* 11 July 1970, p. 1; see also, e.g., "U.S. Underground Espionage Organization in Tientsin Exposed," *New China News Agency* [hereafter *NCNA*] (Peking), 21 March 1951; in *SCMP,* no. 87 (22–24 March 1951), pp. 1–5.

[8] The quotation is from a statement made in the House of Lords by the Marquess of Reading, then British minister of state in the Foreign Office, *Parliamentary Debates* (House of Lords), 5th series (26 June–2 November 1954), 189: 50, cols. 3–4.

[9] See note 6. In the fall of 1971, China announced it would free Van Roosbroeck. "China Frees Belgian Hostage," *Mainichi Daily News,* 28 October 1971, p. 3.

being returned intact have by now become clichés. Businessmen have complained about uncomfortable hotels, ideological harangues, the delays and maneuvers of the Chinese bureaucracy, the boredom of long waits, the unavailability of female companionship, and other difficult aspects of trade with China, but, by and large, they have not expressed concern for their personal security.

Nowhere has this lack of concern been more evident than in Japan. Despite the fact that Japan appears to have had the dubious distinction of leading the world in the number of trade representatives arrested during the Cultural Revolution, the Japanese commercial community had been inundating China with private *ad hoc* trade missions well before the normalization of Sino-Japanese relations in September 1972. And some 2,300 Japanese businessmen —a record number—took part in the Canton Export Commodities Fair in the autumn of 1971.[10]

Although the Japanese press has given enormous coverage to the accelerating interest in trade with China, fear for the safety of Japanese businessmen has not been a prominent concern. This attitude is to be contrasted with that of the London *Times,* which in March 1970, after Shanghai authorities detained two officers of British cargo ships, grimly warned: "Anyone resident in or visiting China, however circumspect, is operating as much at his own risk nowadays as were the earliest explorers in Africa."[11]

Should businessmen who contemplate the China market be concerned about their personal security? Should the eagerness of the Japanese and other competitors flocking to China be attributed to courage, naïveté, need, greed, loss of memory, or other factors? Should one accuse the gray London *Times* of hysterical anticommunism?

As those of us who have interviewed businessmen in the China trade know too well, they are, on the whole, as tight-lipped as they are tough-minded. It is therefore difficult to be certain how most of them evaluate the risk of visiting China and how they weigh it against the potential profits to be made. The following explanation, however, may roughly approximate the unarticulated premises upon which the expanding community of China traders is proceeding.

First of all, many businessmen undoubtedly realize that not all Chinese charges of espionage against their brethren can be attributed to xenophobic officials placing a sinister construction upon innocent actions. Nor can such charges necessarily be dismissed as manifestations of cynical political manipulation that seeks to play upon the masses' traditional suspicion of foreigners in an effort to unify the country and discredit the representatives of foreign capitalism. Scholars have yet to make a systematic inquiry into Chinese

---

[10] "1,457 Japan Firms To Canton Fair," *Mainichi Daily News,* 6 October 1971, p. 6.

[11] "In Peril in Shanghai," *London Times,* 14 March 1970, p. 1.

accusations of foreign espionage, and, given the sensitivity of the subject, it will be difficult to conduct one. It is very likely, however, that in some cases foreign businessmen have in fact been guilty of espionage as charged.

It is common knowledge that intelligence agencies all over the world retain businessmen engaged in foreign trade because of the convenient "cover" that their occupation provides for spying upon other societies. Western countries have frequently resorted to this subterfuge in the Soviet Union and the Eastern European people's democracies. It would be unusual if they neglected this possibility for learning about China.

We know that in China as well as elsewhere the United States has benefited from the intelligence reporting of persons with similar types of "cover," such as foreign students.[12] In addition, the United States Central Intelligence Agency has sought to enlist the services of established American and foreign scholars as informants about China, not only to report on matters that lie within the fields of their professional specialization but also to report on military phenomena that "the Agency" would train them to observe while in China. Moreover, government denials of espionage cannot be taken at face value, as illustrated by the Downey-Fecteau case which involved the airdrop of CIA agents into China.[13]

Thus, sophisticated businessmen can reasonably believe that the risk of their arbitrary arrest and imprisonment during a visit to China is not as great as it might appear, to the uninitiated. It is hard to say, however, by how much the apparent risk is diminished. If we had perfect knowledge, we might find that China's charges were well grounded in most cases, despite the vague hyperbole that the regime often employs to announce convictions for espionage. On the other hand, we might find that in a large percentage of cases the imposition of sanctions was unjust, whether because of exaggerated suspicion or political manipulation.

An important part of the problem, of course, is the extent to which the People's Republic has sought to insulate Chinese society from foreign observers. In order to achieve this goal, it has adopted a correspondingly broad definition of espionage, both in theory and practice. The Act for the Punishment of Counterrevolution, formally promulgated in 1951, is applicable

---

[12] See, e.g., Allyn and Adele Rickett, *Prisoners of Liberation* (New York: Cameron Assoc., 1957), pp. 29–30, 40–42, and 48.

[13] Beginning in 1954, when China announced the conviction of the two Americans for espionage, the United States branded the convictions "a most flagrant violation of justice" based upon "trumped-up charges." See, e.g., 31 *Dept. of State Bulletin,* publication 5683, no. 806 (1954), pp. 856, 857. In early 1973 President Nixon finally acknowledged the CIA's involvement in the case, an admission that shortly thereafter helped to speed Downey's release as the last convicted American held in Chinese prison. See, e.g., Lawrence Fellows, "Downey Back Home To Visit His Mother," *New York Times,* 13 March 1973, pp. 1, 11.

to foreigners as well as to Chinese, in both war and peace; it punishes not only "stealing or searching for state secrets" but also "supplying intelligence to a domestic or foreign enemy."[14] The nature of the "intelligence" to which the law refers is not made clear. No language explicitly limits its scope to state, military, political, or economic secrets. It is possible that the draftsmen of the statute intended the term "intelligence" to embrace only the state secrets whose acquisition they had prohibited. Yet this is far from certain. Moreover, in the context of a closed society where the state virtually plays an all-pervasive role, the definition of "state secrets" tends to become greatly extended in comparison with more open societies.

It would seem clear to all that businessmen who are trained to report troop movements, for example, and who engage in such reporting while in China and tailor their activities to enhance their opportunities for observation will be viewed as spies. But what of those who undergo no training and do not seek enhanced opportunities for observation but who nevertheless are asked to keep their eyes open and who report to their governments about what they have seen and experienced in China? Does it make a difference whether, as in the case of a technician residing in China, this reporting might occur on a number of occasions rather than merely once? Would it matter whether the technician's reporting consisted of nothing more systematic than occasional dinner conversations with acquaintances at his government's mission in Peking? Would it still constitute espionage if reporting did not concern military affairs or other topics that would be sensitive in any society, but everyday matters such as political grumbling or the price of toothpaste?

We cannot answer these questions with precision. We should recall, however, that in the early 1950s China convicted and sentenced to substantial prison terms several young American Fulbright scholars who regularly reported to intelligence officials at the American Consulate General in Peking, and, after it closed, to the British mission there; although the bulk of the information they supplied concerned political, economic, and social conditions at local universities and among intellectuals, occasionally data of military significance were also submitted.[15] A sizable number of foreign religious missionaries were also arrested, some remaining in prison for long periods.[16]

---

[14] See Article 6 (1) of the Act, translated into English in Jerome Alan Cohen, *The Criminal Process in the People's Republic of China, 1949–1963: An Introduction* (Cambridge, Mass.: Harvard University Press, 1968), pp. 299–300.

[15] See Rickett, *Prisoners of Liberation*, pp. viii, x, 16–17, 29.

[16] See, e.g., deposition of Father André Bonnichon, in André Bonnichon, *Law in Communist China* (The Hague: International Commission of Jurists, 1956), pp. 24 *et seq.;* "Espionage Case of American Religious Mission Uncovered in Meihsien," *NCNA* (Canton), 23 April 1951, in *SCMP*, no. 98 (24–25 April 1951), pp. 19–20; "Belgian Catholic Father in Kweisui under Arrest," *NCNA* (Peking), 19 April 1951, in *SCMP*, no. 97 (21–23 April 1951), pp. 13–15. For a fascinating account by a French

Unfortunately, because China does not ordinarily publish its judicial decisions, we have to rely on occasional newspaper dispatches and the New China News Agency (NCNA) news releases for our sources. These sources usually alleged that the implicated missionaries, businessmen, and students had collected political, economic, and cultural information on China, but in addition they amost always included more sinister allegations relating either to the acquisition of military information or the commission of actual acts of sabotage. They often claimed that specific items of incriminating evidence had been introduced against the defendants to support the accusations. For example, when in 1960 China announced the conviction of Father James E. Walsh of the United States, the NCNA stated that the court had found that Walsh had directed the Catholic Central Bureau, an organization through which he "collected important military intelligence about the construction of military airfields in China, the strength, equipment, operations, and air defense measures of the Chinese People's Volunteers units in Korea, and national defense construction. . . . Documentary evidence, secret codes and a letter in secret writing used in carrying out counterrevolutionary activities were submitted as exhibits during the trial."[17] More recent news releases of espionage convictions of some Western technicians alleged that the accused "furtively took photographs of prohibited areas and gathered important intelligence about China's military, political and economic affairs and the Great Proletarian Cultural Revolution. . . ."[18]

It seems clear that businessmen who wish to stay out of prison in China should in no way seek access to military information or convey such information to others. It is also probably fair to conclude, at least as a working hypothesis, that businessmen who eschew all intelligence reporting, as well as traditional forms of espionage, substantially reduce the risk of running afoul of Chinese law.

That risk is further reduced, of course, during periods of relative stability in China, such as the present one, which began at the end of the Cultural Revolution in 1969. As previously mentioned, the largest number of cases in which the personal security of foreigners was threatened occurred during two periods: the era of the consolidation of Communist power in the early 1950s and the Cultural Revolution of the late 1960s. During these periods the leadership in Peking sought to bring about radical transformation of the country. The atmosphere engendered, the power wielded by local groups, and the

national who was arrested in China in 1957 after serving on the staff of foreign diplomatic missions, see Bao Juo-wang and Rudolph Chelminski, *Prisoner of Mao* (New York: Coward, McCann & Geoghegan, 1973).

[17] "U.S. Spy Sentenced in China," *NCNA*-English (Shanghai), 18 March 1960, in *SCMP*, no. 2223 (24 March 1960), pp. 3–5.

[18] "U.S. Imperialist Spy Case Broken by Lanchow's Organs of Dictatorship," *Peking Review*, 12, no. 44 (31 October 1969), pp. 4–5.

ascendancy of extremist policies at both the national and local levels enhanced the likelihood that foreigners would be exposed to arbitrary action. Moreover, both periods witnessed great tensions between China and many other countries, and consequent feelings of fear and hostility toward foreigners in China. It should also be noted that the unsettled conditions prevailing at those times may have encouraged other governments to believe that excellent opportunities for intelligence infiltration existed and may have caused the Chinese government to take extra precautions. Whatever the reasons, foreign businessmen would be wise to avoid visiting China during the periodic upheavals that seem to mark its dialectical progress.

Even at times of over-all stability there may be areas of China administered by radical or antiforeign elements. For a time the post-Cultural Revolution leadership of Shanghai seemed to be somewhat out of step with the trend toward stability and detained a number of foreigners. In one case two ship's officers were held for several weeks for allegedly violating harbor regulations by marking the position of buoys on their charts, an international navigational practice prohibited by the PRC.[19] In another case some elderly foreign residents were arrested for no apparent reason.[20] Obviously, such places ought to be avoided.

The Great Leap Forward of 1958–60 was another era of upheaval at home and tension between China and certain countries. A number of foreigners were prosecuted for espionage at that time, although apparently not so many as in either the early 1950s or late 1960s. Experience during the Great Leap seems to confirm what other eras suggest—that foreigners whose governments are on bad terms with the People's Republic are much more likely to find themselves in difficulty than are other foreigners. For example, in 1958 the Nagasaki flag incident and the breakdown of the fourth Sino-Japanese trade agreement provoked a hard-line Chinese policy toward Japan.[21] One of the ways in which Peking manifested this new policy was by confiscating the boats of a large number of Japanese fishermen who had allegedly violated China's prescribed security zones and by convicting some fishermen of having committed espionage on behalf of American intelligence organizations.[22] Similarly, in 1962, after Sino-Soviet relations had turned hostile, a Soviet national who

---

[19] See note 11 and Garry Lloyd, "China Still Holds British Officers," *London Times,* 14 March 1970, p. 1; and "Release of Detained British Seamen Announced," *Agence France Presse-London,* 26 March 1970, in United States Government, *Foreign Broadcast Information Service* [FBIS], 1, no. 60 (28 March 1970), p. A9.

[20] Davies, "Twisting the Lions' Tails," p. 230; "Traveller's Tales," p. 223.

[21] See Gene T. Hsiao, "The Role of Trade in China's Diplomacy With Japan," in Jerome Alan Cohen, ed., *The Dynamics of China's Foreign Relations* (Cambridge, Mass.: Harvard University Press, 1970), pp. 41, 43 *et seq.*

[22] See, e.g., "Japanese Criminals Sentenced to Jail," *NCNA*-English (Shanghai) (31 October 1958) in *SCMP,* no. 1889 (5 November 1958), pp. 39–40.

ran a Shanghai restaurant was arrested on charges of spying for the United States.[23] By contrast, Pakistanis, Romanians, Albanians, and others whose countries have continued to enjoy good relations with China have apparently not encountered serious difficulty.

Indeed, the Act for the Punishment of Counterrevolution, by punishing the supplying of intelligence "to a . . . foreign enemy," appears to make the existence of espionage depend upon the PRC's relations with the state on whose behalf the intelligence was gathered.[24] With respect to criminal offenses generally, Chinese legal sources have openly instructed judicial decision-makers that one of the factors to be considered in deciding the appropriate punishment for an alien offender is "the situation of the international struggle," that is, the state of relations between his country and the PRC.[25] And Chinese courts have plainly taken this factor into account.[26] Thus, the risk of arbitrary action against foreign businessmen is reduced if they limit their China trips to times when their governments are on good terms with China.

It should be emphasized that the total number of incidents involving sanctions against foreign businessmen appears to be small, both in absolute terms and relative to the many thousands who have gone to China. Any time that a great many foreigners visit a country there are bound to be some incidents. This is an inevitable cost of doing business in another society.

The problem, of course, is not a new one in China's foreign relations. Many of the incidents of the past two decades bring to mind the long series of legal disputes that occurred when Western trading ships began to call regularly at Canton in the century preceding the Opium War of 1839–42. In those days, although China only infrequently exercised criminal jurisdiction over foreign traders and merchant seamen, the instances in which it did so led to a progressive deterioration of its relations with the maritime countries. Ill feeling arose because of disagreement regarding not only the substantive guilt of at

---

[23] See George Volsky, "Mao's Torture Chamber," *Daily Telegraph* (Australia), 3 December 1969, p. 1.

[24] See note 14, *supra*.

[25] See, e.g., Chung-yang cheng-fa kan-pu hsüeh-hsiao hsing-fa chiao-yen-shih pien, *Chung-hua jen-min kung-ho-kuo hsing-fa tsung-tse chiang-i* (Lectures on the General Principles of Criminal Law of the People's Republic of China) (Peking: Legal Publishing House, 1957), p. 214.

[26] See, e.g., Lennart Petri, "Einige Betrachtungen über Recht und Recht-sprechung in der Volksrepublik China" (Some Aspects of Law and Adjudication in the People's Republic of China), *Juristische Blätter* (Vienna), 93, nos. 1–2 (16 January 1971), pp. 29–30. Chinese penal authorities have also given this fact great weight in determining when to release convicted foreign businessmen. For example, the five Japanese trade representatives referred to in note 4 were released "in view of their good conduct while in prison and in consideration of Sino-Japanese friendship," which had begun to flourish after establishment of diplomatic relations. See "Freed Japanese Arrive In HK."

least some of the accused but also because of foreign abhorrence of the adjudication procedures employed by the Chinese authorities.[27]

To be sure, contemporary Chinese criminal procedures differ in some significant respects from those of the Manchu dynasty. Yet foreign traders ought to be warned: although the risk of detention by the police may be small if they visit China during periods of stability, if relations between their country and China are not hostile, and if they avoid intelligence work, the procedures employed in those cases in which businessmen are detained will be nearly as abhorrent to them as earlier Chinese procedures were to their predecessors.

If experience is any guide, the detained person will be kept incommunicado for a period that may range from several weeks to several years. In this period the investigation proceeds, and the prisoner undergoes repeated interrogation, sometimes without adequate food and sleep and without even knowing the charges against him and the bases for them. During this time he will be unable to contact his family, friends, or government, nor will the authorities provide him with any independent source of assistance, such as the services of a local lawyer. Efforts of those on the outside to communicate with him will also be unsuccessful.[28]

Consular access appears rarely to have been granted to foreign missions at the investigation stage. Indeed, in diplomatic correspondence with India in 1963–64, China insisted that international law imposes no obligation to afford consular access to detained aliens who are suspected of crime until after they have been sentenced; and it refused to permit representatives of the Indian government to visit an Indian national held on a charge of rape until all proceedings in the case, including appeal, had been completed.[29] The PRC did not appear to be embarrassed at all by the fact that when India had detained Chinese nationals, the PRC had demanded consular access to them from the very beginning of their detention.[30] This background must be taken into account when evaluating the significance of any agreement that the PRC may make with foreign governments to allow access to their detained nationals

---

[27] See Randle Edwards, "Early Ch'ing Jurisdiction Over European Merchants and Sailors," in Cohen, Edwards and Ch'en, eds., *China's Legal Tradition* (forthcoming).

[28] See, e.g., Rickett, *Prisoners of Liberation*, pp. 65–97; 214–15; and Bonnichon, *Law in Communist China*.

[29] "Note Given by the Ministry of Foreign Affairs, Peking, to the Embassy of India in China, 15 September 1965," *Notes, Memoranda and Letters Exchanged between the Governments of India and China, February 1966–February 1967* [hereafter *White Paper*] (January 1965–February 1966), 12:118–120.

[30] See Jerome Alan Cohen and Shao-chuan Leng, "The Sino-Indian Dispute over the Internment and Detention of Chinese in India," in Jerome Alan Cohen, ed., *China's Practice of International Law* (Cambridge, Mass.: Harvard University Press, 1972), pp. 268, 295 *et seq.*

"in accordance with domestic laws and regulations" or "in accordance with international law."

Chinese authorities may release the detained alien at the close of the investigation of his case, without subjecting him to the formalities of criminal prosecution. Most aliens detained during the Cultural Revolution do not appear to have been prosecuted, even though some were held in prison for years. For example, a number of Japanese business representatives who were detained on espionage charges were released without trial over a four-year period.

If the authorities decide to prosecute, it is possible that after completion of the investigation, they may offer the accused foreigner an opportunity to be defended by a person with legal training. Before the "antirightist" movement of 1957, which put an end to the organized bar that had begun to develop in the mid-1950s, occasionally "people's lawyers" did actually serve as defense counsel.[31] Subsequently, however, their role withered, and in those instances when the PRC reported that the accused foreigner was offered the services of a lawyer, he was usually said to have declined the offer.[32] But even if counsel should be assigned to an accused today, his assistance could only be expected to be decorative. At most he will seek to point out to the authorities reasons why a lenient sentence would be appropriate. There is no likelihood of his waging a vigorous defense against the charges, for the PRC's legal system does not permit any independent challenge to the regime's position.[33]

Whether counsel will be assigned will usually depend upon whether the authorities decide to hold a formal trial. Generally speaking, formal trials, which were being held in increasing numbers before the "antirightist" movement, came to a virtual end by the late 1950s. In some cases the accused is simply informed of his conviction without being given even a *pro forma* opportunity to defend himself before a judicial tribunal. In some cases he is interrogated in a private audience by a judicial official who seeks to verify the results of the investigation before announcing judgment. In neither event is counsel permitted. In either event there may or may not be a subsequent public meeting at which Party and government officials announce the results to the masses. Yet one should not rule out the possibility that there may be a formal European-style trial in which evidence is heard and witnesses as well as counsel appear. Such a trial might or might not be held in public. Although in many instances the authorities do not wish the public to learn of sensitive matters or threats to China's security, in others they may wish to demonstrate governmental vigilance and alert the masses to a foreign menace.

---

[31] See, e.g., Cohen, *The Criminal Process*, p. 13; and Rickett, *Prisoners of Liberation*, pp. 272–75.

[32] See, e.g., note 29, *supra*.

[33] See Jerome Alan Cohen, "Continuity and Change in China: Some 'Law Day' Thoughts," *South Carolina Law Review*, 24, no. 1 (1972), pp. 3, 16–18.

In view of these procedures what advice can one give to a foreigner who becomes caught in the toils of Chinese justice? Honesty would seem to be the best policy. The Chinese have no tradition of protecting an accused against self-incrimination. Rather, their tradition is one of insisting that the accused tell all. An accused who seeks to remain mute will be regarded as unrepentant and defiant and receive harsher treatment than one who talks. One who affirmatively misleads his captors will find himself in a worse situation. Occasionally an accused may brazen out a false story, but generally Chinese investigators, able to mobilize the resources of a totalitarian government and an inquisitorial system, can expose such efforts. In view of the fact that the detained person is completely dependent upon his captors for his release, he is wise to act in a way that enlists their confidence. At least during periods of stability in China and of good relations between the PRC and the government of one's country, Chinese authorities are unlikely to wish to convict innocent persons. They resort to the inquisitorial system in order to achieve greater accuracy than they believe would result from a system that established more of a balance between the authorities and the accused.

Past Chinese denial of exit permits and imposition of house arrest for substantial periods of time ought to stimulate businessmen also to consider the risk of "noncriminal" sanctions. Yet, as the number of eager applicants for the semiannual Canton trade fairs suggests, that risk is currently perceived to be a modest one for short-term visitors to China. This is probably a correct estimate of the situation. Those who contemplate a longer time of residence in China, however—as trade representatives or technical advisers on the installation of factories, for example—might well consider the precedents of China's treatment of the employees of firms that have refused to settle disputes on terms desired by Chinese authorities. Although the risk to such personnel should still be regarded as relatively low, it is probably significantly higher than that to which transients are exposed.

II.   THE SECURITY OF CHINESE ABROAD

Thus far this paper has been preoccupied with the unpleasant, almost morbid, subject of the degree to which foreign traders and business personnel in China ought to fear threats to their personal security. One should not assume from this that the Chinese have not had similar concerns for the safety of their trade representatives and technicians stationed abroad. Because China is a socialist state, these Chinese personnel are usually not private citizens but government employees. Nevertheless, it has not always proved possible to assure their freedom from either the criminal process or mob action.

Perhaps the best-known case of the imposition of sanctions against PRC trade personnel occurred in Brazil in 1964. Two days after a successful military *coup d'état* against the Goulart regime, nine Chinese nationals were detained on charges of carrying out subversive activities, conspiring with the illegal Communist Party of Brazil, and plotting to kill several Brazilian leaders. Seven of the nine persons detained were resident trade representatives: one was deputy representative of the Brazil Office of the China Council for the Promotion of International Trade (hereafter CCPIT) and assistant manager of the China National Textiles Import and Export Corporation; two were members of his office staff; and four were preparing for a Chinese economic and trade exhibition in Brazil. Brazilian police had searched the premises of four of these persons just before their detention. After being held by the authorities for nine months despite a torrent of protests from the PRC, Chinese mass organizations and newspapers, and sympathetic groups from other countries, all nine suspects were convicted of "subversion" on 22 December 1964 and each was sentenced to ten years in prison.[34]

China promptly denounced the convictions as "a shocking frame-up" that was "utterly unwarranted and completely illegal in point of fact, in morals or law." Peking claimed that the act of the Brazilian authorities "unscrupulously tramples on the standards of international law and dignity of justice and is a serious infringement on fundamental rights."[35] The PRC did not argue that the Chinese representatives enjoyed diplomatic immunity from local jurisdiction; these men were not diplomats, Brazil maintained diplomatic relations with the Republic of China on Taiwan rather than with the PRC, and no agreement had been made between the PRC and Brazil conferring immunity on the Chinese representatives. Peking seemed to be arguing that the charges were so blatantly trumped up as to render the conviction a denial of justice and human rights within the meaning of international law. Four months later, after an unsuccessful appeal by the defendants and continuing adverse publicity for Brazil, all nine defendants were deported.[36]

In a number of countries, both communist and noncommunist, the PRC has sought to avoid such incidents by making agreements that insulate resident trade representatives of each party from infringement of their personal security while in the territory of the other party. For example, the 1954 "Agreement between the Republic of India and the People's Republic of China on Trade and Intercourse between [the] Tibet Region of China and India," after providing that each country could establish three trade agencies in the territory of the other, stated that: "The Trade Agents of both Parties shall enjoy freedom from arrest while exercising their functions, and shall enjoy,

---

[34] See Jerome Alan Cohen and Hungdah Chiu, *People's China and International Law* (Princeton, N.J.: Princeton University Press, 1974), pp. 1095–1098; and "China Protests to Brazilian Authorities," *Peking Review*, 8, no. 1 (1 January 1965), pp. 22–23.

[35] *Ibid.*

[36] "Brazil Expels 9 Chinese Convicted As Red Spies," *New York Times*, 18 April 1965, p. 22.

in respect of themselves, their wives and children who are dependent on them for livelihood, freedom from search."[37]

Unlike the Sino-Indian agreement, which conferred only limited immunity upon resident trade agents, the 1958 Sino-Soviet agreement, entitled "The Legal Status of the Office of Commercial Representative of the Union of Soviet Socialist Republics in the People's Republic of China and of the Office of Commercial Representative of the People's Republic of China in the Union of Soviet Socialist Republics," conferred comprehensive protection against the local jurisdiction. Article 2 provided in part:

> The Office of Commercial Representative shall form a component part of the Embassy of its own State.
>
> . . . . .
>
> The Commercial Representative and Deputy Commercial Representative shall enjoy all the rights and privileges accorded to diplomatic personnel.
>
> The premises occupied by the Office of Commercial Representative and its branches shall enjoy inviolability. . . .[38]

These particular agreements have apparently played a useful role in protecting Chinese trade representatives. It is true that in the early 1960s, as a result of the bitter Sino-Indian dispute, Peking charged that India's restrictions had made it impossible for the Chinese trade agency in Kalimpong to perform its functions.[39] But the PRC has not claimed that India violated the resident agent's immunity from arrest during the period when he was able to carry out his functions. Similarly, although Sino-Soviet relations deteriorated badly after the signing of the 1958 agreement, culminating in outrages against diplomats of the other country in both Peking and Moscow, the PRC does not appear to have charged the Soviet Union with having violated the personal immunity of members of the office of the Chinese commercial representative. This is all the more notable in view of the fact that in 1967 the Soviet Union protested against alleged mistreatment of two members of the office of the Soviet commercial representative in Peking who, according to the Chinese version of the events, had been covertly copying wall posters and collecting information about the Cultural Revolution.[40]

---

[37] Article 1(2) of the Agreement between the Republic of India and the People's Republic of China on Trade and Intercourse between Tibet Region of China and India, 29 April 1950; English text in *United Nations Treaty Series* 299:70, 71.

[38] English text in Cohen and Chiu, *International Law*, p. 1084.

[39] See, e.g., "Memorandum Given by the Embassy of China in India, to the Ministry of External Affairs, New Delhi, 2 December, 1961," *White Paper* (November 1961–July 1962), 6:227; "Note Given by the Ministry of Foreign Affairs, Peking, to the Embassy of India in China, 22 September 1962," *White Paper* (July 1962–October 1962), 7: 179–81.

[40] "Soviet Personnel Caught Red-Handed Stealing Information," *Peking Review* 10, no. 29 (14 July 1967), pp. 58–59.

If there is no agreement regulating the status of resident trade representative and if the PRC maintains diplomatic relations with the country in question, the office of the commercial counselor of the Chinese embassy is generally more active in conducting trade negotiations than would otherwise be the case. The staff members of the office are, of course, diplomats and therefore enjoy the personal security that normally accompanies diplomatic status. As the Brazilian case demonstrated, in the absence of diplomatic relations, resident trade representatives lack such protection unless it is specified by agreement.

The PRC's relations with Japan before establishment of diplomatic relations in 1972 illustrate its attempt to endow its trade representatives residing abroad with an approximation of diplomatic immunity through the conclusion of "unofficial" agreements. Although Peking has condemned certain countries with which it maintains diplomatic relations for exchanging trade delegations with its rival on Taiwan as a substitute for diplomatic intercourse, the pre-1972 Japanese case is an example of Peking's resort to a similar expedient. Beginning in 1952 a series of trade agreements was concluded between nongovernmental Chinese and Japanese organizations. Article 10 of the third agreement, signed in 1955, authorized each side to establish permanent commercial agencies in the capital of the other country and provided that the agencies and their personnel would "enjoy the rights accorded to diplomats."[41] Difficulties arose in implementing this agreement, however, because of the Japanese government's determination not to damage its relations with the Republic of China. The Japanese government insisted, for example, that all Chinese Communist commercial personnel who remained in Japan for over two months be fingerprinted like other resident aliens who were not diplomats. This requirement did not infringe greatly on the personal security of the Chinese staff, but Peking understandably regarded it as humiliating and inconsistent with the promised diplomatic treatment. Thus, commercial agencies were never established under the third agreement.[42]

A fourth nongovernmental Sino-Japanese trade agreement was concluded early in 1958 and sought, with the aid of a separate memorandum, to clarify the troublesome question of the immunities and activities of permanent commercial agencies. The signatories were the CCPIT, on the one side, and, on the other, the Japanese Diet Members' Union to Promote Japan-China Trade, the Japan International Trade Promotion Association, and the Japan-China Import and Export Association of Japan. The agreement obligated the signatories to establish permanent commercial agencies in the other's country and "to obtain the concurrence of their respective governments to ensure [the] security of their commercial agencies and their personnel and

---

[41] *Chung-hua jen-min kung-ho-kuo t'iao-yüeh chi* (Collection of Treaties of the People's Republic of China) [hereafter TYC] 1956, 5 (1957), 5:260.

[42] See Cohen and Chiu, *International Law,* p. 1088.

facilities for carrying out their work."[43] The memorandum, which was deemed to be a component part of the agreement, reiterated the obligation to obtain governmental concurrence in guaranteeing the security of the mission members and provided that "any legal dispute . . . should be handled in accordance with the method agreed upon by both sides through liaison." It also stated that both sides would "provide facilities for the personnel of the commercial agency of the other side to enter and leave the country . . . and freedom of travel for trade purposes."[44]

The fourth Sino-Japanese trade agreement was never carried out, however. Peking accused the Japanese government of putting forth a series of pretexts to justify its refusal to implement those provisions of the agreement that, according to the Japanese government, sought to confer "officially privileged status" on the Chinese commercial agency. The dispute centered not on the protection afforded the individual members of the mission but on the right of the Chinese to hoist the PRC's national flag over the mission and the degree of protection to which the flag was entitled. After a Japanese national of anticommunist persuasion pulled down the PRC's flag at a Chinese trade exhibition in Nagasaki, the Japanese government refused to prosecute him for destroying the flag of a foreign government. This led Peking to repudiate the agreement and suspend trade between the two countries.[45]

Provisions for the resumption of trade were not made until late 1962, when the so-called Liao-Takasaki Memorandum, named after its principal "private" negotiators, was signed.[46] This agreement was supplemented in 1964 by another "unofficial" memorandum that authorized the Liao trade office in Peking to open a Tokyo liaison office and the Takasaki trade office in Tokyo to open a Peking liaison office. Apart from prescribing that each side would be responsible for the entry and the safety of the persons staffing the other side's liaison office, the 1964 memorandum said nothing about the privileges and immunities of commercial agents.[47] This represented a far cry, of course, from the attempt in the abortive 1955 agreement to confer "the rights accorded to diplomats" upon the respective commercial agents.

---

[43] Article 11 of the Sino-Japanese Trade Agreement, 5 March 1958, English translation in *NCNA*-English (Peking), 15 March 1958, in *SCMP*, no. 1727 (10 March 1958), pp. 55–60.

[44] Article 1(a) and 1(b) of the Memorandum, *ibid.*

[45] See Hsiao, "China's Diplomacy with Japan," and Gene T. Hsiao, "Nonrecognition and Trade: A Case Study of the Fourth Sino-Japanese Trade Agreement," in Cohen, ed., *China's Practice*, pp. 129, 153.

[46] For the Chinese text of this "memorandum," see *Jih-pen wen-t'i wen-chien hui-pien* (Collection of Documents on Problems Relating to Japan) (Peking, 1963), 4:90.

[47] The Chinese text of the 1964 memorandum appears in *TYC* 1964, 13 (1965), 13:386.

The 1955 Sino-Egyptian trade agreement, which was concluded while Cairo still maintained diplomatic relations with Taipei and before the establishment of diplomatic relations between Peking and Cairo, provided for the reciprocal establishment of governmental trade offices. The two governments agreed "to accord the office of commercial representative of the other party courtesies, security, protection, and all facilities for carrying out their work."[48]

A 1964 agreement between the CCPIT and the Italian Foreign Trade Office established a "nongovernmental" trade office in Rome for China and in Peking for Italy.[49] The terms of that agreement have not been available to me. Although the PRC did not complain of any Italian violation of the agreement in the six years between its signature and the establishment of diplomatic relations between the two governments, during the Cultural Revolution it did protest against what it called "obstructions of the normal functions" of the staff of the Chinese office in Italy.[50]

In March 1972 China sent a seven-man permanent trade mission to Guyana, a state with which it did not maintain diplomatic relations. According to an order published in the official gazette of Guyana, the mission enjoys the same diplomatic immunities and privileges as normal embassies.[51]

The most recent PRC effort to protect permanent commercial representatives in the absence of formal diplomatic relations occurred in early 1973 when Peking and Washington agreed that each would establish an official "liaison office" in the capital of the other, even though Washington and Taipei continued to maintain diplomatic relations. The communique announcing this agreement merely noted that "[d]etails will be worked out through existing channels."[52] Yet in his explanatory press conference, Henry Kissinger stated not only that "[t]his liaison office would handle trade as well as all other matters except the strictly formal diplomatic aspects of the relationship" but also that "[t]he people in the liaison offices will have diplomatic privileges."[53]

---

[48] Article 6. English text in "Sino-Egyptian Trade Agreement Approved," *NCNA*-English (Peking), 14 October 1955, in *SCMP*, no. 1151 (18 October 1955), pp. 64–65.

[49] "Sino-Italian Trade Bureau To Be Established," *Peking Review*, 7, no. 50 (11 December 1964), p. 25.

[50] "Political Provocation," broadcast, *NCNA*-English (Peking), 31 July 1967, printed in *FBIS*, 147, no. 67 (31 July 1967): BBB 4–6.

[51] "Chinese Mission Arrives in Guyana," *Japan Times*, 14 March 1972, p. 10.

[52] "Communique," 22 February 1973, in *Peking Review*, 16, no. 8 (23 February 1973), p. 4.

[53] "Transcript of Kissinger's News Conference in Washington on His Asian Tour," *New York Times*, 23 February 1973, p. 14. The President subsequently extended such privileges to PRC diplomats as authorized by Congress. See P.L. 93–22, 87 stat. 24, 20 April 1973.

The PRC does not appear to have devoted similar attention to the protection of *ad hoc* trade missions sent abroad for short periods. The number of such missions dropped sharply during the years of the Cultural Revolution but has increased of late, providing renewed occasions for concern over the security of these groups. The visit by a Chinese synthetic and chemical fiber survey team to Japan in March 1972 suggests the political and economic difficulties that can be created by failure to afford adequate protection to an *ad hoc* trade mission.

The ten-man fiber survey team, the first Chinese technical mission to visit Japan since the Cultural Revolution, had been invited for forty-five days by a major Japanese company and by the Kansai headquarters of the Japan International Trade Promotion Association. Soon after the arrival of these Chinese guests in Tokyo, Japanese "rightists" staged two demonstrations in front of the Tokyo liaison office of the Chinese memorandum trade office. When the group reached the city of Okayama, according to NCNA a series of "blatant provocations" occurred, including attempts to block the movement of the group and to stage a collision with its car.

NCNA charged that the actions had been taken with "the patronage and connivance of the Japanese authorities," who, under the leadership of Prime Minister Sato, were said to persist in a hostile policy toward China. The Chinese survey team demanded that "Japanese authorities take effective measures against the recurrence of similar incidents."[54] The Chinese memorandum trade office in Peking also began to issue warnings that unless such measures were taken, serious consequences would follow for Sino-Japanese relations. This was understood to mean that the fiber team might cut short its visit, that scheduled visits by similar Chinese shipbuilding and automobile teams might not take place, and that Japan might not achieve its desire to increase the number of personnel staffing the memorandum trade office that each country maintained in the capital of the other. The Japanese government thereafter strengthened its efforts to prevent the recurrence of similar incidents in order to avert the possibility of another suspension of Sino-Japanese trade such as that which began in 1958, and the survey team ended its visit without further difficulty.[55]

III. CONCLUSION

One hopes that the subject of this essay will decline in importance. At present, as China's post-Cultural Revolution contacts with the noncommunist

---

[54] "Rightists Hinder China-Japan Ties," *Mainichi Daily News,* 19 March 1972, p. 3.

[55] "Stop Provocative Acts By Rightist Elements," *Asahi Evening News* (Japan), 23 March 1972, p. 3; "Gov't Orders Curbs On Anti-China Agitation," *Mainichi Daily News,* 25 March 1972, p. 1.

trading world continue to develop favorably, prospects for vindicating this hope seem bright. The moderation currently prevailing in China's domestic and foreign policies makes it unlikely that the foreign businessman who actually minds his business will encounter serious difficulty in China. Similarly, as more and more countries normalize relations with the PRC, China's trade representatives abroad are less likely to run the risk of harm or harassment; some, of course, will enjoy the protection due to diplomats, but even those who do not will benefit from the relaxation of tensions.

Yet the problem is likely to persist. The development of cordial relations will multiply the number of traders and technicians moving between the PRC and other countries, and experience suggests that a variety of ordinary human frailties will inevitably lead to some incidents and misunderstandings. Moreover, foreign governments as well as the PRC may be tempted to use these increasing contacts to conceal subversion and espionage; the present era of good feeling is unlikely to render such activities obsolescent. And, in view of past swings of the pendulum and the succession crisis confronting China's leadership, one can hardly be confident that the present era will endure.

To a certain extent the security of foreign trading personnel in China and Chinese personnel abroad may be enhanced through bilateral agreements. As the pre-1972 Japanese case illustrates, even before establishment of diplomatic relations it may be possible to conclude "unofficial" agreements between "nongovernmental" organizations representing each country. And the 1973 exchange of official "liaison offices" by the United States and the PRC has conferred diplomatic privileges and immunities upon the governmental personnel assigned to the offices, whose functions include facilitation of trade. Although China has shown less interest in making agreements to guarantee the security of *ad hoc* trade missions, such missions could also be granted protection equivalent to that accorded diplomats or whatever lesser degree of protection may be deemed appropriate. Perhaps an agreement, whether denominated "official" or "unofficial," might also be made to protect ordinary businessmen and technicians.

When Japan established formal diplomatic relations with China in 1972, it succeeded in obtaining the PRC's agreement to a mutual pledge to treat their respective embassies "according to international law and practice."[56] Building on this and similar precedents, it may prove possible for the United States to negotiate a joint communique that generally pledges each side to conduct its relations with the other "according to international law and practice." Perhaps the communique might even refer to treatment of trade representatives, businessmen, technicians, and other aliens, but at best such a reference

---

[56] "Joint Statement of the Government of the People's Republic of China and the Government of Japan," 29 September 1972; English text in *Peking Review*, 15, no. 40 (6 October 1972), p. 12.

would probably be rather vague. Following establishment of formal diplomatic relations, and perhaps even before, it may prove possible to negotiate the equivalent of a friendship, commerce, and navigation treaty that could include more detailed reference to the obligation to treat each other's nationals according to some minimal substantive and procedural standards. Or this might be accomplished by an intergovernmental trade agreement or by separate agreements relating to particular matters such as aviation and shipping. It also may prove possible to conclude a consular agreement that prescribes basic guarantees such as the rights of consular officials to receive prompt notice of the arrest or detention of their nationals and to visit and communicate with confined nationals within a prescribed period of time.[57]

Other possibilities for protection may arise from China's eventual adherence to existing multilateral treaties, such as the 1963 Convention on Consular Relations[58] or the 1969 Convention on Special Missions,[59] and from PRC participation in future multilateral treaty-making. Furthermore, as increasing foreign contacts make clear the desirability of China's erecting a more regularized, accessible legal system, the PRC may gradually enact domestic legislation that offers foreigners a greater degree of personal security.

Individual foreign companies may even play a limited role in seeking to minimize the security problems their personnel may encounter in China. For example, a firm that is negotiating a contract for its employees to install a factory in China may attempt to insert a provision in the contract that obligates its Chinese trading partner to make a good faith effort to protect the firm's employees against arbitrary action. And, in order to reduce the number of occasions for dispute with Chinese authorities, firms may wish to write codes of good conduct into their employment contracts with personnel who are to be assigned to work in China.

Yet one must not be too optimistic about the results of all such efforts. The Chinese government will probably remain reluctant to impose a binding system of laws upon itself through either bilateral and multilateral agreements or domestic legislation. In view of the pre-1949 history of foreign interference with China's judicial sovereignty,[60] Peking is also likely to remain extremely sensitive about foreign attempts to stimulate changes in its legal system.

---

[57] See, for example, Article 12 of the Consular Convention between the Government of the United States of America and the Government of the Union of Soviet Socialist Republics, signed 1 June 1964, and the accompanying protocol of the same date; English text in *International Legal Materials*, 3, no. 3 (July 1964), pp. 780–91.

[58] English text in *American Journal of International Law*, 57, no. 4 (1963), pp. 995–1025.

[59] English text in *International Legal Materials*, 8, no. 1 (January 1970), pp. 129–51.

[60] See generally William L. Tung, *China and the Foreign Powers: The Impact of and Reaction to Unequal Treaties* (Oceana: Dobbs Ferry, N.Y., 1970).

Finally, if China should again turn xenophobic and chaotic, treaty commitments and legislative prescriptions are unlikely to afford significant protection in practice. Nevertheless, efforts should be made to improve the existing situation, and the chances for modest progress seem better now than at any other time since the foundation of the PRC.

The Foreign Trade Apparatus

DONALD W. KLEIN

This paper attempts to assess the apparatus developed by the People's Republic of China (PRC) to conduct foreign trade and aid programs.[1] Being neither a lawyer nor an economist, I have not attempted to delve into these areas. Rather, emphasis is placed upon the structure and personnel of the far-flung network, especially the Ministry of Foreign Trade and the commercial and economic sections of the diplomatic establishments abroad.[2]

NOTE: This chapter covers the period from 1949 to 1972.

* Susan Horsey performed yeoman service in the preparation of this article.

[1] Most of the organizational and biographic data for this paper was compiled from my own files and from materials held by the Chinese Leadership Project at the East Asian Institute, Columbia University. The overwhelming portion of the materials is derived from the Chinese press and such obvious works as the *Jen-min shou-ts'e* (People's handbook). Some biographic materials also have been gathered from interviews with foreign diplomats who have dealt with Chinese commercial figures. Since the 1950s both the Japanese and American governments have published extremely valuable organizational directories of Chinese officialdom. These sources provide the researcher with details about the trade apparatus at quite regular intervals. It is also worth noting that the relative "openness" of the foreign trade apparatus facilitates research. For example, commercial officials abroad are regularly included on "diplomatic lists" issued annually by most governments. And, in most cases, trade agreement information appears in the press of the nation with which China is dealing.

One particularly useful work should be noted: Douglas M. Johnston and Hungdah Chiu, eds., *Agreements of the People's Republic of China, 1949–67 : A Calendar* (Cambridge, Mass.: Harvard University Press, 1968). This invaluable book, for example, greatly facilitated gathering the data for section 3, and it was also a valuable aid in preparing other sections of this article.

[2] See the chapter by Victor H. Li for a more detailed discussion of the foreign trade apparatus inside China.

I. The Development of the Foreign Trade Apparatus: The Early Years

When the Chinese Communists assumed power in 1949, foreign trade, like so much else, was in total disarray. Their lack of experience in this field was matched, one presumes, by their distaste for allowing the foreign trade apparatus to remain in the hands of ex-KMT bureaucrats. Foreign trade also was laden with ideological overtones—Shanghai and the other great trade ports symbolized the essence of imperialism and all that connoted for Mao and his colleagues. But at a more immediate and practical level, the PRC could take over the conduct of trade only slowly; moreover, domestic economic tasks were more pressing, and they accordingly were given higher priority.

These priorities were reflected in the structure of the central government established in the fall of 1949. Foreign trade was not given ministerial stature; rather, the Foreign Trade Office was created as one of the subordinate units under the Ministry of Trade. However, a Customs Administration was established at a level one notch below the ministries.

In the winter and spring of 1950 the first steps were taken toward the creation of the foreign trade labyrinth which was to emerge during the next decade. In March six state-owned foreign trade corporations dealing in a wide variety of goods were created, and in the next month the New China News Agency reported that branches of the Bank of China in Hong Kong, Singapore, London, Penang, Kuala Lumpur, Calcutta, Bombay, Chittagong, Karachi, Rangoon, and Jakarta had "restored relations" with the home office in Peking. In other words, these overseas bank branches had "defected" from the Nationalist-controlled banking apparatus.

The low level of foreign trade in the early PRC period can be illustrated by the low monetary value of trade, and by the small number of trade agreements[3] negotiated by Peking. In the first two calendar years of Communist rule, total two-way trade amounted to an annual average of only about $1.8 billion. In the same period only 26 agreements were signed—all but two of them with the USSR or one of the East European Communist countries. Apart from Bank of China officials abroad, the PRC confined itself to dispatching commercial counselors only to the Soviet Union, Poland, and India. Lesser commercial representatives (e.g., commercial attachés, commercial secretaries) were apparently not assigned to any embassy. The few commercial men abroad were partly supplemented by delegations sent to negotiate trade pacts and contracts. But even these were few and far between in this period and were confined almost exclusively to the Communist bloc. Still another

---

[3] The word "agreement" is used throughout this paper in a generic sense, although it is used by the PRC in a more specific sense as a document second only in importance to a treaty. This term also refers to agreements between governmental or quasi-governmental organs, rather than specific contracts between trading companies.

common practice of later years to stimulate trade—the holding of economic and commercial exhibits abroad—was not yet being employed. In short, through the year 1951, foreign trade was a minor league operation.

The year 1952 was the last in what the Communists call the period of reconstruction and rehabilitation, which in turn set the stage for the First Five-Year Plan inaugurated in 1953. To gear up for the five-year plan, a number of institutional adjustments were made in all sectors of the economy, including two such steps in the field of foreign trade.

In April 1952 the International Economic Conference was convened in Moscow. Its purpose was simple: to break through the economic blockade imposed upon the Communist bloc by the United States and its allies as a result of the Cold War in general and the Korean War in particular. The Chinese responded by sending to Moscow a large delegation which included just about every major foreign trade figure in China. The immediate results were meager if measured by the volume of contracts signed with non-Communist nations. But a breakthrough *had* been made, and contacts established.

The Moscow Conference was immediately followed by the establishment in Peking of the China Committee for the Promotion of International Trade (hereafter CCPIT) in May 1952. It was headed by Nan Han-ch'en (concurrently head of the People's Bank of China), and the redoubtable Chi Ch'ao-ting was made the secretary-general. If the CCPIT then seemed like a rather pathetic organization, it soon would demonstrate its ability to conduct trade throughout the world—and especially in those nations without formal diplomatic ties to Peking. This, in short, was and is its mission: to trade in places devoid of official PRC representation. As such, it is usually regarded as the unofficial arm of the Ministry of Foreign Trade (MFT). In fact, in many capitals and commercial centers throughout the world, Nan Han-ch'en and Chi Ch'ao-ting were better known than the "official" trade representatives.

The other major development of 1952 was the establishment in August of the MFT; or, more properly, the division of the old Ministry of Trade into the Ministries of Commerce (for domestic needs) and Foreign Trade. The former trade minister, Yeh Chi-chuang, was given the new Foreign Trade portfolio, and he brought with him as a vice-minister Lei Jen-min, who had been a vice-minister in the Trade Ministry. Two other men were also made vice-ministers, one of whom, Li Ch'iang, concurrently assumed the post of commercial counselor in the Chinese embassy in Moscow. The high level of Sino-Soviet economic ties at this time accounted for Li's Moscow assignment. Thus, he was on hand when later that same month (August 1952), Chou En-lai arrived in the Soviet capital to negotiate a series of agreements which were of critical importance for the First Five-Year Plan.[4]

---

[4] Chou returned home in September 1952, but he left several of his top economic and trade aides in Moscow where they remained for several months. For details, see

In 1952 the foreign trade apparatus abroad also was beefed up slightly. Three commercial counselors were now assigned to Moscow (Li Ch'iang being one of them), and two others were assigned to East Germany and Hungary. Further, for the first time a trade official was posted in a non-Communist country of Europe with the arrival in Stockholm of a commercial attaché, who had concurrent responsibilities in Denmark and Finland. The year 1952 saw no rise in foreign trade, but it provided the first evidence of a trend which lasted a decade: the orientation of trade heavily in favor of fellow Communist nations. Moreover, the pace of trade negotiations clearly indicated an intent to boost trade. The 26 agreements signed in the two-year period 1950–51 could now be contrasted with the 42 negotiated in 1952 alone.

Whatever the importance of institutional and other steps taken through 1952, the expansion of international commerce was severely hampered by the hard political fact that war still raged in Korea. After the truce in July 1953, however, many new opportunities arose, and within a year foreign trade work was moving into high gear. For example, among Chou En-lai's entourage to the famous 1954 Geneva Conference was the acting manager of the most important of the foreign trade corporations, the China National Import-Export Corporation. Midway in the conference Chou arranged for this man to lead an exploratory delegation to London. At almost the same moment K'ung Yüan, head of the Customs Administration and a vice-minister of foreign trade, began a lengthy tour of Indonesia and India. The negotiation of foreign trade agreements reached a new high of 63 in 1954—a level which was to be maintained until the Cultural Revolution a dozen years later.

The growing international importance of the PRC was illustrated again at the 1955 Bandung Conference, which among other things opened up new avenues for trade. Almost coinciding with Bandung was the first major Chinese delegation to Japan—a portent for booming Sino-Japanese trade over the ensuing years. This delegation, led by Vice-Minister Lei Jen-min, was one of the most impressive the Chinese had ever sent abroad and included a score of China's top trade figures. Paralleling these developments was the dispatch of still more commercial counselors abroad. Thus, by 1955 commercial counselors were located in the USSR, Poland, East Germany, Hungary, Czechoslovakia, Romania, North Korea, and North Vietnam within the Communist bloc; elsewhere they were in India, Indonesia, Burma, Pakistan, Sweden (upgraded from commercial attaché), Switzerland, and the United Kingdom. Moreover, in five of these nations, commercial attachés were assigned to assist the commercial counselors.

the biography of Li Fu-ch'un in Donald W. Klein and Anne B. Clark, *Biographic Dictionary of Chinese Communism, 1921–65* (Cambridge, Mass.: Harvard University Press, 1971). This source has lengthy biographies of most of the major figures mentioned in this paper.

By the mid-1950s the basic structure of the MFT had been fleshed out.
Four numbered bureaus (i.e., First Bureau, Second Bureau, etc.) were created
to handle trade, respectively, with the Soviet Union and the three Asian
Communist nations; the East European Communist nations; West Europe
and the Americas; and non-Communist Asian and African nations.[5] In
addition, several other bureaus, offices, and institutes were set up. They are
listed below. With the exception of the Customs Control Bureau (not to be
confused with the more important Customs Administration), all the above
organs were in existence by 1957.[6] This structure lasted until the Cultural
Revolution, with only minor alterations in the interim.[7]

ORGANIZATION OF THE MINISTRY OF
FOREIGN TRADE IN THE MID-1950s

Minister
Vice-Ministers
Assistant Ministers

Customs Administration	Accounting Bureau
	Commodity Inspection Bureau
Legal Office	Customs Control Bureau
Protocol Office	Economic Liaison Bureau
Staff Office	Export Bureau
	Import Bureau
Market Research Institute	Personnel Bureau
	Planning Bureau
First Bureau	Technical Cooperation Bureau
Second Bureau	Transportation Bureau
Third Bureau	Whole Plants Bureau
Fourth Bureau	

---

[5] A decade later, in 1965, a Fifth Bureau was inaugurated. Only one official was
identified with this bureau, and on the two occasions he was mentioned it was in
connection with African nations—suggesting that the Fifth Bureau had been split off
from the Fourth Bureau.

[6] The Customs Control Bureau was not identified until 1962.

[7] As noted below in the text, it is presumed that the Economic Liaison Bureau
formed the basis for the Economic Liaison Bureau with Foreign Countries, which was
created in 1960. The Technical Cooperation Bureau was transferred to the State
Council's Scientific and Technological Commission by 1959, and the Whole Plants
Bureau was transferred around 1962 to the above-mentioned Bureau for Economic
Liaison with Foreign Countries.

Foreign trade organs also were established at the provincial level and in the cities of Peking and Shanghai.[8] The most important of these bureaus appear to be those in Kwangtung and Shanghai, a fact that reflects the importance of the Canton Trade Fair and the role of Shanghai as China's leading port.

Paralleling the consolidation of the MFT, the foreign trade corporation structure was basically set by the mid-1950s and underwent relatively few changes over the subsequent decade. Thus, by 1956 the above-mentioned six corporations had been expanded to sixteen. That number had dropped again to fourteen by 1970. In 1971, however, the corporation structure underwent a major reorganization which reduced the number to seven.[9]

The mid-1950s also witnessed establishment of a college-level program to train foreign trade personnel. By 1954 the Peking Foreign Trade Specialists' School (Pei-ching tui-wai mao-i chuan-k'o hsüeh-hsiao) was in existence. A 1954 guide to higher education[10] lists two departments in this school: the first for foreign trade specialists, and the second for the study of "practical" (ying-yung) foreign languages, namely, Russian, German, English, French, Korean, Vietnamese, Japanese, and Spanish. This school presumably formed the basis for the establishment (no later than December 1954) of the Peking College of Foreign Trade (Pei-ching tui-wai mao-i hsüeh-yüan). A clue to its importance is suggested by the fact that it was headed by Hsieh Hsüeh-kung, then a vice-minister of foreign trade.[11]

Still another important development of the mid-1950s illustrated the always present factor of politics in the management of foreign trade in China. The background to this development began at the Bandung Conference when Chou En-lai met a number of important African, Asian, and Middle Eastern leaders for the first time. For purposes of expanding Chinese political and commercial ties, the most important contact for Chou was Egypt's Nasser. Before the year was out, Peking had signed a commercial agreement with

---

[8] Audrey Donnithorne, China's Economic System (New York: Praeger, 1967), p. 322. In general, little is known about the men who have held the post of director or deputy director of the bureaus, but it is known that the majority of them have had experience in finance or trade work.

[9] These seven corporations are: China National Cereals, Oils, and Foodstuffs Import-Export Corporation; China National Chemicals Import-Export Corporation; China National Light Industrial Products Import-Export Corporation; China National Machinery Import-Export Corporation; China National Metals and Minerals Import-Export Corporation; China National Native Produce and Animal By-Products Import-Export Corporation; and China National Textiles Import-Export Corporation.

[10] T'ou-k'ao ta-hsüeh chih-tao (Guide to universities for those reporting for examinations) (Hong Kong: Hsiang-kang hsüeh-sheng shu-tien ch'u-pan [Hong Kong Student Bookstore Publishers], 1954), p. 27.

[11] In 1969, at the ninth CCP Congress, Hsieh was one of the very few men specializing in foreign affairs or foreign trade who was elected to the Central Committee.

Egypt which provided for, *inter alia,* the establishment of a "commercial representatives' office" in each capital.

This action had a special significance for both Peking and Taipei, for it was the first instance in which either of the "two Chinas" governments had dealt officially with a nation without the other automatically breaking diplomatic ties with that nation. Put another way, it demonstrated that there were pragmatic and political limitations to the alleged inflexibility of the "two Chinas" to countenance any compromise. In any event, the Chinese commercial representative took up residence in Cairo in early 1956—and it was not until several months later that Cairo broke diplomatic ties with Taiwan.

What might be called the "Egyptian formula" was repeated later in 1956 with Syria, Lebanon, and Cambodia. The Commercial Representatives' Office in Syria and the Economic Mission in Cambodia soon led, as it had with Egypt, to the establishment of formal diplomatic relations. (On the other hand, Peking was not able to escalate its commercial office in Beirut to an embassy; the office was soon closed, possibly because of this failure.) In later years, using similar unorthodox methods, Peking opened commercial offices in other nations, all but one of which (Austria) maintained diplomatic relations with Taipei. The slightly altered pattern was to place these commercial offices under the CCPIT. Thus, commercial representatives arrived in Brazil in 1964, and in Chile, Italy, and Austria in 1965. With the fall of the Goulart government, the representative to Brazil was accused of being a spy and was imprisoned for a year. But within a few years Chile, Italy, and Austria established diplomatic relations with Peking.

By far the most important case involving "semi-official" relations is Japan.[12] From the Chinese viewpoint, Sino-Japanese trade had reached very significant proportions by 1957, even though it was conducted by the CCPIT and the various state trading corporations without the benefit of permanent trade missions in each capital. Trade dropped sharply in 1958 as a result of the so-called Nagasaki Flag Incident, and remained at modest levels into the early 1960s. Then, in 1962, Peking's top "Japan expert," Tokyo-born Liao Ch'eng-chih negotiated a special arrangement with a Japanese named Takasaki Tatsunosuke. This came to be known as the Liao-Takasaki (or LT) agreement; and under a 1964 supplementary agreement each side established a "liaison office" in the other's capital. Trade immediately and dramatically rose to new heights, and Japan quickly became China's number one trading partner.

A. *China's Aid Program*

By the middle to late 1950s the various pillars of Peking's trade apparatus— the MFT, the CCPIT, and the corporations—were firmly set in institutional

---

[12] For a more detailed discussion of Sino-Japanese trade relations, see the chapter by Henderson and Matsuo.

form. The remaining task was to formalize the aid program, which is so intrinsically linked to trade. The PRC had been in the aid business from its earliest days, principally in the form of military aid to Korea and Vietnam. More conventional, nonmilitary aid programs took shape from the middle 1950s, with most of the recipients located in South and Southeast Asia. It appears that a decision was taken in 1960 to institutionalize the aid program under a new organization, a step possibly related to the fact that 16 African nations won their independence that year. The new organ—the Bureau for Economic Liaison with Foreign Countries—was almost certainly upgraded from the old Economic Liaison Bureau under the MFT. (The only information about the old bureau is that it was in existence by 1956, when the bureau had a representative in Vietnam.)

The new bureau was set up in January 1960, but it was not until a year later that it was staffed with a director and eight deputy-directors. The backgrounds of these men demonstrated the close tie between Peking's trade and aid programs. Director Fang I, who was to emerge in the ensuing years as the key Chinese aid official, had already spent several years in Vietnam as head of China's aid program there. Four of the eight deputy-directors had had specific and lengthy experience in the foreign trade field. Another deputy-director was an economic planning expert, and two others had wide experience in heavy industry. (The background of the eighth man is unknown.)

In 1964 the bureau was raised to the commission (ministerial) level,[13] with Fang I still at the helm. It appears to be no coincidence that in the same year a new post, the economic counselor *(ching-chi ts'an-tsan)*, was established in Chinese embassies abroad. The Chinese moved quickly to dispatch economic counselors in 1964–66 to Albania, Burma, Mali, Algeria, Cambodia, the Congo (B), Ghana, Indonesia, Korea, Nepal, Tanzania, and Guinea. In 1969–71, after the Cultural Revolution, economic counselors were sent to Zambia, Sudan, Southern Yemen, and Ceylon, and lower ranking economic attachés to Mongolia, Somalia, Mauritania, Uganda, and Romania.[14] We doubtless would know more about the men and the economic counselor/attaché posts were it not for the Cultural Revolution. As it was, a dozen-odd counselors and a handful of attachés had barely reached their new posts when the Cultural Revolution resulted in most of them returning home.

---

[13] The term commission *(wei-yüan-hui)* was retained into 1970, but for reasons unknown it was redesignated a ministry *(pu)* by 1971.

[14] See Appendix A for more details on the assignment abroad of economic counselors. Note that the approximate equivalent of economic counselors had been stationed in Vietnam and Cambodia since 1956, and in Laos since 1961. A slight difference in nomenclature regarding the men in Tanzania and Zambia is explained in table 11 of this appendix.

II. The Foreign Trade Apparatus in Operation: Commercial Representation Abroad

By 1966 (on the eve of the Cultural Revolution) the PRC had commercial officials in virtually all nations with which it maintained diplomatic relations and had economic officials in countries that received Chinese aid. Most of these officials were called home during the Cultural Revolution, but events through 1974 demonstrate that this same network has been restored to 1966 proportions. Indeed, with many nations newly recognizing the PRC in 1970–74, the network has substantially expanded beyond the 1966 level.

Appendix A provides details on China's commercial and economic representation abroad. This data, summarized in table 1, lists the total number of nations where the PRC has (or has had) commercial and economic representatives. It should be noted that before the autumn of 1970 the PRC had diplomatic relations with forty-five nations. Then, beginning with Canada in October 1970, thirty-eight nations established relations with the PRC and another four restored previously severed relations—bringing the total in April 1972 to eighty-seven nations.

These data clearly demonstrate that the post of commercial counselor and/or the CCPIT-sponsored (i.e., ostensibly unofficial) commercial offices have been thoroughly institutionalized within the PRC trade apparatus. (The exceptions —all detailed in Appendix A—are so trifling that they require no discussion.) But what relation, if any, is there between the institutionalization of commercial missions abroad and total Chinese trade? The correlation is positive, but in many ways irrelevant, if one focuses on the 1950s. In those years PRC trade

TABLE 1

Areas in Which the PRC Has (or Had)
Commercial-Economic Representatives (1950–72)

	Commercial Counselors	Commercial Attachés or Secretaries	Economic Counselors	Economic Attachés
USSR and East Europe	9	8	1	2
South and Southeast Asia, Japan, Australia, and New Zealand	9	7	6	5
Asian Communist Countries	3	3	2	3
Middle East	7	8	2	1
Africa	11	11	7	8
West Europe	11	10	0	1
The Americas	5	3	0	0
Totals	55	50	18	20

was mainly with the Soviet bloc, where Peking did have commercial officials and, of course, formal diplomatic relations.

The question becomes more complex in the 1960s and 1970s when PRC trade was dramatically reoriented toward the non-Communist world. More than 50% of total Chinese trade was with Communist nations as late as 1962, but since then it has been increasingly conducted with non-Communist nations. In 1970, for example, about 80% of Chinese trade was with the latter; and among the PRC's 10 leading trade partners in that year, formal relations were maintained with only two, Britain and France. However, in five other countries the PRC had "unofficial" commercial officials. Thus, she had neither diplomatic relations nor commercial representatives in only three nations—Canada, Australia, and West Germany.

The Canadian and Australian cases are almost exclusively accounted for by the PRC's heavy grain purchases during the past decade. In the case of West Germany, it seems that heavy trade is stimulated by a combination of excellence of German products and the vigorous (if technically unofficial) sponsorship of trade with China on the part of the government.[15] In these exceptional instances, the Chinese have displayed a flexibility to suit their needs. Canadian officials in Hong Kong, for example, have had no trouble in making regular visits to China to negotiate their large grain sales, and the Chinese have often reciprocated by sending special trade delegations to Canada.

TABLE 2

RELATIONSHIP BETWEEN THE ARRIVAL OF COMMERCIAL OFFICIALS AND
THE INCREASE (OR DECREASE) OF TRADE (ROUNDED TO $ MILLIONS)

	Trade in Year Before Arrival of Commercial Officials	Trade Two Years after Arrival of Commercial Officials	Increase (or Decrease) in Trade vis-à-vis Nation in Question during Three-Year Span (in percentages)	Increase in Total Chinese Trade during the Three-Year Span (in percentages)
Sweden	$8 (1951)	$2 (1954)	− 75	+ 25
Finland	$1 (1952)	$9 (1954)	+ 800	+ 25
U.K.	$45 (1954)	$74 (1957)	+ 64	+ 24
Switzerland	$34 (1954)	$56 (1957)	+ 65	+ 24
Norway	$2 (1955)	$8 (1958)	+ 300	+ 37
Netherlands	$15 (1957)	$28 (1960)	+ 87	+ 28
France	$80 (1963)	$146 (1966)	+ 83	+ 48
Italy	$42 (1964)	$132 (1967)	+ 214	+ 18
Austria	$4 (1964)	$22 (1967)	+ 450	+ 18

[15] For a more detailed discussion of Sino-West German trade, see the chapter by Arthur Stahnke.

Attempting a further refinement concerning the institutionalization of the foreign trade network abroad, we can ask whether the dispatch of commercial officials or the establishment of a CCPIT commercial office has *boosted* trade. The answer is a qualified yes. Table 2 illustrates this in terms of China's important trade with Western Europe.

In general these same relationships work out for South-Southeast Asia and the Middle East, and they are particularly striking for Japan. On the other hand, in Africa and Latin America, total trade figures are so trifling that attempts at correlations would be more misleading than helpful. At a minimum, then, it seems valid to conclude that commercial officials abroad facilitate a boost in trade.

A. *Where China Negotiates*

Trade-aid agreements constituted 48% of *all* types of international agreements signed by the PRC between 1949 and 1966.[16] This is not to suggest that foreign trade is a "48% component" of the total picture of Chinese international relations. Yet one is struck by the statistical consistency of this percentage on a year-to-year basis. (See Appendix B.) In any case, absolute figures given in table 3 show that China negotiated over 1,000 trade or aid treaties, agreements, protocols, etc., from 1949 through 1970. Slightly more than half (54%) were signed in Peking, and the balance (46%) abroad. That is, some agreements were signed in China by foreign diplomatic or

TABLE 3

RANK ORDER OF TRADE-AID AGREEMENTS, 1949–70
(EXCLUDING MULTILATERAL AND UNKNOWN LOCALE)

Area	No.	Signed in China	Signed Abroad
East Europe	285	156	129
South and SE Asia	210	91	119
Communist Asia	168	118	50
Africa	115	56	59
USSR	68	23	45
Middle East	68	34	34
West Europe	65	40	25
Japan	29	28	1
Americas	27	19	8
Totals	1,035	564	471

[16] In contrast, in the four years from 1966 to 1970—i.e., the period during the Cultural Revolution and immediately afterwards—the percentage rose to 70 percent of all agreements negotiated. As a tentative conclusion, it appears that special priority was given to foreign trade during this period. However, the percentage shields the fact that the *absolute* number of trade agreements dropped somewhat during this period.

commercial officials stationed in Peking; other agreements were signed using a reverse procedure whereby Chinese officials posted abroad signed in foreign capitals; and in still other cases, Chinese or foreign delegations visited each other's capital to conduct trade. Obviously, there are many variations on these three principal themes.

At first glance there seems to be no pattern to this situation, and it is probably true that a more detailed breakdown is easily susceptible to over-analysis. Nonetheless, a few points can be made, particularly if seen in the larger framework of politics and, perhaps, cultural characteristics.

Those areas with the largest disparities in terms of locale of signing are probably the most suggestive. For example, the 2:1 Moscow/Peking ratio is far more striking when one notes that through 1953—i.e., during the Stalin era when the Soviet Union was in a donor position—19 pacts were signed in Moscow and only one in Peking. If in fact the Chinese viewed this as a slight to their national dignity, then they have come a long way toward evening the score; since 1954, 22 agreements have been negotiated in Peking and 26 in Moscow. An exact reversal of this situation exists in China's dealings with its three Asian Communist neighbors—Vietnam, Korea, and Mongolia, all recipients of Chinese aid. Here Peking enjoys (if that is the word) far better than a 2:1 ratio. For Western Europe, if one ignores the 10 agreements reached at or shortly after the 1952 Moscow International Economic Conference (when China was attempting a major breakthrough of the economic blockade), Peking stands ahead at a nearly 3:1 ratio. But the most striking case is Japan, where we find Peking with a 28:1 advantage. Students of Sino-Japanese trade, however, can point to what might be called the "laughing-all-the-way-to-the-bank" role played by the Japanese.

B. Who Signs for China?

Who signs—and who negotiates—the hundreds of trade agreements under discussion? The names and posts of the Chinese signatories are available for the overwhelming majority of these agreements, but we woefully lack information about the actual, across-the-table negotiations and the specific authority vested in Chinese officials to make decisions. Moreover, there are vast disparities in the money value of one agreement as opposed to another: a single contract to purchase Japanese chemical fertilizers can be worth ten times a half-dozen agreements signed with small African nations. Despite these limitations, we can gain some notion of the workings of the overall foreign trade system by examining who, in the sense of their role or post, signs the agreements.

Officials of the MFT have signed by far the largest number of agreements—459 (or 53%) of the total of 864. A breakdown is given in table 4.

TABLE 4

AGREEMENTS SIGNED BY MINISTRY OF FOREIGN TRADE PERSONNEL

	In Peking	Abroad	Total
Minister of Foreign Trade	103	32	135
Vice-Ministers and Assistant-Ministers of Foreign Trade	182	113	295
Foreign Trade Ministry bureau directors and deputy-directors	18	11	29
Totals	303	156	459

The fact that the minister signed so often at home is not surprising, but it is impressive to note how often he went abroad. The hard-core element of the entire foreign trade system probably rests on the shoulders of the 20 different men who have served as the vice-ministers or assistant-ministers. Here again it is impressive to see how frequently these men have gone abroad.

The next highest category is MFA personnel abroad—in virtually all cases the ambassador, the chargé d'affaires a.i., or an embassy counselor (not the commercial counselor). Table 4 reveals that 156 agreements were signed by MFT personnel traveling abroad. An almost identical number (153) were signed by the ambassador or one of his political aides. This is probably a much inflated figure, however, when one examines which men hammered out the detailed agreements; the demands of protocol presumably call for the ambassador's signature, as opposed, say, to that of the commercial counselor. We get some clue to this suggestion in the news dispatches about the agreements, which often mention that the commercial counselor "attended the signing ceremony" or "took part on the Chinese side in the negotiating . . ." of the particular trade pact. Commercial counselors, in fact, have signed only 21 documents—and 15 of these have been in the lower range of importance (i.e., contracts, or exchanges of "letters" or "notes" regarding trade terms).

The next ranking category consists of the premier (Chou En-lai), one of the vice-premiers, or Finance Minister Li Hsien-nien. These men have signed 90 agreements, all but nine of them in Peking. Here again, protocol has clearly played a role in the signings by Chou En-lai or one of his vice-premiers. But Li Hsien-nien (who is also a vice-premier) is a special case. By any standard Politburo member Li is a towering figure in the Chinese political hierarchy, and since 1954 he has been one of the four or five most important economic officials in Peking. He has played an active role in foreign trade since the late 1950s, and he became even more heavily involved during the Cultural Revolution.

Our figures have less significance when we examine the number of times corporation officials or CCPIT men have signed agreements. The figures are only 29 for the former and 23 for the latter. In the case of the CCPIT, as stressed earlier, this is largely a political question—being the unofficial arm of the MFT, it has devoted itself almost exclusively to Japan and those Western European nations which do not have diplomatic relations with Peking.

C. Trade Personnel

Finally, we turn to the question of the men who run the foreign trade system and the lines of authority. It appears that at the highest levels foreign trade cuts across two systems *(hsi-t'ung)*—foreign affairs, and finance and trade. Setting aside such obvious policy-level leaders as Mao Tse-tung and Chou En-lai, two high-echelon figures stand out: Li Hsien-nien and Yeh Chi-chuang. We have already noted the long-time roles of Li and Yeh as Finance minister and Foreign Trade minister, respectively. But it may be of greater use to note their posts on three government committees that have stood at the peak of the finance and trade system since 1949 and which can be regarded as successor committees. These are the Finance and Economics Committee (1949–54), the Fifth Staff Office (1954–59), and the Finance and Trade Staff Office (1959–?). Li was a vice-chairman of the first and director of the latter two. Yeh was a vice-chairman (or deputy-director) of all three.

The configuration of the foreign affairs system is somewhat different.[17] For the first decade there was no government body paralleling the Finance and Economics Committee, nor the Fifth Staff Office. But then the Foreign Affairs Staff Office was established in 1958. K'ung Yüan, a former MFT vice-minister and Customs Administration chief, was made one of the deputy-directors, and three years later foreign aid chief Fang I was added as another deputy-director. Li, Yeh, K'ung, and Fang were all members or alternates of the Eighth Central Committee elected in 1956–58. It would be facile to state that this foursome "controlled" the Chinese trade-aid program, but it seems clear that they have played a critical coordinating role and that their advice was sought at the highest policy levels.[18]

Shifting from policy and senior coordinating levels to day-to-day administration, the most striking characteristics are continuity of service within the trade-aid system and the interlocking network of men. For example, through 1966 the 15 men who had held the post of vice-minister of the MFT averaged over 12 years of experience in foreign trade. This same group visited no less

[17] See Donald W. Klein, "The Management of Foreign Affairs in Communist China," in John M. H. Lindbeck, ed., *China: Management of a Revolutionary Society* (Seattle: University of Washington Press, 1971).

[18] Yeh Chi-chuang died in 1967, and K'ung was a victim of the Cultural Revolution. However, Li and Fang have been very active in recent years. For details, see Chapter 4 of Bruce D. Larkin's *China and Africa, 1949–70* (Berkeley, Calif.: University of California Press, 1971).

than 49 different nations—several of them on more than one occasion. The interlocking nature of the system is illustrated by the 200 men who have been commercial counselors (92), MFT officials (77), and/or corporation officials (94). Table 5 indicates the frequency with which these men have crossed over among these posts.

TABLE 5

MEN WHO HAVE BEEN FOREIGN TRADE MINISTRY OFFICIALS, CORPORATION
OFFICIALS, AND/OR COMMERCIAL COUNSELORS

Only Corporation Officials*	56
Only Foreign Trade Ministry Officials**	42
Only Commercial Counselors	46
Both Corporation and Foreign Trade Officials	17
Both Foreign Trade Officials and Commercial Counselors	25
Both Corporation Officials and Commercial Counselors	28
All Three	7

* Managers and deputy-managers

** Ministers, vice-ministers, assistant-ministers, bureau directors, and bureau deputy-directors.

Arranging the data in another fashion, we find that nearly a quarter (22 of 93) of the commercial counselors have held this post in two nations (and three of the 22 in three nations). Similar trends are also found within the MFT posts in Peking. Of the 77 ministry personnel, 36 have held more than one post within the ministry, and 11 of these 36 have held at least three different posts. We have confined this analysis to the corporations, commercial counselors, and ministry personnel, but it applies with equal force to the CCPIT and the Bank of China. In more human terms, we can note the sequence of posts held by Li Cho-chih from 1953 to date: commercial counselor to Czechoslovakia and then Yugoslavia; manager of the China National Metals Import Corporation in Peking; commercial counselor in London; assistant-minister of foreign trade; manager of the Bank of China branch in Hong Kong. P'ang Chih-chiang serves as a similar example: deputy-director of the ministry's Transportation Bureau; member of the CCPIT's Maritime Arbitration Committee; deputy-manager of the China Foreign Trade Transportation Corporation. Cases like these abound.

III. CONCLUSION

From very modest origins in 1949, the PRC has developed an impressive foreign trade apparatus. The system seems to be well integrated and self-contained. It draws from its own ranks, and only on rare occasions has it been required to absorb personnel from other systems (e.g., propaganda, military). Experience derives principally from an extraordinary number of delegations sent abroad and from the large number of commercial men posted overseas.

There are no striking suggestions that the foreign trade system developed in the 1950s had any particular difficulties in absorbing the newly created foreign aid network in the 1960s.

The Cultural Revolution curtailed trade somewhat, but the available evidence suggests that foreign trade personnel were only marginally affected. Further, the PRC has already expanded its international commercial network as an outgrowth of the establishment of diplomatic relations with many nations in the 1970–74 period.

APPENDIX A

CHINESE COMMERCIAL AND ECONOMIC REPRESENTATION ABROAD (1950–72)

The following tables are arranged so that nations in each geographic area are listed in the order in which Peking sent its *first* commercial official—which in most cases means the commercial counselor. Much of the information is self-explanatory, but by their structure these tables tend to distort or neglect other points. Hopefully, the notes and "comments" appended to each area table will clarify some issues, and demonstrate how closely politics and commerce are related. It should be noted that information at the counselor level is generally excellent, but it is sometimes deficient for the attachés and secretaries. Finally, as stressed in the text, a number of nations have formalized relations with Peking quite recently. If past practice is any guide, the PRC will soon send commercial officials to these nations. To anticipate this probability, the following tables include *all* nations with which China has had diplomatic relations.

TABLE 6

CHINESE COMMERCIAL AND ECONOMIC REPRESENTATION IN
USSR AND EAST EUROPE

	Commercial Counselors	Commercial Attachés or Secretaries	Economic Counselors	Economic Attachés
USSR	1950	...	...	...
Poland	1950	1955	...	...
Germany	1952	1960	...	...
Hungary	1952	1964	...	...
Czechoslovakia	1953	1954	...	...
Romania	1953	1954	...	1972
Yugoslavia	1955	1971	...	...
Bulgaria	1956	1954	...	...
Albania	1962	1962	1964	1968

Comment on table 6 : In the heyday of Moscow-Peking relations (1957–58) China had no less than six commercial counselors in Moscow, but only one since 1962.

TABLE 7

CHINESE COMMERCIAL AND ECONOMIC REPRESENTATION IN
SOUTH AND SOUTHEAST ASIA, JAPAN, AUSTRALIA, AND NEW ZEALAND

	Commercial Counselors	Commercial Attachés or Secretaries	Economic Counselors	Economic Attachés
India	1950	...	...	...
Burma	1955	1957	1964	...
Indonesia[1]	1955	1955	1965	...
Pakistan	1955	1956	...	1965
Nepal	1956	...	1965	...
Cambodia[2]	1959	1959	1956	1956
Ceylon	1957	1957	1971	1970
Afghanistan	1961	1956	...	1966
Laos[3]	...	...	1961	1961
Japan[4]	1964	1964	...	...
Maldives	(diplomatic relations established October 1972)			
Australia	(diplomatic relations established December 1972)			
New Zealand	(diplomatic relations established December 1972)			

[1] The PRC "suspended" relations with Indonesia in October 1967.

[2] The officials listed in the economic counselor and attaché columns were actually the chief and his deputies of the Economic Mission to Cambodia, which was set up two years before an embassy was established. An economic counselor was not sent to Cambodia until 1965.

[3] The officials listed in the economic counselor and attaché columns are actually the chief and his deputies of the Economic and Cultural Mission in Xieng Khouang, Laos, which was set up several months before an embassy was established.

[4] The officials listed in the commercial counselor and attaché columns are actually the chief and his deputies of the Tokyo Liaison Office, described elsewhere in this article. Japan and the PRC established diplomatic relations in September 1972, and by April 1973 a commercial counselor was assigned to Tokyo.

Comment on table 7. The important point here concerns the three key nations of the area—India, Indonesia, and Japan. Bitter disputes with India and Indonesia in the early and mid-1960s brought commercial contacts to a virtual standstill. On the other hand, after rocky relations with Japan in the late fifties and early sixties, trade with Japan surpassed trade with *any* nation by the late 1960s—the lack of formal diplomatic relations until 1972 notwithstanding.

TABLE 8

CHINESE COMMERCIAL AND ECONOMIC REPRESENTATIVES IN
COMMUNIST ASIAN COUNTRIES

	Commercial Counselor	Commercial Attachés or Secretaries	Economic Counselors	Economic Attachés
Vietnam[1]	1955	1956	1956	1959
Korea	1955	1962	1965	1964
Mongolia	1956	1960	...	1969

[1] The officials listed in the economic counselor and attaché columns were actually the representative and his deputies of the Foreign Trade Ministry's Economic Liaison Bureau. "Economic representatives" (rather than economic counselors) have continued to be in Vietnam into the 1970s.

Comment on table 8 : The prime point concerns aid rather than trade. The lack of a top-level economic (aid) official in Mongolia reflects the cooling in Sino-Mongolian relations—after very impressive Chinese aid in the late 1950s (before the establishment of the post of economic counselor). On the other hand, high levels of aid continue to be given to Vietnam and Korea; noteworthy in this regard is the presence of four economic attachés in Hanoi—more than in any other nation.

TABLE 9

CHINESE COMMERCIAL AND ECONOMIC REPRESENTATIVES
IN THE MIDDLE EAST

	Commercial Counselors	Commercial Attachés or Secretaries	Economic Counselors	Economic Attachés
Egypt[1]	1956	1956	...	...
Syria[2]	1956	1956	...	...
Lebanon[3]	1956	1956	...	...
Iraq	1959	1958	...	...
Sudan	1960	1959	1971	...
Yemen	1960	1963	...	1965
Southern Yemen	...	1970	1971	...
Kuwait	...	1971	...	...
Iran	1972	...	...	...

[1] Egypt and Syria merged to form the United Arab Republic in 1958, but the union was dissolved in 1961. The officials listed in the commercial counselor and attaché columns were actually the representative and his deputy of the Office of the Commercial Representative, which was set up several months before an embassy was established. A commercial attaché was in Cairo later in 1956, but the first commercial counselor was not appointed until 1959.

[2] See above re Egypt. After Syria broke away from the UAR in 1961, no commercial counselor was sent there, but a commercial secretary was posted there by 1964.

[3] The officials listed in the commercial counselor and attaché columns were actually the representative and his deputy of the Office of the Commercial Representative. However, unlike the Egyptian and Syrian cases, this did not lead to diplomatic relations, and thus the commercial office was closed. But then in November 1971 Lebanon and the PRC established diplomatic relations.

TABLE 10

CHINESE COMMERCIAL AND ECONOMIC REPRESENTATIVES IN AFRICA

	Commercial Counselors	Commercial Attachés or Secretaries	Economic Counselors	Economic Attachés
Morocco	1959	1962	...	...
Guinea	1961	1960	1966	1968
Kenya	...	1960	...	...
Mali	1961	1961	1964	1964
Ghana[1]	1961	1961	1965	...
Somalia	1961	1964	...	1969
Algeria	1963	1962	1965	1972
Congo (B)	1964	...	1965	1970
Tunisia[2]	1964	...	...	...
Tanzania[3]	1965	1964	1965	...
Zambia[4]	1972	1971	1970	1970
Mauritania	...	1970	...	1970
Uganda	...	...	...	1970
Nigeria	1972	1972	...	...
Zanzibar[5]	...	...	...	...
Burundi[6]	...	...	...	...
Central African Republic[7]	...	...	...	...
Dahomey[8]	...	...	...	...
Equatorial Guinea	(diplomatic relations established October 1970)			
Ethiopia	(diplomatic relations established November 1970)			
Cameroon	(diplomatic relations established March 1971)			
Sierra Leone	(diplomatic relations established July 1971)			
Rwanda	(diplomatic relations established November 1971)			
Senegal	(diplomatic relations established December 1971)			
Mauritius	(diplomatic relations established April 1972)			
Togo	(diplomatic relations established September 1972)			
Malagasy	(diplomatic relations established November 1972)			
Zaire	(diplomatic relations "normalized" in November 1972 and then fully established in January 1973)			
Chad	(diplomatic relations established November 1972)			

[1] Ghana severed diplomatic relations with the PRC in October 1966 but restored them in February 1972.

[2] Tunisia severed diplomatic relations in September 1967 but restored them in October 1971.

[3] There was a commercial counselor in Tanzania by 1965. However, later in the same year an office of economic and commercial representatives was established. Thus, economic and commercial representatives (rather than counselors) are posted there.

[4] The official in Zambia listed under economic counselor is actually designated economic representative. However, an economic counselor was in Zambia by April 1972, possibly in addition to the economic representative.

[5] Zanzibar established diplomatic relations with the PRC in 1963, but a few months later that island nation merged with Tanganyika to form Tanzania.

⁶ Burundi severed diplomatic relations in 1965 but restored them in October 1971.

⁷ The Central African Republic established relations with Peking in 1964, but they were broken in 1966.

⁸ Dahomey severed diplomatic relations with the PRC in 1966 but restored them in 1972.

Comment on table 10 : Although there are more commercial and economic officials in this area than any other, Chinese trade with Africa is extremely marginal. On the other hand, aid is significant—especially the approximately third of a billion dollar loan to build the Tan-Zam railway.

TABLE 11

CHINESE COMMERCIAL AND ECONOMIC REPRESENTATIVES
IN WEST EUROPE

	Commercial Counselors	Commercial Attachés or Secretaries	Economic Counselors	Economic Attachés
Sweden	1955	1952	...	...
Finland	1956	1952	...	...
Denmark	...	1953	...	...
U.K.	1955	1955	...	...
Switzerland¹	1955	1956	...	1968
Norway	1971	1956	...	...
Netherlands	1964	1958	...	...
France	1964	1964	...	...
Italy²	1965	1965	...	...
Austria²	1965	1965	...	...
Turkey	1972	...	...	...
Belgium	1972	...	...	...
San Marino	(consular relations established May 1971)			
Iceland	(diplomatic relations established December 1971)			
Cyprus	(diplomatic relations established December 1971)			
Malta	(diplomatic relations established January 1972)			
Greece	(diplomatic relations established June 1972)			
Germany (West)	(diplomatic relations established October 1972)			
Luxembourg	(diplomatic relations established November 1972)			
Spain	(diplomatic relations established March 1973)			

¹ The presence of an economic attaché is confirmed from official Swiss sources. As stressed in this paper, economic officials deal with aid rather than trade, but this is clearly not the case in Switzerland.

² The officials listed under commercial counselor and attaché columns were, from 1965, the representative and his deputy of the Commercial Representatives' Office of the CCPIT in both Italy and Austria. Italy established diplomatic relations with Peking in November 1970, and Austria established them in May 1971. Subsequently commercial counselors were identified in Italy (July 1971) and Austria (November 1971).

TABLE 12

CHINESE COMMERCIAL AND ECONOMIC REPRESENTATIVES
IN THE AMERICAS

	Commercial Counselors	Commercial Attachés or Secretaries	Economic Counselors	Economic Attachés
Cuba	1961	1965	...	...
Brazil[1]	...	1964	...	...
Chile[2]	1965	1965	...	...
Canada	1971	...	...	...
Peru[3]	1971	...	...	...
Mexico	1972	...	...	...
Argentina	(diplomatic relations established February 1972)			
Guyana	(diplomatic relations established June 1972)			
Jamaica	(diplomatic relations established November 1972)			

[1] The official listed under the commercial attaché column was actually the deputy representative of the Commercial Representatives' Office of the CCPIT in Brazil. As noted in the text, he was imprisoned for a year as a spy, and the office was closed.

[2] The officials listed under the commercial counselor and attaché columns were actually the representative and his deputy of the Commercial Representatives' Office of the CCPIT in Chile. In January 1971 Chile established diplomatic relations with the PRC, and by April of that year a commercial counselor was in Chile—thus replacing the CCPIT office.

[3] The official listed under commercial counselor was actually the representative of the Commercial Representatives' Office of the CCPIT in Peru. This office was established in 1971, but later in the year Peru and the PRC established diplomatic relations; by March 1972 a commercial counselor was in Peru—thus replacing the CCPIT office.

APPENDIX B

TRADE-AID AGREEMENTS IN RELATION TO ALL AGREEMENTS

Year	Total Agreements	Trade-Aid Agreements	Percentage Total of Trade-Aid
1949	5	0	...
1950	30	14	47
1951	27	12	44
1952	66	42	64
1953	69	35	51
1954	107	63	59
1955	113	53	47
1956	149	71	48
1957	134	62	46
1958	118	69	58
1959	115	48	42
1960	139	54	39
1961	162	96	59
1962	121	63	52
1963	155	60	39
1964	198	81	41
1965	163	67	41
1966	108	45	42
1967	50	30	60
1968	38	28	74
1969	34	26	76
1970	67	49	73
Totals	2168	1068	

State Control of Foreign Trade after Liberation

VICTOR H. LI

I. INTRODUCTION

This essay tries both to investigate methodology for the study of China and to examine the workings of the Chinese foreign trade system. The methodological problem lies in the fact that most academics use essentially the same body of primary materials for their work, supplemented by the press and broadcast translation services. The amount of this published material is by no means small, but it still is a finite quantity. I also do not think the recent improvement in United States-China relations will significantly and quickly change the situation.

There is a similar although less precise problem with respect to refugee interview data. While "new" knowledgeable refugees continue to appear, the search for such persons is becoming more difficult. The greater number of scholars engaged in interviewing has increased, so to speak, the competition for resources. From another point of view, many scholars would consider refugee interview data to be too weak a peg on which to hang their research effort, in the absence of substantial support from published materials.

All this is not to say that there are not many areas in Chinese studies still unexplored. Rather, I am suggesting that as the amount of "new" material decreases, we must seek better ways of utilizing the available data. This paper is a tentative step in that direction.

Thus, there already are several works which discuss the organization and structure of Chinese foreign trade, notably the writings of Gene Hsiao, Audrey Donnithorne, and Jerome Cohen.[1] Helpful as these are, after studying them

---

[1] Audrey Donnithorne, *China's Economic System* (New York: Praeger, 1967); three articles by Gene Hsiao, "Communist China's Foreign Trade Organization," "Com-

I still do not have a "feel" for how foreign trade work is handled within China. As Professor Hsiao states, "[s]tudy of organization . . . is only the first step on the long road toward an understanding of Peking's complex legal policy and operation in foreign trade."[2] We still must answer questions such as: What are the range of decisions, both intermediate and final, which are made in the course of managing foreign trade work? Irrespective of the formalities, who actually makes these decisions? On what bases are the decisions made? From what sources comes the impetus for change or suggestion for innovation? Are there aspects of the handling of foreign trade work in China that are unique to the Chinese situation?

In trying to deal with some of these questions, I re-examined materials that already have been gone over by other scholars. I have concentrated on statutory materials in order to see whether a careful textual analysis employing different perspectives and making use of insights derived from the work of others can produce a clearer understanding of the actual process by which foreign trade is controlled and managed within China. Specifically, I picked out from the following legal compendia all items related, even indirectly, to foreign trade. I think I have most, if not all, of the statutory and quasi-statutory materials in this area, with the exception of international trade agreements and items discussing the volume and commodity composition of trade. These collections also included a number of major speeches and JMJP editorials.

The collections are: *Chung-yang jen-min cheng-fu fa-ling hui-pien* (Compendium of laws and directives of the Central People's Government) (hereafter *FLHP*), vols. 1–5 (1949–54), and its successor, *Chung-hua jen-min kung-ho-kuo fa-kuei hui-pien* (Compendium of the laws and regulations of the PRC) (hereafter *FKHP*), vols. 1–12 (1954–61); *Chung-yang jen-min cheng-fu ts'ai ching cheng-ts'e fa-ling hui-pien* (Compendium of laws and directives concerning the financial and economic policies of the Central People's Government) (hereafter *TCCT*), vols. 1–3 (1949–52); *Chung-yang ts'ai-cheng fa-kuei hui-pien* (Compendium of the fiscal laws and regulations of the central government) (hereafter *TCFKHP*), vols. 1–5 (1955–59); *Chung-yang jen-min cheng-fu chin-jung fa-ling hui-pien* (Compendium of the financial laws and directives of the Central People's Government) (hereafter *CJFLHP*), vols. 1–3 (1949–54),

---

munist China's Trade Treaties and Agreements (1949–1964)," and "Communist China's Foreign Trade Contracts and Means of Settling Disputes," *Vanderbilt Law Review*, nos. 20, 21, and 22, pp. 303, 623, and 503; and Jerome A. Cohen, "Chinese Law and Sino-American Trade," in Alexander Eckstein, ed., *China Trade Prospects and U.S. Policy* (New York: Praeger, 1971). See also Alexander Eckstein, *Communist China's Foreign Trade and Economic Growth* (New York: McGraw-Hill, 1966); Arthur Stahnke, ed., *China's Trade with the West* (New York: Praeger, 1972); Feng-hwa Mah, *The Foreign Trade of Mainland China* (New York: Aldine, 1971).

[2] Hsiao, "Foreign Trade Organization," p. 319.

and its successor, *Chung-hua jen-min kung-ho-kuo chin-jung fa-kuei hui-pien*
(Compendium of the financial laws and regulations of the PRC) (hereafter
CJFKHP), vols. 1–4 (1955–57); *Chung-yang jen-min cheng-fu shui-wu fa-ling
hui-pien* (Compendium of laws and directives concerning tax affairs of the
Central People's Government) (hereafter *SWFLHP*) (1952); and *Hua-tung-
ch'ü ts'ai-cheng ching-chi fa-ling hui-pien* (Compendium of laws and directives
concerning the finance and economics of the East China Region) (hereafter
HTFLHP), vols. 1–2 (1952).

The statutory material is supplemented by newspaper articles from the
Union Research Institute files which deal with foreign trade. They provide a
fairly good cross section of the newspapers inside China, particularly the
newspapers of the coastal cities, and of *Ta-kung-pao* in Hong Kong.

I have largely avoided the use of secondary sources, because I wish to know
what can be learned solely from the primary sources. Instead, I have approached
the primary materials from two points of view. First, I treat the work of bringing foreign trade under state control as one aspect of the over-all effort to
establish control over the entire society. In this sense many of the problems
encountered in trying to manage foreign trade work are similar to those
encountered in trying to handle, say, legal work. In both instances, for example,
the Communists lacked personnel at all levels who were both professionally
skilled and politically reliable. Thus, the Communists had to rely to some
degree on private traders and former KMT trade officials; these persons often
came into conflict with the Communist cadres. In addition, the Communists
had difficulty determining what form and style the work of managing foreign
trade should take. Institutions and operating rules frequently were changed
and changed again as they experimented with various ideas and structures.

Second, I focus on the problem of what Franz Schurmann calls the contradiction between the center and the region, and on related questions raised by
Professor Donnithorne in the concluding chapter of her book.[3] I try to describe
in greater detail what is meant by "dual leadership" by indicating what
decisions were made at the local level or, at least, were strongly influenced by
local interests. I also discuss some of the efforts made by the center to establish
control over local interests, and the degree to which and reasons for which
these efforts were successful or unsuccessful.

This paper basically deals with the years 1949–54, although an effort is
made to trace the principal issues into later years. Ideally, of course, one
should try to cover the entire post-Liberation era, but this would be an
enormous undertaking. The early period was chosen for a number of reasons.
First, my search of the statutory collections produced a tremendous amount

---

[3] Donnithorne, *"China's Economic System,"* pp. 497–511; H. Franz Schurmann,
Ideology and Organization in Communist China (2nd ed.; Berkeley and Los Angeles:
University of California Press, 1971), pp. 73–104.

of materials for 1949–54, relatively little material (except for the People's Bank) for 1954–57, and almost none for the subsequent period. Given this situation, the promulgation of the constitution in 1954 marks a convenient cut-off point.

Equally important is my feeling that the early period is neglected by scholars, perhaps out of a sense that it is no longer "timely." Yet in some ways, this is the most interesting time because the Communist leadership was experimenting with various leadership structures and methods and in the process revealed a great deal about its thinking. In addition, many of the major issues of later years—such as center/local tensions—are already apparent in the early years; indeed, it may well be that the later handling of these issues is shaped by the manner in which they arose and were treated in the period immediately after Liberation.

II. THE BASELINE AND EXTERNAL CONDITIONS

The Communists had little experience in foreign trade work before 1949. Although they controlled sizable areas for a number of years, these areas were inland and, from an economic point of view, consisted of locally oriented agricultural societies.

There was some expansion of the foreign trade apparatus after the Second World War as the Communists extended the areas they controlled.[4] During 1945–48 the Northeast Foreign Trade Department, operating through a state-owned trading company, handled the trade between the Communist-controlled portions of Manchuria and the Soviet Union. At about the same time the Kuan-tung Foreign Trade Bureau in Luta established a state-owned trading company to handle trade with North Korea, Japan, and possibly Hong Kong and Macao. Other such companies were formed in the major coastal cities as the Communists completed their takeover.

Although the Communists had not engaged in very much trade themselves, they were quite aware of the importance of foreign trade to the development of the economy, and they were also sensitive to the problems China had had in trading with the West for the past century. For over a hundred years imperialist nations had been stripping China of valuable raw materials and selling back manufactured goods at high prices. In addition, the KMT regime was criticized for importing luxury items rather than capital goods, and for maintaining a large trade deficit which gradually weakened the national economy.[5]

---

[4] Ai T'o-ya, "Foreign Trade Organization of the Communist Bandits," *Chin-jih ta-lu* (Mainland today), 3 February 1962. Despite the anti-Communist source and the polemics, this article is quite thorough and accurate.

[5] Lou Li-ch'i, "New Trend in China's Foreign Trade," *Hsin-hua yüeh-pao* (New China monthly), vol. 1, no. 5 (March 1950).

From the beginning the Communist policy was to encourage foreign trade, since this was an effective method by which China could obtain modern producer goods and technology. The Common Program declared that China would trade with anyone, so long as the principles of equality and mutual benefit were maintained.[6] As described below, measures were taken to control the quantity, balance, and commodity composition of trade. Since imports had to be financed by exports, the government helped to promote exports by emphasizing the planting of exportable agricultural products,[7] and by providing export subsidies in the form of lower tax rates[8] and reduced domestic transportation charges.[9]

The onset of the Korean War and the United Nations embargo brought about a number of important changes. Despite statements that the embargo did not hurt the Chinese economy[10] (and indeed that only Western capitalists suffered by being deprived of the Chinese market), it is clear that at least for the short run, the embargo was damaging. In any case it caused major adjustments in the pattern of Chinese trade. The already limited trade with Western countries dropped sharply, accompanied by a corresponding increase in trade with the socialist countries.[11] In addition, China de-emphasized the role of foreign trade and turned inward to fulfill its economic needs. Agricultural producers were instructed to plant fewer items for export and more items for domestic use;[12] and Chinese consumers of foreign goods were urged to find

---

[6] For a translation of the Common Program, see Albert Blaustein, ed., *Fundamental Legal Documents of Communist China* (So. Hackensack, N.J.: Rothman and Co., 1962).

[7] Nan Han-chen, "The Great Significance and Energetic Direction of Agricultural Fiscal Work," *TCCT*, 3: 240 (10 May 1951). See also, Ch'en Yun, "Report Concerning the Finance Situation and Grain Situation," *TCCT*, 1: 38 (13 April 1950).

[8] Ministry of Finance, "Detailed Rules for the Implementation of the Temporary Regulations on Excise Tax," *TCCT*, 2: 425 (21 December 1950); "Table on the Scope of Reducing Income Tax for Various Businesses," *HTFLHP*, p. 143; "Notice Concerning the Implementation of the Amending of the List for Tax Rebates for Export Goods as of April 29, 1951," *SWFLHP*, p. 94 (12 April 1951).

[9] Ministry of Railroads and Ministry of Trade, "Temporary Methods for Public and Private Enterprises to Apply for Special Rates for the Transport of Export Goods," *HTFLHP*, p. 1,392 (1 July 1950).

[10] Ch'en Ming, "Foreign Trade in Shanghai During the Past Two Years," *Hsin-wen jih-pao* (Shanghai), 29 September 1951; "Our Country's Foreign Trade During the Past Five Years," *JMJP*, 5 October 1954; "The Work of the Nation's Banks in 1950," *TCCT*, 3: 183.

[11] *Ibid.;* Tseng Shan, "Actual Conditions of Financial and Economic Work in Hua-tung," *TCCT*, 3: 30.

[12] *Ibid.;* East China Military Committee, "Directive Concerning the Work of Agricultural Production in 1951," *HTFLHP*, p. 1,140 (13 January 1951).

domestic substitutes.[13] A large part of this effort involved the improvement of internal commerce and transportation. For example, one article described how the trade department of Shansi Province sent people all over the country to promote the distribution of provincial products.[14]

The manner in which trade was conducted, particularly trade with the nonsocialist areas, also was changed in response to the embargo. Before the Korean War trade was carried out both by means of the barter process (the giving of goods for goods) and the exchange process (the sale of goods through the use of cash or bills of exchange).[15] In the very early days barter was favored because China lacked the foreign exchange with which to purchase imports, and because the severe inflation made it difficult to fix a price for Chinese goods. In the North China region, for example, about three-fourths of the trade was conducted through barter transactions.[16] By late 1949 the Chinese began to limit this mode of trade, since it interfered with the country's efforts to accumulate foreign exchange reserves.[17] It also obstructed import/export planning since the Chinese trader often had to take (or provide) "unplanned" goods in order to complete a transaction. The "Temporary Measures for the Control of Foreign Trade" promulgated in 1950 provided that all foreign trade should be conducted through the exchange process, and that barter could be used only with the special permission of the Ministry of Trade.[18]

The imposition of the embargo made it difficult for China to obtain either foreign exchange or the Western goods it desired. To meet these difficulties,

---

[13] GAC, "Temporary Methods for the Distribution and Use of Foreign Exchange," *HTFLHP*, p. 528 (6 October 1960); Ch'en Yün, "The Situation of Financial and Economic Work in the PRC During the Past Year," *TCCT*, 2: 240; *Hsin-wen jih-pao*, 29 September 1951.

[14] "Energetically Promote the Sale of Native Products," editorial, *JMJP*, 10 April 1951 in *TCCT*, 3: 250; see also, *TCCT*, 3: 30; *Hsin-wen jih-pao*, 29 September 1951.

[15] The foreign trade control regulations for Hua-pei, Hua-tung, and Hua-nan can be found in *Hsin-chung-kuo shang-yeh-chia chih tao-lu* (The road for businessmen in New China), March 1950, and also in *Hua-shang pao*, 21 March 1949 and *TKP-HK*, 31 December 1949. See also the foreign-exchange control regulations for Hua-pei, Hua-tung, Hua-nan, Hua-chung, Yünnan Province, and Tientsin in *CJFKHP*, 1: 241–53.

[16] FEC, "Directive Concerning the Amending of the 'Temporary Methods for the Control of Foreign Trade in the North China Region' by Removing the Barter System in Foreign Trade in Article 16," *TCCT*, 1: 414 (12 October 1949).

[17] *Ibid.*, p. 414.

[18] "Temporary Regulations for the Control of Foreign Trade," *FLHP*, 2: 337 (12 December 1950); Ministry of Trade, "Detailed Rules for the Implementation of the Temporary Regulations for the Control of Foreign Trade," *TCCT*, 3: 765 (February 1951).

barter was re-instituted as the principal mode of trade.[19] Imports and exports were divided into three categories according to their strategic importance. In order to export goods of any category, foreign goods of an equal or higher category had to be obtained in return. Moreover, import had to precede export, and export usually was on FOB terms.[20] In this way China could protect herself against loss if any goods were seized by the allies en route.

The effort to switch to barter trade was not entirely successful. The principal problem appears to have been that many exporters did not have the inclination or the know-how to engage in the import business, and vice versa.[21] This problem was aggravated by the constraints imposed by the requirement that certain categories of goods could be exchanged only for certain other categories of goods.

The Chinese tried to meet this difficulty by establishing Barter Exchange Offices under the dual auspices of the local branches of the Foreign Trade Control Bureau (hereafter FTCB) and the People's Bank.[22] These offices enabled a barter transaction to be broken in half. A Chinese merchant, for example, might import goods, and then "sell" to the office the right and duty to export goods of equivalent value from the proper export categories. Another merchant who specialized in export trade then would "purchase" this right, export the appropriate goods, and thus complete the "barter" transaction.

In addition, it appears that, at least by mid-1951, the exchange process again was in common use, although from the materials I have, I cannot tell how much trade was conducted through the barter process and how much through the exchange process. The principle of import preceding export was continued by requiring that Chinese exports could not be shipped until payment was received, and that payment for imports could be made only after the goods had arrived in China.[23] (The only major exception appears to

---

[19] "Temporary Methods for the Control of Barter Trade," and "Detailed Rules for the Implementation of the Temporary Methods for the Control of Foreign Trade," *Hsin-hua yüeh-pao*, 15 April 1951, also in *TCCT*, 3: 344–49; *TCCT*, 3: 183; Lin Chih, "How to Conduct Barter Trade," *Ching-chi-tao pao* (Economic directions) (Hong Kong), 13 March 1951; Yu Feng, "What is an Authority to Purchase?" *TKP-HK*, 17 August 1953.

[20] *TCCT*, 2: 30; *Hsin-wen jih-pao*, 29 September 1951; Huang Shao-lung, "Concerning the Letter of Credit," *Ching-chi-tao pao*, 12 May 1953.

[21] *Ching-chi-tao pao*, 13 March 1951.

[22] See, for example, Ministry of Trade and Chinese People's Bank, "Rules for the Shanghai Barter Exchange Office," *HTFLHP*, p. 774; Chinese People's Bank, "Rules for the Bank of China for Clearing Barter Accounts," *HTFLHP*, p. 776; "Temporary Measures Concerning the Operation of the Barter Exchange Offices," *TKP-HK*, 10 March 1951.

[23] "Adopt the Method of Goods Arriving Before Making Payment," *Hsin-wen jih-pao*, 22 August (?) 1951; "Improve Foreign Trade Arrangements," *TKP-HK*, 17 March 1951; see also, Ch'en T'ien-hsien, "Further Discussion on Methods of

have been the allowing of some exports to be sold on a consignment basis.[24]) As part of this adjustment, the Chinese began to replace the letter of credit with the letter of guarantee for import trade.[25] Under the latter instrument a Chinese bank would guarantee the foreign exporter that payment would be made in China after the goods had arrived in China. This served several purposes. If goods were seized by the allies before arrival in China, the loss would be borne by the foreign party. In addition, since there was some danger that the assets of Chinese banks and companies abroad might be frozen, it was unwise to keep a large amount of money outside the country; making payment in China resolved this difficulty. This instrument also may have been a means of pressuring foreign exporters into buying Chinese goods with the foreign exchange they had earned, since it was difficult to remove foreign exchange from China.

During the early years testing by the commodity inspection and testing office was usually, but not always, required.[26] This was due to the fact that the embargo forced some reliable and established firms out of the China trade, with the consequent filling of the vacuum by a number of small and sometimes not so experienced or scrupulous companies. In order to protect its own merchants, China required that goods must be inspected before payment could be made.

Throughout the 1949–54 period, the Communists were troubled by the lack of cadres who were experienced in foreign trade work.[27] One way to

---

Receiving Payment," *TKP-HK*, 7 March 1958. The last item is one in a long series of articles discussing methods of conducting trade.

[24] "Export by Definite Sale, Export by Consignment, and Import by Definite Sale," *TKP-HK*, 7 September 1952; see also, Shanghai Branch of the Bank of China, "Methods Concerning the Registration, Transfer and Settlement for Import and Export Barter," *Hsin-wen jih-pao*, 6 March 1953.

[25] *Ching-chi-tao pao*, 12 May 1953; "There Usually are Three Forms of Commercial Letters of Credit," *TKP-HK*, 4 February 1955.

[26] "Concerning Payment by Letter of Guarantee," *Ching-chi-tao pao*, 23 May 1953. See also notes 63–65, *infra*.

[27] For discussion of problems involving inexperienced cadres, see "Cooperation between Public and Private Develops Foreign Trade," editorial, *JMJP*, 4 September 1950, in *TCCT*, 2: 893; *TCCT*, 3: 30; *TCCT*, 3: 183; "Decision of the GAC Concerning the Handling of Duties in Dividing Finance and Economic Work Between the Center and the Local Areas," *FLHP*, 2: 109 (24 March 1951); Chang Hsü-yang, "Statement Concerning Foreign Trade Work," *Fu-chien jih-pao*, 11 October 1957; *JMJP*, 5 October 1954; "Central Ministry of Foreign Trade Investigates Basic Construction Work," *JMJP*, 17 November 1953; "A Mistake of One Character," *TKP-Tientsin*, 17 March 1953. See also "Directive of the Ministry of Foreign Trade Concerning Collection Work after the Autumn Harvest," *FLHP*, 4: 156 (6 October 1953); "Correct Organization and Improve Regulation," *Tientsin jih-pao*, 16 May 1952. Li Hsien-nien said in a report to the National People's Congress in 1955 that "in the Ministry of Foreign Trade, errors committed in the course of buying and shipping

overcome this difficulty was to make use of the expertise of the private traders and bankers. During the initial years after Liberation, for example, the private sector handled about one-half of China's trade, including almost all of the trade with nonsocialist countries.[28] Similarly, a number of privately owned banks continued to operate under fairly stringent controls.[29]

The Communists had a very ambivalent attitude toward the private sector. On the one hand, state cadres and enterprises were urged to cooperate with private traders since these persons were best able to promote trade with nonsocialist areas. On the other hand, there was considerable distrust of the private sector, as well as discomfort over the thought that a socialist state had to rely so heavily on capitalist businessmen. Thus, while private traders were praised for their contribution to socialist construction, they were also criticized for subordinating the greater national good to their own desire for profit. And at the same time that numerous regulations were issued to restrict the activities of the private sector, cadres were told to mobilize the private traders to even greater efforts and were criticized for favoring the public sector over the private sector.[30] Similarly, the state banks were criticized for being both too generous[31] and too restrictive[32] in their handling of requests from private traders for loans and for release of foreign exchange. Although the private sector essentially was eliminated within a few years after Liberation, this problem did not entirely disappear. Many of the private traders became employees of the state-owned enterprises, and probably continued to trouble the Communist cadres with their style of and attitude toward foreign trade work.

---

goods led to very great waste." "Report on the Country's Final Accounts for 1954 and Estimates for 1955," *TCFKHP*, 1: 18, 28 (6 July 1955). Part of the waste may have been due to the use of inexperienced personnel. This problem was reduced the following year, and hardly mentioned in 1957. Li Hsien-nien, "Report on the Country's Final Accounts for 1955 and Estimates for 1956," *TCFKHP*, 2: 21 (15 June 1956), and "Report on the Country's Final Accounts for 1956 and Estimates for 1957," *TCFKHP*, 3: 15 (29 June 1957).

[28] *TCCT*, 2: 893.

[29] Chinese People's Bank, "Methods Concerning the Applying for Registration and Examination of Capital for Private Bank and Money Enterprises in the Hua-tung Region," *HTFLHP*, p. 428 (9 September 1949); Hua-pei People's Government, "Temporary Methods for the Control of Private Bank and Money Enterprises in Hua-pei Region," *TCCT*, 1: 267 (27 April 1949); *CJFLHP*, 1: 241–53. Some banks were converted to joint public private exterprises, but this usually did not result in a change of management personnel. See, for example, GAC, "Order Concerning the Strengthening of Leadership and Supervision Over the Bank of China," *TCCT*, 1: 267 (22 March 1950).

[30] *TCCT*, 2: 20; *TCCT*, 2: 893. See also "Actively Organize Public-Private Joint Enterprises to Increase Export of Native Products," *TKP-Tientsin*, 10 October 1954.

[31] Chinese People's Bank, "Directive Concerning Loan Policy and Correcting of Interest for Industry and Commerce," *CJFLHP*, 1: 185 (12 May 1949).

[32] *TCCT*, 2: 893.

III. STATE CONTROL OF FOREIGN TRADE, 1949–54[33]

The state had virtually total control over every aspect of foreign trade. It supervised the work of private and foreign traders by requiring them to apply for a license to do business and a license for each transaction, by defining the categories of goods they could deal in, by restricting the availability of foreign exchange, and possibly by manipulating a variety of taxes and levies.[34] More important, the state set up a number of state-owned corporations that were directly responsible to the Ministry of Trade; by 1954, these corporations were handling 97 percent of China's trade.[35] The state issued plans to these corporations which fixed the quantity, composition, and (to a lesser extent) price of the goods to be traded. It further supervised the work of these corporations through licensing requirements and through financial monitoring operations of the banking system.

A. Administrative Organs

The 1949 "Organic Law of the Central People's Government"[36] created the Government Administration Council (hereafter GAC) as the chief executive and administrative organ of the state. Several advisory-coordinating-policy making committees concerned with various functional areas were established within the GAC. One of these was the Finance and Economic Committee (hereafter FEC) which handled, among other things, matters involving foreign trade. In addition, the GAC set up a number of subordinate organs, including the Ministry of Trade, to actually administer the policies and directives of the GAC. In 1952 the Ministry of Trade was reorganized into the Ministry of Commerce (for domestic trade) and the Ministry of Foreign Trade.[37]

The Ministry of Trade (and later the Ministry of Foreign Trade) was in over-all charge of government organs which regulated foreign trade, and was

---

[33] Parts of the section will be brief, since they have already been discussed at some length by other authors. See note 1, *supra,* especially Hsiao, "Foreign Trade Organization."

[34] On the manipulation of taxes to control foreign trade, see FEC, "Notice Concerning the Date for Implementing the Changing of Tax Collection," *TCCT,* 1: 173; "Two Basic Principles in the Improving of Tax Collection," editorial, *JMJP,* 29 June 1950, in *TCCT,* 1: 177. See also notes 8 and 9, *supra.*

[35] Solomon Adler, *The Chinese Economy* (New York: Monthly Review Press, 1957) p. 224; Hughes and Luard, *The Economic Development of Communist China, 1949–60* (2nd ed.; London: Oxford University Press, 1961), p. 123.

[36] Blaustein, ed., *Fundamental Legal Documents,* p. 104.

[37] GAC, "Decision Concerning the Correcting of the Organs of the Central People's Government," *FLHP,* 3: 35 (10 August 1952).

empowered by the GAC to issue rules defining the duties and scope of activities of these organs.[38] Locally situated foreign trade control organs, however, were under the dual leadership of the ministry and the local government's finance and economic committee.[39]

The ministry also was in charge of the work of the state-owned national foreign trade corporations. It submitted to the FEC plans concerning the quantity and composition of the total trade of these corporations,[40] and plans concerning the amount of foreign exchange that would be needed to conduct this trade.[41] In addition, the ministry had to approve plans submitted by the corporations detailing how they would carry out their work, manage their capital, and control the price of goods. It also had to supervise the implementation of these plans. Local branch offices of the corporations, however, were under the dual leadership of the ministry and the local finance and economic committee[42] (in addition to being a subordinate arm of the national corporation).

Much of the work of overseeing the conduct of foreign trade was handled by the local FTCB. They issued licenses to do business to the traders operating in the local area as well as licenses for each transaction,[43] took charge of goods which arrived in port without an import permit,[44] managed the Barter Exchange Offices in conjunction with the People's Bank, and generally assisted the bank, customs office, and other foreign trade control organs in carrying out their work. From my materials I cannot tell how many FTCBs there were, although it appears that they existed in all the administrative regions *(hsing-cheng ch'ü)* and many of the provinces and major cities.[45] In cases where no FTCB had been established or where special circumstances existed, the

---

[38] GAC, "Decision Concerning the Unification of Financial and Economic Work," *TCCT*, 1: 26 (3 March 1950); also in *HTFLHP*, p. 7.

[39] *FLHP*, 1: 337; *TCCT*, 3: 765. For further discussion of dual leadership, see section IV, *infra*.

[40] GAC, "Decision Concerning Methods for Implementing the Unification of State Trading in the Entire Country," *TCCT*, 1: 403 (10 March 1950).

[41] *HTFLHP*, p. 528.

[42] *TCCT*, 1: 403; see also section IV, *infra*.

[43] *FLHP*, 1: 337; *TCCT*, 3: 765.

[44] Ministry of Trade and Customs Administration, "Temporary Methods for Handling Goods Arriving in Port without a Permit," *HTFLHP*, p. 790 (July 1950).

[45] Each of the administrative regions had promulgated foreign trade control regulations which included the creation of a foreign trade control bureau; see note 15, *supra*. There also are a number of references to bureaus in the larger cities; see, for example, Shanghai Foreign Trade Control Bureau, "Detailed Rules for Carrying Out the Application for Enterprise Registration for Import/Export Factories and Merchants," *HTFLHP*, p. 782 (10 January 1951).

ministry might assign special agents *(t'e-p'ai-yüan)* to take charge;[46] otherwise the work was handled by the local government's department of industry and commerce.

A number of other organs also were involved in foreign trade control work. The first regulation issued by the GAC concerning foreign trade (and indeed, one of the first regulations on any subject) established the Customs Administration.[47] This is not surprising since the Communists regarded the KMT customs apparatus as one of the principal means by which the foreign powers dominated and manipulated China's foreign trade.[48] A Customs Administration General Office was established directly under the GAC. Within a year, twenty-six customs offices, nine suboffices and thirty-five branch offices were set up in the major cities and ports.[49] Interestingly, neither the December 1949 regulation creating the Customs Administration nor the December 1950 directive setting up the local customs offices mentioned the usual dual leadership formula for locally situated customs organs, although a March 1950 notice from the GAC discussing the leadership role of the customs general office did do so.[50] In January 1953 the Customs Administration was placed under the Ministry of Foreign Trade, and local customs offices and FTCBs were merged into a single unit.[51] This time the dual leadership formula was explicitly invoked. In September 1955 the two organs were again separated, and the Customs Administration was made a subordinate organ of the Ministry of Foreign Trade.[52]

The Customs Administration assisted in the drafting of new tariff rates and regulations governing the movement of goods, mail, and travelers across the

---

[46] On the work of the special agents, see "Resolve to Do Well the Work of Organizing Goods for Export," *JMJP,* 12 August 1956; "The Experience and Circumstances of the Northwest Native Products Export Office in Using Contracts to Organize Goods for Export," *TKP-Tientsin,* 3 March 1954; *FLHP,* 5: 156.

[47] GAC, "Provisional Organization Regulations for the Main Customs Administration," *FLHP,* 2: 343 (30 December 1949); also in *TCCT,* 1: 145; see also "Temporary Customs Law of the PRC," *FLHP,* 2: 183 (21 March 1951); also in *HTFLHP,* p. 809.

[48] GAC, "Decision Concerning Tariff Policy and Customs Work," *FLHP,* 2: 347 (27 January 1950); also in *HTFLHP,* p. 952.

[49] GAC, "Directive Concerning the Principles for Establishing Customs Offices and Correcting the Customs Organization in the Entire Country," *FLHP,* 1: 350 (14 December 1950); also in *HTFLHP,* p. 956.

[50] FEC, "Notice Concerning the Direct Leadership by the Customs Administration General Office over All Local Customs Offices in the Entire Country," *HTFLHP,* p. 960 (8 March 1950).

[51] GAC, "Decision Concerning the Carrying Out of Combining Customs and Foreign Trade Control Organs," *FLHP,* 4: 8 (9 January 1953).

[52] State Council, "Notice Concerning the Change in the Responsibilities and Leadership Relationships of All Customs Offices," *FKHP,* 2: 594–95 (5 September 1955).

Chinese border, collected the appropriate tariffs, handled cases where traders and travelers disagreed with the valuation placed on goods by local customs organs,[53] imposed a variety of administrative sanctions on persons who tried to avoid or obstruct tariff collection, confiscated and disposed of smuggled and other illegal goods,[54] and compiled national foreign trade statistics.[55] It also set up a licensing system for customs brokers[56] and took over a number of warehouses to hold imports awaiting inspection and exports which had already been inspected.[57] The 1949 regulation gave the Customs Administration jurisdiction over matters concerning harbors and waters.[58] In March 1950, however, it was forbidden to patrol the national borders or operate armed vessels. This probably was a reaction to the overly extensive quasi-military activities of the administration's KMT predecessor. Jurisdiction over harbors and waters was transferred to the Ministry of Communication or to the local city's harbor affairs bureau.[59] Later that year a harbor affairs control organ was established in the Ministry of Communication with a general bureau at the central level and bureaus in the cities and ports.[60] These bureaus took over all work involving the control and use of water ways and harbor facilities. They also coordinated the work of personnel from customs, public security, and the health department in making inspections of newly arrived ships.[61]

---

[53] Customs Administration General Office, "Temporary Methods Concerning Cases Appealing Valuations of the Tariff by Category Made by the Customs Offices," *TCCT*, 2: 525 (26 October 1950); chap. 17, *FLHP*, 2: 183.

[54] Customs Administration General Office, "Temporary Methods Concerning Handling by Customs Offices of Import Goods Where There is Obstruction in Reporting or Paying or Where Payment is Not Timely," *HTFLHP*, p. 962 (1950); FEC, "Temporary Methods for the Handling of Confiscated Goods by the Customs Offices," *HTFLHP*, p. 977 (20 March 1953).

[55] Art. 7 (7), *FLHP*, 2: 183.

[56] Shanghai Customs Office, "Temporary Methods for the Control of Customs Brokers," *HTFLHP*, p. 985 (14 November 1949).

[57] Shanghai Customs Office, "Temporary Methods for the Supervision of Warehouses for Export Goods," *HTFLHP*, p. 991 (6 January 1951); Shanghai Customs Office, "Temporary Methods for the Control of Warehouses for Imported Goods Which Have Not Yet Paid Tax," *HTFLHP*, p. 994 (16 November 1949).

[58] Art. 7, *FLHP*, 2: 343.

[59] *FLHP*, 2: 347.

[60] FEC, "Directive Concerning the Unifying of Control of Ocean Affairs and Harbor Affairs," *HTFLHP*, p. 1, 441 (26 July 1950); Customs Administration Main Office, "Methods for Transferring Ocean Affairs and Harbor Affairs," *TCCT*, 2: 909 (6 September 1950).

[61] "Temporary Regulations for the Control of the Transport Industry," *TCCT*, 3: 724 (17 July 1951); GAC, "Temporary Articles on the Control of Waters and Harbors of the PRC," *FLHP*, 5: 133 (21 January 1954).

During the period immediately after Liberation, commodity inspection and testing was handled both by the Ministry of Trade and by local testing bureaus.[62] This work was brought under central control in late 1951 when the GAC authorized the Ministry of Trade to set up local level Commodity Inspection Bureaus, and to establish standards and methods for carrying out tests.[63] A 1953 regulation created a general bureau at the central level and increased the number of local bureaus.[64]

In like manner the department of industry and commerce of various local level governments began to register trademarks after Liberation. The GAC issued a series of directives in 1950 which permitted trademarks to be registered with the central government's Private Enterprise Bureau, and which annuled all KMT trademarks and ordered all locally registered trademarks to be reregistered with the central government.[65]

Two other bodies ought to be mentioned, although strictly speaking they are mass organizations rather than governmental units. The China Committee for the Promotion of International Trade (hereafter CCPIT) was established in 1952. As its name implies, its task was to promote trade, particularly with countries with whom China had no diplomatic relations. It also operated a foreign trade arbitration committee and a maritime arbitration committee to handle disputes arising in the course of trade.[66] The Federation of Industry and Commerce also was established in 1952. Through its local branches the federation helped the industrial and commercial sectors to understand and to follow government policies, and also conveyed reactions and suggestions from these sectors back to the government.[67]

---

[62] See, for example, Ministry of Trade, "Temporary Methods of the Commodity Inspection Bureau for the Inspection of Commodities Shipped Out of a Different Port," *HTFLHP*, p. 1,012 (18 October 1950); "Temporary Articles for the Inspection of Import and Export Commodities for the Hua-pei Region," *Hsin-hua yüeh-pao*, March 1950.

[63] FEC, "Temporary Articles for Commodity Inspection," *Tientsin jih-pao*, 24 November 1951.

[64] For a translation of this regulation, see *Trade with China: A Practical Guide* (Hong Kong: *Ta Kung Pao*, 1957), p. 95.

[65] GAC, "Temporary Articles for Trademark Registration," *TCCT*, 2: 206 (28 July 1950); FEC, "Detailed Rules for Carrying Out the Registration of Trademarks," *TCCT*, 2: 211; FEC, "Methods for Handling the Trademarks Registered by the Former KMT Reactionary Government's Trademark Bureau," *TCCT*, 2: 215. See generally, Hsiao, "Foreign Trade Organization."

[66] For a short discussion of these tribunals, see Hsiao, "Settling Disputes," and Victor H. Li, "Legal Aspects of Trade with Communist China, *Columbia Journal of Transnational Law*, no. 3 (1964), p. 57.

[67] GAC, "Notice on the Organizing of the Federation of Industry and Commerce," *FLHP*, 3: 94 (16 August 1952).

B. State Trading Corporations

As discussed earlier, the Communists operated several state-owned foreign trade corporations on a regional level before and just after Liberation. In March 1950 the GAC issued a "Directive Concerning the Detailed Methods for Unifying State Trading" which set up six national foreign trade corporations, each controlling one specialized area of trade.[68] One corporation handled imports, and the other five exported, respectively, hog bristles, native products, oil and fats, minerals, and tea. From time to time thereafter new corporations were formed specializing in still other areas. The income of these corporations resulting from foreign transactions *(wai-hsiao)* belonged entirely to the central government; for domestic transactions 20 percent of the income *(nei-hsiao)* went to the local government and to the place where the activity was situated.[69]

Branch offices of the national corporations were set up at the administrative region level.[70] In some cases, apparently where the amount of trade was not too great, the national corporation merely established a department to handle trade for a particular region rather than set up a branch office.[71]

Finally, there were ambiguous entities called "port corporations" *(k'ou-an kung-szu)*. On the whole these corporations appear to have been branches of the national corporation situated at the major ports.[72] Yet, in some instances, they appear to have been separate entities which were independent from the national corporations. For example, one article described how a regional organ of the National Native Products Export Corporation, acting "on behalf" of the port corporations in Tientsin, Hankow, Tsingtao, Shanghai, and Canton, signed contracts with local producers of native goods.[73] It would seem that if the port corporation were part of the national corporation, the contracts could have been signed directly by the national corporation rather than "on behalf" of the port corporations. The article further described how the agreement of the producer, the regional organ of the national corporation, and the port corporation was needed before the contract price could be altered. Again the concurrence of the port corporation to the change would not be needed if it

---

[68] *TCCT,* 1: 403.

[69] State Council, "Orders Concerning the Improvement of the System of Commercial Control," *FKHP,* 6: 355 (11 November 1957).

[70] Art. 4, *TCCT,* 1; 403.

[71] *TKP-Tientsin,* 4 March 1954.

[72] See, for example, *TKP-HK,* 10 October 1954, "The China National Chemicals Import and Export Corporation and Its Port Corporation," *Tui-wai Mao-i* (Foreign Trade), no. 1 (January 1963), p. 5. *FKHP,* 6: 355 (11 November 1957); refers to "purchase and supply stations" *(ts'ai-kuo kung-ying chan)* set up by national corporations in major cities and ports. These may be the "port corporations."

[73] *TKP-Tientsin,* 3 March 1954.

were a subordinate arm of the national corporation. Thus, it may be that the national corporation was the purchasing agent who gathered together all the native products, and the port corporation actually made the sales to the foreign buyers. Alternatively the port corporation may be an agent of the national corporation, with the former collecting export items for the latter to sell abroad,[74] or a "purchase and supply station" gathering a wide variety of goods for both domestic and foreign trade on behalf of several national corporations.[75] It also may be that the term "port corporation" is used, perhaps informally or incorrectly, for some or all of these possibilities.

The national corporations, although independent accounting units,[76] operated under a wide variety of state controls. Basically they were bound by the import/export plans issued by the GAC.[77] In 1957 the planning system was amended such that the State Council issued four plans dealing with income, expenditures, total personnel, and profits.[78] The corporations had to submit plans of their own to the Ministry of Trade (or Ministry of Foreign Trade) detailing how they would carry out their work, handle their finances, and manage their capital;[79] they also had to submit plans to the Ministry of Finance indicating the expected income and expenditures.[80] In addition, the Ministry of Trade had a contractual arrangement with the People's Bank whereby each corporation and branch corporation had an account with an office of the bank, and all but a few minor financial transactions were handled by the bank (see below).

At the time the national corporation was first set up, it had to submit to the ministry for approval an organizational and personnel plan for the central office. It appears that thereafter the national corporation had considerable leeway in organizing and staffing the regional and city branches.[81] As with all other organs the locally situated branches were under the dual leadership of the central office of the corporation and the local level people's government.

---

[74] But cf. Frank Münzel, p. 285, *infra*, who believes that these "enigmatic intermediaries" are independent entities. Audrey Donnithorne appears to think that the port corporations are branches of the national corporations. Donnithorne, *China's Economic System*, p. 326.

[75] *FKHP*, 6: 355.

[76] Act. 10, *TCCT*, 1: 403.

[77] *Ibid.; TCCT*, 1: 26; GAC, "Decision Concerning the Unification of the Work of Controlling Financial Income and Disbursement for the Year 1950," *TCCT*, 1: 99.

[78] *FKHP*, 6: 355.

[79] Art. 8, *TCCT*, 1: 403.

[80] *Ibid.*

[81] Arts. 8 and 9, *TCCT*, 1: 403; *Tientsin jih-pao*, 13 June 1952; *Tientsin jih-pao*, 16 May 1952.

C. *The People's Bank*

The People's Bank played an extremely important role in the implementation of state control over foreign trade. It controlled coinage and foreign exchange, handled the bank accounts and financial affairs of the organs and enterprises engaged in foreign trade, and compiled numerous reports and statistics on trade. Being directly responsible to the GAC, it constituted another separate channel for central control and communication. Given its sheer size—the bank employs over 300,000 persons (although many of these probably are tellers at local offices), making it one of the largest Chinese bureaucracies[82]—and the multitude of functions it fulfilled, this institution has received surprisingly little scholarly attention.

In the period immediately after Liberation, the People's Bank supervised foreign trade work principally through its control of foreign exchange. It designated a number of other banks, many of them branches of the Bank of China, to act as its agents for the purchase and sale of foreign exchange.[83] These designated banks formed exchange offices to handle the actual transactions. Daily opening prices for various foreign currencies were fixed by the office with the approval of the People's Bank. Thereafter, it appears that individual transactions were carried out in a more or less free-market manner.

When an exporter made a sale, he would present the foreign exchange he earned together with the export permit from the local FTCB to a designated bank. The bank then would sell the foreign exchange for RMB at the exchange office. Conversely, an importer needing foreign exchange would present his import permit to a designated bank, which then would purchase the required amount from a seller at the exchange office.

The scope of the bank's activities increased substantially in late 1950. In October all foreign exchange was placed under central control.[84] Foreign currency exchange rates were fixed by the People's Bank, and conversion to or from RMB was made directly by the People's Bank or a designated bank without going through the exchange office. Later that year the bank became the principal accounting agent for all state organs and enterprises and also issued new rules which improved the work of handling and clearing accounts.[85] In addition, the FEC ordered all independent accounting units to open accounts with the bank and to deposit therein all except a small amount of

---

[82] Donnithorne, *China's Economic System,* p. 407.

[83] *HTFLHP,* p. 528; *HTFLHP,* p. 774.

[84] *HTFLHP,* p. 528.

[85] Chinese People's Bank, "Decision Concerning the Complete Developing of Internal Payments," *TCCT,* 1: 306 (17 September 1949); GAC, "Decision Concerning the System of Settlements, the Approval of Budgets, the Carrying Out of Capitalization Plans, and the Control of Cash," *TCCT,* 2: 271 (1 December 1950); Ministry of Trade and the Chinese People's Bank, "Directive on the Promulgation of the Third Contract for a Trade Depository," *CJFLHP,* 1: 81 (10 February 1951).

cash on hand.[86] Thereafter, financial transactions were conducted by means of accounting adjustments made by the bank to the accounts of the respective parties. The bank had the authority to make these adjustments on its own where one party failed to make the requisite payments to another.

The supervisory role of the bank was also enhanced in late 1950. The FEC ordered that the bank should receive copies of the income and expenditure plan, the capital construction plan, and sometimes the production plan of all state organs and enterprises.[87] In handling the financial affairs of these bodies, the bank had the duty to make sure that the various plan obligations were being fulfilled. Discrepancies were reported vertically to the central level bank office, and also horizontally to the local government's finance and economic committee. In some instances the bank could withhold payments for a period of time until the discrepancy was cleared up. The bank also controlled the granting of loans and credit and supervised the manner in which these funds were spent.[88]

The bank had to compile numerous reports on all aspects of its work. In foreign trade matters, for example, it had to submit trade statistics every day, every ten days, and each month. In addition, it submitted reports on the foreign exchange situation every ten days, and a report on "the condition of important products in the international market" every week. There also were regular reports on the bank accounts and financial transactions of the organs and enterprises involved in foreign trade.[89] These reports gave the central authorities an additional and independent source of information about the operation of the foreign trade apparatus.

IV. The Implementation of State Controls

The problem of how the system of state control over foreign trade actually operated is too vast a subject to be covered by one paper. I do not discuss here

---

[86] FEC, "Methods for Implementing the Control of Cash," *TCCT*, 2: 549 (25 December 1950).

[87] *Ibid.*; *CJFLHP*, 1: 26. The Ministry of Finance also had its own investigation organ; Ministry of Finance, "Methods for Establishing Finance Investigation Organs," *TCCT*, 2: 298 (12 October 1950).

[88] Chinese People's Bank, "General Principles of the Chinese People's Bank on Loans," *CJFLHP*, 1: 93 (23 January 1951); also in *TCCT*, 3: 221; see also, Chinese People's Bank, "Regulations of the Chinese People's Bank for Trade Loans," *TCCT*, 3: 229 (23 January 1951); Chinese People's Bank, "Notice Concerning Problems in Establishing the Methods for Planning and Credit for the First Quarter of 1955," *CJFLHP*, 3: 29 (6 December 1954).

[89] Chinese People's Bank, "The Statistical Reporting System of the Main Office of the Chinese People's Bank," *CJFLHP*, 1: 338 (1951); Chinese People's Bank, "Directive Concerning Unified Rules for Enterprises Reporting to the Bank," *CJFLHP*, 3: 35 (26 January 1954). See also *FLHP*, 2: 337; *Hsin-hua yüen-pao* (March 1950).

the problems involving the manner in which trade was conducted between a Chinese and foreign party. I also do not discuss foreign trade planning or the role of foreign trade in the Chinese economy, except where these questions help illustrate some other aspect of the implementation of foreign trade controls.

Instead, I focus on the manner in which state control was divided between the central and the local levels, and give some reasons why this pattern of apportionment prevailed. In doing so I concentrate on the relationship between the center and the region and deal only in passing with the relationship among various bodies within the center and with the relationship between the region and lower governmental units.

A.   Centralization of State Control

Prior to Liberation the center formulated unified economic policies, but left much of the actual management of economic affairs to local governments.[90] This situation changed gradually after Liberation, and in March 1950 a concerted effort was made to unify under central control the work of economic management. A series of GAC directives[91] ordered that all tax proceeds should be turned in to the central government, with the exception of certain specified minor taxes and certain local surcharges which could be added to the central taxes. In addition, the capital investment budget and the income and expenditure plan of all governmental organs and enterprises were brought under central control. Various costs and expenses also were apportioned between the central and local levels. The bank was given an important role in assuring that the wishes of the center were being followed. The entire effort to improve central control was reviewed a year later.[92]

As discussed earlier, the asserting of central control over foreign trade followed the same pattern. During the period immediately after Liberation, the regional governments handled most of the foreign trade work. Almost all regions had their own regulations concerning the control of traders and individual transactions, the inspection of commodities, the registration of trademarks, the management of harbors and waterways, and the collection of tariffs. Many regions also operated state-owned trading companies. The central government did interfere on occasion, such as the time it amended the

---

[90] *TCCT*, 2: 20.

[91] *TCCT*, 1: 26; *HTFLHP*, p. 73; GAC, "Decision Concerning the Improving of the Finances of Cities and Local Areas," *CJFLHP*, 1: 69 (31 March 1951). Income and expenditure also were placed under central planning control. *TCCT*, 1: 99; *TCCT*, 2: 271; *HTFLHP*, p. 55. The handling of bank accounts, foreign exchange, and cash on hand also were placed under central control. *TCCT*, 2: 549; *HTFLHP*, p. 528.

[92] *FLHP*, 2: 109; GAC, "Decision Concerning the Separation of the System of Income and Disbursement for the Year 1951," *TCCT*, 3: 121 (29 March 1951).

foreign trade rules of the North China region to replace barter trade with trade using the exchange process. It should be noted, however, that the orders of the center were not always followed. A newspaper report published a month after the North China rules were "amended" showed that while barter transactions had declined, they had by no means been eliminated.[93] In addition, if this action by the central government indicated a national policy of restricting barter, the policy was contravened by the "Swatow Foreign Trade Control Measure" issued soon thereafter which encouraged the use of barter.[94]

Beginning in late 1949 the central government took a series of steps to bring foreign trade entirely under its control. Within a short time it had created the foreign trade corporations and had established central organs to handle customs, commodity inspection, trademark registration, and harbors and waterways management. Each of these organs in turn issued sets of rules to govern its subordinate bodies throughout the country. Borrowing heavily from regional regulations and practices,[95] the center also took charge of foreign trade planning, licensing of traders and individual transactions, and handling of foreign exchange.

There were limits, however, on the extent to which central control could be asserted. On a theoretical level the Communists may have felt that it was inherently impossible for the center to lay down a single set of rules to govern the foreign trade of the entire country. In theoretical terms principles or rules in the abstract had little significance, and they took on meaning only when they were applied to and interacted with actual situations. The same rule applied to different situations called for different courses of action and produced different results; conversely, depending on the actual situation, it would be correct sometimes to do one thing and sometimes another. This produced a dilemma for the center in trying to establish detailed operational rules for the control of foreign trade work: how could these rules avoid being so general as to be nothing more than lofty phrases, and yet at the same time not be so specific as to impose uniform solutions on situations that by definition required the application of different methods? One possible answer was a system of decentralized control in which the center set general policy, but local levels were allowed considerable leeway in applying these policies.

On a more practical (though not necessarily more important) level, China may have been too vast and diverse a country with too limited a system of communications to be effectively governed from the center. This was especially true during the time when both rules and institutions were still at the developmental stage, and where the government as a whole, as well as individual cadres, was still unfamiliar with their work. For foreign trade the difficulties

---

[93] *TKP-HK,* 16 November 1949; see also notes 16 and 18, *supra.*

[94] *TKP-HK,* 22 November 1949.

[95] See, for example, *Hsin-hua yüeh-pao* (March 1950).

were further increased because of its close ties with agricultural production. Most exports were agriculture-related products, and the total exports in turn determined the amount of foreign exchange available for the purchase of imports. Agriculture, however, was extremely difficult to plan for and to control.[96] Aside from continually changing weather conditions, the existence of many, many producers all over the country meant that there would be a great deal of local variation, and that an inordinate amount of effort would be required to coordinate the work of all persons and organs concerned. This problem was aggravated by the country's poor transport system. Professor Donnithorne also suggests that foreign trade was a residual item in over-all economic planning;[97] to the extent that this was true, it made even more difficult the task of determining the kind and quantity of goods that could be exported and imported.

All in all, it seems to me that in the early years the center, particularly the GAC, tried too hard to control directly all aspects of foreign trade. The involvement of the GAC is understandable for matters affecting major trade items such as tax rebates for textile exports.[98] It still is understandable, although less so, for less important matters such as the prohibition of the export of bean cakes and cigarette paper in order to protect the domestic fertilizer and tobacco industries.[99] But when the FEC and GAC (not to mention the Customs Administration, the Ministry of Trade, and the South Central region's finance and economic committee) took a direct hand in the granting of an export subsidy to the firecracker industry of Tung-huan *hsien* in southern Kwangtung, one wonders whether these bodies were inundated with minutiae, or whether they merely rubber stamped decisions made at other levels and places.[100]

---

[96] See, for example, *SWFLHP*, p. 94; *Fu-chien jih-pao*, 11 October 1957; *TCCT*, 2: 942.

[97] Donnithorne, *China's Economic System*, p. 323.

[98] Ministry of Trade and Customs Administration Main Office, "Notice Concerning the Rebate of the Excise Tax for Raw Materials for Export Textile Goods," *SWFLHP*, p. 98 (8 May 1951).

[99] FEC, "Decision Concerning the Prohibiting of the Export of Beancakes and Cigarette Paper," *TCCT*, 2: 906 (5 November 1950).

[100] Ministry of Finance, "Notice Concerning the Permitting of the Excise Tax for Raw Materials for the Firecracker Exports of Tung-huan *Hsien*," *SWFLHP*, p. 96 (3 August 1951). One gets a similar feeling on seeing GAC directives concerning inspection of persons and goods crossing the national boundary. GAC, "Temporary Rules Concerning the Inspection of Trains, Trainmen, Passengers, and Luggage Entering and Leaving the Country," *HTFLHP*, p. 1,436 (24 May 1951); GAC, "Temporary Rules Concerning the Inspection of Ships, Sailors, Passengers, and Luggage Entering and Leaving the Country," *HTFLHP*, p. 1,450 (27 November 1950).

B.   Dual Leadership—Explicit Sharing of Control with the Local Level

The regional level was able to influence foreign trade work both through explicit grants of authority from the center and through more subtle means of asserting and protecting its interests. The former method usually took the form of placing the locally situated trade organs (such as the FTCB or the regional branches of state trading corporations) under the dual leadership *(shuang-ch'ung ling-tao)* of their vertical administrative superiors and of the regional government.

The basic formula for dual leadership was that the upper level vertical organ "led" *(ling-tao)* and the regional government "guided, supervised, and assisted" *(chih-tao, chien-tu, ho hsieh-chu)* the work of the local unit.[101] There were a number of variations on this formula. For example, foreign trade work was conducted under the "unified direction" *(tung-i chih-hui)* of the Ministry of Trade, while the regional governments supervised and assisted.[102] When the Customs Administration was first set up in 1949, local customs offices operated under the "direct leadership" *(chih-chieh ling-tao)* of the general office and the "guidance" of the local level government.[103] After the merger of the Customs Administration with the Ministry of Foreign Trade in 1953, the general office retained "direct leadership" while the local governments were empowered to "guide, supervise, and investigate" *(chien-ch'a)* the work of the local offices.[104] The local branches of the Harbors Affairs Control Bureau were under the "unified leadership" *(tung-i ling-tao)* of the general bureau and the "guidance and supervision" of the local governments.[105] Finally, there were references to the local governments "leading" the work of purchasing local products for export;[106] in these cases it seems that *ling-tao* was not used as a technical term but rather in a more colloquial sense.

Under the dual leadership formula the primary authority rested with the vertical "leader," while the horizontal unit that guided, supervised, etc., occupied a secondary position.[107] Leadership by the upper level enabled it to issue rules and regulations that bound the lower level, and to fix the financial plan and business *(yeh-wu)* plan of the lower level.[108] In addition, the leadership unit usually could determine the organizational structure and could appoint the personnel of the lower level.[109] (This was not always true since

---

[101] *FLHP*, 2: 109; *TCCT*, 1: 403.

[102] *TCCT*, 1: 26.

[103] *HTFLHP*, p. 960.

[104] *FLHP*, 4: 8.

[105] *FLHP*, 5: 133; see also, *HTFLHP*, p. 1,441.

[106] *FLHP*, 4: 156; *TKP-Tientsin*, 3 March 1954; *Fu-chien jih-pao*, 11 October 1957.

[107] *FKHP*, 6: 355.

[108] *TCCT*, 1: 403; *TCCT*, 1: 26; *HTFLHP*, p. 960; *FLHP*, 4: 156.

[109] *HTFLHP*, p. 960.

in the case of the Harbor Affairs Control Bureau, the center was merely taking over existing structures and personnel, and in other instances, such as the creation of local branches of the state trading corporations, the local governments were authorized to appoint the personnel.[110])

The function of the regional government in the dual leadership system was to make sure that locally situated central organs "completely carried out the nation's unified policies, methods, plans, and important regulations."[111] Basically, this involved making sure that the centrally issued business and financial plans of the local organs were being properly carried out.[112] In addition, the regional government coordinated the work of all regional level units and submitted "opinions" to the upper level vertical organ about the appointment and transfer of the personnel of the local organ.[113]

But what exactly did all this mean in practice? Except for some general references to "supervising the work of lower level organs," the materials I examined seldom mentioned any participation of the regional government in foreign trade planning or in implementing the import plans. While this may indicate merely the narrowness of my materials—for example, I did not use periodicals such as *Chi-hua ching-chi* which concentrate on planning—it seems to me that the lack of mention reflected the limited involvement of the regional government in these matters.

Thus, the *implementation of import plans* consisted almost entirely of negotiations for and purchases of foreign goods by state trading corporations. The regional government really was not a part of this process, except in the sense that the ultimate consumer of the foreign goods may have been a regionally situated enterprise and that the failure to obtain these goods would affect over-all regional production. Supervision of the implementing of import plans, that is, making sure that the necessary goods were purchased in a timely manner at an appropriate price, was best handled by the FTCB, which issued permits for all transactions, and by the Bank, which controlled the financial affairs of the trading corporation.

Foreign trade planning was a somewhat different matter. While this work was handled by the center, plans were not formulated by fiat or in the abstract, but rather through a process of negotiation and bargaining among various interest groups within the center as well as between the center and local producer or consumer units. Obviously, the regional government was concerned with planning decisions that affected locally situated units; much less clear was the extent to which it could lobby for and influence the formulation of trade plans.

---

[110] *TCCT*, 1: 403.

[111] *FLHP*, 2: 109.

[112] *Ibid.; TCCT*, 1: 403.

[113] *TCCT*, 1: 403.

On the whole, it seems to me that the center exercised great control over *import planning*. The planning agency had before it all the applications for foreign goods, and also knew or could estimate the total value of imports for that year. Consequently, it could make careful decisions assigning priorities to the various requests. Even so, the extent of central discretionary power depended to some degree on the type of goods to be imported. This power was great for capital goods since the center was relatively free to decide, subject to some unknown amount of regional lobbying, what to invest in and where to make the investments. Central control was less extensive in the import of raw materials since factories were already in existence that needed certain amounts of supplies in order to maintain production.[114] For items that could be used by many areas, such as chemical fertilizers, regional lobbying may have been more intense.

The center had less control over *export planning*, although this again depended on the category of goods. Manufactured items were subject to fairly strict central control since the quantity and type of goods to be exported could be determined accurately beforehand. Much of the exports of the 1949–54 period, however, were agricultural products. Because of the extremely large variety of goods involved, the uncertainties both in quality and quantity of agricultural production, and the vagaries of the international market, it was difficult to formulate plans for these exports except in general gross terms. Consequently, local foreign trade organs had to be given considerable discretionary power to decide what and how much to buy, and what price to pay.[115] If an item was in great supply or was selling particularly well abroad, these organs could purchase more than the export plan called for. They also could influence the production of export goods by giving price incentives for some items, and by requesting the center to adjust the production plans of local units. Indeed, two recurring complaints by local producers were that the foreign trade organs would refuse to purchase more than the planned or contracted amount, leaving the producers with an expensive and difficult task of disposing of surpluses, and that these organs would claim that an item was of too poor quality, and hence, would reject it or refuse to pay the full price. Because of the substantial impact of these activities and decisions on local affairs, the local government naturally would play a much more important role. In addition, as mentioned above, the local government received 20 percent of the income produced from "domestic transactions" of locally situated foreign trade corporations; presumably, these transactions largely involved purchases of locally produced goods for export.

In view of the above discussion, it appears that the role of the regional

---

[114] See, for example, the raw materials needed for the textile industry, *SWFLHP*. p. 98.

[115] *TKP-Tientsin*, 3 March 1954; *Fu-chien jih-pao*, 11 October 1957; *FLHP*, 4: 156.

government in "guiding, supervising, and assisting" the work of locally situated foreign trade organs was limited primarily to helping *implement the export plan*. More precisely, the center fixed the export plans for industrial goods, and the regional government checked to make sure that local industrial exterprises fulfilled their production plans. In the agricultural sector export plans were formulated by the center and the local foreign trade organs, with some participation from the regional government; there were continuous adjustments of these plans, depending on local agricultural conditions.

Thereafter, the regional government took almost complete charge of (that is, "led") the implementing of these plans. It (together with various subordinate level governments) sponsored meetings where the export plan was explained to local producers and where contracts were signed between these producers and state trading corporations.[116] Most important, it assumed responsibility for seeing that these contracts would be fulfilled by organizing production and by taking charge of harvesting and delivery.[117] The extensive role of the regional government in this aspect of foreign trade work was due in part to its familiarity with local conditions and its ability to coordinate the activities of numerous local level units. In addition, foreign trade organs lacked the manpower to handle the work of overseeing implementation; the Native Products Export Corporation, for example, had only fifty-eight cadres to handle all its work in the North China region.[118]

The regional government performed one other major function, the "leading" of political and educational work.[119] In general, this referred not to the fulfillment of production and business plans in a quantitative sense, but rather to the manner in which and methods by which the plans were fulfilled. In the usual course political work appears to have consisted of little more than exhorting the masses to exert themselves and urging the foreign trade cadres to act in a kindly and enlightened manner.[120] This work took on great importance, however, during rectification campaigns. Although there seem to have been very few foreign trade cadres who were actually purged, their attitudes and work styles did come under close public scrutiny and criticism during these times. And campaigns occurred frequently: during the early years, there were nation-wide campaigns in 1950, 1953, and 1954–55 and still others for particular local areas.[121] In addition, as the Party took a more active and direct

---

[116] *TCCT*, 3: 40; *FLHP*, 4: 156.

[117] *Ibid.*

[118] *TKP-Tientsin*, 3 March 1954.

[119] *FLHP*, 2: 109; *TCCT*, 2: 403.

[120] *FLHP*, 4: 156.

[121] *TCCT*, 3: 30; *Tientsin jih-pao*, 5 May, 11 June and 11 August 1952; *TKP-Tientsin*, 17 March 1953; *JMJP*, 5 October 1954; *Fu-chien jih-pao*, 11 October 1957. See generally note 27, *supra*.

role in administration in the late 1950s, political work correspondingly increased in scope and importance.

Finally, there were several efforts to place locally situated commercial organs under the direct and sole leadership of the local government.[122] These actions, however, generally did not affect the foreign trade sector.

C. Decision-making by Locally Situated Central Organs

The previous subsection discussed those aspects of foreign trade control work which were granted by the central to the regional government under the dual leadership formula. This section deals with the powers that were retained by the central government and exercised through the locally situated branches of central foreign trade organs. It proceeds on the premise that these organs had loyalties and involvements with both the center and the local area, and asks whether they were upholding central or local interests in their decision-making. I must stress that I am talking about the *relative* strength of the ties to the center and to the local area, and not about a breakdown of center-local relationships. Parts of this discussion are sketchy and conjectural, both because of the nature of the subject matter and because of the nature of the materials used.

To begin with, what was the allocation of decision-making power between the center and its locally situated branches? The center retained control of planning for import/export and for short-term bank credits. (It should be remembered, however, that the planning decisions flow directly from the data that is available to the planners; much of this data is supplied by locally situated organs.[123] Moreover, these organs could act as advocates for particular projects, and thereby influence the decision of the planners.[124]) The center also controlled the business and financial plans of the subordinate organs and appointed some of the leading personnel. In addition, it decided a variety of matters such as which items should be given export subsidies or should be placed under unified sale and purchase.

At the local level the FTCB, acting within the confines of the import/export plan and its own business plan, issued permits for all foreign trade transactions. It granted licenses to do business to traders, although this meant very little after the state trading corporations took over most of the foreign trade. The FTCB, together with the bank, also controlled foreign exchange. Actual trading was conducted by branches of the state trading corporations. They purchased goods for export, sold these to foreign traders, and purchased

---

[122] *FKHP*, 6: 355.

[123] See, for example, *TKP-Tientsin*, 3 March 1954; *CJFLHP*, 3: 29.

[124] For example, the local governments probably were influential in getting the tax rebates for the textile and firecracker industries. *SWFLHP*, pp. 96 and 98.

foreign imports. The bank handled all financial transactions, and also supervised the implementation of the financial plans of all local organs. In addition, within the limits set by the central bank's loan plan, the local bank extended credit to local enterprises. The Commodity Inspection Bureau inspected and certified all imports and exports; and the customs office collected tariffs and controlled the actual movement of goods in and out of the country.

One method of determining the amount of central control over locally situated organs (or conversely, the extent of local autonomy and discretionary power) is to examine the scope of the regulations and directives issued by the central organ. The simplest case was the Commodity Inspection Bureau which had virtually no discretionary power. The very detailed and precise rules issued by the center determined what goods were to be inspected, how the inspection was to be carried out, and what standards were to be applied.[125]

The customs office occupied a midway position. Tariff rates and customs fees were set by the center. Appeals from valuation decisions of the local customs office were also heard at the central level. Otherwise, this office handled the imposing of administrative sanctions on persons who violate customs regulations and the disposing of fines and confiscated property.[126] It also could make its own arrangements for matters such as customs inspections, establishing of warehouses, and licensing of customs brokers.[127]

The FTCB and the local branches of the state trading corporation had the widest discretionary power. For imports, the trading corporation was usually instructed to purchase a particular quantity of a particular item, but was allowed considerable leeway in negotiating the price and other contract terms, as well as in deciding which foreign seller to deal with. The FTCB had similar leeway in issuing permits for individual transactions. The scope of discretionary power was even greater in export trade. As described above, the FTCB and the foreign trade corporation could exceed the export plan, and indeed were urged to do so. They also were allowed to take steps to encourage or discourage the production of certain items. Similarly, wide discretionary power was granted in nontrade matters. For example, the rules governing the licensing of traders and the handling of goods which arrive without an import permit were phrased most generally and allowed the local bureau to set its own standards and procedures.[128]

---

[125] See notes 62–64, *supra.*

[126] *HTFLHP,* pp. 960, 962, and 977.

[127] See notes 56 and 57, *supra.*

[128] *HTFLHP,* p. 790. With respect to the question of the granting of discretionary power to locally situated organs, the most interesting institution to study is the bank. This would, however, be an enormous task, since the quantity of available material, e.g., CJFLHP and CJFKHP, is formidable. At first glance, there appears to be a vast array of rules governing how each type of transaction and situation was to be handled. The only areas left to the local bank's discretion were the naming of "designated banks"

To the extent that local organs, particularly the FTCB and the branches of the state trading corporations, had discretionary power, did they tend to exercise this power in favor of central or local interests (again recognizing the difficulty in making a sharp distinction)? One factor affecting which may shed some light on this question is the backgrounds of the personnel who staffed these organs. The presumption is that persons with strong local ties would be more likely to decide in favor of local interests. The determining of the degree of local ties is very tenuous, of course, in the absence of a great deal of concrete biographical data. For lack of something better, I focus on who first appointed a person to his post in foreign trade control work.

Using this criterion, the Customs Administration was very centrally oriented. In 1949 the GAC abolished all but a few locally organized customs organs and sent out a number of central cadres to set up the new customs office. Afterwards, these persons stayed on to head the new offices. The center also retained control of subsequent appointments to all important positions in customs offices.[129]

On the other hand, the FTCB was staffed mostly by persons first appointed by the regional government. As discussed earlier, all the administrative regions and many of the major cities had established similar organs after Liberation. When all foreign trade work was unified under the Ministry of Trade in March 1950, the ministry took over leadership of these organs, but apparently without changing the personnel. In setting up additional FCTB thereafter, the ministry may have co-opted the personnel from the provincial and city governments' commerce and industry departments who up to that time were handling foreign trade matters. Moreover, the regional government could offer "opinions" about the appointment of personnel to locally situated central organs. Similarly, branches of the state trading corporations also were

---

and the operating of the Foreign Exchange and Barter Exchange Offices in the early years, and the deciding of how much credit an enterprise should receive within the limits of the loan plan (see notes 82 and 87, *supra*). Upon further examination, however, the local bank seems to have had considerable decision-making power. There was explicit recognition of the fact that differing local conditions had to be handled in different ways, and the fact that until the national banking regulation system was "completed" local banks had to make most of their own decisions. See especially, Chinese People's Bank, "Notice Allowing Each Branch to Handle in an Appropriate Manner the Problems Involving Commercial Loans in the Transitional Period Before the Total Revision of the Methods of Credit and Settlement," *CJFKHP*, 3: 43 (28 September 1956); Ministry of Commerce and Chinese People's Bank, "Directive Concerning the Elimination of Using Commercial Credit to Make up for Financial Deficits," *CJFKHP*, 1: 144 (28 May 1955); Chinese People's Bank and Supply and Market Cooperative, "Joint Directive Implementing the 'Temporary Methods of the Chinese People's Bank for Giving Loans to Basic Level Supply and Market Cooperatives to Purchase Agricultural Products,'" *CJFKHP*, 1: 208 (26 May 1955).

[129] *FLHP*, 2: 343; *HTFLHP*, p. 960.

staffed by locally oriented persons. The directive setting up these corporations specifically left the appointment of regional branch personnel to the regional government.[130] In addition, it is likely that many of these employees were formerly private traders who had operated in the local areas.

As events actually transpired, however, it appears that having strong "local ties" (as defined here) did not incline a person to decide in favor of local interests. Thus, despite the apparent "local orientation" of the personnel of the FTCB and the branches of the state trading corporations, there was frequently criticism for ignoring or resisting the wishes of the local government.[131] The basic problem was that many foreign trade cadres felt their work involved "special conditions" and therefore required special handling. In particular, they regarded foreign trade work as one of the most important economic tasks for the country. Imports were greatly needed to improve production, and exports were needed to finance the purchase of imports. In addition, they stressed the highly centralized nature of this work. Trade planning had to be controlled by the center in order to assure that the most urgent national needs received the highest priority handling. Hence, it appears that "localism" was overcome by "professionalism."

As a consequence of these attitudes, foreign trade cadres tended to regard the foreign trade "system" as independent from other units or systems. Thus, suggestions or objections from local governments could be ignored on the excuse that local foreign trade organs were bound by directives issued by their superiors at the center.[132] These organs also resisted interference from other nonforeign trade central organs. For example, the Ministry for Purchase of Agricultural Products and the local government together had decided to raise the local price for hog intestine sheaths, an item used in both domestic and foreign trade. The local foreign trade organs at first attempted to continue paying the old price, since an increase would adversely affect the exportability of this product. This attempt was unsuccessful, and the increased price had to be paid; soon thereafter, however, these organs found a means by which to reduce the price once more.[133] A variation of this problem was the tendency of foreign trade cadres to be excessively zealous, particularly in dealing with exports. They often were so convinced of the importance of their work that they insisted their plan quotas be fulfilled and overfulfilled, even where this damaged the local economy or the local producers.[134]

---

[130] *TCCT*, 1: 403.

[131] *FLHP*, 3: 109; *FLHP*, 4: 156; *JMJP*, 5 October 1954; *Fu-chien jih-pao*, 11 October 1957. See also, *FKHP*, 6: 355 which gave a share of the foreign exchange earned from exports in order to encourage export work.

[132] *Fu-chien jih-pao*, 11 October 1957.

[133] *Ibid.*

[134] *Ibid.*

V. Conclusion

This essay discussed the foreign trade control system in the early and mid 1950s. There have been few changes since that time, although the volume of trade has increased several fold and the main direction of trade has shifted from the communist to the noncommunist countries. Central control is still maintained by the Ministry of Foreign Trade operating through the various subordinate organs and using the planning, licensing, and other restrictions described above. The only structural change (and one that affects foreign trade only indirectly) was the creation in the 1960s of the Ministry for Economic Liaison with Foreign Countries to handle the aid program.[135]

Some of the changes that have taken place resulted from the increased dealings with Western countries. As the volume and complexity of trade grew, it became necessary to regularize some of the trading relationships. Thus, as described in other chapters, the Chinese entered into a number of agreements concerning the volume and composition of trade, settlement of payments, trademark registration, etc. In addition, the CCPIT played a major role in developing trade with countries with which China did not have diplomatic relations, as well as in promoting trade generally.

Other changes were related to the decentralization efforts of the late 1950s.[136] In particular, the supply and market cooperatives which had acted as the intermediate link between the producers and the appropriate foreign trade export corporations were eliminated. Thus, these corporations had to find new ways of reaching their suppliers.

Finally, we might speculate about a question of considerable importance: did the foreign trade cadres become very much more locally oriented with the passage of them? On the one hand, foreign trade work might be so specialized and so directly tied to the center that these cadres remained centrally oriented. On the other hand, further research might show that as politics took command in the late 1950s and again in the late 1960s, local officials might have taken much more seriously their job of "leading" the political work of the foreign trade organs. In addition, the foreign trade system may have stopped expanding after the late 1950s. Consequently, foreign trade cadres may have become less concerned with upward career mobility, something controlled by the center; instead, they may have worried more about career security and the avoidance of attacks and criticisms. Since political work and rectification campaigns were handled mostly by the local Party and government, these cadres may have decided that their own interests were best safeguarded by the development of strong local ties and relationships.

---

[135] See Donald Klein, p. 315.

[136] See generally, Donnithorne, *China's Economic System*, pp. 324–29.

The Old Canton System of
Foreign Trade

RANDLE EDWARDS

I. INTRODUCTION

Western businessmen going to the Canton Trade Fair for the first time generally have reported that nothing in their experience has fully prepared them for trading with the Chinese. Though all have been briefed to expect tough negotiations in a distinctive atmosphere, most are still somewhat surprised by the nature and scope of the ground rules imposed on them by their Chinese hosts. They might be even more surprised if they were aware that the practice of concentrating foreign trade at Canton has a tradition going back more than a thousand years and that many of the rules they are subject to had counterparts in the Imperial era.

Some of the unique flavor of the China trade—past and present—is suggested by two cases which illustrate the way the Chinese authorities of both periods have attempted to extend their supervision even over the private lives of visiting foreign traders. In an incident occurring in 1830 the Chinese authorities threatened to suspend the entire British trade with China because an English merchant had violated the rule against bringing wives to Canton.[1]

---

[1] Hosea B. Morse, *The Chronicles of the East India Company Trading to China, 1635–1834*, 5 vols. (1926, 1929; reprint ed., Taipei: Ch'eng-wen, 1966), 4, pp. 234–39; and William F. Hunter, *The 'Fan Kwae' at Canton* (1882; reprint ed., Taipei: Ch'eng-wen, 1970), pp. 119–20; compare the official Chinese version of the handling of this case, in *Ch'ing-tai wai-chiao shih-liao : Tao-kuang ch'ao* (Historical materials concerning foreign relations in the Ch'ing period: the Tao-kuang reign) (1931–33; reprint ed., Taipei: Ch'eng-wen, 1968), pp. 310–12, 316–17, 331. For detailed scholarly studies of the old Canton commercial system, see Earl H. Pritchard, *The Crucial Years of Anglo-Chinese Relations, 1750–1800*, Research Studies of the State College of Washington, no. 4, pp. 3–4 (September–December 1936); Louis Dermigny, *La Chine et l'Occident :*

This sanction was avoided only when the English agreed to send the offending spouse to Macao. And, as recently as the spring of 1972, the hopes of a Dutch corporation for landing a lucrative trade contract in China were extinguished when its representative at the Canton Fair was expelled from China for making advances to a hotel waitress.[2]

Both of the above cases involve rules which, to the Western observer, may appear absurdly puritanical and totally irrelevant to the main concern of furthering mutually profitable trade relations. But both also persuasively convey the central message that outsiders wishing to do business with China generally must do so on conditions unilaterally prescribed by China. These include not only the terms of the trading arrangement but also the terms of entry, residence, and travel. How can the similarities between these two cases be explained and what is their significance for our attempt to understand the Chinese system of regulating foreign trade today?

Although no one would argue that Chinese values and institutions have not been profoundly changed since the establishment of the People's Republic of China, in Peking's present-day foreign trade policy and practice one can detect resonances of the old policies espoused by the Manchu courts in the period before the beginning of Western domination in the mid-nineteenth century. This resemblance stems in part from certain geopolitical constants that influence China's choice of the most appropriate path toward economic development. But it also reflects a conscious government policy of isolation, or "self-reliance." One aim of this policy is to prevent a repetition of the subjugation and exploitation which China suffered for a century under the treaty system (1842–1943)[3] which had been imposed on a weak Manchu dynasty by Westerners of an earlier era intent on opening up the "vast China market." In addition, present Chinese leaders, like many of their predecessors, regard self-strengthening and self-development to be the principal means of solving China's social ills. Consequently, while some foreign inputs are helpful, the type and quantity of such inputs must be limited so that they do not "corrupt" the proper development of Chinese society. The result of these several shaping forces is the distinctive system of regulating foreign trade that has been adopted by Peking today.

This essay seeks to place the foreign trade system of the People's Republic

---

Le commerce à Canton au XVIIIe sicèle 1719–1833, 4 vols. (Paris: S.E.V.P.E.N., 1964); and Michael Greenberg, British Trade and the Opening of China 1800–1842 (Cambridge: The University Press, 1951).

[2] Talk at East Asian Legal Studies, Harvard Law School, May 1972 (the speaker has requested to remain anonymous).

[3] For a thorough description and analysis of the formative early years of the treaty period, see generally John K. Fairbank, Trade and Diplomacy on the China Coast, 2 vols. (Cambridge: Harvard University Press, 1953); see also Wesley R. Fishel, End of Extraterritoriality in China (Berkeley: University of California Press, 1952).

of China in historical perspective. Understanding of China today obviously cannot be attained without an awareness of the fundamental significance of the continuing revolution which has been guided by Marxism-Leninism-Maoism. But communist ideology alone does not explain why China has adopted particular policies and institutions to control its relations with foreigners. History too can provide valuable insight into the reasons why the Chinese seem especially suspicious and fearful of alien participation and subversion of Chinese social and political institutions.[4] In this brief essay, we will analyze certain key features of foreign trade policy and organization, actual trade practice, and major problems of the old China trade, comment on apparent analogues in today's China trade, and conclude with some reflections on the legacy of China's early foreign trade practices.

II. Ch'ing Foreign Trade Policy and Procedures

After installing themselves on the Chinese imperial throne in Peking in 1644, the Manchus were preoccupied until the mid 1680s with the problem of establishing actual control over the territory they claimed and with the task of forming appropriate institutions for maintaining their domestic rule within China. Just as today, Ch'ing China's economic and political center of gravity was strictly internal. With a huge agrarian population, the governments of both imperial and revolutionary China have been preoccupied with the enormous task of feeding and governing the largest population of any nation in the world.

The Manchu court, in theory, deemed foreign trade to be of merely peripheral importance; trade was tolerated by the emperor primarily as a source of exotic foreign handicrafts. For much of the early Ch'ing period, foreign trade was completely prohibited.[5] And even after its resumption in the latter part of the seventeenth century, China's foreign trade was of so little significance for another fifty years or so that the European governments were not concerned enough to try to take forceful measures to improve the conditions of trade.[6] Nor was the emperor's share of the revenues and "unofficial rakeoff" from foreign trade large enough to motivate him to give serious attention to its regulation. It was only in the mid-eighteenth century that the foreign trade at Canton assumed such proportions that the respective

---

[4] For a study of the policies and rules established to control this alien threat, see my unpublished paper "Early Ch'ing Control of Aliens," presented at the Conference on Local Control and Social Protest During the Ch'ing Period, Honolulu, Hawaii, 27 June–2 July 1971.

[5] Mark Mancall, "The Ch'ing Tribute System: An Interpretive Essay," in J. K. Fairbank, ed., *The Chinese World Order* (Cambridge: Harvard University Press, 1968), pp. 63–89.

[6] See generally Morse, *Chronicles*, vols. 1 and 5.

governments became seriously concerned with the terms upon which the trade was conducted and the general conditions under which alien traders were required to live while on Chinese soil.

After suppressing the serious anti-Manchu Revolt of the Three Feudatories in the early 1680s and successfully completing a subsequent half-century of military campaigns against marauding Mongol nomads in central Asia and a hostile uprising in Tibet, the Ch'ing empire in the mid-eighteenth century was at the height of its power and prosperity. At this time the Manchu court turned to face the maritime threat posed by the rapidly growing European trade at Canton and Macao. As the value of this trade grew during the first half of the eighteenth century, the European traders became increasingly unhappy over the vagaries of their personal position and the uncertain protection afforded for their sizable financial investment. The Chinese central government had in effect allowed a combination of official and private merchant interests at Canton to regulate the conditions of the foreign trade in order to squeeze from it the maximum personal return for themselves.[7] The imperial court was indifferent so long as it received Western handicrafts and other curios together with a small portion of the foreign trade revenue. Centrally promulgated tariff laws were honored only in the breach.

The court began to give serious attention to the need to elaborate a foreign trade policy and establish effective control regulations only when the European trading community at Canton began submitting demands directly to Peking in the 1750s. This action violated a fundamental rule of traditional Chinese foreign relations which prohibited direct foreign contact with Peking, with the exception of envoys from tributary states, who came very infrequently in accordance with a schedule prescribed by the Chinese court.[8] The English traders had knowingly violated this prohibition in a fit of desperation over the grasping exactions of corrupt local officials and over their failure to secure meaningful support from their own home governments (which, it should be noted in their defense, lacked both diplomatic relations with Peking and any significant military presence in Asia).

In 1759 James Flint, an Englishman who had served for many years in China as interpreter-translator for the British East India Company (hereafter EIC), headed a private mission to the Ch'ing court to seek redress for a long list of grievances suffered by the British merchants at Canton. The immediate result of the mission was three years' house arrest in Macao for Flint, the dismissal of the Chinese official in charge of foreign trade, and an ineffectual

---

[7] Edward L. Farmer, "James Flint Versus the Canton Interest (1755–60)," in *Papers on China,* no. 17, pp. 38–66 (Harvard University, East Asian Research Center, 1963).

[8] See Ssu-yü Teng and John K. Fairbank, "On the Ch'ing Tributary System," in *Ch'ing Administration: Three Studies* (Cambridge: Harvard University Press, 1960), pp. 107–218.

imperial order to eliminate corruption and arbitrariness in the administration of the customs tariff.[9] But by far the most important effect of this early Western effort to pierce the veil surrounding Peking was to focus imperial attention on the potential danger to Chinese military security and political stability posed by the European presence in Canton. The ensuing debate at the highest levels of the Ch'ing administration led to the enactment of a series of laws establishing the rigid system of control of European commerce and residence known as the "Canton System."[10]

Included in these control measures was the confinement of foreign trade to the single port of Canton and restriction of the Western traders to the "foreign factories," a rectangular area that measured only 1100 by 700 feet. With the exception of a visit under escort to a public park three times each month, they were required to remain within these compounds for the duration of the four- or five-month trading season. They had to then depart for home or for Macao to await the arrival of the ships in the fall. Other rules included prohibitions on bringing any foreign women to Canton, on foreigners hiring Chinese language teachers, and on direct communications with the Chinese authorities. It was during this period that the Englishman, referred to in the introduction, was found "guilty" of smuggling his wife into Canton.

In addition to restriction on their personal lives, the traders' freedom to do business was similarly curtailed. Foreign traders were prohibited from trading with anyone but a licensed hong merchant (see below). Nor were they allowed to go into the Chinese interior or to communicate with European priests in Peking for fear that they would obtain and misuse secret political, cultural, or economic information. Moreover, iron, saltpetre, books, and other items considered of military value were completely prohibited from export.[11]

The assumption underlying all these regulations was that any alien presence in China for whatever purpose represented a potential threat to the political and social order. Trade could be allowed only under conditions that would reduce such danger to an absolute minimum. The official justification for permitting foreign trade stressed the utter dependence of the foreign barbarians

---

[9] An English language translation of this edict is contained in Lo-shu Fu, *A Documentary Chronicle of Sino-Western Relations (1644–1820)*, 2 vols. (Tucson: The University of Arizona Press, 1966), 1: 222–24. In 1829 the British East India Company's governing body in China, the Select Committee, made another effort to send the emperor a letter requesting redress of grievances connected with the Canton trade. The letter was returned unopened by the governor-general, who refused to transmit it. Morse, *Chronicles,* 4: 217–18.

[10] See Pritchard, *The Crucial Years,* pp. 119–41; Fairbank, *Trade and Diplomacy,* pp. 39–53; and Immanuel Hsü, *The Rise of Modern China* (New York: Oxford University Press, 1970), pp. 183–213.

[11] *Ta-Ch'ing lu-li hui-t'ung hsin-tsuan* (New edition of the complete statutes and substatutes of the Ch'ing), 5 vols. (1873; reprint ed., Taipei: Wen-hai, 1964), 3: 1711, 1726.

on commerce with China.[12] But the needs of these poor barbarians were secondary in importance to the dictates of state security. This was made quite clear on the not infrequent occasions when the entire foreign trade was suspended for long periods to secure foreign compliance with Chinese control regulations.[13]

The Ch'ing emperors styled their general policy of alien control as one of simultaneously "soothing and restraining the outer barbarians," and thereby keeping disruption of the Chinese order by resident aliens to a minimum.[14] The posture of strictness was implicit in requiring the European countries to operate within the assumptions and rules of the traditional Chinese "tribute system" of foreign relations.[15] All countries bordering on China, as well as any other country desiring contact with China, were required to accept the status of an inferior vassal state and to comply with the protocol of the Chinese court, including the "kowtow."[16]

The "soothing" of aliens was handled in several ways. Foreigners were beneficiaries of a limited guarantee by the Chinese government of the private debts of Chinese merchants, a security gratuitously conferred upon the alien to compensate for his inability to remedy grievances in the Chinese courts or through diplomatic channels.[17] This official policy of protecting the legitimate interests of the alien merchants is succinctly expressed by the Ch'ien-lung emperor in the following excerpt from a 1777 decree ordering the punishment of a Chinese merchant who had cheated the English traders at Canton:

Foreign merchants risk their lives to sail across two oceans to make money. We naturally should trade with them honestly so they can take home sufficient profits. . . . The Middle Kingdom's reign and the pacification of the foreigners depend entirely upon justice and fairness so that they may be grateful and respect us. . . . If when they have grievances and appeal to our government . . . we show partiality to our people and fail to alleviate the foreigner's difficulties, then, since they cannot go to Peking to present further accusations, they have no recourse but to store up and suppress hatred for us in their hearts.[18]

Apart from commercial matters, the Ch'ing government showed its solicitude toward the resident foreign community by the measures it took to protect aliens and by its regular practice of administering swift and stern punishment to any Chinese subject found guilty of crimes against foreigners' life or

---

[12] See imperial edict of 1761, in Fu, *A Documentary Chronicle,* 1: 228–29.

[13] George T. Staunton, *Miscellaneous Notices Relating to China* (London: John Murray, 1850), pp. 89, 141–42, 219.

[14] Fu, *A Documentary Chronicle,* 1: 188, 223, 229.

[15] Teng and Fairbank, "On the Ch'ing Tributary System."

[16] In practice, however, the strict statutory protocol was not always enforced to the letter. See Fairbank, ed., *The Chinese World Order.*

[17] Greenberg, *British Trade,* p. 69; also see Staunton, *Notices,* pp. 132–33.

[18] Fu, *A Documentary Chronicle,* 1: 278.

property.[19] A corollary principle was that violations of Chinese law by foreigners were usually adjusted locally or even disregarded. The only exceptions to the latter practice were the homicides of Chinese, an offense which vitally threatened the ever tense balance between the Chinese and the resident alien community. In such cases the Chinese authorities sought to prosecute the alien offender in accordance with Chinese law.[20]

In keeping with the tribute-system principle of avoiding a show of genuine official interest in foreign trade revenue, the function of implementing the above policies was assigned in the first instance not to regular civil officials but to private Chinese businessmen known as hong merchants.[21] Prosperous traders who were granted licenses as foreign traders by the Board of Revenue in Peking, the hong merchants (who never totaled more than thirteen firms and were usually fewer) together enjoyed a monopoly of the trade in the major export items of tea and silk. They were considered quasi officials and, as such, were collectively responsible for compliance by the foreigners with all Chinese laws, criminal as well as commercial. Each foreign ship had to be "secured" by one of the hong merchants. For any failure of the foreign ship to pay port duties or for any violation of the Canton-System rules by any member of the ship's crew, the "security merchant" was held responsible. Should he ultimately be unable to secure compliance from the alien who was responsible, the hong merchant's property would be confiscated and he would be exiled to Chinese Turkestan without much hope of return.

The legally precarious status of such an important functionary inevitably imparted an atmosphere of tension and conflict into the relationship between the Chinese and European merchants. The foreign traders themselves were, of course, extremely low on the Chinese social scale, being both barbarians and lowly merchants in a country where trade was considered not a vital social function but a parasitic drain on the labor of the good peasant. Given such a pecking order, it is not surprising that under the Canton System all communications from the foreigners were required to be forwarded indirectly through the hong merchants. Because of the hong merchant's fear of criminal punishment, this procedure was at best barely satisfactory for ordinary matters and a dismal failure when the foreign merchant wished to complain about corruption or unfair business practices on the part of the hong merchants

---

[19] Morse, *Chronicles*, 4: 176–77.

[20] See my "Early Ch'ing Criminal Jurisdiction over Western Merchants and Sailors" (unpublished paper presented at the Conference on China's Legal Tradition, Bellagio, Italy, 7–14 August 1969).

[21] Ann B. White, "The Hong Kong Merchants of Canton" (Ph.D. diss., University of Pennsylvania, 1967), University Microfilm, ed., 1968. Also see Liang Chia-pin, *Kuang-tung shih-san hang k'ao* (A study of the thirteen hongs at Canton) (1937; reprint ed., Taichung, Taiwan: Tunghai University Press, 1960).

themselves.[22] The foreigners could avoid this difficulty only by employing Chinese to help them obtain information and convey letters to the officials, by occasionally succeeding in establishing direct contact with the governor-general and the commissioner of foreign trade, and, as a last resort, by refusing to trade until the Chinese authorities would hear their case and give appropriate remedies.

Yet the Canton System, as modified by the above practices, represented a successful *modus vivendi* which allowed a large and mutually profitable trade to grow up at Canton between merchants of countries with very different cultures and sharply contrasting legal concepts and political systems. Some of the reasons for this success will be discussed in the following section on contracts during the Canton period. Before launching into that discussion, however, it will be useful to comment briefly about the collapse of the Canton-System *modus vivendi*.

The dynamic balance between the Chinese and foreign interests at Canton, which generally satisfied the Chinese minimum requirement of preservation of local order and made possible a flourishing foreign trade, depended on the ability of the hong merchants and the EIC to control their respective country-men engaged in trade. But with the growth in numbers and power of the free British traders like Jardine and Matheson in the early nineteenth century and the abolition of the EIC monopoly in 1833, not to mention the unsettling presence of the aggressive American traders at Canton, there was no longer a single power figure on the Western side to ensure compliance with the Canton System.[23] And on the Chinese side the booming opium trade had created powerful vested interests which were not responsive to the directions of either the officials or the hong merchants.[24] The resulting chaos and mutual dissatisfaction set the stage for escalating conflict, which boiled over when British demands for a new era of free trade and equal state-to-state relations were forced upon China by the Opium War and the resulting treaty settlements.[25]

---

[22] Morse, *Chronicles*, 5: 77–78; *Chinese Repository* (Macao or Canton, monthly, ed. by E. C. Bridgman and S. W. Williams 1832–51), vol. 2 (1835), pp. 579–584.

[23] Staunton, *Notices*, pp. 15–17 of the Introduction. The hong merchants had feared that the termination of the East India Company's charter would result in disorder and endanger their lives as well as their fortunes; thus, they had petitioned both the Chinese governor-general and the Select Committee to seek an extension of the charter. Morse, *Chronicles*, 4: 245–47.

[24] See Hsin-pao Chang, *Commissioner Lin and the Opium War* (Cambridge: Harvard University Press, 1964), especially pp. 46–50.

[25] See generally Chang, *Commissioner Lin*, and Fairbank, *Trade and Diplomacy*.

III. NEGOTIATION AND ENFORCEMENT OF CONTRACTS UNDER
THE OLD CANTON SYSTEM

A Western businessman going to the modern Canton Trade Fair for the first time is probably concerned about the fact that China and his own country do not share a common set of procedures and principles governing the conclusion of trade contracts and the resolution of trade disputes. Further, he should be advised that China has not promulgated a domestic civil or commercial code, and that even if there were such codes they would be of little use to him because the contracts concluded by China's foreign trade enterprises usually preclude resort to regular courts. Moreover, when arbitration is provided for in the contract, it is seldom resorted to because the Chinese make it clear that the only practical way to resolve differences is through "friendly negotiations."

Despite the above factors, the Western businessman is likely to end up signing a contract disproportionately favorable to the Chinese party, containing many legal provisions he never would have accepted in a Western business context. And, perhaps surprisingly, the transactions will usually be concluded to the mutual satisfaction of both contracting parties. Why would an intelligent European or American executive accept such an unusual arrangement and why does it work? The simple answer that most businessmen give is that the Chinese are exceptionally reliable and trustworthy.

Again one can turn the clock back to the early nineteenth century and be faced with a similar scene. Ch'ing China had no civil or commercial courts accessible to aliens, nor any systematic commercial or civil law. And as the Ch'ing court did not recognize the sovereign equality of any other state, the Western trader at Canton a century and a half ago lacked both diplomatic protection and appeal to regular courts of law.

Yet, despite this insecure and threatening situation, the annual total value of the Canton foreign trade at the beginning of the nineteenth century exceeded $20 million and the annual tariff revenue from tea imported into Great Britain constituted more than 10 percent of the total annual revenue of the British crown.[26] Individual British, American, and European traders commonly made upwards of half a million dollars in ten years and retired to a life of leisure.[27]

In addition to the official policy of accommodating foreign desires for a fair profit, the prosperity of the old Canton trade was also facilitated by the fact that the individual hong merchants had a world-wide reputation for generosity, honesty, and dependability. As neither the Western governments nor the Chinese government and legal system could be called upon to provide the

---

[26] Greenberg, *British Trade*, p. 3.

[27] Jacques Downs, "The American Community in China, 1785–1839" (unpublished manuscript).

ground rules and ultimate sanction of force necessary to lend predictability to foreign-trade transactions, the Western traders had to rely on their own combined economic strength and upon the establishment of a relationship of mutual trust and confidence with their Chinese counterparts. Such relationships did, indeed, exist, despite some of the disharmonies indicated below. Western commercial records are filled with testimonials to the high character of the hong merchants.[28] Mutual respect, combined with a common economic interest in the trade, enabled the merchants of both sides to evolve a local system of trading principles and practices that gave Canton the reputation of being the most efficient port in the world in the early 1800s.[29]

Scholars of legal history are interested in the role trade contracts played in the growth of the bustling commerce at Canton. Some historians have suggested that written contracts were not used in the early Western commercial contact with China.[30] From commercial records it seems clear, however, that written contracts were employed by English merchants in the China trade at least as early as 1699.[31] And, in 1704, we find an English ship captain recommending that all agreements be reduced to writing. His comment, "For, tho' they may be Rogues enough in their Hearts, they don't care to appear so in writing," seems a universally applicable observation on the value of the written form.[32]

The bulk of the Canton foreign trade in the latter half of the eighteenth century involved the export of tea and silk to Europe, and a large part of this trade was governed by written contracts between the monopolistic EIC and the small group of Chinese foreign traders. Before leaving Canton at the end of each trading season, the agents of the EIC would hold a conference with the assembled hong merchants to negotiate contracts for the purchase of tea and silk for the next season.[33] The purpose of these contracts was to fix the quantity, quality, and price of the export goods to be purchased the following year from each hong merchant.

---

[28] For example, see Morse, *Chronicles*, 2: 88, 392.

[29] Greenberg, *British Trade*, pp. 60–61. A strong argument for retention of the old Canton system was made in 1831 by one of the leading American China merchants, Robert Bennett Forbes, who asked: " . . . who would barter the present free trade in all descriptions of goods for a regular commercial system of duties, entries, permits, etc., myriad of forms, like those in London? The facilities of trade have always been remarkable here and those who have had most experience are perfectly willing to put up with a continuation of the same." Letter to T. H. Perkins, dated 12 December 1831 (from *R.B. Forbes Letterbook* in the Museum of the China Trade, Milton, Mass.).

[30] For example, see Greenberg, *British Trade*, p. 61.

[31] Morse, *Chronicles*, 1: 90–91.

[32] *Ibid.*, p. 105. For additional references to the use of written contracts in the China trade throughout the eighteenth and into the nineteenth century, see *ibid.*, 1: 249–50, 279, and 2: 392.

[33] *Ibid.*, 2: 392.

The EIC commercial representatives in China learned early that the hong merchants were very skillful in using the terms of the contract to bind the hands of the EIC, and equally adept at avoiding being so confined themselves. For example, in 1734 the EIC Canton agents reported that they had required from each hong merchant "a contract signed by himself that if any dispute should hereafter arise we might produce it before the Mandarines & thereby do ourselves Justice."[34] But, despite these precautions, a disagreement soon arose when the EIC agents claimed that pieces of silk cloth did not conform to contract specifications for weight, color, or quality. The Chinese merchants insisted upon being paid the full contract price for the delivered goods. After the dispute had dragged on for more than two months, the EIC agents attempted to obtain a formal hearing before the Chinese civil authorities but were told not to disturb the officials "on such trifling occasions." The incident was finally settled only when the authorities applied behind-the-scenes pressure on the Chinese merchants, forcing them to compromise and allow the foreign merchants to recover part of the amount claimed.

Although there was no governmental or private tribunal willing and competent to adjudicate or arbitrate commercial disputes between Chinese and Western merchants in the pre-Opium War era, trade continued to grow, using the contract as the principal instrument setting forth the terms of agreement and the consequences of noncompliance. In 1830, however, the Select Committee of the EIC decided not to sign any more formal advance contracts for the purchase of tea. They gave the following justification for their decision:

The futility of all attempts to make a formal deed binding upon those who had interests at variance with its tenor has been frequently apparent, whereas we were obliged to adhere to an agreement which was occasionally enforced to our disadvantage, but was never available to our benefit. . . . We are quite secure in the full amount of our wants being easily met and a simple declaration of those wants will prove as effective as any contracts could be."[35]

The Select Committee was exaggerating when it claimed that it had always strictly complied with its contractual obligations. Just the previous year the committee had purposely delayed, from November until February, unloading the EIC ships which had arrived at Whampoa, in an effort to coerce the Chinese authorities to revise radically the Canton System regulations.[36] The hong merchants were caught in the middle and lost considerable sums of money since they had made substantial subcontracts with tea merchants to provide teas for delivery to the EIC in November. The president of the Select Committee, Mr. Plowden, acknowledged the validity of the hong merchants' claim and called upon the entire committee to give the hong merchants some assurance

---

[34] *Ibid.*, 1: 226–27.

[35] *Ibid.*, 4: 224.

[36] *Ibid.*, 4: 199–221, 215–16.

that the EIC would fulfill its contractual obligations. However, the majority of the committee overruled him and informed the Chinese merchants that they must suffer the consequences of the refusal of the Chinese government to modify the Canton system as demanded.[37]

As in the 1734 case discussed above, the products sold by the hong merchants occasionally did not conform to contract specifications. And, as there did not exist any official commodity inspection organ to issue certificates of quality, the EIC practice throughout most of the eighteenth century was as follows. Damaged teas would be destroyed in Europe, substandard teas would be reclassified and accepted as a lower grade, and grossly substandard (or "rubbish") teas would be sent back to China and returned to the seller. In most cases, the hong merchant would accept the unilateral determination of the EIC, "trusting to the honour of the Court [the governing body of the EIC, resident in London] and of the Council [collective decision-making organ of the EIC in China, predecessor to the Select Committee]."[38] In the late eighteenth century, the EIC began the practice of assigning an expert tea taster to its Canton staff;[39] this measure helped avoid the expense of shipping "rubbish" teas to England and back.

When the EIC notified the responsible hong merchant that some of his export goods departed from contract specifications in any of the ways described above, the latter would compensate the former by replacing the substandard commodity with commodities conforming to contract specifications; by repayment of the portion of the contract price represented by the inferior goods; or by giving the buyer a discount on subsequent purchases.[40] In addition, some contracts contained clauses providing for punitive damages.[41] Even in the absence of such a provision, on at least one occasion the Chinese seller agreed to pay an additional assessment of 50 percent of the contract price of "rubbish" teas, to compensate the buyer for shipping expenses.[42] However, as the value of rejected teas multiplied with the over-all rapid growth of the tea trade in the late eighteenth and early nineteenth centuries, the hong merchants became less willing to acknowledge in their entirety the claims submitted by the EIC. Accordingly, the latter was forced to accept only partial compensation.[43]

The contract price for tea and silk exports, as agreed upon in the "forward" contracts between the EIC and the hong merchants, generally reflected the

---

[37] Ibid., 4: 215–216.
[38] Ibid., 2: 88–89, 181, 193, and 3: 28; see also Staunton, Notices, p. 169.
[39] Morse, Chronicles, 2: 181.
[40] Ibid., 2: 88–89.
[41] Ibid., 1: 91, and 2: 35.
[42] Ibid., 2: 193.
[43] Ibid., 3: 28.

current market price but obviously might vary widely from the market price nine months later when delivery was to be made. When the hong merchant was forced to pay to the local tea and silk brokers a much higher price than anticipated in order to fill the advance contracts, he was usually successful in getting the EIC to agree to some upward revision of the total contract price. Similarly, in a falling market, only the strongest of the hong merchants was in position to force the EIC or the major American merchants to pay the price agreed upon almost a year before.[44] This mutual willingness to adjust the pricing terms reflected a common interest in preserving a profitable trading relationship.

The Ch'ing tried to restrict the outflow of Chinese silver[45] and to conduct foreign trade on a barter basis.[46] Both policies were increasingly invoked, to no avail, by the Ch'ing emperors in the early nineteenth century. They vainly strove to reverse the trend away from the huge import surplus and silver drain of the early 1800s. This drain had been caused chiefly by the rise of illegal opium imports from India, which had to be paid for with Chinese silver coins.[47] Related to these protectionist policies was a broad rule prohibiting Chinese merchants from accepting foreign financing.[48] Despite the fact that many Chinese merchants were found guilty of violating this law and were severely punished, the practice continued to flourish as the only way for the Chinese party to finance the major tea and silk transactions with the EIC and other big traders.

The European traders at Canton, private as well as the monopolistic companies, paid for part of their purchases of tea and silk with imports of Western goods. In the EIC's trade, the barter method was commonly used to pay for one-third or more of the Chinese export commodities in any year.[49] The use of this method of payment, though an apparent response to the official Chinese preference for barter, was in fact chosen by the local agents of the EIC as the only way to promote the sale of British manufactured goods on the Chinese market.[50]

---

[44] Downs, *The American Community in China,* chap. 3, p. 11.

[45] *Ta-Ch'ing lü-li* (reprint), 3: 1751. The rationale behind this prohibition, and the problems encountered in enforcing it, are examined in a memorial submitted to the emperor in 1814, in *Ch'ing-tai wai-chiao shih-liao: Chia-ch'ing-ch'ao* (Historical materials concerning foreign relations in the Ch'ing period: the Chia-ch'ing reign) (1931–33; reprint ed., Taipei: Ch'eng-wen, 1968), pp. 392–94.

[46] *Ta-Ch'ing hui-tien shih-li* (Ch'ing administrative statutes with precedents), 24 vols. (Kuang-hsü edition 1899; reprint ed., Taipei: Chung-wen shu-chü, 1963), 10: 8278–79.

[47] Morse, *Chronicles,* 4: 259–60.

[48] Fu, *A Documentary Chronicle,* 1: 225.

[49] Morse, *Chronicles,* 1: 114, 124, and 2: 281.

[50] Greenberg, *British Trade,* pp. 7, 59.

When barter reached its practical limits, the balance of the purchase price had to be paid in silver coin.[51] In the early years the EIC ships themselves were obliged to import silver bullion in large quantities directly from England. From the latter part of the eighteenth century they were able to use silver obtained by private traders from India. Indian products, including raw cotton, were sold for cash on the Canton market. The private traders then generally turned over the silver to the EIC trade representatives in China in return for bills of exchange on London.[52]

The ramifications of this complex means of financing the old Canton trade are worth careful analysis. Its intrinsic complexity inevitably led to periodic conflicts between the foreign merchants and the Chinese authorities. In the late eighteenth century between six and ten Chinese hong merchants handled from ten to twenty million dollars worth of export and import commodities each year.[53] As noted above, each spring the EIC made advance contracts with these hong merchants to deliver several million dollars worth of tea and silk in the fall. Although they entered into these undertakings with complete awareness of the need for cash, the hong merchants were perennially short of necessary capital. Their financial squeeze was the direct result of several facts of life in the treaty ports. First, there were no banks serving the foreign trade; second, the merchants were required to pay the imperial customs from their own cash reserves; and third, they were subjected to numerous illicit exactions by the local officials.[54] Forced contributions to emergency governmental expenses, such as for disaster relief or for mobilizing the militia to suppress local uprisings, depleted remaining liquid assets.

For these reasons, the Canton trade came to be increasingly financed by the foreign traders themselves. In the spring the EIC would advance more than a million dollars in cash to several hong merchants to enable them to purchase tea from the producers and meet the contracts for fall deliveries.[55] Such extension of credit, while seeming generous to the Chinese side, contained seeds of disaster for both parties. The EIC would also sell the bulk of its imports on account, thus further increasing the cash debt of the merchants. And in order to secure a sizable contract for the sale of tea to the EIC, the hong merchant would have to agree to accept imports of English woolens as

---

[51] Morse, *Chronicles*, 1: 114.

[52] *Ibid.*, 2: 9, 27, 40–41, 83; 3: 54–55, 76, 205; 4: 189, 260; and 5: 115.

[53] *Ibid.*, 2: 201; Greenberg, *British Trade*, p. 3. By 1832 the value of China's annual foreign trade at Canton had climbed to more than $55 million. Morse, *Chronicles*, 4: 339–40.

[54] Greenberg, *British Trade*, pp. 61–69.

[55] For example, see record of the advances made by the EIC to the various hong merchants in 1791 and 1792, in Morse, *Chronicles*, 2: 184, and 193, respectively; also see *ibid.*, 8, 28, 89–90, and 126–127.

partial payment.[56] Since the Chinese domestic market for woolens was never strong (in fact it existed only because of the EIC's dumping policy), the hong merchants often found part of their assets tied up in costly stocks of unmarketable foreign goods. Even when they were able to sell the unwanted woolens, they were likely to use the money received to pay customs duties or old debts, instead of applying it to repay the huge advances under the tea contracts.[57] The frequent result was the financial collapse of the hong involved. From the institution of the Canton System in 1760 until its termination with the outbreak of the Opium War in 1839, dozens of hong merchants went out of business, owing millions of dollars to the EIC, foreign free traders, and Chinese tea and silk dealers in the countryside.[58]

As the Canton System regulations had prohibited hong merchants from borrowing from foreigners and because resort to the Chinese authorities was fraught with many financial and personal risks, foreign merchants and the still solvent hong merchants (who were collectively responsible for the debts of the defunct member of the closed fraternity) usually attempted to arrange a private plan to pay off all the creditors.[59] Another reason why a private arrangement was preferred was that the government's debt guarantee covered only the principal (plus accrued interest not in excess of the original sum owed) outstanding with respect to foreign goods purchased on account by a Chinese hong merchant.[60] Also, several years usually elapsed from the time the Chinese government order to repay a foreign merchant was issued until the time of payment of the final installment on the amount found due.

Thus, private settlement of these debts was obviously desirable to both Chinese and foreign merchants because it averted government penalties and exactions. In some privately adjusted cases the debtor would even remain in the foreign trade business, but usually he would have to dispose of all his assets to help pay the debt; he then would retire quietly, happy to escape the legal penalty of banishment for "collaborating with foreigners and cheating them out of their money."[61] However, where a bankrupt's assets were insufficient even to pay his overdue imperial customs duties, there was no

---

[56] Staunton, *Notices*, pp. 162–63; Morse, *Chronicles*, 2: 28, 260–61, and 5: 159.

[57] See discussion of the 1795 case involving the bankruptcy and subsequent suicide of the hong merchant, Munqua, in Morse, *Chronicles*, 2: 273.

[58] See generally Morse, *Chronicles*, vols. 2–5; see also the interesting analysis of the causes and effects of the hong merchant debts, in Greenberg, *British Trade*, pp. 61–69.

[59] Morse, *Chronicles*, 2: 300, and 3: 183.

[60] Fu, *A Documentary Chronicle*, 1: 291–92.

[61] This is the short title of the *li* (substatute) which was generally cited by the Ch'ing officials when sentencing hong merchants for financial crimes involving aliens; the same law was applied to punish any Chinese who dared to teach the Chinese language, or draft documents, for the Westerners. This is the first substatute under the *lü* (statute) entitled *P'an-chieh chien-hsi* (Interrogation of spies). *Ta-Ch'ing lü-li* (reprint), 3: 1700.

recourse but to report the matter to the officials. The debtor would be put in chains (and ultimately exiled), his property confiscated and sold to pay the state and the creditors, and the other hong merchants ordered to repay the rest of the debt to the foreign merchants.[62] On occasion the debt was initially repaid from customs revenues, because default by a Chinese merchant was regarded as having brought shame upon the entire Chinese body politic and exposed the government and the people to ridicule by the barbarians.[63] The remaining hong merchants would share the responsibility of repaying the government.

A few perceptive English observers who were involved in the early Canton trade recognized that the Ch'ing state guarantee of the private foreign debt—a protection the foreign merchant lost under the modern treaty system—served as a *quid pro quo* for the tight restrictions imposed on alien residents in China.[64] But an increasingly vocal majority of Western merchants were either unaware of the Chinese government's commitment to underwrite the private foreign debt or dissatisfied with the limited coverage and slow operation of the debt-repayment procedure. They consequently persisted in complaining about the recurring problem of bankruptcy of hong merchants and the lack of a body of commercial law and of competent and accessible courts. The increasingly unsatisfactory resolution of these debt disputes, together with conflict over criminal jurisdiction and over the opium trade, led the majority of the Western merchant community in Canton to demand a fundamental revision of the rules of Sino-Western commercial intercourse.[65]

IV. THE TREATY SYSTEM

The principal aims of the British policy in waging the Opium War (1840–42) included improving the conditions of trading with China, placing Sino-Western relations on an equal state-to-state basis, and protecting English nationals from China's "barbaric" laws and corrupt officials. The British, American, and French treaties concluded with China between 1842 and 1844 attempted to accomplish all of these aims.[66] They opened additional ports to foreign trade and residence, and required Chinese local officials to communicate

---

[62] See reports of handling of cases occurring between the 1770s and the 1830s, in Morse, *Chronicles*, 2: 270–72, and 4: 219–20; Fu, *A Documentary Chronicle*, 1: 276–77, 280–81, 317–19; and *Ta-Ch'ing lü-li* (reprint), 2: 1372, 1378.

[63] Fu, *A Documentary Chronicle*, 1: 318.

[64] Staunton, *Notices*, pp. 132–33; Greenberg, *British Trade*, p. 69.

[65] John K. Fairbank, Edwin O. Reischauer, and Albert M. Craig, *East Asia: The Modern Transformation* (Boston; Houghton Mifflin, 1965), pp. 134–36.

[66] *Ibid.*, pp. 134–46, 166–73; also see generally, George W. Keeton, *The Development of Extraterritoriality in China*, 2 vols. (London: Longmans, Green, and Company, 1928).

with Western consuls as equals. The treaties also established the institution of extraterritoriality. In criminal cases occurring on Chinese soil, Western treaty nationals were judged by their own laws, administered by officials appointed by their own governments. Later treaties, concluded in 1858 and 1860, forced China to allow the stationing of foreign diplomats in Peking.

Despite the fact that periodic treaty revisions fostered the growth of Western power and influence, Western commercial principles and practices never became fully operative in China. This was so even in the treaty ports such as Shanghai, which was virtually ruled by a coalition of Western consuls.[67] The Ch'ing customs administration was, of course, satisfactory to the Western states—it was headed by a British subject and Europeans and Americans filled the important positions. The bulk of its revenues was remitted to Western governments as war indemnity.

In the actual legal adjudication of disputes, Chinese law applied in all cases in which the defendant was Chinese. In Shanghai this meant the case would be tried by the Mixed Court, with a Chinese judge presiding and a Western lawyer observing as assessor, with power only to register a protest.[68] Over the years these assessors began to intervene more and more, in spite of the lack of sound treaty authority for their participation in judicial decision-making. The result was the growth of a body of judge-made "Chinese" commercial law strongly influenced by Anglo-American law. But, since this body was not comprehensive or systematic, the Western businessmen in the treaty ports never ceased complaining about the lack of a codified Chinese commercial law.[69]

Much later, a draft of such a code was produced.[70] It was part of the legislation which the collapsing Ch'ing empire's reformers desperately offered to foreigners in their attempt to abolish the "unequal treaties" and recover China's national sovereignty. Like many of the other reforms of this period, this code was never promulgated because of political upheaval. It remained for later regimes, first the Nationalists and then the Communists, to exert order and control over the laws and institutions of China's foreign trade.[71]

---

[67] A. M. Kotenev, *Shanghai: Its Mixed Court and Council* (1925; reprint ed., Taipei: Ch'eng-wen, 1968), pp. 1–22.

[68] *Ibid.*, pp. 45–68.

[69] Keeton, *The Development of Extraterritoriality,* 2: 364–67.

[70] Legal History Research Office, Bureau of Codification, State Council, *Ch'ing-shih-kao hsing-fa-chih chu-chieh* (The treatise on criminal law in the draft history of Ch'ing, annotated) (Peking: Fa-lü ch'u-pan-she, 1957), pp. 40–41, note 6.

[71] See generally Warren L. Shattuck, Richard Cosway, and Herbert Ma, *Trade and Investment in Taiwan: The Legal and Economic Environment in the Republic of China* (Taipei: Mei-ya, 1973).

V. CONCLUSION

It would be erroneous to conclude that there are no important distinctions between the foreign trade posture of the conservative Ch'ing court and the revolutionary regime in Peking today. Nevertheless, the above sketch of key principles and practices in the old China trade and the speculations advanced with respect to the origin and significance of similar themes and modes of action in the conduct of the PRC's foreign trade suggests several striking resemblances between the situation of Western businessmen involved in the China trade today and their counterparts who traded at Canton more than a century ago. To mention but a few, much of current China trade is still conducted in Canton during specified times of the year. Contact between Western businessmen and the bulk of Chinese society is strictly limited—and this presumably limits the degree to which foreign influences might disrupt the Chinese political and social order.

The central problem faced by both today's and yesterday's Western businessman engaged in the China trade has been the lack of a commercial code or a systematic body of commercial custom and the unavailability of regular courts competent to construe and enforce foreign trade contracts. This has meant that the foreign businessman either has had to abandon the idea of trading with China or else rely upon mechanisms other than clear and enforceable legal rules to provide him with the degree of predictability sufficient to warrant his risking the time and money involved in developing a trading relationship with Chinese enterprises.

The quandary of the Western businessman sailing in a sea uncharted with familiar legal guidelines seems in both eras to have been adequately resolved by the establishment of a functional substitute which has usually furnished as much predictability as is found in a Western market governed by published legal norms administered by courts. In both the old and new Canton trade, the Western and Chinese traders have relied—with generally satisfactory results—upon mutual good faith and mutual interest in preserving a valuable relationship. Additional security has been provided in both periods by the fact that both the Manchu court and the PRC leadership have considered national prestige to be involved even in ordinary international commercial relationships. The state thus has in effect "guaranteed" the equitable performance of contractual obligations while at the same time virtually precluding a formal legal resolution of trade disputes.

Lest the Western businessman get too enthusiastic about the "unlimited potential" of the China market, he should remember that in Peking's attitude toward foreign trade today there are two elements which history has shown impose real obstacles to the growth of China's foreign trade. First, it is deemed both unnecessary and undesirable for China to become dependent on foreign imports. Second, political considerations prevail in case of a conflict between the implementation of foreign trade contracts and the realization of important foreign policy goals such as the preservation of political orthodoxy or border security.

Another consideration which calls for a cautious estimated of China trade prospects is that, unlike the Manchu court, which was essentially passive in its domestic and foreign economic policies, the PRC considers foreign trade as simply another tool to be employed in the task of socialist construction of the country. Although the Chinese leadership now is encouraging trade with the West, future changes in its assessment of the needs of domestic construction could lead to an abrupt curtailment of its foreign trade activities.

Italian-Chinese Commercial Agreement

Article 1. In so far as is possible and in conformity with regulations actually in existence in its own country, each contracting party binds itself to grant favorable treatment for goods imported from the territory of the other party and for goods exported to the territory of the other party, particularly for the goods indicated on lists "A" and "B" which are annexed to this agreement.

Article 2. This agreement does not exclude the exchange of goods not indicated in lists "A" and "B."

Article 3. All payments between the Republic of Italy and the Chinese People's Republic must be made through the Bank of Italy or through Italian banks authorized by that bank to deal in foreign currencies and through the Chinese People's Bank, and all payments must be in accordance with regulations actually in effect in the two Countries and with customary practice.

Article 4. (1) The two contracting parties reciprocally grant most favored nation treatment to each other in matters of customs rights, additional taxes, and every other supplementary obligation as well as in matters of formality, regulations, and customs procedures.

(2) The foregoing paragraph does not apply: A) to advantages, favors, privileges, and exemptions granted or which will be granted by each of the two contracting parties to bordering Countries (including border traffic); B) to advantages, favors, privileges, and exemptions granted or which will be granted by each of the two contracting parties to interested Countries in the course of the actual or future participation in customs unions or similar institutions.

Article 5. The two contracting parties bind themselves to do all that is possible such that the prices of the goods traded by virtue of this agreement are fixed on the basis of those used for the same goods in the principal international markets.

Article 6. The two contracting parties agree to establish a mixed commission to examine the application of the present agreement and to study the development of commercial trade and cooperation between the two Countries. The commission will meet at least once each year, alternately at Rome and Peking.

ARTICLE 7. If necessary with respect to their respective international obligations, the two contracting parties agree to enter into consultations intended to establish fair provisions, but which nevertheless do not compromise the fundamental purposes of the present agreement.

ARTICLE 8. This agreement will enter into force upon the date it is signed and will be effective until 31 December 1974. It may be renewed yearly subject to written agreement between the two contracting parties meeting at least three months prior to the date of termination.

ARTICLE 9. All obligations deriving from the application of the present agreement during its validity will be fulfilled also after its termination, on the ground of the provisions contained in the agreement itself.

List "A." Chinese exports to Italy: silk and silk products, textile products; embroidered objects; frozen pork meat; egg products; canned goods and food products; rosin and other natural products; furs, leather and other animal products; products of light industry; stationery articles and sporting goods, machine tools; sundry machinery; precision instruments; ferrous metals and scrap iron; non-ferrous minerals and mineral products; chemical and pharmaceutical products; artisan's tools.

List "B." Italian exports to China: textile products; machine tools for metal or woodworking; tractors, other agricultural machines; construction and road machines, conveyor belts; apparatus for freezing and conditioning; machinery for the electric industry and electrical materials (including generators, turbines, alternators, cables, etc.); motors of all types, compressors and pumps; motor vehicles, their components and parts; materials and apparatus for lifting, moving, and storing; ball and roller bearings; equipment and material for the petroleum industry; telecommunications apparatus and apparatus for air and rail traffic control; precision and measuring instruments and apparatus; ferrous and non-ferrous metals; cinematographic and photographic materials and apparatus; chemical and pharmaceutical products (including fertilizers, antiparasites for agricultural use, dyes, tires); artificial and synthetic textile fibers and their yarns (unspun fiber, etc.); plastic materials and synthetic resins.

TRADE AND PAYMENTS AGREEMENT
BETWEEN
THE GOVERNMENT OF THE KINGDOM OF DENMARK
AND THE GOVERNMENT OF THE PEOPLE'S REPUBLIC OF CHINA

The Government of the Kingdom of Denmark and the Government of the People's Republic of China, desirous of promoting trade relations and maintaining economic cooperation between the two countries on the basis of equality and mutual benefit, have agreed as follows:

ARTICLE 1. The two Contracting Parties will mutually accord one another as favourable a treatment as possible with respect to the issue of import and export licences and with the greatest goodwill consider and decide on the proposals which they submit to one another and which aim at facilitating and furthering their mutual economic relations.

ARTICLE 2. (a) The Government of the People's Republic of China will in accordance with rules in force permit the exportation to Denmark of the commodities specified in List A attached to this Agreement. The Government of the Kingdom of Denmark will give favourable consideration to licence applications for such commodities.

(b) The Government of the Kingdom of Denmark will in accordance with rules in force permit the exportation to the People's Republic of China of the commodities specified in List B attached to this Agreement. The Government of the People's Republic of China will give favourable consideration to licence applications for such commodities.

ARTICLE 3. The two Contracting Parties will also give sympathetic consideration to applications for the import and export of commodities which are not mentioned in the Lists A and B attached.

ARTICLE 4. All payments between the Kingdom of Denmark and the People's Republic of China shall, subject to foreign exchange laws and regulations in force in the respective countries, be effected in Danish kroner through "Transferable Kroner Accounts" opened by Chinese banks in Danish banks or in transferable pound Sterling or in other mutually acceptable currencies.

The People's Bank of China and the Danmarks Nationalbank will make mutual arrangements for the implementation of these payments provisions.

ARTICLE 5. This Agreement shall come into force on the date of its signature and its validity is for one year. If neither Party notifies the other to terminate this Agreement in writing at least three months before its expiration, the validity of this Agreement shall tacitly extend for a period of one year, further extensions shall be effected in a similar manner.

After its termination all obligations arising from this Agreement shall be liquidated in accordance with the provisions thereof.

Done at Peking on the 1st of December 1957, in two original copies in the Danish, the Chinese and the English languages, and the three texts being equally authentic. In case of conflicting views with regard to the interpretation, the English text shall be valid.

For the Government of	For the Government of
the Kingdom of Denmark:	the People's Republic of China:
sign. K. Knuth-Winterfeldt.	sign. Lu Hsu-chang.

NOTE. List A specifies Chinese goods which may be exported to Denmark: animal by-products; foodstuffs; cereals and fodder; spices; oils and other vegetable products; handicrafts; chemicals; textiles and fibers; machinery; minerals and metals; and sundries. List B specifies Danish goods which may be exported to China: machinery and industrial equipment; transportation equipment; metals and tools; electrical and telecommunication equipment and instruments; instruments; chemical products; medicine and medical instruments; foodstuffs; textiles; and others.

LETTER OF THE CHINESE GOVERNMENT TRADE DELEGATION

Peking, 1st of December, 1957.

Mr. Chairman,

I have the pleasure to acknowledge the receipt of your letter dated 1st of December, 1957, which reads as follows:

"Our Governments being desirous of establishing an Agreement on mutual most-favoured-nation treatment with respect to the levying of customs duties and other charges, customs clearance formalities and navigation, I have the honour to confirm that the Danish Government agrees to the following:

(a) Denmark and the People's Republic of China will grant each other unconditional and unrestricted most-favoured-nation treatment in all matters concerning customs duties, surtaxes and other subsidiary charges as well as customs clearance formalities, regulations and procedures.

(b) Either Contracting Party will accord the other Contracting Party most-favoured-nation treatment of crews from ships of either Contracting Party during stays in ports of the other Contracting Party.

The provisions of the above paragraphs shall not, however, apply to:

1. Favours, granted or to be granted hereafter by Denmark or the People's Republic of China to an adjoining State to facilitate frontier traffic.

2. Advantages, favours, privileges and immunities which the Government of the People's Republic of China has granted or may grant to any neighbouring country.

3. Advantages, favours, privileges and immunities which the Government of Denmark has granted or may grant to Finland, Iceland, Norway or Sweden or all or several of these countries.

4. Advantages, favours, privileges and immunities resulting from any existing or future customs union or similar international agreement to which either of the Contracting Parties is or may become a Party.

(c) Ships flying the flag of either Contracting Party shall enjoy, when entering into, berthing at and sailing from the ports of the other Party, most-favoured-nation treatment in all respects.

(d) The Contracting Governments shall refrain from adopting any measure or any action of a discriminatory nature tending to restrict the liberty of ships of either country to take part in normal competition with ships of any third country."

I have the honour to confirm you that the Government of the People's Republic of China agrees to the contents stated in your letter.

I avail myself of this opportunity to express to you, Excellency, the assurance of my highest consideration.

Vice-Minister,
Ministry of Foreign Trade,
People's Republic of China,
Chairman of the Chinese
Government Trade Delegation.
sign. Lu Hsu-chang.

His Excellency Kield Gustav Count Knuth-Winterfeldt, Envoy Extraordinary and Minister Plenipotentiary, Chairman of the Danish Government Trade Delegation.

REGULATIONS GOVERNING THE OPENING OF RENMINBI ACCOUNT
WITH THE BANK OF CHINA, HEAD OFFICE, BANKING DEPARTMENT

The opening of a Renminbi account with the Bank of China, Head Office, Banking Department, Peking (hereinafter called "the First Party") by (hereinafter called "the Second Party") shall be governed by the following regulations:

(1)   Credits to the Renminbi account shall be limited to:

(a) Purchase of Renminbi against Italian Lire to be used as working balance, but such a working balance shall not exceed RMB. . . .

(b) Proceeds of Chinese imports and related charges.

(c) Purchase of Renminbi against Italian Lire to be used for payment of Chinese exports and relative charges of the basis of a contract concluded with a Chinese National Import and Export Corporation.

(2)   Debits to the Renminbi account shall be limited to:

(a) Payment of Chinese exports and related charges.

(b) Payment of non-commercial expenses with China.

(c) Payment within Italy.

(d) Conversion into Italian Lire.

(3)   The Renminbi account may be used for passing the receipts and payments between all the domestic branches of the First Party and the domestic branches of the Second Party in

(see list as follows)

(4)   On receipt of a statement of account of the Renminbi account from the First Party each month, the Second Party must, within a month, inform the First Party by letter of any outstanding items and whether the balance standing at the end of the month is correct.

(5)   These regulations shall enter into force on the opening of the Renminbi account and have been agreed to and confirmed by the following officials of the Second Party whose authorized signatures are affixed hereunder:

REGULATIONS GOVERNING RENMINBI EXCHANGE BUSINESS
BETWEEN THE BANK OF CHINA,
HEAD OFFICE, BANKING DEPARTMENT, PEKING, CHINA
AND

———

In its purchase or sale of spot or forward Renminbi from or to the Bank of China, Head Office, Banking Department, Peking (hereinafter called "the First Party"),   (hereinafter called "the Second Party") must observe the following regulations:

(1) A purchase of spot or forward Renminbi by the Second Party from the First Party must be made against Italian Lire and is limited to payment of Chinese exports and related charges on the basis of a Chinese export contract concluded with a Chinese National Import and Export Corporation. Spot Renminbi bought may be used as a working balance in a Renminbi account.

(2) A purchase of spot or forward Renminbi by the Second Party from the First Party must be effected by cable. The cable must show a test number, the amount of Renminbi to be bought and its equivalent in Italian Lire, and the date or period of delivery. The date of delivery for a purchase of spot Renminbi is 2 or 3 working days after the date of the despatch of the cable. The period of delivery for a purchase of forward Renminbi is based on the period of the relative contract, but it must not exceed six months.

(3) On receipt of a cable from the Second Party for a purchase of spot or forward Renminbi, the First Party shall, if agreeable to the purchase, immediately confirm to the Second Party by cable. A deal in the purchase and sale of Renminbi is thus concluded between the two sides, and both sides must make payment to each other in accordance with the deal. If it is necessary, the First Party has the right to inquire of the Second Party by cable the purpose of the purchase, for instance, the contract concerned. On receipt of the cable of inquiry, the Second Party must immediately reply by cable, so that the First Party may ascertain whether the purchase conforms to section (1) of these regulations.

(4) A sale of spot Renminbi by the Second Party to the First Party must be effected by cable. The cable must show a test number, the amount of Renminbi to be sold and its equivalent in Italian Lire, and the date of delivery. The date of delivery shall be 2 or 3 working days after the date of the despatch

of the cable. If, on receipt of the cable, it is found that there is a sufficient balance in the Renminbi account of the Second Party, the First Party shall notify the Second Party of the amount of Italian Lire, the First Party will pay and the date on which payment will be made. A deal in the purchase and sale of Renminbi is thus concluded between the two sides, and both sides must make payment to each other in accordance with the deal.

(5) A sale of forward Renminbi by the Second Party to the First Party must be based on a Chinese import contract concluded with a Chinese National Import and Export Corporation and must be effected by cable. The cable must show a test number, the amount of Renminbi to be sold and its equivalent in Italian Lire, and the period of delivery. The period of delivery is based on the period of the relative contract, but it must not exceed six months. On receipt of the cable, the First Party shall, if agreeable to the sale, confirm to the Second Party by cable. A deal in the purchase and sale of Renminbi is thus concluded between the two sides, and both sides must make payment to each other in accordance with deal. If it is found necessary, the First Party has the right to inquire of the Second Party by cable the purpose of the sale, for instance, the contract concerned. On receipt of the cable of inquiry, the Second Party must immediately reply by cable, so that the First Party may ascertain whether the sale conforms to the stipulations of this section.

(6) The exchange rate for spot Renminbi against the Italian Lira is the same as that for forward Renminbi against the Italian Lira. The exchange rate for forward Renminbi and forward charges shall be fixed by the First Party and shall be notified to the Second Party. When the Second Party sells or buys spot or forward Renminbi to or from merchants, it should also use the aforesaid exchange rates, but it may appropriately charge commission.

(7) The exchange rates and forward charges for the purchase and sale of spot and forward Renminbi by the Second Party from or to the First Party shall be based on those notified by the Bank of China as ruling at the time when the First Party despatches its cable of agreement to the sale or purchase following the receipt of a cable from the Second Party.

(8) In the event of an amendment to or a change in these regulations, the First Party shall notify the Second Party.

(9) These regulations shall enter into force on 25 July 1971 and have been agreed to and confirmed by the following officials of the Second Party whose authorized signatures are affixed hereunder:

APPROVED.

MT Contract Form for Japan Export

Contract No.:   MT (70)

Date of Contract:

Place of Contract: Peking

Buyers: China National Machinery Import and Export Corporation
                  Erh Li Kou, Hsichiao, Peking
                  Cable Address: MACHIMPEX PEKING

Sellers: (Friendly Firm K.K.)

In performance of the Details of Agreement for Memorandum Trade for the year 1970, based on the three political principles and the principle of inseparability of politics and economics which were confirmed by the communique announced on April 19, 1970, by the representatives of both the Japanese and Chinese Memorandum Trade Offices, and the four conditions of Sino-Japanese trade enunciated by the Chinese government, and through friendly negotiations, both parties agree to sign this contract, the terms of which are as follows:

1.

Name of Commodity and Specifications	Unit	Quantity	Unit Price	Total Amount

Total Amount:

2. *Country of Production:* Japan

3. *Manufacturer:*

4. *Port of Loading:*

5. *Port of Destination:*

6. *Loading Date:*

7. *Marking:*

Sellers shall clearly mark on each box the gross weight, net weight, packing number, content and other markings as stipulated below.

8. *Insurance:*

Insured by Buyers.

9. *Technical Materials:*

Sellers shall send all documents listed below to Buyers　　　days prior to loading.

10. *Quality Guarantee:*

The Sellers guarantee that all cargo under this Contract conforms to provisions of articles 1 and 2 of this Contract with regard to quality specifications and technical requirements. The guarantee period shall be　　　months after arrival of the goods at the port of destination. But it shall not exceed　　　months after the date of loading. Sellers shall be responsible for damages occurring within the guarantee period as the result of defects of design or construction on the part of the manufacturers when Buyers use the goods under conditions consistent with handling stipulated by the instruction manuals. Sellers shall be responsible for repair, replacement of parts, or substitution of goods without charge, upon demand of the Buyers, substantiated by certificates issued by the Chinese commodity inspection agency. Sellers shall remit promptly in cash consequent transportation expenses for replacement of the defective goods from the place of use, inspection costs, and loss of interest to Buyers.

In case Sellers have a protest against Buyers' claim, they shall submit a reply within two weeks of receipt of Buyers' claim. If that period expires, Buyers' claim shall be considered valid.

11. *Inspection and Compensation:*

(1) Sellers shall, prior to shipment, conduct an inspection concerning the quality specifications and the quantity of the cargo and issue an inspection certificate through the manufacturer or a Japanese commodity inspection agency pre-selected by mutual consent of Sellers and Buyers; moreover they shall explain the technical standards and conclusion of the inspection.

(2) Buyers shall conduct an inspection, entrusted to the Chinese Commodity Inspection Bureau, concerning specifications and quantity, after the cargo arrives at the destination port, and in case cargo damage or failure to conform with contract specifications or quantity is observed, the Buyers may, within　　　days of arrival at the destination port, claim compensation supported by an inspection certificate issued by the Chinese Commodity Inspection Bureau. Sellers, based on Buyers' claim, shall be responsible without compensation for lowering of commercial value, for supplementing shortages and for replacement of portions not conforming with this Contract's provisions, and moreover they shall make prompt exchange remittances in

cash to Buyers to cover consequent freight for replacement cargo to port of destination, Buyers' inspection expense and loss of interest. If Sellers have a protest against Buyers' claim, they must submit an answer within two weeks after receipt of Buyers' claim.

(3) Reinspection shall be conducted in accordance with the provisions of article 10 of this Contract.

12. *Payment Terms:*

Buyers shall, within twenty days after receipt of cable notice from Sellers of the export license number and loading (for each lot), open an Irrevocable Letter of Credit at the Bank of China, making the Sellers the beneficiary and payable at sight and posted in English pounds. Sellers will receive payment of the price of the cargo by forwarding to the opening bank, as required in the provisions of the Letter of Credit, various documents as provided in article 16 of this Contract. The effective period of the Letter of Credit shall be up to 15 days after loading date.

13. *Shipping Terms:*

(1) In case of FOB terms, they shall be implemented as specified below:

(a) Sellers shall give notice to Buyers by cable 30 days prior to the shipping date stipulated by this Contract confirming contract number, description of goods, quantity, gross weight including packing, and measurements (concerning cargo in which the weight of any one crate exceeds 5 tons, all crates must be individually listed, including weight with packing, and measurements), and Sellers shall facilitate Buyers' arrangement of shipping space.

(b) Buyers shall entrust the arrangement of shipping space and carriage under the contract to the China National Chartering Corporation in Peking.

(c) Buyers shall notify Sellers by cable of the name of the vessel, loading port and cable address and address of vessel's agent 10 days prior to said vessel's entry at port. Sellers shall promptly contact vessel's agent and facilitate the vessel's loading.

(d) In case Sellers' goods are unavailable for shipment on schedule, even though Buyers' chartered vessel arrives at loading port on time, Sellers shall be liable for demurrage and dead freight. In case the vessel does not arrive within twenty days after the loading date forwarded by Buyers, all necessary warehouse costs at loading port from the 21st day shall be at Buyers' expense, and Sellers shall receive from Buyers such expenses in accordance with receipts for the warehouse charges of the port of shipment.

(e) FOB Terms of Delivery: Sellers shall bear 50 percent of all cargo risks and loading charges until goods are taken overside. Loading charges shall mean all costs incurred during the period cargo is alongside until inside the vessel's hold (that is, from a place possible for Buyers' onboard cranework to the designated space within the vessel's hold), including heavy cargo crane rental charges on land or on sea needed for heavy cargoes at time of loading. However, this does not include on board stowage cost, fixing cost, packing cost, or hatch opening and closing costs.

(2) In case of C & F conditions, they shall be implemented as specified below:

(a) Sellers shall be responsible for shipping commodities, within the time period, on vessels voyaging directly from the loading port to the Chinese port as stipulated in article 6 of this Contract. Transshipment enroute may not be done.

(b) Carrying vessels shall not call at ports in the United States or in the Taiwan area before arrival at Chinese ports; also American vessels shall not be used.

(c) If Sellers' chartered vessel is a Japanese ship, the said vessel shall abide by the navigation regulations for Japanese ships in Chinese waters enforced by the Government of the People's Republic of China.

14. *Shipping Notices:*

(1) After completion of loading the goods, Sellers will immediately notify Buyers and the China National Foreign Trade Transportation Corporation (cable address: ZHONGWAIYUN) in the port of destination, as to contract number, description of goods, quantity loaded, gross weight (of which, concerning cargo exceeding either 9 tons in weight, 3,400 mm in width or 3,250 mm in length of both sides, weight including packing and measurements for each package shall also be listed separately), invoice amount, vessel name and departure date.

(2) In case Buyers were unable to secure insurance in time, because Sellers failed to cable loading notice on time, Sellers shall be responsible for all damage or all losses arising therefrom.

15. *Packing:*

Goods shall be packed in strong, seawaterproof, shockproof and rustproof wooden crates, suitable for long distance sea voyages and capable of withstanding carriage. Losses resulting from insufficient packing shall be Sellers' responsibility.

16. *Loading Documents:*

In order to receive the price of the goods, Sellers shall present to the paying bank, after completion of loading, the documents listed below:

(a) Clean, on-board ocean Bills of Lading in triplicate originals negotiable for the value of the goods. "Freight Payable at Destination" ("Freight Prepaid," for C & F terms) to be clearly written in, and blank endorsed and addressee left blank, distinctly marked to notify China National Foreign Trade Transportation Corporation at Port of Destination.

(b) Commercial invoices in quintuplicate. They will be distinctly marked with contract number, description of goods, quantity, unit price and total amount. In the event of partial shipment, lot numbers will also be noted.

(c) Packing list in duplicate.

(d) Quality inspection certificate and certificate of quantity and weight: One each, issued by the manufacturer or by the Japanese commodity inspection agency previously agreed to by mutual consent of both Buyers and Sellers.

(e) Instruction manual explaining in detail the handling process and technical materials specified in article 9 of this Contract, one each, or one certificate affirming that the aforementioned written items have been duly enclosed within the packing of the goods.

Sellers shall send on the vessel to agent at destination port a non-original copy of the above documents (a), (b), (c) addressed Buyers' cargo reception agent at the port of destination, China National Foreign Trade Transportation Corporation, and shall airmail one copy each to Buyers, and to the China National Foreign Trade Transportation Corporation at the destination port within 3 days after the vessel's departure.

17. *Force Majeure:*

Sellers shall not be responsible, in case it becomes impossible to deliver the goods or to deliver the goods on time due to Force Majeure, for example, wars, major floods or storms, fire, snow or earthquakes, which arise within the loading period stipulated by this Contract, whether during production, loading or carriage. But after Sellers have been able to learn of the occurrence of an incident, they shall promptly notify Buyers by cable and within fifteen days after cabling submit to Buyers documents of proof issued by a registered notary public or the Chamber of Commerce and Industry of the area in which the Force Majeure incident occurred. In such event, Sellers shall take all necessary measures to make up for the goods not yet delivered, and at the same time must inform Buyers in detail of the nature of measures effected.

It shall be the Buyers' option, based on the actual circumstances, to mutually agree with Sellers or to cancel the Contract. In case of Force Majeure extending ten weeks or more, Buyers shall have the right to cancel the Contract for the goods involved.

18. *Penalty for Delays in Delivery:*

In case of delays in delivering for which Sellers are responsible, excluding those caused by Force Majeure, Sellers shall pay a penalty of 1 percent of the total value of the goods to Buyers for every two weeks. All delays under a period of two weeks are computed as two weeks. The penalty shall be increased another 1 percent every subsequent two weeks of delay. However, the total amount of penalty shall be limited to 5 percent. The Sellers shall pay the penalty to Buyers in cash, but Sellers must submit documents on the manufacturer's production progress 14 days prior to the delivery date provided by the Contract, and indicate also a new delivery date. In case delay exceeds ten weeks, Buyers shall have the right to cancel for the delayed goods, bypassing arbitration, and a penalty of 5 percent of the total price of the said goods shall be promptly paid by the Sellers to the Buyers.

19. *Arbitration:*

All disputes arising during performance of this Contract, or in connection with this Contract shall be settled by mutual discussions between both parties as signatories hereto. When mutual discussion has been concluded and no solution could be found, it can be submitted to arbitration. Arbitration shall be conducted in the country where defendants reside; in China, the Foreign Trade Arbitration Committee of the China Committee for the Promotion of International Trade shall conduct the arbitration in compliance with the Commission's arbitration regulations; in Japan, the Japanese International Commercial Arbitration Association shall conduct the arbitration in compliance with the association's arbitration regulations. Appointment of arbitrators shall not be restricted to the list of arbitrators of the Japanese International Commercial Arbitration Association, but shall be People's Republic of China nationals, Japanese nationals, or nationals from a third country selected by the mutual consent of both parties. Arbitration awards shall be final decisions, and both parties signing this Contract shall fully abide by the decisions. Both parties shall obtain approval from their respective Governments and expedite the conduct of the arbitration and the travel of essential participants, as well as guaranteeing their safety. The losing party shall bear all expenses thereof, unless otherwise specifically decided by the arbitral committee.

20. *Documentation:*

This Contract becomes effective promptly upon being duly signed by the Sellers and the Buyers, but the contract documents shall be made out in both

Japanese and Chinese, with two copies for each and each with equal force, and both signing parties shall have one copy of each for proof.

21. *Supplementary Conditions:*

(1) All damages, expenses, claims for compensation, or penalties held against Sellers as provided in Articles 8, 11, 17 and 19 of this Contract shall be remitted by Sellers directly to Buyers, and reduction of the price of the goods shall not be permitted.

(2) Concerning other items, they shall be handled in accordance with the Details of Agreement of the 1970 Memorandum Trade, with the three political principles and the principle of the inseparability of political and economic affairs acknowledged in the joint communique published by the representatives of China and Japan's Memorandum Trade Offices, as well as the Four Conditions for China-Japan Trade enunciated by the Chinese Government.

Buyers: China National Machinery   Sellers:
         Import and Export
         Corporation

FRIENDLY EXPORT FROM JAPAN

Sino-Japanese Friendly Firm Trade Agreement

Contract No:

Contract Date:

China Import Export Corporation (hereinafter referred to as Buyer) and Friendly Firm K.K. (hereinafter referred to as Seller) agree to conclude this agreement in order to expedite friendly relations and economic interchanges between the Japanese and Chinese peoples, and based on the three political principles, three trade principles, and the principle of inseparability of politics and economics, and the four conditions of Sino-Japanese trade as enunciated by the Chinese government, and through friendly negotiations between them.

The terms of this agreement are as follows:

1. *Name of Commodity and Specifications:*

2. *Quantity:*

3. *Unit Price:*

4. *Total Amount:*

5. *Packing:*

6. *Port of Loading, Port of Discharge, Marks:*

7. *Time of Loading:*

8. *Insurance, Producing Country and Manufacturer:*

   (1) Insurance: (Buyer to arrange insurance).

   (2) Producing Country and Manufacturer.

9. *Payment Terms:*

   After the contract is concluded, Buyer shall open, through the Bank of China, an irrevocable letter of credit in favor of Seller, and Seller will receive payment of the cost of goods from the opening bank against the documents mentioned in each item specified in Provision 1 of the Delivery Clause of this agreement. Validity of the letter of credit is for fifteen (15) days after the loading of the goods.

10. *Other Terms:*

Other related matters will be treated pursuant to the provisions of the Delivery Clause (details are noted on the reverse side). The said Delivery Clause constitutes an indivisible portion of this agreement. When the Delivery Clause conflicts with relevant provisions of the Supplementary Clause under Article 11 of this agreement, the provisions of the Supplementary Clause shall control.

11. *Supplementary Clause:*

(1) This agreement was concluded by negotiations held between the representatives of both Buyer and Seller at the Chinese Export Goods Fair in the Spring of 1971.

(2) This agreement, written in Chinese, is made in duplicate, and one each will be kept by both parties.

(3) After signing of this agreement, all the matters relating to the performance of this agreement will be handled directly by   Branch Office of China National Import Export Corporation and Seller.

Buyer: China National Import   Seller: Friendly Firm K.K.
   Export Corporation

Address: Address:

Cable Address: Cable Address:

DELIVERY CLAUSE

1. *Shipping Documents:*

(1) To receive the price of the goods, Seller shall submit the following documents to the paying bank:

(a) A clean on-board ocean bill of lading with blank endorsement, in triplicate, marked: Notify China National Foreign Trade Transportation Corporation. In the case of FOB terms, "Freight Forward" shall be noted and in the case of C & F terms, "Freight Prepaid" shall be noted.

(b) Invoices with the contract number clearly entered, in quadruplicate.

(c) Packing lists/statements of weight in quadruplicate.

(d) One each of certificates of quality, quantity, weight and inspection issued by the Japanese Commodity Inspection Agency or the manufacturers.

(e) One copy of shipping cable that Seller sent to Buyer upon loading of goods.

(2)   Besides the said copy of the shipping cable, Seller will deliver 2 copies of the documents stated in the preceding clause to the China National Foreign Trade Transportation Corporation as agent of consignee located at the port of destination, by entrusting such documents to the vessel.

Further, within 2 days after the vessel's departure, 2 copies shall be sent by airmail to Buyer and 1 copy to the China National Foreign Trade Transportation Corporation located at the port of destination.

2.   *Shipping Terms:*

(1)   In case of C & F terms of delivery:

(a)   Seller is responsible for shipping the goods, within the period specified in Article 7 of this agreement, from the port of loading directly on a Chinese vessel to a Chinese port. Seller shall not transship the goods in transit nor utilize any vessel of U.S. nationality.

(b)   No cargo vessel shall anchor at any U.S. port, or anchor at Taiwan or in the vicinity of Taiwan before arriving at the port of discharge as specified in Item 2, Article 6 of this agreement.

(c)   In case a Japanese vessel is used, it must comply with the People's Republic of China's regulations for Japanese vessels navigating in Chinese waters.

(2)   In case of FOB conditions of delivery:

(a)   Buyer or Buyer's chartering agent, China National Chartering Corporation (Cable address: SINOFRACHT PEKING), will arrange for the vessel to carry goods under this agreement. Seller is responsible, within the period for loading provided in Article 7 of this contract, and for preparing the goods for loading on the designated vessel on the date indicated by Buyer or Buyer's chartering agent.

(b)   Fifteen (15) days before the loading of the goods, Buyer or Buyer's chartering agent shall notify Seller by cable the name of the vessel, date of loading, port of loading, contract number, name of commodity, quantity and name of shipping agent, so that Seller can prepare for the loading of the goods. When any alterations are made to the above-mentioned name of vessel, date of loading, quantity etc., Buyer or Buyer's chartering agent must immediately notify Seller of such changes.

(c)   Even though the vessel chartered by Buyer has arrived at the port of loading, when Seller cannot load the goods by the date of notice, any dead freight and demurrage arising from such delay shall be borne by Seller. When the vessel chartered by Buyer does not arrive at the port of loading on the stipulated date, any warehouse charges and insurance premiums lost, counting from the 16th day after the expiration of the

loading date, shall be borne by Buyer. Any relevant expenses that Seller pays to Buyer, or Buyer to Seller, shall be paid against formal receipts.

3. *Shipping Notice:*

(1) Seller shall give notice, by cable at least 10 days before the loading of goods, concerning the contract number, name of commodity, quantity of goods prepared for loading, amount of money, name of vessel, port of loading and expected sailing date to Buyer or Buyer's cargo agent at the port of discharge, China National Trade Foreign Transportation Corporation.

(2) After the completion of cargo loading, Seller shall give cable notice of the contract number, name of commodity, quantity loaded and total quantity, number of cases, invoice amount, name of vessel, port of shipping, sailing date and port of discharge, separately to Buyer and Buyer's consignee, the China National Foreign Trade Transportation Corporation.

(3) Shall seller fail to give Buyer loading notice by cable at an appropriate time so that he can not insure the goods, all losses thus incurred shall be Seller's responsibility for reimbursement.

4. *Inspection:*

(1) The cargo to be delivered under this contract shall be inspected before delivery with regard to quality, specifications, quantity/weight by a Japanese commodity inspection agency or the factory that produced the goods, and it shall issue an inspection certificate. The said inspection certificate constitutes one of the documents required for Seller to receive payment of the price of the cargo.

(2) Seller shall guarantee that the cargo delivered is perfect and in conformity with the quality and specifications of this contract, and after the goods arrive at the discharge port, Buyer will entrust the China Commodity Inspection Bureau located in the district to re-inspect for quality, specifications and quantity/weight. Should the quality and specifications of the cargo not conform with this contract or should the quantity/weight not conform with the invoice, Buyer shall return the cargo or file claims, within 60 days after the cargo arrival at the discharge port, in accordance with the inspection certificate by the China Commodity Inspection Bureau, except in cases where responsibility lies with the shipping company or insurance company. Any expenses or losses (including inspection charges) incurred from returning the cargo or filing of claims shall be borne by Seller.

5. *Force Majeure:*

Seller need not bear the responsibility for inability to deliver the goods on time, or for cases where it is impossible to deliver the goods, due to Force

Majeure accidents, for example, war, grave floods, fires, natural calamity, whether or not the goods are in the process of manufacture, loading or in transit. However, Seller must definitely notify Buyer by cable immediately upon knowing the occurrence of such accidents, and also send, within 15 days after such dispatch of cable, evidentiary documents issued by the Chamber of Commerce in the district where the Force Majeure accidents occurred, or by a registered notary public, to Buyer by registered airmail, to enable him to examine and verify them. Under such circumstances, Seller must definitely take necessary steps to send the undelivered cargo thereafter. When Force Majeure accidents continue over one month, Buyer has a right to cancel the contract.

6. *Penalties for Delayed Delivery:*

In case Seller should delay the delivery of goods, Buyer may either cancel the contract, or on obtaining the understanding of the Buyer, Seller has the right to delay delivery of the cargo, on condition that he pays a penalty. In case the delay is less than two weeks, Seller shall pay 1% of the total price of the delayed goods as a penalty and the penalty shall increase by one percent for every two weeks delay thereafter. However, the maximum amount should not exceed 5% of the total price of the delayed goods. The fines shall be deducted by the ban of payment at the time of paying the cost of goods.

7. *Arbitration:*

All disputes which may arise from performance of the contract or in relation to this contract shall be settled by friendly negotiations between the signing parties. If, as a result of negotiations between them, settlement is impossible, arbitration may be initiated. The place of arbitration shall be the country of defendant. In the case of China, arbitration shall proceed at the Foreign Trade Arbitration Committee of the China Committee for the Promotion of International Trade (CCPIT), pursuant to the arbitration regulations of the said Commission. In the case of Japan, arbitration shall be conducted at the Japanese International Commercial Arbitration Association pursuant to the arbitration regulations of the said Association. As for the selection of arbitrators, they need not be on the list of arbitrators issued by the Japanese International Commercial Arbitration Association, but they must be persons with the nationality of the People's Republic of China or Japan, or of a third country as may be agreed by both parties. The arbitration awards shall be final and binding upon the signing parties.

Both parties, with the understanding of their respective governments, shall extend to the other party all the conditions for convenience or operation and the processing of the arbitration, as well as entry and departure of the other party's staff, and guarantee their security. The arbitration fees shall be borne by the losing party, unless otherwise specified by the arbitration committee.

STANDARD PURCHASE CONTRACT

No.

Peking, Date:

The Buyers:

Erh Li Kou, Hsi Chiao, Peking.

Cable Address:

The Sellers:

This Contract is made by and between the Buyers and the Sellers; whereby the Buyers agree to buy and the Sellers agree to sell the undermentioned commodity according to the terms and conditions stipulated below:

1. *Commodity, Specifications, Quantity and Unit Price:*

2. *Total Value:*

3. *Country of Origin and Manufacturers:*

4. *Packing:*

To be packed in strong wooden case(s) suitable for long distance ocean transportation and well protected against dampness, moisture, shock, rust and rough handling. The Sellers shall be liable for any damage of the commodity and expenses incident thereto on account of improper protective measures taken by the Sellers in regard to the packing.

5. *Shipping Mark:*

On the surface of each package, the package number, measurement, gross weight, net weight and the wordings "DO NOT STACK UP SIDE DOWN", "HANDLE WITH CARE", "KEEP AWAY FROM MOISTURE" the lifting position and the following shipping mark shall be stenciled legibly with fadeless paint:

6. *Time of Shipment:*

7. *Port of Shipment:*

8. *Port of Destination:*

9. *Insurance:*

To be covered by the Buyers after shipment.

10. *Terms of Payment:*

The Buyers, upon receipt from the Sellers of the shipping advice specified in Clause 12 hereof, shall, in 15–20 days prior to the date of delivery, open an

irrevocable Letter of Credit with the Bank of China,   in favour of the
Sellers, for an amount equivalent to the total value of the shipment. The
Credit shall be payable against the presentation of draft drawn on the Opening
Bank and the shipping documents specified in Clause 11 hereof. The Letter
of Credit shall be valid until the 15th day after shipment.

11. *Documents:*

(1) The Sellers shall present the following documents to the paying bank
for negotiation:

(a) One full set of Clean "On Board" ocean Bills of Lading marked
"FREIGHT TO COLLECT" and made out to order, blank endorsed, and
notifying the China National Foreign Trade Transportation Corporation at the port of destination.

(b) Five copies of Invoice, indicating contract number and shipping mark
(in case of more than one shipping mark, the invoice shall be issued
separately).

(c) Two copies of Packing List with indication of shipping weight, number
and date of corresponding invoice.

(d) Two copies of Certificate of Quality and Quantity issued by the
Manufacturers as specified in Item (1) of Clause 16.

(e) Certified copy of cable to the Buyers, advising shipment immediately
after the shipment has been made.

(2) The Sellers shall within 10 days after the shipment is effected, send
by airmail one copy each of the above-mentioned documents with the
exception of Item (e) of this Clause; one set to the Buyers and the other set
to the China National Foreign Trade Transportation Corporation at the port
of destination.

12. *Terms of Shipment:*

(1) The Sellers shall, 30 days before the date of shipment stipulated in the
Contract, advise the Buyers by cable/letter of the Contract No., commodity,
quantity, value, number of package, gross weight and measurement and date
of readiness at the port of shipment for the Buyers to book shipping space.

(2) Booking of shipping space shall be attended to by the Buyers' Shipping
Agents Messrs. Sinofracht Chartering and Shipbroking Corporation, Peking.

(3) Sinofracht, Peking, or their Port Agents (or Liners' Agents) shall send
to the Sellers 10 days before the estimated date of arrival of the vessel at the
port of shipment, a preliminary notice indicating the name of vessel, estimated
date of loading, Contract No. for the Sellers to arrange shipment. The Sellers
are requested to get in close contact with the shipping agents. When it becomes
necessary to change the carrying vessel or in the event of her arrival having to

be advanced or delayed the Buyers or the Shipping Agency shall advise the Sellers in time. Should the vessel fail to arrive at the port of loading within 30 days after the arrival date advised by the Buyers, the Buyers shall bear the storage and insurance expenses incurred from the 31st day.

(4)   The Sellers shall be liable for any dead freight or demurrage, should it happen that they have failed to have the commodity ready for loading after the carrying vessel has arrived at the port of shipment on time.

(5)   The Sellers shall bear all expenses and risks of the commodity before it passes over the vessel's rail and is released from the tackle. After it has passed over the vessel's rail and been released from the tackle, all expenses of the commodity shall be for the Buyers' account.

13.   *Shipping Advice:*

The Sellers, immediately upon the completion of the loading of the commodity, shall notify by cable the Buyers of the contract number, name of commodity, quantity, gross weight, invoiced value, name of carrying vessel and date of sailing. If any package of which the weight is above 9 metric tons, width over 3400 mm or height on both sides over 2350 mm the Sellers shall advise the Buyers of weight and measurement of each package. In case the Buyers fail to arrange insurance in time due to the Sellers not having cabled in time, all losses shall be borne by the Sellers.

14.   *Technical Documents:*

(1)   One complete set of the following technical documents written in English, shall be packed and despatched together with each consignment.

  (a) Foundation drawings.
  (b) Wiring instructions, diagrams of electrical connections and/or pneumatic hydraulic connections.
  (c) Manufacturing drawings of easily worn parts and instructions.
  (d) Spare parts catalogues.
  (e) Certificate of quality as stipulated in Item 1 of Clause 16.
  (f) Erection, operation, service and repair instruction books.

(2)   The Sellers shall in addition send to the Buyers by airmail the respective technical documents as stipulated in paragraphs a, b, c, d and f of Item 1 of this Clause within . . . months after the signing of this Contract.

15.   *Guarantee of Quality:*

The Sellers shall guarantee that the commodity is made of the best materials, with first class workmanship, brand new, unused and complies in all respects with the quality, specifications and performance as stipulated in this Contract. The Sellers shall guarantee that the goods, when correctly mounted and properly operated and maintained, shall give satisfactory performance for a period of . . . months counting from the date on which the commodity arrives at the port of destination.

16. Inspection:

(1) The Manufacturers shall before making delivery make a precise and comprehensive inspection of the goods as regards the quality, specification, performance, and quantity/weight, and issue certificates certifying that the goods are in conformity with the stipulations of this Contract. The certificate shall form an integral part of the documents to be presented to the paying bank for negotiation of payment but shall not be considered as final in respect of quality, specification, performance and quantity/weight. Particulars and results of the test carried out by the manufacturers, must be shown in a statement which has to be attached to the Quality Certificates.

(2) After arrival of the goods at the port of destination the Buyers shall apply to the China Commodity Inspection Bureau (hereinafter called the Bureau) for a preliminary inspection in respect of the quality, specifications and quantity/weight of the goods and a Survey Report shall be issued therefore. If any discrepancies are found by the Bureau regarding specifications or the quantity or both, except when the responsibilities lie with the insurance company or shipping company, the Buyers shall within . . . days after arrival of the goods at the port of destination, have the right to reject the goods or to claim against the Sellers.

(3) Should the quality and specifications of the goods be not in conformity with the contract, or should the goods prove defective within the guarantee period stipulated in Clause 15 for any reason, including latent defect or the use of unsuitable materials, the Buyers shall arrange for a survey to be carried out by the Bureau, and have the right to claim against the Sellers on the strength of the Survey Report.

17. Claims:

(1) In case that the Sellers are liable for the discrepancies and a claim is made by the Buyers within the time-limit of inspection and quality guarantee period as stipulated in Clause 15 and 16 of this Contract, the Sellers shall settle the claim upon the agreement of the Buyers in one or the combination of the following ways:

(a) Agree to the rejection of the goods and refund to the Buyers the value of the goods so rejected in the same currency as contracted herein, and to bear all direct losses and expenses in connection therewith including interest accrued, banking charges, freight, insurance premium, inspection charges, storage, stevedore charges and all other necessary expenses required for the custody and protection of the rejected goods.

(b) Devalue the goods according to the degree of inferiority, extent of damage and amount of losses suffered by the Buyers.

(c) Replace new parts which conform to the specifications, quality, and performance as stipulated in this Contract, and bear all the expenses and direct losses sustained by the Buyers. The Sellers shall, at the same time, guarantee the quality of replaced parts for a further period according to Clause 15 of this Contract.

(2) The claims mentioned above shall be regarded as being accepted if the Sellers fail to reply within 30 days after the Sellers receive the Buyers' claim.

18. *Force Majeure:*

The Sellers shall not be held responsible for the delay in shipment or non-delivery of the goods due to Force Majeure, which might occur during the process of manufacturing or in the course of loading or transit. The Sellers shall advise the Buyers immediately of the occurrence mentioned above and within fourteen days thereafter, the Sellers shall send by airmail to the Buyers for their acceptance a certificate of the accident issued by the competent Government Authorities where the accident occurs as evidence thereof. Under such circumstances the Sellers, however, are still under the obligation to take all necessary measures to hasten the delivery of the goods. In case the accident lasts for more than ten weeks the Buyers shall have the right to cancel the Contract.

19. *Late Delivery and Penalty:*

Should the Sellers fail to make delivery on time as stipulated in the Contract, with exception of Force Majeure causes specified in Clause 18 of this Contract, the Buyers shall agree to postpone the delivery on condition that the Sellers agree to pay a penalty which shall be deducted by the paying bank from the payment under negotiation. The penalty, however, shall not exceed 5% of the total value of the goods involved in the late delivery. The rate of penalty is charged at 0.5% for every seven days, odd days less than seven days should be counted as seven days. In case the Sellers fail to make delivery ten weeks later than the time of shipment stipulated in the Contract, the Buyers shall have the right to cancel the Contract and the Sellers, in spite of the cancellation, shall still pay the aforesaid penalty to the Buyers without delay.

20. *Arbitration:*

All disputes in connection with this Contract or the execution thereof shall be settled friendly through negotiations. In case no settlement can be reached, the case may then be submitted for arbitration to the Arbitration Committee of the China Committee for the Promotion of International Trade in accordance with the Provisional Rules of Procedures promulgated by the said Arbitration Committee. The Arbitration shall take place in Peking and the decision of the Arbitration Committee shall be final and binding upon both parties; neither party shall seek recourse to a law court or other authorities to appeal for revision of the decision. Arbitration fee shall be borne by the losing party.

21. *Supplementary Condition:*

This Contract is made in two original copies, one copy to be held by each Party in witness thereof.

The Buyers: The Sellers:

CONTRACT FORM FOR ITALIAN EXPORT

No.

Peking. Date:

This Contract is made by and between the CHINA NATIONAL MACHINERY IMPORT AND EXPORT CORPORATION at Erh-Li-kou, Hsi Chiao, Peking, China, (Cable Address: "MACHIMPEX" PEKING) hereinafter called the Buyers and the   , hereinafter called the Sellers; whereby the Buyers agree to buy and the Sellers agree to sell the commodities on the terms and conditions stipulated below:

1. *Commodity, Specifications, Quantity and Unit Price:*
[description of goods sold and price]

2. *Total Value:* FOB Trieste.

3. *Country of Origin and Manufacturers:* Italy.

4. *Packing:*
To be packed in strong wooden case(s) or in carton(s), suitable for long distance ocean freight transportation and to change of climate, well protected against moisture and shocks.

One full set of service instructions for each instrument shall be enclosed in the case(s).

The Sellers shall be liable for any damage of the commodity and expenses incident thereto on account of improper packing and for any rust attributable to inadequate or improper protective measures taken by the Sellers in regard to the packing.

5. *Shipping Mark:*
The Sellers shall mark on each package with fadeless paint the package number, gross weight, net weight, measurement and the wordings: "KEEP AWAY FROM MOISTURE," "HANDLE WITH CARE," "THIS SIDE UP," etc., and the shipping mark:

6. *Time of Shipment:*

7. *Port of Shipment:* Trieste Italy.

8. *Port of Destination:* Durres Albania.

9. *Insurance:* To be covered by the Buyers after shipment.

10. *Payment :* for/by L/C

(1) In case by L/C: The Buyers, upon receipt from the Sellers of the delivery advice specified in Article 12 hereof, shall, 15–20 days prior to the date of delivery, open an irrevocable Letter of Credit with the Bank of China, Peking, in favour of the Sellers, for an amount equivalent to the total value of the shipment. The Credit shall be payable against the presentation of the draft drawn on the opening bank and the shipping documents specified in Article 11 hereof. The Letter of Credit shall be valid until the 15th day after the shipment is effected.

(2) In case by Collection: After delivery is made, the Sellers shall send the following documents, from the Sellers' Bank through Bank of China, to the Buyers for collection.

(3) In case by M/T or T/T: Payment to be effected within seven days after receipt of the shipping documents specified under Article 11 of this contract.

11. *Documents :*

The Sellers shall present to the paying bank the following documents for negotiation:

(1) In case by sea: 3 Negotiable copies of clean on board ocean Bill of Lading marked "FREIGHT TO COLLECT," made out to order, blank endorsed, and notifying the "MAKINAIMPORT" at Tirana, Albania.

In case by air freight: One copy of Airway Bill marked "FREIGHT PREPAID" and consigned to the Buyers.

In case by post: One copy of Parcel Post Receipt addressed to the Buyers.

(2) 5 copies of Invoice with the insertion of Contract No. and the Shipping Mark (in case of more than one shipping mark, the invoice shall be issued separately).

(3) 2 copies of Packing List issued by the Manufacturers.

(4) 1 copy of Certificate of Quantity and Quality issued by the Manufacturers.

(5) Certified copy of cable/letter to the Buyers, advising shipment immediately after shipment is made.

(6) The Sellers shall, within 10 days after the shipment is effected, send by air-mail one copy each of the above-mentioned documents (except Item 5)— One set to the Buyers and the other set to the China National Foreign Trade Transportation Corporation at the port of destination.

The Buyers: The Sellers:

China National Machinery Import
and Export Corporation

12. *Terms of Shipment:*

(1) In case of FOB Terms.

(a) The Sellers shall, 30 days before the date of shipment stipulated in the Contract, advise the Buyers by cable/letter the Contract No., commodity, quantity, value, number of package, gross weight and date of readiness at the port of shipment for the Buyers to book shipping space.

(b) Booking of shipping space shall be attended to by the Buyers' Shipping Agents Messrs. China National Chartering Corporation, Peking, China. (Cable address: Zhongzu Peking)

(c) China National Chartering Corporation, Peking, China, or their Port Agents (or Liners' Agents) shall send to the Sellers 10 days before the estimated date of arrival of the vessel at the port of shipment, a preliminary notice indicating the name of vessel, estimated date of loading, and Contract No. for the Sellers to arrange shipment. The Sellers are requested to get in close contract with the shipping agents. When it becomes necessary to change the carrying vessel or in the event of her arrival having to be advanced or delayed the Buyers or the Shipping Agency shall advise the Sellers in time.

Should the vessel fail to arrive at the port of loading within 30 days after the arrival date advised by the Buyers, the Buyers shall bear the storage and insurance expenses incurred from the 31st day.

(d) The Sellers shall be liable for any dead freight or demurrage, should it happen that they have failed to have the commodity ready for loading after the carrying vessel has arrived at the port of shipment on time.

(e) The Sellers shall bear all expenses, risks, of the commodity before it passes over the vessel's rail and is released from the tackle. After it has passed over the vessel's rail and been released from the tackle, all expenses of the commodity shall be for the Buyers' account.

(2) In case of C & F Terms:

(a) The Sellers shall ship the goods within the shipment time from the port of shipment to the port of destination. Transshipment is not allowed. The carrying vessel shall not fly the flag of the USA nor shall her captain be USA nationality nor shall she call en route at any port of the USA or in the vicinity of Taiwan.

(b) In case the goods are to be despatched by parcel post/air-freight, the Sellers shall, 30 days before the time of delivery as stipulated in Article 6, inform the Buyers by cable/letter the estimated date of delivery, Contract No., commodity, invoiced value, etc. The sellers shall, immediately after despatch of the goods, advise the Buyers by cable/letter the Contract No., commodity, invoiced value and date of despatch for the Buyers to arrange insurance in time.

13. *Shipping Advice:*

The Sellers shall, immediately upon the completion of the loading of the goods, advise by cable/letter the Buyers of the Contract No., commodity, quantity, invoiced value, gross weight, name of vessel and date of sailing, etc. In case the Buyers fail to arrange insurance in time due to the Sellers not having cabled in time, all losses shall be borne by the Sellers.

14. *Guarantee of Quality:*

The Sellers guarantee that the commodity hereof is made of the best materials with first class workmanship, brand new and unused, and complies in all respects with the quality and specification stipulated in this Contract. The guarantee period shall be 12 months counting from the date on which the commodity arrives at the port of destination.

15. *Claims:*

Within 90 days after the arrival of the goods at destination should the quality, specification, or quantity be found not in conformity with the stipulations of the Contract except those claims for which the insurance company or the owners of the vessel are liable, the Buyers shall, on the strength of the Inspection Certificate issued by the China Commodity Inspection Bureau, have the right to claim for replacement with new goods, or for compensation, and all the expenses (such as inspection charges, freight for returning the goods and for sending the replacement, insurance premium, storage and loading and unloading charges, etc.) shall be borne by the Sellers. As regards quality, the Sellers shall guarantee that if, within 12 months from the date of arrival of the goods at destination, damages occur in the course of operation by reason of inferior quality, bad workmanship and the use of inferior materials, the Buyers shall immediately notify the Sellers in writing and put forward a claim supported by Inspection Certificate issued by China Commodity Inspection Bureau.

The Certificate so issued shall be accepted as the base of a claim. The Sellers, in accordance with the Buyers' claim shall be responsible for the immediate elimination of the defect(s), complete or partial replacement of the commodity or shall devaluate the commodity according to the state of defect(s). Where necessary, the Buyers shall be at liberty to eliminate the defect(s) themselves at the Sellers' expenses. If the Sellers fail to answer the Buyers within one month after receipt of the claim aforesaid the claim shall be reckoned as having been accepted by the Sellers.

16. *Force Majeure:*

The Sellers shall not be held responsible for the delay in shipment or non-delivery of the goods due to Force Majeure, which might occur during the process of manufacturing or in the course of loading or transit. The Sellers shall advise the Buyers immediately of the occurrence mentioned above and within fourteen days thereafter, the Sellers shall send by airmail to the Buyers for their acceptance a certificate of the accident issued by the Competent Government Authorities where the accident occurs as evidence thereof.

Under such circumstances the Sellers, however, are still under the obligation to take all necessary measures to hasten the delivery of the goods. In case the accident lasts for more than 10 weeks, the Buyers shall have the right to cancel the Contract.

17. *Late Delivery and Penalty:*

Should the Sellers fail to make delivery on time as stipulated in the Contract, with exception of Force Majeure causes specified in Clause 16 of this Contract, the Buyers shall agree to postpone the delivery on condition that the Sellers agree to pay a penalty which shall be deducted by the paying bank from the payment under negotiation. The penalty, however, shall not exceed 5% of the total value of the goods involved in the late delivery. The rate of penalty is charged at 0.5% for every seven days, odd days less than seven days should be counted as seven days. In case the Sellers fail to make delivery ten weeks later than the time of shipment stipulated in the Contract, the Buyers shall have the right to cancel the contract and the Sellers, in spite of the cancellation, shall still pay the aforesaid penalty to the Buyers without delay.

18. *Arbitration:*

All disputes in connection with this Contract or the execution thereof shall be settled friendly through negotiations. In case no settlement can be reached, the case may then be submitted for arbitration to the Arbitration Committee of the China Committee for the Promotion of International Trade in accordance with the Provisional Rules of Procedures promulgated by the said Arbitration Committee. The Arbitration shall take place in Peking and the decision of the Arbitration Committee shall be final and binding upon both parties; neither party shall seek recourse to a law court or other authorities to appeal for revision of the decision. Arbitration fee shall be borne by the losing party.

19. *Special Provisions:*

(1) Supplement to term 4 of this contact: Buyers should agree to the main body unpacked, but sellers should guarantee the safety during the sea transportation, preventing against rust, etc.

(2) 8 complete sets of following technical documents shall be sent by sellers (5 sets to be sent to C.N.M. I & E Corp., 3 sets to be sent with machine). Technical literatures: Parts lists, Service, Maintenance and Operating instruction, and other necessary documents and so on.

IN WITNESS THEREOF, this Contract is signed by both parties on the date as above-mentioned in two original copies; each party hold one copy.

MT CONTRACT FORM FOR JAPAN IMPORT

Contract No.: MT(72)
Contract Date:

This agreement, made at   ,   , this   day of   , 1972, by and between "Japanese Friendly Firm, Inc." (herein called Buyers) and (State Corporation) of the People's Republic of China (herein called Sellers) witnesseth:

Whereas both parties hereto desire to implement the provisions of the Sino-Japanese Memorandum Trade Agreement of 1972 in accordance with the joint communique signed at the conference of December 21, 1971, by the representatives of the Memorandum Trade Offices of China and Japan and in compliance with the three political principles governing the relations between China and Japan, the principle of inseparability of politics and economics, and the four conditions of Sino-Japanese trade enunciated by the Chinese Government.

Now, therefore, it is hereby mutually agreed, through amicable discussions by and between the parties hereto, as follows:

1. *Name of Commodity:*

2. *Quantity:*

3. *Specifications:*
   Tolerance of impurity: 2% maximum.

4. *Unit price:* (1)
   (2)

5. *Total amount:*

6. *Latest date of loading:*

7. *Packing:*
   Shipment shall be made in bulk, superimposed with a layer of said commodity contained in used and/or mended jute bags by way of cargo-weight, provided, however, that the volume of such cargo-weight shall not exceed 5% of the total volume of the shipment. The effective weight of the shipment shall include that of the jute bags.

8. *Port of loading :*

(1) In the case of F.O.B. terms, the Seller shall have the option of loading the cargo at any one of the ports named below:

Dairen, Ch'in Huang-tao, Hsin Kang, or Ch'ing-tao.

(2) In the case of C.I.F. terms, the Buyer shall have the option of taking delivery of the shipment at two ports out of the following six ports of Japan: Tokyo, Yokohama, Nagoya, Osaka, Kobe or Moji.

9. *Payment Terms :*

In accordance with the provisions of this agreement, the Buyer shall open, through a bank acceptable to both parties hereto twenty-five (25) days prior to the scheduled date of shipment, an irrevocable, assignable, divisible, and pound sterling denominated commercial letter of credit in favor of China National Cereals, Oils and Foodstuffs Import and Export Corporation, or its branches in an amount corresponding to the value of each monthly shipment as prescribed in this agreement which will be available at sight in London [for the full amount against usual shipping documents]. Said letter of credit shall be valid for fifteen (15) days after shipment. The number of letters of credit [to be established under this agreement] shall bear the symbol "MT-(72)-." And the Seller shall have the option of increasing or decreasing the quantity or value of the shipment specified in the letter of credit by a margin of five (5) per cent as the case may be.

10. *Shipping documents :*

The Seller shall submit the following documents to the bank of payment:

(1) commercial invoice, original and two copies

(2) clean bill of lading, three copies of the original and four copies

(3) inspection certificate relative to the quality and quantity of the export commodity shipped, one original and two copies

(4) in the case of C.I.F. terms, the insurance policy, one original and two copies

11. *Inspection of Commodity :*

(1) Inspection of the quality and quantity of the commodities to be shipped under this agreement shall be conducted by the Chinese Commodity Inspection Bureau at ports of loading, and the inspection certificate issued by this Bureau shall be acceptable as a basis for payment. (Inspection fees shall be borne by the Seller.)

(2) When the cargo arrives at the port of discharge, the Buyer shall commission a Japanese commodity inspection agency to reinspect the cargo (inspection fees thus incurred borne by the Buyer). In case the findings of the

inspection at the port of discharge are at variance with the quality or quantity specified in the agreement, the Buyer shall have the right to demand [from the Seller] compensation for the damages thus found within thirty (30) days after the arrival of the shipment at the port of discharge, provided, however, that in case such damages were caused by Force Majeure or other causes attributable to the insurance company or the shipping firm, the Seller shall not be liable for such damages.

12. *Shipping Terms:*

(A) In the case of F.O.B. terms: Chartering of a vessel or vessels by the Buyer [for the purpose of shipping the commodities under this agreement] shall be subject to the consent of the Seller. In case the Buyer charters a Japanese vessel, the vessel must observe the maritime regulations of the Government of the People's Republic of China governing the navigation of vessels in Chinese territorial water. The Buyer shall advise the Seller by cable, two weeks prior to the estimated date of arrival of the vessel which the Buyer plans to charter under this agreement, of her name, nationality and the estimated date of her arrival and shall obtain the consent of the Seller before finalizing the charterage of the vessel. Warehouse charges and other related expenses incurred on account of delayed arrival of the vessel beyond scheduled date of arrival shall be borne by the Buyer. Loading time shall be computed at a rate of 260 metric tons per fair working day per hatch. The method of computation and payment of demurrage or bonus for accelerated loading shall be based on the Temporary Law concerning the Computation of Demurrage and Bonus for Accelerated Loading/Discharging of Foreign Vessels at Chinese Ports promulgated on January 1, 1962, by the Ministry of Transport of the People's Republic of China. And any demurrage or bonuses incurred thereunder shall be payable in pounds sterling.

(B) In the case of C.I.F. terms:

(1) With the exception of tankers, chartering of ordinary cargo vessels shall be undertaken by the Seller. Upon receipt of a notice of arrival of the vessel from her master or from her shore agent, the Buyer shall forthwith commence unloading of the cargo.

Discharge of cargo shall be conducted at the standard rate of discharge stipulated in the charter party which the Seller concluded with the shipowner. In case the discharge was actually carried out at a rate higher or lower than that specified in said charter party, a demurrage or bonus for accelerated discharge shall be computed in accordance with the rate of demurrage or bonus for accelerated discharge stipulated in the charter party. And the demurrage or bonus for accelerated discharge shall be paid in pounds sterling directly to the Buyer or the Seller as the case may be.

In the case of shipments on C.I.F. terms, cargoes shall be discharged at two ports. In case cargoes should be discharged at more than two ports at the request of the Buyer, the extra expenses incurred in connection with calling at and discharging the cargoes at the third and additional ports shall be borne by the Buyer. (These expenses shall be computed in accordance with the relevant clauses of the charter party concluded between the Seller and the shipowner.)

(2)   The Buyer shall advise the Seller by cable of the ports of discharge two weeks prior to the estimated date of arrival of the vessel at the port of loading.

(3)   The Seller shall advise the Buyer by cable, within forty-eight (48) hours after the shipment of the cargo, of the contract number, name of the commodity, its quantity, the amount of invoice, name of the vessel, and the name of the ship's agent at the port of call.

(4)   The Seller shall have the option of increasing the monthly quantity of shipment by a volume equivalent to five (5) per cent, and the price of the extra quantity thus increased shall be computed and settled in accordance with the contract price of the commodity.

13.   *Insurance :*

(1)   In the case of F.O.B. shipments, the cargo shall be insured by the Buyer, and all risks involved after the cargo is moved inside the ship's side-railing shall be for the account of the Buyer.

(2)   In the case of C.I.F. shipments, the Seller shall insure the cargo for 110 per cent of its invoiced value covering war risk and all other risks. In case the Buyer wishes to protect the cargo with additional insurance coverage or increase the amount of the insurance, he shall notify the Seller of such additional coverage or increase. The premium on the increased insurance amount consented to by the Seller shall be for the account of the Buyer.

14.   *Arbitration :*

Any and all disputes arising in the course of performance of, or in connection with, this contract shall be resolved through mutual discussion between the parties hereto. In case a dispute proves not amenable to resolution through mutual discussion, such a dispute may be referred to arbitration to be held in the country of defendant. In case an arbitration hearing is to be held in Japan, such a hearing shall be held by the Japanese International Commercial Arbitration Association in accordance with the arbitration procedure of the Association. Appointment of the arbitrators shall not necessarily be restricted to those contained in the list of arbitrators of the Association. They shall be appointed from among nationals of the People's Republic of China, Japan, and those of third countries who are acceptable and consented to by both parties hereto.

In China, the arbitration hearing shall be conducted by the Foreign Trade Arbitration Committee of the China Committee for the Promotion of International Trade in accordance with the arbitration procedure of the same Committee.

Awards handed down by said Association or by said Committee shall be final and binding on both parties hereto. Expenses incurred in connection with such arbitration hearings, other than those specified by the Arbitration Association or the Arbitration Committee, shall be borne by the losing party. Each of the parties hereto shall, with the consent of its government, give every facility to the personnel of the other party to facilitate the execution of their work connected with arbitration and their travel. It shall further guarantee the personal safety of the arbitration-related personnel of the other party.

15. *Force Majeure:*

In case the Seller is prevented from delivering the goods, in part or in whole, according to the delivery schedule for causes beyond its control, the Seller shall be permitted to postpone the delivery of the goods in part or in whole or to cancel the agreement in its entirety: provided, however, that the Seller shall submit to the Buyer a statement issued by the China Committee for the Promotion of International Trade at testing to the circumstances under which the accident had occurred.

16. *Penalty:*

In case the Seller is prevented from performing its obligations, in part or in whole, arising under this agreement on account of the failure of the Buyer to open the stipulated letter or letters of credit as prescribed in this agreement or to dispatch a vessel or vessels within the time limits of shipment or on account of any other violation or non-performance of this agreement by the Buyer, the latter shall be liable for the damages thus sustained by the Seller. The amount of compensation shall be three (3) per cent of the total amount of this agreement or of such part of the agreement which [the Buyer] failed to perform. In case the Seller failed to deliver the goods in part or in whole [for reasons ascribable to it] other than those beyond its control, the Seller shall be liable for the demages caused to the Buyer thereby. The amount of compensation shall be three (3) per cent of the total amount of this agreement or of such part of the agreement which the Seller failed to perform.

17. This agreement shall be performed by trading firms recommended by the Buyer and approved by the Seller, and quotas for each of these trading firms under this agreement shall be recommended by the Buyer and established by the approval of the Seller.

The quotas for each of the trading firms shall be allocated in accordance with the Schedule appended hereto. And the Schedule shall constitute an integral part of this agreement.

18. In witness whereof, this agreement shall be prepared in the Japanese and the Chinese languages and executed in duplicate on this   day of   , 1972, and one copy to be retained by each of the parties hereto. The agreement, prepared in both languages, shall have the same force.

Seller: Buyer:
Representative: Representative:
Address: Address:
Telephone No.:   Telephone No.:

SINO-JAPANESE FRIENDLY FIRM TRADE AGREEMENT
(FRIENDLY IMPORT TO JAPAN)*

Contract No.:

Contract Date:

This agreement, made at Peking, this   day of   , 197 , by
and between the China National Cereals, Oils and Foodstuffs Import and
Export Corporation (herein called the Seller), and (Friendly Firm K.K.),
(herein called the Buyer), witnesseth:

Whereas the parties hereto are desirous to promote the friendly relations
and economic exchanges between the peoples of Japan and the People's
Republic of China on the basis of the three political principles governing the
relations between China and Japan, the principle of inseparability of politics
and economics all governing Sino-Japanese relations, and of the four
conditions of Sino-Japanese trade proposed by the Government of the People's
Republic of China, and following amicable negotiations, the parties hereto
have mutually agreed as follows:

ARTICLE 1.   1.1   Matters relating to the merchandise covered by this
agreement, its name, quantity, specifications, unit price, total amount,
packing, dates of shipment, port of loading, etc. shall be governed by the
provisions contained in the exhibit(s) appended to this agreement. And the
said exhibit(s) shall constitute an integral part of this agreement.

ARTICLE 2.   2.1   Terms of Payment: The Buyer shall establish, twenty-
five (25) days prior to the first day of the month in which the shipment is to
be effected under this agreement, through a bank agreed to by both parties
hereto, an irrevocable, assignable and divisible letter of credit which will be
available at sight in London [for the full amount] in pounds sterling by telegraphic transfer. The validity of the letter of credit shall be extended fifteen
(15) days after loading and be terminated in China.

2.2   [The Buyer] agrees that the quantity and price of the cargo entered
into the letter of credit may be either increased or decreased by five (5) per cent
at the option of the Seller. The beneficiary of the letter of credit shall be those
stipulated in [said] exhibit(s).

ARTICLE 3.   3.1   In the case of an agreement based on F.O.B. terms, and
in case the Buyer charters a Japanese vessel, the vessel shall observe the

NOTE: From *Nitchu boeki hikkei,* p. 64.

Regulations of Navigation in Chinese Territorial Water applicable to Japanese vessels as prescribed by the Government of the People's Republic of China.

3.2   The Buyer shall, two weeks prior to the vessel's arrival at the port of loading during the loading period stipulated in this agreement, notify the Seller by cable of the name of the vessel, her nationality and the scheduled date of arrival and after obtaining the consent of the Seller, the matter shall be finalized. In case the vessel dispatched by the Buyer fails to arrive at the port of loading on schedule, the extra warehouse charges and the fees for waiting time, etc. (incurred on account of the vessel's delay) shall all be borne by the Buyer.

3.3   In the case of an agreement based on C.I.F. or C & F terms, where the Seller is to arrange a carrying vessel, if the Buyer fails to open a letter of credit covering such a shipment as prescribed by this agreement, the Seller may at its discretion refuse to load the cargo altogether or postpone the shipping period to the extent the opening of the letter of credit has been delayed. All expenses and losses incurred on account of such delay or failure shall be borne by the Buyer.

ARTICLE 4.   4.1   Terms of Shipment:

(1)   The Seller shall notify the Buyer by cable of the contract number, the name of the cargo, its quantity, invoice amount and the name of the carrying vessel, within forty-eight (48) hours after the completion of loading of the export cargo.

(2)   The Seller shall have the right to increase or decrease the quantity of each shipment by a quantity equivalent to five (5) per cent of the contract quantity. And the difference between the quantity covered by the letter of credit and that which was actually shipped shall be settled on the basis of the contract price.

ARTICLE 5.   5.1   In the case of an agreement based on C.I.F. terms, the Seller shall insure each of its shipments at 110 per cent of the gross invoice value covering "with average" and war risk. In case the Buyer wishes to increase the kinds of coverage or the amount of said insurance, he shall notify the Seller to that effect and bear the amount of premium increased thereby.

ARTICLE 6.   6.1   Documents: The Seller shall submit to the bank the following documents: one original and two duplicate copies of the invoice, three original copies and four duplicate copies of clean bills of lading, and one original and two duplicate copies of the inspection certificate of export merchandise as to its quality and weight. And in the case of agreed C.I.F. terms, the Seller shall submit one original and two duplicate copies of the insurance policy. [In addition to the above specified documents.]

ARTICLE 7.   7.1   Inspection: With respect to the inspection of the quality and weight of the merchandise shipped under this agreement, a quality and weight inspection certificate issued by the Chinese Commodity Inspection Bureau stationed at the port of loading shall constitute proof of delivery of the cargo. However, the Buyer shall have the right of reinspecting the cargo at the port of destination after its arrival. In this case, the expenses incurred in connection with such reinspection shall be borne by the Buyer.

ARTICLE 8.   8.1   Claims and Damages: In case the Buyer has any complaint regarding the quality or weight of the cargo after it has arrived at the port of destination, the Buyer may file with the Seller, within thirty (30) days after the arrival of the vessel at a Japanese port, a complaint substantiated by an inspection report issued by a Japanese commodity inspection agency (the inspection fees to be borne by the Buyer) (in the case of frozen foods or perishable goods, reinspection must be conducted within three (3) days after the cargo has been unloaded at the port of destination). Provided, however, that the Seller shall not be held liable for damages caused by Force Majeure or for reasons ascribable to the insurance company or the shipowners.

ARTICLE 9.   9.1   In case the Seller has been prevented from performing its contractual obligations arising under this agreement, in whole or in part, owing to the failure of the Buyer to establish letters of credit as prescribed in this agreement or to his failure to dispatch vessels as prescribed in the case of an F.O.B. agreement, and the Seller sustains damages on account thereof, the Buyer shall be liable for such damages. And the amount of compensation payable by the Buyer shall be three (3) per cent of the total amount of the contract or of such part of the contract which the Seller has been prevented from performing, as the case may be.

9.2   In case the Seller has failed to deliver the cargo in whole or in part as prescribed in this agreement, the Seller shall, except in the cases of Force Majeure, compensate the Buyer for the damages caused thereby. And the amount of compensation payable by the Seller shall be three (3) per cent of the total amount of the contract or of such part of the contract which the Seller failed to deliver, as the case may be.

ARTICLE 10.   10.1   Force Majeure: In case the Seller is unable to deliver the goods according to the schedule for reasons which are beyond his control, the Seller may postpone the delivery of the goods in whole or in part or cancel the agreement in its entirety: provided, however, that the Seller must hand over to the Buyer a document issued by the China Committee for the Promotion of International Trade attesting to the existence of circumstances in which [alleged] accidents have taken place.

ARTICLE 11.   11.1   Arbitration: Any and all disputes arising in the course of performance of this agreement or in connection therewith shall be resolved through mutual discussions between the parties hereto. In case the parties hereto fail to reach a resolution through mutual discussions, such disputes shall be referred to arbitration.

11.2   Arbitration hearings shall be held in the country of the defendant's residence. In case the country of the defendant's residence is China, the Foreign Trade Arbitration Committee of the China Committee for the Promotion of International Trade shall conduct hearings in accordance with the Committee's procedural rules for arbitration.

In case the country of the defendant's residence is Japan, the Japanese International Commercial Arbitration Association shall conduct the arbitration hearing in accordance with its procedural rules for arbitration.

11.3   Appointment of arbitrators shall not necessarily be confined to those contained in the list of arbitrators of the Japanese International Commercial Arbitration Association. However, they shall be chosen from among the citizens of the People's Republic of China and those of Japan or from among citizens of third countries to whom both parties hereto have agreed.

11.4   An award given by the Arbitration Court referred to in the preceding paragraphs shall be final and binding on both parties hereto.

11.5   In order to facilitate the execution of matters relating to the arbitration by the other party, the host party shall, after having obtained the consent of his government, offer all facilities and convenience for the travel of the other party's personnel and guarantee their personal safety.

11.6   Unless otherwise stipulated by the Arbitration Committee or Association, arbitration expenses and fees shall be borne by the losing party.

IN WITNESS WHEREOF, each of the parties hereto has caused this agreement in the Chinese original to be executed in duplicate by its duly authorized representatives on this   th day of   of 197   , one of which shall be retained by each of the parties hereto.

Seller: Buyer:
Cable Address: Cable Address:

Exhibit No.   of Contract No.

                                                            Date:

1. Name of the Merchandise

2. Specifications

3. Quantity

4. Unit Price

5. Total Amount

6. Packing

7. Port of Loading

8. Port of Destination

9. Period of Shipment: from   to

10. Mark: (to be decided by the Seller)

11. Beneficiary of Letters of Credit:

       Branch

       China National Cereals, Oils and Foodstuffs Import and Export Corporation

12. Remarks:

Seller:_____   Buyer:_____

_____   _____
         (signature)   (signature)

PURCHASE CONTRACT
CHINA NATIONAL CHEMICALS IMPORT & EXPORT CORPORATION

Contract No.

Peking, May 14, 1969.

The Buyers, CHINA NATIONAL CHEMICALS IMPORT & EXPORT CORPORATION, Erh Li Kou, Peking, Cable Address: SINOCHEM PEKING

The Sellers,

Cable:

This Contract is made by and between the Buyers and the Sellers; whereby the Buyers and the Sellers agree to sell the under-mentioned goods subject to the terms and conditions as stipulated hereinafter:

1. *Name of Commodity and Specification:*

PURE BENZENE

(Details of the chemical composition)

2. *Quantity:*

3. *Unit Price:*

4. *Total Value:*

5. *Packing:* In bulk.

6. *Country of Origin & Manufacturer:* Italian origin.

7. *Terms of Payment:*

After conclusion of business the Buyers shall open with the Bank of China, Peking, an irrevocable letter of credit in favour of the Sellers payable at the issuing Bank against presentation of the shipping documents as stipulated under Clause 3 (A) of the Terms of Delivery of this Contract after departure of the carrying vessel. This said letter of credit shall remain in force till the 15th day after shipment.

8. *Insurance:* To be covered by the Buyers.

9. *Time of Shipment:* In one lot only.

10. *Port of Loading:* Venice.

11. *Port of Destination:* Dairen.

12. *Shipping Mark(s) :*

On each package shall be labelled conspicuously port of destination, package number, gross and net weights, measurements and the shipping mark shown on the right side. (For dangerous and or poisonous cargo, the nature and the generally adopted symbol shall be marked conspicuously on each package.)

13. *Other Terms :*

a) Other matters relating to this Contract shall be dealt with in accordance with the Terms of Delivery as specified overleaf, which shall form an integral part of this Contract; b) This Contract is made out in Chinese and English, both versions being equally authentic.

14. *Supplementary Condition(s) :*

(Should any other clause in this Contract be in conflict with the following Supplementary Condition(s), the Supplementary Condition(s) should be taken as final and binding.):

as per Attached List

The Sellers   The Buyers

Terms of Delivery

1. *Terms of Shipment :*

For C & F Terms: The Sellers shall ship the goods by a direct vessel sailing from the port of loading to China Port within the time as stipulated in Clause (9) of this Contract. Transhipment en route is not allowed without the Buyers' consent.

The contracted goods shall not be carried by a vessel flying the flag of the United States of America. The carrying vessel shall not call or stop over at the port/ports of the United States of America and shall not call or stop over at the port/ports of Taiwan and/or the port/ports in the vicinities of Taiwan prior to her arrival at the port of destination as stipulated in the Clause (11) of this Contract.

For FOB Terms: The shipping space for the contracted goods shall be booked by the Buyers or the Buyers' shipping agent, China National Chartering Corporation (Address: Erh Li Kou, Peking. Cable Address: ZHONGZU PEKING). The Sellers shall undertake to load the contracted goods on board the vessel nominated by the Buyers on any date notified by the Buyers, within the time of shipment stipulated in the Clause (9) of this Contract. 15 days prior to the date of shipment, the Buyers shall inform the sellers by cable of the contract number, name of vessel, date of loading, quantity and the name of shipping agent, so as to enable the latter to contact the shipping agent direct and arrange the shipment of the goods. Should it become necessary for the Buyers to replace the named vessel with another one, or should the named vessel arrive at the port of shipment earlier or later than the date of arrival as previously notified to the Sellers, the Buyers or their shipping agent shall advise the Sellers to this effect in due time. Should the Sellers fail to load the goods within the time notified by the Buyers or board the vessel booked by the Buyers after its arrival at the port of shipment, all dead freight, demurrage, etc., shall be borne by the Sellers. Should the arrival of the carrying vessel booked by the Buyers be incidentally delayed or for reasons of similar nature which would render the Sellers unable to load the goods on board the vessel at the time originally scheduled by the Buyers' shipping agents, the loss incurred by the Sellers in storage and insurance premium calculated from the 6th day after the expiry of the laydays shall be borne by the Buyers. Payments for charges or expenses to be effected by the Sellers to the Buyers or vice versa shall be made against formal invoices.

2. *Advice of Shipment:*

Immediately after completion of loading of goods on board the vessel the Sellers shall advise the Buyers by cable of the contract number, name of goods, quantity or weight loaded, invoice value, name of vessel, port of shipment, sailing date and port of destination.

Should the Buyers be made unable to arrange insurance in time being to the Sellers' failure to give the above mentioned advice of shipments by cable, the Sellers shall be responsible for any and all damaged and/or loss attributable to such failures.

3. *Shipping Documents:*

(A) The Sellers shall present the following documents to the paying bank for negotiation of payment:

(a) Full set of clean on board "freight prepaid" for C & F Terms or "freight to collect" for FOB Terms, ocean Bills of Lading made out to order and blank endorsed, notifying the Branch of China National Foreign Trade Transportation Corporation at the port of destination.

(b) Five copies of signed invoice, indicating contract number and shipping marks.

(c) Two copies of packing list and/or weight memo.

(d) One copy each of the certificates of quality and quantity of weight, as stipulated in the Clause 5 of the Terms of Delivery.

(e) One duplicate copy of the cable advice of shipment, as stipulated in the Clause 2 of the Terms of Delivery.

(B) The Sellers shall dispatch, in care of the carrying vessel, one copy each of the duplicates of Bill of Lading, Invoice and Packing List to the Buyers' receiving agent, the Branch of China National Foreign Trade Transportation Corporation at the port of destination.

(C) Immediately after the departure of the carrying vessel, the Sellers shall airmail one set of the duplicate documents to the Buyers and two sets to the Branch of China National Foreign Trade Transportation Corporation at the port of destination.

4. *Dangerous Cargo Instruction Leaflets:*

For dangerous and/or poisonous cargo, the Sellers must provide instruction leaflets stating the hazardous or poisonous properties, stowage, storage and handling remarks, as well as precautionary and first-aid measures and measures against fire. The Sellers shall airmail, together with other documents, three copies each of the same to the Buyers and the Branch of China National Foreign Trade Transportation Corporation at the port of destination.

5. *Inspection:*

It is mutually agreed that the certificate of quality and quantity or weight issued by the Manufacturer or public surveyors shall be part of the documents to be presented to the paying bank for negotiation of payment. However, the inspection of quality and quantity or weight shall be made in accordance with the following:

(A) For General Cargo: In case the quality, quantity or weight of the goods be found not in conformity with those stipulated in this Contract after re-inspection by the China Commodity Inspection Bureau within 60 days after arrival of the goods at the port of destination, the Buyers shall reject the goods delivered and/or lodge claims against the Sellers for compensation of losses, with the exception of those claims for which the insurer or owners of the carrying vessel are liable. In such case, the Buyers shall send samples of the goods in question to the Sellers along with the Survey Report, if sampling is feasible.

(B) For Pharmaceuticals: Pharmaceuticals are imported into China subject to laws and regulations of the People's Republic of China. Disqualified pharmaceuticals are prohibited to be imported. It is mutually agreed that for the quality of the contracted goods in this category, the Survey Report issued by the China Commodity Inspection Bureau after inspecting the goods within 60 days from the date of arrival at the port of destination shall be taken as final and binding upon both Parties. The Sellers shall take back all the disqualified goods and compensate the Buyers for the value of the goods plus all losses sustained due to rejection of the cargo, such as freight charges, storage, insurance premium, interest, inspection charges, etc.

Should the quantity weight be found not in conformity with those stipulated in this Contract after inspection by the China Commodity Inspection Bureau, the Buyers shall have the right to claim against the Sellers for compensation of losses within 60 days after the arrival of the goods at the port of destination on the bases of the Survey Report issued by the said Bureau.

6. *Force Majeure:*

The sellers shall not be held responsible for late delivery or non-delivery of the goods owing to generally recognized "Force Majeure" clauses. However, in such case, the Sellers shall immediately cable the Buyers the accident and airmail to the Buyers within 15 days after the accident, a certificate of the accident issued by the competent government authorities or the chamber of commerce which is located at the place where the accident occurred as evidence thereof. With the exception of late delivery or nondelivery due to "Force Majeure" except, in case in Sellers fail to make delivery within the time as stipulated in the Contract. If the "Force Majeure" cause lasts over 60 days, the Buyers shall have the right to cancel the Contact or the undelivered part of the Contract.

7. *Arbitration:*

All disputes in connection with the Contract or the exception thereof shall be amicably settled through negotiation. In case no settlement can be reached between the two Parties, the case under disputes shall be presented to the Foreign Trade Arbitration Committee of the China Committee for the Promotion of International Trade for arbitration. The arbitration shall take place in Peking, China, and shall be executed in accordance with the Provisional Rules of Procedure of the said Committee and the decision made by the Arbitration Committee shall be accepted as final and binding upon both Parties. The fees for arbitration shall be borne by the losing Party unless otherwise awarded.

PURCHASE CONTRACT

An AGREEMENT is made this   Day of
between Messrs.

(hereinafter called the Sellers) and Messrs. CHINA RESOURCES COMPANY, Bank of China Building, Hong Kong, Cable Address: CIRIMP HONGKONG (hereinafter called the Buyers) WHEREBY IT IS AGREED that the Sellers undertake to sell and the Buyers undertake to buy the undernoted goods on terms and conditions stipulated herebelow:

Description of Goods:

    One set

Total Price:

Manufacturers:

Time of Shipment:

    To be made from U.K. Port not later than the end of March, 1972.

Payment: To be made to the Sellers 30 days after receipt of the goods.

Insurance: All risks including war risk.

Documents:

    The Sellers shall send the Buyers 5 copies each of Invoice and Packing list and two copies of the insurance policy.

Seller's Guarantee:

The Sellers guarantee that the goods supplied are of genuine quality, freshly manufactured and brand new, up to standard in all respects and in good condition. In case of discrepancy with regard to quality, survey result made by the Chinese Commodity Inspection Bureau shall be accepted by both the Sellers and the Buyers as final.

Sellers   Buyers

DISTRIBUTORSHIP AGREEMENT
CHINESE COMMODITIES EXPORT FAIR
CHINA NATIONAL CHEMICALS IMPORT & EXPORT CORPORATION
TRADE DELEGATION, KWANGCHOW, CHINA

Date:

Kwangchow.

This Agreement is made by and entered into between China National Chemicals Import & Export Corporation, Shanghai Branch, Shanghai, China (hereinafter referred to as Party A) and (Italian Company) Party B, whereby Party A appoints Party B to act as their distributors for the under mentioned commodity in the designated territory upon the terms and conditions hereafter set forth:

1. *Name of Commodity:*

(hereinafter referred to as specified commodity)

2. *Territory:*

The territory covered by this Agreement is confined to Italy only. Party A agree not to sell any of the specified commodity to other firms or importers for the sales in the said territory. Party B shall handle with efficiency and diligence so as to secure the maximum volume of sales. Party B agree not to handle any of the specified commodity from any source other than China.

3. *Minimum Turnover:*

Party B undertakes to place with Party A orders amounting to a minimum quantity of each for Party B and of the specified commodity and shall try their best to reach the quantity during the period of one year of this Agreement. The amount of the order placed during the first six months of the Agreement should not be less than half of the minimum quantity as above mentioned.

4. *Price:*

Price should be fixed 15 days before each quarter of the year for the supply of the coming quarter through negotiation between Party A, and Party B. Party B should cooperate with USVICO and negotiate with them the prices for the sales in the market in order to avoid any competition.

5. *Payment:*

Upon confirmation of order, Party B shall open confirmed irrevocable letter of credit available at sight in the name of Party A as the beneficiary. The L/C shall reach Party A 30 days ahead of each shipment.

6. *Market Report:*

Party B undertakes to supply each quarter of the year to Party A a comprehensive market report of the specified commodity of this Agreement. Party B shall keep Party A duly advised of any information or events of urgent character.

7. *Validity of the Agreement:*

This Agreement is to remain valid for a period of one calendar year, commencing January 1, 1970, and terminating on December 31, 1970, and shall automatically become null and void at the expiration of the said period. If either Party considers it necessary to extend the Agreement, the proposing Party may take the initiative to conduct negotiation with the other Party and to so inform the other Party one month prior to its expiration.

8. In the event of the breach of any of the provisions of this Agreement by either Party, the other Party may at its option cancel this Agreement forthwith, by giving notice in writing to the defaulting Party of its intention to so cancel it.

Party A: Party B:
China National Chemicals Import
and Export Corporation
Shanghai Branch

SALES CONFIRMATION

Date:

Sellers: China National Native Produce & Animal By-Products
Imp. & Exp. Corp., Tientsin

Signed At: Kwangchow

Address: 66, Yen Tai Street, Tientsin   Cable Address: BYPRODUCT

Buyers:

Address: Cable Address:

The undersigned Sellers and Buyers have agreed to close the following transactions according to the terms and conditions stipulated below:

1. *Name of Commodity :* NORTH CHINA RAW GOATSKINS.

2. *Specifications :*   1st./2nd./3rd. Grade 20/70/10%, about 70% Black Mixed, average weight about 190 lbs. per 100 skins.

3. *Quantity :*   Skins.
with   % more or less both in amount and quantity allowed at the Sellers' option.

4. *Unit Price :*   At   RMB per skin CIF Genoa.

5. *Total Value :*   RENMINBI

6. *Packing :*   In bales.

7. *Time of Shipment :*   Per steamer during November/December, 1970.

8. *Loading Port & Destination :*
From Tientsin to Genoa, transhipment and partial shipments allowed.

9. *Insurance :*
To be effected by Sellers covering All Risks and War Risk for 110% of invoice value as per Ocean Marine Cargo Clauses of the People's Insurance Co. of China. (Excluding SRCC.)

10. *Terms of Payment :*
By Confirmed, Irrevocable, Transferable and Divisible Letter of Credit to be available by sight draft, to reach the Sellers before November 5th, 1970, and

to remain valid for negotiation In Tientsin until the 15th day after the aforesaid Time of Shipment.

11. *Shipping Mark:* Sellers' shipping mark.

12. Quality, quantity and weight certified by the China Commodity Inspection Bureau or the Sellers, as per the former's Inspection Certificate or the latter's certificate, are to be taken as final.

13. In case shipment is not effected within the time stipulated above, an automatic extension of 10 days is allowed both for the time of shipment and that of the expiration in the relative L/C.

The Sellers   The Buyers

The Brokers

Bill of Lading

The China Shipping Company
Bill of Lading
Direct or with Transhipment

Vessel: "Kosovo" Voy.   Port of Discharge: Napoli

Nationality: Port of Loading: Hsinkang

Shipper: China National Chemicals Imp. & Exp. Corp.

Consignee: Unto Order   or assigns

Notify:

Shipped on board the vessel named above in apparent good order and condition (unless otherwise indicated) the goods or packages specified herein and to be discharged at the above mentioned port of discharge or as near thereto as the vessel may safely get and be always afloat.

The weight, measure, marks, numbers, quality, contents and value, being particulars furnished by the Shipper, are not checked by the Carrier on loading.

The Shipper, Consignee and the Holder of this Bill of Lading hereby expressly accept and agree to all printed, written or stamped provisions, exceptions and conditions of this Bill of Lading, including those on the back hereof.

Particulars furnished by the Shipper

Marks and Numbers	No. of Packages	Description of Goods	Gross Weight	Measurement
NAPOLI	5,000 Bags	Paraffin FREIGHT PREPAID	kilos	

Total Packages (in words) SAY TOTAL BAGS ONLY

Freight and Charges:

In witness whereof, the Carrier or his Agents has signed TWO Bills of Lading all of this tenor and date, one of which being accomplished, the others to stand void.

Freight payable at Tientsin   Date   at Tientsin.

Shippers are requested to note
particularly the exceptions and conditions of this Bill of Lading with
reference to the validity of the insurance upon their goods.   For the Master.

CERTIFICATE OF QUALITY AND QUANTITY

Messrs.
China National Machinery
Import & Export Corporation
Peking—China

Milan,

Certificate of Quality and Quantity.
Re: Contract No.

Dear Sirs,

This is to certify that we have inspected and tested at our Works in Milano, the following machine:

[Description of machine]

and we confirm that the commodity is made of best material with first class workmanship, brand new, unused and complies in all respects with the quality specifications and performance as stipulated in contract.

We guarantee that the goods, when correctly mounted and properly maintained, shall give satisfactory performance for a period of 12 (twelve) months from the date of which the commodity arrives at the port of destination.

Always at your disposal, we remain,

Yours faithfully,

QUALITY CLAIM

China National Chemicals Import and Export Corporation

Codes Used	Er-Li-Kou, Hsi Chiao	Cable Address
Acme	Peking	"Sinochem"
Bentley's Ind		Peking

Your Ref.
Our Ref. 105/293T

August 4th, 1970.

Milano.

Quality claim on Pure benzene
Contract

Reference is made to 10,451.374 metric tons of pure benzene shipped per M/V Laoshan.

The tanker arrived at Dairen on June 11th, 1970, and upon discharge an inspection was carried out by the Dairen Commodity Inspection Bureau.

It was found that the quality of the goods does not conform to contract stipulation, for details please see the attached Inspection certificate No. 7245.

You are requested to put forward your opinion of compensating us for the loss so that we might pass it to our users for study.

At the same time please remit us the inspection fee RMB.8,573.69.

Looking forward to receiving your early reply.

China National Chemicals
Encl.   Import & Export Corp.

INSURANCE POLICY ON CARGO

The People's Insurance Company of China
Head Office Peking, China
Established 1949

Policy No.

Sum Insured

Rate as arranged

Premium as arranged

Claim, if any,
payable at

by

Whereas it has been proposed to THE PEOPLE'S INSURANCE COMPANY OF CHINA by, as well in their own name as for and in the name and names of all and every other person or persons to whom the subject matter of this policy does, may, or shall appertain in part or in all to make with the said Company the Insurance hereinafter mentioned and described. Now this policy witnesses that in consideration of the said person or persons effecting this Policy paying to the said Company the premium above mentioned the said Company takes upon itself the burden of such Insurance to the amount of

and promises and agrees with the Insured, their Executors, Administrators and Assigns in all respects truly to perform and fulfil the Contracts contained in this Policy. And it is hereby agreed and declared that the said Insurance shall be and is an Insurance (lost or not lost) upon

Marks and Numbers	Quantity	Property Insured	Valued at
Conveyance(s) sailing on or about:		Voyage: At and from to	

And the said Company promises and agrees that the Insurance aforesaid, unless otherwise stated, shall commence upon the said Goods and Merchandises from the time when the Goods and Merchandises shall be laden on board the said Ship or Vessel, Craft or Boat as above and continue until the said Goods and Merchandises be discharged and safely landed at as above. And that it shall be lawful for the said Ship or Vessel in the voyage so Insured as aforesaid to proceed and sail to and touch and stay at any Ports or Places whatsoever without prejudice to this Insurance. And touching the Adventures and Perils which the said Company is contented to bear and does take upon itself in the Voyage so insured as aforesaid: they are of the Seas, Fire, Jettisons, Barratry of the Master and Mariners and of all other like Perils, Losses, and Misfortunes that have or shall come to the Hurt, Detriment or Damage of the aforesaid subject matter of this Insurance or any part thereof. And in case of any Loss or Misfortune it shall be lawful to the Insured, their Factors, Servants and Assigns, to sue, labour and travel for, in and about the Defence, Safeguard and Recovery of the aforesaid subject matter of this Insurance, or any part hereby Insured. And it is expressly declared and agreed that the act of Insurer or Insured in Recovering, Saving, or Preserving the Property Insured shall not be considered as a waiver, or acceptance of abandonment.

IN WITNESS WHEREOF this Policy has been signed by the said Company at this   day of   in the year One thousand Nine hundred and,

Examined

The People's Insurance Company of China

The People's Insurance Company of China
Ocean Marine Cargo Clauses
(1/1/1972)

With a view to developing friendly trade dealings between China and the peoples of various countries in the world and according to the principle of equality and mutual benefit, this Company writes Ocean Marine cargo Insurance, the clauses being as follows:

1. *Scope of Cover*

This insurance is classified into three forms—Total Loss Only (T.L.O.), With Average (W.A.) and All Risks. Where the insured goods sustain loss or damage, this Company shall undertake to indemnify therefor according to the risks insured and the Provisions of these Clauses.

(1) Total Loss Only (T.L.O.)

This Company shall be liable for

(a) Total loss of the Insured goods caused in the course of transit by natural calamities—heavy weather, lightning, floating ice, seaquake, flood, etc. or by accidents—grounding, stranding, sinking, collision or derailment of the carrying conveyance, fire, explosion and falling of entire package or packages of the insured goods into sea during loading or discharge, etc.;

(b) Sacrifice in and contribution to General Average and Salvage Expenses arising from the foregoing events.

(2)   With Average (W.A.)

This Company shall be liable for

(a) Total or partial loss of the insured goods, caused in the course of transit by natural calamities—heavy weather, lightning, floating ice, seaquake, flood, etc. or by accidents—grounding, stranding, sinking, collision or derailment of the carrying conveyance, fire, explosion and falling of entire package or packages of the insured goods into sea during loading or discharge, etc.;

(b) Sacrifice in and contribution to General Average and Salvage Expenses arising from the foregoing events.

(3)   All Risks: In addition to the liability covered under the aforesaid Total Loss Only and With Average insurance, this Company shall also be liable for total or partial loss of the insured goods caused by shortage, shortage in weight, leakage, contact with other substance, breakage, hook, rainwater, rust, wetting, heating, mould, tainting by odour, contamination, etc. arising from external causes in the course of transit.

Goods may be insure on Total Loss Only or With Average or all Risks conditions and may also be insured against additional risks upon consultation.

2.   *Exclusions*

This Company shall not be liable for

(1)   Loss or damage caused by the intentional act or fault of the Insured:

(2)   Loss or damage falling under the liability of the Consignor or arising from normal losses of the insured goods:

(3)   Loss or damage caused by strikes of workers or delay in transit:

(4)   Risks covered and excluded in the Ocean Marine Cargo War Risk Clauses of this Company.

3.   *Commencement and Termination of Cover*

This insurance shall take effect from the time the insured goods leave the Consignor's warehouse at the place of shipment named in the Policy and shall continue in force in the ordinary course of transit including sea and land transit until the insured goods are delivered to the Consignee's warehouse at the destination named in the Policy. The Cover shall, however, be limited to sixty days upon discharge of the insured goods from the sea-going vessel at the final port of discharge.

4.   *Survey of Damage to Goods and Presentation of Claim*

(1)   The Insured shall take delivery of the insured goods in good time upon arrival thereof at the destination or port of destination named in the Policy and shall undertake to:

Apply immediately for survey to the surveying agent of the claims settling agent stipulated in the Policy should the insured goods be found to have sustained loss or damage. In case this Company has no surveying agent or claims settling agent locally, a local competent surveyor may be applied to for survey;

Obtain forthwith from the Carrier or relevant Authorities (Customs and Port Authorities, etc.) Certificate of Loss or Damage and/or Short-landed Memo and lodge a claim with the Carrier or the party concerned in writing should the insured goods be found short in entire package or packages or to show apparent traces of damage.

(2) The Insured shall submit the following documents when presenting a claim to this Company;

Original Policy or Certificate of Insurance, original or copy of Bill of Lading, Invoice, Packing List and Tally Sheet;

Certificate of Loss or Damage and/or Short-landed Memo, Survey Report and Statement of Claims.

When third party liability is involved, the letters and cables relative to pursuing of recovery to the from the third party and the other essential certificates or documents shall be submitted in addition.

(3) The time of validity of a claim under this Insurance shall not exceed a period of nine months counting from the time of completion of discharge of the insured goods from the sea-going vessel at the final port of discharge.

This Company shall undertake to indemnify the Insured for the reasonable expenses incurred by him for having immediately taken effective measures in salving and preventing further loss of the insured goods after damage was sustained but the amount of such indemnity together with the amount of the claim shall not exceed the insured amount of the damaged goods.

5. *Treatment of Dispute:*

All disputes arising between the Insured and this Company shall be settled by friendly negotiations of the principles of seeking truth from facts and of fairness and reasonableness. Where a settlement fails after negotiation and it is necessary to submit to arbitration or take legal actions, such arbitration or legal action shall be carried out at the place where the defendant is domiciled.

The People's Insurance Company of China
Ocean Marine Cargo War Risk Clauses
(1/4/1972)

1. *Scope of Cover*

This Company shall undertake to indemnify for the loss of or damage to the insured goods consequent upon the undermentioned causes:

(1) Loss or damage caused by war, hostile acts or armed conflicts;

(2) Loss or damage caused by seizure, detainment, confiscation or blockade arising from the events in (1) hereinabove, but such loss or damage shall be dealt with only on expiry of six months from the day when the loss or damage arises;

(3) Loss or damage caused by conventional weapons of war, including mines, torpedoes and bombs.

This Company shall further be liable for

Sacrifice in and contribution to General Average and Salvage Expenses arising from the events enumerated in (1) and (3) hereinabove.

2. *Exclusion*

This Company shall not be liable for loss or damage caused by atomic or hydrogen bombs or nuclear weapons of war.

3. *Commencement and Termination of Cover*

This insurance shall attach from the time the insured goods are loaded on the sea-going vessel or lighter at the port of shipment named in the Policy until the insured goods are discharged from the sea-going vessel or lighter at the port of destination, named in the Policy, but in case the insured goods are not discharged from the sea-going vessel or lighter the longest duration of this insurance allowable on the insured goods upon arrival at the port of destination shall be limited to 15 days counting from midnight of the day of their arrival at such port.

This insurance shall cease to attach when the insured goods are discharged from the sea-going vessel or lighter at the port of transhipment, but in case the insured goods are not discharged from the sea-going vessel, the longest duration of the insurance allowable on the insured goods upon arrival at such port shall be limited to 15 days counting from midnight of the day of their arrival at such port. The insurance shall reattach when the insured goods are loaded on the on-carrying sea-going vessel at the port of transhipment.

4. *Automatic Termination of Cover*

Should the insured goods be used for serving a war of aggression launched by imperialism, this insurance shall terminate automatically from the time of the outbreak of such war. Note: These Clauses are the clauses of an additional insurance to the Ocean Marine Cargo Insurance. In case of conflict between any clauses of these Clauses and the Ocean Marine Cargo Clauses, these Clauses shall prevail.

THE PEOPLE'S INSURANCE COMPANY OF CHINA
HULL CLAUSES

With a view to meeting the requirements for the development of the shipping enterprise and according to the principle of equality and mutual benefit, this Company writes Hull Insurance, the Clauses being as follows:

1. *Scope of Cover*

This insurance is classified into Total Loss Cover (Time and Voyage) and Comprehensive Cover (Time and Voyage). This Company shall undertake to indemnify the insured for loss of or damage to the ship insured according to the risks insured and the provisions of these Clauses.

(1) Total Loss Cover: This Company shall be liable for total loss of the insured ship caused by:

(a) Natural calamities and/or accidents;

(b) Latent defects in Hull Machinery;

(c) Negligence of the Master, Crew, Pilots or ship repairers.

(2) Comprehensive Cover: This Company shall be liable for total or partial loss of the insured ship caused by:

(a) Natural calamities and/or accidents;

(b) Latent defects in Hull and Machinery;

(c) Negligence of the Master, Crew, Pilots or ship repairers.

This company shall further be liable for the following liabilities and expenses arising from the foregoing events:

(i) Contribution to General Average;

(ii) In case of collision, the indemnity assumed by the insured ship towards the loss to the other ship in collision and the goods abroad such other ship, dock, wharf or other fixed structures, and delay to or loss of use of such other ship or fixed structures and salvage expenses incurred in connection therewith, but in no case shall the amount so indemnified exceed the insured amount of the insured ship;

(iii) Salvage expenses;

(iv) Expenses for pursuing recovery from third parties, reasonable expenses for ascertaining the loss or damage within the scope of Cover and the expenses for examining the ship's bottom after grounding.

Partial losses caused by the events in sub-sections (a) to (c) under section (2) hereinabove shall be subject to the deductible franchise stipulated in the Policy for each and every voyage (a voyage is meant a sailing from port of sailing to port of destination).

Ships may be insured for Total Loss Cover or Comprehensive Cover on application and may also be insured against additional risks upon consultation.

2. *Exclusions*

This company shall not be liable for

(1) Loss or damage caused by unseaworthiness of the insured ship;

(2) Loss or damage caused by the negligence of the Shipowner and his representative and by the intentional act of the Shipowner and his representative and Master;

(3) Maintenance repairs to the hull and machinery of the insured ship, expenses for painting, wear and tear and corrosion;

(4) Risks covered and excluded in the Hull War Risk Clauses of this Company;

(5) Demurrage of the insured ship and other indirect expenses;

(6) Expenses for removal or disposal of obstructions.

3. *Trading Limit*

The Prior agreement of this Company shall be obtained in case the insured ship sails out of the trading limit stipulated in the Policy, and an additional premium may be charged by this Company when so required.

4. *Period of Insurance*

(1) Time Insurance: Longest duration one year, the time of commencement and termination being subject to the stipulation in the Policy.

In the event that the insured ship is sold or transferred during the currency of insurance, the insurance shall become terminated forthwith unless such sale or transfer is agreed to by this Company in writing. Where the insured ship is sold or transferred in the course of a voyage, the insurance may be extended until the completion of such voyage.

(2) Voyage Insurance: To be subject to the voyages stipulated in the Policy. The time of commencement and termination to be dealt with according to the following provisions:

(a) With no cargo on board: To commence from the time of unmooring or weighing anchor at the port of sailing until the completion of casting anchor or mooring at the port of destination.

(b) With cargo on board: To commence from the time of loading at the port of sailing until the completion of discharge at the port of destination, but in no case shall a period of thirty days be exceeded, counting from midnight of the day of arrival of the ship at the port destination.

5. *Cancellation of Insurance and Return of Premium*

   (1) Time Insurance:

   (a) Where the insured ship is sold or transferred or the insurance thereon is cancelled during the currency of insurance, a premium to be calculated pro rata daily shall be returned to the Insured.

   (b) Where the insured ship undergoes repairs in dock or shipyard or is laid up in port for a period exceeding thirty consecutive days, 50% (fifty percent) of the premium, to be calculated pro rata daily, for the period during which the insured ship is under repairs or laid up shall be returned to the insured.

   (2) Voyage Insurance: In no case shall the insurance be cancellable once it commences.

6. *Treatment of Loss*

   (1) In the event of accidents to the insured ship which fall under the scope of Cover, the Insured shall notify this Company immediately and take all possible measures to minimise the loss to the insured ship. The prior consent of this Company shall be obtained before repairs are carried out. This Company shall be entitled to make deductions of unreasonable repairing costs and other expenses.

   The Insured shall cause the insured ship to undergo periodic overhaul and repairs and be well kept, so as to make her in good technical condition.

   (2) Where the insured ship is in collision with other ships, the Insured shall obtain the prior agreement of this Company on the liability resting with both parties and the amount of recovery which be ascertained with the party concerned.

7. *Claim and Subrogation of Rights*

   (1) In the case of a total loss of the insured ship, the full insured amount of the insured ship shall be indemnified.

   (2) Where no news is received of the whereabouts of the insured ship over a period of six months after the date on which she is expected to arrive at the port of destination, it shall constitute an event of missing of ship.

   Where the insured ship is missing or it is estimated that the aggregate of the amount of loss to the ship, salvage expenses, cost of repairs and other necessary disbursements will exceed the insured value of the insured ship, it may be deemed a total loss, and the full insured amount of the insured ship shall be indemnified.

   (3) In the case of a partial loss to the ship, this Company shall be liable for the reasonable costs of replacements and repairs.

   (4) In the case of loss of or damage to the insured ship, should the insured amount be lower than the sound value of the ship, the contributions to the

general average and the salvage expenses to be paid by this Company shall be calculated in the proportion that the Insured amount bears to the sound value.

(5) In submitting his claims for loss, the Insured shall, in case third party liability is involved, subrogate the right of recovery from the third party and transfer the necessary documents to this Company.

8. *Treatment of Disputes*

All disputes arising between the Insured and this Company shall be settled by friendly negotiation on the principle of seeking truth from facts and of fairness and reasonableness. Where a settlement fails after negotiation and it is necessary to submit to arbitration or take legal actions, such arbitration or legal actions shall be carried out at the place where the defendant is domiciled.

HULL WAR RISK CLAUSES

1. *Scope of Cover*

This Company shall be liable for loss of or damage to the insured ship, expenses and liabilities caused by:

(1) War, hostile acts or armed conflicts;

(2) Seizure, detainment, confiscation or blockade arising from the events in (1) hereinabove, but such claim shall be dealt with only on expiry of six months from the day when such events arise;

(3) Conventional weapons of war, including mines, torpedoes or bombs.

2. *Exclusions*

This Company shall not be liable for loss of or damage to the insured ship caused by:

(1) Requisition, pre-emption, detainment or confiscation by the government of the country of which the insured is a national;

(2) Atomic or hydrogen bombs or nuclear weapons of war.

3. *Termination of Cover*

(1) Should the Insured ship be used for serving a war of aggression launched by imperialism, this insurance shall terminate automatically from the time of the outbreak of such war.

(2) In respect of time insurance this Company shall be entitled to issue to the Insured, at any time, notice of cancellation to terminate such war risk insurance upon expiry of fourteen days from the day on which such notice is issued.

NOTE: These Clauses are the additional clauses to the Hull Clauses of this Company. In case of conflict between any clauses in these Clauses and the Hull Clauses, these Clauses shall prevail.

THE PEOPLE'S INSURANCE COMPANY OF CHINA
INSURANCE CERTIFICATE

This Certificate is also a Policy

Assured's Name   China National Chemicals Imp. & Exp. Corp.

We have this day noted a risk as hereunder mentioned in your favour, subject to all clauses and conditions of the Company's printed form of Policy and to the special terms outlined herein (where latter shall override the policy terms in so far as they may be inconsistent therewith).

Marks & Nos.	Quantity	Description of Goods	Amount insured
Napoli	5,000 Bags	Paraffin	RMB

Total Amount Insured: RENMINBI ONE HUNDRED TWENTY NINE THOUSAND TWO HUNDRED AND FIFTY YUAN ONLY.

Premium: as arranged   Rate as arranged

Per conveyance S.S. "Kosovo"   Sig. on or abt. 1971,7,31

From Hsinkang to Napoli

Conditions   Covering all Risks from warehouse to warehouse
& or   inland Italy Naples subject to The Ocean Marine
Special Coverage   Cargo Clauses—All Risks of The People's Insur-
                          ance Company of China.

                          Including risks of War subject to The Ocean
                          Marine Cargo War Risks Clauses.

Claims, if any, payable to the Holder of the appertaining documents and on surrender of this Certificate.

In the event of accident whereby loss or damage may result in a claim under this Certificate immediate notice must be given to the nearest Company's Agent as mentioned hereunder.

This certificate is issued in duplicate

Claim payable at destination

Date: 30th July, 1971.   Tientsin

Index

Academy of Sciences (of China), 80

Accounts: in RMB, 187, 281–82, 384; of China Products Company, Ltd. (HK), 214–15; with socialist countries, 271; with capitalist countries, 272; with the People's Bank, 346. *See also* Bank of China

Accounting, incasso system of, 93–94

Adenauer cabinet, 121

Administration: of shipping, in China, 254–56

Administrative Case Litigation Law of Japan, 65

Africa: Chinese trade with, 20, 26, 261, 318; Chinese commercial and economic representation in, 315, 326

Agents: governmental control of trading, 125; in Sino-German trade, 138; sole *(Alleinvertreter)*, 162; and continental law, 162n; rights of, in Liao-Takasaki Memorandum, 302; port corporation as, 345; purchasing, 345

—in Hong Kong: of PRC state trading corporations, 199; as wholesalers, 199; unincorporated partnerships as, 199, 200; China Resources Co. as, 200

Agreements: on repatriation of nationals between U.S. and China, 16; between Soviet Union and Manchuria, 71, 333; on International Railway Freight Communication, 91; Sino-West German, 131, 245; over-all need for, in Sino-U.S. trade, 244; Sino-Italian, 245; Sino-

Indian, 299–300; Sino-Egyptian, 303; negotiation of, 311; monetary values of disparities in, 319; signators of, 319–21; Distributorship, 427–28. *See also* Memorandum Trade

—bilateral: commercial effects of, 177; and security of trading personnel, 305

—Trade and Payments (TPA), 179–81; definition of, 150; terms of, 150–51, 151–53, 272–73; in Sino-Danish trade, 143, 149, 150, 162–63; in Sino-Italian trade, 173, 174–75, 303, 379–80

—on marine transport (MTAO), 179–81; Sino-Soviet, 87; Sino-Italian, 187n

Agricultural products: American, exported to China, xii, 222; Chinese, export of, 78, 334, 350, 353

Agricultural Products, Ministry for Purchase of, 358

Aichi, Kiichi, 45

Aid: and trade, 26, 315, 321–22; agreements on, 318, 329

—Chinese: to Albania, 21; on Tanzam Railway, 26; military to Korea, 315; military to Vietnam, 315; nonmilitary to South and Southeast Asia, 315; and Bureau for Economic Liaison with Foreign countries, 315, 359, and Cultural Revolution, 315–16

—Soviet: to Manchuria, 71; to PRC, 72–73, 106; to Third World, 81, 112; during Korean War, 82; confusion of, with trade, 83–84; Soviet views on, 84–85